ELIZA]
OF THE T

THE UNFOLDING
OF HER MESSAGE

Volume 2
In the Infirmary & After her Death

Joanne Mosley

First published 2012 by:

TERESIAN PRESS
Carmelite Priory
Boars Hill
Oxford OX1 5HB
priory@carmelite.org.uk

ISBN 978-0-947916-12-1
(vol. 2)

A catalogue record for this book is available from the British Library.

For permissions to use copyright material,
see Acknowledgements at the end of this volume.

Cover photograph © Carmel of Dijon
Photograph of early 1903,
not long after Elizabeth had taken her vows

Cover design by Bill Bolger

Typeset and printed by Joshua Horgan, Oxford

In memory of
Mother Germaine de Saint-Seine
(1870-1934)
Prioress and Novice Mistress of the Dijon Carmel
who accompanied Elizabeth as her message unfolded
and was the first to make it known

CONTENTS

VOLUME 2
IN THE INFIRMARY & AFTER HER DEATH

PART III   IN THE INFIRMARY

PART IV   AFTER HER DEATH

Appendices

Part III

IN THE INFIRMARY

October 1906, about four weeks before her death

the Blessed Virgin is…there to teach me to suffer as He did (LR 41)

Chapter 15

PREPARING FOR ETERNITY

A Cloister within a Cloister

Elizabeth's entrance to the infirmary was the beginning of a new life. When she had entered Carmel, almost five years previously, she had entered a cloister within the city of Dijon. Now, as she left her cell for the infirmary, she was as if entering a cloister within a cloister: a confined space away from the community, a place where prayer was even more intimate and her focus even more exclusively on Jesus alone. She herself saw it as an 'even more profound solitude', where she had 'nothing to do but love' (L 278). And she said to her mother in those early weeks: 'If you knew how happy I am in the solitude of my little infirmary; my Master is here with me, and we live night and day in a sweet heart-to-heart. I appreciate the happiness of being a Carmelite even more' (L 267). To her young friend Françoise de Sourdon, she wrote in similar vein, for again the two things uppermost in her mind were *happiness* and the *heart-to-heart*: 'it is so good to be His... The two of us are so happy together here in the solitude of my little infirmary; it is a heart-to-heart that lasts night and day, and it's delightful!' (L 270; cf. PN 17:3).

The 'heart' was a place of prayer and love, a place that could know sweetness and delight. But a different matter from her heart and soul was her body. It was a place of ravages – though still, too, a place of love: a body offered to God as 'an extension of His passion' (L 259). Just after Elizabeth's death, Françoise de Sourdon would look at her friend's body which had been consumed by illness, and would later comment perceptively: 'Elizabeth's love of God was all-consuming' (ETB, p. 719).

Elizabeth herself was in no doubt that it was love that had brought her to the infirmary. Sister Marie of the Trinity would recall that as soon as Elizabeth arrived there, 'she told us that she was so highly aware that her body was entirely a secondary cause and that God had his sights on her soul, and she was aware of an inexpressible love that was on her' (ETB, pp. 658–9). Sharing the sufferings of Jesus, in those words of St Paul which she found so inspiring (cf. Ph 3:10; HF 28), in her remaining few months she would give glory to God as she lived out, in her afflicted body, her vocation to be 'a praise of his glory' (cf. Eph 1:12). So this new stage of her life was not an end but a beginning. And if her flesh was weak, her spirit was more than willing: even in the extremes of weakness, there is an inner dynamism and energy about the whole of Elizabeth's time in the infirmary, right up to the day she died, just under eight months later.

The Mysterious, Silent Cell

Her final journey began, as we have seen, straight after the feast of St Joseph[1] – the saint whose name she had drawn as her patron for 1906, the 'Patron of a Good Death'. Now, she was filled with the knowledge that he was 'coming to fetch [her]' (ETB, p. 652). The physical journey itself, on the day she left for the infirmary, was to the other end of the first floor of the Dijon Carmel. The shape of this route could be described as a capital 'L'. The vertical stem was the long corridor containing most of the sisters' cells; near the top on the right-hand side, and looking onto the large courtyard, was the cell Elizabeth had occupied for nearly five years and was now leaving for good. Eight doors down, still on the right – or on her left, if we follow Elizabeth's slow progress down the corridor – was the office of the prioress, Mother Germaine. Immediately after this came the corner: the landing beneath the bell tower, straight ahead of which was the chapter room where Elizabeth had taken her vows, imbued with a sense of 'offering her body as a living sac-

---

[1] See Chapter 14, n. 7.

rifice to God' (cf. Rm 12:1) – an offering that was now coming
to its fulfilment.

But at this point, she turned left, into what we might term
the shorter, horizontal bar of the 'L'. Firstly, she passed through
the terrace: a pleasant space used as a promenade by sisters
staying in the infirmary. To her left, the terrace looked down
onto the large courtyard and was open to the air. To her right, it
had windows opening onto the choir, so that sisters who were too
ill to go downstairs could follow the Offices which were recited
several times a day; the choir, with its very high walls, occupied
both floors of the monastery, so Elizabeth would have been listening to the community from above. After the terrace came a
few small rooms. And finally, the far tip of the 'L' which, as in
fashionable handwriting, finished with a flourish. In this upward
curve, as Elizabeth turned left again, there were a pharmacy and
two infirmary cells, both of them corner rooms. She was given
the smaller one, on the left after the pharmacy, and it faced out
onto the large courtyard, diagonally opposite the window out
of which she had looked for the last five years.

Here, in the infirmary cell that would be hers until the day
she died, Elizabeth was installed in the small plain bed with
iron-railed bedstead and white sheets. The bed was directly on
her right as she came in, and it ran alongside the right-hand
wall. But although she faced one of the windows, what commanded Elizabeth's view most of all was the large wooden cross
to the left of it, hanging high on the wall. It was an empty cross
– for, as she would write that August: 'He…has substituted me
for Himself on the Cross so that "I may suffer in my body what
is lacking in His passion for the sake of His body, which is the
Church"' (LR 41; cf. Col 1:24). This spiritual scenario would set
the scene for Elizabeth's life in the infirmary. She would write
to her sister:

> I wish I could invite you here near me; it is so mysterious, so
> silent, this little cell with its white walls that set off a black
> wooden cross without a Corpus. It is mine, the place where

I must immolate myself at every moment to be conformed
to my crucified Bridegroom. Saint Paul said: 'what I want is
to know Him, Christ, to share in His sufferings, to become
like Him in His death.' (L 298; cf. Rm 8:29)

While the first window gave onto the opposite wing of the monastery, Elizabeth's best view of all – looking out over the large
inner courtyard and the cloisters – came from the window on
the wall to her left. Next to it stood an earthenware stove. As for
the wall facing her, beneath the black wooden cross to the left
of the window was a small wooden chair; while a rather more
comfortable armchair was directly at the foot of her bed, facing
the stove and the window with the view. Directly ahead of her,
in the right-hand corner of the room, there was a small table on
which would be placed her breviary, her profession crucifix and,
at a future stage, her much-loved statue of Our Lady of Lourdes
which she would name 'Janua Coeli', 'Gate of Heaven'. Above
the table there would soon be a framed picture of the Calvary
scene, with Mary, John and Mary Magdalene standing beneath
the Cross; this had been a gift from Madame Guémard, and it
was to come with Elizabeth to the infirmary. Finally, to the left
of the bed was a tiny bedside cupboard; this was probably where
she would keep the little box containing her writings – her notebooks and poems and prayers. Indeed, it was in the infirmary
that Elizabeth would be at her most prolific.

A New Community

Elizabeth was not just inhabiting a cloister within a cloister, so to
speak, but also joining a community within a community as she
became part of a small group of companions, all centred around
the infirmary, for the remaining eight months of her life.

She had a next-door neighbour, the long-standing occu-
pant of the large infirmary cell: Sister Marie of the Incarnation
who was seventy-six and had already been there for two years
when Elizabeth entered Carmel. This white-veil sister, who was
paralysed, was the one who had celebrated her Golden Jubilee

on the Thursday after Easter in 1903, when news had arrived during Benediction that the public chapel was to be closed to the public with immediate effect. Elizabeth, we have seen, had dedicated a poem to her for that day (P 87), in which she called herself the 'littlest bride' in the Dijon Carmel, and this eldest one 'Grandmama'! In these verses, Elizabeth had said that she longed to go to heaven; she must have been envious of this elderly nun who would naturally have been expected to be the first of them, by far, to reach the end of her life. But as mentioned earlier, incredibly they would die within only five days of each other – Elizabeth, in fact, being the one who would depart first. This sister, of whom it would be said that she was 'always forgetful of herself' (ETB, p. 584), would follow the final months of Elizabeth's long and painful agony.

There was also an unofficial patient: Sister Anne-Marie of the Child Jesus, who was thirty-three. About three years earlier, her health had taken a turn for the worse. Alas, she had soon decided that she was more ill than she actually was, and that she could no longer continue with her lay sister's domestic duties! She often frequented the infirmary for rest, and after Elizabeth's death would be moved into the small infirmary cell, where she insisted on having her meals brought up to her! The doctor was not fooled and often refused to see her, saying it was 'a waste of time' (ETB, p. 586). But Sister Anne-Marie may well have been in good faith and genuinely deluded that she was dying. For she also suffered from illusions in her spiritual life, believing herself to be gifted with great mystical graces, which was not at all the case. However, at the time of Elizabeth's illness, she was still held in high regard by several of the nuns. Mother Marie of Jesus, the former prioress, thought of Elizabeth and Sister Anne-Marie as two saintly sisters. Sister Aimée even thought that the latter was holier than Elizabeth – an assertion with which Mother Germaine, to her credit, disagreed entirely! Nonetheless, this over-pious sister proved to be helpful company for Elizabeth who would include her in preparing gifts for Mother Germaine (cf. L 284; P 107, n. 1); and Elizabeth would also share her spirituality with her, so that Sister Anne-Marie would even sign herself on one occasion as 'Praise of glory'. 'The holy Master is leading us to Calvary' (P 102), Elizabeth would say – the 'us' referring to them both. Indeed, the Master did lead Sister Anne-Marie to her death... thirty-seven years later!

Through a strange but welcome parallel with her time spent in community, Elizabeth's two immediate superiors were Mother Germaine and Sister Marie of the Trinity, her most valued confidantes over the last few years. This sub-prioress, who had also been Elizabeth's 'Angel' – not to mention 'first portress', overseeing her work at the turn – had, by a curious coincidence, been appointed 'second infirmary sister'. Elizabeth could not have escaped her, had she wanted! Fortunately, she didn't wish to, and she continued to confide in her.

But best of all was when Mother Germaine came to see her. Each day, according to custom, the prioress would give a blessing, morning and evening, to the sisters in the infirmary, and would also pay each of them a visit. The morning visits in particular were of great significance to Elizabeth. Unable to walk to the Communion grille of the infirmary, and often too weak even to be carried there, she was able to receive the Real Presence only five times during her first fifty days in the infirmary – and this, ironically, after the decree of Pope Pius X, on December 20, 1905, allowing daily Communion. It was, at that time, the custom in the Dijon Carmel that a priest could not enter the enclosure to bring Communion to the sick – unless, of course, it was the 'Viaticum' for a nun who was dying. So Mother Germaine hit on an ingenious solution: sensitive to how deprived Elizabeth must be feeling, she would come to kneel at her bedside to make her thanksgiving after receiving Communion; and Elizabeth, strongly aware of the Real Presence dwelling in the prioress in those most privileged moments immediately after Mass, would prepare herself 'as if she were really about to receive the hidden God' (PG, p. 155), as the prioress would write later. Indeed, it seemed to Elizabeth that she was receiving Communion in Mother Germaine's soul (cf. L 271). This morning visit, Elizabeth used to say, was 'the sunshine of [my] day' (PG, p. 155).

Apart from her two superiors, there were three sisters Elizabeth saw on a daily basis: these were the ones assigned to work, or help out, in the infirmary. The 'first infirmary sister' was Sister Anne of Jesus who was sixty-four. A practical, decisive woman – she had been bursar when the monastery was being built – she was much suited to nursing: the letter sent to Lisieux in August 1901, with a commentary on each sister in the community photographs, describes Sister Anne as 'a consummate nurse, a true doctor!' (ETB, p. 579). There was one problem, however: she was extremely deaf. Possibly because she could not hear the things Elizabeth said, she would at some point begin to steal a glance into the patient's writing box, looking through her personal papers; this probably occurred after a few weeks, when Elizabeth became able to leave her cell. One day, Elizabeth noticed what was happening and asked Mother Germaine what she should do about it. The prioress told her that she must in future lock the box. The next time Sister Anne of Jesus tried to open the lid, she found it locked. And although she did not fail in her duties or consideration towards her patient, from that time on she maintained a certain reserve towards her – something that the sensitive Elizabeth could not fail to have noticed and experienced as painful.

Then there were two white-veil nuns. One was the delightful, smiling Sister Marthe of Jesus, who that April would turn forty-four. While she helped out a little in the infirmary, her main role was that of the monastery cook; and with her thoughtful, sensitive nature, she prepared dishes according to the needs of each invalid and carried in their meals. Elizabeth called her 'Darling little Mama' (L 283) and 'Little Mama whom I love' (L 281). Sister Marthe would later say that Elizabeth 'was so affectionate and delicate in her gratitude for the least service one gave her that it was a joy to go to her' (L 281, n. 1).

Last, but definitely not least, was the thirty-six-year-old Sister Marie of the Holy Spirit. She would leave the convent five years later, but while she was there she rendered Elizabeth the most valuable of services. While nervous by nature, she was physically most robust and proved able, single-handedly, to carry Elizabeth to the Communion grille on those days when the invalid felt strong enough to leave her bed. Elizabeth, she would say, 'clasped me to her heart, telling me that [Our Lord] was imprinted in me, so grateful she was to me' (L 271, n. 7).

Elizabeth was grateful to everyone. This is what she would write to Madame de Sourdon about the prioress and all who were helping her: 'If you knew what a Mother I have at my side: a true mama, her heart has the tenderness, the delicacy known only to the hearts of mothers. As for my infirmarians, they rival each other in charity. What a Carmel!' (L 268).

Medical Matters

This, then, was Elizabeth's new community, as it were. But she continued to have contact with visitors from outside: Madame Catez and Guite, who would come to the infirmary parlour usually every other Saturday, and occasionally friends who came to see her. Elizabeth would see her mother and sister for the first time around the end of April, when she would be carried into the infirmary parlour and placed on a small bed by the grille; 'you can guess the joy of that meeting' (L 271), she would write to Canon Angles.

The 'outside' person she undoubtedly saw the most, though, was the community's physician, Dr Barbier. He was not, it appears, a believer, but Elizabeth formed a spiritual bond with him; this may possibly have begun as a sharing of her faith, but it was always a genuine mutual respect and friendship. Whenever Dr Barbier was away, a Dr Lucien, who appears to have been a younger colleague, would stand in. He saw Elizabeth once while she was still in community and suffering with her stomach; and about four times during the last few weeks of her life. Both he and Dr Barbier were highly impressed with Elizabeth as they witnessed her courage in suffering and radiance in her faith. Dr

Lucien would leave this memorable portrait of Elizabeth, which he gave for the beatification Process:

> I can see her still, on her bed of suffering, holding her crucifix in her hand, contemplating it with love, kissing it, and telling me of her happiness that she would see him before long. She offered up her sufferings for her neighbour, she had concern for my soul and warned me very solemnly that here below all is vanity. She promised that as soon as she was in heaven she would greet my late parents, in particular my mother; and she asked me: 'Do you want me to be your children's guardian angel?' (ETB, p. 709)

Later, we will also come across some other doctors. These were sent in for two consultations at the initiative of Guite's husband Georges. In fact, when Canon Angles first learnt of Elizabeth's serious illness, he remarked that she was lucky to have an intelligent and devoted brother-in-law who would surely be of help to her (cf. ETB, p. 661). Elizabeth did not relate much with these particular doctors, one of whom was a stomach specialist, for they examined her as a group and discussed her case amongst themselves. No one diagnosed Addison's Disease, but this is not unduly surprising as it was very little known at the time.[2] Also, no mention was ever made in the community of tuberculosis – the usual cause of Addison's Disease – although Mother Germaine would later say that Dr Barbier took precautions against TB in the case of Elizabeth's illness.

What *was* evident to everyone, though, was Elizabeth's main symptom (other than exhaustion): her severe stomach pains, and virtual inability to eat. So severe was the situation that, throughout Elizabeth's entire time in the infirmary, the contents of about one glass of milk practically made up what she called her four 'meals' (PG, p. 213) of the day. In addition, she would eat small amounts – minuscule amounts – of ice cream, cottage cheese, cake and chocolate: her friends would send her,

---

[2] See Chapter 13, section 'The Doctor's Diagnosis'.

and even make her, lots and lots of chocolate, each of them trying to find a consistency that she would be able to digest. Elizabeth would say: 'I do what I can not to let [my stomach] die of hunger' (L 309).

The community were now beginning to see the danger Elizabeth was in. They would soon make contact with other Carmels, asking them to join them in prayer to Margaret of Beaune, a seventeenth-century Carmelite whose Cause for beatification was currently being brought forward in Rome. Beaune was near Dijon, and we remember that Elizabeth had visited the Carmel there with her friend Marie-Louise Hallo in the spring of 1901. For Venerable Margaret to be beatified, a miracle was needed. So the Carmelites now began to pray novenas for Elizabeth's cure, and she was given a relic of Margaret to wear. Mother Germaine knew well that Elizabeth longed to go to heaven – so she put her under obedience to pray to be cured! But it would soon become only too clear that Elizabeth was instead following Venerable Margaret on the path of suffering.

The First Attack

Palm Sunday fell on April 8, and that day Elizabeth had some relief from her symptoms. It was a feast day to which she was very devoted; for like Teresa of Avila, she felt the cruel irony of the crowds in Jerusalem waving their palm leaves to hail Jesus as their King, but who were nowhere to be seen when he needed a place to rest that night. Instead, his faithful friends, Lazarus, Martha and Mary, welcomed him to their home in Bethany – a place that held many resonances for Elizabeth, ever-aware of the significance of her name as 'House of God'. She had once said to Jesus: 'I offer you the cell of my heart, may it be your little Bethany; come and rest in it' (IN 5). For this reason, she was particularly sorry not to be able to receive Communion on Palm Sunday.

But in the evening during Compline, Elizabeth suddenly fainted and lost consciousness. As she seemed to be at the point of death, word was sent hurriedly to Father Maurice Donin of

St Peter's parish, calling him urgently to the Carmel. Before he arrived, Elizabeth regained full consciousness. And she believed that these were her last moments on earth. As she would write to her friend Germaine de Gemeaux: 'I thought the hour had finally arrived when I was going to fly away into the infinite realms to contemplate unveiled this Trinity that has already been my dwelling place here below' (L 278). Yet this was not a moment of unmitigated joy: for, as she would explain to her mother, she was awe-struck at this 'solemn moment', and acutely aware of being 'so little and empty-handed' (L 266) – words that would have come to her from Thérèse's *Act of Oblation*: 'In the evening of this life, I shall appear before You with empty hands' (SS, p. 277). In this state of mind, Elizabeth was filled with gratitude for the comforting presence of Mother Germaine who took her hands in hers and helped to prepare her for death.

When Father Donin arrived, the immediate danger had passed, although he still found Elizabeth suffering and struggling to breathe. He had brought with him the holy oil to anoint her for 'Extreme Unction', and the Communion Host for the 'Viaticum' which would be her food for the journey out of this life. First, he asked her if she was able to accept her sufferings. Elizabeth seemed absolutely astonished that he should speak only of *accepting* them. She answered: 'Oh! I am *happy* to suffer' (ETB, p. 659), emphasising the 'happy'.

The priest had also come prepared to give an exhortation, as was the custom when assisting at the bed of a dying person. But he now realised that there was no need for him to say anything of the sort. On the contrary: it was he who was edified. He saw her hands clasped together in prayer as she calmly responded to the words of the prioress; and he noted with admiration Elizabeth's 'constancy, courage, surrender of self to God and union with Christ' (PG, p. 287). Before leaving, he would say to the prioress: 'How sweet death is in Carmel! If I were younger I would become a religious' (PG, p. 151). He would even write to Elizabeth's mother, the next year, to say that meeting her daughter had been 'one of the graces of [his] priestly life' (PG,

p. 286), and he added: 'never has such an unearthly radiance been more visible to me' (PG, pp. 286–7).

He now anointed Elizabeth and gave her Communion. At the moment of Extreme Unction, Mother Germaine gazed on her and thought how 'beautiful' she looked, 'her eyes ablaze' (L 266, n. 3), as she took her profession crucifix and exclaimed: 'O Love! Love! Love!' (PG, p. 151). For it seemed to Elizabeth that this was the very moment at which Jesus would 'break [her] bonds', and she felt 'so happy to die a Carmelite' (L 278).

But it was not to be. Not yet. Later, when alone, Elizabeth drank in the 'calm and silence' of that night on which she had received 'the visit of [her] Master' (L 278). It gave her particular joy to know that on Palm Sunday evening, at the hour when he had gone to stay with his friends in Bethany, Jesus had come to rest in 'His *little house*' (PG, p. 151) – 'Elizabeth', his Bethany!

Mirroring Holy Week

Elizabeth was still radiating the joy of this experience the next morning, Monday of Holy Week. Meanwhile, that same morning Madame Catez took herself to Mass at the Carmel.[3] She made sure to cough, so that Elizabeth would hear her from the other side of the grille! But her daughter was not, of course, there. Until now, only Guite had been aware of the situation; the extent of Elizabeth's illness had been kept from their mother for the time being, as Madame Catez herself had not been well. But two hours after she returned home, Guite arrived in tears and broke the news that Elizabeth was seriously ill. Madame Catez, almost out of her mind with terror, ran straight back to the Carmel, where the prioress explained everything. Elizabeth's mother was now facing her own martyrdom. But with great courage she wrote to Elizabeth that week, saying 'that she was resigned to the

---

[3] The Carmelites' chapel had not yet officially reopened since its closure, on Government orders, in April 1903; the reopening would be announced in the weekly Catholic newspaper of Dijon on May 12, 1906. However, since the Law of Separation of Church and State in December 1905, private worship was no longer restricted: see L 165, n. 6; L 285, n. 7.

Will of God and that she agreed to drink the cup [of suffering]' (L 266, n. 2). Elizabeth would reread this letter often, and it was a great consolation for her.

It was to Canon Angles, instead, that Madame Catez poured out her devastation. He received her letter the next day and wrote back straightaway, leaving no doubt about how he really viewed Elizabeth: 'May the good God leave this angel, whom we love so much, to her family! May he leave to France this saint, at a time when it is in such need of saints!' (ETB, p. 661). The distraught mother wrote to him again the following week, having been told that Elizabeth had said to the physician: 'Doctor, why aren't you letting me leave for heaven?' (ETB, p. 661). The Canon's reply shows not just his high esteem for Elizabeth but also his paternal pride in her: 'How I wept on reading that line! And how these words are truly from my Elizabeth, my little saint!' (ETB, p. 661, n. 2).

For Elizabeth, who so longed to be united with Christ in his Passion, it should not surprise us that Holy Week saw the addition of acute pain to her existing sufferings. Contemplating how Jesus himself had suffered, she united herself to him as a fellow victim chosen for sacrifice. Her patience in suffering was remarkable, as were her joy and her complete self-surrender. Good Friday, especially, was an extremely painful day. Sister Marie of the Trinity exclaimed: 'To what degree she was associated with the sufferings of Christ, especially on Good Friday!' (ETB, p. 660). Once more, in fact, Elizabeth appeared to be in an alarming condition.

But throughout the night from Good Friday to Holy Saturday, she felt a change being worked in her. And the next morning, she was astonished to find that, having been unable to move all week, she could now sit up and kneel on her bed. She even felt like eating again – whereas she had been unable to consume anything at all. When Sister Marie of the Holy Spirit came into her cell, Elizabeth declared: 'I am cured' (ETB, p. 660); and she wanted to go and receive Communion. It was the morning on which the Church sang the first 'Alleluia' of

Easter. And the community, who had been praying so much for her cure, were filled with joy on hearing the good news which they learnt just before going to the Office in choir. Meanwhile, on the other side of the choir grille, Madame Catez was kneeling in the chapel and giving thanks that her daughter's life had been spared.

'A beautiful, luminous dream'

On Easter Sunday, Mother Germaine installed herself at Elizabeth's bedside, pen at the ready, and took down to dictation a letter to Madame Catez. This was the first of Elizabeth's many letters from the infirmary, most of which she would eventually be able to write by hand herself, even if several of them were in pencil and in a shaky handwriting. Well aware that her time was running out, Elizabeth would make sure to write to her family and friends as much as possible, assuring them of her affection and sharing with them her spiritual ideals. One practical thing she did stress, though – both to reassure her mother, and to give voice to her overflowing gratitude towards Mother Germaine – was just how much the prioress was taking care of her: 'thanks again for your treats,' Elizabeth wrote to Madame Catez, 'those ices that are my only consolation; if you could see with what happiness Our Mother brings them to me and how she herself has me take them like a little child...' (L 266). This must have caused the scribe to smile! And a few days later: 'You can't imagine the care she lavishes on me, with all the tenderness and delicacy of a mother's heart!' (L 267). Curiously, this new period in Elizabeth's life was very much like her earliest days in the convent, when as a new postulant she had exclaimed about how the prioress was caring for her 'like a real baby' (L 85), seeing to her every need.

But most of all, in these days of April 1906, Elizabeth wished to communicate, to those closest to her, the experience of her recent brush with death. We learn quite a bit from these letters about her state of mind during the immediate aftermath, because a number of themes keep recurring. One of them is the feeling of having been *in a dream – a dream of great beauty*. This is how she expressed it to Madame de Sourdon: '[these days] have drawn me still closer to God, to the invisible world. I feel as if I'm coming out of a beautiful, luminous dream' (L 268). To Françoise she spoke of 'the thought of this first face-to-face with Divine Beauty' (L 270). And to Canon Angles she wrote:

> To you, who have always been my confidant, I know I can tell everything: the prospect of going to see Him whom I love in His ineffable beauty, and of being immersed in the Trinity that was already my Heaven here below, fills my soul with immense joy. Oh! what it costs me to return to earth; it seems so ugly to me, coming out of my beautiful dream. (L 271)

United in Love

While Elizabeth invariably gave spiritual advice to her mother to console her, she was able to speak more on equal terms with her sister, so to Guite she let her heart overflow. In a letter to her at the end of the month, she spoke of her beloved ideal of being a praise of God's glory, and gave full expression to her longing to go to heaven; this she conveyed with Thérèse's image of the 'Divine Eagle' (cf. SS, p. 200) and the expression 'the secret of His Face' which Elizabeth would have encountered in John of the Cross (cf. LF 2:17):

> at times it seems to me that the Divine Eagle wants to swoop down on His little prey and carry her off to where He is: into dazzling light! You have always put your Sabeth's happiness before your own, and I am sure that if I fly away, you will rejoice over my first meeting with Divine Beauty. When the veil is lifted, how happy I will be to disappear into the secret of His Face, and that is where I will spend my eternity, in the bosom of the Trinity that was already my dwelling place here below. Just think, my Guite! to contemplate in His light the splendours of the Divine Being, to search into all the depths of His mystery, to become one with Him whom we

love, to sing unceasingly of His glory and His love, to be like Him because we see Him as He is!... (L 269)

With such a vision of beauty and glory before her, inevitably Elizabeth could not manage to hide from her mother how sorry she was not to have gone to heaven! 'I'll confess in a whisper,' she wrote, 'my great disappointment at not going to Him whom I love so much' (L 266).

However, this longing for heaven was joined with another theme in these letters: that had she died, she and those close to her would have been *even closer*. 'If I had gone to Heaven,' she said to her mother, 'how I would have spent my life with you! I would never have left you; I would have made you feel the presence of your little Sabeth' (L 266). And to Françoise: 'Heaven would only have made the fusion of our souls more true. You've often said I was like a little mother to you, and I do in fact feel that my heart holds a maternal affection for you; just think what it would be like if I were in the great Furnace of love... how I would have watched over [you]' (L 270). These words, like other letters at this time, highlight how Elizabeth felt that *being in heaven would give her a protective role* towards her family and friends. 'I will be your little protectress' (L 268), she wrote to Madame de Sourdon; and to Madame Catez: 'I would have so loved to protect [my little nieces] if I had flown away' (L 266); she would also, she said, have been so happy to be the 'Angel' of Guite and Mother Germaine (cf. L 269; L 271).

Preparing for Heaven

This brush with death, occurring so soon after Elizabeth's arrival in the infirmary, had quite a providential timing. For it made Elizabeth aware, more than ever before, of how precious each moment was. Not so much in order to appreciate every moment she had left to live: rather, so as to *make use of every moment in preparing for death*. Notably, Elizabeth did not speak of 'death' but of 'eternity'. 'Oh, little Mama,' she wrote to Madame Catez, 'let us prepare for our eternity, let us live with Him, for

He alone can accompany and help us on this great journey' (L 267). And again: 'Let's thank God for these days, however painful they are to your heart; I have a real sense that they are passing over us, dear Mama, like a wave of love; let's not waste any of it' (L 266).

This also meant *seeing the value of suffering*, and in a letter to Madame de Sourdon Elizabeth explained why: 'God has made me understand in His light what a treasure suffering is, and we will never understand enough the extent to which He loves us when He gives us trials; the cross is a token of His love!' (L 268). She made the same point again to her mother: 'He is a God of love; we cannot comprehend the extent to which He loves us, *above all when He sends us trials*' (L 267). The reason for this, we can be sure, is that Elizabeth knew that *suffering increases the likeness to Christ*. That is why she did not put up any resistance to God but gave him free rein to carry out his work in her. As she said to Canon Angles: 'my Master's happiness is mine, and I surrender myself to Him so He can do whatever He wants in me' (L 271).

An especially important theme that emerges – one that was central to Elizabeth's spirituality – is her message of *heaven in faith*: that there is no need to wait until eternity before living the life of heaven. Elizabeth began once more to express this notion, which was already so dear to her, about three weeks after the attack of Palm Sunday evening. For by the end of April, she had come to accept that her departure, while not far off, was none-theless not quite as imminent as she had thought. So, focusing on the life of heaven through faith (rather than expecting to depart for the real heaven at any moment), she said to Madame de Sourdon around the end of the month: 'Saint Paul tells me that in my soul, through faith, I possess in substance these splendours [of Heaven], these divine riches that I thought I was going to contemplate in the great brightness of God' (L 268; cf. Hb 11:1). And on May 9, she would write to Canon Angles: 'Only in God is everything pure, beautiful, and holy; fortunately we can dwell in Him even in our exile!' (L 271).

A Testament Letter

Around the end of April, Elizabeth wrote a magnificent letter to Guite (L 269) who would later describe it as a testament letter (cf. L 269, n. 1). Elizabeth makes her a solemn bequest as she speaks of living, as in heaven, in union with the Trinity:

> I leave you my devotion for the Three, to 'Love'. Live within with Them in the heaven of your soul; the Father will overshadow you, placing something like a cloud between you and the things of this earth to keep you all His, He will communicate His power to you so you can love Him with a love as strong as death; the Word will imprint in your soul, as in a crystal, the image of His own beauty, so you may be pure with His purity, luminous with His light; the Holy Spirit will transform you into a mysterious lyre, which, in silence, beneath His divine touch, will produce a magnificent canticle to Love... (L 269)

Here, we see the finesse of Elizabeth's expression, as she uses a musical image to describe the person transformed by God's creative action: that of a 'lyre' whose strings are moved by the Holy Spirit; and the effect is that the strings begin to play a song – the song of praise of God's glory. At this point, Elizabeth leaves Guite her own vocation as 'Praise of Glory':

> you will be 'the praise of His glory' I dreamed of being on earth. You will take my place; I will be 'Laudem Gloriae' before the throne of the Lamb, and you, 'Laudem Gloriae' in the centre of your soul; we will always be united, little sister. (L 269)

Elizabeth now expresses her final wishes for Guite: 'Always believe in Love. If you have to suffer, think that you are even *more loved*, and always sing in thanksgiving' (L 269). And she makes this request: 'Teach the little ones to live in the sight of the Master' – adding her personal wish that Sabeth, in particular, might have her aunt's 'devotion to the Three'. Elizabeth will be with them, in spirit, at their First Communions. And as a final farewell: 'A Dieu, little sister, how I love you… Perhaps I will go soon to be lost in the Furnace of love; whether in Heaven or on earth, we must live in Love to glorify Love!' (L 269).

'Pray for me…'

Elizabeth asked her sister: 'Pray for me', and she truly meant it for she added: 'I have offended my Master more than you think; but above all thank Him; say a Gloria every day' (L 269). It is no coincidence that she asked Guite to say this particular prayer – it was, after all, the perfect prayer for a 'praise of glory'. But Elizabeth, like all the saints, was well aware of the infinite difference between herself and God, and of the numerous graces she had received and not made fruitful. On May 9, she would write this heartfelt plea to Canon Angles:

> Since you are His priest, oh, consecrate me to Him like a little sacrifice of praise who wants to give glory to Him in Heaven, or on earth as much suffering as He wishes. And then, if I go, you will help me get out of purgatory. Oh, if you knew how deeply I feel that everything within me is soiled, everything is miserable, I really need my good Mother to help free me of it. (L 271)

'Oh! what a Mother!' she continued, on the subject of Mother Germaine. 'For the body, a true mama; for the soul, the image of the God of mercy, peace, and love' (L 271). This is reminiscent of what Elizabeth had said to him about the prioress, the previous year: 'I am so full of [miseries], but God has given me a Mother, the image of His mercy, who, with a single word, can calm all the anguish in the soul of her little child' (L 225). If Mother Germaine was her spiritual mother, Canon Angles was her spiritual father; and she described herself as his 'little child' (L 271; L 208), too. It is also revealing that these two spiritual parents would *both* be her 'priest'; for as we shall see, this was a role which Elizabeth would also attribute to her prioress.

Jesus had 'set his face towards Jerusalem' (Lk 9:51), as he made his way towards his Passion and death. Elizabeth likewise, we can see, was looking courageously at the path ahead as she ended her letter with these words: 'Pray that I might give Him *everything* in the sufferings He sends me and that I might already live by love alone' (L 271). Finally, asking the Canon to bless her '*for eternity*', she signed herself: 'M. E. of the Trinity, praise of His glory'.

Chapter 16

THE HOST, THE ALTAR, THE PRIEST

'Whatever He wants...'

In her letter to Canon Angles on May 9, Elizabeth had said: 'I surrender myself to Him so He can do whatever He wants in me. Since you are His priest, oh, consecrate me to Him like a little sacrifice of praise who wants to give glory to Him in Heaven, or on earth as much suffering as He wishes' (L 271). This remarkable statement reflects not only Elizabeth's generosity but also her main disposition: total surrender to God. As she lay on her bed, weak and in pain, she submitted to whatever came to her, seeing everything as God's will. Not once did she give her mother a word of hope that she might be cured, because Elizabeth knew instinctively that she was going to die.

This attitude was in marked contrast to the anger outside the convent walls. Rumours were circulating among Elizabeth's friends that Dr Barbier, the convent's physician, was failing in his care of her. In particular, her brother-in-law, Georges Chevignard, was consumed with rage. He railed to his sister Madeleine: 'You don't let a girl of twenty-six die without treating her' (ETB, p. 663, n. 1). He would rather have had her taken out of the monastery and given vigorous specialist treatment. Elizabeth was not taken out of the convent. But what did happen, as we have seen, is that Georges brought together three doctors, one of whom was a stomach specialist, and arranged for them to examine her in the Carmel.

One of the two consultations arranged by Georges took place on May 4, almost a month after Elizabeth's Palm Sunday attack. Mother Germaine wrote that morning to Madame Catez: 'This morning we are awaiting, quite *at peace*, the visit of this

23

poor medical trinity' (ETB, p. 663)! This sceptical tone – which the prioress would surely not have used, had she been afraid of dashing the mother's hopes – may well reflect this lady's own belief that the visit would not achieve anything. It could also suggest that this was the doctors' second visit and that the first one had been less than promising (hence the word 'poor') – although the visit in May is likely to have been the first of the two.[1]

At any rate, the consultation did not prove helpful. The doctors seem to have been at a loss: deciding first in favour of an operation, then against it. They also appear to have been impersonal and uncaring in their attitude – looking on Elizabeth as simply a medical case, and discussing her fate like judges as they stood over her. After one of these consultations, Elizabeth said: 'While the doctors were deliberating together, I united myself to the Divine Master before the tribunals when the judges were debating whether He should live or die' (PG, pp. 152–3).

After they had decided in favour of an operation, she remarked with a quiet smile: 'Yes! An operation – the doctors talk of nothing else' (PG, p. 152). But on this subject she was serene – again because of her belief that all events were the expression of God's will. So she said, with reference to the doctors: 'I leave myself in their hands as in the hands of God' (PG, p. 152). A few days later, the doctors abandoned the idea of an operation – possibly sending word to the monastery, for it would doubtless have been too soon to hold a second consultation just days after the first. As soon as the prioress heard, she came to impart the good news to the patient. But she saw, to her surprise, that Elizabeth's face gave not a hint of the relief she must surely have been feeling. The sub-prioress mar-

---

[1] Although these doctors are not named, three separate names of doctors (other than those we have previously met) appear in various accounts of Elizabeth's illness, and may well be those of the group who came in May: Drs Morlot, Gautrelet and Dubard. Their second consultation appears to have taken place in late July or early August, and follow-up treatment given in August and September.

velled at such self-possession, and felt that the only explanation was the extent to which Elizabeth was 'possessed by God'
(ETB, p. 663).

The prioress herself was 'happy' (ETB, p. 663) about the
decision not to operate. So, too, were the community. In fact,
having already prayed a great deal to Margaret of Beaune for
Elizabeth's cure, they now attributed the doctors' decision to
her intercession! Why? The nuns probably knew instinctively
that an operation would have been painful and of no real help
in Elizabeth's case. But there is possibly another reason for their
reaction: the path was left open for a miraculous, not a surgical,
cure.

The Second Attack

Dr Barbier, for all the criticisms about him outside the walls, was
highly regarded by Mother Germaine, and not without cause.
Perhaps only too well aware that he could not effect a cure,
he concentrated on helping Elizabeth to be as comfortable as
possible. Considerate and sensitive, he encouraged her to eat
whatever she could manage, for he felt that the best help for a
stomach was whatever it felt able to digest; and whenever she
could eat a little more, he raised the portions slightly. So by the
end of April, while Elizabeth had inevitably become still thinner,
there was also some improvement since the beginning of the
month. She was now eating slightly more and especially took to
'Bruges bread', a type of brioche which had the advantage of
being a form of food (the only form) in which she was able to
absorb eggs.

Then, on Sunday, May 13 came a second attack, which
lasted from four in the morning until two in the afternoon. As
on April 8, Elizabeth lost consciousness – and, as she said later,
'Heaven seemed to open again' (L 275). Her life was spared
once more; but when she came round, it was to find herself
in a far worse state of health than before. The prioress told
Madame Catez only enough details to keep the mother abandoned to the will of God; over the next few days, for example,

she sent her little health bulletins containing the more encouraging pieces of news: on the 14th, that Elizabeth had slept better that night; on the 15th, that she was suffering a bit less from her stomach; on the 16th, that while Elizabeth's insomnia had been a bit worse, she had not spent such a bad night. The full reality – which Mother Germaine explained to Canon Angles – was that Elizabeth was now afflicted with an extremely painful inflammation in her stomach like 'a fire consuming her inside' (L 271, n. 1). The consequences were terrible: a scorching thirst that could not be quenched, because the slightest drop of water caused acute sufferings to her stomach. It was a veritable torment, and yet Elizabeth remained so serene that Mother Germaine was able to say to the Canon: 'in the midst of all that, what peace, what beautiful serenity! She suffers as she has lived, like a saint' (L 271, n. 1).

From this time on, another verse from Scripture began to be important to Elizabeth: 'God is a consuming fire' (Hb 12:29; cf. Dt 4:24). She would put it as the epigraph to her next letter to Canon Angles at the beginning of June – and in Latin, which for her always denoted a quotation of special importance: 'Deus ignis consumens' (L 275). And writing on June 3, to thank a Dominican sister in Dijon who had sent her some sweets to give her energy, Elizabeth would write: 'I am delighted to immolate myself to Love for you, so that this God whom Saint Paul calls "a consuming Fire" might transform and divinise your whole being' (L 274).

This verse must have been of great help to Elizabeth at this time. It would have enabled her, feeling her stomach consumed as if by fire, to use her physical symptom as a springboard to the spiritual realm; and the spiritual realm she would have had in mind was the action of the Holy Spirit. In this letter to the Dominican sister, Elizabeth speaks of praying to the Holy Spirit – not surprisingly, in one sense, because she was writing on the feast of Pentecost; but the notion of being divinised suggests also the influence of John of the Cross (cf. SC 22:3; 27:7), who describes the Holy Spirit as the 'living flame of love' (cf. LF 1:1).

Notably, in his work of that title, he quotes the words 'God is a consuming fire' (LF 2:2), and then follows this by speaking of the 'fire of God' which 'divinises' the soul (LF 2:3). Elizabeth in fact mentions John of the Cross explicitly in this letter, referring to him as 'the great doctor of love' (L 274).

A Poignant Visit

On May 17, four days after her severe attack, Elizabeth was carried to the infirmary parlour for her second visit from her mother and Guite, the first having taken place around two weeks earlier. The prioress sat with her and, while waiting for them to arrive, began writing to Canon Angles. She had in her hand the letter Elizabeth herself had written to him on May 9 (L 271), but this was Mother Germaine's first opportunity to add some lines of her own before she sent it off. She described the poignant scene: 'This morning I am writing to you beside our little saint whom we have just put [on] a bed in front of the parlour grille to give one last consolation to her dear family. It is probably the last time these beautiful, deserving souls will see each other on earth' (L 271, n. 1). It was with these considerations in mind that, in April, the prioress had had a photograph taken as a keepsake for the family: it showed Elizabeth in bed in the infirmary cell, with her black veil spread out on either side of her, which she was wearing for the occasion; and behind her head had been placed the large picture, from Madame de Sourdon, of the Annunciation – a striking symbol of the 'incarnation' of Christ that was taking place in Elizabeth (cf. PT).

The prioress continued her letter: 'The dear little one has been much more ill since Sunday [May 13]... Since then, what sufferings throughout this poor body! Her mother does not know the whole truth of her crucifying condition; her heart is broken enough already' (L 271, n. 1). Elizabeth, too, lying on the little bed in the infirmary parlour and waiting for her visitors to arrive, was acutely aware of her mother's distress. Madame Catez was herself unwell at the time, and Elizabeth would actually say to a friend of her mother's: 'I wonder if I should pray for her cure, for she will suffer so much from my death' (ETB, p. 662). She knew what a devastating trauma it had been for her mother when she had entered Carmel; and the impending definitive separation could well be a shock too great for her to bear.

The visitors arrived, to find Elizabeth emaciated but shining with joy. The prioress watched Madame Catez carefully, and saw that she could not take her eyes off her daughter's radiant face. Elizabeth knew that she had to prepare her mother and sister for their imminent loss, so it is very likely for this reason that she made no secret of her disappointment at not yet having departed for heaven.

Finally, as she felt that this could well be their last-ever meeting, Elizabeth asked to see them separately. And in these poignant and solemn exchanges, as described later by the prioress, she 'urged them to sanctify their souls, and prepared them for the coming sacrifice by leading them to where she dwelt herself – beneath the divine Light' (PG, p. 161).

The Priesthood of Mother Germaine

The prioress continued her letter to Canon Angles by describing Elizabeth's worsened symptoms, and then wrote these striking words: 'I feel as though I have a priesthood to exercise with the Divine Master over this holy little victim of Love' (L 271, n. 7). This might have sounded rather unusual (or even presumptuous) to say to a priest. But Mother Germaine would have felt that he understood exactly what she meant. For she was speaking of a spiritual notion of the priesthood that derived from, but was not exclusive to, the ordained priesthood – and which, as we shall see, denoted the sacrificial offering of Jesus in the Eucharist. As she also said in this letter: 'Elizabeth reminds us of the Divine Master on the Cross' (L 271, n. 1).

The prioress would later describe her, in equally loaded terms, as 'bound upon the altar of sacrifice' (PG, p. 160). This was the impression made upon her when seeing Elizabeth lying in pain on her bed, which was the 'altar of sacrifice' (cf. PG,

p. 218); and the word 'bound' brings to mind Abraham binding his son Isaac when he was about to offer him to God on a mountain in the land of Moriah (cf. Gn 22:9) – the Old Testament prefiguration of the hill of Calvary.

This language of exercising a priesthood was something that Mother Germaine would undoubtedly have shared with Elizabeth, who herself would say that her suffering was a 'Mass' (L 309) and her bed an 'altar': 'this little bed that is the altar on which I am being immolated to Love' (L 294). When Mother Marie of Jesus came on a visit from Paray in August, Elizabeth would say to her: 'When I lie down on my little bed, I imagine I am climbing onto my altar and I say to Him: "My God, do not hesitate!"' (L 306, n. 1).

But for Elizabeth to be the sacrificial victim, there was need of a 'priest' who would carry out the sacrifice. It had been Abraham in the case of Isaac; God the Father who had given his Son Jesus; and for Elizabeth, the father figure of the priest was actually that of a mother: 'Our dear Mother [Germaine], who is also our consecrating Priest' (L 306), she would say.[2] She was able to 'consecrate', for in her role as prioress she was the superior given to Elizabeth by God so as to offer her to God. And it was not difficult for Elizabeth to *see* the priestly image in action throughout her years in Carmel: each morning and evening, for example, when the prioress gave each sister a blessing and they would kneel, according to custom, and kiss Mother Germaine's scapular.

In June, Elizabeth would call her a 'Priest' for the first time (cf. P 100); and as the year wore on, she would explore this role more and more – culminating, as we shall see, in her farewell letter to Mother Germaine, *Let Yourself Be Loved*. But it was one thing just to *call* the prioress a 'priest': if we look more closely at

---

[2] Elizabeth actually writes 'Pontiff' ('Pontife') in this letter, as she does in a poem of October (P 121); but more usually, she refers to Mother Germaine as a 'Priest' ('Prêtre'): cf. P 100; P 113; L 320; L 321; LL 1. An article on Elizabeth and the priestly mission, by Didier-Marie Golay, OCD, can be found in *Carmel*, no. 122, 2006, pp. 67–80.

Elizabeth's writings, we can discern some of the nuances as to her understanding of Mother Germaine's priesthood towards her. And we shall see, in particular, that Elizabeth draws on the three essential aspects of the sacrifice of the Mass.

The 'Priest' and the Mass

In the first place – the most fundamental one – Mother Germaine as 'Priest' was offering her as a *sacrifice*; and Elizabeth, as 'victim', was identifying herself with the Eucharistic Host. In letters to Canon Angles, Elizabeth explicitly asks him to consecrate her at Mass *with* the Host (cf. L 256); but she also asks him to consecrate her *as* a host (the French word, 'hostie', meaning both Eucharistic 'host' and 'sacrificial victim') – 'please consecrate me at Holy Mass,' she would say, 'as a sacrifice [*hostie*] of praise to the glory of God' (L 294). Mother Germaine was preparing Elizabeth for suffering and death: a process lasting throughout Elizabeth's illness. But we can see this captured in miniature in the events of Palm Sunday evening when it was thought that Elizabeth was about to die. In those solemn moments, Mother Germaine had helped prepare her for death by her words, but revealingly she had also taken Elizabeth's hands between her own. This was the formal gesture for when the prioress received the vows of a nun, and it recalls the day of Elizabeth's own vows. Symbolically, as we have seen, Elizabeth climbed each stair to the chapter room as if ascending the mountain of sacrifice – her thoughts imbued with the words of St Paul: to offer herself to God 'as a living sacrifice' (cf. Rm 12:1). And at the summit, it was the prioress, conducting and presiding over the ceremony, who had performed the sacrifice and handed her over to God. Elizabeth, we know, saw herself as a 'praise of glory' – or, notably, as a *sacrifice of praise* to his glory (cf. L 294). And after Elizabeth's death, Mother Germaine would describe her own role towards Elizabeth as that of a priest offering up this 'praise of glory' as a sacrifice – again with the gesture of the hands: 'In these last days,' the prioress would later write, recalling the final weeks of Elizabeth's life, '*Laudem gloriae*, having become a "sacrifice of praise", liked to call her "priest" the one between whose hands her self-offering had been made and through whom the supreme sacrifice was being consummated' (S1, p. 182, n. 145).

A second aspect of the priest's role at the Eucharist is that when he offers up the sacrifice of Jesus, it is *to God the Father.* In a letter to a future priest, the Abbé Beaubis – in which Elizabeth had said notably, '"Apostle, Carmelite", it is all one!' – she described the contemplative prayer of the Carmelite nun in terms which evoke the sacrifice of the Mass: 'it is, so to speak, God whom we are offering to God' (L 124). Here, she was speaking of the way in which prayer is a receiving of the Spirit from God and a giving it back to him, in the mutual communication to and from God (cf. L 185). She was not referring here to the role of the prioress specifically. But in the light of Mother Germaine's priesthood towards her, she would have been aware of the prioress offering God to God: in that she was offering, to God the Father, Elizabeth who was united with Jesus, the Eucharistic Host (cf. L 256). Besides, Mother Germaine herself was attuned to this notion of identification with the Host; the previous year, for example, she had asked André Chevignard that at his First Mass after ordination he might 'consecrate the Carmelites as hosts' (L 232, n. 12).

A third way in which Mother Germaine was a priest to Elizabeth is linked to the moment when the priest, having consecrated the Host, gives it *to the people.* Elizabeth saw this giving of God as her own role, too: 'The Carmelite is an invaded soul, / Full of God so as to give Him always' (P 83). She especially saw it as the role of Mother Germaine: 'how she gives God (to others), don't you agree?' (L 158), she once wrote. And in a poem to the prioress she would say: 'How much, at each instant, you give the good God... / Just to look at you, [I] think [I] am seeing Him' (P 108). As Elizabeth's illness progressed, she would become more and more aware that her body was being given for the needs of others and for the Church, and she would be inspired by these words of Catherine of Siena: 'May my life distil drop by drop for you, O Christ, and for the Church, Your sweet spouse' (ESS, p. 39). As a Carmelite, Mother Germaine was well aware that Elizabeth's self-offering was for others; and she would describe this in sacrificial terms after Elizabeth's death: '[she]... had immolated herself for the holy Church and its blessed priesthood' (S1, p. 196). This passage occurs, furthermore, in what would become a bestselling biography: Mother Germaine's last gift of Elizabeth to the world.

Finally, while Elizabeth identified herself with Christ as 'victim', Mother Germaine's priesthood over her was ultimately associated with that of Jesus, the High Priest. As Elizabeth wrote: 'God is pleased to immolate His little sacrifice... His love is the priest' (L 309).

A Tabor Experience

When Elizabeth had tried to prepare her mother and sister for the coming sacrifice, she endeavoured, as we have seen, to lead them to where she dwelt herself: 'beneath the divine Light' (PG, p. 161). Sacrifice and light belong together, just as the Passion is inseparable from the Resurrection. And light *precedes* the Passion, too, as when Jesus, before making his way to Jerusalem and Calvary, was transfigured on Mount Tabor (cf. Lk 9:29.51). The disciples who witnessed God's glory there were strengthened by it; they were better able to come back down the mountain to face the dark and harrowing times ahead.

On May 24, Elizabeth herself had a life-changing Tabor experience that would strengthen her for the coming trial. It was the feast of the Ascension – commemorating Jesus' return to the house of the Father (cf. Jn 14:2; ETB, p. 668), and marking the beginning of the community's 'Cenacle' retreat: the sisters would enter into retreat in the evening. Early that Thursday morning, Elizabeth received one of the greatest mystical graces of her life. She already loved the verse from John's Gospel on the indwelling of God in the soul (Jn 14:23). But that morning, 'in the depths of [her] soul', she suddenly heard these very words: 'If anyone loves me, my Father will love him; we will come into him and we will make our dwelling in him' (S1, p. 164).[3] And at the same time, she 'saw' the three divine Persons – they were 'holding their council of love within me' (S1, p. 164), she would say to Mother Germaine.

Meanwhile, the prioress happened to be late for her usual visit that morning. Elizabeth, however, had 'lost all idea of time' (PG, p. 182), as she would say, and was quite unaware of the delay. But when Mother Germaine at last entered the infirmary cell, she was not greeted with an expression of impatient anticipation: instead, she was struck by Elizabeth's face that seemed 'completely transfigured' (S1, p. 164). The word 'transfigured' was an astonishingly accurate perception: this had indeed been a Tabor experience – a 'transfiguration' – for in a real sense, Elizabeth had *seen* the glory of God.

She now explained to the prioress what had happened. And as with any genuine mystical grace, her explanation shows that God's revelation of himself is beyond human expression: 'I could not say how the Three divine Persons revealed Themselves' (S1, p. 164), she said simply.[4] And yet, she *had* seen their presence within her, holding their council of love – 'and it seems to me that I can still see Them thus' (S1, p. 164), she added. Mother Germaine would call this episode an 'intimate manifestation

---

[3] This is a literal translation from Elizabeth's account of this experience as related in the *Souvenirs*, Mother Germaine's biography of her. When Elizabeth quotes this verse in her writings, however, she uses the more usual phrasing: 'we will come *to* him' (cf. L 184; L 273; HF 9; LR 28). Interestingly, the account in the biography does not include the part of the verse about keeping God's word. This is either a simple omission by Mother Germaine, or possibly Elizabeth heard primarily the message of love: for when, writing *Heaven in Faith* that August, she quotes the verse in full, she comments: 'It is love that attracts, that draws God to His creatures' (HF 9).

[4] 'The mystics are unable to express clearly what they experience in their mystical activities. It is only by means of examples, comparisons and metaphors, or circumlocution that they are able to give some notion of what transpires during these operations... The reason is that [this] transcends the discursive power of human reason. Mystical experiences are intuitive, and as such they can be experienced, but they cannot be expressed in human language': see Aumann, *Spiritual Theology*, *op. cit.*, p. 334.

of the Holy Trinity' which, she said, 'crowned [Elizabeth's] life of persevering recollection with the grace of the Mystery [of the Trinity] which she ceaselessly adored within herself' (PG, p. 183). The prioress might also have said, as did Teresa of Avila: 'God gives Himself [in visions] to those who give up all for Him' (BL 27:12). For exactly a week earlier, Mother Germaine had written to Canon Angles: '[Elizabeth] has loved [God] alone and has surrendered everything to Him' (L 271, n. 1).

Interestingly, Elizabeth's vision of the Trinity bears striking resemblance to one experienced by Teresa of Avila – with the very same biblical verse being heard. And curiously, Teresa's vision took place in the same liturgical season: five days after Ascension Thursday. As Teresa's description is also an explanation of this kind of vision, the further details which she adds seem relevant to Elizabeth's own experience:

> When the soul is brought into [the seventh] dwelling place, the Most Blessed Trinity, all three Persons, through an intellectual vision, is revealed to it through a certain representation of the truth. First there comes an enkindling in the spirit in the manner of a cloud of magnificent splendour; and these Persons are distinct, and through an admirable knowledge the soul understands as a most profound truth that all three Persons are one substance and one power and one knowledge and one God alone. It knows in such a way that what we hold by faith, it understands, we can say, through sight – although the sight is not with the bodily eyes nor with the eyes of the soul, because we are not dealing with an imaginative vision. Here all three Persons communicate themselves to it, speak to it, and explain those words of the Lord in the Gospel: that He and the Father and the Holy Spirit will come to dwell with the soul that loves Him and keeps His commandments. (IC VII:1:6; cf. ST 13:1)

The mystical grace of Ascension Day had lasting effects on Elizabeth's life. One of them was a different way of perceiving the Trinity who dwelt within her: when Mother Germaine asked her to pray for an intention, Elizabeth would say that she would 'speak to [her] almighty Council' (S1, p. 164) about it – 'council' being the very way in which she had seen the 'Three' communicating among themselves within her. And more and more from this time, she would speak of her 'intimacy' (L 273; L 278) with God.

Elizabeth also became more detached from people, and more completely attached to God. Whereas she had previously been disappointed whenever Mother Germaine's visit was delayed, she was now perfectly able to reassure her: 'Do not feel anxious any longer about disappointing me. When you cannot come, you will know that I am with my Divine Guests. I cannot and ought not to care for anything else except to live in intimacy with Them. I feel so clearly that They are there' (PG, p. 183). At this, she clasped her hands over her heart. This was a gesture Elizabeth had used before entering Carmel, when she had enthused to her fellow 'postulant outside the walls', Marguerite Gollot, about the indwelling of God (cf. PD, p. 193). At that time, she had been speaking from a state of fervour for God's presence; now, she was speaking from a mystical experience of the reality itself.

Most importantly, Elizabeth was now overwhelmed by God's love, which strengthened her for her sacrifice and determined her, more than ever, to be given for the Church as a 'victim of Love' like Teresa of Avila. In her next letter to Canon Angles, she would write:

> You would think He had only me to love and think about from the way He gives Himself to my soul, but this is so I, in return, might surrender myself to Him for His Church and all His interests, so I might care for His honour like my holy Mother Teresa. Oh! ask that her daughter might also be 'Charitatis victima'! (L 275; cf. ST 31; L 169, n. 4)

'Think that you are with Him...'

About three days after this event, Elizabeth wrote to her mother with some instruction on prayer – for, she said, 'I am *the little mama of your soul*' (L 273). She did not mention her extraordinary experience; but the whole letter is imbued with it, though filtered in a way that would help her mother most. It is no surprise that the epigraph she puts at the beginning is the very verse from St John she had heard God speak to her (Jn 14:23). Inevitably, Madame Catez would have seen this as simply a quotation – Elizabeth refers to it as a 'beautiful thought' she has quoted – and could never have imagined just how these words had been imprinted on her daughter's soul. Elizabeth now emphasises this message of the indwelling God, linking it to another verse in John's Gospel that was a particular favourite – the command of Jesus to remain in him (cf. Jn 15:4):

> You can believe my doctrine, for it is not mine; if you read the Gospel of John, you will see over and over again that the Master insists on this commandment: 'Remain in me, and I in you', and also that beautiful thought at the beginning of my letter, in which He speaks of making His home in us. (L 273)

Elizabeth would have longed for her mother to be given something of the grace that she herself had received when the Three Persons had 'revealed' themselves to her; and so she says, using the same word: 'I am asking the Holy Spirit to reveal to you this presence of God within you' (L 273).[5] We cannot but notice Elizabeth's humility and discretion. She does not say something like: It was revealed to me in a vision last Thursday! Instead, she points to the only true authority, one that was infinitely greater than whatever she herself might say: 'You can believe my doctrine, for it is not mine; if you read the Gospel of John...' And she continues by pointing her mother to St John's letters, and then to her other beloved authority, St Paul:

> Saint John, in his epistles, wants us to have 'fellowship' with the Holy Trinity; that word is so sweet, and it is so simple. It is enough – Saint Paul says this – it is enough to believe: God

---

[5] The official translation has 'show', but Elizabeth literally wrote 'reveal' (cf. OC, p. 681), which is how she had described the way the Trinity had manifested itself to her (cf. S1, p. 164).

is spirit, and we approach Him through faith. Realise that your soul is the temple of God, it is again Saint Paul who says this; at every moment of the day and night the three Divine Persons are living within you. You do not possess the Sacred Humanity as you do when you receive Communion; but the Divinity, that essence the blessed adore in Heaven, is in your soul; there is a wholly adorable intimacy when you realise that; you are never alone again! (L 273; cf. 1Jn 1:3; Hb 11:6; 1Cor 3:16)

Between the lines, this passage is a heartfelt plea to her mother not to fall into despair when she will be left bereaved. More than ever, Elizabeth, in this rich letter, is urging her to this 'intimacy' of communion with God – knowing that he alone will fill the void left by her death. And should it prove difficult for her mother to envisage God *within* her soul, Elizabeth makes this practical suggestion: 'If you'd prefer to think that God is close to you rather than within you, follow your attraction, as long as you live with Him' (L 273).

Realising, though, that Madame Catez needed a structure and set prayers, Elizabeth now gives her advice that is both practical and accessible. What she says next, especially in the light of her recent mystical experience, sounds like a rapid descent to earth from the lofty heights: 'I hope,' she says, 'you are making your *three* prayers, *five* minutes each'. Elizabeth had made her a little chaplet of beads, so that her mother could count how many times in the day she had been attentive to God! But Elizabeth homes in on the essence:

Think that you are with Him, and act as you would with Someone you love; it's so simple, there is no need for beautiful thoughts, only an outpouring of your heart. (L 273)

Finally, in words that reflect her recent vision of the Trinity, and also prepare her mother to have the true perspective, Elizabeth exclaims: 'Oh! the earth and the things here below are nothing in comparison with eternity!'

'Love, to be true…'

This letter to Madame Catez can be complemented by the
even richer one that Elizabeth wrote, about a fortnight later, to
Germaine de Gemeaux (L 278); it contains yet further insights
and is tailored to this young woman who felt strongly drawn to
the contemplative life. Here, Elizabeth repeatedly stresses the
importance of sacrifice and of following the will of God; for
without that, she knew that no amount of prayer would be ade-
quate – and that true contemplative prayer would not even be
possible. Indeed, the deluded Sister Anne-Marie, the unofficial
patient in the infirmary, had great ardour for prayer; but crucially, as mentioned in her obituary circular, she did not follow
Jesus with courage or perseverance, nor did she practise obedience (cf. ETB, pp. 585–6) – which would, of course, have meant
renouncing her own will. Elizabeth now wrote to Germaine:

> be faithful to your resolutions, practise the way of sacri-
> fice and renunciation, for this must be the great law for all
> Christian life, and with even more reason for a soul who,
> like yours, aspires to follow the Master very closely, whatever
> His plans for her might be. Live always with Him within;
> that requires great mortification, for to unite oneself to
> Him constantly like that, one must be able to give Him
> everything. When a soul is faithful to all the least desires of
> His Heart, Jesus, in return, is faithful in protecting it, and
> He establishes between them so sweet an intimacy… (L 278)

Elizabeth also spoke to her about listening to the voice within.
As with her letter to Madame Catez, this is another veiled reference to her recent experience. Here, too, Elizabeth longed for
her friend to have a share in the grace she herself had received.
So while she had said to her mother: 'I am asking the Holy
Spirit to reveal to you this presence of God within you' (L 273),
she now writes to Germaine: 'I am asking Him always to be
the Master who instructs you in the secret depths of your soul'
(L 278).

The letter now turns to the theme of detachment and separation as Elizabeth continues: 'Little Germaine, be wholly attentive to His voice and remember that when He has thus found a
place in a heart, it is to live there *"alone and set apart"*.' Notably,
Elizabeth is not saying this only because her friend wishes to
become a nun – that is, *literally* 'set apart' – for her teachings
are, to quote her own words in this letter, 'for all Christian life'.
So she comments: 'You understand in what sense I mean this:
I am not speaking of religious life, which is a great separation
from the world, but of the detachment, the purity that places a
veil over all that is not God and allows us to adhere constantly
to Him through faith' (L 278).

At this point, Elizabeth speaks of the three Persons of the
Trinity as they relate to us. She describes their action on the
soul in terms reminiscent of the mystery of the Annunciation,
but applies it to the transformation of the soul in God; and she
writes in a contemplative spirit akin to that of John of the Cross,
who is also the source of her words 'alone' and 'set apart':[6]

> May the Father overshadow you, and may that shadow be
> like a cloud that envelops you and separates you; may the
> Word imprint His beauty within you, in order to contem-
> plate Himself in your soul as if in another Himself; may the
> Holy Spirit, who is Love, make your heart a little hearth that
> rejoices the Three Divine Persons through the ardour of its
> flames... (L 278; cf. L 269)

And then, Elizabeth returns to the crucial criterion, as she
adds: 'but do not forget that love, to be true, must be sacrificed:
"He loved me, He gave Himself for me", there is the culmination of love' (L 278; cf. Gal 2:20). At this point, she gives the
down-to-earth, practical pieces of advice that are needed for
the daily challenge: 'learn how to forget yourself always'; 'be
very faithful to your duties and all your resolutions'; 'Live more

---

[6] In the French, Elizabeth writes: 'seul' and 'séparé', which are both found
in SC 35:5; see also L 220, n. 4.

by will than by imagination'; 'Oh! how our soul needs to draw strength in prayer'. And she defines prayer as 'that intimate heart-to-heart in which the soul flows into God and God flows into it to transform it into Himself'; this, she adds, 'is my only occupation in my little [infirmary] cell, which is a true paradise' (L 278).

Finally, thinking that this was her last-ever letter to Germaine – there would actually be one more, in October – Elizabeth put this farewell to what was intended as a testament letter: 'A Dieu, my dear little Germaine, "may our life be hidden with Christ in God". I leave you that thought from Saint Paul that says so much to my soul, and I am for all eternity your sister' (L 278; cf. Col 3:3).

'A river of peace'

Around the beginning of June, Elizabeth felt slightly stronger. This meant that she was not too weak to be carried to the Communion grille, and the timing was excellent. We have already come across Pius X's decree, authorising daily Communion, issued on December 20, 1905. It had been published in the Catholic newspaper of Dijon on April 21, 1906 and had recently begun to be applied in the Dijon Carmel. So Elizabeth was now carried each morning to the grille, where she sometimes encountered Father Donin, the priest who had been so inspired when giving her Extreme Unction on Palm Sunday evening. Now, when he held the Host out to her, he saw how Elizabeth raised herself with a 'quick, decided movement', so that it seemed to him 'as if all her physical force returned to her that she might meet our Lord as He came to her' (PG, p. 287). Then, she was carried back to bed – or, as she wrote to Madame Hallo: 'I come back with my Master to make my thanksgiving in my little bed' (L 276).

Elizabeth was currently managing to eat a tiny amount of Bruges bread each hour, and a few more of the chocolates which Guite had sent her: 'I give all these treats to my Master,' she commented to Madame Catez, 'I don't have any more scruples like that' (L 285). And when thanking Mother Jeanne, the Dominican who had sent her some sweets, Elizabeth said humorously: 'My wretched, recalcitrant stomach enjoyed His Majesty the Bonbon completely' (L 274)! Often now, unless it was too windy, Elizabeth was carried back down the corridor and around the corner, to sit on the terrace and take advantage of the fresh air, for the weather was warm at this time of year. There were also a few things on the horizon to look forward to: a succession of feast days and celebrations which, that year, were crowded into the first half of June.

The first of these was Trinity Sunday, June 10; needless to say, this was a most special time for Elizabeth. For this feast day, she wrote two poems, one for each of her superiors. These were the first poems she had written since her arrival in the infirmary, other than a short verse for Guite around the end of April (P 97): four beautiful lines inviting her to live with God in 'a profound mystery, an eternal silence', and in this way already begin her heaven. These latest two poems, like the one for Guite, were both in pencil, no doubt because Elizabeth was too weak to manage a pen; it would be the only time she ever wrote a poem for the prioress that was not in ink.

The poem for Mother Germaine (P 98) contains sixteen lines and creates a little story using the Trinity as a setting, for it is in the bosom of the Three, Elizabeth says, that she receives a magnificent present. In this tale, she sees the Father's heart directed to the prioress with a burning arrow – recalling the Transverberation of Teresa (cf. BL 29:13). Jesus takes the arrow out of the furnace and hands it to Elizabeth as a pledge of his love. He then instructs her to give a message to Mother Germaine: 'Tell her "that *she is loved*", O praise of glory'. Elizabeth had the intuition to know that the prioress needed to hear this message, as well as the boldness to express it to her; she would repeat it, loud and clear, in *Let Yourself Be Loved*. Elizabeth may well have felt that the prioress was burdened with her responsibilities (cf. CW I, p. 176) and that she was possibly overlooking the reality of this important lesson from Scripture (which Elizabeth quotes

as an epigraph for this poem): 'We have believed in God's love
for us' (1Jn 4:16).

The second poem (P 99) was for Sister Marie of the Trinity
who, like Elizabeth, had a feast day on Trinity Sunday. This time,
the Trinity is not used as the framework for a point to be made
but is itself the central message. Elizabeth rarely used images in
her writings, though a favourite one of hers, thanks probably
to the influence of Thérèse or John of the Cross (cf. SS, p. 77;
LF 1:30), was that of the ocean. This poem is about a 'river', but
there is the feel of an ocean in her description of the water's
grandeur and depth. The eight resonant lines give the impression of eight wide steps, descending further and further into the
depths of contemplation:

> May the grace of God flood you and invade you,
> Spreading out in you like a river of peace.
> May [God's grace] bury you under its tranquil streams
> So that nothing from outside may ever touch you, even
>   lightly.
> In this depth, this calm and this mystery
> You will be visited by the Divinity.
> That is where I fête you in silence, O my Mother,
> Adoring, with you, the Holy Trinity. (P 99)

And Elizabeth signed it with the name which, by now, would
have been known as hers in the community: 'Laudem gloriae'.[7]

'There are no more sacrifices...'

On the Tuesday, Guite brought her young daughters to see
Elizabeth. Madame Catez had already left for Paris, where she
was spending a few days with the Hallo family so as to attend
the three days of celebrations, from the 11th to the 13th, in
honour of the Carmelites of Compiègne; they had been beatified a fortnight earlier, on May 27. These were the sixteen

---

[7] At some point during Elizabeth's time in the infirmary, Sister Aimée noticed
that the prioress and a few of the sisters were calling Elizabeth 'Laudem': cf.
PD, p. 198.

Carmelite nuns executed at the guillotine during the Terror
that followed the French Revolution; in fact, even before their
arrest, they had offered their lives to God.[8] The Hallos lived
in the Rue Vavin, so it would have been a short but agreeable
walk alongside the Luxembourg Gardens to the church of St
Sulpice; this was the venue for the June triduum, as it had been
the family parish of the prioress of the martyred Carmelites,
Teresa of St Augustine.

Elizabeth's heart seemed to miss a beat when she considered the privilege of shedding one's blood for Christ. She
even said to her mother: 'Oh! what happiness if your daughter
could also give her God the witness of her blood! That would
be worth the pain of staying on earth and seeing her dream
of Heaven vanish. But she has found that Heaven on earth'
(L 280). We might think that at this point she would speak of
her terrible sufferings – the equivalent of martyrdom. But this
would have been too harrowing for her mother to hear; and
besides, Elizabeth was not in the habit of turning in on herself.
So instead, she spoke of 'Heaven on earth', which was love: 'you
see,' she explained, 'there is a phrase from Saint Paul that is
like a summary of my life and could be written on every one of
its moments: "Propter nimiam charitatem". Yes, all these floods
of graces are because He has loved me exceedingly' (L 280; cf.
Eph 2:4). Again, as in her poem to Mother Germaine for the
feast of the Trinity (P 98), Elizabeth placed the emphasis not on
loving but on *being loved*; the knowledge of being loved by God
must surely have overwhelmed her even more since her vision
on Ascension Day.

The beatification of the martyrs of Compiègne would have
caught the attention of the French public at this time of conflict
between Church and State. Canon Angles, we recall, had written
in April that this was 'a time when the saints are so necessary
[to France]' (ETB, p. 661) – and how relevant in the case of

---

[8] See the excellent account by William Bush: *To Quell the Terror: The Mystery
of the Vocation of the Sixteen Carmelites of Compiègne guillotined July 17, 1794*,
Washington, DC: ICS Publications, 1999.

saints who had been martyred by the French State! May was also the time of the next elections, and these kept the anticlerical majority in power. One day around this time, Madame Catez told Elizabeth – in her perennial hope of bringing her daughter home again – that if the Carmel had to go into exile abroad, she would be too ill to travel and that she, her mother, would have to prevent her from leaving. Elizabeth replied with serenity, all the while taking care not to raise unfounded hopes of a cure that would only be dashed: 'Oh well, Mama, if it is the will of God, I will go to die in your house' (ETB, p. 662).

As we have seen, one good effect of the Law of Separation was that private worship was no longer under Government control. So for the first time in three years, the public could attend the Corpus Christi octave in the Carmelite chapel and pray before the Blessed Sacrament there throughout those eight days; this may be the reason why the chapel's reopening was mentioned in the Dijon Catholic paper on May 12, 1906, to give a month's notice of the octave. Elizabeth reminisced to her mother about how she 'used to love spending hours and entire days' (L 285) before the Blessed Sacrament. But this year, she was too weak to do so. Instead of expressing disappointment, though, she made this astonishing statement: 'But I love the will of my adored Master even more, and there are no more sacrifices for me' (L 285).

By 'no more sacrifices' Elizabeth meant that as she saw the will of Jesus in every event, he was just as present to her, even when she could not physically be before the Real Presence. Moreover, she knew he would compensate her for this, as she explained: 'if I cannot go to Him, He comes to me to embrace my soul with the tenderness of a mother' (L 285). Even before entering Carmel, Elizabeth had shown this kind of spiritual maturity when she was too unwell to go to Communion: 'the good God has no need of the Sacrament to come to me' (L 62; cf. IN 10). For his coming to her gave her everything she needed, and most of all himself. Continuing her letter, she said to her mother: 'Your daughter is truly a happy creature, a child spoiled by God' (L 285). Given the intensity of her sufferings, she could have felt justified, at a non-spiritual level, in finding herself not 'spoiled' but severely in want. Her words speak reams about the richness of her spiritual life.

In Honour of Mother Germaine

The climax of that week – probably one of the high points of Elizabeth's whole year – was Mother Germaine's own feast day on June 15. It was said that Elizabeth always took more pleasure in this day than in her own feast day (cf. PD, p. 196); but this year made it particularly special as Elizabeth knew it was the last time she would be there to celebrate it. So she threw herself into assiduous planning. Firstly, she asked Canon Angles to say Mass for Mother Germaine: 'I need your chalice' (L 275), she told him! She also asked Marie-Louise Hallo (cf. L 277) to have a Mass said for the prioress at Montmartre, by which Elizabeth meant the basilica of the Sacred Heart.

Then, in the secrecy of the infirmary cell when Mother Germaine was absent, she was joined by Sister Anne-Marie in preparing some gifts. One was a joint four-page letter (L 284) in which Elizabeth listed, in festive violet-coloured ink, all the prayers they would offer for their prioress. Elizabeth included this sister in her own spirituality, describing them as 'the two Praises of Glory' (L 284). The letter expressed gratitude to God for the gift of the prioress – 'so good a Mother' – and carried this solemn Latin title: 'PROPTER NIMIAM CHARITATEM' – 'BECAUSE OF HIS EXCEEDING LOVE' (Eph 2:4).

The other joint venture was a poem (P 101) to be performed, as we shall see; they each composed two eight-line verses – Elizabeth's being the second and fourth – and wrote them out in their own hand, Elizabeth again using violet ink. They also called in Sister Geneviève, with her gift of calligraphy, to write out the epigraph; this was another Scripture passage vital to Elizabeth: 'God has predestined us by a decree of his will so that we might be the praise of his glory' (Eph 1:11–12). And Marie-Louise Hallo, with the help of her brother Charles, was asked to create items for a display (cf. L 277): all of them were to be symbolic and made according to Elizabeth's detailed instructions.

On the evening of the 14th, some of the sisters carried Elizabeth on a chaise longue down the corridor and into the chapter room where, for the very first time since moving to the infirmary, she had the joy of being surrounded once more by the whole community. Normally, she was too weak to bear being in the presence of a large group; but that evening, she managed to join them to sing in honour of the prioress on the eve of her feast day.

The following evening, Elizabeth delighted in the 'private' celebrations (L 286; L 288) – 'intimate' ones, she said literally – when Mother Germaine came to join her and Sister Anne-Marie in the little infirmary cell. The prioress walked in, to be greeted with an elaborate display consisting of a bouquet, cards, letters and gifts, including some from Elizabeth's family. At some point, the two invalids sang or recited their verses. Elizabeth's are reminiscent of when she had used the Trinity as a framework to introduce a story or message (cf. P 98). She follows the same strategy in this new poem (P 101), in a way that is as contrived as it is touching: the 'mystery of the Three', she says, is reproduced by Mother Germaine, Sister Anne-Marie and herself! There is, however, some logic shown in this, in that the second and third persons emanate from the first. In the final stanza, Elizabeth delivers her message to the prioress: 'He wants to enclose you "in this fortress", / This deep abyss of holy recollection' (P 101). This was the first time in Elizabeth's writings – along with a letter that same day (L 284) – that she had used the image of the 'fortress' of recollection. It comes from the last chapter of *The Spiritual Canticle*, where John of the Cross describes the soul, transformed by mystical marriage, enclosed with the Bridegroom in the fortress of interior recollection (cf. SC 40:3).

As the prioress examined the gifts – thanks, in large part, to Marie-Louise Hallo – she would have been struck by their symbolism which expressed the essence of Elizabeth's spiritual life as well as her own inclusion in it. One of these was a picture. Elizabeth had asked Marie-Louise if Charles could draw the Trinity and three souls, the three who would be celebrating the private feast – but the soul of Mother Germaine, she had said, must be depicted as 'more beautiful' than the others! These souls were seen holding a harp, singing the praise of God's glory. There was also an accompanying inscription from Ephesians 1:12, which Elizabeth herself had translated from French into Latin, and which she had asked Charles Hallo to correct.

The next gift symbolised the priesthood of Mother Germaine. Marie-Louise, as instructed, had made a proper-sized chalice out of gold cardboard, and it contained three 'hosts'. One of them represented Guite and her daughters; another, Sister Anne-Marie; and the third one, Elizabeth herself. Naturally, unlike the picture of the three 'souls' praising God's glory, none of these three 'hosts' could represent Mother Germaine: for the prioress herself had the role of the priest. And this was Elizabeth's most earnest message in the important long poem (P 100) she gave her, which was not a joint venture but a gift from herself alone. It is entitled, 'The Dream of a Praise of Glory: Intimate Reminiscences'.

Elizabeth's 'Souvenirs'

With these 'Reminiscences' – or, as Elizabeth wrote, 'Souvenirs', which would one day be the title of Mother Germaine's biography of her – Elizabeth gives her the supreme expression of her thanks, as she tries to convey all that the prioress means to her. She begins by saying, in the first verse, that she had looked forward to celebrating this feast day from on high, but had managed to get only a glimpse of heaven. It will, she says, be 'an immense happiness' for her to be able, in heaven – 'in the centre of His Heart' – to overwhelm Mother Germaine with graces.

Then come the second and third stanzas – the two central ones – concerning the priestly role of the prioress. In the second one, Elizabeth recalls the unforgettable hours of Palm Sunday

evening. And it is here that she calls Mother Germaine a 'Priest'
for the very first time in her writings:

> Never will I forget the adorable hours
> When you prepared me for the divine Rendez-vous.
> I formed with you ineffable plans
> While I was awaiting the '*Veni*' of the Bridegroom.
> And He consecrated you so that you might be the Priest,
> The One who performs sacrifices and who would offer me
>   to Love.
> It is you who gave to Him, who handed over to Him, my
>   being
> So that He might consume it both night and day! (P 100)

Elizabeth then turns to the reverse mirror image, as it were: no
longer Mother Germaine *giving her to God*, but the prioress *giving
God to her*. Here, in the third stanza, we have Elizabeth's recollections of how the prioress used to come into the little infirmary
cell every morning, immediately after receiving Communion,
so that Elizabeth might share, through faith, in receiving the
Real Presence:

> Mother, do you remember that the River of life
> Always passed through you to flow into me?
> Under its overflowing streams I was buried,
> When I took Communion 'in your heart' through faith.
> At each new dawn, in a profound silence
> You came to bring me my Master and my Saviour.
> May He express to you the love and the gratitude
> Which your little child keeps in the depths of her heart.
>   (P 100)

The fourth verse, like the first one, expresses her desire to
draw down graces on her prioress – which is 'the dream of my
heart' – and speaks of living heaven in faith. Then comes the
final stanza, the fifth, which marks the ultimate act of Mother
Germaine's priesthood towards her. Elizabeth recalls: 'From my
first day I have done everything with [you]' – a reference to how

she has been Mother Germaine's first postulant, first novice, and the first Carmelite to be professed at her hands. And now, there is only one thing left:

> And it is in [your] arms that I want to fall asleep
> To go and contemplate the eternal Splendour
> And to sing the Sanctus which will never cease! (P 100)

Chapter 17

WALKING TO HEAVEN

A Queen and Martyr

In the middle of June, a few days after the celebrations for the feast of St Germaine, Elizabeth began to feel somewhat stronger. She wrote to her mother on the 19th: 'Today I'm coming myself to tell my dear Mama that her little patient still feels better, has more strength for sitting up in bed, and her head is fairly sound; it's her legs that don't want to hold her up' (L 287).

If only her legs *could* carry her! Elizabeth so wished that she might be able to relieve the infirmary sisters of some of the numerous tasks they had to carry out for her – and Elizabeth needed *everything* done for her. She would also have loved to be before the Blessed Sacrament during the octave of Corpus Christi. But on June 18, as she was now feeling a little more resilient, she was carried to the terrace, where she was able to spend an hour and a half in the morning on a chaise longue, and the same amount of time in the evening. There, with the terrace windows opened onto the choir, she was able to remain in prayer, united with her community at the Offices, and hear the singing of Benediction.

The next morning, Elizabeth was even able to attend the whole of Mass in the infirmary tribune and spend another hour straight after it, 'on the same level and quite close to the Blessed Sacrament' (L 287). To understand this, we need to visualise her surroundings. The chapel was very high, extending from ground level right up to the ceiling of the first floor of the monastery. Any member of the public praying before the tabernacle, which was on the main altar, could look up and see directly above it – at first-floor level – a large painting of Christ in the Garden of Olives. Perhaps less obvious to a visitor's eyes were the two tall, narrow rectangular grilles: one on either side of the painting as the wall curved round to left and right. These marked the two infirmary tribunes. The one on the right contained the Communion grille; there, Elizabeth received the Host when the priest mounted the inner staircase after Mass. The one on the left was where Elizabeth would often pray: overlooking the tabernacle, but with her own face obscured from public view by its tall grille.

Inside was a tiny room with a wooden step on which one could kneel at the grille and look down towards the tabernacle; or, if kneeling was difficult, there was a small low wicker chair just behind the step; or, as in the case of June 19, she had been carried in and placed on a chaise longue. Whenever there was solemn exposition of the Blessed Sacrament, the monstrance containing the Host was raised high up above the tabernacle, so that it was indeed right next to Elizabeth that day, practically on a level with her as she sat in the first-floor tribune. In her description to her mother, she said that this made her feel 'like a queen at the right hand of her Spouse' (L 287). She was echoing here the words of the Psalm, 'On your right stands the queen' (Ps 44:10) – a line which she would quote the next month in her *Last Retreat* (cf. LR 13), when she would also call Mary the 'Queen of martyrs' (LR 41). As Elizabeth's illness progressed, she would say: 'My Master asks me to go to my passion with the majesty of a queen' (ESS, p. 40).

It may well have been on this day, June 19, that Elizabeth began to associate the notion of the queen and the martyr. For not only was she, in the tribune, 'at the right hand' of Jesus, aware of herself as a suffering bride; she also reflected, that day, on the Order of Carmel 'made famous by so many saints and martyrs', and on how she, too, wished to follow the path of martyrdom:[1]

Oh! how happy I would be if my Master also wanted me to pour out my blood for Him! But what I ask of Him especially

---

[1] Elizabeth would especially have had in mind the recently beatified martyrs of Compiègne, and in this letter she mentions a little book on them which is a gift from Madame Hallo: cf. L 287, n. 7.

is that martyrdom of love that consumed my holy Mother Teresa, whom the Church proclaims a 'victim of charity'; and since the Truth has said that the greatest proof of love is to give one's life for one's beloved, I am giving Him mine; it has been His for a long time, so He can do with it whatever He wishes, and if I am not a martyr by blood, I want to be one by love! (L 287; cf. Jn 15:13)

On Reading and Writing

A new symptom was coming to light, as Elizabeth's voice was becoming much weaker. This caused problems of its own because her voice could hardly carry when she had to communicate through a closed grille. One such difficult scenario was confession: 'it is all I can do to tell my sins' (L 287), she wrote to her mother. Another was parlour visits, though fortunately not in the case of her family whom she was allowed to see with the grille open; this made it possible for her to be heard even though speaking softly.

However, if the spoken word was drying up, the written word was proliferating. Mother Germaine lifted all the usual rules on correspondence where Elizabeth was concerned, and around this time gave her permission to write one letter a day; the prioress felt that two, however, would tire her. So as Elizabeth was writing to Madame de Vathaire on the 20th, Mother Germaine herself wrote to Madame Catez that day. The prioress had a brainwave. As the lady was still in Paris for a few days, staying with the Hallos, Mother Germaine asked her to bring back a special present for her daughter: 'Along with prayer,' she said, 'what makes her happy are books that speak of God in the movement of her soul; these fill her solitary days. Now among these books one captivates her, but I cannot let her have it because it is the only one in the Community and has many friends. It is...' (L 288, n. 7). The title of this book was *Ruysbroeck the Admirable.*[2]

---

[2] Blessed John Ruysbroeck is known as 'the Admirable Doctor'; also, 'the Divine Doctor'.

Blessed John Ruysbroeck, the fourteenth-century Flemish mystic, would be a major influence on Elizabeth in these last months of her life. His appeal would be similar to that of John of the Cross. For as the prioress had said so perceptively: Elizabeth loved writings that spoke of 'God in the movement of her soul'. This word, 'movement', reflects the *dynamism* of the indwelling God, for Elizabeth was always aware that the three indwelling Guests were *alive* and *active* in her. And she, too, was vitally alive on the inside: for all the weakness of her body, her reading of this book would not be simply to pass the time during her 'solitary days', but itself a dynamic input into her continually evolving spirituality.

On Saturday, June 23, Madame Catez arrived for her fourth fortnightly visit to the infirmary parlour. She brought with her not one spiritual book but two, the second being the *Maxims* of John of the Cross which was a gift from Madame Hallo. But after the visit, Elizabeth first plunged into Ruysbroeck. The next day, she was already writing enthusiastically to Guite, calling this book as admirable as its title and quoting these lines of Ruysbroeck – the first of many quotations from him that summer: 'The one who is holiest is the one who is most loving, the one who gazes the most toward God and most fully satisfies the sight of His gaze' (L 288).

While Ruysbroeck's contemplative writings resemble those of John of the Cross, his impact on Elizabeth also has something in common with St Paul. Elizabeth would describe her new book as 'magnificent' (L 300), the same word she had used when speaking of the letters of St Paul (cf. L 191). And she would also immerse herself in Ruysbroeck, as in St Paul, finding favourite quotations and weaving them together. A striking parallel can be seen from her last two 'Intimate Notes': the first of these was her 'retreat devotion' of 1905 (IN 16), a mosaic of quotations mostly from Philippians; and in the summer of 1906, she wrote a piece of almost identical format and length (IN 17), this time comprising passages from Ruysbroeck.

There are obvious differences, though, between the two great authors. Ruysbroeck was a spiritual writer who focused on contemplation and the encounter with God in the depths of the soul; St Paul gave Elizabeth an insight into such things as God's plan of salvation, the mystery of Christ, her identity as God's 'temple', and the call to be a praise of glory. St Paul, we could say, gave her theology as well as spirituality. Another difference is that Elizabeth admired Ruysbroeck's writings, but she loved St Paul as much as his works – her 'dear Saint Paul' (L 239) who had a 'great, generous heart' (L 264). There is no evidence that the personality of Ruysbroeck himself impinged on Elizabeth: she met him instead at the level of his *ideas* – though this would, nonetheless, prove to be an extremely deep encounter.

The 'Abyss' of Love

One idea that resonated for Elizabeth in the writings of Ruysbroeck was the image of the 'abyss'. She had used it several times before, over the years, and was familiar with it from the Psalms, Catherine of Siena, John of the Cross and Thérèse; later that summer, she would also meet the 'double abyss' in another mystical writer, Angela of Foligno. But during the coming weeks, it was a word that would occur regularly in her writings, thanks to her reading of Ruysbroeck – for this book, she would say, 'always speaks of [the] interior "abyss"' (L 292).[3]

The notion of the 'abyss' corresponded well with Elizabeth's inclination towards the movement of descent into the depths of her soul; in this connection, she loved to interpret these words of Jesus to Zacchaeus: 'Hurry and come down' (Lk 19:5; cf. HF 7). She shared her discovery with Guite: 'I'm reading magnificent things in the book from Mama (tell her that); it always speaks of that interior "abyss" in which we must immerse and lose ourselves, that abyss of love we possess within us where beatitude awaits us if we are faithful in returning there. Little sister, union

---

[3] See L 292, n. 2, for an excellent note by Conrad De Meester, OCD on Elizabeth's use of the term 'abyss'.

in that very simple movement, in that descent toward our interior abyss' (L 292). And: 'I have so many desires for your soul, or rather I have only one, that you love, that you be all love, that you move only in love, that you give happiness to Love; that He might hollow out His abyss in your soul and that you might always be present to Him there' (L 288). The 'abyss' in the soul, then, is the result of God's action of 'hollowing out' a space for himself, creating a deep place where a person may be totally present to him. And, as we can see, Elizabeth sees the 'abyss' – the inner dwelling enabling union with God – as a springboard into exploring how to live by love.

As this letter continues, we get an indirect glimpse into how Elizabeth, worn out after yet another night of insomnia, may have waited for the dawn to rise on those beautiful June mornings, and let her heart rise, too:

> Little praise of glory, let us sing our hymn to Love together day and night; with David let us say: 'I want to awake the dawn!', that is: before the dawn appears, I am already loving… It is so simple to love, it is surrendering yourself to all His desires, just as He surrendered Himself to those of the Father; it is abiding in Him… it is suffering for Him, gathering up with joy each sacrifice, each immolation that permits us to give joy to His Heart. (L 288; cf. Ps 56:9)

Elizabeth, though, never loses sight of the relationship with God as a two-way movement. Love, she had recently written, quoting John of the Cross, makes the soul 'in some way the equal of God' and 'establishes unity' (L 274; cf. SC 28:1; 36:1). To suffer was, for Elizabeth, to show her love for God as she allowed herself to be moulded into the likeness of Christ; and likewise, she felt that by sending her suffering, God was showing his love for her. Writing to Madame Hallo, to thank her for the copy of the *Maxims* by John of the Cross, Elizabeth echoes his *Spiritual Canticle* as she describes her own illness as one of love: 'this sickness…seems a little mysterious to me, and I call it the sickness of love, for is it not He…who is working on us, who is consuming us! I am still on my little bed, wholly abandoned to my Master, wholly joyful beforehand for all that He will do' (L 289; cf. SC 11:13; 10:1).

'Earthly offices'

Elizabeth's letters at this time, around the end of June and the beginning of July, are marked with a sense of imminent death and a longing to go to heaven soon: 'Death is so sweet for a Carmelite that its perspective gave me only joy' (L 290), she wrote to Cécile Lignon as she recalled the attack in which she had expected to die; and to Louise Demoulin, she spoke of 'His Heaven that I so desire' (L 291). Elizabeth was not writing in reply to Louise, but sending a farewell letter which she wrote of her own initiative. It is one of the starkest:

> He loves brave and generous hearts... And then remember that love must end in sacrifice... May His holy will be the two-edged sword that immolates you at every moment; go [and] learn this science near Jesus in the agony of the garden, when His crushed soul cried out: 'May Your will be done and not mine.' (L 291; cf. Mk 14:36)

These words reflect the virile courage which Elizabeth was exercising during her own 'agony'. Not least because, unlike some of her other letters which speak of suffering, this passage does not appear to have been written with the recipient's own situation in mind. Especially as Elizabeth seems not to have heard from Louise for a while: 'It has been a long time since I have seen you,' she writes, and she informs Louise that she has been in the infirmary for the last three months. Finally, she says: 'I hope I will soon go to see Him in His light, in His beauty, to sing the canticle of the Lamb with the procession of virgins' (L 291).

Uplifting this may have been. But all this talk about wanting to die was getting a bit much for Mother Germaine! In fact, the prioress could not help feeling that Elizabeth's longings for heaven were getting in the way of the community's prayers for her! Worse still: 'heaven seemed to side with [Elizabeth]' (PG, p. 172). So around the beginning of July, she gave Elizabeth a talking-to. She told her that she should try and wish to be cured – indeed, *pray* to be cured. She also knew just how to strike her conscience: if, she said, Elizabeth regained her health, then she could spend her future years working zealously for the community, and that would show proof of her gratitude for the graces she had received in religious life (cf. PG, p. 172).

This struck a chord. Elizabeth duly obeyed: she prayed to be cured. But no sooner had she done so, than she was astonished to hear a voice speak within the depths of her soul – an intimation from God which filled her with peace and joy. It said: 'Earthly offices are no longer for you' (PG, p. 172). Elizabeth now reported back to the prioress! She even requested that the community stop praying for her cure. They duly obliged – but only in Elizabeth's hearing! In reality, they continued as assiduously as before, with novena after novena to Venerable Margaret of Beaune.

This was not the first time Mother Germaine had tried to counteract Elizabeth's impatience, only to be overruled by divine intervention. In the autumn of 1901, the still-new postulant could not wait to become a novice, and she had longed to receive the habit and the white mantle soon – which was somewhat premature! Then, during the octave of the feast of Teresa of Avila, as we have seen, Elizabeth received an intimation that this would happen on December 8, feast of the Immaculate Conception, when she would have been in Carmel for only four months. Elizabeth informed the prioress, but Mother Germaine told her that the community might actually vote to postpone her clothing! However, the community, knowing nothing of Elizabeth's intimation, eventually settled on December 8, after circumstances beyond their control had ruled out the date they had previously chosen. Now, at the end of June 1906, when Elizabeth told Louise Demoulin about her longing to go to heaven, she remarked: 'He has fulfilled all my desires' (L 291).

It is possible that Elizabeth herself may have made the connection between these two events: the entrance to the novitiate and the entrance to heaven. Because she would soon describe her longing for heaven as a longing for being clothed with the *heavenly* mantle. She would write to Canon Angles in early July: 'she, the Immaculate One, gave me the habit of Carmel and I am asking her to clothe me again in that "fine linen robe" in which the bride is dressed to present herself at the marriage feast of the Lamb' (L 294; cf. Rv 19:8–9). This idea would even take hold of Mother Germaine, as Elizabeth would write the next month: 'Our Mother did me so much good by telling me...that on the 8th of December, if the Blessed Virgin sees I am ready, she will clothe me in her mantle of glory' (L 306). Meanwhile, Elizabeth nourished her desire for heaven as she read *The Living Flame*:

> I believe love does not allow us to pause for long here on earth, and besides Saint John of the Cross says so defini- tively; he has a wonderful chapter in which he describes the death of souls who are victims of love, the last assaults He gives them, then all the rivers of the soul, which are so immense they already resemble seas, go to lose themselves in the Ocean of divine love. (L 293; cf. LF 1:30)

'*Our* Master'

Around the beginning of July, Clémence Blanc left the monas- tery. It was 'for special reasons' (PG, p. 197), whatever this might mean; but it was not a decision she was happy with, and she nurtured the hope that she might be able to return to Carmel. Elizabeth extended her role of 'Angel' outside the cloister, in that Clémence now went to stay with Guite for a while. Guite was on holiday with her mother and daughters and Madame Guémard who was a family friend. They were at Sainte Marie- sur-Ouche, about thirteen miles west of Dijon, staying in school rooms belonging to the Providence Sisters. This community, like so many others, had been forced by the Government to close their school; they were now using the premises as guest rooms. One of the sisters, Marie-Philippe, showed great kind- ness to Madame Catez who was suffering from stomach troubles at the time, and Elizabeth wrote to thank her (cf. L 303). This was an ideal holiday: it was close enough to Dijon for Georges to commute between work and family; and also for Elizabeth's mother to make her regular visits to the Carmel, every other Saturday. It was ironic that her earlier desire to see her daughter every two weeks, instead of the customary four, should at last have proved possible thanks to such distressing circumstances.

Clémence sent Elizabeth two postcards, including one of the convent accommodation, on which she marked the bedroom and the place in the garden occupied by Madame Catez. Most of all, though, she expressed her anxiety about her vocation. She even asked if Elizabeth could pray for a 'sign' as to whether she might be able to return to the convent. Elizabeth was well aware of the girl's distress and longed to alleviate it; but she realised she must help her kindly but firmly: 'despite my intense desire to make you happy, I cannot [ask God for a sign], for that is not my grace, and it seems to me that it would mean putting aside abandonment' (L 293).

Instead, Elizabeth directed the girl's thoughts towards the essential dispositions she needed at this time of uncertainty and thwarted desires. And the most important thing, she wrote, was that Clémence should know that she was loved by God: 'that you are loved, very much loved by *our* Master and that He wants you for *His own*. He is divinely jealous for your soul, with the jealousy of a Bridegroom' (L 293). Sensitive to the girl's situation of exclusion, Elizabeth showed her that they were still united as sisters following Christ – '*our* Master', she writes. And even when Elizabeth refers to him as 'Bridegroom', she is not speaking of being bound to Christ in religious vows: she is alluding to a state of union with God that applies just as much in the world as in the cloister. So she urges Clémence to find the most important cloister of all: the interior space in which to love God intimately. 'Keep Him in your heart "alone and set apart",' she advises; 'may love be your cloister; you will carry it everywhere and thus you will find solitude among whole multitudes' (L 293).

In this heartfelt letter, Elizabeth is doubtless drawing on her own memories of the painful days, and years, when she was on the outside of the convent. But having learnt from her own experience, she urges Clémence to do the will of God by pleasing him. It will be a daily commitment – so that 'we can say at the end of every day: "Because I love my Father, I always do what pleases Him"' (cf. Jn 8:29). If they both do this, she tells her, then God 'will really be able to consume us' (L 293). In other words: God will carry out his plan if no resistance is put up; and for Clémence this would mean, paradoxically, letting go of her own plans for her future, however holy they must have seemed to her.

Conformed to his Passion

On July 7, Elizabeth began a novena of prayer for Mother Germaine: during the next nine days, leading up to the feast of Our Lady of Mount Carmel, she and Sister Anne-Marie would offer up their Communion each day for the prioress. Elizabeth conveyed this information to Mother Germaine in a poem she wrote for her (P 102). It is imbued with the background of Elizabeth's intense sufferings, for she describes the path of herself and Sister Anne-Marie as the road to Calvary: 'The holy Master is taking us to Calvary... / We are climbing this austere mountain, / Going together to our passion' (P 102).

A day or two later, Elizabeth confided in Canon Angles about the relentless progression of her illness – a letter that was all the more poignant as she reminded him that she was soon to turn twenty-six. She was on her 'little bed that is the altar', she told him, and there she was being sacrificed 'to Love' (L 294). Her thoughts were consumed with the longing to be in the likeness of the crucified Christ and to walk, with Jesus, the road to Calvary.

It is here, for the first time in her writings, that Elizabeth highlights the words from St Paul which she had come upon that spring when opening his letters at random, and which she had taken as her future programme: *to share the sufferings of Christ and be conformed to his death* (cf. Ph 3:10). She had included the verse as part of a longer passage from Philippians in her 'retreat devotion' of 1905 (IN 16). But here, she singles out this ideal – or more specifically, conformity to Christ's death – for not only does this phrase appear on its own, but it is made to stand out even more through the solemn use of Latin. It is a heartfelt outpouring, as well as a harrowing description of her illness:

> Oh, ask that my likeness to the adored Image might be more perfect each day: 'Configuratus morti ejus.' That is what haunts me, what gives strength to my soul in suffering. If you knew what a work of destruction I feel throughout my whole being; the road to Calvary has opened, and I am quite joyful to walk it like a bride beside the divine Crucified... please consecrate me at Holy Mass as a sacrifice of praise to the glory of God. Oh, consecrate me so completely that I may be no longer *myself but Him...* (L 294)

Walking to Calvary

Elizabeth speaks here of being joyful to 'walk' the road to Calvary. In literal terms, though, she was of course still unable to use her legs. But on July 8 or 9, maybe just hours after writing to Canon Angles, there came an astonishing breakthrough. Feeling extremely tired, she happened to remark to Mother Germaine that she was fading away. The prioress was not at all pleased! Her reaction recalls their earlier exchange, when she had reprimanded Elizabeth and told her to start praying to be cured. This time, she retorted that instead of talking about fading away, she should try and start walking!

Alone once more, and willing as ever to obey the prioress, Elizabeth managed with some effort to sit on the edge of her bed. She tried to stand up, but it was very painful and the task proved impossible. She made a few more attempts – all with the same result. Then she had a sudden inspiration. This is how she explained what happened next, when she wrote to announce the news to her mother on July 11: 'I prayed to Sister Thérèse of the Child Jesus, not to cure me but to give me the use of my legs, and I was able to walk' (L 295). A miraculous cure! Or so it would seem. But Elizabeth was not letting her mother in on the whole story.

There is a clue beneath the surface of her words: 'I prayed to [her], not to cure me but to give me the use of my legs'. Elizabeth had actually formulated two separate requests: she wished to regain the use of her legs – and *not* be cured! There was a specific motivation behind this prayer, and Elizabeth disclosed the whole picture to Mother Germaine who would later explain it in the biography. Elizabeth, suspecting that the community were still praying for her cure – although she had asked them not to, once she felt convinced that her cure was not the will of God – had turned to Thérèse of Lisieux to pray for the opposite intention. She felt that Thérèse, who herself had been 'homesick for heaven' (PG, p. 172), would understand her only too well. So when the prioress told Elizabeth to start trying to walk, Elizabeth had a brainwave: she asked Thérèse 'as a guarantee against her fears, that she might be able to walk' (PG, p. 173). And when she found she *was* able to walk again, 'she felt certain she would not recover' (PG, p. 173). In other words, we have a huge paradox: the sudden improvement in her health – the ability to walk again – was the very sign she had asked for, to show her that she would *not* be cured! Elizabeth, we could say, was walking her way to heaven. The community, of course, oblivious to what had gone on behind the scenes, attributed the miracle to the intercession of Venerable Margaret of Beaune. In hindsight, they might have been more successful making novenas to Thérèse!

It was four months since Elizabeth had last walked. And now, she could move around! 'It is a real miracle,' she said with astonishment, 'for I could no more walk than fly!' (ESS, p. 41); and she wrote to Madame Catez: 'I can't get over it, for I'm no stronger than before, when I couldn't even sit up' (L 295). Her muscles were still weak, though, and she described her efforts with the eye of a comedian: 'You'd really laugh if you saw me like a little old lady bent over my stick. Our good Mother takes me by the arm onto the terrace. I'm quite proud of my comings and goings; I'm longing to give you a demonstration; you'd surely get a good laugh, for I'm very funny' (L 295). About a week later, Elizabeth was able to dispense with the stick; and just before the end of the month, she walked all the way to the door of Mother Germaine's office, a distance of about thirty yards – where it was surely not just to turn back again, but to pay the prioress a surprise visit.

To sustain this amount of exercise, Elizabeth would have needed an increase in her food intake, which unfortunately her stomach did not allow. But she still managed to get to the tribune several times a day, as well as to the terrace. The procedure was generally the same: she would emerge from her cell early in the morning after a night of insomnia, leaning on the arm of an infirmary sister. On reaching the armchair on the terrace, Elizabeth would thank her with a smile that moved the sister deeply. Then she would immediately close her eyes and enter into prayer, uniting herself to that of the community. During the day, any nuns who happened to pass by would say to each other: '*Laudem Gloriae* is absorbed in contemplation again' (PG, p. 174). It reminded the sub-prioress of Elizabeth as a postulant, when in the refectory – and indeed everywhere – she could be seen closing her eyes and immersing herself in prayer.

Madame Catez provided Elizabeth with a little table, on which she placed her copy of Ruysbroeck, and of course her breviary so that she could join in the Offices as and when they took place. Curiously, her love for the Divine Office deepened yet more, and in a new and liberating way. She remarked one day to Sister Marie of the Trinity: 'My attraction for the divine praise is increasing more and more; if I went back to the choir, I would no longer commit the faults I did before. Then I was as though somewhat constrained, now I feel free' (ESS, p. 33). And on another occasion: 'with what zeal I would apply myself to the least ceremonies! And with more freedom than before' (ESS, p. 32). Sister Thérèse, the postulant who would leave in September for health reasons, would later recall this memorable scene: 'I remember having met her sometimes on the terrace where…she was sent to say her Office. Always I admired this great invalid, hardly able to stand up, but with a firm and mortified attitude, reciting her breviary in perfect recollection, while her face already reflected the features of the dying Christ' (ETB, p. 676).

'Janua Coeli'

One night, shortly before the feast of Our Lady of Mount Carmel, Elizabeth was given a special grace that filled her with a renewed love for Mary. The picture from Madame Guémard, depicting Mary, John and Mary Magdalene at the foot of the Cross, still hung on the wall of the little infirmary cell. Elizabeth had looked at it often. But on this particular night, around the second week of July, she happened just to glance at it – and her heart was immediately touched by the figure of Our Lady of Sorrows. She became aware of 'an affectionate reproach and a tender, maternal urging to ask more of a mother's love' (PG, p. 174). When Elizabeth explained this to the prioress, she admitted to not having thought so frequently of Mary in recent times. But now, her love of Mary redoubled.

It was now that she thought of asking Madame Catez to bring back the statue of Our Lady of Lourdes: the one which had been Elizabeth's own as a young girl, and which she had been allowed to have in her cell throughout Advent in 1903. Elizabeth had a particular idea in mind: just as Mary had been the guardian of her coming into the world, she likewise needed Mary to help her in 'going out' of it (PG, p. 174; cf. Ps 120:8). So when the statue of Our Lady of Lourdes arrived, Elizabeth gave her a new name to reflect this solemn role – which, characteristically, was marked with the seal of Latin: 'Janua Coeli' ('Gate of Heaven'). Mother Germaine called the statue Elizabeth's 'wall and bulwark' (cf. PG, p. 176; Is 26:1); it would even be left to stand on guard, as it were, outside the door of the tribune when Elizabeth was praying inside. As Sister Agnes would remark: 'When you saw *Janua coeli* anywhere, you knew that Sister Elizabeth was there' (ETB, p. 677).

This little statue, about eighteen inches high, indeed became her inseparable companion. Elizabeth was as courageous in her illness as it was possible to be; but deep down, she felt vulnerable and in need of a motherly presence. This statue of Mary gave her a kind of physical comfort. She carried it with her almost everywhere, and one sister would recall poignantly: Elizabeth 'took it in her arms when she was suffering too much' (ETB, p. 677).

Perhaps most of all, Elizabeth knew her weakness and inadequacy before God, and needed even more the security of her heavenly Mother. To a great extent, the prioress was fulfilling this role for Elizabeth on earth, and the Virgin Mary was in many ways a continuation of her maternal protection. Just before she died, Elizabeth would say anxiously to Mother Germaine: 'When the end comes, you won't be there to give me your hand.' But the prioress knew just what to answer: 'Yes, but *Janua coeli* will be there.' And Elizabeth replied, reassured: 'Yes, *Janua coeli* will certainly let her little Praise of glory pass through' (ETB, p. 677).

It was full of love for Mary that Elizabeth celebrated the feast day of Our Lady of Mount Carmel on July 16. That year it was particularly festive. The chapel was now open to the public; the statues had come out of hiding and returned to their places; and the feast was attended by the new Bishop of Dijon, Pierre Dadolle, who celebrated the morning Mass and presided at afternoon Benediction. But the greatest feast for Elizabeth was in her heart as she was seeing the Virgin Mary with new eyes. That day, she wrote to Guite, full of emotion:

> Oh! never have I loved [the Blessed Virgin] so much! I weep for joy when I think that this wholly serene, wholly luminous Creature is my Mother and I delight in her beauty like a child who loves its mother; I feel strongly drawn to her, I've made her Queen and Guardian of my heaven, and of yours, for I do everything for both of us. (L 298)

And in a short poem to the prioress on this feast day, she referred to herself and Sister Anne-Marie as 'praises of love' of their 'immaculate Queen' (P 103) – a parallel title to being praises of the glory of God.

Preparing her Family

'I am selfish, for I am perhaps going to hurt you...' (L 298). The 'perhaps' was an understatement, for with these words to Guite in her letter of July 16, Elizabeth said openly: 'I don't think I will live much longer'. She was being 'selfish', she said, for she wished to speak to her about going to heaven, and 'I love to lead you above what dies, into the bosom of infinite Love' (L 298). In reality, Elizabeth was not being selfish at all, but trying to prepare her sister for the coming separation. For her imminent death was now inevitable. When, that same day, Elizabeth had written to a nun in Paray-le-Monial, 'I think I will soon leave [Carmel] for Heaven' (L 297), Mother Germaine had added: 'and I think so too' (L 297, n. 4).

Elizabeth's letters during her illness bring to mind, in a way, the final discourses of Jesus to his disciples (Jn 14–17), in that he knew his time was running out and he was trying to impart everything to them with urgency, as one friend speaking to another: 'I call you friends, because I have made known to you everything I have learnt from my Father' (Jn 15:15). Elizabeth, too, was doing this, and possibly nowhere more so than in her very long letter to Guite on the feast of Our Lady of Mount Carmel, in which she not only gives her advice but also speaks to her as someone on the same spiritual plane: 'the abyss of your misery... attracts the abyss of His mercy, oh! you see, He is making me understand that so well, and it is for both of us' (L 298).

Elizabeth urges Guite to rise above her feelings and says, in this eloquent phrase: 'you must cross out the word "discouragement" from your dictionary of love' (L 298). The more God seems hidden, she says, 'the more you must rejoice, for then you are giving to Him'. This is a lesson of pure faith, as she adds: 'What does it matter what we feel; *He*, He is the Unchanging One, He who never changes: He loves you today as He loved you yesterday and will love you tomorrow.' And she goes the extra mile in faith: 'I am happier at not enjoying His presence so I can make Him enjoy my love' (L 298).

In this letter, Elizabeth quotes the verse from St Paul, so important to her in the last year of her life, on sharing in Christ's sufferings and being conformed to his death (Ph 3:10). But she interprets 'death' with relevance to her sister, in terms of the spiritual life and the efforts to be made: 'By this is understood that mystical death by which the soul annihilates itself and forgets itself so completely that it goes to die in God in order to be transformed in Him' (L 298). However, at the literal level, it still applied to Elizabeth sacrificing herself 'at every moment to be conformed to my crucified Bridegroom'. And this brings us to a new stage in her letters to her family.

Up to now, it had been relatively easy to allude to her future death, as this could be expressed in a beautiful, uplifting way: as heaven, eternity, dazzling light, praising God's glory before his throne... There was also, of course, the physical side of her illness, though Elizabeth tended to minimise the details – saying to her mother, for example, 'my stomach is less tired out' (L 285), instead of stating the more obvious fact of how much she was suffering. And on this subject, she had urged her mother to 'be at peace' (L 285).

In the middle of July, however, Madame Catez wrote to her of her fears that Elizabeth 'might be a victim marked out for suffering' (L 300). In response, Elizabeth did not deny what was making her mother afraid. Instead, she tried to show her that this was not something to be feared:

> I beg you not to be sad about it, that would be so beautiful; I don't feel worthy of it; think now, to have a share in the sufferings of my crucified Bridegroom, and to go with Him to my passion to be a redemptrix with Him... Rejoice in your mother's heart when you think that God has predestined me and has marked me with the seal of the Cross of His Christ. (L 300)

Elizabeth knew that in preparing her family, she would need them not only to become reconciled to her death as such, but also to accept her actual sufferings which could not escape their notice and which she knew it would be harrowing for them to contemplate. So her letters to them at this time say much about the positive aspects of suffering. On July 11, she had written to Madame Catez: 'If we knew how to appreciate the happiness of suffering, we would yearn for it; keep in mind that it is thanks to it we can give something to God' (L 295). And five days later, she wrote to Guite: 'He is...drawing me very much toward suffering, the gift of self; it seems to me that this is the culmination of love' (L 298).

'You cannot cure her'

Elizabeth could never quite get over the care being lavished on her. 'Oh! what a Carmel!' (L 308), she exclaimed, not for the first time. She was especially moved by the attentiveness of the prioress – though Sister Marie of the Holy Spirit, who was close to Elizabeth in the infirmary, felt that Mother Germaine did not do more for Elizabeth than for any other sick sister (cf. ETB, p. 700, n. 2). Nonetheless, there was a very deep bond between them; it had existed already but was enhanced yet further during Elizabeth's time in the infirmary.

In a letter to her mother on her twenty-sixth birthday, Elizabeth's appreciation for the prioress overflowed: 'How she cares for me and anticipates my every need; I had told her I had a bad taste in my mouth and she got some new candy for me to bring me more relief, and it's like that with everything; she has the intuitions of a mother' (L 300). And eight days later: 'if you saw her kindness to your child, to both of us! You see, we'll never love her enough' (L 301). Or again, to Marie de Benoist, a postulant in Paray who knew both Elizabeth and the Dijon Carmel well: 'Ah! if you could see her at the bedside of her child! I could never say all that she is for me' (L 297).

This made it all the more upsetting for Elizabeth that her brother-in-law had a poor opinion of how she was being cared for in her illness. It was probably towards the end of July that Georges felt the need to arrange another consultation, so the doctors – who may be the same ones as in May – examined her for a second time. Surgery as such had been ruled out; but that summer, possibly as late as September, Elizabeth had to undergo what she called 'painful operations' (PG, p. 186). They were without doubt the worst torments of her entire time in the infirmary. This treatment was the terrible stomach pump.

Before the doctors arrived, Elizabeth would prepare herself in the spirit of 'martyrdom' (PG, p. 186) – this dread itself being a considerable source of suffering, as she knew what was coming. Then, when it was time, she kissed her crucifix and 'submitted calmly and peacefully' (PG, p. 187), to quote the prioress. This was incredibly heroic, for the pain was sheer agony; Mother Germaine called it a 'veritable torture' (PG, p. 186) – and we recall that just a drop of water was enough to cause her stomach excruciating pain.

The fact that the stomach pump was used at all – let alone repeatedly – may well show that the Carmelites were doing everything to show willing. They would have felt under scrutiny, and if they had refused admission to the doctors sent by Georges, the rumours would doubtless have stepped up, saying that the nuns were denying Elizabeth proper treatment. Mother Germaine had made sure to invite Georges up to the infirmary parlour in the last week of July, so that he could observe the invalid's improvement in walking. And when Dr Gautrelet arrived one day, Elizabeth 'welcomed [him] as warmly as possible so he won't have a poor impression of Carmel' (L 305). Relating this to her mother, she added: 'I love my Carmel so much, I want all who come near me to share my feelings.'

With these new doctors, though, there seem to have been no 'shared feelings', but rather misunderstandings and some friction. Elizabeth reported to Madame Catez on August 2 that Dr Morlot had 'upset' (L 302) Mother Germaine and hadn't been back. But if that at least may have been good news, less cheering was the fact that 'good Doctor Gautrelet' *had* come back! He brought with him a recipe for recovery: 'a good stew with bacon'. 'I don't think he's the one who will bring me back to life,' Elizabeth commented to her mother. '…I'll bet you have about as much of an appetite for that as I do!' (L 305). She tried it; it made her sick – and the new diet was abandoned.

This was very different from the trusting relationship with the community's regular physician, Dr Barbier, who always maintained that Elizabeth should eat only what she could comfortably manage, and his colleague Dr Lucien who asked her to promise to try and eat something more substantial. When this caused acute sufferings, Mother Germaine called him back two days later and asked him, at Elizabeth's bedside, to relieve her of her promise. He did so immediately, realising that 'eating [was] for her a source of violent sufferings' (ETB, p. 709). Dr Gautrelet, however, seemed to have no idea that Elizabeth's stomach could not accept a bacon stew. And one wonders whether these outside doctors misunderstood her completely and thought she was simply refusing to eat. Dr Dubard, who saw her around this time, gave this summing-up after his visit: 'You cannot cure an invalid like her; she does not want to live; she thinks only of heaven: she will die of it' (ETB, p. 708).

'The fullness of peace'

The end of July brought the feast days of St Anne on the 26th and St Martha on the 29th. This gave Elizabeth the joy of writing testament poems for those sisters who had become such a large part of her life this year. In her poem for Sister Anne, the 'first infirmary sister', Elizabeth thanked her for her 'tender charity' and looked ahead to being reunited with her 'in the holy Trinity'. Always attuned to the action of each of the divine Persons individually, Elizabeth expressed this wish for her:

> May the Father overwhelm you with great generosity,
> May the Word imprint Himself in the centre of your heart,
> And may the Spirit of love consume you unceasingly...
>   (P 104)

For Sister Marthe, the cook who helped out a little in the infirmary, Elizabeth shared with her what she saw as Christ's own 'plans of union' (P 105) for Sister Marthe – which, we can see, are the same as Elizabeth's own desires for herself: he has predestined this sister to be 'pure and holy in His presence' (Eph 2:4) and he wants her to be in the likeness of Christ. This poem is imbued with the theme of beauty, echoing *The Spiritual Canticle*: 'that you may reflect His splendour, His beauty,' she writes; and further on: 'I dream of seeing you beautiful with His beauty' (cf. SC 36:5). So Elizabeth urges her: 'surrender yourself unceasingly' to his love, which is 'the consuming Fire which divinises everything' (P 105; cf. LF 2:2–3). At this point, Elizabeth shows clearly how the prayer of recollection is nothing less than an openness to God that will allow a person to be transformed into him:

> In the centre of your soul, in a profound silence,
> Under the unction of the Holy One recollect yourself often;
> Then you will reach this resemblance,
> You will no longer be you, but Christ alone. (P 105)

The third poem (P 106) was for the postulant Sister Marie-Joseph, who as a white-veil sister was also celebrating her feast on St Martha's day. Elizabeth saw this poem as an important duty: 'Since I am your Angel'. It reads like a digest of the most important themes of Elizabeth's own spirituality, as though she is trying to convey everything to her at once. She stresses the transformation that is happening in the heart at 'every instant'; and she invites her to 'remain in silence' under the touch of the Holy Spirit, so that 'He may imprint on you the image of the Saviour'. Elizabeth urges her always to believe in love; and she will pray for her, from heaven, that she may 'do something divine with everything'.

It is worth exploring what Elizabeth meant by this last expression, and fortunately her writings give us the clue. First and foremost, it meant doing everything while being *consciously* united with God; we see this from her comment on living in union with God, when writing to her mother in September: 'everything lies in the intention: how we can sanctify the smallest things, transform the most ordinary actions of life into divine actions!' (L 309). It also meant, for Elizabeth, doing the will of God, which she understood as the same thing as doing everything in union with him. This is how she explained it one day when correcting Sister Madeleine, an extern sister who had refused to do what she was asked: 'the Will of God and God are the same thing. They cannot be separated. If...[you obey], you will do the Will of God and you will do something divine; whereas, if you carry on doing what you want, you will do your own will and you will do something human' (PD, p. 197).

In the concluding lines of the poem, Elizabeth speaks of suffering like Christ. However, she does not speak of his suffering as such, but rather depicts his *strength* in suffering. This is an important passage, as it reveals exactly the image of Christ which Elizabeth had before her eyes at this time of her own great pain (cf. LR 3). The paradox – which she was surely experiencing for herself at first hand – is that even in 'anguish' it is possible to find 'peace':

> Under the hand which sacrifices you, oh, be calm and
>   serene,
> Like your beloved Christ who in all His suffering
> Always remained the Strong One, possessing the fullness
>   of peace
> Even in agony and anguish of heart. (P 106)

Finally, Elizabeth passes on to her recipient the secret of becoming a praise of glory: '[being] truly a reproduction of Him, / You will in this way be able to give immense glory to the Father'.

'On the threshold'

On the night of August 1, Elizabeth's thoughts returned to her family home and to the very last evening the 'trio' had spent together in Prior Street. With joy, she reminisced over the five years she had spent in Carmel, and she shared this the next day in a letter to her mother:

> Last night I was recalling that last evening, and as I wasn't able to sleep, I settled myself close to my window and stayed

there until almost midnight, in prayer with my Master. I spent a heavenly evening; the sky was so blue, so calm, you could feel such a silence in the monastery; and I went back over these five years, so filled with graces. (L 302)

That same day, she wrote to Father Vallée to mark the anniversary: 'Five years ago today I knocked on the door of Carmel, and you were there to bless my first steps into holy solitude; now I am knocking on the eternal gates, and I ask you to bend once again over my soul and bless it on the threshold of the Father's House' (L 304).

But Elizabeth was not yet 'on the threshold'. The 'road to Calvary [had] opened' (L 294) – and in the three months that remained to her, Elizabeth would walk it with every fibre of her being.

Chapter 18

THE SONG OF THE LYRE

To *Be* a Praise of Glory

When Madame Catez had been asked to obtain the Ruysbroeck anthology, it had been meant as a surprise for her daughter. And Elizabeth had immersed herself in his writings with delight, just as a fish might take to water, for they corresponded so well with her own spirituality. Now, a few weeks later, she decided that she would like to share some of this wonderful book with Guite and in turn give her a surprise by writing something for her – something much longer than just a letter. So at the beginning of August, she asked the prioress for permission. Mother Germaine was happy about this and allowed her to use the notebook with a black hardback cover which Elizabeth had in mind. Over the course of ten days, with her favourite books by her side – especially the writings of St Paul, Ruysbroeck and John of the Cross – Elizabeth would fill seventy pages of the notebook, about seven inches by four. Without thinking that she was writing a spiritual treatise – for it was intended simply as a souvenir for her family – she produced what would be the first of her four main works: *Heaven in Faith.*

It is often thought that this piece is the record of a 'retreat' which Elizabeth made. It was not exactly that because Elizabeth was not, strictly speaking, on retreat. Also, her aim was to share her key spiritual ideas with her sister. This is quite different from a retreat where Elizabeth would start out, not with preconceived ideas but as an empty page, so to speak – open to the inspirations of God and to whatever he might reveal to her during that time. She does, though, refer to *Heaven in Faith* as a 'retreat' (HF 28); and she divides it into ten 'days', according to the usual length of time a Carmelite would have had for a private retreat. She also avoided interruptions as much as possible, and exceptionally wrote no daily letters at this time – nothing after August 2 until the evening of the 13th. It is very possible that she began the ten days on Saturday, August 4, directly after her mother's seventh visit to the infirmary parlour.

While Elizabeth shares with Guite some of her favourite passages from Ruysbroeck (and others), *Heaven in Faith* is far more than a collection of lines from other authors, even if the quotations in it are very abundant. Not only does Elizabeth comment on them when weaving them together; but also, as the piece progresses, she writes some remarkable meditations of her own, such as her sections on the Virgin Mary and on the meaning of a 'praise of glory'. The work also conveys her most essential ideas, such as indwelling prayer and remaining in God – so that the central theme, as Mother Germaine would say so well, is 'How to Find Heaven on Earth' (CW I, p. 90); this is the title the prioress would give it before it was eventually published as *Heaven in Faith*.

This work would make an excellent catechism, as it were, of the spiritual life. Not only does it have both breadth of ideas and depth of treatment; it is also applicable to everyone, as an invitation to a union with God that can be lived as much in the world as in the cloister. As Elizabeth herself writes, quoting Ruysbroeck and at the same time anticipating the call of Vatican II to universal holiness:[1] 'Whatever may be our way of life or the clothing we wear [secular or religious], each of us must be the holy one of God' (HF 24).

For this reason, a full discussion of *Heaven in Faith* is given separately, in Chapter 32, as a synthesis of Elizabeth's message. But for now, the work might be summed up in a nutshell as follows. The *object* of the retreat, Elizabeth states, is to become more like Jesus – 'and even more, to become so one with Him that we may say: "I live no longer I, but He lives in me"' (HF 28;

---

[1] Cf. *Lumen Gentium* (*Dogmatic Constitution on the Church*), # 39–42.

cf. Gal 2:20). The *means*, she shows, is union with God through encountering him in prayer: in his indwelling presence in the centre of the soul. And the height of this likeness and union is to be a *praise of glory*.

We often think of 'praise' as a prayer or a hymn. But as we have seen again and again, in Elizabeth's writings, she discovered in Scripture that we are called to *be* a praise of God's glory (cf. Eph 1:12). It is a whole way of life – what we might call singing praise with our whole self, not just our voice. As St Augustine has written: 'Praise God with the whole of yourselves; it is not only your tongue and your voice that should praise him, but your conscience, your life, your deeds.'[2] And praise, as he shows, has the nature of song: 'Sing with your voices, sing with your hearts, sing with your lips, sing with your lives.'[3] So it is not surprising that *Heaven in Faith* is a lyrical work. In fact, it becomes stunningly beautiful when, in the climax, Elizabeth gives a long description of a 'praise of glory', developing an image she has mentioned before in this connection (cf. L 269) – that of the lyre:

> A praise of glory is a soul of silence that remains like a lyre under the mysterious touch of the Holy Spirit so that He may draw from it divine harmonies... she always sings, she always adores, for she has, so to speak, wholly passed into praise and love... (HF 43–44)

Heaven in Faith is a marvellous blend of ideas and music; it is worth remembering that Guite was a fellow musician, and that this connection may have brought out such a musical self-expression in Elizabeth's writing. Perhaps the best way to describe the work is to call to mind the impression Elizabeth made on the community's physician, Dr Barbier; after visiting her one day, he exclaimed: 'what intelligence and what poetry!' (S1, p. 153).

---

[2] From his Discourse on Psalm 148, in *Divine Office*, vol. II, p. 601.
[3] From St Augustine, Sermon 34, in *ibid.*, p. 538.

The Divine 'Visit'

Around the same time, Elizabeth wrote a short piece (IN 17) that resembled a 'retreat devotion'; this format, as we have seen, comprised one or two pages which a sister would read out, to give the community some idea of the flavour of her recent retreat. As this entry in Elizabeth's personal notebook is almost entirely a mosaic of quotations from Ruysbroeck, she may well have written it in July when she began to be immersed in his writings; but it is also possible that she wrote it now, as if to mark an at least unofficial retreat during this first fortnight of August – not that she would read out this particular piece. Elizabeth's choice of quotations provides a very good insight into the impact this author was making on her during the last few months of her life. We can see just how much Ruysbroeck corresponded with Elizabeth's own spirituality: he did not take her in a completely new direction but gave her added insights and enrichment.

This 'Intimate Note' is all about the centre of the soul where God dwells, and an inspiring invitation to enter there. For while the language is so lofty that at first sight a reader of Ruysbroeck might simply admire it – it is perhaps no surprise that he is called 'the Admirable Doctor'! – Elizabeth is an example of someone who took the contemplative life *seriously*, as something to be followed, not simply admired. Her soul was as 'refreshed' as the one she describes here: a soul which always lives *within* – in contact with God who is 'infinite Love'.

The most recurrent theme in this piece is that God *visits the soul continually*. Here, we see the dynamic movement of God, which is reminiscent of that of 'spiration' in John of the Cross, in which it is God himself, as Holy Spirit, who is the means by which the soul communicates with the Father and the Son (cf. SC 39:3). Elizabeth had once written of contemplative prayer: 'it is, so to speak, God whom we are offering to God' (L 124). And in this passage from Ruysbroeck, she shows how he speaks of God visiting the soul – while, at the same time, being continually there. She quotes: 'it is God in our depths, who receives God coming to us.'

Elizabeth also found in Ruysbroeck a theme so dear to her from John of the Cross: the transformation of the soul in God. As she says here, God creates his likeness in us. Again, she speaks of this divine 'visit': after creating his likeness in us, 'He wants to visit this image' – to enrich it with his marvellous gifts and the greatest virtues.

In the final lines, Elizabeth highlights the divine reality taking place in the present, at each moment: she emphasises Ruysbroeck's word 'now', and quotes him saying that in every moment contained in the word 'now', 'God is born in us'. We can see from this how Ruysbroeck was a deep inspiration for Elizabeth, who longed to be 'another humanity' (PT) for Christ – one in whom he is born anew – and to be transformed by the 'creative Action' (PT) of the indwelling Trinity.

Sustained in Suffering

When Elizabeth emerged from the ten days of writing *Heaven in Faith*, she had been reflecting on what it meant for her to be a 'praise of glory'. And she would spend the remaining weeks of her life exploring, more and more, how to live fully this vocation that was hers. She also said to the sub-prioress around this time: 'To be a praise of glory sustains me in all my difficulties' (ESS, p. 36) – 'difficulties' being an understatement for atrocious suffering.

In August, her stomach pains and headaches reached new levels of intensity. It was pain, too, that now dominated her nights of insomnia. All this became almost overwhelming, even for Elizabeth's courage and patience. Helpless, and in desperate need of the strength which only prayer could give her, she would take herself to the tribune so as to be close to God's presence in the tabernacle. Many times, Mother Germaine would find her there, bent over double in agony. One day, she looked inside, but as it was dark she could not see Elizabeth. So she called out: 'Laudem Gloriae'. As her eyes grew accustomed to the dim light, she suddenly caught sight of Elizabeth huddled over with pain. Elizabeth tried to sit up and even managed a smile as she answered, with tears in her eyes: 'I came to take refuge beneath the prayer of my Master, for I needed His divine strength: I am suffering so much!' (S1, p. 160).

On another occasion, one of the sisters met Elizabeth on the landing of the infirmary and thought she looked 'like a ghost'. This sister asked her for some information; and Elizabeth gave it to her, she thought, 'with her usual sweetness, as if she were quite well' (PG, p. 176). Later, she was no doubt horrified to learn that at the time of this exchange, Elizabeth had been on her way to the tribune 'to seek for strength to endure an almost unbearable attack' (PG, p. 176).

The same sister, when walking past the tribune, used to cast a glance inside. At first, it seemed empty. But she discovered that if she came quite close, she could see Elizabeth crouched on the floor in a corner where she could not normally be seen. It seemed to her that Elizabeth was 'a personification of prayer and pain' (PG, p. 176). What these episodes reveal is not only the terrible extent of Elizabeth's sufferings, but also her courageous desire to conceal her pain from others as much as possible. If she was unable to hide it through self-control, then she simply hid herself.

The prioress felt that it was 'unceasing prayer' (S1, p. 160) that was sustaining Elizabeth in her courage. But while Elizabeth drew her strength from God, we must not underestimate how much she also needed the support of human beings. There is no doubt that Mother Germaine, above all, was a gift to her from God – every bit as pivotal as Mother Agnes in Lisieux had been for her younger sister Thérèse. Two letters to Madame Catez around this time contain descriptions by Elizabeth of how the Dijon prioress was caring for her every need, both material and spiritual. 'Our good Mother takes such good care of me…,' Elizabeth writes, 'she knows only how to bring me relief, to urge me to take some nourishment, and, you know, mothers have an intuition about their children that others don't have. I wish I could tell you with what delicacy she lavishes her maternal care on me, but you know it, don't you' (L 308). Elizabeth's next letter to Madame Catez gives a snapshot, as it were, of Mother Germaine giving her the spiritual support she needed to cope with her pain, and of how the prioress sustained her by reminding Elizabeth of the fruitfulness of her suffering for the Church:

> The bride belongs to the Bridegroom, and mine has taken me, He wants me to be another humanity for Him in which He can still suffer for the glory of His Father, to help the needs of His Church; this thought has done me so much good... My darling Mother talks about it often with me and tells me such beautiful things about suffering... I close my eyes and listen, and I forget that it's she, for it seems it's my Master who is beside me, coming to encourage me and teach me to carry His Cross. (L 309)

As the prioress helped her to offer her life to God, Elizabeth may well have thought often about Mother Germaine's 'priesthood' over her (cf. P 100, n. 4; L 271, n. 1). As we have seen, this carried a whole symbolism: with Elizabeth as a 'host', her suffering as a 'Mass', and her bed as an 'altar'. As with the words from the Psalm – 'The Lord will help him on his bed of pain' (Ps 40:4) – so these associations helped Elizabeth as she faced each painful night ahead. In August, she shared some of this with her former prioress who was on a visit to the Dijon Carmel. Mother Marie of Jesus would later recall Elizabeth telling her what happened when she got into bed each night: 'When I lie down on my little bed, I imagine I am climbing onto my altar and I say to Him: "My God, do not hesitate!"' This courageous offering of herself must have taken all her moral strength. For Elizabeth then admitted: 'Sometimes anguish comes'. But she would gradually banish it, and: 'I very quietly calm down and tell Him: "My God, that doesn't count"' (L 306, n. 1).

It was when writing to the prioress of Paray, in anticipation of this visit, that she described Mother Germaine as 'our consecrating Priest' (L 306). Elizabeth saw such spiritual priesthood as belonging, in a very special way, to the Virgin Mary offering her Son to the Father; and Elizabeth invited her own mother, Madame Catez, to share in this priestly role:

> don't forget you've promised me, at the Elevation of Holy Mass, to place yourself with the Virgin at the foot of the Cross to offer *your children* together to the heavenly Father, 'whose entire will is one of love'... (L 308)

'A few lines from you'

As for priests themselves, Elizabeth was always eager to receive advice and inspiration from them. She was extremely happy to have the opportunity, that month, of speaking with Father Vergne on his visit to the Carmel. This Jesuit, we have seen, was the priest who had had serious reservations about Elizabeth taking her vows in a state of anguish, but who had left without informing the prioress as he had not understood that profession was due to take place the following morning. Now, he misunderstood again. Behind the grille, Elizabeth was drinking in all the 'magnificent things' (L 308) he was saying to her. Suddenly, he stopped and sent her away! When he heard her straining to speak – for her voice by that time was barely audible – he thought he was tiring her and ended the exchange!

Fortunately, Elizabeth still had the use of her pen. And on August 2, she wrote to Father Vallée for advice. Firstly, she asked for his prayers: 'that I...may ascend my Calvary as a bride of the Crucified' (L 304). It was the crucified Christ on whom Elizabeth was focused, in this last year of her illness, and she continued by quoting one of her favourite verses from Scripture: 'Those whom God foreknew, He also predestined to be conformed to the image of His Divine Son' (Rm 8:29). 'Oh! how I love that thought of the great Saint Paul!' she commented. 'It gives rest to my soul.' Finally, she asked the Dominican for his counsel: 'Dare I tell you what I wish? I would be so happy to receive a few lines from you in which you would tell me how I might accomplish the divine plan: to be conformed to the image of the Crucified' (L 304).

Father Vallée sent his reply to her from Belgium on August 5, and she would have received it a few days later. In this letter, he directed her thoughts not so much towards suffering as towards *love*: 'We have known the love God has for us, *and we have believed in it*... To believe that we are loved like that is our great act of faith; it is the way to repay our crucified God love for love; it is the "mystery hidden" in God's heart for all ages and finally penetrated, and our whole heart thrills under the life which overflows into it – and for which it was made' (HF 20, n. 11a). Elizabeth took this to heart and would quote it – possibly from memory, as the wording would not be identical – when she wrote *Heaven in Faith* (cf. HF 20). And when writing to her mother at the end of August, she began with an epigraph which is also a borrowing from Father Vallée's letter: 'The entire will of God for our souls is one of love' (L 308; cf. L 308, n. 2).

On August 13, a few days after Elizabeth heard from him, we see her adopting his balanced perspective as she presented suffering as inseparable from God's love. It was a love, she pointed out to Madame Catez, that gave her strength:

> I would like to take on all your sufferings; that is the first impulse of my heart; but I think that would be selfish, for suffering is so precious a thing, and then, what I want is to obtain for you the grace to endure it faithfully without wasting any of it; the grace, too, to love it and receive each suffering as a pledge of the heavenly Father's love. I read something so beautiful in Saint Paul: he wishes for his followers 'that the Father might strengthen them inwardly so Christ might dwell in their hearts through faith and they might be rooted in love'... Oh, may the Master reveal to you His divine presence, it is so pleasant and sweet, it gives so much strength to the soul; to believe that God loves us to the point of living in us... (L 305; cf. Eph 3:16–17)

A Very Special Visit

Two lines later, Elizabeth came to a halt. It was by now too dark to continue writing, so she decided to resume the next day. In the interval, she received a very special visit that Monday evening. Some time before nine o'clock, during the hour of great silence between Compline and Matins, Mother Germaine came into her little cell, knelt next to the bed, and massaged Elizabeth's legs.

When she recounted the visit in her letter to her mother the next day, Elizabeth would express how she had identified Mother Germaine with Jesus: the prioress had been simultaneously like 'a mother rocking [her child] to sleep' and like Jesus 'washing the feet of His apostles' (L 305). That day, too, she wrote a poem for Mother Germaine (P 108) to express how much this visit had moved her. She does it in a striking way: not simply comparing the prioress to Christ, but recounting the visit as that of *Jesus himself* coming into her room, kneeling by her bed and touching her. She then speaks of how she responded to this touch of Christ: peace flooded her heart, and 'I closed my eyes tightly in the divine embrace / So as better to see, within, the Face of the Lord' (P 108).

Elizabeth now delivers a message to the prioress: 'Mother, to the little one who loves you, if you knew / How much at every moment you give the good God...' And she continues by saying that, just to see the prioress is to see the God of peace and mercy. This is how the poem ends, and Elizabeth is saying something important. On the one hand, we know that the prioress, by virtue of her office, was standing in the place of Christ for the sisters in her community. But Elizabeth is also expressing her own long-held belief that a Carmelite may 'give God' by being filled with his presence and letting it overflow to others. Yet this poem goes further still: it shows that to give God is not just to pour out his presence, great as that is. It is to be *identified with him*. And this was Elizabeth's ultimate ideal: that the Father might look at her and see in her the image of his Son (cf. PT). This is the very point she had made when writing to Canon

Angles in July: 'consecrate me at Holy Mass…so completely that I may be no longer *myself but Him*, so the Father, in looking at me, may recognise Him' (L 294).

Elizabeth, we have often seen, loved to write poems to express her gratitude and appreciation, as well as to pass on a particular message. For the recipient, a poem, more than a letter, would give the sense of a keepsake, something with a lasting quality. That August, Elizabeth wrote another poem for Mother Germaine (P 107); and here we see how, the closer she was to heaven, the more Elizabeth felt protective towards those she loved. To her mother, she had recently called herself '*the little mama of your soul*' (L 273); and to the prioress, she now said that she wished to be Mother Germaine's 'Angel in Heaven!' – which, in the convent's terminology, would have carried the instant association of the prioress as Elizabeth's novice or postulant! This may possibly explain Elizabeth's exclamation mark which was perhaps tongue-in-cheek.

John of the Cross had described the sense of God's absence as a 'deadening north wind', contrasted with the action of the Holy Spirit as the 'south wind…that [wakens] love' (SC 17:3). And he had commented: 'thus the bride has immense longing that the north wind be stilled and the south wind come and breathe through her garden' (SC 17:8). So Elizabeth, probably thinking of this passage, writes that if she herself is faithful to God while still on earth, 'I will be able to hold back the breeze / That is blowing through your garden!' Elizabeth did not always give titles to her poems, but this one has a title, expressing her feelings for the prioress in a nutshell: 'The Ineffable Desire of a Grateful Heart' (P 107).

Towards Freedom

In August, Pius X gave his final decision to the French Government as to the proposed 'associations of worship'. As we have seen, if the Church did not agree to these groups of elected lay people administering its property, then church buildings would no longer be able to be used, and everything the Church owned would pass into the hands of the State. The decision lay with the Pope, and he was acutely aware that to reject the associations could entail much suffering and even the destitution of the French clergy. Most of the French bishops were against the Government's proposed associations. But they were also afraid of the consequences of a complete break with the State, so some of them suggested a compromise solution: the establishment of a different type of association, canonico-legal ones, which would still be within the framework of the law but would be under the control of the Church hierarchy.

Pius X, however, was unwilling for the Church to be compromised. When a cardinal asked him how the Archbishop of Paris could possibly manage without a palace and a substantial budget, the Pope replied: 'If he cannot do so, I will appoint a Franciscan in his place – a man who will have taken a vow of poverty'![4] In the end, it was a matter of one single principle. The Pope identified it clearly, saying privately: 'Always we come back to that one word – liberty.'[5] And on August 10, 1906, he issued the encyclical *Gravissimo Officii Munere*, which forbade both the 'associations of worship' and the suggested compromise: the canonico-legal form of association. The Government's response to this was the law of January 2, 1907, on the public exercise of worship. As a result, the threats contained within the Law of Separation were carried out completely, and the Church's property passed into the hands of the State. Those words from Philippians that meant so much to Elizabeth could be perfectly applied to the French Church at this time: 'For love of Him I have forfeited everything' (Ph 3:8).

The Church had defended its freedom. And yet, the consequences would not be the disaster expected: not only did church buildings continue to be made available for worship, but most importantly the Church in France had something of a religious revival from within. Lay Catholics became ever more aware of

---

[4] In Daniel-Rops, p. 174.
[5] In Burton, p. 181.

being united to their priests. And while there were fewer vocations to the priesthood, they were authentic ones: men motivated by apostolic zeal, as there was no longer any place for those who had been attracted by worldly security. It has been said by one historian that the French Church now became more apostolic and more heroic.[6]

'I desire...'

Elizabeth herself was mirroring the Church as she herself entered into an ever-greater freedom. Or, as she expressed it to the sub-prioress around this time: 'now I feel free' (ESS, p. 33). Elizabeth was referring to praying the Divine Office when she said this, but what she was really saying was that she had a greater *inner* freedom. In August she wrote a magnificent poem (P 109), a prayer to Jesus which shows Elizabeth gravitating towards freedom – longing to be free of herself so as to plunge into the depths of God. The tone is set by the first four lines, containing an image from Thérèse well-known to Elizabeth – the 'drop of dew lost in the ocean' (SS, p. 256):

> O Lord, I would like to flow into your bosom
> Like a drop of water in an immense ocean.
> Deign to destroy in me what is not divine
> So that my soul, free, may cast itself into your Being. (P 109)

This poem is fired by an inner momentum, a passionate movement in which Elizabeth longs to go out of herself and lose herself in God. And she continues, with urgency: 'I must...' What she must do, she says, is 'penetrate... / This unfathomable abyss and this profound mystery' – by which she means the mystery of God himself. And the reason? 'In order to love you, O Jesus, as you are loved in Heaven'.

With these words, Elizabeth introduces another key theme of the poem: to live the life of heaven. We have encountered this in her writings many times before. But there is a difference about

---

[6] Cf. Daniel-Rops, p. 175.

the way Elizabeth is expressing herself now. She is speaking as someone standing on the threshold of heaven – as someone whose soul is already in heaven, even if her body is still on earth. In October, one sister would say perceptively of Elizabeth: 'Her feet rest on this world; her heart, her soul, and her spirit are in heaven' (PG, p. 203). We might even say that, through faith, Elizabeth was already seeing the dazzling light of eternity, as we glimpse from the beginning of the second verse:

> I desire to live in your Furnace of love
> Under the radiance of the brightness of your Face
> And to live from you alone, as in the divine Dwelling,
> In this sweet peace which no good surpasses... (P 109)

This, says Elizabeth, will enable the transformation in God to take place, so that in this peace 'I will become like another you'. But there is one condition: 'That I will have forfeited everything for you' (Ph 3:8). Elizabeth would include these words from Philippians in her *Last Retreat*, later that month; there, she would express in practical terms what she must give up and be detached from: not only 'natural' but 'supernatural' gifts. 'Laudem Gloriae,' she would write, '...must also be able to say with St. Paul, "For love of Him I have forfeited everything"; that is: because of Him, that I may adore Him always, I am "alone, set apart, stripped" of all things, both with regard to the natural as well as the supernatural gifts of God' (LR 25).

Elizabeth now moves onto love, the main theme of the third stanza of her poem, for it is by loving that she can go out of herself:

> One no longer lives in oneself when one truly loves,
> For one feels the need to forget oneself unceasingly.
> The heart has rest and relaxation
> Only when it has found the object of its tenderness.[7] (P 109)

---

[7] These two lines are thought to be an echo of a saying attributed to St Albert the Great: cf. P 109, n. 8. They also recall the well-known words of St Augustine: 'our heart is restless until it rests in you' (cf. *Confessions* I:1).

Elizabeth continues: 'That is why, Jesus, in my love for you / I no longer desire anything but your holy presence.' The presence of God had been the hallmark of Elizabeth's spirituality over the years, and in her reading of Ephesians she found the notion of being pure and holy in his presence (cf. Eph 1:4). In a recent letter to a Carmelite novice – a friar from a community exiled abroad, whom Mother Germaine had presumably put in touch with her – Elizabeth had linked these words of St Paul to the heritage of Elijah: 'Saint Paul, whose magnificent epistles I am reading a great deal, says "God chose us in Him before creation so we might be immaculate and holy in His presence, in love." To live in the presence of God is a heritage Saint Elijah bequeathed to the children of Carmel, he who, in the ardour of his faith, cried out: "He lives, the Lord God, in whose presence I am"' (L 299; cf. 1Kgs 17:1). As the third verse of Elizabeth's poem comes to an end, it contains a desire that is quite moving, as it gives a glimpse into how Elizabeth was hiding her pain, which only God could see. Yet she is perhaps, in fact, going even further than speaking of her suffering as hidden from others; she may well be expressing a desire for a self-forgetfulness so great that her pain will be hidden even from herself, as she will 'go out' of herself:

> At every moment of the day I want to go out of myself
> And under your gaze alone, immolate myself in silence.
> (P 109)

In the fourth and final verse, Elizabeth begins by asking that God might 'bury' her in 'the profound calm of [His] eternal Being'; and a few lines later she will speak of 'hiding' herself. These two notions – 'buried' and 'hidden' – were practically interchangeable for Elizabeth, who had written 'buried' when quoting this line from Colossians: 'your life is hidden with Christ in God' (Col 3:3; cf. L 158). In fact, the present poem was a gift for Sister Marie-Xavier, for whom those very words of St Paul would, thanks to Elizabeth, become extremely important. At the end of October, this sister would ask her for a name for herself that would give her strength and direction, the way

Elizabeth was sustained by her own motto of 'Laudem Gloriae'. In reply, she would receive a note from Elizabeth on which was written a Latin phrase taken from this same verse of Colossians: 'Abscondita in Deo' ('Hidden in God'). There is another hint, too, of the presence of Sister Marie-Xavier in the poem. This was the nun who had once confided in Elizabeth that she suffered from distractions in prayer. So it is perhaps no coincidence that when Elizabeth says, in the first verse, that she wishes to love Jesus as he is loved in heaven, she explains: 'Without anything from outside being able to distract me' (P 109).

The final verse, while its theme is consistent with the rest of the poem, has a change of impetus. It has less of the feel of Elizabeth almost bursting out of herself and flying off to heaven. Instead, the words 'already in this life' suggest a sense of peaceful patience. It is almost like the difference between the two poems Elizabeth wrote on December 8, 1897, when she was longing to enter Carmel. In one poem, she had asked impatiently: 'When will I be able to give myself to you?' (P 44); and in the other she had written calmly: 'my heart is always with Him' (P 43). Now, she says with a calm that contrasts with the impatience of longing to depart for heaven: 'bury me so that, already in this life, / I may be able to remain, through everything, as in Heaven, / "In your Love" and your infinite peace' (P 109; cf. Jn 15:9). As Elizabeth knew so well, to live with the indwelling God is the most essential thing of all, so she concludes her poem with these marvellous lines:

> It is not outside that I must seek you...
> In the centre of my heart I have only to hide myself
> And lose myself forever in your divine essence. (P 109)

A Novitiate for Heaven

Elizabeth wrote another poem at this time, and it carries a note at the beginning: '*Remember 8 December, 1901!...*' Referring in this way to her clothing day, Elizabeth reminds Mother Germaine, who is the poem's recipient, of the day the prioress 'betrothed' her to God. 'But now,' says Elizabeth, speaking of herself in the third person: 'there appears the eve of the wedding, / And it is again you / Who are uniting her to her King' (P 110). This poem is not dated but may well have been written around the middle of August. For as we have seen, when Elizabeth wrote to Mother Marie of Jesus on the 14th, she spoke of the parallel between departing for heaven and being clothed in the white mantle of Carmel: 'on the 8th of December,' Mother Germaine had told her, 'if the Blessed Virgin sees I am ready, she will clothe me in her mantle of glory' (L 306). There is another parallel with religious life, too: Mother Germaine had done her much good, Elizabeth remarked, 'by telling me that this retreat would be my novitiate for Heaven' (L 306).

What Elizabeth meant by 'this retreat' was not the ten days in the first half of that month, when she had written *Heaven in Faith* for Guite. Rather, when that time had come to an end, Elizabeth had asked Mother Germaine if she might have her own private retreat. And the prioress had given her permission to have a whole sixteen days – beginning on the evening of August 15, and ending on the morning of the 31st. This, Elizabeth wrote to Mother Marie of Jesus who would see her that month for the last time, would be 'my great journey'. And she announced it to her in this way: 'I leave with the Blessed Virgin [in the evening] of her Assumption to prepare myself for eternal life' (L 306). Or, rather, not to prepare herself, but to let *God* prepare her: 'His whole work,' she said, 'is to prepare me for eternal life' (L 306). Eternity is a recurrent theme of this letter and also prominent in the opening lines of both her works that month (cf. HF 1; LR 1). In fact, as this letter reveals, eternity or blessedness was the all-consuming topic of her prayer at this time: 'Beatitude attracts me more and more,' she wrote to her former prioress; 'between my Master and me that is all we talk about' (L 306).

But with stark courage, Elizabeth was focused on the immediacy of the present moment, on the *preparation* for eternity – the path of Calvary which would bring her to complete identification with Jesus:

> I so want the Father to be able to recognise in me the image of the One crucified by love, since Saint Paul, my dear saint, says that in His foreknowledge God has predestined us to this resemblance and conformity. (L 306)

Elizabeth had hoped, in her *Prayer to the Trinity*, that the Father, looking at her, would see the image of his Son. And she had wished to be 'another humanity for Him in which He can renew His whole Mystery' (PT). Mother Marie of Jesus, we recall, had tried to persuade Elizabeth to enter the Carmel of Paray-le-Monial, justifying herself by saying that Elizabeth loved the Sacred Heart. But Father Vallée had pointed out judiciously: 'It is her Christ in his entirety that she loves' (ETB, p. 397, n. 2). This remark was something of a prophecy: for Elizabeth was indeed embracing Christ's 'whole Mystery' – Christ 'in his entirety'. She was living, in her own body, both the Passion and the Resurrection; the hardships of life on earth and the beauty of heaven; the agony and the glory.

Just hours before her retreat began, Elizabeth wrote a short note to Sister Agnes: 'This evening, Laudem gloriae is entering the novitiate for Heaven to prepare to receive the habit of glory' (L 307). This 'glory' is what she would 'praise' as she let herself be shown how to attain full identification with Jesus:

> This is what I am going to be taught: conformity, identity with my adored Master, the One crucified by love. Then I will be able to fulfil my work as praise of glory and sing even now the eternal Sanctus while waiting to go and chant it in the divine courts of the Father's house. (L 307)

Her letter also reveals her aspirations on the eve of her retreat: to let a 'loving gaze of faith' separate her from everything; to keep her whole self for Jesus; and to 'sing to the Lord on [her] lyre: "I shall keep my strength for You"' (L 307; cf. Ps 58:10).

Elizabeth's whole being was a song. The soul of this richly gifted musician was being moved by the Holy Spirit like the strings of the lyre forming 'divine harmonies' (HF 43) – words which she may have written only two days earlier, which is about the time when she completed her *Heaven in Faith*. Then, she had continued: the soul 'knows that suffering is a string that produces still more beautiful sounds; so it loves to see this string on its instrument that it may more delightfully move the Heart of its God' (HF 43).

As we have seen, Elizabeth had highlighted the parallel between her clothing as a Carmelite and her clothing for heaven (cf. L 306). But she also saw a parallel between the summons to heaven and the moment at her profession when she had been called to become a bride of Christ: the 'Veni' – 'Come' – on which her sights were now firmly fixed. She wrote to Mother Marie of Jesus:

> my little soul...will sing His canticle of praises while she waits for the Bridegroom to say to her: 'Come, my praise of glory, you have sung enough here on earth, now chant your canticle in My eternal courts, beneath the rays of light streaming from My Face.' (L 306)

Chapter 19

THE LAST RETREAT

A Lived and Written Retreat

To speak of Elizabeth's 'last retreat' means two separate things: a lived retreat and a written work. For Elizabeth herself, those sixteen privileged days of August, from the evening of the 15th until the morning of the 31st, were first and foremost a lived experience. In many ways, it was the opposite of the first half of the month: her goal then had been to produce something in writing for her sister: this, as we have seen, is the work known as *Heaven in Faith*. Now, though, Elizabeth was entering deeply into a time of intense personal preparation, or what the prioress had described as her 'novitiate for Heaven' (L 306). And the work that grew out of it – the *Last Retreat*, as we know it today – was her personal notebook, a means of articulating to herself her own discoveries as each day passed. She was single-minded in her aim: *to learn how to live fully her vocation as a 'Praise of Glory'* (cf. LR 1; LR 9).[1]

Elizabeth spent her time in almost complete silence – praying and reading. She often sat on the terrace. However, unlike retreats of previous years, it simply was not possible to have absolute solitude and silence. There were not only the comings and goings of the infirmary sisters, but occasional visits from Dr Barbier. And on Saturday, August 25, Madame Catez came for her eighth visit to the infirmary parlour. Elizabeth had not told her family that she was on retreat, for knowing that she would not live much longer, she did not want to deprive them of

---

[1] See the helpful introduction to the *Last Retreat* by Conrad De Meester, OCD, in CW I, pp. 131–40.

seeing her. There was also a last meeting with Mother Marie of Jesus from Paray-le-Monial who happened to be in Dijon during those days.

It was only when the day was over, and there were no more interruptions, that Elizabeth could write up her notebook. She did this during her nights of insomnia, and in such violent pain that she felt she could faint – she was almost overcome with agony. There, in the little infirmary cell, by the light of a small lamp, she recorded the fruits of her inner explorations.

Although Elizabeth would no doubt have chosen to write up this retreat notebook anyway, the *Last Retreat* was actually written under obedience. Mother Germaine knew that she herself would need something to put into the obituary essay known as the 'circular': a biographical notice distributed to the other French Carmels and to friends, whenever a sister died. The prioress had already looked through the black notebook Elizabeth had handed her, containing *Heaven in Faith*, but it was not as personal as Mother Germaine might have liked. For one thing, it was written specifically for Guite and was therefore expressed in general terms, rather like the letters Elizabeth wrote to give spiritual advice. Another aspect is that her own words in *Heaven in Faith* were, in places, virtually submerged beneath quotations from her favourite authors, especially extended passages from Ruysbroeck; this was no coincidence because she had particularly wanted to share his works with Guite in that piece, as the anthology of his works had been a gift from Madame Catez. So just before Elizabeth began her retreat, the prioress asked her to 'note down any spiritual insights that she received' (CW I, p. 131) – which was actually an unusual request to make. Elizabeth 'understood', Mother Germaine would say later, and 'smilingly agreed' (CW I, p. 131)! The prioress also seems to have suggested that Elizabeth might quote other authors a bit less, and write more from personal experience, conveying her own ideas to a greater extent. When Mother Germaine eventually saw the finished piece, she would be delighted with the outcome.

This inspiring work, then, is not so much a treatise as a diary or spiritual autobiography. In her letters, for example, containing advice for others, Elizabeth often linked two or more biblical verses, and her correspondents just saw the end result. But in the *Last Retreat*, we see her thought processes in action as she selects the relevant verses or ponders their meaning: 'If I compare these two [passages], I conclude from them that...' (LR 6); or: 'I think that is what St. Paul means when he says...' (LR 33). The word 'I' appears often, and it is a genuine expression of her personal quest; so, too, is 'she' (referring to a 'praise of glory') or 'the soul', both of which apply to the writer herself.

The style is Elizabeth's own voice, rather than a mosaic of excerpts from other authors. The one exception is Scripture, from which she includes numerous passages. These do not lessen her personal input, though, but strengthen it: they reveal how Elizabeth was pondering the word of God and incorporating it into her life, for it is Scripture that reveals her 'vocation' (cf. LR 36–37) to her. But just as her letters are a sharing with others of her own spirituality and discoveries, so this work, too, is relevant to everyone – compellingly so, as we can identify with a fellow seeker, someone searching to discover God's will in her life. Indeed, as Elizabeth says of God's work in her: 'This is Christ's work in every soul of good will' (LR 31).

The *Last Retreat*, as said, is concerned with how to be a praise of glory. There are, broadly speaking, three aspects that emerge: God has predestined us to be a praise of his glory; we live this vocation by being in the likeness of Christ; and finally, we can live the life of the blessed in heaven – the perfect expression of a praise of glory – already here on earth. This continual theme – of union with God *on earth as in heaven* – would lead Mother Germaine, when speaking of this work, to call Elizabeth a 'soul of one idea' (CW I, p. 136).

The *Last Retreat* could be called something of a masterpiece, except that Elizabeth was not trying to produce a work of art. But each of its sixteen sections is inspiring, memorable and life-giving. And the style of writing could be described as a sumptuous bouquet: the thoughts bound together tightly, like a vast number of rich blossoms – and after we have read each of them, we can still smell their perfume. Another image that comes to mind is that of a deep and luscious well, from which a reader, thirsting for God, can drink of a life-giving source.

Yet the very beauty of this work carries the risk for readers of never moving beyond the savouring of individual sentences. While that itself may be extremely enriching – and at one level is entirely legitimate – it does not allow us to see into the full riches of this piece. Behind the 'poetry' that was Elizabeth, there was also a formidable 'intelligence'.[2] Behind the lyric we find the logic.

Foundations and New Horizons

Given the torturing pain she was in, the fact that there is any structure in the work at all is a tremendous tribute to Elizabeth's will power and forgetfulness of self. The prioress would later say of Elizabeth during these days: 'Never did we discover her being turned in on self' (CW I, p. 137). What we must also keep in mind is that the counterpart to forgetting herself was a continual remembering of God – as well as of the goal to which she was called, and which she was exploring here with every fibre of her being.

The work's structure is not obvious, like that of an academic treatise. Rather, it has a definite though discreet outline, like the branches of a tree that carry the foliage, yet are mostly hidden by it. There is no evidence that Elizabeth planned it out in advance. In fact, this would have run contrary to her own disposition of total openness – she who wished to 'spend [her] life in listening' (PT) to God. As she says at the outset, in only her third sentence: it is Jesus who will 'teach her to fulfil the work which will be hers for eternity and which she must already perform in

---

[2] To recall the words of Dr Barbier, who had said of Elizabeth: 'what intelligence and what poetry!' (S1, p. 153).

time' (LR 1). But she was clear-sighted, and was probably aware – especially in the wake of having written *Heaven in Faith* – that she was putting together a whole work rather than merely making entries in a diary. For not just the overall piece but also each individual section or 'day' holds together all the material in it. There are no outpourings of random thoughts, nor any wandering digressions. Rather, each section is a treatment of a theme, like a self-contained unit. One sign of how aware Elizabeth was of constructing individual essays, as it were, is that she wrote 'continued' at the beginning of the eleventh 'day', to show that it was a continuation of the theme she had begun to discuss in the tenth.

The work's sixteen sections are, as mentioned, called 'days', each of which is a meditation of about two or three paragraphs. The notion of 'days', though, does not necessarily indicate a chronological account of her retreat, like writing up a diary each day without fail from the 16th to the 31st of August, the way a nun might chronicle her private retreat; hence, 'day' will be used here (in quotation marks) to refer to a section of the work rather than to a particular date. It is probable that Elizabeth did actually write one section each day of the retreat, though we cannot be absolutely certain of this as she did not hand the notebook to Mother Germaine until September 24.[3] What we do know is that the sections fit remarkably well together as a whole; it has been rightly said by Conrad De Meester that Elizabeth's interior life at this time is illustrated by 'the *totality* of thoughts expressed in the *Last Retreat*' (CW I, p. 133). The work brings together her ideas and is nothing less than a synthesis of her spirituality. However, it would be only one half of the picture if

---

[3] It is most unlikely that Elizabeth added anything more to the contents after September 14, as the words of Angela of Foligno – prominent in her letters as from that date – do not appear in the *Last Retreat*. Elizabeth probably wrote the work during the retreat, and made minor revisions either at the time or afterwards: there are numerous small corrections and additions, which also suggests that the notebook was Elizabeth's one and only draft: see CW I, pp. 131–2 & 139, n. 12.

we simply thought of Elizabeth as *looking back* and assembling ideas she had already formed.

The other half of the picture is that, during the retreat, Elizabeth was constantly *in progress*. Unlike *Heaven in Faith*, in which she was conveying the essential ideas of her spiritual life to her sister, the *Last Retreat* is the record of a search: Elizabeth yearning to discover the riches of her vocation to be a praise of glory. She especially pondered Scripture, which helped to keep the process constantly moving. Many, but not all, of the biblical quotations were already among Elizabeth's favourites, and she wrote the *Last Retreat* with these verses at her fingertips. But while it is rarely if ever the case that she was discovering passages here for the first time, she was nonetheless pondering them anew, examining more fully how she could incorporate them into her life. This is why, even when her style is occasionally at its loftiest, Elizabeth's ideas are never mere theory but always based on, and tuned into, experience.

On this retreat, Elizabeth's own experience was taken one stage further, when she received a particular grace from God. Mother Germaine would later recount it in the biography: 'During those blessed days, Sister Elizabeth was drawn towards Calvary; her beloved Master spoke to her of His Passion, not in words, but by opening up new horizons to her on the love hidden in the Cross, He made her understand that her dreams of union would find their realisation in suffering. The generous child, enraptured with love more than ever, became intoxicated with the divine chalice whose bitterness became changed for her into infinite sweetness' (S1, p. 164).[4] This makes it clear why Elizabeth was able to embrace her pain and not just bear it: for suffering, too, was part of her calling.

The essence of the whole piece, as we have seen, is Elizabeth's search for how to be a praise of glory.[5] And if we look closely,

---

[4] Elizabeth herself expresses this most strongly in the fifth 'day' of the *Last Retreat*, which possibly corresponds to a date around August 20.

[5] In *Heaven in Faith*, the main focus is expressed as the goal of resemblance to, and union with, Christ (cf. HF 28).

we begin to see the foundational, underlying structure, for this aim appears prominently at the most important staging points: the beginning, the middle and the end – that is, the first 'day' (cf. LR 1), the eighth (cf. LR 20), and the concluding sixteenth 'day' (cf. LR 44). We should not, of course, overdo the notion of 'divisions', for in Elizabeth's writings they are often barely discernible, and 'structure' is a word that somehow strikes a jarring note with her flowing soul. But when we look at the arrangement of the sixteen 'days', it does seem helpful to note that after every four 'days', Elizabeth begins something new, so that the sixteen 'days' are actually four blocks, so to speak.

'Days' one to four are concerned with the notion of likeness to Christ, and of Elizabeth preparing herself for transformation into him. 'Days' five to eight contain a commentary on extended passages from the Book of Revelation – the life of the blessed in heaven, who were her model for praising God's glory. 'Days' nine to twelve explore the command, in Scripture, to be holy as God is holy (cf. Lv 11:44; 1Pt 1:16; Mt 5:48). And 'days' thirteen to sixteen discuss the notion of a praise of glory with reference to specific guides: her great teacher, St Paul; and her ultimate models, Jesus and Mary. There is also a sense in which the work falls into two halves: with a glimpse of the adoration of God in heaven powerfully portrayed at the end of the eighth 'day', the halfway mark; and at the end of the sixteenth, the closing lines of the whole work, where adoration is depicted with regard to the heaven of the soul. Finally, there is a key focus that holds everything together: for soon after the opening of the *Last Retreat*, and again close to the end, we find the image of the suffering Christ which Elizabeth was constantly keeping before her eyes (cf. LR 3; LR 41).

Not just in structure, but even more so in essence, Elizabeth's work is profoundly Christocentric. It focuses on the suffering Christ in particular, but also penetrates into likeness to the Father and to the whole Trinity (cf. LR 26; LR 44), to which Jesus is *the* gateway. Alive with the quest to achieve a resemblance to Christ that would make her into a perfect praise of God's glory, Elizabeth now described, as never before, the means for fulfilling this vocation. Yes, this work is a great piece of spiritual writing, perhaps even a classic. But for Elizabeth herself, it was mostly an aid: to help her discern the path she must follow – and live to the full – in the crucial remaining weeks of her life.

'DAYS' ONE TO FOUR: LIKENESS TO CHRIST

Formed into Christ

We can visualise Elizabeth as she entered the place of her retreat on the evening of August 15. It would not have been a different room from usual, but a secret and sacred space: it is the 'inner cellar', she says. To understand what this 'cellar' meant for Elizabeth, we can go to her source which imbues her opening lines: *The Spiritual Canticle*. In this work, John of the Cross describes the inner cellar as 'the last and most intimate degree of love in which the soul can be placed in this life' (SC 26:3). We are here in the innermost depths of the soul – the place in which 'is wrought the perfect union with God, called spiritual marriage' (SC 26:4).

Like the bride of the Song of Songs, Elizabeth says: 'Nescivi' ('I knew not').[6] This, her very first word of the *Last Retreat*, sets the tone for her single-minded search. It is a deliberate *unknowing* of anything that is not Christ (cf. SC 26:14), and she translates 'Nescivi' with a line from the poem of *The Spiritual Canticle*: 'I no longer knew anything' (LR 1; cf. SC, stanza 26). But in the same spirit, Elizabeth shows just how much she wants to *know*: 'I do not want to know anything except "to know *Him*, to share in His sufferings, to become like Him in His death"' (LR 1; cf. Ph 3:10). To be *identified with Christ* was her main ideal, *the key to becoming a praise of glory*:

> 'God has...predestined [us] to become conformed to the image of His divine Son', the One crucified by love. When I

---

[6] Sg 6:11 in the Vulgate, from which this Latin word is taken; Sg 6:12 in the Hebrew Scriptures.

am wholly identified with this divine Exemplar, when I have wholly passed into Him and He into me, then I will fulfil my eternal vocation: the one for which God has 'chosen me in Him' 'in principio', the one I will continue 'in aeternum' when, immersed in the bosom of my Trinity, I will be the unceasing praise of His glory, Laudem gloriae ejus. (LR 1; cf. Rm 8:29; Eph 1:4.12)

In line with her major theme of *heaven on earth*, Elizabeth saw perceptively that her vocation was 'eternal': it was to be lived not just in heaven but also on earth ('in time'). So in her opening lines she gives her definition of 'time', one which also appears at the beginning of *Heaven in Faith*: 'eternity begun and still in progress' (LR 1; cf. HF 1).

Elizabeth knew that to fulfil her vocation she needed help. On one level, she had saints who could *teach* her: John and Mary Magdalene, she said, 'penetrated deeply this mystery [of Christ]' (LR 2); St Paul, too, could explain some of this mystery to her, for to him 'understanding of it...was given' (LR 2; cf. Eph 3:3–4). But only the Virgin Mary, Elizabeth felt, could *form* her, for she alone 'penetrated the depths of the mystery of Christ' (LR 2):

> This Mother of grace will form my soul so that her little child will be a living, 'striking' image of her first-born, the Son of the Eternal, He who was the perfect praise of His Father's glory. (LR 2)

It was the perfect solution. For Elizabeth, to grow in the likeness of Christ – who is 'the perfect praise of His Father's glory' (LR 2) – meant letting herself be formed as Christ was: by his own mother. We also see here a striking similarity – but a difference, too – with her *Prayer to the Trinity*. There, Elizabeth had identified *with Mary* at the Annunciation, praying that Christ might be formed within her. She now expresses it more as identification *with Jesus* being formed by Mary. But these are essentially the same thing: it is Elizabeth's longing to become another Christ, who will live in her and transform her into himself.

This passage shows us, too, how Elizabeth, who in July had rediscovered Mary with wonderment, is taking her as her guide and constant companion. She does not describe her here as merely an instrument who will form her; rather, Mary appears as a beacon of light, a joy to Elizabeth's soul: 'how all the saints remain in the shadows when we look at the Blessed Virgin's light! This is the unspeakable "secret" that she kept in mind and pondered in her heart which no tongue can tell or pen describe!' (LR 2; cf. Lk 2:19.51).

A Unified Soul

Elizabeth begins the second 'day' with an inspiring depiction of the soul of Christ in his sufferings: 'in the midst of all His anguish He always remained the calm and strong One' (LR 3). This was the image she held before her eyes and was already imitating so well. For others could see that Elizabeth had complete self-possession, despite her pain – and this is how Elizabeth describes here the state of living with Christ in one's suffering: 'complete self-possession in the presence of the peaceful One' (LR 3).

Elizabeth is especially struck when considering his strength – a strength in silence – which, for her, fulfils the Carmelite *Rule* (# 21): 'My Rule tells me: "In silence will your strength be"' (LR 3; cf. Is 30:15). Elizabeth explains this as to have a very focused disposition of soul: it is 'to unify one's whole being by means of interior silence' (LR 3); and the quality of this kind of focus is 'to collect all one's powers in order to "employ" them in "the one work of love"' and 'to have this "single eye" which allows the light of God to enlighten us' (LR 3). Elizabeth writes, literally, 'irradiate us', and an image which comes to mind is that of making oneself into a direct channel through which God can pour his light into us in torrents.

All this requires some effort on our part – something which Elizabeth now describes with the image of the lyre, reminiscent of the climax of *Heaven in Faith* (cf. HF 43) where she had described a praise of glory:

A soul that debates with its self, that is taken up with its feelings, and pursues useless thoughts and desires, scatters its forces, for it is not wholly directed toward God. Its lyre does not vibrate in unison and when the Master plays it, He cannot draw from it divine harmonies, for it is still too human and discordant. The soul that still keeps something for self in its 'inner kingdom', whose powers are not 'enclosed' in God, cannot be a perfect praise of glory... Instead of persevering in praise through everything in simplicity, it must continually adjust the strings of its instrument which are all a little out of tune. (LR 3)

A key word here is 'simplicity', a virtue for which Mother Germaine had a great love. Elizabeth describes the souls in heaven as 'simple' (LR 4) and conveys simplicity in the best sense of the word: as a 'beautiful inner unity' which is 'indispensable' (LR 4). Another key word – recurring in this second 'day' no fewer than five times! – is 'Nescivi'. Elizabeth applies it firstly to Mary Magdalene (cf. LR 4), and then to the soul who has 'entered into the "fortress of holy recollection"' (LR 5; cf. SC 40:3). Elizabeth holds onto this word of unknowing, like a weapon in the battle for maintaining inner silence:

'Nescivi'! Yes, [Mary Magdalene] knew nothing but *Him*! There could be noise and excitement around her: 'Nescivi'! They could accuse her: 'Nescivi'!... Then disturbances from without and tempests from within may arise; [the soul's] self-esteem may be wounded: 'Nescivi'! God may hide Himself, withdraw His sensible grace: 'Nescivi'. (LR 4–5)

An Extension of his Glory

The third 'day' is a particularly important section of the *Last Retreat*, for here Elizabeth goes to the heart of what it means to be a praise of glory, and she connects this with heaven: both life in heaven, and especially life in 'the heaven of our soul' (LR 8) – an expression used by Teresa of Avila when speaking of the prayer of recollection (cf. WP 28:5). In these last few weeks before her

death, Elizabeth's thoughts about heaven inspired her more and
more with how to live on earth. For by pondering the place to
which she would soon be called, she became increasingly aware
of the 'heaven' that was within her; the blessed on high were
perfect models, then, for how she could best live within herself.

Elizabeth begins by linking two phrases from Ephesians,
identifying two things to which we have been called: to be a
praise of God's glory (cf. Eph 1:12), and to remain in his presence in love (cf. Eph 1:4). The first, she points out, is the goal;
the second, the means of attaining it (cf. LR 6). Moving onto
the souls in heaven, Elizabeth takes the theme of simplicity and
develops it one stage further than her reflections the previous
day: she sees their contemplative gaze on God as *the means by
which they are transformed*. In this way, they become 'an unceasing praise of glory' (LR 7). As Elizabeth knew well, they were
not praising God's glory simply by singing hymns or psalms,
but were praising him with their whole being: they had let their
entire selves be formed in the image of God, and he 'contemplates in them His own splendour' (LR 7).

Elizabeth now thought what 'immense joy' it would give to
'the Heart of God' if she imitated the blessed in the 'heaven of
[her] soul' (LR 8). By contemplating him, she could be transformed into him just as they have been! She would return to the
'image and likeness' (LR 8; cf. Gn 1:26) of God in which human
beings had originally been created. Looking at it from God's
own perspective, she comments:

> Such was the Creator's dream: to be able to contemplate
> Himself in His creature and see reflected there all His
> perfections, all His beauty as through a pure and flawless
> crystal. Is not that a kind of extension of His own glory?
> (LR 8)

As always, Elizabeth did not shy away from hard work: she knew
that this requires detachment – especially detachment from
oneself – because this 'permits the divine Being to be reflected
in [us]' (LR 8). So sensitised was she to the heart of God that she

longed to reach this state for *his* sake: 'this [song of the praise of glory] thrills God to His very depths' (LR 8; cf. Rv 14:3).

Faith – a Light in Darkness

We can be in no doubt that the fourth section was written the day after the third, as it begins with the word 'Yesterday'. Yesterday, St Paul. Today, St John. Yesterday, she had learned from St Paul about the 'occupation of the blessed' (LR 8). Today, she is learning from St John about the heavenly Jerusalem, 'the holy city' (LR 9; cf. Rv 21:2). This notion of a dwelling place would have filled Elizabeth with delight. She, who from the age of ten had considered herself a 'House of God', now pondered on her soul as this 'interior city' and wondered how it might have 'some similarity and likeness' (LR 9) to the holy city of heaven.

Up to now, the *Last Retreat* has been full of light, with Elizabeth often speaking of brightness and radiance. But she now considers light in its special role as the light of faith in darkness. As we have seen before, Elizabeth did not merely *write about* the things of God, but sought to *live* them. So, instead of just describing the heavenly Jerusalem, she sought in Scripture how to live the life of the blessed in heaven. And the Book of Revelation nourished her thoughts on the role of faith: for in the heavenly city, she read (cf. Rv 21:23), there are 'no lights' – Jesus himself is 'its only light' (LR 9). For this to take place in her own soul, Elizabeth makes this decision: 'I must extinguish every other light and, as in the holy city, the Lamb must be "[my] only light"' (LR 9).

The thought of Jesus as a light in darkness immediately, then, suggests to Elizabeth the role of faith: 'Here faith, the beautiful light of faith appears. It alone should light my way as I go to meet the Bridegroom' (LR 10). Elizabeth realises that extinguishing other lights will mean: 'putting all my powers in darkness and emptiness; then I will meet my Master' (LR 10).

This gives Elizabeth another aspect of how she might become a praise of glory: by being 'unshakable in her faith' (LR 10; cf. Hb 11:27); and, above all, by channelling her faith into believing in God's love for her (cf. LR 10; 1Jn 4:16) – being 'unshakable in her faith in His "exceeding love"' (LR 11; cf. Eph 2:4). Elizabeth says that she would feel 'embarrassment' (LR 11) – literally, she says: 'shame' – if her varying states of soul should affect her when she has considered the words of Hebrews on faith (cf. Hb 11:1):

> What does it matter to the soul that is absorbed in recollection of the light which these words create in it, whether it feels or does not feel, whether it is in darkness or light, whether it enjoys or does not enjoy. (LR 11)

Rather, she wishes, as Ruysbroeck had once said, to raise God up 'on the highest summit of the mountain of [her] heart' (LR 11), where she can be united with Jesus, above and beyond all things.

'DAYS' FIVE TO EIGHT: LIFE IN HEAVEN

Communion with the Passion of Christ

The fifth 'day' is one of the high points of the *Last Retreat*. It opens with a long quotation from Chapter 7 of the Book of Revelation, describing the great multitude in heaven before Christ, the 'Lamb' (Rv 7:9.14–17). As we have seen, Mother Germaine would later say that Elizabeth received a great grace during these days to embrace suffering, and to go beyond its bitterness (cf. PG, p. 182). Nowhere is this expressed more than in this fifth 'day', which itself is a magnificent section reaching into the core of the paschal mystery: it is the Passion that leads to the resurrection, and the multitude before the Lamb are those who have 'washed their robes...in the Blood of the Lamb' (LR 12; cf. Rv 7:14). Elizabeth comments:

> Before contemplating 'with uncovered face the glory of the Lord', they have shared in the annihilation of His Christ; before being 'transformed from brightness to brightness in the image of the divine Being', they have been conformed to the image of the Word Incarnate, the One crucified by love. (LR 12; cf. 2Cor 3:18)

Elizabeth now draws out the implications for the heaven of her soul, which she also calls her 'inner sanctuary', her 'temple' (LR 13; cf. 1Cor 3:17). To serve God in his temple day and night means, for her – and here she emphasises the word – being 'resolved to share *fully* in [her] Master's passion' (LR 13). Or, as she says literally, *'effectively'* – which is eloquent about the *reality* of suffering. In recent days, Elizabeth had been writing of the blessed in heaven, those who are now 'glorified' (HF 27; LR 7); but Elizabeth knew it was the Passion that could 'make the glory of His grace blaze forth' (LR 13; cf. Eph 1:6).

At this point, we encounter what we know from Mother Germaine to be the great grace of her retreat. Elizabeth first portrays the crucified Christ in his majestic silence: 'her crucified, annihilated, humiliated King,…always so strong, so calm, so full of majesty as He goes to His passion' (LR 13); and she longs to be his queen sharing in his sufferings. At the beginning of her retreat, she had expressed her heartfelt wish that 'the Master' would 'teach her' how to be a praise of glory (cf. LR 1). She now explains what 'her holy Master makes her realise':

> He wants to associate His Bride in His work of redemption and this sorrowful way which she follows seems like the path of Beatitude to her, not only because it leads there but also because her holy Master makes her realise that she must go beyond the bitterness in suffering to find in it, as He did, her rest. (LR 13)

This was a great grace indeed. As she expresses it a few lines later: 'she no longer suffers from suffering' (LR 14). That is why Elizabeth can embrace suffering: 'Then the Lamb can *"lead her to the fountain of life"*, where He wills, as He wills, for she does not look at the paths on which she is walking; she simply gazes at the Shepherd who is leading her' (LR 14; cf. Ps 22:2).

This is why Elizabeth could find 'her rest' in suffering. And she feels with delight that the Father, seeing her soul 'so conformed to the image of His Son' (LR 14; cf. Rm 8:29), will himself be full of joy and able to transform her into a praise of glory: 'His fatherly heart thrills as He thinks of consummating His work, that is, of "glorifying" her by bringing her into His kingdom, there to sing for ages unending "the praise of His glory"' (LR 14; cf. Jn 17:4; Eph 1:12).

The Sacrifice and the Beauty

Elizabeth begins her sixth 'day' by quoting another memorable passage from Revelation describing the blessed in heaven: this time, the multitude of one hundred and forty-four thousand, singing the 'new song' and bearing on their forehead the name of both the Father and the Son (Rv 14:1–4). To bear the name of the Lamb, she writes, is to be conformed to his suffering – to wear, like those in heaven, a robe 'stained with the blood of their constant sacrifice' (LR 15; cf. Rv 19:13; 7:14). To bear the name of the Father is to reflect his beauty: 'He radiates in them the beauty of His perfections. All His divine attributes are reflected in these souls, and they are like so many strings which vibrate and sing "*the new song*"' (LR 15).

At first sight, these seem to be opposites: sacrifice and beauty. But it is again the paradox of the paschal mystery. This double movement corresponded to the dual nature of Elizabeth's own life at this time: held down by suffering, yet rapidly approaching the throne of the Lamb in heaven. Her goal, her only goal, was resemblance to God. So we see that to follow Jesus in his sufferings – which, in appearance, is not beautiful – is nonetheless to reflect 'the beauty of [the Father's] perfections' (LR 15). In this sense, there is no essential contradiction between the Passion and the resurrection.

The blessed in heaven, as Elizabeth sees in the passage from Revelation, are able to bear the name of the Father and of the Son because they are '*virgins*' (Rv 14:4). Elizabeth interprets this in its broadest, and truest, sense. She knew that it did not apply only to consecrated virgins, but to all who are 'pure as the light' (LR 15). To be virginal, she says, means: to be 'free, set apart, stripped; free from all save their love, set apart from everything, especially themselves, stripped of all things both in the supernatural order as well as in the natural order' (LR 15). Here, she is using a striking phrase which she had quoted in a letter just over two years earlier, said to be by Monsignor Gay: that God is free from everything *except his love*; that he *cannot* stop loving us (cf. L 199). Elizabeth, too, wishes to rise to this challenge of being free from everything, except from love – which will mean dying to herself in order that she might live for God. 'Quotidie morior' (LR 16), she says, quoting St Paul (1Cor 15:31) – that is, 'I die every day'. But to 'die' in this way, by 'going out from self' (LR 16), is all about living – and the capitals in the passage below are Elizabeth's own emphasis:

> we must be dead! Without that we may be hidden in God at certain moments; but we do not LIVE habitually in this divine Being because all our emotions, self-seekings and the rest, come to draw us out of Him... O blessed death in God! O sweet and gentle loss of self in the beloved Being which permits the creature to cry out: 'I live, no longer I, but Christ lives in me.' (LR 16; cf. Gal 2:20)

The Day and the Night

It was the opening words of a Psalm that gave Elizabeth inspiration for the seventh 'day': 'The heavens proclaim the glory of God... Day unto day takes up the story and night unto night makes known the message' (Ps 18:2–3). In this next section of her *Last Retreat*, Elizabeth explores how her own life may tell of the glory of God. Again and again, we see her spirituality to be so whole and balanced, involving not just spiritual *ideas* but every aspect of her life and being: she knew that we are called to *be* a praise of glory (Eph 1:12), not merely to speak of it. Our *lives* have to be the proclamation of his glory; and these words in the Psalm helped Elizabeth to draw out new dimensions of how her life could do this. Once more, we have the paradox of the paschal mystery: the light and the darkness.

Elizabeth begins with the *day*. For her, this means first of all the enlightenment which she receives from God: 'All God's lights, all His communications to my soul are this "day which passes on to day the message of His glory"' (LR 17; cf. Ps 18:3). Then, there is what she herself can contribute, as she listens to what he is telling her: 'my fidelity in corresponding with each of His decrees, with each of His interior commands, makes me live in His light; it too is a "message which passes on His glory"' (LR 17). And she thrills to know, as she reads in another Psalm, that to contemplate God will itself make her 'radiant' (LR 17; cf. Ps 33:6).

Then there is the *night* – for that, too, can tell of the glory of God. Elizabeth finds this 'very consoling', for it embraces human nature at its most helpless. She writes with wonder:

> My weaknesses, my dislikes, my mediocrity, my faults them-selves tell the glory of the Eternal! My sufferings of soul or body also tell the glory of my Master! (LR 18)

Elizabeth will mingle her blood with that of Christ, so that her own blood, united to his, 'is in some way made infinite and can give magnificent praise to the Father'. 'Then,' she adds, 'my suf-fering is "a message which passes on the glory" of the Eternal' (LR 18).

She ends with another line from Psalm 18, giving her expla-nation in brackets: 'There (in the soul that tells His glory) He has pitched a tent for the Sun' (LR 19; cf. Ps 18:5). Elizabeth, this 'House of God', was always alert to her soul being a *place* where Jesus could dwell. So she thrills to this mention of a 'tent' – his dwelling place in her soul. She knows she must make herself 'empty of all' except 'His love, His glory' (LR 19). Then the tent can become 'His bridal chamber', and he will cast himself into it – into her! The sun, says Elizabeth with joy, is the 'consum-ing fire' (cf. Hb 12:29) that will transform her into him and make her 'a "praise of glory" of the Father!' (LR 19). This Psalm showed Elizabeth the power of the God who was living in her soul, this God in whom light is joined to heat: the light of God bringing enlightenment (cf. LR 17); the heat being the dynamic force of transformation – forming her into her ultimate ideal, a 'praise of glory' (cf. LR 19).

Adoration – 'a word from Heaven!'

The eighth 'day', which brings us to the midway point of the *Last Retreat*, is a climax in its own right – equalled only by the visionary quality of the closing words of the sixteenth and final 'day'. For here, Elizabeth glimpses into heaven with the insight of one already on the threshold of eternity.

Fittingly, she begins with another extended quotation from Revelation: the inspiring scene, from Chapter 4 of that book, of the blessed in heaven who prostrate themselves in adoration, casting their crowns before his throne and singing, 'Holy, holy, holy...' (LR 20; cf. Rv 4:8.10–11). Elizabeth finds this inspirational. She formulates a question and is intensely interested in finding an answer to it: 'How can I imitate in the heaven of my soul this unceasing occupation of the blessed in the Heaven of glory?' (LR 20). Yet again, this brings her to paradox. For while she seems, on the one hand, to be as if soaring heavenwards, she expresses this 'occupation of the blessed' in words from St Paul which convey the solidity of being bound to the earth: 'rooted and grounded in love' (Eph 3:17); and she comments: 'such, it seems to me, is the condition for worthily fulfilling [my] work as praise of glory' (LR 20).

'Holy, holy, holy...' These are words from Revelation (Rv 4:8), from the *Te Deum*, and from the Mass. Elizabeth almost certainly has the Mass in mind as she calls this formula a 'Sanctus' (LR 20); and she also echoes the liturgy of the Mass when describing how to be rooted in love: such a soul, she writes, does everything 'in Him, with Him, by Him and for Him' (LR 20). Elizabeth is a soul of absolutes. For her, there is no room for *anything* – not even a fraction of a second, or a fragment of a thought – to be taken away from Christ:

> this soul, by each of its movements, its aspirations, as well as by each of its acts, however ordinary they may be, 'is rooted' more deeply in Him whom it loves. Everything within it pays homage to the thrice-holy God: it is so to speak a perpetual Sanctus, an unceasing praise of glory! (LR 20)

Elizabeth now comes to what thrills her heart most: the inner reality of *adoration* – 'a word from Heaven!' (LR 21), she exclaims. She notes especially – with her keen eye for learning what Scripture can teach her – that first of all the soul, like the blessed in heaven, should prostrate itself. This brings to Elizabeth's mind a phrase from Ruysbroeck: about a soul which 'has plunged so low that no one will look for it there' (LR 21). Why plunge this low? Not just to see how low it can go! Rather, for the fruitful consequences: no one, she points out, will follow that far – and so, the soul which lowers itself is left free for God alone. 'Then' – and this is the big 'then' – 'it can "adore"' (LR 21). At this point, it is as though Elizabeth breathes a blissful sigh of satisfaction as she envisages the soul which has reached a state in which it is able to be immersed in adoration. Elizabeth almost goes out of herself, in her sheer joy at contemplating a life spent adoring God:

> Adoration, ah! That is a word from Heaven! It seems to me it can be defined as the ecstasy of love. It is love overcome by the beauty, the strength, the immense grandeur of the Object loved, and it 'falls down in a kind of faint' in an utterly profound silence, that silence of which David spoke when he exclaimed: 'Silence is Your praise!' Yes, this is the most beautiful praise since it is sung eternally in the bosom of the tranquil Trinity... (LR 21; cf. Ps 64:2)[7]

This, Elizabeth sees, is the way in which she can live 'in an anticipated Heaven' (LR 21), as she expresses it – a striking phrase that she will use again, shortly before her death (cf. L 333). That is: she will be 'beyond all that passes, beyond the clouds, beyond

---

[7] The wording of the quotation from the Psalm is from the Hebrew version: see *The New Jerusalem Bible: Standard Edition*, London: Darton, Longman & Todd, 1985, p. 877. Quite often, with quotations from the Psalms, Elizabeth's wording differs from that in our own Bibles; this depends on the translation she was using, her source sometimes being the works of John of the Cross: see, for example, LR 43, n. 9.

[herself]!' (LR 21). She will cast down her crown before God, like the blessed in heaven, and in this way be a soul who 'loses sight of self, and finds its beatitude in that of the adored Being, in the midst of every suffering and sorrow' (LR 21). In short: 'it has left self, it has "*passed*" into Another' (LR 21).

'DAYS' NINE TO TWELVE: 'BE HOLY'

The Desire of the Creator

As with the previous block of four 'days' – when the first, second and fourth had begun with a quotation from Revelation – so now Elizabeth follows that same pattern, but this time with the theme being the command of God to be holy and perfect like himself. 'Be holy for I am holy' (Lv 11:44.45; 1Pt 1:16). These are the words with which Elizabeth begins her ninth 'day'. And she sees them as nothing other than 'the very same wish expressed on the day of creation when God said: "Let us make man in Our image and likeness"' (Gn 1:26). Elizabeth comments: 'It is always the desire of the Creator to identify and to associate His creature with Himself!' (LR 22).

Here, we have a perspective that characterises Elizabeth's writings: whatever we are called to do – whether it be to praise God's glory, to imitate Christ, to live in his presence, to be holy – this is, she shows, *the desire of God himself.* In this section, teeming with biblical quotations, Elizabeth draws extracts especially from Sts Peter, Paul and John, and focuses on our call to share in God's own nature (cf. 2Pt 1:4; Hb 3:14; 1Jn 3:2–3). But the key to everything is her initial quotation from Leviticus (quoted in 1 Peter): to 'be holy'.

To this, Elizabeth joins an equivalent command of Jesus: 'Be perfect as your heavenly Father is perfect' (LR 22; Mt 5:48). Elizabeth's interpretation of this has nothing to do with a narrow-minded sense of 'perfection': a religious perfectionism that may manifest itself as rigid observance of rules, possibly leading to scrupulosity. In fact, she explains perfection as living in God's presence, as she brings in this passage from Genesis: 'Speaking

to Abraham God said: "Walk in My presence and be perfect'"
(LR 23; Gn 17:1). Elizabeth comments with joy:

> This then is the way to achieve this perfection that our
> Heavenly Father asks of us!... 'God has chosen us in
> Him before the creation of the world, that we might be
> holy and immaculate *in His presence* in love.' (LR 23; cf.
> Eph 1:4)

Once more, Elizabeth has an eye to the effort required – what is
often called the ascetical work. She always considered such effort
amply worth it, for it would lead to nothing less than union with
God: 'This is the way set forth; we have only to strip off self to
follow it as God wills! To strip off self, to die to self, to lose sight
of self. It seems to me the Master meant this when He said: "If
anyone wants to follow Me, let him take up his cross and deny
himself"' (LR 24; cf. Mt 16:24). This brings Elizabeth back to
the spiritual notion of 'death' as she ends her ninth 'day' with a
verse from Hosea which she doubtless came across in *The Living
Flame*: '"O death," says the Lord, "I will be your death"' (LR 24;
cf. Hos 13:14; LF 2:34). Elizabeth then rephrases this as follows:
'O soul, my adopted daughter, look at Me and you will forget
yourself; flow entirely into My Being, come die in Me that I may
live in you!' (LR 24).

Eternal Present, Eternal Solitude

Elizabeth begins her second section on the theme of holiness,
the tenth 'day' of the retreat, by recalling again these words
of Jesus: 'Be perfect as your heavenly Father is perfect' (LR 25;
Mt 5:48). Once more, this has nothing to do with perfectionism.
And her emphasis, here, is seen to lie with the simple word 'as':
for likeness to God is her goal. So she focuses in particular on
this command of Jesus as a call to resemble the Father – to be
perfect like the Father. And she identifies what, to her, are the
Father's two prominent characteristics: he lives in an eternal
present, and he lives in an eternal solitude. Both these things
evoke for Elizabeth her ideal of a unified being.

As we have seen before, Elizabeth was working out how to *live* her ideal of being a praise of glory: for she knew that she still had time – a small but crucial amount of time – left to her, in which to prepare herself for the ultimate call of praising God's glory in heaven. So she considers how she might live the eternal present which is, she says, an 'attitude of adoration' (LR 25). St Paul gives her the key – or half the key: 'For love of Him I have forfeited everything' (Ph 3:8). The other half is provided by John of the Cross.

In her *Last Retreat*, Elizabeth quotes quite sparingly, with the exception of passages from biblical writers. John of the Cross, however, is one author who appears from time to time, not least in the opening, with the 'inner cellar' and the bride who sings, 'Nescivi' (cf. LR 1; SC 26:3; Sg 6:11). But it is in this tenth 'day', most of all, that his presence is felt, especially that of his ascetical teachings. So Elizabeth complements those stark words from St Paul (cf. Ph 3:8) with even starker ones from John of the Cross: to forfeit everything, she says, is to be 'alone, set apart, stripped' of all things (LR 25; cf. SC 35:5; 40:2). Writing in the spirit of John's teachings – which Elizabeth sees ultimately as a path to freedom – she paraphrases this as being 'destroyed and freed' (LR 25) from self.

The next month, Elizabeth would write to her young friend, Françoise de Sourdon, assuring her that she would not be 'commonplace' – literally, 'banal' – if she lived in God's presence and avoided acting only 'naturally': that is, to the exclusion of the supernatural life (cf. GV 8). In this tenth 'day' of the *Last Retreat*, Elizabeth again links being 'banal' ('trivial', in the English standard translation) with staying on the natural level alone: 'a soul that is not thus "destroyed and freed" from self will of necessity be trivial and natural at certain moments, and that is not worthy of a daughter of God, a spouse of Christ, a temple of the Holy Spirit' (LR 25). To be free of self seems an impossible task to achieve. But there *is* a way. Elizabeth's explanation is a huge affirmation of faith, and of the powerful transforming effect of contemplative prayer:

To guard against this natural life the soul must be wholly vigilant in her faith with her gaze turned towards the Master. (LR 25)

Halfway through this section, Elizabeth repeats Jesus' command for us to be perfect like our heavenly Father (cf. LR 26); and as if starting her discussion again, she now considers what she defines as the second characteristic of the Father, whom she describes in words which she attributes to Dionysius: 'God is the great solitary' (LR 26). She continues:

> My Master asks me to imitate this perfection, to pay Him homage by being a great solitary. The divine Being lives in an eternal, immense solitude. He never leaves it, though concerning Himself with the needs of His creatures, for He never leaves Himself... (LR 26)

This whole notion filled Elizabeth with delight: she, too, wishes that 'nothing may draw me out of this beautiful silence within' (LR 26); and at the same time, she sees that contemplation is no impediment to charity: God is concerned with us, but this does not mean that he goes out of himself. For Elizabeth, to remain within this inner silence requires the same apprenticeship as needed for living in an 'eternal present': 'the same solitude, the same withdrawal, the same stripping of self!' (LR 26). Once again she draws on John of the Cross, who speaks of the 'four passions' of the soul which must not be allowed to distract us from God (cf. SC 20:4.9–13). Elizabeth finds this a helpful pointer for how to maintain inner solitude and silence:

> If my desires, my fears, my joys or my sorrows, if all the movements proceeding from these 'four passions' are not perfectly directed to God, I will not be solitary: there will be noise within me. There must be peace... (LR 26)

Elizabeth gives other examples, too, of things that distract us from God: 'our feelings, our memories, our impressions' (LR 26). Elizabeth longs to make a 'break' with 'the *self*'. This would give her the 'beauty' that would charm 'the King' (cf. Ps 44:12) – and it would likewise increase her resemblance to God: 'For beauty is unity, at least it is the unity of God!' (LR 26).

Enclosed in God

At the beginning of her eleventh 'day' Elizabeth writes 'continued', for she is aware of having broached the subject only from the angle of *the person* aspiring to live in solitude and silence. Now she will speak of when *God himself* steps in, and the soul is ready to be enclosed within God's own silence:

> The Creator, seeing the beautiful silence which reigns in His creature, and gazing on her wholly recollected in her interior solitude, is enamoured of her beauty and leads her into this immense, infinite solitude, into this 'spacious place' sung of by the prophet, which is nothing else but Himself... (LR 27; cf. Ps 17:20)

The 'prophet' is in fact a reference to the Psalmist – in keeping with her times for, as seen before, David was often called the king of the prophets in her day (cf. LR 34, n. 12). But a few lines later Elizabeth does quote a prophet, and she draws on the riches contained in this contemplative verse from Hosea: 'I will lead her into solitude and speak to her heart' (LR 27; cf. Hos 2:14). Elizabeth had written, in her *Prayer to the Trinity*: 'I want to spend my life in listening to You'. Enclosed in the great solitude of God himself, she could be in a place where all this would be fulfilled: 'The soul has entered into this vast solitude in which God will make Himself heard!' (LR 27).

She now takes a verse from Hebrews – one that speaks of the word of God spoken to us in Scripture – and interprets it as applying to the words spoken by God in the silence of prayer. More than this, she is affirming prayer as a vital means of opening oneself to the direct action of God:

> 'His word,' St. Paul says, 'is living and active, and more penetrating than a two-edged sword: extending even to the

division of soul and spirit, even of joints and marrow.' It is
His word then that will directly achieve the work of stripping in the soul; for it has this particular characteristic, that
it effects and creates what it intends, provided however that
the soul consents to let this be done. (LR 27; cf. Hb 4:12)

Elizabeth now says: 'it is not enough just to listen to this word, we
must keep it!' (LR 28); and she quotes the biblical verse she has
in mind here (Jn 14:23). For Elizabeth, this particular passage
from John's Gospel held enormous resonances. She would inevitably have been overwhelmed whenever she thought back to
her mystical experience on Ascension Day, when she had heard
these very words of Jesus spoken within her: 'If anyone loves
me, my Father will love him; we will come into him and we will
make our dwelling in him' (S1, p. 164; cf. Jn 14:23). And at that
very moment, Elizabeth 'saw' (PG, p. 183) the Trinity within
her. This experience may well explain why Elizabeth could easily
identify the word of Scripture with the word of God spoken in
the silence of contemplation. So, on quoting this very verse from
John's Gospel, she now comments: 'It is the whole Trinity who
dwells in the soul [which] loves them in truth, that is, by keeping
their word!' (LR 28).

Elizabeth now repeats once more Jesus' call to perfection (cf. Mt 5:48; LR 28). The first time, as we have seen, she
focused on perfection as *living in God's presence* (cf. LR 23); the
second time, on *resemblance to the Father* (cf. LR 25); and now,
on this being *a command of Jesus, an expression of his will* (cf.
LR 28). Elizabeth is resolved to do everything according to
the will of God. She wishes for her own will to be 'enclosed in
God's will' (LR 28) – an expression of Ruysbroeck; and quoting
St Paul, she aspires to be 'moved by His Spirit' (Rm 8:14; cf.
3A 2:10). This will bring about her resemblance to the Father:
'I will do only what is divine, only what is eternal, and, like
my Unchanging One, I will live even here below in an eternal
present' (LR 28).

The Work of Immense Love

In the twelfth 'day', Elizabeth comes to the summit of the call to holiness. This important section is an attempt to penetrate the mystery of Christ, who is not just our model but also, crucially, the one who will carry out the great work of making us holy. 'This is Christ's work in every soul of good will,' she writes, 'and it is the work that His immense love, His *"exceeding love"*, is eager to do in me' (LR 31; cf. Eph 2:4).

Firstly, though, she begins by recalling the words from John's Prologue on Christ taking flesh and dwelling among us (cf. Jn 1:14), and she repeats those of Leviticus, quoted by St Peter: 'Be holy, for I am holy' (LR 29; Lv 11:44.45; 1Pt 1:16). Combining the two passages, Elizabeth points out the indispensable role of the Incarnation as she comments:

> But He remained hidden in His inaccessible [light] and the creature needed to have Him descend to it, to live its life, so that following in His footsteps, it can thus ascend to Him and become holy with His holiness. (LR 29; cf. 1Tm 6:16)

Elizabeth now explores Scripture in order to learn about Christ. In particular, she immerses herself in St Paul. We might well ask: Why not the Gospels? Towards the climax of the *Last Retreat*, Elizabeth will indeed go straight to the Gospels to 'study this divine Model' (LR 37). But at this point, she is looking for a specific type of knowledge: a way of *fathoming the mystery of Christ*. St Paul, she writes, had been given an understanding of this mystery (cf. LR 29; Eph 3:4). And Elizabeth ('Laudem Gloriae') thrills to Paul's words: that Christ is our 'hope of glory' (LR 29; Col 1:26). 'So,' she adds, 'it is from the great Apostle that I am going to learn how I may possess this knowledge which, in his expression, "surpasses all other knowledge: the knowledge of the love of Christ Jesus"' (LR 29; cf. Eph 3:19).

'First of all,' says Elizabeth, beginning to quote a list of phrases from Colossians: '[St Paul] tells me that He is "my peace",...making peace through the Blood of His Cross' (LR 30;

cf. Eph 2:14; Col 1:20). As she considers the implications for the
human race, one point follows on after the other. Nine points in
all: he gives us peace; he gives us access to the Father; he recon-
ciles all things to himself; he fills us with his fullness; he buries
us with him in baptism; he gives us new life; he forgives us our
sins; he wins the victory over all 'Principalities and Powers' – and
all this in order 'to present you holy, pure, and without reproach
before Him' (LR 30; cf. Eph 2:18; Col 1:19–22; 2:10.12–15).

We gain an insight, at this point, into Elizabeth's reading
of Scripture: firstly, seeking to learn about Christ; and then,
drawing out the implications for her own life – both her inner
life, and the daily living that ensues from it. For she now goes
back over those nine points in Colossians and shows how Jesus
will bring these theological realities into effect in her own soul
– and 'in every soul of good will' (LR 31):

> He wants to be my peace so that nothing can distract me
> or draw me out of 'the invincible fortress of holy recollec-
> tion'. It is there that He will give me 'access to the Father'
> and will keep me as still and as peaceful in His presence as
> if my soul were already in eternity. It is by the Blood of His
> Cross that He will make peace in my little heaven, so that it
> may truly be the repose of the Three. (LR 31; cf. SC 40:3)[8]

Taking up now the remaining points, Elizabeth continues by
saying that Jesus will fill her with himself, bury her with him, and
make her live with him. And faced with her weaknesses, he will
lift her up, forgive her, and free her 'from everything that is an
obstacle to the divine action' (LR 31). She even discerns a parallel with the 'Principalities and Powers', for Jesus will triumph
over the 'powers' of her soul and she will pass into him. Then,
at last, she will be able to say: 'I no longer live. My Master lives in

---

[8] This passage is a second version, which Elizabeth immediately pasted over
the first. The main change is that she had initially written: '...to be my peace
so that nothing may draw me out of the bosom of the Father...' Elizabeth
may have felt that this wording bore too great a resemblance to the union of
Christ with his Father (cf. Jn 1:18): see LR 31, n. 14.

me' (LR 31; cf. Gal 2:20). And ultimately, as she concludes with joy: 'I will be *"holy, pure, without reproach"* in the Father's eyes' (LR 31; cf. Col 1:22).

'DAYS' THIRTEEN TO SIXTEEN: MIRRORS OF GLORY

A Programme of Life

Continually open to being guided and taught, Elizabeth turns to her favourite biblical author: 'it is St. Paul who instructs me' (LR 32), she writes in the opening line of this thirteenth 'day'. The whole of this section is a meditation on a passage from Colossians (Col 2:6–7) which she explores in depth, as a guide for living the life of Christ. Leading into this, though, she firstly recalls one short phrase from Ephesians: 'to restore all things in Christ' (LR 32; cf. Eph 1:10). Elizabeth wishes, she says, that she may 'personally realise this divine plan' (LR 32). By this she would have meant gathering together into Christ every aspect of herself ('all things'). St Paul teaches her how to do this, for the passage from Colossians, she says, gives her 'a rule of life' (LR 32):

> Walk in Jesus Christ, be rooted in Him, built up in Him, strengthened in faith, growing more and more in Him through thanksgiving. (LR 32; Col 2:6–7)

Elizabeth will quote this passage to others, giving different explanations of each of its phrases according to the person concerned: Françoise de Sourdon (cf. GV 10–12) and Mother Germaine (cf. L 316). This fact itself shows the riches Elizabeth would continue to discover in this passage, for she knew that it could be pondered again and again, and each time be a source of new insights for living the life of Christ. Here, she applies it to her own inner life – which is why themes from previous sections of the *Last Retreat* reappear now, held together within the framework of this 'rule of life'. But far from this being a summing-up of those themes, it is part of Elizabeth's ongoing search; and she says that with this passage, St Paul is coming to her aid and drawing up a rule of life for her (cf. LR 32). It is an insight into her reading of Scripture as addressed to her personally.

To '*walk in Jesus Christ*' is, for Elizabeth, to 'leave self, lose sight of self, give up self', so as to 'enter more deeply into Him with every passing moment' (LR 33). The very notion of entering *deeply* into Christ shows Elizabeth that this is how she can be '*rooted*' in him (Col 2:7). And she comments with panache: 'to every event, to every circumstance we can fling this beautiful challenge: "Who will separate me from the love of Jesus Christ?"' (LR 33; cf. Rm 8:35). Nothing, she knows, will be able to separate her from Christ, for such is the nature of being rooted.

In Carmel, Elizabeth pondered short Scripture texts each day from her *Manual*. The current section of the *Last Retreat* is possibly a typical example of how she would explore a small passage in depth, drawing out dimensions which a more rapid reading might well overlook. So, whereas the notion of being 'rooted' could be thought of as simply a concept, Elizabeth, on the contrary, contemplates its reality – the extraordinary hidden activity, beneath the depths of the soil, where nourishment streams powerfully through roots and pours life into a plant:

> When the soul is established in Him at such depths that its *roots* are also deeply thrust in, then the divine sap streams into it and all this imperfect, commonplace, natural life is destroyed. Then, in the language of the Apostle, 'that which is mortal is swallowed up by life'. (LR 33; cf. 2Cor 5:4)

In this way, Christ will absorb Elizabeth into himself: this is a state of being stripped of self, and fed with Christ's life alone. And that, she can see, will transform everything – absolutely everything – so that both 'exterior encounters' and 'interior difficulties' (LR 33) become means of union with Christ and not obstacles to it. But while rootedness suggests depths, being *built up in Jesus Christ* suggests heights, which Elizabeth now explores:

> And now what does it mean *to be built up in Him?* The prophet also sings 'He has set me high upon a rock, now my head

is held high above my enemies who surround me'; I think
that this can well be taken as a figure of the soul 'built up
in Jesus Christ'. He is that rock on which it is set high above
self, the senses and nature, above consolations or sorrows,
above all that is not *Him* alone. And there in complete self-
control, it overcomes self, it goes beyond self and all else as
well. (LR 34; cf. Ps 26:5–6)

The clarity of Elizabeth's thinking is quite phenomenal, given
the atrocious pain she was in. Here as elsewhere, her penetrating thought and enthusiasm in pondering point after point
– hundreds of them in the *Last Retreat* – could easily give the
impression that this work was written by someone in full health.
It is only when we come across such discussions as the one just
quoted that we cannot help perceiving, between the lines, a
description of the strategy she was using to cope with her illness.
For she will write, the next month, about the necessity of forgetting self and going beyond nature, so that suffering can be
seen through the eyes of faith and even be welcomed with joy
(cf. GV 6–8); and tellingly, the last paragraph of the *Last Retreat*
speaks explicitly of rising above nature and going beyond pain
(cf. LR 44).

Even Elizabeth's nights of insomnia are possibly discernible
in this thirteenth 'day', when she speaks of the soul never being
allowed to 'doze' (LR 34). As we know from the accounts of
the time of her illness, her terrible insomnia was matched, and
outdone, by her spiritual watchfulness. And vigilance – which is
also a hallmark of the Carmelite *Rule* (cf. # 10) – is the theme of
the next point of her programme: 'Next St. Paul advises me to
be strengthened in faith: in that faith which never lets the soul doze
but keeps it wholly vigilant beneath its Master's gaze' (LR 34).

Elizabeth now comes to St Paul's invitation 'to grow in Jesus
Christ through *thanksgiving*' (LR 35). It is his final piece of advice:
'for everything should end in this!' (LR 35). She will make this
point to Françoise de Sourdon the next month, when commenting on the same passage from Colossians: '[Thanksgiving] is

the last word of the programme and is but the consequence of it' (GV 12).

Recalling, now, how Jesus said: 'Father, I thank You!' (Jn 11:41), Elizabeth hears these words as a *song*, and wishes to make it her own: 'My Master sang this in His soul and He wants to hear the echo of it in mine!' (LR 35). Aspiring to sing with *her whole life*, she will sing the 'new song' from the Book of Revelation (cf. Rv 14:3). Or rather, she will make herself into the instrument on which *God himself* will play the song; and in this way, she will truly be the praise of his glory:

> I think that the 'new song' which will most charm and captivate my God is that of a soul stripped and freed from self, one in whom He can reflect all that He is, and do all that He wills. This soul remains under His touch like a lyre, and all His gifts to it are like so many strings which vibrate to sing, day and night, the praise of His glory! (LR 35)

Offering herself with Christ

The fourteenth 'day' of the *Last Retreat* is a magnificent portrayal of Jesus, which also reveals how Elizabeth is striving to identify with his dispositions; and, between the lines, we see just how much her life has been identified with his.

Firstly, though, she begins by quoting the long passage from Philippians (Ph 3:8–10.12–14) which had been her 'retreat devotion' in 1905 (IN 16). She has often quoted separate verses from it, for it expresses so many of her own longings: to have a knowledge of Christ that surpasses all else; to share his sufferings and be conformed to his death;[9] and now, as her life on earth is drawing to a close, something that speaks to her with keener

---

[9] It is notable that the words 'that I may know...the power of his resurrection' (Ph 3:10) – which occur in Philippians immediately before the mention of sufferings and death, and which Elizabeth included when quoting the passage in her retreat devotion of 1905 – are omitted from the *Last Retreat* (cf. LR 1; LR 36); this is without doubt because Elizabeth, at this stage of her illness, is focused on imitating Christ in his sufferings and death.

relevance than ever before: 'I run straight to the goal..., to the prize of the heavenly vocation to which God has called me in Christ Jesus' (LR 36; cf. Ph 3:12).

It is again St Paul, she says, who 'teaches' her that she must be conformed to the image of Christ (cf. LR 37; Rm 8:29); and Elizabeth turns her sights to imitating Jesus because this, she sees, is the way to become a praise of glory and 'respond to the dignity of this vocation' (LR 37). She writes: 'It is important then that I study this divine Model so as to identify myself so closely with Him that I may unceasingly reveal Him to the eyes of the Father' (LR 37). In the twelfth 'day', Elizabeth had gone to the letters of St Paul to fathom the *mystery of Christ*. Now, she immerses herself most of all in the Gospels, so as to enter into the *dispositions of Jesus*.

The key to everything in his life, Elizabeth finds, is his offering of himself to do the Father's will. And Elizabeth unites herself to Christ, even adapting the biblical verse to the plural 'we' – which she emphasises – so that the words from Hebrews refer to both Jesus and herself: 'Here *we* are, O Father, we come to do your will!' (LR 37; cf. Hb 10:9). Elizabeth stresses this vital disposition, for she knows that the quality of this offering determined everything that followed in the life of Jesus: 'His life was as it were but the consequence of it!' (LR 38).

Elizabeth, too, we remember, had offered her life without any consolation. She had taken her vows – which had been for life – while still in the trial of spiritual darkness, and she may well have been thinking of this now: for it is perhaps no coincidence that she speaks of herself repeatedly, in this fourteenth 'day', as being the 'bride' of Christ. On the day she had taken her vows 'in pure faith' (ETB, p. 522), knowing only that she was sacrificing herself for God, her soul had been at peace. That is what Elizabeth describes now: knowing the *peace* and *joy* of being crucified with Christ (cf. LR 38). And there is a whole life of dying to self in daily living, by embracing the will of God at every moment. It was the 'food' (Jn 4:34) of Jesus – and, Elizabeth adds: 'It should also be that of the bride' (LR 38). She recalls the words of the Psalm, 'Your decrees are my inheritance forever; they are the joy of my heart' (LR 38; cf. Ps 118:111); then she comments: 'my Master sang this in His soul, and it should echo resoundingly in that of the bride!' (LR 38). Indeed, his prayer of self-offering to do the Father's will (cf. Hb 10:9) 'should,' she says, 'be like the bride's heartbeat' (LR 37).

Although it was a few years since Elizabeth had played the piano, music still had a privileged capacity to bring out the beauty of her soul. Three times, in three successive 'days', she describes the words and thoughts of Jesus as *songs* being sung in his soul (cf. LR 35; LR 38; LR 41).[10] Praise, too, was itself a musical concept for Elizabeth. This was equally true of making her whole life into a 'praise of glory', even if it concerned such ugly things as nausea and pain. Likewise, to sing of following God's decrees is to evoke a reality that is potentially just as unmusical and prosaic: 'constant fidelity', and being 'stripped and set free of self' (cf. LR 38). Ultimately, Elizabeth will offer a 'sacrifice of praise' (LR 38; cf. Hb 13:15).

Then, at last, comes 'her hour of humiliation, of annihilation' (LR 39). Elizabeth may well have written this passage on the actual fourteenth day of her retreat. For on August 29, the date in question, Elizabeth wrote to her mother – the only letter she wrote during this retreat – and spoke here, too, of the 'hour'. What Elizabeth says in that letter helps complete the picture of how she was living her own 'hour': 'When a great suffering or some very little sacrifice is offered us, oh, let us think very quickly that "this is our Hour", the hour when we are going to prove our love for Him who has "*loved us exceedingly*"' (L 308; cf. Jn 12:27; Eph 2:4).

Elizabeth now focuses all her attention on meditating on the Gospel accounts of the *Passion*. The *silence* of Jesus strikes her as much as his *words*. Elizabeth was walking with Jesus to the end, conforming herself to him even in his Passion, and she now

---

[10] Elizabeth may have taken this expression from the poem by John of the Cross, 'The Living Flame of Love', of which the subtitle begins: 'Songs of the soul...'

makes his last words, as well as his silence, her own. This is how she speaks of herself, the 'bride' (cf. LR 38):

> 'Jesus autem tacebat' ['Jesus, however, was silent']; and she will be silent... And when the hour of abandonment, of desertion, and of anguish comes, the hour that drew from Christ this loud cry, 'Why have You abandoned Me?', she will recall this prayer: 'that they may have in themselves the fullness of My joy'; and drinking to the dregs 'the cup prepared by the Father', she will find a divine sweetness in its bitterness. Finally, after having said so often 'I am thirsty', thirsty to possess You in glory, she will sing: 'Everything is consummated; into Your hands I commend my spirit.' (LR 39)

When finally she reaches this point, the Father, she says, will 'bring her into His inheritance' (LR 39; cf. Col 1:12), and she will be clothed entirely with Christ. Elizabeth sums up this whole section in words of John the Baptist about Christ which can be said to apply to Elizabeth's entire life and spirituality: 'He must increase and I must decrease' (LR 39; Jn 3:30).

Mary, 'so beautiful to contemplate'

Elizabeth now turns her eyes to the greatest model among creatures: the Virgin Mary, 'the great praise of glory of the Holy Trinity' (LR 40). When Elizabeth rediscovered her love for Mary, shortly before the feast of Our Lady of Mount Carmel in July, she exclaimed to her sister: 'Oh! never have I loved her so much! I weep for joy when I think that this wholly serene, wholly luminous Creature is my Mother and I delight in her beauty like a child who loves its mother' (L 298). Elizabeth's heart continued to overflow, as we can see only too well from 'day' fifteen, which is a most stunningly beautiful portrait of Mary – she who 'responded fully' to the call to be *pure, immaculate, and without reproach* (LR 40; cf. Col 1:22) in the eyes of God.

If Elizabeth aspires to 'decrease' (LR 39; Jn 3:30), Mary has done more than this: she has virtually disappeared. Earlier in August, Elizabeth had said that Mary's life is 'so lost in God that there is hardly anything we can say about it' (HF 39). Now, in the *Last Retreat*, she describes Mary as lost to the human eye, and like a mirror that reflects its subject:

> Her soul is so simple. Its movements are so profound that they cannot be detected. She seems to reproduce on earth the life which is that of the divine Being, the simple Being. And she is so transparent, so luminous that one would mistake her for the light, yet she is but the 'mirror' of the Sun of Justice... (LR 40)

For Elizabeth, the hallmark of Mary is that everything took place *in her heart*; 'with her,' she writes joyfully, 'everything took place within!' (LR 41). So it is not surprising that Elizabeth had a perfect affinity with Mary; or rather, it is also true to say that the image of Mary which Elizabeth found in the Gospels was coloured by her own soul and that she herself brought out this affinity. So, recalling the relevant words in Luke – 'the Virgin kept all these things in her heart' (Lk 2:19.51) – Elizabeth comments: 'her whole history can be summed up in these few words!' (LR 40).[11] We have seen how Elizabeth summed up Jesus' whole life in terms of his *offering of himself* to do his Father's will (cf. LR 38). Elizabeth would not have said that Mary offered herself to God any less than Jesus did, and this section indeed shows Mary giving herself entirely – it is just the emphasis that is different. The rest of her portrayal of Mary, then, is the story of *an interior life*.

The first episode Elizabeth touches on is the Visitation. She does not focus on the visit itself, or on Mary's charity to her cousin – as she had done when writing about this scene for Guite (cf. HF 40). Rather, when writing about what resonates with her own life, Elizabeth focuses on the journey to the hill country of Judea when Mary is alone: that is, Mary as a

---

[11] Elizabeth writes 'histoire' in the French, meaning 'history' or 'story'; she was most likely thinking of the latter, as in the phrase 'story of a soul' ('histoire d'une âme').

contemplative, gazing on the Word who dwells within her. This description is the fruit of Elizabeth's own contemplation as she writes: 'I imagine her passing by so beautiful, so calm and so majestic, so absorbed in recollection of the Word of God within her' (LR 40). When Elizabeth moves onto Mary's being with her cousin, she then contemplates Mary *as if alone*. The Virgin, she says, could sing: 'The Almighty has done great things for me...' (LR 40; cf. Lk 1:49). And these great things are nothing less than achieving the goal which Elizabeth had constantly before her eyes during this retreat: Mary, she writes, was always 'forgetful [of self]', 'freed from self' (LR 40).

Elizabeth now passes on to the description of Mary on Calvary. It is a parallel to the Passion of Jesus, but once more it is marked chiefly by a focus on interiority: 'This Queen of virgins is also Queen of martyrs; but again it was *in her heart* that the *sword pierced*' (LR 41; cf. Lk 2:35). Elizabeth's contemplation of the soul of Mary in suffering is not only beautiful and inspiring, but a gateway for glimpsing the soul of Christ in his Passion:

> Oh! How beautiful she is to contemplate during her long martyrdom, so serene, enveloped in a kind of majesty that radiates both strength and gentleness... She learned from the Word Himself how those must suffer whom the Father has chosen as victims, those whom He has decided to associate with Himself in the great work of redemption, those whom He 'has foreknown and predestined to be conformed to His Christ', crucified by love. (LR 41; cf. Rm 8:29)

Anyone can say beautiful things about suffering. But we know that Elizabeth's words are truly authentic: we have only to recall that she was almost fainting in agony while writing the *Last Retreat*; and every word, we might say, is itself 'both strength and gentleness' (LR 41). This now brings us to what was surely giving Elizabeth the greatest strength in her own sufferings. Firstly, she draws out these Gospel words for herself personally: 'my Master says to me: "Ecce Mater tua." He gives her to me for my Mother...' (LR 41; cf. Jn 19:27). And we see that Mary is given to her to be with her, just as Mary had been with Jesus 'at the foot of the Cross, *standing*, full of strength and courage' (LR 41). At this stage of her terrible illness, Elizabeth is *physically* in the place of Christ; so she turns to Mary to learn how to be *spiritually* in his place, too:

> And now that He has returned to the Father and has substituted me for Himself on the Cross so that 'I may suffer in my body what is lacking in His passion for the sake of His body, which is the Church', the Blessed Virgin is again there to teach me to suffer as He did, to tell me, to make me hear those last songs of His soul which no one else but she, His Mother, could overhear. (LR 41; cf. Col 1:24)

Towards the end of her portrait of Jesus in the previous section, Elizabeth had made her own the words he spoke just moments before he died: 'Everything is consummated' (Jn 19:30; cf. LR 39). She now recalls them again as she anticipates the end of her own life, the solemn entry into heaven. At that final moment, Elizabeth will not be alone, for Mary will be with her to take her there:

> When I shall have said my 'consummatum est', it is again she, 'Janua coeli' ['Gate of heaven'], who will lead me into the heavenly courts, whispering to me these mysterious words: '*I rejoiced in what was said to me, let us go to the house of the Lord!*' (LR 41; cf. Ps 121:1)[12]

In the Heaven of her Soul

The last day dawned. And in this final 'day', Elizabeth's pen flows towards her goal – tumbling rapidly as a waterfall, and joyous as a whole city's church bells! The sixteenth 'day' is a mixture of her hopes and aspirations, combined with the sheer

---

[12] Elizabeth quotes these words in Latin only (my English translation, here, follows the version she is using), and she enlarges her handwriting to emphasise them. This is a Psalm which the Sisters recited three times a day when processing into choir: see LR 41, n. 1.

joy of knowing that *her vocation to be a praise of glory is one that she can already live now.* This magnificent, concluding section is itself like a hymn to the glory of being in the presence of God.

Elizabeth's opening lines reveal her impatient longing: 'When will I appear before His face?...' (LR 42; Ps 41:3). 'And yet,' she continues, writing of herself, '...Laudem Gloriae has found while waiting to be brought to the holy Jerusalem, "beata pacis visio" ["blessed vision of peace"] – her retreat, her beatitude, her anticipated Heaven in which she begins her life of eternity' (LR 42). For Elizabeth is in God, and her soul is at peace (cf. LR 42; Ps 61:2).

'This is the mystery my lyre sings of today!' (LR 42), she exclaims. The Scripture passage that speaks to Elizabeth most strongly here – apart from the Psalms, which themselves are so much in keeping with the theme of praise – is the command of Jesus to Zacchaeus: 'Hurry and come down, for I must stay in your house today' (LR 42; Lk 19:5). This, right at the end of her life, bears witness to the constancy with which Elizabeth has embraced her identity, from early childhood, as a 'House of God'.

The *descent* spoken of by Jesus will not, of course, be literally that of Zacchaeus: climbing down from a sycamore tree! Elizabeth, though, sees that the passage applies to her and asks: 'but where?' To the place, she answers, that is 'the innermost depths of my being'; and she must be 'withdrawn from self', 'stripped of self' – 'in a word, *without self*' (LR 42).

Elizabeth now repeats the invitation of Jesus to Zacchaeus, giving just the essential, which lends this a sense of urgency and energy: 'I must stay in your house!' (LR 43). Elizabeth, we can be sure, felt personally called by this command – and here, she recalls the expression 'House of God'; she gives it in the context of St Paul's Letter to the Ephesians, but still in line with her charism of dwelling in the Trinity:

It is my Master who expresses this desire! My Master who wants to dwell in me with the Father and His Spirit of love, so that, in the words of the beloved disciple, I may have 'communion' with Them. 'You are no longer guests or strangers, but you already belong to the House of God,' says St. Paul. This is how I understand 'belong to the House of God': it is in living in the bosom of the tranquil Trinity, in my interior abyss, in this 'invincible fortress of holy recollection' of which St. John of the Cross speaks! (LR 43; cf. 1Jn 1:3; Eph 2:19; SC 40:3)

Elizabeth now envisages, with awe, the indwelling of God within her. Here, in the sixteenth 'day', she echoes the description contained in the eighth: that of adoration, which is the climax to the midway point of the *Last Retreat*. There, she had written of the blessed prostrating themselves before Christ (cf. LR 20–21; Rv 4:10). Now, she quotes from a Psalm: 'My soul falls down in a faint for the courts of the Lord' (LR 43; Ps 83:3; cf. SC 11:4).

This faint, Elizabeth feels, should be her own attitude – in fact, the attitude of 'every soul that enters into its interior courts to contemplate its God and to come into closest contact with Him' (LR 43). Notably, Elizabeth does not consider this faint as a loss of life – rather, and most strikingly, she sees it as life that leaves the soul and 'flows into its God' (LR 43).

Throughout the *Last Retreat*, as we have seen, Elizabeth has spoken again and again of being stripped of self, or freed from self. Such a notion may sound difficult, even off-putting. But when described by Elizabeth, it becomes beautiful. Nowhere more so than here, when we see her in admiration of this ideal: 'Oh! How beautiful is this creature thus stripped, freed from self!' (LR 44). It is her ultimate task, while still on earth and preparing herself to enter 'the place which is [her] goal' (LR 44; Ps 83:6). That 'goal', that final destination, is *the Trinity*.

Elizabeth is almost overwhelmed with awe at the grandeur of those whom she has so often called her 'Three' – doubtless especially now that she knows her own moment of death to be approaching. She describes them in Latin, with the utmost solemnity, to convey the grandeur of 'the unfathomable Trinity' into whose presence she is to be brought: 'Immensus Pater, immensus Filius, immensus Spiritus sanctus!'[13] It is an extraordinary journey: this rising of the creature above herself and above nature, and beyond every joy and pain, until she penetrates '"*into the interior*" of Him whom [she] loves' (LR 44). And she can, and must, do all this 'without leaving the holy fortress' of her soul!

Elizabeth comes now to the climax, the final words, of her *Last Retreat* – the fruit of sixteen days of intense searching, in which every word has been *lived* – and to the moment when she will pass out of herself and into God, as a perfect praise of his glory:

> It is also without leaving [her innermost depths] that the soul will live, like the immutable Trinity, in an *eternal present*, 'adoring Him always because of Himself', and becoming by an always more simple, more unitive gaze, 'the splendour of His glory', that is, the unceasing praise of glory of His adorable perfections. (LR 44)

---

[13] These words come from the Athanasian Creed – a long confession of faith in the three Persons of the Trinity – which the Carmelites recited at the Office of Prime on Trinity Sunday, and on the ordinary Sundays of the year: see ETB, p. 574, n. 1.

Chapter 20

THE HOME OF THE HOUSE OF GOD

In the House of Carmel

Elizabeth emerged from her last retreat on August 31. It was a special feast day, celebrating the dedication of churches of the Carmelite Order. Since the age of ten, Elizabeth had known herself to be a 'House of God'. So it is not surprising that she had a special devotion for the feasts of dedication of churches, the places in which God dwells. On that particular day, she renewed her consecration to the three divine Persons – they who had revealed their presence within her on Ascension Day. Mother Germaine considered that this vision of the indwelling Trinity had been 'the supreme dedication' (PG, p. 183) of Elizabeth, and saw this feast on the last day of August as, above all, a thanksgiving for it. Elizabeth's affinity with the feasts of dedication of churches was not lost on the prioress who would later describe her as a little 'tabernacle' (PG, p. 183). And in the month of September which was now beginning, the notion of the *dwelling place* would take on new dimensions for Elizabeth, strengthen her in her suffering, and bring new riches to her spiritual life. Uncannily, she would eventually die on the Church's greatest feast of dedication: November 9, that of the Lateran Basilica.

Meanwhile, Elizabeth gave herself to everyday life in her earthly dwelling place: the monastery in the Boulevard Carnot. Despite her extreme weakness, she continued to follow the Carmelite daily routine as much as her failing strength allowed. This was thanks, in large part, to Elizabeth's ever-increasing ardour for observing the Carmelite 'Rules' (S1, p. 167). What Mother Germaine appears to be referring to here is not just the

137

Rule of St Albert, written for the Carmelite Order, but also the observances and customs of the monastery: the prioress mentions, for example, Elizabeth's eagerness to observe 'the most minute details' (PG, p. 186).

Importantly, Mother Germaine would also say that even though Elizabeth was captivated by the visions of heaven described in the Book of Revelation, there was nothing of an exalted enthusiasm in her: rather, she was led by faith, which made her appreciate, still more, the path of daily fidelity (cf. ETB, p. 690). Elizabeth knew that God had given her the *Rule* as the divine instrument to bring her to holiness (cf. L 169). In July, when she had written to a Carmelite novice friar, she had listed various aspects of the charism of the Order and some of the main teachings of the saints. But she especially highlighted the Carmelite *Rule*: 'above all, let us know how to prove our love to God by fidelity to our holy Rule; let us have a holy passion for it; if we keep it, it will keep us and make us saints, that is, souls such as [St Teresa] wanted, *able to serve God and His Church*' (L 299).

In fact, we find an astonishing shift in Elizabeth's perspective. Since her youth, she had longed to go to heaven. We recall how she had once confided to Mother Marie of Jesus that she wished she could go to heaven even before entering Carmel – and how the then prioress had told her off for being lazy (cf. L 55)! Now, while Elizabeth's longing for heaven was very strong, she nonetheless said to Mother Germaine that the only thing that would reconcile her to being cured was if she were able to follow the *Rule* as perfectly as possible, and so make her self-offering more complete (cf. PG, pp. 185–6). Elizabeth was indeed putting this into practice. When one of the nuns, probably Sister Anne-Marie, wanted to talk during a time of silence, Elizabeth now had the courage to insist on observing silence at that time (cf. ETB, p. 692). And as soon as the bell rang for an Office, Elizabeth would take her stick at that very moment, and begin making her way to the tribune where she would follow the services in union with her sisters who were in choir.

Of all the Offices, it was Lauds that thrilled Elizabeth most. It was, so to speak, her very own: the Office of Praise, which carried her name. Lauds took place until about twenty past ten each night, and she would follow it while sitting by the window of her cell, gazing up at the stars, and letting her soul ascend with the canticles of praise 'into the presence of the "Three"' (PG, p. 185). During the warm summer months, she had stayed there in silent prayer for the first few hours of the night, as she was unable to sleep anyway. But when the cool autumn evenings arrived, she had to give up these long vigils. However, she continued to rise for Lauds each night, right up to the last week of her life. Elizabeth called this Office her 'nocturnal Lauds' (S1, p. 167); she even found that its calming effect helped her to fall asleep soon afterwards.

'Nothing made her suffer'

Elizabeth was amazed that she still had the strength to keep walking and moving around, for her food intake was next to nothing, as it had been for several months. She would have some soup, to which milk was added, but each spoonful gave her pain. She did not dare to increase the amount: because as soon as she tried to force down a bit more, it set off another 'attack' (L 309). Friends and family continued to send in varieties of chocolates, in the hope she could keep them down. Suchard was too rich, but a brand called 'Klauss' made her 'less nauseated' (L 309); and in this way she managed, just, to consume sufficient calories to keep going.

There were, however, other factors – interior ones – that enabled Elizabeth to keep going. In fact, her state of health gave her no choice other than to develop discipline, and even heroism, in following the Carmelite life. Absolutely everything was an arduous task, due to the terrible pain and relentless insomnia. This meant that her will was constantly being strengthened, so that she could say from experience, in a letter to her mother that month: 'try to put joy – not the joy you can feel but the joy of your will – into every irritation, every sacrifice' (L 317).

Nowhere, perhaps, was her will more evident than on the night when, exhausted and in terrible pain, she felt 'tempted' to miss Compline and go back to bed. Suddenly, she had an impulse to do the opposite. As she explained it afterwards to the prioress: 'I left my armchair and knelt to pray with stronger faith on account of my lack of courage' (PG, p. 186). Her good will and act of faith were rewarded with so much strength that she had no trouble whatsoever in postponing her rest until after Compline that night.

But what seems most extraordinary of all is the fact that Elizabeth forgot herself to such an extent that she seemed to cope as if unaffected by her state of health. Sister Aimée would describe her as 'dead to herself rather than mortified' (ETB, p. 708), and she would give this striking testimony about Elizabeth during her illness:

> It was a state, a state of sacrifice, a state of immolation. Nothing annoyed her, nothing surprised her. In a certain sense you could say: nothing made her suffer, neither the light, nor draughts, nor mishaps... She seemed not to notice the lack of sleep or food. A few months before her death, ill, exhausted, she was walking on a terrace, leaning on the arm of the prioress, walking at the same pace, without thinking for a moment that it was beyond her strength. I had to intervene. Then the prioress told her to show me her tongue which was red and inflamed and, she added, the whole of her insides was the same. [Elizabeth] smiled as if none of this related to her. (ETB, p. 708)[1]

Mother Germaine would say that Elizabeth 'had lost her instinct of self-preservation, even before she entered Carmel' (ETB, p. 708). This is reminiscent of how Elizabeth, on her last holiday

---

[1] The dating of this episode, 'A few months before her death', probably refers to late August or early September, because the episode suggests a time when Elizabeth had built up sufficient strength in her leg muscles to walk at a normal pace (after her first tentative steps in the second week of July), but also a time when her exhaustion was extreme.

in the south of France, had been warned by Father Vaux, a relation of her 'aunts', that the Carmelite life would be too severe
for her health – and she had simply replied: 'Oh well, I'll die
then' (ETB, p. 337). This utter simplicity would lead her to say,
in the last few months of her life: 'It is as simple to suffer as to
enjoy' (ESS, p. 41). And in a letter she wrote less than a fortnight
before her death, we see the secret of this serenity in suffering:
'forget self, give up self, ignore self, look at the Master, look only
at Him, accept as coming directly from His love both joy and
suffering; this places the soul on such serene heights!...' (L 333).
The sub-prioress could not help thinking of St Francis of Assisi:
Elizabeth seemed to her to be 'sovereignly detached...and sovereignly free' (ETB, p. 708).

'Children playing with ashes'

Elizabeth had always been rightly seen as a person of prayer, but
the emphasis now seemed to be shifting in that she became outstanding for her courage and strength. The prioress noticed that
this change of emphasis reflected itself in the way she was influ-
encing the other sisters. Previously, Mother Germaine would
recall, Elizabeth 'drew souls to recollection; now her influence
led them to practise the most heroic virtues' (PG, p. 188). To
Sister Marie of the Holy Spirit, Elizabeth said: 'How we deceive
ourselves regarding genuine union with God! Souls that think
they have reached it because they enjoy sensible consolations are
like children playing with ashes that the wind carries away' (PG,
p. 188). To one novice she said: 'We must accept our difficulties
rather than wish to be freed from them' (PG, p. 188). However,
she did not just leave it at that, but with excellent pedagogy
explained the positive reason: 'accepting them frees us' (PG,
p. 188). And she went on to say: 'In the same way we must be
willing to undergo the consequences of our faults or faithless-
ness as being due to God, Who will know how to derive from
them glory to Himself and profit to us' (PG, p. 188). And she
told Sister Marie-Joseph, whose 'Angel' she was, that when she
was blamed she should not only submit but even be glad and say,

'Thank you' (PG, p. 188). Elizabeth, we know, always practised what she preached: we recall how she had once thanked Sister Ignace for telling her that her singing was soulless (cf. ETB, p. 579)!

This last piece of advice has a slight echo with the famous austere saying of John of the Cross, which in earlier years was an ideal Elizabeth had been hoping to acquire (cf. L 207). This was *the desire to suffer and be despised*, because in this way she would resemble Christ more fully. Sister Marie of the Trinity would later say that Elizabeth had indeed come to embrace this ideal: 'The need to suffer, [and] to resemble [Christ] in his sufferings, was joined by the ardent desire of being, like him, a subject of shame and contempt' (ETB, p. 692, n. 4). It was in a similar frame of mind that Elizabeth confided to her one day: 'You know how much I love my vocation. It seems to me that if our Mother said to me: You are unworthy to wear the holy habit, then dismissed me from the Order, I would experience great joy at being treated as I deserve' (ESS, p. 37).

As we know, Elizabeth was not, of course, put to the test; but one day, she received a prophetic intimation of a similar kind about this very sister. These were rare occurrences in her life, for Elizabeth lived by faith like anyone else. But we have come across an earlier example, when she was still living at home and informed Madame Catez that she had learned, in prayer, that a family friend had died – which was before the news actually arrived (cf. ESS, p. 8). Now, Elizabeth said to the sub-prioress: 'I do not know how it will happen: whether it will be after a revolution or something else, but you will help to reestablish another Carmel, and there will be great suffering in your life' (ESS, p. 34). And as it happened, Sister Marie of the Trinity *was* sent to another Carmel: to Toulon, which proved to be a time of great trial to her. We have no way of knowing, but perhaps Elizabeth's sharing with her about suffering and being despised had been a help to this sister who maybe remembered her words when she needed them. For she did need them: she was somewhat unappreciated for much of her time in Toulon and would have felt lost without the support of Mother Germaine; and when she died, in 1954, it was after years of physical suffering.[2]

The Greatness of Our Vocation

In the second half of August, Marie-Louise de Sourdon had come to the Carmel to ask if she might see Elizabeth. As Elizabeth was too weak to hold a conversation through the closed grille, Mother Germaine had instead promised that a letter would be sent to her sister Françoise. Elizabeth knew that this would be the last one she would ever send her. So in early September, over several days when she felt almost too weak to keep going, she pushed her pencil across the ruled writing paper, eventually filling twelve small sides by around September 9. This letter is now known as one of her main spiritual works: *The Greatness of Our Vocation.*[3]

Elizabeth was not just writing a farewell letter. She was also answering Françoise's questions, especially on how to acquire humility and deal with one's pride. So this is not a work that deals with union with God or the heights of contemplation; rather, its content is influenced by the genuine questioning of a reader who had not yet matured in the life of faith. The work is practical, helpful and often inspiring. It tells Françoise how to live in Christ in a daily battle with herself, keeping her eyes fixed on the greatness to which she is called. It is also filled with human love and affection, which is immediately obvious from the opening words: 'Here comes Sabeth at last to sit down by her dearest Framboise and visit – with her *pencil!*' (GV 1). This is soon followed by: 'How I love our evening rendez-vous' (GV 1) – which brings to mind that Elizabeth had continued to meet Françoise in spirit at eight o'clock each evening, as arranged, for at least the last five years (cf. L 310, n. 2). The tone then

---

[2] For details of her time in Toulon, see an article by Conrad De Meester, OCD, in Clapier (ed.), p. 691.

[3] This title was given to the letter by Conrad De Meester, based on ideals expressed by Elizabeth in a previous letter to Françoise (cf. L 238) and a phrase contained in the *Last Retreat* (cf. LR 36): see CW I, p. 122.

becomes earnest, for this loyal friendship was towards the girl seven years her junior, who had always been her 'child'. 'It seems to me,' Elizabeth writes, 'that I am like a mother bending attentively over her favourite child: I raise my eyes and look at God, and then I lower them on you, exposing you to the rays of His Love. Framboise, I do not use words when I speak to Him of you but He understands me even better for He prefers my silence' (GV 1). And now, Elizabeth begins to answer the girl's questions: 'Let's treat humility first...' (GV 2).

When Françoise had once written to Elizabeth about the tantrums she was having, we remember that Elizabeth had replied, with a sigh: 'you have my nature' (L 98)! Now, what she says about the battle with pride sounds very much like Elizabeth's own daily struggle with anger in her own youth: 'Little Framboise, pride is not something that is destroyed with one good blow of the sword!... we must put it to death each day!' (GV 2). But Elizabeth gives the reason behind it: she says to Françoise that nothing can disturb the humble person, and therefore to kill one's pride is a path to peace. Imbued with the spirit of Thérèse, and also quoting Ruysbroeck, Elizabeth says that this makes us feel our 'weakness' before God, and that this itself becomes our greatest pleasure (cf. GV 2).

Elizabeth now interprets for her young friend the command of Christ to take up one's cross and deny oneself in order to follow him (cf. GV 3; Mt 16:24). She admits that this sounds very 'austere'. But it 'takes on a delightful sweetness when we consider the outcome of this death – life in God in place of our life of sin and misery' (GV 3). Moreover, she writes, it brings us to likeness with Christ, to which God has predestined us (cf. GV 3). And she gives a little piece of advice that might well have hit home to this slightly immature girl: 'Oh! you see, if we would think more about the origin of our soul, things here below would seem so childish' (GV 3). Elizabeth contrasts this with the freedom of the 'children of God' (GV 4; cf. Rm 8:21).

It is in this sentence that Elizabeth slips in a phrase that was almost certainly intended to make Françoise sit up and take notice: 'the soul that is aware of its greatness' (GV 4). This girl, who has just been told to lower herself to be humble, and to kill off her pride, is suddenly being shown that to be humble is to be 'great'! Elizabeth knew that this would speak to Françoise, this girl of lofty spirit to whom she had once written: 'I understand that you need an ideal, something that will draw you out of yourself and raise you to greater heights' (L 128).

We have seen, again and again in Elizabeth's life, how every circumstance was grist for the mill in developing her spirituality. This even included the symptoms of illness, just as the notion of God as a 'consuming Fire' really began to speak to her earlier in the summer, when she first experienced inflammation in her stomach – 'the sense of a fire consuming her inside' (L 271, n. 1). Now, as she felt herself wasting away from lack of nourishment, she had an idea about how to present to her friend the means of overcoming pride: starvation! And she writes, almost with humour: 'If anyone were to ask me the secret of happiness, I would say it is to no longer think of self, to deny oneself always. That is a good way to kill pride: let it starve to death!' (GV 4).

With psychological insight, Elizabeth now advises Françoise on how to avoid pride, as well as the discouragement if she fails: 'What God asks of you is never to entertain deliberately any thought of pride, and never to act on the inspiration of pride, for this is wrong. And yet, if you find yourself doing either of these, you must not become discouraged, for again, it is pride which is irritated' (GV 5). Instead, Françoise should show her 'misery' to God – for 'He so loves to see a soul recognise its weakness' (GV 5). Elizabeth is not suggesting humiliating oneself, but humbling oneself – and being accepted in love.

All along, we see Elizabeth trying to help her friend to see things in a new, and generally reversed, perspective. Françoise has proud thoughts – so she should practise humility. If she lowers herself through humility, this will bring her to greatness. If she fails, this is no cause for discouragement, because God loves it when we know our weakness. And now, Elizabeth shows that by denying our own self, we will actually become our higher and freer self. 'I truly believe,' she writes, 'that God wants your life to be spent in a realm where the air breathed is divine' (GV 6). And she would like to say to those who live only for trivialities: 'what are you doing with these bonds that chain you to yourself and to things less than yourself? It seems to me that the happy ones of this world are those who have enough contempt and forgetfulness of self to choose the Cross as their lot!' (GV 6).

This brings Elizabeth to the greatest paradox of all: the 'joy' to be found in 'suffering' (GV 6). She is not writing as a masochist but as a witness to union with Christ, and she is speaking from the experience of the 'way of Calvary I climb each day' (GV 7). This is the midway point of the work, and it stands out with central importance as she opens up, with unusual candour for her letters, as to how she is experiencing this time of great suffering. She first begins with the words of St Paul: 'In my own flesh I fill up what is lacking in the passion of Christ for the sake of His body, which is the Church' (GV 7; Col 1:24). 'The thought pursues me' (GV 7), she says with ardour. Elizabeth sees herself as an 'apostle', precisely because she 'finds...happiness in this [thought]' (GV 7). And this happiness, for Elizabeth, is a deep-rooted joy: 'I confess that I experience a profound inner joy in thinking that God has chosen to associate me in the passion of His Christ' (GV 7). At this point, she gives a most moving, yet harrowing description of the ravages being caused in her by her illness. But what shines through is that it has become second nature for her to view everything 'in the light of faith':

> Have you ever seen those pictures depicting death reaping with his sickle? Well, that is my condition; I seem to feel myself being destroyed like that. Sometimes it is painful for nature and I can assure you that if I were to remain at that level, I would feel only my cowardice in the face of suffering. But that is looking at things from the human point of view! Very quickly 'I open the eye of my soul in the light of faith.'

And this faith tells me that it is love who is destroying me, who is slowly consuming me; then I feel a tremendous joy, and I surrender myself to Him as His prey.[4] (GV 7)

Elizabeth's radiant joy during her illness was itself a striking witness to the fact that physical suffering does not have to make one unhappy. The example of her very being shows that it is possible to be simultaneously happy and in pain, for the happiness she speaks about is 'a profound inner joy' – whereas physical pain, as such, is external to the soul. A few paragraphs later, Elizabeth writes: 'I wonder how a soul that has sounded the depths of love the Heart of God has "*for it*" could be anything but joyful in every suffering and sorrow' (GV 12).

She now turns her sights to another of her friend's misconceptions. Françoise, as we have seen, had high ideals. As she did not wish to live just an easy life, she assumed that this was pride. Elizabeth corrects her on this point (cf. GV 6) and then explains that even an apparently ordinary life does not have to make us 'commonplace', which seems to have been one of the girl's fears. Elizabeth warns her dear 'Framboise' ('Raspberry') against seeing everything at the level of nature:

> Framboise, to attain the ideal life of the soul, I believe we must live on the supernatural level, that is, we must never act 'naturally'. We must become aware that God dwells within us and do everything with Him, then we are never commonplace, even when performing the most ordinary tasks, for we do not live in these things, we go beyond them! A supernatural soul never deals with secondary causes but with God alone. (GV 8)

Elizabeth now issues a challenge to see, with the eyes of faith, the sublime things that have taken place already in Françoise and of which the girl is probably unaware. She exclaims: 'baptism... has stamped you with the seal of the Holy Trinity!'; 'how often

---

[4] The quotation is from Father Vallée's rendering of a sentence by Catherine of Siena: cf. L 199, n. 9; cf. GV 7, n. 21a.

you have been justified by the sacrament of penance and by all those touches of God in your soul, without you even being aware of it!' (GV 9). Then, there is her future destiny: 'what awaits you in eternity!' (GV 9) – our degree of glory depending, she adds, on the degree of grace in us at the moment of death.

Elizabeth now ends with a mini-manual, so to speak, as she quotes an all-encompassing passage from St Paul, which she had applied to herself in the *Last Retreat* (cf. LR 32–35): 'Walk in Jesus Christ, rooted in Him, built up on Him, strengthened in faith and growing in Him in thanksgiving' (GV 10; cf. Col 2:6–7). This time, she develops a commentary on it that is tailor-made for Françoise. *Walk in Christ*: 'Yes,…you need this broad road, for you were not made for the narrow paths of here below!' (GV 10). *Rooted*: 'uprooted from self' (GV 10). *Built up on Christ*: 'high above everything that is passing, there where everything is pure, everything is luminous' (GV 10). *Strengthened in faith*: 'never act except in the great light of God, never according to impressions or your imagination' (GV 11); and most of all, she must have faith 'in His love, His *exceeding* love' (GV 11; cf. Eph 2:4). *Thanksgiving*: 'That is the last word of the programme and is but the consequence of it' (GV 12). But there are some more last words in her message, and again they come from St Paul: that God has chosen Françoise to be holy and pure in his presence in love (cf. Eph 1:4); and that she should be reassured in the light of struggles and temptations, for: 'When I am weak,…it is then I am strong, for the strength of Jesus Christ dwells in me' (GV 12; cf. 2Cor 12:10.9).

Elizabeth herself was very, very weak. So she realised she must now sign off and come to the closing lines of her letter (GV 13). She found it incredibly hard to say goodbye to this young girl who had captured her heart when Elizabeth herself had been a teenager. 'I cannot bring myself to leave you,' she wrote. But it was half-past seven in the evening, and Elizabeth was at the end of her strength. And so she had to say: 'I cannot go on.' Françoise must 'guess' the rest 'in the silence of our rendez-vous'. Elizabeth came to her final words: 'I send you a kiss. I love you as a mother loves her little child. A Dieu my little one. "In the shadow of His wings may He guard you from all evil".'

'Where did He dwell?'

Mother Germaine was all too aware of the intensity of Elizabeth's physical suffering. But even in this appalling pain, Elizabeth did not seek to be relieved of it. Crucially, she knew that her pain was of *use* to the Church (cf. L 294; Col 1:24), so when the prioress offered to give her something that might bring some relief, Elizabeth replied simply:

> It is not worth it, I am at the end of my career; God is making me understand that as I am soon to see him face to face, *Laudem gloriae*, far from taking her rest, must extract from her being all the prayer and suffering possible. (S1, p. 168)

Mother Germaine realised that she must try to help Elizabeth immerse herself yet more in the mystery of the Passion. For this, she had a stroke of genius: she gave Elizabeth the *Book of Visions and Instructions* by a thirteenth-century Italian mystic, Bl Angela of Foligno. In *The Greatness of Our Vocation*, which Elizabeth completed around September 9, she had quoted from this book. But it was not until the 14th, or just before, that she came across a phrase which would prove to be life-transforming, and which she would quote again and again over the next few weeks (cf. L 311, n. 3). It spoke to her most powerfully in the heart of her pain: 'Where then did He dwell but in suffering?' (L 311, n. 3).[5]

On that day, the feast of the Exaltation of the Cross, Madame Catez paid her ninth visit to the infirmary parlour. Elizabeth was bursting with her new discovery, and not wanting her mother to leave empty-handed with nothing for Guite, she took a piece of paper and wrote down, there and then, a message to be taken back to her sister:

---

[5] In the translation Elizabeth was reading, the word is 'douleur', which literally means 'pain', on the physical level, and 'sorrow', on the emotional one. It can equally be rendered as 'suffering', as it is in the translation of Elizabeth's letters.

I've read something so beautiful, listen: 'Where then did Jesus Christ dwell but in suffering?' O little child, it seems to me that I have found my dwelling place: it is the immense suffering that was also the Master's; in a word, it is He Himself, the Man of sorrows. (L 311)

That very day, when Mother Germaine was writing to Marie Bouveret – a former aspirant to the Carmel – she, too, quoted those words from Bl Angela, adding that they came at the end of 'a superb chapter in which she speaks of the painful life of Christ' (L 311, n. 3). It is not known whether the prioress or Elizabeth discovered the phrase first; but as they both wrote enthusiastically about it (cf. L 311; L 311, n. 3), there was, most importantly, an extremely favourable environment in which Elizabeth could share it with her and receive so much strength from it in her own pain. In fact, this sentence delighted Elizabeth so much that one sister, aware of this, would repeat these words to her whenever they met. At this, she said, Elizabeth 'used to speak to me in feeling accents of the Saviour's Passion, and of her joy at dwelling with Him through suffering' (PG, p. 171).

'This is where I want to live'

On this feast of the Exaltation of the Cross, Mother Germaine went into her office and found that Elizabeth had already been there and had left her a surprise gift, all of it made by Elizabeth herself. What immediately caught her eye was a little cardboard cut-out of a fortress with a drawbridge, about four inches by just under two and a half. On one corner of the tower was a small flag, on which Elizabeth had written two messages in red ink, one on either side: 'Citadel of suffering and of holy recollection' and 'Dwelling of Laudem gloriae while waiting for the Father's House' (L 307, n. 2). The door of the fortress was closed, but Elizabeth had pasted near it a picture of Our Lady of Lourdes representing *Janua Coeli* – Gate of Heaven.

At the foot of the drawbridge was a poem, on which there was a little picture of Mary Magdalene at the feet of the crucified Christ, the picture surrounded by the words '*Amor meus crucifixus*' ('*My crucified Love*'). The ground-breaking words of Bl Angela are the starting-point of the three verses, and the poem as a whole shows just how much those words had taken root in Elizabeth. Here, she refers to Angela as a 'saint', which is how she was commonly known. The poem is addressed to Mother Germaine:

> One saint wrote, when speaking of her Master:
> 'Where then did He dwell, if not in suffering?'
> That is where I want to live, O my Mother, O my Priest,
> So as to exalt, very high, the Cross of my Saviour.
>
> But I have need of you: in the shadow of your wing
> I will be able to penetrate into this divine palace,
> Into this fortress, into this citadel
> Where the soul takes her rest in invincible peace.
>
> David said of Christ: 'His suffering is immense',
> In this immensity, I am setting up my dwelling.[6]
> There I want to sacrifice myself in a sacred silence
> So as to be transformed into a 'victim of love!...'
>   (P 113; cf. Lm 2:13)

We see, here, Elizabeth's fertile creative mind, for she has already moved on from the *fact* of Christ dwelling in suffering. She is now exploring the various *dimensions* of where he dwells; and

---

[6] In the light of the words of Angela of Foligno which so inspired her, Elizabeth uses three different terms for 'dwelling', each with its own flavour. Usually when describing the soul as a dwelling place for God, Elizabeth uses the word 'demeure' – echoing St Teresa's *Interior Castle* which is known as *The Book of the Mansions* (literally: *Dwelling Places*) – in French: *Le Livre des Demeures*; as such, it is a place where one *lives* and *remains*, and Elizabeth will use 'demeure' in a letter of September 18 in connection with Bl Angela's words (L 312). In the current poem, and another one ten days later (P 115), Elizabeth uses 'séjour' which has a similar meaning: literally, a place to *stay*. A word she has used only once before (cf. L 239), and will use more often as from this time, is 'habitation' – a place where one *resides* (cf. P 114; P 120; L 311). This is derived directly from Bl Angela's question, 'Where then did He dwell ['habitait']...?'

in her poems around this time, she brings in specific types of dwelling place, each with its own resonance. There is the *palace* (P 113) – the dwelling of the King; and we know that Elizabeth perceived herself as the queen at his side, so the 'palace' would be for her a place of union with him. Then there are the *fortress* and *citadel* (P 113) – places which give security and protection and enclose her in God, in deep recollection (cf. SC 40:3). Sacrifice, she would write to Sister Marthe, is the Bridegroom's *wedding chamber* (P 114; cf. LF 4:13) where he will make this sister 'more virginal', more pure of heart – and by implication, his true bride. And as self-lowering allows us to remain in his presence, even this may be a *residence* and *royal palace* (P 120).

But the key to what inspired Elizabeth most of all is revealed in that initial letter to her sister on September 14: that Elizabeth's 'dwelling place' is not only Christ's suffering – it is no less than 'He Himself, the Man of sorrows' (L 311). For Elizabeth, suffering was not, then, just a *dwelling* place but a *meeting* place. This brings her to the closest possible union with Christ, and here she explores a whole new set of dimensions – of how to inhabit suffering *with him*.

In her letters at this time, she frequently quotes the groundbreaking words of Bl Angela, and then explains what they mean to her. To a family friend, Madame Gout de Bize, Elizabeth comments: 'Every soul visited by suffering, therefore, dwells with Him' (L 315). It is a being-with of great intimacy, as she expresses it to her mother: 'Every soul crushed by suffering, in whatever form it may occur, can tell itself: I dwell with Jesus Christ, we are living in intimacy, the same dwelling shelters us!' (L 314). And to another family friend, Madame d'Anthès, she writes: 'Any soul immersed in suffering, then, lives beside Him' (L 312).

But for Elizabeth, it was not just a living *with* or *beside* Jesus, however intimately: it was a living *in* him. This is how she expresses it in another poem she wrote for the prioress on September 14, describing herself in the third person and introducing further types of dwelling place, this time buildings with a more monastic flavour: 'In the Man of sorrows she has enclosed herself / That is her hermitage, and her beloved enclosure' (P 112). And in a short poem around this time, full of movement and dynamism, Elizabeth says that Jesus takes the initiative in enclosing her: he calls her 'my other self' and says to her: 'I am coming to enclose you, more than ever before, / In this fortress where my extreme love / Thirsts to overwhelm you with its sweetest gifts' (P 111).

'I did not suspect…'

Mother Germaine made an inspired choice when she gave Elizabeth the writings of Angela of Foligno. For the impact of this one phrase – 'Where then did He dwell but in suffering?' – caused a remarkable change in Elizabeth's inner life. It is an understatement to say that she had, for years, been longing for heaven. Yet this longing now began to be almost outweighed by the desire for suffering. This is how Elizabeth explained it, when writing to her mother on September 21:

> More and more I am drawn to suffering; this desire almost surpasses the one for Heaven, though that was very strong. Never has God made me understand so well that suffering is the greatest pledge of love He can give His creature… [Angela of Foligno] says that the sign by which we recognise that God is in us and His love possesses us is that we receive not only patiently but gratefully whatever wounds us and makes us suffer. To reach that state, we must contemplate the God crucified by love, and that contemplation, if it is true, never fails to end in the love of suffering. (L 314)

The key point is that Elizabeth's love of suffering was drawn entirely from her love of Christ – it was not a sign of masochism. As she explained to her mother, a few days later: 'I cannot say I love suffering in itself, but I love it because it conforms me to Him who is my Bridegroom and my Love' (L 317). That is why she could tell the sub-prioress that she wanted to reach heaven 'not only with the purity of an angel…but transformed into Jesus crucified' (PG, p. 168). Indeed, the very fact that she was beginning to be attracted more to suffering than to heaven likewise came from her longing to resemble Jesus, as she reveals in these striking words to Sister Marie of the Trinity: 'Suffering has a growing attraction for me; the desire of it almost overmastered the Lord of Heaven, strong as He is' (PG, p. 168).

The other point to keep in mind is that Elizabeth never considered that God was treating her cruelly; on the contrary, she saw that he was treating her as he did his Son. This is why she could see her suffering as 'the greatest pledge of love' (L 314), as she wrote to her mother; and she made the same point to Madame de Sourdon three days earlier, on September 18: 'Never have I understood so well that suffering is the greatest pledge of love that God can give His creatures, and I did not suspect that just such sweetness was hidden at the bottom of the chalice for the one who drank it to the dregs' (L 313); 'it is a fatherly hand,' she said, 'a hand of infinite tenderness that metes out suffering to us' (L 313). With such words as 'Never have I understood so well' and 'I did not suspect', we can see that this discovery of the words of Angela of Foligno does indeed mark a turning-point for Elizabeth in this month of September 1906. The sub-prioress would call it 'a new stage' (ETB, p. 689) in Elizabeth's life – even if, we can be sure, it resonated with what Elizabeth was already living.

Inevitably, to reach this state was a work of grace, for nature itself could only recoil at such horrendous pain. Elizabeth was managing to withstand and even love her suffering through contemplating the crucified Christ, which made her want to give herself as he had done (cf. L 314; L 133). And she explained: 'living in continual contact with God' enabled her to 'see everything in His light, the only true one' (L 315).

The more Elizabeth's illness progressed, the more she found she was given strength. 'Do not fear suffering...,' she wrote to Sister Marthe, 'He will strengthen you' (P 114). And Elizabeth wrote to Madame Gout de Bize: 'the great, true happiness I have found in Carmel increases in proportion to the suffering' (L 315) – a point, she said, that she often repeated to Mother Germaine. She also gives an awesome insight into how she was overcoming the distress of suffering by relying on will rather than natural sensations, and by submitting her will to God's will: 'Undoubtedly our nature can be distressed in the face of suffering – the Master willed to know that humiliation – [but] the will must come to dominate all these sensations and say to the Heavenly Father: "May Your will be done and not mine"' (L 315).

Elizabeth also quotes a saying which shows how suffering can leave positive traces on the soul: 'suffering passes away, but the experience of having suffered endures forever' (L 312). These last words recall the risen Christ – free from the pain, yet bearing the marks of his Passion (cf. Jn 20:27). He had referred to the Passion as his 'hour' (cf. Jn 12:27; 13:1), and Elizabeth saw her own troubles in the same way. 'The Master called the hour of His passion "His hour",' she said; and she urged her mother to regard both great sufferings and little sacrifices as '"our Hour", the hour when we are going to prove our love for Him who has "*loved us exceedingly*"' (L 308; cf. Eph 2:4). While Elizabeth was going through her own 'hour' of great suffering, she kept her eyes fixed on 'the supreme hour when He passed from this world to His Father' (L 315). She was fully aware of being in the process of preparation for eternal life: 'It seems to me that something similar is taking place in [me]. The evening of [my] life has arrived, the evening that precedes the eternal day' (L 315).

The 'eternal day' was itself a dwelling place – the goal of her destination. She had often spoken of the afterlife as 'Heaven'. But for the first time, she speaks of it in three biblical terms (cf. Jn 14:6; 8:12; 1Jn 4:16) which, in a slightly different order, would be the last words Elizabeth was ever heard to speak: 'Life...Light...Love' (L 313).

Comfort and Sacrifice

Elizabeth wrote to her mother, explaining a little paradox about the prioress: 'This good Mother, who is so inspiring about the ways of immolation, thinks of nothing but giving me comfort' (L 309). Elizabeth often pointed this out to Mother Germaine! But knowing that obedience came first, she accepted everything she was given and appreciated the endless kindnesses. Elizabeth was feeling the cold quite badly by the second week of September. She was wearing two shawls, and also asked her mother to send in her 'little cape from the Pyrenees' (L 309). Meanwhile, the prioress sent to their supplier for a brown quilted material, lightweight but warm, that was the same colour as the Carmelite habit. There was an earthenware stove in the infirmary cell, and Elizabeth at first asked for it not to be lit: she was afraid that if she grew accustomed to the warmth, she would no longer be able to stand the temperature in the tribune – and more than anything, she wanted to be able to keep visiting the Blessed Sacrament. But by the end of September, the prioress gave orders for the stove to be lit.

Plenty of practical gifts were pouring in from the outside, too. Madame Catez made her a petticoat, the recalcitrant stomach was greeted with 'varieties of chocolate' and 'delicate candies' (L 317), and Guite's husband sent in a case of milk. To her mother, Elizabeth commented: 'Be careful about what you say to Georges about me' (L 309) – for he was presumably not of the opinion that Elizabeth herself often expressed: 'If you only knew how well cared for I am in my dear Carmel' (L 315).

While Elizabeth declined anything that might bring her some alleviation, she was not opposed to the relief of pain in principle. Rather, she saw it as a question of what each person is called to. She said to the prioress that for anyone who had tasks to carry out, pain relief was often necessary. But Elizabeth, near the end of her days and with no other work to do, felt that she was called to devote herself to 'prayer and suffering' (PG, p. 186). That, then, was her own task, and it speaks reams about the heroism of her every moment. But because she knew it was the loving Father who was sacrificing her, she did not even find the time long. This is how she explained it to her mother, around the second week of September:

God is pleased to immolate His little sacrifice, but this Mass He is saying with me, for which His love is the priest, may last a long time yet. To the little victim in the Hands of the Master who is sacrificing her, time does not seem long and she can say that, even if she passes through the way of suffering, she is still following the path of *true* happiness,...a happiness no one can take from her. (L 309)

Celebrating Mother Germaine

Later that month, Elizabeth was delighted to have new cause for celebrating the prioress. On the 24th it would be the twelfth anniversary of Mother Germaine's profession. Elizabeth had been building up to this, and in one of the poems she had given her on September 14, Elizabeth had announced a generous gift which she would be gathering up for her over the next ten days: 'From Laudem gloriae, receive then in advance / Her unceasing prayer, and all her suffering. / She is your little victim/host [*hostie*], she is offering herself for you' (P 112).

Now, on the day itself, Elizabeth gave her a poem entitled 'Remember!...' (P 116). Inviting Mother Germaine to look back to when she took her vows twelve years earlier, Elizabeth is without doubt drawing on memories of her own profession: 'The beautiful "*Amo Christum*" made you thrill... / Like a pure holocaust, ah, you came to offer yourself! / And your soul was singing, radiant and vibrant, / The divine "*Suscipe*" sacrificing you irrevocably' (P 116). In this poem, Elizabeth evokes another dwelling place, as she describes the soul of Mother Germaine as a walled enclosure like the city of Sion: '[The Father] placed, within your walls, as He did for Sion, / His tenderness, His peace, His strength, His power' (cf. Ps 147:13–14). Then, in the last verse, Elizabeth returns to the present day, describing God's continued presence in the soul of the prioress:

> Contemplating His love residing in your soul,
> God feels drawn there more and more strongly
> And the double current, all limpid and calm,
> Is established between you continually! (P 116)

Elizabeth could not expend herself enough for Mother Germaine. For there were several more gifts from her to the prioress, including another poem (P 115), which is deep and contemplative while still characteristic of a celebratory set piece. It is the story of the 'humble boat' of 'Laudem gloriae'. In the first stanza, Elizabeth evokes the beauty and serenity of the 'peaceful night' and 'profound silence' while the boat drifts gently on the 'immense Ocean'. Suddenly, deep waves rise up and the 'frail' boat disappears beneath them.

On the feast of the Exaltation of the Cross, Elizabeth had written of setting up her dwelling in the 'immensity' of suffering (P 113); and, as she wrote at around the same time, 'this suffering was as immense as the sea' (L 314; cf. Lm 2:13). But while, in this new poem, Elizabeth uses the image of the ocean, she enters into another 'immensity' which the opening words of the second verse announce: 'It was the Trinity...' And she writes: 'I have found my centre in the divine Abyss!' We have here the whole movement of her soul: casting herself into the depths of the Three (cf. PT), and disappearing (cf. L 172) – which has more than a hint of her imminent departure for heaven. Mother Germaine, reading this poem, would have been only too aware that very soon she would see Elizabeth no longer:

> I shall no longer be seen on the shore,
> I am plunging into the Infinite, that is my whole destiny,
> My soul takes its rest in this immensity
> And lives with its Three as if in eternity! (P 115)

And this is where Elizabeth wishes to remain: in the Trinity, '*this spacious place*' (cf. Ps 17:20). But while she is ostensibly speaking of prayer in *this* life – her great theme of *heaven on earth* – she is also trying to prepare Mother Germaine for their imminent separation. For returning to the anniversary celebrations, Elizabeth tells her, in this third and final stanza, of a plan her heart has formed: '*Your feast will last* right up to the solemn day / When Laudem gloriae departs for Heaven, / But so as to begin again, more beautiful than on earth, / In the divine secret of the Face of the Father!' (P 115).

Elizabeth felt so united with the prioress that it seemed to her inevitable that when she was in heaven she would keep Mother Germaine's memory alive. Elizabeth even expresses this union in a way more usual for describing union with God: as an *indwelling* in the heart. This is what she writes in another short poem (P 117), possibly given to Mother Germaine that same day, the 24th, or maybe six days later on the anniversary of the death of Thérèse, which was held as a feast day in the Carmel of Dijon. Elizabeth begins: 'O my Mother, I will soon go [to sing] near Thérèse', and in the last four lines she speaks of a new place of dwelling for herself – lodgings in the heart of the prioress:

> If you wish, we will make a mysterious exchange:
> At the moment of departure, in the fire of Love,
> You will ascend to the Heavens, I will be your praise there,
> And you will give me lodgings in your heart night and
>   day! (P 117)

We have seen how Elizabeth considered herself to be a spiritual mother – *'the little mama of your soul'* (L 273) – to Madame Catez. Now, more and more, she was discreetly taking on this role in relation to Mother Germaine. Elizabeth could not very well say it openly – this was, after all, the prioress! But she had a clever idea: again for the anniversary celebrations of Mother Germaine, she wrote her a letter (L 316), but this time as if coming directly from the Virgin Mary.

On the first page was a picture of the Virgin and Child Jesus, surrounded by the quotation: 'Ecce Mater tua' – 'Behold your Mother' (Jn 19:27). Then, speaking as Mary herself, Elizabeth gave the prioress the same passage of St Paul which she had explained for Françoise in *The Greatness of Our Vocation*: to walk in Christ, be rooted in him, built up on him, strengthened in faith... (cf. Col 2:6–7; GV 10–12). The commentary this time, though, was not all about being uprooted from self –

advice more tailored to Françoise de Sourdon. Instead, she gave Mother Germaine a much more contemplative interpretation of the passage: *walking* 'the luminous Road'; being *rooted* 'in the depths of the Abyss'; being *built up* on God who is a 'Rock' and 'Fortress'; and being *strengthened in faith*. With this last point, Elizabeth invites the prioress to *believe in love* – to have 'faith in the immense Love that is rushing from the great Furnace into the depths of your soul' (L 316). 'My daughter...,' says Elizabeth daringly to her Mother Superior, 'with what *particular tenderness* you are loved' (L 316). But she could of course get away with it, because it was all said in the person of the Virgin Mary – a strategy, the prioress felt, that displayed 'great tact' (PG, p. 201).

Then there were the presents: a scapular accompanying this letter, which Elizabeth herself had made, putting the greatest care into it despite her exhaustion. Mother Germaine would later recall how Elizabeth's 'charming little attentions' and her notes for her sisters in Carmel – she would single out this very letter as an example – brought 'both light and life' (PG, p. 201) to their recipients. And finally, on that September 24, there was without doubt the greatest gift of all. Elizabeth handed Mother Germaine a little package wrapped in poor-quality brown paper and carrying the title: 'The last retreat of Laudem Gloriae' (CW I, p. 132). The prioress was delighted with the work which she felt could have been called, '*Intimate Reminiscences*', for it seemed to her that the pages allowed one to 'read into [Elizabeth's] soul' (S1, p. 165).

'This holy place'

Five days later came the sixteenth anniversary of the clothing ceremony of Sister Louise de Gonzague, who had been Elizabeth's 'first officer' in the habit room. Elizabeth wrote her a poem, addressed from the 'place' of her suffering, and says in the opening lines: 'I am thinking of you very much on the Mount of Calvary, / ...this holy place' (P 118).

It was the feast of St Michael, September 29, and Elizabeth's ever-active mind grasped the significance of his name which means, in Hebrew, 'in the likeness of God'. No theme could have delighted Elizabeth more, and several times she repeats this question: 'Who then is like God?...' This is how she begins her answer:

> 'Who then is like God?...' A magnificent motto
> For every being who dwells in annihilation
> And distils her life in order to help the Church
> In profound silence and in recollection. (P 118)

This is the first (and only) mention in Elizabeth's writings of the idea, from Catherine of Siena, of a life being 'distilled' for the Church. It would become extremely important to Elizabeth in her final days, when she would often repeat: 'May my life distil drop by drop for you, O Christ, and for the Church, Your sweet spouse' (ESS, p. 39). It also ties in perfectly with Elizabeth's personal longing to 'extract from her being all the prayer and suffering possible' (S1, p. 168).

Humility – or lowering oneself to the point of disappearing – provides the second and main theme of this poem. To be like God is to resemble Christ who annihilated himself before the Father, she says – and 'in our turn we want to disappear'. But where? It is not, this time, a descending into the depths of the 'immense Ocean' of the Trinity (cf. P 115). Rather, it is the 'double abyss': 'Oh,' she exclaims, 'let us rush to the depths of the "double abyss": / "The immensity of God, our own nothingness"' (P 118). The two phrases Elizabeth quotes here come from her recent reading of Angela of Foligno. The 'double abyss', in particular, caught Elizabeth's heart because it expresses not just infinite depths ('abyss'), but also an intimate exchange with God ('double'). It is, in the words of Bl Angela, a 'tête-à-tête' (P 118, n. 7), and it corresponds to Elizabeth's longed-for 'face-to-face' (cf. L 332). The way to get there is by humbling oneself, as Angela of Foligno explains: '...the double abyss, where the divine Immensity is in a tête-à-tête with the nothingness of man. And the light of the double abyss, this light, is humility' (P 118, n. 7). Elizabeth's body may have been almost too weak to take a step, but her soul was soaring – rushing to that double abyss where she would meet God who was coming swiftly to meet her:

> He so loves to find the soul in this attitude
> Of annihilation, of humiliation:
> He flings Himself towards her with His plenitude
> So as to consummate the divine union. (P 118)

The Palace of Pain and Bliss

So long as she had been able to hide her illness, Elizabeth had said nothing of it to her sisters in community or in her letters. It was really only now, at the point of death, that she allowed herself to say openly, writing here to family friends: 'I am very ill' (L 313); 'Yes, I am very ill these days' (L 318). But 'illness' refers only to her physical state, her symptoms, whereas 'suffering' says so much more, with all its resonances of spiritual fruitfulness and union with Christ. This is what Elizabeth wrote to her mother at the end of September:

> I am very absorbed in the passion, and when you see all He suffered for us in His heart, in His soul, and in His body, you have, as it were, a need to give all that back to Him in return; it's as if you wish to suffer all that He suffered. (L 317)

When Elizabeth said, 'I am very absorbed in the passion', what she meant in particular was that she was absorbed in reading Angela of Foligno who was continuing to enrich her own suffering; and we can see, from the quotations in Elizabeth's letters, that she was reading or rereading a small selection of pages from Bl Angela's *Book of Visions and Instructions*. It is also worth noting that the spiritual impetus, in the last few months of Elizabeth's life, seems to have come from four medieval mystics: Ruysbroeck, on the life of God in the soul; Angela of Foligno, on the Passion; Catherine of Siena, with the notion of a life being distilled drop by drop for the Church; and right at the end, as we shall see later, St Gertrude, with her prayer of praise and her passionate longing for union with Christ.

Over the years, there had been great maturing in Elizabeth, and her faith and courage had been strengthened to a remarkable degree. After just a few months in Carmel, she had longed to 'set up [her] tent' (P 74) on Tabor with Jesus; but now, less than five years later, she could say from the midst of her pain: 'I am asking the Master to set up a tent there [on Calvary] next to His own' (L 317). Elizabeth said this to her mother at the end of September, and her request was answered almost immediately.

On the last day of September, Elizabeth's pain was so bad that she wrote a note to the prioress at 11 p.m., saying: 'Your little praise of glory is suffering very much, very much; it is the "exceeding love", the divine dispensation of pain' (L 319; cf. Eph 2:4). Elizabeth, seeing always the connection between her suffering and God's love for her, is in fact describing exceeding *pain*. But this note is not about pain alone: she asks to offer it up as 'a novena of suffering' for the forthcoming anniversary of Mother Germaine's election as prioress. And Elizabeth positions herself in yet another dwelling place, one of *shelter*: 'I have taken complete refuge in the prayer of my Master' (L 319), she writes. But the next month, on an even more terrible night, it seems there was nowhere to hide.

Again, it was 11 p.m., after the prioress had come to visit and give her the night blessing. Elizabeth wrote Mother Germaine the most desperate note she had written since the evening before her profession, when her soul had been 'overwhelmed with anguish' (L 152). Now, in October 1906, longing for the help and presence of the prioress, the word 'anguish' appears twice; and while it is accompanied by 'peace' at the beginning of the letter, by the end it has reached a crescendo pitch when it is inseparable from 'fear'. This is the letter in its entirety, ending in the midst of the emotion and, like the previous note, without a signature:

My darling Mother, my beloved priest,
    Your little praise of glory cannot sleep, she is suffering; but in her soul, although the anguish penetrates there too,

she feels so much peace, and it is your visit that has brought her this Heavenly peace. Her little heart needs to tell you this, and in her tender gratitude she is praying and suffering unceasingly for you! Oh, help me climb my Calvary; I feel the power of your priesthood over my soul so strongly, and I need you so much. My Mother, I feel my Three so close to me; I am more overwhelmed by happiness than by pain: my Master has reminded me that it is my dwelling place and I am not to choose my sufferings; so I immerse myself with Him into immense suffering, with much fear and anguish. (L 320)

As Elizabeth lay there, with the pain cascading down on her, she must have felt that it was drowning out everything else. And yet, still she held onto her 'happiness' which, like the pain, 'overwhelmed' her. Together, they formed the dwelling place that would be hers for the remaining weeks of her life – the address at the top of her letter:

From the palace of pain and bliss.[7]

---

[7] In the French, Elizabeth writes 'douleur' and 'béatitude'. As we have seen (cf. n. 5 above), the first term means, in the physical sense, 'pain', and in the emotional sense, 'sorrow' – hence, 'Notre Dame des Douleurs' ('Our Lady of Sorrows'); it can also mean 'suffering', which is why Elizabeth, after quoting Bl Angela, for example, uses the more common word for 'suffering' – 'souffrance' – as a synonym for 'douleur' (cf. L 315). The second term means 'beatitude' or 'bliss'; it is deeper and more solemn than 'bonheur', the usual word for 'happiness', which Elizabeth uses within the letter.

Chapter 21

CLOTHED FOR A NEW LIFE

'Clothed with the Man of sorrows'

'While waiting for my habit,' Elizabeth had written to her mother at the end of September, 'I look like a Poor Clare, in a housecoat of grey flannel' (L 317). Then, on Thursday, October 4, she received her new brown quilted habit. And an inspiration came to her: she asked Mother Germaine if she might take this opportunity to renew the ceremony of her clothing, when she had received the Carmelite habit for the first time.

The prioress agreed, and it took place that afternoon near the tribune. Elizabeth put on her new habit and managed to observe every detail of the ceremony, even the great prostration when she lay on the floor with her arms outstretched in the form of a cross. She had always thrilled at the thought of being set apart for God, given to him as a sacrifice, and in the last few weeks of her life this is a recurrent theme: a sense of being handed over totally in a definitive consecration. This ceremony, then, with the same prostration as when she first received the Carmelite habit and also when she took her vows, could well have brought to Elizabeth's mind her profession and the priesthood of Mother Germaine who had offered her – and would offer her again – to God.

For that same day, Elizabeth gave her a poem (P 121), in which she speaks of the prioress as priest and herself as sacrificial victim.[1] Equally prominent in it is Elizabeth's identification with

---

[1] This poem (P 121) as well as a letter (L 321) are provisionally dated by Conrad De Meester as October 4, but with the additional possibility, for the letter, of October 9, the fifth anniversary of Mother Germaine's election as prioress: cf. P 121, n. 1; L 321, n. 1. As the themes in both pieces are

the crucified Christ. As she says of God the Father: 'He is identifying me / With the Man of sorrows'. This was, in fact, a 'clothing' in its own way: Elizabeth loved St Paul's words about being 'clothed' with Jesus Christ (cf. Gal 3:27; LR 39; PT), and she would be filled with joy when, just before her death, a sister said to her: 'You are clothed with the Man of sorrows' (PG, p. 218).

The poem's appearance on the page is very striking. Unlike any other piece Elizabeth ever wrote (except for the words on the flag sticking out of the cardboard citadel!), it is in red ink. This was almost certainly in order to reflect the sacrificial theme. On the first page is a picture: the Father giving his crucified Son, and between them the Spirit in the form of a dove. In front of this can be seen a priest at the altar, raising up the Host at the moment of consecration in the Mass. And Elizabeth begins the poem with these words: 'O my Mother, it is you, this Pontiff at the altar / And Laudem gloriae is the little host.' She then goes on to remind the prioress how she had offered her as a sacrifice at Elizabeth's profession. Then, she says, it had been the 'wholly luminous day' of the Epiphany, and the sacrifice had been the gift of Elizabeth to the infant Jesus lying in the manger. But now, as she says starkly, Jesus is asking for a 'new sacrifice'. And she addresses Mother Germaine with a thinly veiled reference to Abraham preparing to sacrifice his son Isaac: 'But [Christ] wants still more, and your maternal hand / Is going to sacrifice to Him your wholly little child.' As this shows so well, the poem is concerned with the parallel between Elizabeth's vows – when she died to herself so as to be given totally to God – and her imminent death and departure for heaven which will be the ultimate fulfilment of her profession.

At the same time, this poem is meant to be an affirmation of Mother Germaine in that Elizabeth repeats, from a recent letter

---

primarily the priesthood and the offering of sacrifice – and the priesthood of the prioress in particular – the poem and letter almost certainly belong together, deriving from the same occasion. Further support for the date of October 4 comes from the fact that the election anniversary on the 9th is commemorated by Elizabeth with a separate poem (P 122).

(cf. L 316), the message of how much the prioress is loved by God. Elizabeth says of her own profession: 'This offering pleased Him, because *He loves you* so much'; and of her imminent departure for heaven: 'Your God, because He loves you, is accepting your sacrifice/host [*hostie*]'. This poem, then, is focused not so much on Elizabeth herself being sacrificed, but on how Mother Germaine's offering of that sacrifice is acceptable to God. The poem spells it out loud and clear: 'if God took me and accepted me, / It is because it is you who had presented me'.

Finally, looking ahead to her death, Elizabeth tries to console and prepare the prioress:

What happiness, then, I had to be offered by your hand!
That is why God is taking me, is sacrificing me,
Why He is leading me to Calvary and why He is
      identifying me
With the Man of sorrows, my divine Model.

Mother, you must regard as a *pledge* of love
The departure of Laudem for the holy Homeland. (P 121)

The First of Many Feasts

When Elizabeth renewed her clothing ceremony, it was a day of celebration in the Carmel. October, while in many respects the most harrowing month for Elizabeth in terms of her illness, was also marked with a whole series of joyous festivities, one following on from another. First came October 4, which marked the anniversary of the death of Teresa of Avila in 1582.[2] And Elizabeth received a favour from St Teresa that day, which has something uncannily in common with her original clothing date

---

[2] Feast days often mark the day a saint died – or, if that date has already been taken, the free day nearest to it is chosen. Teresa of Avila died on a most unique day: October 4, 1582 was the last day on which the Julian calendar was in use; it was replaced, the next day, by the Gregorian calendar. Ten days were 'lost' that year, meaning that she died on the old October 4, and the next day – subsequently her feast day – was the new October 15. This explains why the two celebrations for Teresa in the Dijon Carmel were eleven days apart.

in 1901. We have already seen how Elizabeth, as a postulant, had wished to receive the habit very soon after entering Carmel, and how she had confided this longing to St Teresa and then received an interior intimation that this would take place on the feast of the Immaculate Conception – which, as we know, would turn out to be the case although it had at first seemed unlikely.

Now, on October 4, 1906, Elizabeth longed to join her sisters in choir that evening. It was almost seven months since she had last been on the ground floor, and in all this time she had been with the whole community only once: on June 14, when she had been carried the few yards from the infirmary to the chapter room, for the eve of the prioress' feast day. So it seemed most unlikely that Elizabeth would be able to withstand the exertion of being taken downstairs and of joining in the community's celebration there. But she confided this wish to Teresa of Avila, and against all likelihood it was granted. The ever-sturdy Sister Marie of the Holy Spirit picked her up and carried her down the stairs in her arms like a child.

Elizabeth now entered the choir, for the first time since the feast of St Joseph, or the following morning, in mid-March.[3] It was dark in the half-light of the October evening, and the sisters could hardly make her out. But what they saw moved them deeply. Frail and trembling, she sat there, lost to everything around her, absorbed in fervent prayer and knowing that this was the last time she would ever pray in this sacred place. Then, for the second time that day, she made the prostration – before the grille, following the prescribed custom. Despite being extremely shaky, she felt a sense of calm inner joy as she did so. Finally, serene and radiant, she left her sisters. She had renewed the gift of herself. And as Mother Germaine would say so well, Elizabeth was now to 'complete the gift so sincerely renewed' (PG, p. 202).

Although near the end of her days, Elizabeth felt that this giving of herself was like entering 'a new life'. This is what she had written to the prioress that very day:

---

[3] See Chapter 14, n. 7, on the likelihood of this date.

+ My beloved priest,

I do not know what is happening. My Master caught hold of me and made me understand that today the Mother and child are beginning a new life, 'wholly present to Love, wholly within pure Love'. At Mass, the Sovereign Priest is going to deliver up His priest and His two victims, and it will be full possession by Love! Oh, I cannot say what I feel, my Mother. How great it is! (L 321)[4]

Plotting Together

When Madame Catez paid her tenth visit to the infirmary parlour in early October, she was shocked to see the difference in her daughter. It was quite obvious that Elizabeth was dying, and the mother now harboured no illusions of a cure. But what also struck her powerfully was the inner energy, so to speak. For she would say: '[Elizabeth's] eyes that were so beautiful were more luminous than ever: her life was concentrated in them' (ETB, p. 696). And quite incredibly, Elizabeth now used some of this lively animation to devote herself to a little matchmaking!

Mother Germaine had no idea what was happening under her very nose! It was, as we know, a custom of the monastery that the prioress would read all correspondence between a nun and her family and friends, and that an additional sister must be present at every parlour visit. But the prioress had relaxed the rules in the case of Elizabeth and Madame Catez. Surely she could trust this saintly Carmelite who was expressing her dying words to a grieving mother... Instead, Madame Catez and Elizabeth were 'plotting together' (L 322) – and Elizabeth slipped her a letter for forwarding to a third party which the prioress absolutely must not see!

---

[4] For the most likely dating of this letter as October 4, see n. 1 above. The phrase 'His two victims' suggests the inclusion of Sister Anne-Marie who would have taken part in the community's celebrations that day and whom Elizabeth included in her other festivities during her time in the infirmary. The 'Sovereign Priest' is, of course, Christ; and the 'priest' refers to Mother Germaine.

This was the plan: Madame Gout de Bize was looking for a husband for her daughter Jeanne, a young woman of twenty-four known by the nickname of Jaja! Family photographs had been sent to Elizabeth; she found Jaja's expression 'charming' (L 318) and felt quite drawn to her. In fact, she said that she felt haunted by the picture (cf. L 318). So much so that she worked out who might be a most eligible suitor: 'I know a person who is so noble, of so fine a character, so worthy of your Jaja' (L 318), Elizabeth had written to Madame Gout de Bize on the last day of September. She even offered up her sufferings for the happy outcome, and said that she hoped this would help. Or rather, she did not say, 'I hope', but literally in the French – and in capital letters – 'I WANT' (OC, p. 766)! Which is a rare glimpse of the headstrong Elizabeth as in the days of her youth. She then placed Jaja's photograph at the foot of the statue of Our Lady of Lourdes and made a novena to Mary for the feast of Our Lady of the Rosary, which in those days was celebrated on the first Sunday in October; that year, it happened to fall on the 7th.

On the feast day itself, Elizabeth wrote again to Madame Gout de Bize. And once more, it was a letter to be passed on surreptitiously, care of her mother. This time, Elizabeth's letter revealed the name: 'Monsieur Robert de Saint-Seine' – none other than the younger brother of Mother Germaine! Hence the secrecy! The man in question, she continued, was 'someone with such a fine character and such lofty sentiments, so profoundly Christian' (L 322). But maybe she also guessed what would impress that lady most: 'he is one of those young men of a "stock" one scarcely finds any more' (L 322). Unfortunately, there was a potential snag, of which Elizabeth was only too well aware: the young man had an officer's salary – but no fortune. Hoping that this would not prove an obstacle, Elizabeth made sure to point out in an important postscript that he was one of 'the lords of Burgundy'; and she referred her friend to Madame Catez, saying: 'I'll leave the earthly side to *Mama*' (L 322)! As for Elizabeth, her interests were exclusively those of the heart: 'oh,' she exclaimed, 'how well [his heart] would go with the heart of my Jaja!...' (L 322).

But Madame Gout de Bize said 'no'. The problem? As Elizabeth wrote sadly to her mother: 'Alas, that wretched money, as soon as it's lacking...' (L 325). Elizabeth felt the disappointment keenly. Not only had this match been her 'dream' (L 318), but it was now a cause of embarrassment as the prioress had meanwhile been filled in! 'Our Mother's brother can do much better!' (L 325), wrote Elizabeth to Madame Catez, saying of the prioress: 'Don't feel sorry for my dear Mother, she was half expecting it and sees only God's will' (L 325). So Elizabeth now contented herself with matchmaking Mother Germaine and Madame Gout de Bize as bosom friends! As she wrote to Jaja's mother: 'your hearts are so well made to *go together*' (L 330)! The prioress, whose breeding (or 'stock') was clearly evident, wrote the lady a most gracious note, declaring her heart to be 'wholly yours' (L 330, n. 5)! But when Elizabeth's letters were returned to the convent after her death, Mother Germaine did her best to try and erase her brother's name!

Elizabeth was not just disappointed about the failure of her plan. She must also have been disillusioned at the ways of society and the unhappiness they caused – for her aim had been for Jaja to find 'happiness' (L 318).[5] Thanks to the mother's refusal, Jaja would remain single until the age of thirty-seven, tragically dying in childbirth the following year. And how often Elizabeth had written letters of condolence to Madame de Sourdon about the failed marriage prospects of her daughter Marie-Louise, which appear to have been a major concern to the mother. Yet in 1903, the girl had had a suitor with great 'qualities' who unfortunately had had to be turned down because he did not have the 'qualifications' (L 167). By which, Elizabeth did not mean

---

[5] Elizabeth was concerned, more than once, with helping a friend to find a husband. She prayed for this intention for Marie-Louise de Sourdon (who would eventually get married in May 1907), and also for Anne-Marie d'Avout to whom she said at their last parlour meeting when she was already very ill: 'I will send you a fine husband' (L 315, n. 8).

academic ones: 'I imagine,' she wrote, '[the name] is what he lacks' (L 167). It must have made Elizabeth marvel even more about how Jesus – God himself! – weds us to himself, with all our unworthiness and wretchedness. As she wrote at this very time: 'I live with my crucified Bridegroom' (L 323a).

'Have you not seen the priest...?'

A few days after Elizabeth's new 'clothing', a picture was taken of her as she sat on the terrace. This was the very last photograph taken of Elizabeth during her lifetime. Her companion, 'Janua Coeli', can be seen beside her: the statue of Our Lady of Lourdes standing on a little high table slightly behind her right shoulder. Elizabeth is holding a rosary given to her by Antoinette de Bobet. And on her lap is the volume of John of the Cross containing *The Spiritual Canticle* and *The Living Flame of Love*; the book is open at a page of *The Living Flame*. Perhaps the most noticeable thing of all is Elizabeth's intent gaze: she is looking ahead and slightly to the left. This may well be deliberately symbolic: for her eyes are turned towards the office of Mother Germaine.

October 9 marked five years since Mother Germaine's election as prioress – 'the glorious day when you became my Mother!' exclaims Elizabeth in a poem she gave her to commemorate the anniversary of the event (P 122). This is, Elizabeth says, the sign of God's excessive charity towards herself: 'I really was "loved too much"' (cf. Eph 2:4). This is no exaggeration. In fact, we might well wonder what Elizabeth's Carmelite life would have been, had she never had a Mother Germaine. She was a mother to Elizabeth in the very best sense: loving, firm, forming her to an inner strength and freedom, and sensitive to the subtlest inspirations of Elizabeth's soul. One sister would later say of Mother Germaine: 'No one in the community knew Elizabeth as she did' (PD, p. 203). In fact, as suggested before, the bond between them calls to mind Thérèse and her sister Pauline who was her second mother (cf. SS, p. 34) during her childhood and, as Mother Agnes, her prioress in Carmel. Mother Germaine may even have had this parallel relationship in mind. For later that month, she would ask Elizabeth how she envisaged her future mission in heaven, and if it would be like that of Thérèse (cf. CW I, p. 32) – a topic also discussed between Thérèse and Mother Agnes before Thérèse's death (cf. LC, p. 238). And Mother Germaine would write to this same prioress of Lisieux, who had brought out Thérèse's *Story of a Soul*, about her own proposed work: the biography of Elizabeth.

This poem was the last one Elizabeth would write for Mother Germaine, and it expresses the union between them. This relationship – one of priest and sacrificial victim – was part of God's plan at the beginning of time, when 'thinking of the moment of my sacrifice / [He] already consecrated you... / His love united His victim and His priest' (P 122).[6]

But most of all, we can see Elizabeth trying to console Mother Germaine for her imminent loss, assuring her that they will never be separated. So Elizabeth continues, explaining that this union between them, which originated at the beginning of time, will last forever: '"And from eternity to eternity" / His gaze will see them always united.'

In the final verse, Elizabeth expresses their bond with the striking image of the Eucharistic Host, carried along the city streets by the priest when taking Communion to the sick:

> Throughout the cities, have you not seen the priest
> Carrying, hidden on him, the sacrament of the Master?
> Ah, is that not how, on your maternal heart,
> Laudem gloriae will spend her whole Heaven? (P 122)

'Held firm in pure love'

That very day, Elizabeth was writing to explain the same bond, but in more universal terms: she was not speaking now of the

---

[6] This could also be translated as 'His victim and her priest' – that is, Elizabeth's (the victim's) 'priest', which would still refer to Mother Germaine as the French pronoun 'son' ('His'/'his' or 'her') could denote either. Elizabeth probably intended the meaning 'His', as in the letter: 'His priest and His two victims' (L 321).

union between the prioress and herself in particular, but of that between the living and the dead in general. She was replying to Madame de Sourdon who had recently lost her sister, Madame de Maizières, and had asked Elizabeth to 'get into contact' with the deceased. Naturally, Elizabeth was 'astonished' and wondered if she had understood rightly! But she took the opportunity, in her reply, to explain just how much we are united, through faith and prayer, with those who have gone before us. 'I unite myself with the dear deceased,' she wrote, 'I enter into communion with her, I find her once more in Him by whom alone she lives: and so each time I draw near to God, faith tells me that I am also drawing close to her' (L 323).

This letter becomes increasingly inspiring and insightful as Elizabeth explains how our union with the departed is just as close, whether the deceased is in purgatory or in heaven:

> Now, whether she is already in the City of saints or still in that place where the soul completes the work of being purified to contemplate the divine beauty and be transformed in His own Image, as Saint Paul says: in whichever of these she may be, she is held firm in pure love, nothing distracts her from God, and that is what makes me feel closer to the dead than to the living. For, dear Madame, when we want to find a beloved soul again, do we know if at every moment it is dwelling in God? Alas, here below, so many things make us wander!... (L 323; cf. 2Cor 3:18)

This is an important statement and it would explain why Elizabeth placed so much stress on giving friends set times for a 'rendez-vous' with her in prayer – times when she could be sure that both she and the other person were meeting each other in God. It is in God, she knew, that we can meet others at the deepest level, for we are all in him. But if one person is focused on God, and the other person is not, the current of communication is lessened. With the dead, however, there is no such problem: they are 'held firm' in him and are focused on him all the time – 'nothing distracts' them from God. So even in purgatory, they are fulfilling Elizabeth's long-held ideal of prayer: '*May nothing* be able to distract me from you' (IN 5); 'May I never leave You...alone, but be wholly present... I want to gaze on You always' (PT).

Having explained that God himself is the place, so to speak, in which to meet other people again, Elizabeth now speaks of how the Cross is her own 'beloved dwelling place' and also a meeting place, for she dwells there with him: 'on my cross...I taste unknown joys. I understand that suffering is the revelation of Love, and I rush to it: it is my beloved dwelling place where I find peace and rest, where I am sure to meet my Master and dwell with Him' (L 323). The Cross may seem an unlikely place of 'rest'. But Elizabeth is surely thinking of the whole attitude of surrender and submission implied by the Cross. Expressing this in terms of the image of the Cross itself, she had written, in her poem to Sister Louise ten days earlier, of 'Him whom [the Cross] supports' (P 118) – a notion drawn from Angela of Foligno. And when Elizabeth spoke with Father Vallée later that month, he would say afterwards that she wished, more and more, to lie down on the Cross.[7]

Elizabeth knew that her death was rapidly approaching, and she admitted to Madame de Sourdon: 'I don't think He will be much longer in coming to seek me' (L 323). This reveals, characteristically, how she saw death in terms of her *relationship* with God: she does not say that she is simply going to 'die', in that impersonal word; rather, to use her expression here, Jesus will come and 'seek' her. Mother Germaine added a postscript to the letter, saying: 'she is really going downhill, the little saint. Another month, six weeks perhaps...' (L 323, n. 7). The prioress was more accurate than the community's physician (cf. ETB, p. 698): it would be one month exactly.

---

[7] Cf. Sesé, p. 176. Sesé dates this final meeting between Elizabeth and Father Vallée as towards the end of October 1906; however, Conrad De Meester points out that the Dominican met Elizabeth in the infirmary parlour during one of the days when he was preaching at the Carmel: October 13 or 14 (cf. ETB, p. 696).

'Eternally living and present'

The next day, October 10, Elizabeth wrote to her friend Germaine de Gemeaux and gave her an insight into the 'joy' she was finding in pain. Out of context, this sounds off-puttingly masochistic, but in its real context it is an authentic witnessing to how even the worst circumstances, humanly speaking, are made bearable and even joyful by union with Jesus:

> I am tasting, experiencing unknown joys. The joy of pain, oh! little Germaine, how pleasant and sweet it is!... Before I die, I dream of being transformed into Jesus Crucified, and that gives me so much strength in suffering... Little sister, we should have no other ideal but to be conformed to that divine Model; then what eagerness we would have in sacrifice, in contempt of ourselves, if the eyes of our heart were always focused on Him. (L 324)

But the kernel of this letter is advice about Germaine's own discouragement. Since her earliest years, Germaine had wanted to become a nun. Now, however, she was acutely aware of a sense of being too wretched and unworthy to be accepted for religious life. Elizabeth speaks with the authority of one who is drawing close to heaven: 'Little sister of my soul, in the light of eternity God makes me understand many things, and I come to tell you as if it were coming from Him...' And this is what she says: as for Germaine thinking herself unworthy to be a nun, Elizabeth warns her against such discouragement which she calls 'a huge temptation'. More than this: Elizabeth invites her friend not just to banish discouragement, but to be encouraged by her 'miseries' which can, and should, be a path to confidence in God. She writes:

> If your nature is a subject of combat, a battlefield, oh, do not be discouraged, do not become sad. I would gladly say to you: love your misery, for that is where God exercises His mercy, and when the sight of it throws you into sadness that makes you withdraw into yourself, that is self-love! When

you find yourself faltering, go [and] take refuge in the prayer of your Master; yes, little sister, on His Cross He saw you and prayed for you, and that prayer is eternally living and present before His Father; that prayer will save you from your miseries. The more you feel your weakness, the more your confidence must grow, for you must depend on Him alone. (L 324)

All this teaching is pure Thérèse. Elizabeth, too, would have been excellent in forming novices in the spiritual life, for she put things in exactly the right perspective: knowing that there is a place for our own efforts, and also a point at which we must refer everything to the mercy of God. And ultimately, that we must have the faith to know that everything has been ordained by him – that Christ's prayer for us is 'eternally living and present before His Father'.

'My consoling ideal'

Elizabeth ended her letter to Germaine by recalling the example of the Carmelite martyrs of Compiègne. As we have seen, their beatification on May 27 was the reason why Madame Catez had visited Paris in June, for three days of celebrations at the church of St Sulpice. Now, the Dijon Carmel was to hold its own triduum, ending on Monday, October 15, the feast of Teresa of Avila. The link between St Teresa and the sixteen nuns of Compiègne ran deeper than the mere overlapping of dates on the calendar. When Elizabeth had written to her mother of the Carmelite martyrs, she had spoken in the same breath of Teresa's 'martyrdom of love' (L 287).

The triduum at the Carmel was a grand occasion. The chapel was decorated with splendour; there were numerous Masses, and a 'concert' (L 325) during Benediction on the Saturday evening; Father Vallée preached at Benediction on the first two evenings; and Bishop Dadolle celebrated Mass on the final morning and was the preacher in the evening. Mother Germaine wrote a report for the local Catholic newspaper; she signed herself anonymously as 'A witness', and passed her article to Elizabeth. After reading it, Elizabeth turned it over, took up her pencil, and... the reverse side of the paper would itself be a witness – to the draft of her final poem!

Elizabeth attended the festivities in her little tribune. During the many Masses, she united herself with the Eucharistic Host; and when the Blessed Sacrament was exposed for adoration, Elizabeth, who was at almost exactly the same level, thought once more of those words in the Psalm: 'The queen stands at the right of the King' (Ps 44:10; S1, p. 180; cf. L 287). It seemed to Elizabeth, that day, that as the queen at the side of the King, she was in a position to 'draw many graces from His heart' (PG, p. 203).

More and more, Elizabeth was perceiving herself as the queen at the side of Jesus, the King. This had nothing, of course, to do with a superior attitude. Rather, it conjured up for her a whole majestic bearing, and suggested to her the dignity of one who suffers in the likeness of Jesus and in union with him. One day she said: 'My Master asks me to go to my passion with the majesty of a queen' (ESS, p. 40). Sister Agnes, struck by the way Elizabeth was bearing her illness, felt that her whole attitude in suffering was summed up by this phrase (cf. ESS, p. 40).

Elizabeth learned this attitude by contemplation. Gazing on Mary, the 'Queen of martyrs', she discovered what majesty was all about. In her *Last Retreat* in August, she had written: 'How beautiful she is to contemplate during her long martyrdom, so serene, enveloped in a kind of majesty that radiates both strength and gentleness...' (LR 41). Mary was constantly before her eyes, especially in her martyrdom on Calvary as she stood there, close to her crucified Son. This gave Elizabeth both strength and peace in her own illness, and she said these marvellous words to the sub-prioress: 'Mary standing at the foot of the Cross is my consoling ideal' (ESS, p. 44).

On the Saturday evening, the first day of the triduum, Madame Catez came to attend the 'concert' at which Guite was performing, and was given a bird's eye view from the visitors' tribune. Mother Germaine then came into Elizabeth's own tribune and opened the 'grille' for her, drawing back the veil-covered frame in front of it. From her place, Elizabeth had the joy of seeing her mother almost opposite her; they were like two women in their theatre boxes, and Elizabeth felt a surge of joy. Writing to her the next day, to inform her that she had actually *seen* her, Elizabeth spoke of her own feelings when comparing herself with her sister that night: 'I felt *my happiness* more than *ever*. I was suffering a lot, I was thinking that soon perhaps earth would no longer be for me, for truly my poor body is very sick, and I said to myself: "You are the happy one."' (L 325).

Elizabeth had also learnt something from listening to Guite accompanying her husband on the piano during their rehearsal one evening. Elizabeth had noticed how her sister kept her piano accompaniment in the background, in order to bring his cello performance to the fore. It was a lesson Elizabeth decided to apply to her own life as much as possible, for it was, she saw, yet another way in which to praise God's glory. As she said to Mother Germaine: 'I ought to be, like [Guite], an instrument from which the divine Master can draw the melodies He loves best, effacing myself to give Him all the glory, only seconding His action by co-operation with His grace' (PG, p. 203).

'Love by my side'

It was during these days that Elizabeth spoke to Father Vallée for the very last time. Mother Germaine took him upstairs to the infirmary parlour, where he found Elizabeth on a little bed. Her veil was lowered over her face, which was the custom when seeing a priest, but it was clear that Elizabeth was having difficulty breathing beneath the veil. So the prioress lifted it – and Father Vallée had the privilege of seeing Elizabeth's face one last time.

It was not entirely a beautiful expression: there was anxiety in the eyes, which showed him how much she was suffering. But he could see that the anxiety belonged entirely to the physical level: it was otherwise clear to him that her soul was in deep peace. His overriding impression was that she was completely detached from herself. And he would later comment: 'Nothing drew her attention back to herself. She thought only of surrendering herself, of lying down more and more on the Cross.'[8]

Elizabeth now spoke of suffering and asked him if she might ask for *more* suffering – or possibly, for more *capacity* for suffering.[9] And she explained: 'Suffering increases my capacity for the grace of my Christ.'[10] We recall how she had written to Father Vallée in August, asking for advice as to how she might 'be conformed to the image of the Crucified' (L 304); and as we have seen, he had directed her thoughts, first and foremost, to faith in God's *love* (cf. L 308; HF 20, n. 11a). Now, meeting her in the parlour that October, he again urged her to embrace a wider perspective than an exclusive focus on suffering (cf. PG, p. 204). He told her to leave the initiative to Christ who loved her; to be ready to obey Christ's will without anticipating anything; and simply to abandon herself joyously, surrendering herself to all Christ's desires.[11]

His words had an impact. We remember how, at their first meeting before she entered Carmel, Elizabeth had seemed to him 'like a tidal wave' (ETB, p. 325) of enthusiasm when he spoke to her of the love of Christ. Now, despite her extreme weakness, something similar happened. Towards the end of their exchange, she made little cries of exclamation, saying: 'O! Love, do not delay, complete what you have begun!'[12] – an echo of the poem 'The Living Flame' by John of the Cross: 'now consummate! if it be your will: / tear through the veil of this sweet encounter!' (LF, stanza 1).

---

[8] In Sesé, p. 176.
[9] Father Vallée, in his account of this meeting, paraphrases Elizabeth's words, saying that she asked him 'if she could beg for more suffering': see *ibid.*, p. 176. However, in the light of a letter she wrote on about October 10, discussed below, it appears that her concern was to ask for more *capacity* for suffering (cf. L 323a).
[10] In Sesé, p. 176.
[11] Cf. *ibid.*, p. 176.
[12] In *ibid.*, p. 176.

Soon after this meeting, Elizabeth told the prioress about the effect on her: 'I feel Love by my side, like a living being who is saying to me: "I want to live in communion [*société*] with you; for that, I want you to suffer without thinking that you are suffering, simply surrendering yourself to my action"' (S1, p. 181); and in her letters, she now began to speak of 'a Being who is Love' (L 327; cf. L 329; L 330). Mother Germaine would later sum up the effect of this interview on Elizabeth: 'From that time her soul, turned towards the regions raised above all suffering, seemed to grow daily more full of light, and, notwithstanding her pain, our little sister appeared to dwell already in the heaven of glory' (PG, p. 204). As for the impression made on Father Vallée, he would write: 'You could see her shining faith in her gaze, in her face. She was so intelligent! She seemed to embrace this whole mystery of death which was clasping her!...'[13] But most of all, it was Love that was clasping her and surrounding her. And this too, for Elizabeth, was a clothing – being clothed with Jesus himself, as she had written to Mother Germaine three weeks earlier: 'The abyss of His love surrounds [you] like a garment: it is the Bridegroom!' (L 316).

There was yet another grace for Elizabeth during the triduum for the martyrs of Compiègne. On the final day, the feast of Teresa of Avila, the Bishop of Dijon preached at evening Benediction and linked the two Carmelite celebrations together, describing St Teresa as a 'martyr' because 'she gave the greatest possible gift... supreme love' (PG, p. 204). His homily was, apparently, most remarkable and it moved many hearts. As Elizabeth left her tribune, she felt the irresistible desire to give her whole love by making an absolute sacrifice of herself. The Bishop came to meet her at the grille of the infirmary parlour, and there he gave her his blessing. The prioress would later say that Elizabeth looked on this as her 'final consecration to the Trinity' (ETB, p. 696).

---

[13] In *ibid.*, p. 178.

'That transforms everything'

Elizabeth had asked Father Vallée if she might pray for an increase in suffering – by which, as we have seen, she may have meant an increase in her capacity for suffering. In fact, this had already been the intention of her prayer for the last few days. For around October 10, she had written to Madame de Vathaire: 'pray that God might increase my capacity for suffering' (L 323a). Most people would say this only in the hope of bearing their suffering more easily. And as her suffering would inevitably increase as her illness progressed, right up to the point of death, she *needed* to be able to bear yet more, and to bear it well. Yet in the light of Elizabeth's heroic desire to 'extract from her being all the prayer and suffering possible' (S1, p. 168), she was probably asking for her capacity to be increased so that she might indeed suffer even more.

If this was a prayer for increased suffering, then it was soon answered. For only about a week later, she wrote to Madame Farrat: 'I have been suffering more for several days' (L 326). In this third week of October, Elizabeth's stomach, already barely functioning, now took yet another turn for the worse. Her letters to her mother reveal that she now has 'continual nausea' (L 327) and that 'everything makes me a little sick' (L 325). Her friends now excelled themselves, seeking out as many different brands of chocolates as they could find; 'Kalougas' were particularly 'soothing', and her 'poor stomach tired of everything' (L 326) was glad of their variety of flavours: pistachio, coffee, fruit... Some people even made their own for her, which elicited Elizabeth's congratulations: 'I award you a diploma in candy making' (L 328a), she wrote to Anne-Marie d'Avout. And to her mother: 'you rival the "*specialists*"!' (L 327). A few people even made pretty presentation boxes, and the poignant irony is that the infirmary cell of this dying nun must have looked, at times, like the scene of one big birthday party. Elizabeth felt it was a shame to give all those sweets to a mouth that couldn't even taste them. And she was struggling to keep

up with Mother Germaine's instructions: to eat eight chocolates a day.

The continual nausea was accompanied by vomiting, and
a sense that the chocolates were burning her stomach. All this
would have been enough to make her life a constant misery.
But the eyes of her soul, as luminous as her physical eyes (cf.
ETB, p. 696), looked beyond it. In her range of vision there
were always two imposing objects: heaven, which once more she
described as 'Light' and 'Love' (L 326; cf. L 313); and Christ, who
was *everything* to her. This is what allowed Elizabeth to rise above
the physical symptoms, as we see from a letter to Madame Catez:

> There is a Being who is Love and who wishes us to live in
> communion with Him. Oh Mama, it is delightful, for He
> is there keeping me company, helping me to suffer, urging
> me to go beyond my suffering to rest in Him; do as I do, you
> will see how that transforms everything. (L 327; cf. 1Jn 1:3)

'A thousand little services'

Elizabeth was continually going beyond her suffering in this
month of October, even though by now her exhaustion was
extreme. Despite this, she spent most of her daytime hours out
of bed and made longer and more frequent visits to the tribune
to pray before the Blessed Sacrament – she begged to be allowed
to spend at least half an hour there. And right up to just before
her death, she would do whatever she could to make life as easy
as possible for the sisters looking after her. When she felt too ill
to do much, she would still help in whatever way she could, such
as arranging the flowers for the sacristy. As Mother Germaine
would say, Elizabeth rendered 'a thousand little services to those
around her' (PG, p. 195). Quite incredibly, in any job she carried
out Elizabeth still showed exactly the same neatness and applica-
tion that had characterised her whole life.

But never, perhaps, did Elizabeth manage to go beyond her
suffering as she did for Sister Marie-Joseph in the second and
third weeks of October. By now, this sister was the only remain-

ing postulant from the initial group of three, as Clémence Blanc had left around July, and Sister Thérèse in September. This left the one lay sister, and her clothing ceremony was soon due to take place; Elizabeth, as her 'Angel', was keen to help with the preparations and even took on herself the making of her white bridal outfit. The prioress would say that 'her great charity sustained her' (PG, p. 205). This was very true: for Elizabeth knew that her contributions would give great delight to the little novice. Mother Germaine also gives a most harrowing picture of Elizabeth at work: 'the exhaustion of her poor body, which was almost reduced to a skeleton and required all her mental energy to urge to the slightest movement, showed that the end was not far off. Her fingers could hardly hem the linen and often fell helpless on her little table' (PG, p. 205). At which, Elizabeth would smile – and somehow manage to carry on.

She also sent notes, either enlisting help or expressing her thanks for it: to Sister Louise, for example, her 'first officer' in the habit room; to Guite, who would be participating in the music at Benediction which preceded the ceremony; and to Madame Catez, who sent in the collar as well as an iron for use on the morning itself. Elizabeth had already inspected the postulant trying on the headdress, and wrote to Madame Catez with joy: 'our little Sister is superb' (L 327). Mother Germaine noted with admiration that Elizabeth did everything with 'exquisite taste' and showed forethought about even the 'smallest details' (PG, p. 205). Elizabeth was only too happy to do this, her aim being that everything should go smoothly for Sister Marie-Joseph on the day itself.

'Place me on your heart'

Finally came the great day: Monday, October 22. In addition to preparing clothes for the new novice, Elizabeth had also written a poem for her (P 123). It is an important one because here, at the end of her life, Elizabeth sums up how to live the Carmelite vocation. The poem refers, throughout, to these words from the Song of Songs: 'Place me on your heart' (Sg 8:6) – this book

being an allegory of the intimate love between God and the
soul, and much loved by Carmelites throughout the centuries.[14]
Elizabeth's poem is about intimacy with Jesus, and the demands
of his love. This, then, is her very last poem – quoted here in
full – and it is her message of how to follow Christ to the end:

> To respond, O my Sister, to the call of your Master,
> Arise in strength and surrender your whole being,
> Then recollect yourself well, beneath [His] excessive love,
> So that He may consume you both night and day.
>
> Is it not for that reason that He is taking you completely,
> That He is putting you in chains in Carmel, that He is
>   making you a prisoner?
> At the eve of this beautiful day, listen to Him, my Sister,
> Here He is, saying to you: 'Place me on your heart.'
>
> To place Him on your heart, an adorable mystery,
> Is to keep Him within you as in a sanctuary
> And to live with Him alone, in an intimacy
> That demands, O my Sister, great fidelity.
>
> To place Him on your heart is to love Him for Himself
> In detachment and forgetfulness of yourself,
> It is to gaze at Him unceasingly in simplicity,
> Fully embracing His entire will.
>
> To place Him on your heart like a bouquet of myrrh,
> Is to lead your life in the spirit of martyrdom.
> May your rule, O my Sister, if you keep it in truth,
> Immolate you to our God, who is Light and Charity.
>   (P 123)

---

[14] It is, notably, the basis for *The Spiritual Canticle* by John of the Cross and
the subject of a short work by St Teresa, *Meditations on the Song of Songs*. And
Thérèse of Lisieux once said: 'If I had time, I would comment on the Song of
Songs; I discovered in this book such profound things about the union of the
soul with her Beloved': in Pierre Descouvemont, *Thérèse of Lisieux and Marie of
the Trinity: The Transformative Relationship of Saint Thérèse of Lisieux and her novice
Sister Marie of the Trinity*, New York: Alba House, 1997, p. 66.

Elizabeth united herself to the ceremony while in her usual place in the tribune. The recent preparations had set her thinking back to the past, and to her own clothing day in 1901: 'that has brought back some memories!' (L 327), she had written to her mother, a few days previously. But now, as Elizabeth considered what was taking place in choir at that moment, she was overcome with happiness, thinking of the future: of another ceremony in a few days' or weeks' time, when she herself would be laid in that very place where the young novice now lay prostrate, clothed for a new life.

Chapter 22

THE FIRE OF LOVE

'A novena of suffering'

It was eleven o'clock in the evening of that same day, October 22. Sister Marie-Joseph had gone up to her cell after her first full day in the Carmelite habit, and Mother Germaine had gone from one door to the next, blessing the sisters before they retired for the night. Elizabeth took a piece of paper and began a note to the prioress with these harrowing words: 'My beloved priest, Your little victim is suffering very, very much, it is a kind of physical agony. She feels so cowardly, cowardly enough to scream!' (L 329). But, she continued, speaking now through the eyes of faith, 'the Being who is the Fullness of Love visits her, keeps her company, makes her enter into communion with Him, while He makes her understand that as long as He leaves her on earth, He will measure out suffering to her.' Finally, Elizabeth's generous spirit brought out an idea which had come to her at the end of September under similar circumstances – 'a novena of suffering' (cf. L 319):

> Darling Mother, if you will allow it, I feel moved to prepare for your feast on All Saints, so you might be rooted in pure love like the glorified, by beginning a novena of suffering for you during which we will go to visit you every night, while you're asleep, with the Fullness of love! Excuse Laudem gloriae, she loves you so much. Next to Him, you are everything to her. (L 329)[1]

---

[1] The 'we' – who will 'go to visit' Mother Germaine – refers to Elizabeth and God, for she knew herself to be subsumed within him: cf. L 329, n. 7.

This 'novena of suffering' could well describe the next stage of Elizabeth's illness: the nine days of intense pain from the 22nd to the 30th inclusive before her final collapse, when she would no longer be able to leave her bed. On this very Monday evening of October 22, just hours after the clothing ceremony of Sister Marie-Joseph, Elizabeth's sufferings stepped up a notch and became more cruel than before.

God's Action

Firstly, there was Elizabeth's constant source of trouble: her stomach. Not only was she now coughing up blood, but the pain itself reached new heights. One sister asked her if she was suffering a great deal, and Elizabeth mimed a reply: her ever-tranquil face became distorted in agony and she made violent gestures with her hands as if someone were ripping out her insides. Then, just as suddenly, her face regained its usual serene smile (cf. ETB, p. 698). To the sub-prioress, she put it into words one day: 'It seems to me that wild animals are devouring my stomach' (ETB, p. 697). All this speaks reams about Elizabeth's courage and self-composure: anyone else in this degree of pain could easily, and understandably, have a face distorted in agony all the time.

Incredibly, there was an even greater source of suffering. The inflammation now became intense and took hold of her entire body, so much so that Mother Germaine would say: 'she was literally scorched' (PG, p. 206). A priest who was passing through Dijon said Mass one day that week at the Carmel and went upstairs to the infirmary tribune to give Communion to Elizabeth. He had been warned that her tongue was inflamed. But being told was one thing; seeing was another. When she opened her mouth to receive the Host, her tongue seemed to him 'as red as fire' (PG, p. 206), and he was so shaken that his hand trembled as he placed the Communion wafer on her tongue.

With the inflammation of her whole mouth, the palate as well as the tongue, speaking became excruciating. Still, she managed to speak words of affection to friends who visited her in the parlour and who went away weeping. But while her body was on fire, 'her face was radiant with joy' (PG, p. 206). This comment by Mother Germaine is extremely apt: it was not just the internal organs that were burning, it was the whole of Elizabeth's inner life. In fact, the priest had felt the same thing, as he would write to the Carmel after Elizabeth's death: 'Our Lord seemed to intimate to me that the love which inflamed the soul of His saintly victim was burning her more fiercely than the heat which consumed her poor body' (PG, p. 206).

Just as in the earlier stages of her illness, so Elizabeth continued to draw strength from the letters of St Paul. At this time, one phrase stood out for her more than ever before: 'God is a consuming fire' (Hb 12:29). We have already seen how important this notion was to Elizabeth. In earlier years, it denoted for her the work of the Holy Spirit in the innermost part of the soul (cf. PT). After the onset of the inflammation in May, it again meant a lot to her (cf. L 274; L 293), and she may well have linked her physical symptoms with the fire of God's action within her. Now, it became a vital support. Night and day, unable to forget the inflammation which raged throughout her body, she did not try to resist the pain or to rail against it. Instead, she experienced it as a symbol of the great spiritual reality taking place within her: it was *God* who was consuming her; it was a fire of *love*. Sister Marthe, watching Elizabeth in great pain with the inflammation, overheard her repeat these words: 'God is a consuming fire; God is a simple Being, He is love, so all His acts are love. And I like to think that it is His love that is consuming me' (ESS, p. 42). As her mouth continued to dry up and her thirst became truly terrible, Elizabeth would focus on the thirst of the crucified Christ: 'God is a consuming fire,' she said; 'it is His action that I am enduring. Our Lord forgets nothing that can make me resemble Him' (ESS, p. 42; cf. Jn 19:28). She would even manage to joke about her condition, saying: 'My Mother, it is very bad, but I think that the first thing I'll do when I get to heaven will be to drink' (ESS, p. 43).

'She is extraordinary'

Dr Barbier was stunned. 'Never have I seen such strength and serenity in suffering,' he said; 'she is enduring a veritable martyrdom' (ETB, p. 699). Sister Agnes, too, was very surprised, even though she knew Elizabeth's resilience; but these sufferings were so terrible that she would have expected them to erode at least some of Elizabeth's 'strength of soul and character' – yet there was not the slightest sign of anxiety to be seen, and she only ever saw Elizabeth 'calm and strong' (ETB, p. 697). Dr Barbier, who had wide experience of treating the sick, was endlessly amazed: 'Ah! you don't see things like this in the world,' he said. 'People who are ill are always occupied with themselves, turned in on themselves. As for her, she is always into St Paul' (ETB, p. 698)! Elizabeth enjoyed sharing with the doctor the fruits of her latest reading. Moreover, the pain did not prevent her mind from being as alert and receptive as ever, and she always had something new to say. So that Dr Barbier, on his arrival, would sometimes greet her with the question: 'Well, Sister, what does St. Paul say today?' (PG, p. 168).

If he was surprised by this unheard-of heroism in pain and illness – 'She is amazing... She has a capacity for suffering!' (ETB, p. 698) – he was even more astonished by her attitude towards death. Sister Aimée once said, with a paradox worthy of St Paul himself: 'You couldn't do anything better to help her to live than to tell her she was going to die' (ETB, p. 698)! But it was logical, too: for the prospect of meeting Jesus face to face gave Elizabeth the strength to keep coping. One day, when the doctor showed his surprise at her happiness, Elizabeth asked him if he knew a certain young woman in the town and how she was longing to be united with her fiancé. 'Yes, I know her!' he replied. 'Well then,' continued Elizabeth, 'for me, it's the same thing' (ETB, p. 698). On leaving the convent one day, he exclaimed to the extern sister: 'She is extraordinary' (ETB, p. 699).

Recalling the Past

It was about this time, about three weeks before Elizabeth's death, that Mother Germaine was sitting beside her, absorbed in writing, when Elizabeth suddenly said: 'I'm happy to think that you will write my circular' (CW I, p. 31). The prioress looked up, to see both the usual smile and a thoughtful gaze, then replied soberly that there might not be much to say about someone who had been in Carmel for only five years. Not that she was declaring Elizabeth to be an inexperienced Carmelite! Rather, as Elizabeth would have read between the lines, what that meant was that the prioress simply did not know what to say. After all, was it not for that reason, among others, that Mother Germaine had asked for the notes from Elizabeth's last retreat in August? So she replied: 'I will help you.' The offer was quickly accepted: 'Very well. I will take you at your word. I am counting on you.' And Elizabeth answered her: 'We will do it together' (CW I, p. 31).

And so, around this fourth week of October, Elizabeth found herself with a new job and a new routine. She would regularly make her slow but purposeful way to the office of the prioress for their collaborative project. Here, they were less likely to be disturbed than in the infirmary. It was also more practical, as Mother Germaine had her desk before her, and her writing materials to hand. Elizabeth, barely able to speak, sat as close to the prioress as possible to answer her questions.[2]

As prioress and novice mistress, Mother Germaine knew Elizabeth's inner life extremely well: Elizabeth had confided in her freely and openly throughout her time in Carmel. But *before* she entered the monastery – that was an area the prioress knew less well. She wanted to know more about Elizabeth's youth,

---

[2] While it would seem that Elizabeth's offer to help with the circular was the cause of these meetings, it is not impossible that Mother Germaine had already begun to conduct these interviews and that it was during one of them that Elizabeth spoke of her joy that the prioress would be writing her circular – a possible clue being that Elizabeth's spontaneous utterance interrupted the prioress while she was writing: cf. ETB, p. 705.

and in particular how she had first received the call to Carmel (cf. ETB, p. 704). No doubt Elizabeth had explained all this to Mother Marie of Jesus in the two years when she was a 'postulant outside the walls'. But now, as she recalled the events of the past for Mother Germaine, she looked back with joy over the years of graces she had received. Even before her First Communion, she explained, she had been 'resolved to keep my love and life for Him alone' (PG, p. 16). She recounted her vow of virginity which she had taken just before her fourteenth birthday. Then there was the great day, soon afterwards, when just after receiving Communion she had heard the word '*Carmel*' spoken in her soul (cf. PG, p. 17). And then, the long years of waiting to enter... Mother Germaine listened avidly and took notes.

From time to time, there came a knock at the door. The prioress did not ignore it but let whichever sister it was come in and say what she needed. The visitors were slightly surprised to find Elizabeth there, but her whole demeanour was so discreet that they never felt awkward or self-conscious. There *was* one sister, though, who objected: Sister Anne-Marie, the unofficial patient! She was offended – probably jealous – that her companion was spending so much time in these tête-à-têtes with the prioress. In fact, during the beatification Process, Sister Agnes would be asked about the 'particular friendship' between Elizabeth and Mother Germaine. She retorted that one could not possibly give such an interpretation to 'the expressions of benevolence, [and] maternal affection shown by a prioress to one of her dying daughters'; and she added – which possibly suggests Sister Anne-Marie as the origin of this rumour: 'to imagine that is pure jealousy' (ETB, p. 700, n. 2).[3]

---

[3] After Elizabeth's death, Sister Anne-Marie's jealousy of her would become well-known, and she believed – and presumably hoped – that her statements at the beatification Process would prevent Elizabeth from being beatified: cf. ETB, p. 586, n. 1. If this seems rather surprising, it should be noted that this sister was weak-minded and had, by the time of the Process, been influenced by a later prioress who considered Mother Germaine a rival and who herself had never known Elizabeth: see Chapter 30, section 'At the Tribunals'.

As we have seen, Sister Marie of the Holy Spirit, who saw Elizabeth often during her time in the infirmary, would testify that Mother Germaine was just as good to all the sisters who were ill and did not give Elizabeth special treatment over the others (cf. ETB, p. 700). In fact, throughout her years in Carmel, Elizabeth never received special treatment – unless we count the attentive work of the prioress to overcome Elizabeth's extreme sensitivity! While Mother Germaine would later repent of the severe reprimands she had given her when a novice – 'The poor little thing!... how I made her suffer' (PD, p. 205) – Elizabeth, on the contrary, had come to appreciate the value of this training. In these last few days of her life, and possibly during one of these sessions with the prioress, Elizabeth expressed her gratitude for the firm formation she had received: 'I needed it,' she said, 'and I thank you for it' (ESS, p. 37).

Mother Germaine may well have been aware that their working arrangement could give rise to jealousy or gossip. Had they not been engaged in this task, she would almost certainly have confined their meetings to the infirmary. And Elizabeth, in her spare moments, would have taken herself to the tribune as usual, to pray before the Blessed Sacrament which was her abiding source of strength. But there was work to be done. Mother Germaine, at her desk, was not unlike that other well-known scribe: Mother Agnes, pen poised at a certain famous bedside, taking down the 'last conversations' of Thérèse.

'Veiled, hidden, wholly interior'

One day, Mother Germaine raised the subject of Elizabeth's future mission, just as Mother Agnes had discussed it with her own dying sister. This was no coincidence: the prioress of Dijon was already looking on Elizabeth as another Thérèse – which says a great deal about her esteem for Elizabeth, given Mother Germaine's veneration for the Carmelite of Lisieux. She asked Elizabeth how she would 'spend her eternity' and 'if, like "Little Thérèse", she would "come back down" to earth for the good of souls' (ETB, p. 703; cf. SS, p. 263). 'Oh! no, indeed,' replied

Elizabeth – expressing an idea that may have been one of Thérèse herself, that of the 'rocket' – 'as soon as I reach the threshold of Paradise, I will rush like a little rocket into the bosom of "my Three"; a Praise of Glory can have no other place for eternity and I will plunge ever deeper into it...' (CW I, p. 32).[4] Then there was a pause, during which the prioress looked at Elizabeth who had her eyes closed and her hands joined together. After a while, she continued: 'However, if God grants my request, I think that in Heaven my mission will be to draw souls into *interior recollection...*' (CW I, p. 32). She then explained that she would help souls to go out of themselves and cling to God, and to remain in an inner silence that would allow him to give himself to them and transform them into himself (cf. ETB, p. 703; L 335).

Elizabeth, like Thérèse, wished to help souls after her death. So, any differences she expressed here are simply a matter of approach or of temperament. While Thérèse had wished to send clear signs of intervention – what she termed 'a shower of roses' (cf. LC, p. 256) – Elizabeth wanted to help people just as much, but in a way that would, she said, be different from that of Thérèse because it would be 'veiled, hidden, wholly interior' (ETB, p. 703); and she specified this several times. Also, while Thérèse envisaged her mission as a *coming to others*, Elizabeth wished to *draw others to where she was* – enclosed in God.

We have seen the same contrast in their respective poems on living by love, when they speak of Mary Magdalene at the feet of Jesus. Thérèse writes of the woman of great passion covering Jesus' feet with her tears and her perfume, and drying his feet with her flowing hair (cf. PN 17:12). Elizabeth, on the other hand, visualises the Magdalene silent and peaceful, sitting at his

---

[4] Thérèse may have described her spirituality with the image of a rocket: for her sister Céline may well have been recalling Thérèse's own description of her way of spiritual childhood, perhaps from a conversation, when she wrote: 'No longer, however, can it, strictly speaking, be called a way because by its swift and direct current we are raised like a rocket to the very Heart of God Himself': in Sister Geneviève of the Holy Face (Céline Martin), *My Sister St. Thérèse*, Rockford, IL: Tan Books & Publishers, 1997, p. 106.

feet and drinking in every word (cf. P 94). But at the most essential level, the reality of their mission was the same: Elizabeth and Thérèse would have gone away only in appearance; they would be in God and interceding so as to draw down graces on the world. This is how Elizabeth expressed it to Clémence Blanc: 'Your little Angel is sending you a note from her heart before going away to Him who was already her All here on earth... In Heaven, I will be your Angel more than ever' (L 331).

Battle in the Wilderness

While Elizabeth's days were filled with prayer and suffering and the work with Mother Germaine, her nights took on an importance all of their own in this last week of October. Assailed with unbearable pain, Elizabeth's spirit engaged in a desperate struggle to remain under the influence of grace. Her seemingly endless nights were an empty wilderness and a battlefield; and like Jesus in the desert, she came face to face with a deadly temptation.

During one awful night in particular, her sufferings reached the point where they were totally overwhelming. So far, she had always managed to follow the promptings of grace; but now, she could feel the response of nature rising to the fore. This led her into a deep struggle – not trying to fight the trouble directly, but to keep her eyes on God. When morning came, this is how she described it to Sister Marthe:

> I felt nature taking over; then I awoke my faith and said to myself: 'That is not how a Carmelite must suffer'; then, looking at Jesus in agony, I offered him these sufferings to console him, and I felt myself strengthened. This is what I have always done in my life; at every trial, large or small, I look at similar things which Our Lord has endured, so as to lose my suffering in his and myself in him. (ETB, p. 707)

If we read between the lines, however, this says next to nothing about the nature of the trial, and it leaves one wondering what

Elizabeth meant by the word 'That', in her enigmatic statement: 'That is not how a Carmelite must suffer'. But there are clues.

As it happens, Elizabeth confided in Dr Barbier about this. And as she used this very phrase, we suddenly find out how to fill in the missing details of her night of struggle. He came in, that day, to be greeted with this harrowing account: 'I suffered so much this night that I was tempted to throw myself out of the window; but I said to myself: that is not how a Carmelite must suffer' (ETB, p. 697). On hearing this, Mother Germaine may well have had a sudden shock, not least because she herself had a similar exchange with Elizabeth – and it most likely took place the evening before, with the idea of the window beginning to lodge itself in Elizabeth's mind.

They had been talking together one evening, and Elizabeth had said, as she always did, that she was happy to suffer. She also looked as serene as ever. But just as the prioress was leaving the room, Elizabeth pointed to the window near her bed and asked: 'My mother, is your mind at rest leaving me all alone like this?' (ETB, p. 698). Mother Germaine had no idea what she meant, and looked at her in surprise. Elizabeth continued: 'I am suffering so much that I now understand suicide' (ETB, p. 698). Immediately, though, she reassured the prioress: 'But be at peace: God is there, and he is watching over me' (ETB, p. 698).

The temptation Elizabeth experienced brings to mind that of Jesus in the desert. At every assault, he responded with a word of God (cf. Mt 14:4.7.10). Elizabeth, in a similar way, countered each negative thought with positive thoughts and words that came to her. In the evening conversation with the prioress, it was faith in his presence: 'God is there…' And during the terrible night itself, it was the memory of her vocation and all it implied: 'That is not how a Carmelite must suffer'. As she had written, long ago: 'A Carmelite…is a soul who has *gazed on the Crucified…* and has wanted to give herself as He did!' (L 133).

The Divine Furnace

One night, the divine strengthening came – just as Jesus, having fought against temptation in the desert, was strengthened by the visit of angels sent by God (cf. Mt 4:11). Elizabeth was yet again in a state of weakness and 'powerlessness' – 'when suddenly,' as she explained to the prioress the next morning, 'I felt myself as if invaded by Love. No expression allows me to convey what I experienced; it was a fire of infinite sweetness, and at the same time it seemed to me that it caused me a mortal wound. I think that if it had continued any longer, I would have succumbed' (ETB, pp. 701–2).

This was a mystical experience on a level with the vision of the Trinity dwelling within her soul on the feast of the Ascension (cf. PG, pp. 182–3).[5] But this new touch of God adds a new dimension: it is the experience of God's *fire* and, inseparably linked to this, it is the fire of his *love*. Mother Germaine could not help thinking of the teachings of John of the Cross. She would say, in the biography, that this had been an experience of God's 'living flame of love' (PG, p. 206). And a few lines later, quoting passages from John's work of that title, she would sum up Elizabeth's life in terms of the burning action of the 'flame of the Holy Spirit' (LF 1:36; cf. PG, p. 207), and the souls who die of love, their own love flowing into God's love like rivers entering the sea (cf. LF 1:30; PG, p. 207); Mother Germaine would also repeat John's prayer for an imminent death and encounter with God: 'Tear, then, the thin veil of this life…' (LF 1:36; cf. PG, p. 208). Elizabeth's mention of a 'wound' also recalls the Transverberation of Teresa (cf. BL 29:13). But in particular, it echoes the experience of Thérèse after she had offered herself to Merciful Love: she, like Elizabeth, felt a 'fire' and a 'sweetness', and she felt she might die if she continued being 'on fire with love' (LC, p. 77).

---

[5] Note that this time, too, Elizabeth was unable to describe fully her experience in human language ('No expression allows me to convey…') – a sign of a genuine mystical experience: see Chapter 16, n. 4.

Elizabeth's mystical experience possibly took place on October 27. For her letters as from the 28th bear traces of it, or of some of the relevant ideas from John of the Cross with which Mother Germaine would describe it (cf. PG, pp. 207–8), and which she may well have discussed with Elizabeth. The letters speak of *fire* – the 'Furnace of love'[6] (L 335; L 336); *water* – waves of love, and a flowing into God (cf. L 332; L 333); and a pressing sense of *the imminent encounter with God* (cf. L 332; L 333). To Sister Marie-Odile in Paray-le-Monial, Elizabeth spoke of 'keeping a rendez-vous with you in the Furnace of love' (L 335). And this is how she wrote to Marthe Weishardt, a former novice of the Carmel who had entered six years before Elizabeth:

> How closely your little soul sister is united to you during these wholly heavenly days, in which 'exceeding love' is overflowing in waves within her heart! Oh, you see, sometimes I think He is going to come and take me to carry me off where He is in dazzling Light. Even now in the night of faith, the union is so profound, the embraces so heavenly! What will it be, in that first face-to-face, in God's great light, that first meeting with divine Beauty! Thus will I flow out into the infinity of Mystery and contemplate the wonders of the Divine Being. (L 332)

This 'overflowing' with love is linked to another new element in Elizabeth's letters during these days: the heart of Jesus at the time when he himself was approaching death and living the fullness of love (cf. Jn 13:1). Elizabeth had always striven, as the 'bride' of Christ, to 'identify [herself] with all the movements of [His] soul' (cf. L 156); and she continued to do this, following the last days of his life as her own life was drawing to a close. As she wrote to Antoinette de Bobet, around the end of the month:

---

[6] Elizabeth was familiar with this expression – 'Foyer de l'amour', meaning literally 'Hearth of love' (or 'Home of love') – from the writings of Thérèse, who links it with 'the burning Abyss' of God's love (cf. SS, p. 200); Elizabeth had in fact used it a few times before: cf. L 190, n. 3.

Never was the Heart of the Master so overflowing with love as at the supreme moment when He was going to leave His own! It seems to me as if something similar is happening in His little bride at the evening of her life, and I feel as if a wave were rising from my heart to yours! (L 333; cf. L 331)

Beauty and Silence

Just before the end of October, Elizabeth said to Mother Germaine: 'If our Lord offered me the choice of dying either in an ecstasy or in the abandonment of Calvary, I should prefer the latter – not on account of its merit, but that I might glorify and resemble Him' (PG, p. 212). As we have seen, throughout her illness Elizabeth kept her gaze on the *crucified* Christ and longed to be like him. But now, we see another image of Christ simultaneously holding its place in her mind. This is the *risen* Christ, the *beautiful* Christ, into whose image she also dreamed of being transformed: she describes him, in a letter to Clémence Blanc, as 'Ideal Beauty'; and she quotes St Paul, saying: 'we will be transformed into the same Image, from brightness to brightness' (L 331; cf. 2Cor 3:18).

In letters Elizabeth wrote during these last few days of October, she focuses on the beauty of heaven in a way that recalls the aftermath of her Palm Sunday attack when it seemed she was about to die (cf. L 268; L 269). In one sense, this is inevitable: even if she was living a Calvary, she was writing farewell letters and surely friends would prefer to be left with a vision of heaven, not an account of suffering! Moreover, for all she knew, she might no longer be on earth by the time they received her letters. But Elizabeth never said something conventional just to suit the occasion. Everything she said or wrote was genuine, springing from her continually evolving soul. And as such, her references to heaven give a great insight into what was filling her mind at this moment, less than a fortnight before her death.

Light and beauty are the themes which pervade these letters, as attributes both of God and of heaven. Elizabeth prays that Clémence might be 'beautiful with His beauty, luminous with His light';[7] and she looks forward to 'contemplating Ideal Beauty in its great brightness' (L 331). To Marthe Weishardt, as we have seen, she speaks with awe of the prospect of her 'first meeting with divine Beauty', the same words she had used when writing to Guite soon after her Palm Sunday attack (cf. L 269). She describes this meeting to Marthe as 'that first face-to-face, in God's great light' – all of which will take place in heaven which she defines simply as 'where He is in dazzling Light' (L 332).

God, beautiful and luminous, forms one half, so to speak, of Elizabeth's picture of heaven. The other is the assembly of the saints 'beneath the radiant light of God's Face': they are, she says, 'the choir of virgins, that generation that is as pure as light', and there 'we will sing the beautiful canticle of the Lamb, the eternal Sanctus' (L 331). This 'eternal Sanctus', which she has mentioned a few times before (cf. L 250, n. 18), is the never-ending 'Holy, holy, holy...' sung before God in heaven. As we see in the *Last Retreat*, the eighth 'day' and climax to the first half of the work gives a glimpse of the adoration of God in heaven and begins with these very words: 'And they do not rest day and night, saying, Holy, holy, holy is the Lord God Almighty' (LR 20; cf. Rv 4:8).

In her letter to Marthe Weishardt, Elizabeth also speaks of the 'Canticum magnum', the 'great Canticle' (L 332; cf. LR 3), and may be referring here to the 'new song' in the Book of Revelation (cf. Rv 5:9; 14:3). But what is most revealing is how Elizabeth envisages the song of praise in heaven. She writes: 'Let us hide ourselves in eternal silence' (L 332). And while she is speaking here of prayer while on earth, 'eternal silence' is, for her, likewise the silence of eternity which is present even in the great singing of the Sanctus, as she had written in August:

> Adoration, ah! That is a word from Heaven!... It is love overcome by the beauty, the strength, the immense grandeur of

---

[7] This phrase has strong associations with an outpouring by John of the Cross on divine beauty (cf. SC 36:5), although Elizabeth additionally combines beauty with light.

the Object loved, and it 'falls down in a kind of faint' in an utterly profound silence, that silence of which David spoke when he exclaimed: 'Silence is Your praise!' Yes, this is the most beautiful praise since it is sung eternally in the bosom of the tranquil Trinity... (LR 21; cf. Ps 64:2)[8]

'Let yourself be loved'

Elizabeth asked Mother Germaine for some writing paper. She did not say why; it was to be a secret. When she was alone again, she took two long, narrow sheets of ruled paper; they were roughly the same length as today's 'A4' paper but half the width. Placing one sheet on top of the other, then folding them in two, she created a little booklet of eight small sides, on which she wrote in ink and at length despite her overwhelming exhaustion.

This marvellous letter, written in the last few days of October, is now known as one of Elizabeth's major spiritual writings: *Let Yourself Be Loved*. It is a testament letter for Mother Germaine, and Elizabeth would not give it to her straightaway. The surprise would come only after Elizabeth's death, when the prioress would find it, open the envelope addressed to her, and begin to read these moving words: 'My Cherished Mother, my Holy Priest, when you read these lines, your little Praise of Glory will no longer be singing on earth, but will be living in Love's immense furnace...' (LL 1).

These lines would without doubt bring tears to the eye of the prioress. But there is a purpose behind them. If Elizabeth will be 'living in Love', this is stated simply as credentials: 'so you can believe [me] and listen to [me] as "the voice" of God' (LL 1). Straightaway, this sets the tone of seriousness, for it is a letter with a message. This is no time for just expressions of affection, however much the affection shines through each line: 'Cherished Mother,' she writes, 'I would have liked to tell you all that you have been for me, but the hour is so serious, so solemn...' (LL 1).

---

[8] On the quotation from the Psalm, see Chapter 19, n. 7.

Elizabeth's mention of being a 'voice' of God recalls the role of John the Baptist (cf. Jn 1:23) and of every prophet who speaks on God's behalf. That is what Elizabeth herself is doing here: she wishes, she says, to reveal to the prioress what God, in prayer, 'makes [me] understand' (LL 1). At this point, Elizabeth increases the size of her handwriting to put the four words which form the essence of her message: '*You are uncommonly loved*' (LL 2).

For the last few weeks, Elizabeth had been telling the prioress repeatedly, in letters and poems (cf. L 316; P 98; P 121), just how much she, Mother Germaine, was loved by God. But now, Elizabeth conveys this with a command. There is one significant word occurring six times in this piece, and on four of these occasions Elizabeth makes it stand out with larger letters or a capital. It is the word 'Let'. This is how she introduces her message: 'He does not say to you as to Peter: "Do you love Me more than these?" Mother, listen to what He tells you: "*Let* yourself be loved more than these!"' (LL 2).

This is a marvellous reversal of perspective. Elizabeth knew, from her own experience, that what gave her happiness was not simply to love God, but especially to know how much God loved *her*. And that to love God actually comes in second place: as a *response* to his love. Many times, during this last year of her life, Elizabeth focuses on the great act of faith expressed in the First Letter of John – to *believe* in God's love (cf. 1Jn 4:16) – which she quotes again and again in her writings. And it is at the heart of this letter, too: 'Mother, *let* yourself be loved more than the others; that explains everything' (LL 3). In other words, once the prioress knows how much she herself is loved by God, everything else will fall into place.

Elizabeth knew exactly what was needed for the prioress, which is why she homes in on these words of Jesus addressed to Peter: 'Do you love me...?' (Jn 21:15). For Mother Germaine had been chosen, like Peter, to lead a flock. She was an exceptionally good prioress and would be elected as many as seven times in all. And yet, for all her gifts, inwardly she lacked confidence and seems to have been anxious about the burden of responsibility. After her death in 1934, when *Let Yourself Be Loved* finally came to light in the community – for it had been known to its recipient alone – the writer of her Circular would say perceptively of Mother Germaine: 'it seems that our venerated Sister Elizabeth of the Trinity had received an intimate revelation (enlightened by God) on the state of suffering that her beloved Mother was experiencing, the Lord having permitted this richly endowed soul to feel in her depths only poverty, humility and fear' (CW I, p. 178, n. 9).

Elizabeth now spells out her message in an inventive way. Not only does she adapt the words of Jesus, so as to include the word 'Let' – which she says three times in quick succession – but she also extends his words, which she addresses to Mother Germaine as if coming from the voice of Jesus directly:

> *Let* yourself be loved more than these! That is, without fearing that any obstacle will be a hindrance to it, for I am free to pour out My love on whom I wish! '*Let* yourself be loved more than these' is your vocation. It is in being faithful to it that you will make Me happy for you will magnify the power of My love. This love can rebuild what you have destroyed. *Let* yourself be loved more than these. (LL 2)

Associated with his Work

We come now to another switching of perspective. While Mother Germaine is her 'Mother' and 'Priest' (LL 1), Elizabeth – while remaining her 'child' (LL 1) and 'little host' (LL 4) – will, at the same time, exchange roles with her when in heaven: 'This time I will be your little Mother' (LL 4); 'I understand also that in Heaven I will fulfil in my turn a priesthood over your soul' (LL 3). Elizabeth will be able to help her, she says, because: 'It is Love who associates me with His work in you' (LL 3).

The basis of this whole way of seeing is that all people are united with God – and, in him, united with each other.

So Elizabeth is not just speaking of how she, in union with God, will help Mother Germaine; she is also expressing her union with the prioress. This recalls her idea of the 'mysterious exchange', which was the subject of a poem Elizabeth had given her about a month earlier (P 117). Inspired by words of St Paul – that nothing, not even death, can separate us from Christ (cf. Rm 8:38–39) – Elizabeth had rewritten them with reference to Mother Germaine, and put them (in Latin) as an epigraph at the beginning of her poem: 'I am certain that neither death nor height nor depth will be able to separate me from my mother!' (P 117). So that, at Elizabeth's death, Mother Germaine would in a way ascend to heaven with her, being united with her; and, as Elizabeth had said, 'you will give me lodgings in your heart night and day!' (P 117). This is the idea that Elizabeth now develops in *Let Yourself Be Loved*:

> If you will allow her, your little host will spend her Heaven in the depths of your soul: she will keep you in communion with Love, believing in Love; it will be the sign of her dwelling in you. (LL 4)

This passage, then, reveals something about the 'veiled, hidden, wholly interior' (ETB, p. 703) character of the posthumous mission Elizabeth was envisaging: through her union with God, she would be associated with his work, even his dwelling within a person's soul. And so she continues: 'I will come to live in you' (LL 4). Wanting to share *everything* with her prioress, she exclaims: 'Oh, in what intimacy we are going to live... I will sing in your name the eternal Sanctus: I will do nothing before the throne of God without you' (LL 4). There are two more reasons why Mother Germaine will be with her. One of them may allude to a private promise: 'I also ask you not to do anything without me,' writes Elizabeth; 'you have granted me this' (LL 4). But the main reason is that the prioress has *formed* her: 'you know well that I bear your imprint and that something of yourself appeared with your child before the Face of God' (LL 4).

The idea of bearing someone's imprint was of vast importance to Elizabeth, whose main aspiration was to praise God's glory by being in the likeness of Christ (cf. LR 1) so that the Father might '[see] in her only the "Beloved in whom You are well pleased"' (PT; cf. Mt 17:5). Or, as she says in a poem, using that very term: 'May I bear the imprint / Of this God who is all Love' (P 88). As for being in the image of another person, Elizabeth saw this, quite logically, as relevant to the relationship of parent and child. Not just in terms of the physical likeness but, more importantly, the spiritual one. So, after the death of Madame de Rostang, Elizabeth had said to Yvonne, consolingly: 'you are truly her daughter, and before leaving this earth she was able to see that you bore her imprint' (L 242). Elizabeth had also spoken in this very way to Mother Germaine: 'Remember your first-born. / Her soul bears your imprint' (P 90). To be her living image, then, would express a genuine *formation*, and it would be the greatest compliment Elizabeth could pay her.[9]

We now come to another exchange of roles. Elizabeth declares to this novice mistress who has given her so much instruction: 'I will instruct you' (LL 4). We have seen, in her correspondence over the years, Elizabeth sharing her spiritual discoveries. And in her recent letters, they seem even more luminous for she is, as it were, seeing everything 'in the light of eternity' (L 333). But what greater vision to come when she will be in heaven! Elizabeth's generous soul longs to share heaven itself: she will 'instruct' Mother Germaine 'so that my vision will benefit you, that you may participate in it, and that you, too, may live the life of the blessed!' (LL 4).

---

[9] Edith Stein was similarly inspired at the thought of being a living image of her Mother in Carmel, Teresa of Avila. She would quote Luis de León who said of Teresa: 'I neither saw nor knew the saint during her lifetime. But today, albeit she is in heaven, I know her and see her in her two living reflections, that is, in her daughters and in her writings': in Edith Stein, *The Hidden Life*, *op. cit.*, p. 65.

God will be 'magnified'

We now reach the most solemn part of this letter. It is, quite literally, a testament – and this is Elizabeth's official bequest to her prioress:

> I bequeath to you this vocation which was mine in the heart of the Church Militant and which from now on I will unceasingly fulfil in the Church Triumphant: '*The Praise of Glory of the Holy Trinity*'. (LL 5)

When Elizabeth first discovered her vocation to be a 'praise of glory', she found in St Paul that it is a vocation to which everyone is called (cf. Eph 1:12). That is why she can say boldly that it is the vocation of the prioress, just as she had ended *Heaven in Faith* by giving Guite the name of 'Laudem Gloriae' for all eternity (cf. HF 44). There is never any question, though, of Elizabeth trying to impose her own path on others. Rather, she knows that everyone is called to be the praise of God's glory in whatever way God himself chooses. She does, however, express her intuition about the way in which Mother Germaine is called to live this out: 'Mother, "*let* yourself be loved more than these": it is in that way that your Master wills for you to be a praise of glory!' (LL 5).

Elizabeth now continues her instruction, countering the discouragement she must have sensed at times in the prioress: 'it is He alone who wants to work in you, even though you will have done nothing to attract this grace except that which a creature can do: works of sin and misery... He loves you like that' (LL 5). This is the spirit of Thérèse, and we can say that Elizabeth is repaying the prioress who would certainly have inculcated it in her, for this letter is here relaying back to her, as it were, the fruits of those lessons. Just as Mother Germaine had helped her to live by faith during the arduous novitiate, Elizabeth now describes to the prioress the invisible work of transformation taking place in our soul at every moment, and encourages her always to have faith in it – and to have faith that it is a work of God's love:

He will do everything in you. He will go to the end: for when a soul is loved by Him to this extent, in this way, loved by an unchanging and creative love, a free love which transforms as it pleases Him, oh, how far this soul will go!... But in the hours when you feel only oppression and lassitude, you will please Him even more if you faithfully *believe* that He is still working, that He is loving you just the same... (LL 5–6)

This, says Elizabeth, is 'the fidelity' which God asks of the prioress: she must 'remain in communion with Love, flow into, be rooted in this Love who wants to mark your soul with the seal of His power and His grandeur' (LL 6). Interestingly, this mention of 'grandeur' or 'greatness' is coupled with the reassurance that if the prioress remains vigilant in love, she will 'never be commonplace' (LL 6). This attempt to reassure her that she will not be 'commonplace', and to make her recognise the potential 'grandeur' of her soul, may suggest that Mother Germaine perhaps needed this reassurance just as much as Françoise de Sourdon had done (cf. GV 4; GV 8). Ultimately, to live all this will be to give glory to God: for if the prioress believes in his love, God will be '*magnified*' in her (cf. LL 6) – and this evokes the soul of the Virgin Mary singing her *Magnificat* to the praise of God (cf. Lk 1:46–55). Finally, Elizabeth urges Mother Germaine: 'Live in the depths of your soul!' (LL 6).

Elizabeth had now imparted all she needed to say. It was time to hand over to another 'voice' (cf. LL 1; LL 6). On a much smaller piece of paper, about four inches by two and a half, she pencilled in the lines; then, with her pen, she copied out a long quotation from the revelations to Angela of Foligno and framed the text in ink. It was a message of love, spoken in the voice of God and addressed to Mother Germaine: 'Believe His "voice",' writes Elizabeth, 'and read these lines as if coming from Him' (LL 6). And when the prioress picked up this small piece of paper, she would see these words: 'Oh! I love you, I love you more than anyone else in this valley!... Love Me! All your life will please Me, provided that you love Me!... I will do great things in you; I will be made known in you, glorified, and praised in you!...' (LL 7).

Elizabeth had only a very small envelope. So she had to fold her little booklet in two; then, taking the long quotation, she trimmed the edges of the paper. Finally, she gave her little missive the most solemn treatment possible: she sealed the envelope with red wax. On the front, she wrote: 'Secrets for our Reverend Mother'. Then she put it away in her little writing box.

'If I started my life over again...'

With just two days to go before her final collapse, Elizabeth devoted herself to writing more testament letters. Much shorter than *Let Yourself Be Loved*, they are nonetheless memorable and important, giving glimpses into Elizabeth's mind during these last few days of her life. In a magnificent letter to Antoinette de Bobet, Elizabeth impresses on her friend the only true perspective – the one that has become ever-clearer to Elizabeth now that she is leaving this life:

> Dear Antoinette, in the light of eternity the soul sees things as they really are. Oh! how empty is all that has not been done for God and with God! I beg you, oh, mark everything with the seal of love! It alone endures. How serious life is: each minute is given us in order to 'root' us deeper in God... (L 333; cf. Col 2:7)

Antoinette was the woman who feared she was too worldly to meet Elizabeth's gaze! But Elizabeth is not preaching at her: she is simply sharing her conviction, which has struck her forcibly at the end of her life, of the importance of every moment. As she wrote to Sister Marie-Odile on October 28: 'it seems to me I now see everything in God's light, and if I started my life over again, oh, I would wish not to waste one instant!' (L 335).

But the highlight of Elizabeth's letter to Madame de Bobet is what she leaves her in her spiritual bequest. It is an extremely moving and beautiful description of Elizabeth's knowledge of the indwelling God, and of how an awareness of this presence within her has transformed her whole life:

> My beloved Antoinette, I leave you my faith in the presence of God, of the God who is all Love dwelling in our souls. I confide to you: it is this intimacy with Him 'within' that has been the beautiful sun illuminating my life, making it already an anticipated Heaven; it is what sustains me today in my suffering. I do not fear my weakness; that's what gives me confidence. For the Strong One is within me and His power is almighty. (L 333)

What Elizabeth shares here is an inestimable gift. It is the gift she hoped to continue sharing from heaven, as we see from her letter to Sister Marie-Odile. Of all the letters she received from Elizabeth, she would save this one alone – simply because it was the last. Although the loss of the others is regrettable, the saving of this particular one is most providential – for it is here, on October 28, that Elizabeth describes her 'mission':

> I think that in Heaven my mission will be to draw souls by helping them go out of themselves to cling to God by a wholly simple and loving movement, and to keep them in this great silence within that will allow God to communicate Himself to them and transform them into Himself. (L 335)

Elizabeth promises to watch over this sister, and even at this late stage of her illness she has not lost her humour: 'if by chance, in the radiance of His Light, I see you leave that sole occupation [of love], I will come very quickly to call you to order; you would want that, wouldn't you?' (L 335). Elizabeth enclosed a note for this nun's own sister who was also in the Carmel of Paray-le-Monial but whom she knew less well. Elizabeth expresses her 'last wish' for Sister Anne, which she 'promises to help her achieve': 'Yes, surrender yourself to this Fullness of Love, this "living Being" who wants to live in communion with you!' (L 336).

Towards the end of her letter to Sister Marie-Odile, Elizabeth asks for her prayers. Here, we see right into the fears which Elizabeth was facing. She would have been only too well aware that her sufferings had increased relentlessly over the last eighteen months, to the point where they were now uncontrollable – yet the awful thing was that they would inevitably continue to increase before she reached the point where she actually died of the illness. Would she be able to bear it? And then, there must have been at least some anxiety about meeting Jesus face to face. Even though this was Elizabeth's greatest source of joy, it was still a momentous and potentially frightening moment, for she had received so many graces, and had she been faithful to them all? This is how she ends her letter, with a heartfelt request:

> Pray for me, help me prepare for the wedding feast of the Lamb. Death entails a great deal of suffering, and I am counting on you to help me. In return, I will come to help you at your death. My Master urges me on, He speaks to me of nothing but the eternity of love. It is so grave, so serious; I wish to live each moment fully… Beloved little sister, let us live by love so we may die of love and glorify the God Who is all Love. (L 335)

'At the eve of my life'

On Monday, October 29, Madame Catez, Guite, and her two daughters Sabeth and Odette, came to the infirmary parlour. It was the last time they would see Elizabeth alive. Her mother looked at her in the armchair, and thought she looked overwhelmed by suffering. But ironically, she also found her able to speak more easily, and they had quite a long conversation. Elizabeth began to make her final requests to them, one of which was to ask Guite to remain just as attached to the Carmelite convent after her death. All the same, Madame Catez still held out hope that this would not be their final meeting. But Elizabeth surely *knew*.

Guite had the two little girls kneel before the grille. Then Elizabeth took her crucifix and 'with a majesty that had something solemn about it' (ETB, p. 710), to quote her mother, she held it up and blessed them. If Madame Catez had any illusions that she would see Elizabeth again, she must have felt a sword twist in her heart when Elizabeth gave her this final instruction: 'Mama, when the extern sister comes to inform you that my suffering is over, you will fall on your knees saying: "My God, you gave her to me; my God, I give her back to you; may your Holy Name be blessed!"' (ETB, p. 710).

We can imagine how distressed her family were after this visit. And Elizabeth, too. As she left the parlour, she struggled to rise above her emotions. Suddenly, she received an inner prompting which reminded her of her vocation to be a praise of God's glory. Afterwards, Sister Marie-Xavier came to see her and Elizabeth told her about this struggle: 'If you knew,' she said, 'what strength I find in my name (Laudem Gloriae). Seeing Mama and Guite so disconsolate, I would have been tempted to dwell for a short time on the thought of them. But in the depth of my heart my Master called me: "Laudem, Laudem, where are you?" Immediately, turning back to Him, I confided these dear ones to Him and resumed my life of prayer and recollection' (ESS, p. 36). This sister was most impressed and thought Elizabeth heroic. She was also slightly envious and asked her: 'Since you have such strength in this name, ask Jesus for one for me.' Elizabeth replied: 'Yes, I will think about it and I will pray' (ETB, p. 710).

The next day, October 30, was the last day Elizabeth was able to get up. She was at the end of her strength. But when, later in the day, Mother Germaine suggested that she might lie down and rest, back came this courageous reply: 'Oh, no! I am so exhausted that I am afraid I should never be able to sit up again' (PG, p. 211). By now, all Elizabeth was eating was a little bit of barley sugar, and even that she could hardly keep down. Drinking, too, was a major problem because each drop of water caused incredible pain on impact with her inflamed stomach.

That same day, Dr Barbier told Georges Chevignard that his sister-in-law was becoming 'weaker and weaker' and that the decline was '*slow* and progressive' (ETB, p. 698) – 'slow' being not exactly accurate, as she had only ten days left to live.

Elizabeth stayed in the infirmary all day and completed her final tasks. She wrote her last testament letter: a will. As we have seen, on August 1, 1901, the eve of her entrance to Carmel, Elizabeth had written her real will which made Guite her sole heir. Now, she wrote another one, appointing Madame de Sourdon as her 'sole heir' – but this was a will with a twist. With a touch of humour, but possibly more than anything as a gesture of friendship, Elizabeth wrote: 'I the undersigned declare that although I possess nothing, since I have previously disposed of everything that belonged to me, I nevertheless appoint as my sole heir Madame la comtesse Georges de Sourdon, resident of Dijon' (L 338). In fact, this did not in any way revoke the earlier will: for everything, Elizabeth admitted here, had already been 'disposed of' – that is, in the will for Guite! But this letter may also have been a genuine bequest: entrusting her mother to this close family friend at a time of great distress – just as Elizabeth also wrote to Madame Hallo, at this time, 'entrusting to you my dear Mama' (L 341). Indeed, as Elizabeth's death drew nearer, Madame de Sourdon would go to stay with Madame Catez in Prior Street, so that she would be with her to support her when the news arrived. Between the lines, this fictitious will also speaks reams about Elizabeth's total gift of herself. At the end of her life, she could indeed say, in spiritual terms: 'I possess nothing'. Or, in the words of St Paul: 'For love of Him I have forfeited everything' (Ph 3:8; cf. L 256).

One more thing remained. Elizabeth had thought and prayed, and she had received a name for Sister Marie-Xavier. She tried to write an explanation, to say that it was Jesus himself who had given her this name, and that great beauty was contained in it. But finding herself too weak to put any soul into what she was writing, she tore the note up. Instead, she contented herself with simply putting the three words that made up the name, and asked for the piece of paper to be left at the sister's door.

Sister Marie-Xavier picked it up with anticipation. And she read: 'Abscondita in Deo' (L 339). 'Hidden in God' – this formula came from the verse of St Paul: 'Your life is hidden with Christ in God' (Col 3:3). A great favourite with contemplatives, it nonetheless took this sister by surprise! 'Me, Abscondita!' she thought, rather pleased, 'so impulsive, so enthusiastic, so expansive, so communicative...' (ETB, p. 710)! And she couldn't wait to go to the infirmary to learn more from Elizabeth. But she soon discovered that the illness had taken a greater hold, and she felt unable to ask her – indeed, she felt she might never be able to speak to her again.

Some time during the course of the day, Mother Germaine came in to visit Elizabeth. The prioress noticed that although she was very pale, 'an expression of happiness, though, was lighting up her face' (S1, p. 185). As it happened, Elizabeth had been looking at a picture of St Teresa on the wall, and had had a moment of discouragement: 'thinking of her glory, I said to myself that in heaven her poor child would be very far from her' (S1, p. 186). She recounted this to the prioress and then told her that, at that very moment, she had heard it said in the depths of her soul 'that the glory of St Teresa was a reward less for her great works than for her love' (S1, p. 186). Elizabeth was much consoled by this.

She had had a similar experience when a postulant. We have seen that there was a picture in her cell of Teresa in ecstasy, with a caption from the saint's words: 'There are people, Lord, who serve you better than I. But that there may be people who desire your glory more ardently, that I will never suffer!' (ETB, p. 431). Elizabeth had been encouraged by this, realising that Teresa's greatness came from her *love* and that she, Elizabeth, could also say in truth that she loved Jesus very much (cf. ETB, p. 431).

Love of Jesus had been a constant in Elizabeth's life. As she sat there in the infirmary cell, looking back over the years, she took her profession crucifix, pressed it to her heart and said: 'we have loved each other so much' (S1, p. 186). She was, in effect, summing up her life which was now drawing to a close. And when she told the prioress about the words she had heard spoken within her that day, she said: 'This light comes to confirm, at the eve of my life, all my attractions of grace… I wish to live only for love' (S1, p. 186).

Chapter 23

THROUGH DARKNESS INTO LIGHT

A Brief Prelude

Elizabeth's last few days on earth, her passage from this world to the next, call to mind the image of someone gradually emerging from a tunnel. Her agony would begin in the thickest darkness. Then, as the days progressed, it was as if she had one foot in the dark, the other in the light, and that both were held in tension. Gradually, the first glimmer of dawn would break onto the horizon – until finally, she slipped into eternal light, on the Friday morning of November 9, 1906.

The last two days of October form a brief prelude to her final agony. On the evening of the 30th, Madame Catez came to the monastery with a pair of shoes for her daughter, as well as some ice for her to sip. Having seen Elizabeth the previous day, she knew that the end was not far off. So she was also visiting to ask for news. She handed the gifts to Sister Aimée, who was second portress sister, and waited until she returned.

Elizabeth was in her armchair when Sister Aimée came into the infirmary cell. She took the shoes and tried them on – just as a person would in good health, the sister noted with surprise; she also dipped her fingers in the ice and moistened her tongue. Before going back to Madame Catez, the portress sister asked Elizabeth for advice about some things that were causing her concern. She noticed, again with surprise, that Elizabeth managed to overcome her exhaustion and summon up the energy to speak 'affectionately, yet with simple and deep gravity' (PG, p. 210). At last, not wanting to keep the mother waiting too long, Sister Aimée asked what message she should take back with her. Perhaps she thought it would be something like, 'Thank you for the shoes.' Instead, she had the shock of her life. For Elizabeth replied: 'Tell her I am dying; I can't go on any more' (S1, p. 186).

At around ten o'clock that evening, Mother Germaine had a sudden intuition that Elizabeth needed her. She went to the infirmary cell and found her in a dire state. Elizabeth was overcome with a fit of shaking and thought she was about to die; she was all the more distressed at the idea that this might happen when the prioress was absent. Mother Germaine gave her something to calm her, and Elizabeth settled down. She also had the reassurance of knowing that the prioress was now spending her nights in the little pharmacy which connected to Elizabeth's cell by an adjoining door. She had moved in two days before, so that she would be able to hear every sound. Elizabeth was delighted to have her so close by.

That very night, Mother Germaine awoke on hearing a noise. It was around three o'clock in the morning. She rushed next door and found Elizabeth in acute pain, thinking the end had come. Elizabeth poured out her soul, and for the prioress this was 'an hour never to be forgotten' (PG, p. 211) – a deep sharing that would have reminded them both of Palm Sunday evening when Elizabeth had had her first attack and was waiting for the parish priest to arrive. Listening to her speaking now, Mother Germaine felt that Elizabeth's gaze was already catching a glimpse of heaven.

The next day, Wednesday, October 31, Elizabeth's weakness was extreme and she received the anointing and viaticum for the second time. From then on, she expected to die at any moment. But it would be another nine days, of unparalleled pain – a magnified form of her 'novena of suffering' (cf. L 329). The new month would begin, however, with a burst of joy.

Awaiting the Call

Elizabeth had always loved the feast of All Saints. That day, she received Communion for the very last time: her tongue was so dried up that she would never again be able to swallow even a particle of the Host. At ten o'clock in the morning, she suddenly took a turn for the worse, and the prioress thought it was the end. The community gathered round her bed and recited the prayers for the dying. After a while, Elizabeth recovered from her collapse. Looking round, and seeing that all the sisters were there, she asked their forgiveness. One sister asked her a question, and Elizabeth's reply was like her final bequest to the community:

> Everything passes!... at the evening of life, love alone remains... We must do everything out of love; we must forget ourselves unceasingly; the good God so loves it when we are forgetful of ourselves... (S1, p. 187)

Then she added with regret: 'Ah! if only I had always done so!...' (S1, p. 187).

At midday, the bells rang out the Angelus from all the churches in Dijon. Elizabeth was filled with joy and exclaimed: 'O my mother, these bells make my heart swell with joy; they are ringing for the departure of *Laudem Gloriae*! Already for my profession, all these bells of the city rang out, and hear how they are resounding again for my passage from the Church Militant to the Church Triumphant; they will make me die of joy, these bells! Let's go then!...' (S1, p. 187). And she stretched out her arms towards heaven as if to fly away. The parallel with the day of her profession was as strong in her mind as ever; she was, as she had said a few days earlier, awaiting 'the Bridegroom's "Veni"' (L 332). And like Teresa of Avila on her own deathbed, Elizabeth was declaring herself a daughter of the Church.[1]

To Elizabeth's joy, the bells pealed all day, celebrating the feast of the saints. She hoped and even expected that by the

---

[1] That is, in seeing herself as passing 'from the Church Militant to the Church Triumphant' – both her life and her death being defined in terms of belonging to the Church. A few days earlier, Elizabeth had used these solemn titles for the very first time, to describe her transition from earth to heaven (cf. LL 5). St Teresa, on her deathbed, described herself as 'a daughter of the Church': see Tomás Álvarez, OCD, *Estudios Teresianos*, vol. III, Burgos: Editorial Monte Carmelo, 1996, pp. 284–6.

evening she would have joined them in heaven. She had always loved the readings for the feast of All Saints, almost all of which were taken from the seventh chapter of the Book of Revelation, with the vision of the 'great multitude' (Rv 7:9) of saints adoring God. To hear these readings on that very day, when she was nearly at the point of death, would have seemed to Elizabeth like the call to enter heaven. So it was most likely on November 1 that Elizabeth wrote her farewell letter to Madame Hallo, containing these very themes.[2] As before, when Elizabeth had been too weak to hold a pen, Mother Germaine took down the letter to dictation:

> + My second Mama,
>   My hand can no longer hold a pen, but the heart of your daughter still leads it, passing through the heart of her Mother. I believe that the great day, so ardently desired, of my meeting with the only beloved, *adored*, Bridegroom is here.
>   This evening I hope to be in 'that great multitude' that Saint John saw before the throne of the Lamb, serving Him day and night in His temple. I am keeping a rendez-vous with you in that beautiful chapter of Revelation and in the last, which carries the soul off so well up above the earth into the Vision in which I am going to lose myself forever!... Pray very much for your little Elizabeth; do not leave her waiting too long for the divine fusion. (L 341; cf. Rv 7; 22)

This extract shows how, right at the end of her life, Scripture was still providing Elizabeth with inspiration and strength, and accompanying her at each stage of her journey. She hoped to be,

---

[2] Although the letters to Madame Hallo and her son Charles (L 341; L 342) are the last two in the *Complete Works*, it is known only that they were written in 'November'. As Elizabeth speaks to Madame Hallo of expecting to join the 'great multitude' of the saints in heaven by that evening (cf. L 341), this would suggest the date of the feast of All Saints as a strong possibility; and it would imply that L 340 to Dr Barbier, written during the 'first days of November', was actually Elizabeth's final letter.

as she said, in 'that great multitude' (cf. Rv 7:9–12): the crowd of the redeemed – the saints who, wearing white robes and holding palm branches, sing forever the praises of God. We also see that Scripture was a new place of 'rendez-vous'. For it was there, in the vision of eternity, that her friends would be able to glimpse into heaven and, in this way, meet Elizabeth once more.

It was in this letter that Elizabeth entrusted her own mother to Madame Hallo. She also dictated a shorter note to Charles Hallo, the brother of Marie-Louise. We remember that the Catez 'trio' had been with Monsieur Hallo when he died in 1897, and how he had said to Madame Catez on his deathbed: 'I have loved your daughters very much' (ETB, p. 168). Elizabeth, herself now at the point of death, reminded Charles of the memory of his 'venerable father' and of how he must follow him in 'the valiant faith that keeps the will always faithful' (L 342). She may well, at this moment, have been thinking of her own father, Joseph Catez, whom she was soon to join. Elizabeth now put herself entirely at Charles' disposal: 'You will have battles to fight, my little brother, you will encounter obstacles on the path of life, but do not be discouraged, call me' (L 342).

Just as, in community, it had been said of Elizabeth that she had a *need* to give pleasure (cf. ETB, p. 531), it was just the same when she anticipated helping others from heaven. So she continued to Charles: 'Yes, call your little sister; in this way you will increase her happiness in Heaven' (L 342). She had said the same thing to Madame Hallo: 'How I will think of you, dear Mama, and of my little sister Marie-Louise in the light of that Furnace of love! You will be very present to me there, and my happiness will grow in interceding for you whom I love so much' (L 341).

Elizabeth was already contemplating her future mission. About a week earlier, she had written to Madame Gout de Bize: 'in the Furnace of love, I will be *actively* thinking of you' (L 330) – an echo of the words of Thérèse: 'I really count on not remaining inactive in heaven' (LT 254). And Elizabeth's desire to draw people close to God is alive to the last: 'When I am close to

God,' she said to Charles, 'recollect yourself in prayer and we will meet each other in an even deeper way' (L 342). Finally, she left him a medal from her rosary – 'wear it always,' she said, 'in memory of your Elizabeth who will love you even more in Heaven!' (L 342).

The day of great joy came and went. And now began her final trial.

Engulfed in the Night

The physical symptoms alone were overwhelming. For months, Elizabeth had been severely deprived of food and sleep; more recently, it had been painful even to drink. The last sip she had taken from her mother's ice, three days earlier, had proved to be 'her last meal on earth' (PD, p. 199), to quote Sister Aimée who had watched her take it. And in the remaining nine days of her life, Elizabeth would consume neither a crumb of food nor a drop of water. As she burned up inside, all the sisters could do was moisten her lips. The scorching thirst was sheer torture, but when someone remarked that this was how Jesus had suffered on the Cross (cf. Jn 19:28), Elizabeth exclaimed: 'Oh! yes; it's delightful; He is infinitely thoughtful, and forgets nothing that can associate me with His sufferings!' (S1, p. 188).

This is what sustained Elizabeth throughout: knowing that her suffering was forming her into the likeness of Christ. She reacted with a joyful 'Oh! yes', when a sister said to her: 'You are clothed with the Man of sorrows; you are indeed conformed to Jesus crucified' (S1, p. 192).

The physical sufferings were joined now by another aspect of his Passion. As the prioress would later say: '*darkness...* enwrapped her during those first days of agony' (PG, p. 220). Mother Germaine, with her deep understanding of the spiritual life, had made a striking comment at the end of Elizabeth's novitiate: 'She has profited from her trial so perfectly that I would not be surprised if God should leave her in her beautiful peace right to the end, the work of destruction is done'

(ETB, p. 522). He *did* leave her 'right to the end' – but just as for Jesus (cf. Lk 4:13), that 'end' itself included the final hour of trial. Elizabeth said to the prioress: 'Oh, my Mother, it is like believing that there is no God!' (ESS, p. 39). And as if to strengthen this spiritual darkness, she was now sent a *physical* night: her eyes became bloodshot and almost impossible to open – quite literally, she could no longer see. In every sense, she was engulfed in the night. This is how she described the state of her whole self:

> It seems as though my body were suspended and my soul in darkness... (PG, pp. 212–3)

Elizabeth could not have expressed more accurately the experience of Christ on the Cross in which she was now sharing: he hung there – suspended – while 'there was darkness over the whole land' (Mk 15:33), and believing that the Father had abandoned him. Mother Germaine, who hardly ever left her side, was aware of Elizabeth's 'helplessness and crucifying feelings of abandonment' (PG, p. 212). But Elizabeth said to Sister Marthe, with great realism and generosity of spirit: 'If I had died in my former state of soul, death would have been too sweet. I depart in pure faith, and I prefer it, for I resemble my Master more closely, and it is more real' (PG, p. 213).

For a long time, Elizabeth had been firmly resolved to believe that all things come to us through God's love. This, the prioress believed, was what now gave Elizabeth 'the strength of martyrs' (PG, p. 212). Indeed, when Elizabeth had said that she felt suspended and in darkness, she had immediately added:

> ...but it is the action of Love, and knowing that, my heart rejoices. (PG, p. 213)

The two parts of this utterance combine to characterise the whole of Elizabeth's final agony: it has a *double character*, one of simultaneous contrasts. Overcome by suffering, she rejoiced through faith to see the action of God. And while bodily illness held her captive on her Calvary, her soul was free to rejoice.

The darkness of faith was soon joined by a fear of death. Elizabeth was in awe at the power and justice of God, as the prospect of the great encounter – and the inevitable sense of the unknown – dawned on her with its full weight of reality:

> what a serious thing it is when we come to this state! The thought of heaven thrills my soul, I seemed to have dwelt there for a long time, yet it is quite unknown to me!... Oh! how we ought to pray for the dying! I would willingly spend my eternity near them to help them. There is something terrifying about death... I have an indescribable feeling, an intuition of the justice and sanctity of God. I realise that death is a punishment, and I feel so insignificant, so wanting in merit... How we ought to encourage those in their last agony!... (PG, p. 218)[3]

'The priest should be here'

Throughout this acutely difficult time, Elizabeth had others who encouraged her in her own last agony. There was the community chaplain, Father Courtois, who frequently heard her confession and spoke comfortingly to her. He could not, though, give her Communion: as we have seen, she would not have been able to swallow even one particle of the Host. A sister said to her that it must be hard being deprived of God. Elizabeth gave this profound reply, which in fact conveys the essence of the Eucharist:

> I find Him on the cross; it is there He gives me His life. (PG, p. 214)

The 'priest' whom Elizabeth most needed by her side, though, was Mother Germaine; and Elizabeth, knowing the end to be

---

[3] Thérèse, too, had been beset with anxiety just before dying and felt keenly how much those in their final agony have need of prayers. During her last afternoon on earth, she had said, agitated and appearing 'close to despair', 'How we ought to pray for the agonizing!': in Father Marie-Eugène of the Child Jesus, *Under the Torrent of His Love: Thérèse of Lisieux, a Spiritual Genius*, New York: Alba House, 1995, p. 56.

very near, was anxious that she must not die without the prioress being present. Whenever Mother Germaine was unable to be there, Elizabeth would say to the sub-prioress:

> The victim is about to be sacrificed, and cannot do without *the priest*. (PG, p. 217)

Once, when she felt at the point of death, she asked for the prioress. As Elizabeth could not see, the nun who was with her at the time – and possibly thinking she could spare the exhausted prioress – actually pretended to be Mother Germaine! Elizabeth was no more fooled than she had been as a very young child when her doll had been disguised as the baby Jesus. 'That is not right,' she reprimanded the sister. 'I am going to die and the priest should be here to offer his sacrifice' (ESS, p. 45).

The 'priest' herself, Mother Germaine – looking at her racked with pain, and seeing the bed as 'a genuine altar of sacrifice' (PG, p. 218) – was reminded of how, as a young girl, Elizabeth had offered herself as a '*victim* for the sins of the world' (PG, p. 218).[4] The prioress felt that these 'prayers had been heard', and that Jesus 'the High Priest was completing the oblation of His innocent victim' (PG, p. 218).[5]

---

[4] Mother Germaine may have been recalling, here, one of Elizabeth's reminiscences which she had been sharing with her in recent weeks: cf. ETB, pp. 703–5. The prioress may well, though, have been thinking of one particular passage from Elizabeth's *Diary*, as she later quotes it in the *Souvenirs*: 'My God, in union with Jesus crucified, I offer myself as victim...' (PG, p. 47; cf. D 126). She may also have had in mind an earlier passage from the *Diary*, where Elizabeth prays to Jesus: 'I take on myself the sins of the world... I am your victim' (D 7).

[5] In connection with Elizabeth's being a '*victim*' for 'the sins of the world', Mother Germaine mentions her 'sufferings', together with her 'innocence' (PG, p. 218). The combination of all these elements is significant: they reflect the Passion of Jesus who, an innocent Victim, took the sins of the world on himself. This also calls to mind something which was said by Thérèse of Lisieux on the day she died: 'Never would I have believed it was possible to suffer so much! never! never! I cannot explain this except by the ardent desires I have had to save souls' (LC, p. 205).

'Thirty or forty years more'

One day, moments before Elizabeth spoke about the 'terrifying' nature of death, she grasped Mother Germaine's hand and said imploringly: 'Do not leave me, I stand in great need of your aid to finish climbing my Calvary' (PG, p. 218). During those terrible nine days and nights, Mother Germaine hardly left her side at all. But even then, Elizabeth was haunted by thinking of the moment when she would have to let go, forever, of that reassuring hand: 'Oh! to think that the time will come when I must traverse that mysterious, solemn passage alone!' (PG, p. 218). Fortunately, the prioress knew exactly how to reassure her: 'But our Lady will be there,' she said consolingly, 'and will take you by the hand; you will have nothing to fear with such a Mother.' 'Yes, that is true!' Elizabeth replied. '*Janua coeli* will be sure to let little *Laudem Gloriae* pass through...' (PG, p. 218).

Another source of help at this time was when someone offered to read her 'The Exercises of St Gertrude'. Elizabeth was grateful to anyone who would recite these prayers to her, and if the sister stopped reading Elizabeth would often try to whisper: 'Gertrude!' (PG, p. 215) so that she might resume. The thirteenth-century Cistercian mystic expresses, here, her passionate longing for union with Jesus, the Bridegroom: 'O Love! Love! do not delay in accomplishing for me the solemnity of the eternal marriage!... O Love! hurry to satisfy my desire... complete what you have begun' (S1, pp. 189–90). But the climax came, for Elizabeth, at this particular point in the prayers: 'Praise yourself in yourself; praise yourself in me and through me'. At this, Elizabeth trembled with emotion and murmured: 'Oh! that's [exactly] it!' (S1, p. 190). For this was the perfect expression of a 'Praise of Glory': a person in and through whom God would be praised.

After one particularly bad attack, Elizabeth thought of a saying of Catherine of Siena: 'May my life distil drop by drop for You, O Christ, and for the Church, Your sweet spouse' (ESS, p. 39). And with enormous generosity of soul – still wishing to 'extract from her being all the prayer and suffering possible' (ESS, p. 38) – Elizabeth cried out that she was willing for this state to continue for years, if necessary:

> O Love! Love! You know how much I love You, how much I desire to contemplate You; You know, too, how much I am suffering, nevertheless, thirty or forty years more if You wish it, I am ready. Spend all my substance for Your glory, let it distil drop by drop for Your Church. (ESS, p. 39)

'Oh, what a vocation!'

Incredibly, although her sufferings had not abated, Elizabeth sometimes managed to become her old self again and be responsive to the people around her. Sister Marie of the Trinity would describe her, at these times, as 'smiling to everyone and to each one, forgetful of herself, preoccupied with others, always considerate' (ETB, p. 715). And Sister Aimée would describe her as 'always lovable, thoughtful, delightful, affectionate' (ETB, p. 713). Whenever Mother Germaine came into the room, Elizabeth greeted her with a smile of 'indescribable sweetness' (PG, p. 217). It was at such moments, especially, that Elizabeth felt the sacrifice of not being able to open her eyes, though sometimes she managed to peer through half-closed eyelids. She so loved to see the face of the prioress, and one day betrayed her disappointment. Inclining her head in a little gesture of sadness, she said with regret: 'I can no longer make out your features!' (ETB, p. 715).

On Monday, November 5 – the half-way point of the final agony – Sister Marie-Xavier was alone in the room with her. This nun was astonished when Elizabeth clasped her hand and murmured, in a gasping, almost dying voice: 'You are *Abscondita*, are you not?' 'Yes!' she replied. 'Well! it is He Himself Who gave you that name; I understood it. Oh, what a vocation!' (PG, pp. 216–7). The nature of this vocation was what Elizabeth had tried to put in writing on October 30, the day she had been too weak to express herself as she would have wished; she had also, at the time, wanted to explain the 'beauty' (L 339, n. 1) of this calling. So she explained it now: '*Abscondita in Deo* means separation from all earthly things, a continual ascension to Him. What mortification, what prayer, what self-effacement that name requires! I cannot tell you all, but I will help you from heaven' (PG, p. 217); and each time Sister Marie-Xavier came back to the infirmary cell, Elizabeth would repeat this promise, saying: 'I will help you' (PG, p. 217). Then suddenly, playfully, Elizabeth told her to take the sweets which had been left by her bedside. 'That,' she said, 'is for the baptism of Abscondita!' (PD, p. 203).

That week, Elizabeth bequeathed another name. Almost three years earlier, Sister Aimée had first pointed out to Elizabeth the phrase from Ephesians which would come to define Elizabeth's entire spiritual vision: 'praise of glory'; then, at Elizabeth's request, she had shown it to her in the Latin. Later, when Elizabeth had entered the infirmary, Sister Aimée noticed that the prioress and some of the sisters were calling Elizabeth by the nickname of 'Laudem'. Sister Aimée said nothing, but possibly she felt left out: 'Elizabeth,' she would say later, 'had received a great grace which I did not have, a grace that was greater than mine' (PD, p. 198). Perhaps Elizabeth had sensed something of these feelings. For in this final week of her life, and without doubt to express her deep gratitude, she gave Sister Aimée the two things that meant most to Elizabeth herself: 'I leave you our Mother,' she said to her, 'and my name of Laudem Gloriae' (ESS, p. 43).

At times, Elizabeth could be heard praising God. She also said consoling things to her sisters, as and when her voice allowed. And whenever she was able to receive visits, it was always a pleasure to go and see her. Mother Germaine would say: 'We used to love to visit her and collect the sayings which seemed addressed to us from the threshold of eternity' (PG, p. 219). The nuns even felt that Elizabeth could see into their souls. Given the acuteness of her sufferings, the sisters were astonished by her presence of mind.

Strength for the Trial

Elizabeth was aware that Mother Germaine was wearing herself out, for she was with her almost every moment of the day and night. Sometimes Elizabeth managed to catch a glimpse of the drained features, and she told her to take food and rest. One day, she said that as soon as she got to heaven she would pray for Mother Germaine's health. The prioress, who was nothing if not spiritual, replied in surprise that it would be better to pray first for her soul. Elizabeth's answer shows how perfectly balanced was her own way of seeing: 'It's true, the soul comes before the body,' she said; 'but, in heaven, I think that one can take care of many things at once, for heaven is UNITY' (S1, p. 191).

Elizabeth was keen to show her gratitude to the person who had taken such care of her own body: Dr Barbier. At some point during the first few days of November, she decided to write to him, and in her letter (L 340) would speak explicitly of her 'mission'. So now, for the very last time,[6] Mother Germaine took up her position as scribe, beginning the letter with a little cross:

+

My good Doctor,

My heart is borrowing the hand of my Mother to tell you again one last time how grateful it is to you for the good care you have lavished on me during these months of sufferings that have been months of blessings, profound joys unknown by the world.

I also want to tell you that it is my turn now; I feel my mission is beginning on your behalf. Yes, God is entrusting you to your little patient, and she is to be the invisible Angel, close to Him, who will lead you, by the path of duty, to the goal of every creature born of God. In this last hour of my exile, in this beautiful evening of life, how solemn everything looks to me in the light coming to me from eternity...

---

[6] See n. 2 above.

I wish I could make souls understand, tell them the vanity, the emptiness of anything not done for God. At least I am sure you understand me, dear Doctor, for you have always understood me; I felt it very much and it made me so happy in the depths of my heart.

Elizabeth now asked him to think back often to the things they had spoken about; and she added, beautifully: 'let your soul resonate under the action of the grace they will bring to it'. The aim, she said, was that this might lead him to 'conform [his] will faithfully to what God asks', which can be discerned, she wrote, in God's Law and his Church. Finally, she gave him the only gift she could possibly have chosen – the one that was so perfect for him, after all their months of sharing:

It made me so happy to see you appreciate my dear Saint Paul that I am asking you, so as to complete my happiness, to accept as a last goodbye from your little patient, a last testimony of her affectionate gratitude, the book of those Epistles from which my soul has drawn so much strength for the trial. We will meet in the light these pages bring to those who read them with the faith of the children of God; in this light that for me will soon have no shadow, I will remember you and will pray to Him, who was so merciful to me, to keep you for Himself until all eternity, where I want to meet you one day, good Doctor. A Dieu, and thank you again. I am signing by this little cross.

+

A Soul and a Body

As the end approached, the pain reached heights that few can imagine. The raging inflammation now attacked her head with ferocity. Elizabeth felt her brain was on fire, and the sisters feared the onset of meningitis. They placed ice on her head – it melted instantly. All throughout her illness, Elizabeth had somehow managed not to let the pain overcome her. But now, the pain was quite literally overwhelming and she appeared to be murmuring away, barely audible. She also looked 'unrecognisable', so much was she 'ravaged with the pain'.[7] In this extremity, Mother Germaine knew that nature could take over: a soul could be at the mercy of those visceral feelings which come from a body in agony. And yet, she would say, Elizabeth's soul still 'mastered her physical state' (PG, p. 214). Her speech became almost indistinguishable, and the prioress leaned close to her, trying to catch something of what she was saying. And she heard, with admiration, that although Elizabeth 'could hardly control her thoughts' (PG, p. 214), she was still expressing her love of God – it was clear to the prioress that 'divine union had become so habitual to her that it was maintained in spite of everything' (S1, p. 189). The same impression was made on another sister, who leant close to Elizabeth to say something consoling – and instead, went away edified.

The love of God had so taken possession of Elizabeth that it simply poured out of her, even when she could barely influence what she was thinking or saying. God had answered her prayer fully: 'I ask You to "clothe me with Yourself", to identify my soul with all the movements of Your Soul, to overwhelm me, to possess me, to substitute Yourself for me that my life may be but a radiance of Your Life' (PT). We recall how, in her first few days in Carmel, Elizabeth had been asked in the postulant's questionnaire what dispositions she would like to have at the moment of death. And she had replied: 'I would like to die while loving, and thus to fall into the arms of Him whom I love' (IN 12). That moment was rapidly approaching as God was bringing to fulfilment this long-held desire. When Mother Germaine came to write the biography, she would sum up Elizabeth's life with these words: 'She has loved much' (S1, p. 183; cf. Lk 7:47).

---

[7] From a letter by Mother Germaine, of November 21, 1906, in Poinsenet, p. 268.

A Soul Ascending

It seemed to Mother Germaine that after the period of nearly eight months when Elizabeth had been virtually alone in the infirmary, the community were, so to speak, returning to her (cf. PD, p. 205). Moved, and in awe, they were constantly coming to the little cell. The impressions Elizabeth made on them are expressed in various ways: she had the charming simplicity of a child (cf. PG, p. 219); she was a champion athlete finishing her race (cf. PG, p. 215; cf. 2Tm 4:7); she was a queen, majestic in suffering (cf. PG, p. 216). Sometimes her expression reminded them of the Holy Face and inspired in them a reverent recollection as they gazed on her and must have simultaneously thought of the Passion of Christ (cf. PG, p. 219). Sister Marie of the Trinity spoke of 'the descent from the cross' (PG, p. 217) and Sister Aimée of a soul 'ascending' (cf. PD, p. 199). This apparent contrast was captured by Mother Germaine who described Elizabeth as dead in appearance yet alive to God (cf. PG, p. 214). The sub-prioress felt the same, as she contemplated a body 'that was no more than a ruin' and at the same time a soul 'grappling with the whole great mystery of the Beyond' (ETB, p. 715). Occasionally, Elizabeth opened her eyes, joined her hands and looked at a fixed point, as if in ecstasy; on seeing this, Sister Marie of the Trinity felt moved to the depths.

These impressions extended even to veneration. The community saw her as a saint – so much so that objects were continually being sent up to the infirmary, with the request that Elizabeth might touch them. Sister Marthe was overwhelmed by a sense of the presence of God in her. She could not help kissing Elizabeth's hands – she felt that in doing so, she was kissing the hands of Jesus. Elizabeth understood: 'It is for Him!' (PG, p. 215), she said.

One day, the infirmary sister, seeing her in torture, asked: 'You can bear no more, my poor little sister?' Elizabeth cried out her agreement: 'Oh, no! I can bear no more!' (PG, p. 219). The sister asked if she wished to go to heaven. Elizabeth replied:

'Yes!' And then she expressed her impatience – not to be done with the suffering, but to see Jesus face to face: 'Until now,' she said, 'I have abandoned myself to Him, but I am His bride, and now I have the right to say to Him: "Let us go!" We love one another so dearly, we are impatient to see one another. Oh! how I love Him!' (PG, pp. 219–20).

'The joy of paradise'

One day, very close to the end, Mother Germaine came into the little infirmary cell and knew straightaway from Elizabeth's expression that the spiritual darkness of the first few days 'had given way to light' (S1, p. 193). She soon discovered that Elizabeth had been given to understand certain things, of which she was not allowed to speak. But after a while, Elizabeth told the prioress of a dream she had had which had enchanted her. There was a palace, entirely of white and gold, and in it a bride: a girl incredibly tall, but so perfectly proportioned that she was graceful – and who had, said Elizabeth, an incomparable majesty (cf. S1, p. 193). The prioress asked if perhaps it was Laudem Gloriae herself? Elizabeth smiled and said she didn't know. 'I did not see her face,' she replied; 'but she was beautiful!... she was beautiful!... and this dream has placed in my heart the joy of paradise' (S1, p. 193).

Another morning, Elizabeth leaned forward and peered through her half-closed eyelids as though trying to examine an object she had just noticed. 'I see a palm leaf' (S1, p. 193), she said, in answer to Mother Germaine's question. And she put out her hand as if to take hold of it. 'A palm leaf?' said the prioress, no doubt hoping to hear more. 'Yes!' Elizabeth answered, 'a beautiful palm leaf.' 'Would it be for you?' asked Mother Germaine. As before, Elizabeth did not know. But generous and spontaneous to the end, she added: 'I am not selfish, and I want some of them for all my sisters, too' (S1, p. 194).

The bride and the palm – rich in resonances for Elizabeth as the Book of Revelation was already opening its promises to her. The 'great multitude' in adoration – wearing white and holding palms (cf. Rv 7:9). The wedding feast of the Lamb, for which the bride was being made ready (cf. Rv 19:7). And then there was the 'new song' (cf. Rv 5:9; 14:3)...

Mother Germaine came in one day and had an amazing sight. Elizabeth, the former pianist, was moving her fingers over an imaginary keyboard. Ever-intuitive, the prioress did not ask what she was playing but whether she was *hearing* something. 'Oh, my Mother,' Elizabeth replied with joy, 'they are divine harmonies' (ESS, p. 43). This great interpreter of Chopin and Liszt was now interpreting the harmonies of God. But for the ears of those who were still on earth, they could be heard only as silence.

On another occasion, Elizabeth made a gesture to show she was surrounded with brightness as she exclaimed: 'It is full of light!... It is grand!... It is...' (S1, p. 194). At this, she broke off: 'she was not permitted,' the prioress would later write, 'to explain the secrets heard in those regions so near to the vision of God' (PG, p. 220).

The Song of her Soul

Two days before her death, Mother Germaine would say, Elizabeth 'found strength to express her happiness' (PG, pp. 220–1). On Wednesday, November 7, Dr Barbier paid Elizabeth his final visit. He did not yet know about her letter and her gift of the writings of St Paul: they would be sent to him a week after her death. He took her pulse and Elizabeth asked for his findings. He replied that it was extremely weak, and gave her to understand that she might live only another couple of days. On receiving such news, most of his patients would have been upset, to say the least! But Elizabeth burst out with joy:

> In two days I shall probably be in the bosom of my 'Three'; is not that joy enough? *Laetatus sum in his quae dicta sunt mihi!* ['I rejoiced in what was said to me!'] It is our Lady, full of light, pure with the divine purity, who will take me by the hand to lead me into heaven – that realm of dazzling brightness! (PG, p. 221; cf. Ps 121:1)

The doctor was stunned. Then Elizabeth, with a supreme effort that brought tears to several eyes, spoke to him with joy about God's having adopted us as his children. In her spontaneous rejoicing, she had quoted to the doctor the first line of Psalm 121 as she 'rejoiced in what was said' to her. What the doctor had said to her *literally* was that she was soon going to die. Possibly, she now explained to him what had *really* been said – this being revealed in the next line of the Psalm: 'Let us go to God's house' (Ps 121:1).[8]

This final explosion of joy had used up her remaining strength. After the visit, Elizabeth fell into a permanent silence. At times, though, her lips still seemed to be moving. Mother Germaine listened closely and managed to catch these words: 'I am going to Light, to Love, to Life!...' (ETB, p. 716).[9] These were the last words Elizabeth was ever heard to say – or to chant. The prioress thought they sounded like a song (cf. S1, p. 194).

'To behold my glory'

The final night, from Thursday to Friday, brought the sufferings to a climax, for a new and vicious symptom was added: asphyxiation. Mother Germaine and Sister Marie of the Holy Spirit watched over her the whole night, and witnessed her terrible fight for breath. By early morning, however, her acute sufferings had subsided. To Mother Germaine, she seemed to be

---

[8] Throughout her time in Carmel, this Psalm had been linked, for Elizabeth, with entering into a sacred place, for the Carmelites of Dijon recited it three times a day as they entered the choir for Offices: cf. LR 41, n. 13.

[9] 'Light', 'Love' and 'Life' are sometimes quoted in a different order as Elizabeth's final words (cf. S2, p. 263), which perhaps reflects the fact that she may have repeated them over and over again, perhaps in a varying order. The one given here is contained in the account by Mother Germaine in the first edition of the biography and in the Circular (cf. S1, p. 194; ETB, p. 716, n. 1), and it is also how the words would be printed on Elizabeth's memorial card (cf. ETB, 716, n. 1). It is worth mentioning in passing that these three words are applied to the crucified Christ in a book on Mary Magdalene which Elizabeth had read in her youth – though there is no evidence that she had this book in mind: cf. ETB, p. 716, n. 1.

calm and silent as she 'peacefully awaited the coming of the divine Bridegroom' (PG, p. 221).

At about a quarter to six, Elizabeth suddenly indicated that she would like very much to get up; this was not unusual, felt Sister Marie, in those who were ill. So, together with the prioress, she began to move her. She lifted her under the arms, and Mother Germaine picked her up from under the knees. Just then, Elizabeth's head drooped onto the chest of Sister Marie who realised, with alarm, that Elizabeth was about to leave them. They immediately put her back on the bed, saw that she was still breathing, and made her as comfortable as possible, propping her up with a pillow so that she was almost in a sitting position.

The community were immediately alerted; as it happened, it was the time they would normally get up. Probably, like Sister Agnes, they looked up to find Sister Marthe saying: 'She's dying' (ETB, p. 717). Elizabeth's bed, normally in the corner of the little infirmary cell, had been pulled out to make room for the sisters to gather round her. Elizabeth was leaning towards her right, her head was tilted back and her eyes, which for the past week had been closed almost constantly, were now wide open – 'luminous, alive' (ETB, p. 718), the sub-prioress would say. Her 'radiant' gaze (PG, p. 222) was fixed on a point just above their heads – 'a little above me, kneeling close to her,' Mother Germaine would write.[10] Elizabeth seemed to her to be 'in ecstasy rather than in agony' (S1, p. 194). But so very peaceful. So much so that her passing would be barely perceptible.

For about half an hour, the community knelt around her bed, reciting the prayers for the dying. Then, according to custom, the prioress read out the priestly prayer of Jesus, his final discourse at the Last Supper. By now, it was around a quarter past six.

Elizabeth had been born while the prologue from the first chapter of John's Gospel was being read at the Mass that was

---

[10] In a letter of November 21, 1906, in Poinsenet, p. 268.

said for her safe delivery – on Christ coming into the world and revealing his glory (cf. Jn 1:14). And while the seventeenth chapter was being read for her safe departure – with Jesus' prayer that all might be with him where he is, to behold his glory (cf. Jn 17:24) – 'Laudem Gloriae' left the world and departed for heaven.

Part IV

AFTER HER DEATH

Mother Germaine, Elizabeth's prioress,
novice mistress and first biographer

God has given me a Mother, the image of His mercy (L 225)

Chapter 24

'A NEW LIGHT IS SHINING'

Hearing the News

In the darkness and quiet of the early November morning in the Carmel of Paray-le-Monial, Mother Marie of Jesus, Elizabeth's first prioress, was making her way to morning prayer. At that same moment, the nuns of her former monastery were in the infirmary at Dijon, gazing on Elizabeth as she passed away. Just then, Mother Marie pushed open the door to the choir, and as she stepped inside had a shock: she heard a voice speaking within her! It announced: 'Sr. Elizabeth is dead.'[1] Like the young Samuel in the Old Testament (cf. 1Sm 3:4.6.8), perhaps she found it too much to grasp at the first hearing. For she was given the words once more: 'Sr. Elizabeth is dead.' At that very instant, she felt Elizabeth's presence with such intensity that she knew the message was true. She must then have remembered how Elizabeth had once promised her that she would be the first to hear the news.

The second person to hear was Elizabeth's own mother. On the Boulevard Carnot in Dijon, the figure of an extern sister could be seen emerging through the great portals of the Carmelite monastery onto the dark pavement. It was just over five years since Madame Catez, sobbing as if bereaved, had made her slow, unsteady way from that very door back to Prior Street, having just left her elder daughter behind the monastery walls. 'We went to Mass and she didn't come back' (ETB, p. 402), the dazed mother had said to a neighbour when she got home. But today, the extern sister had the daunting task of telling her that her elder daughter had departed for good.

---

[1] De Bono, p. 104, n. 498.

Madame Catez was not alone that morning. A few days earlier when the end was known to be imminent, her close friend Madame de Sourdon, as we have seen, had gone to stay with her to support her when the dreaded moment came. And that Friday morning, November 9, 1906, the doorbell finally rang. There stood the veiled figure in the brown Carmelite habit, bearing the bad news. Madame Catez had known what to expect. But as the news hit home, waves ran through her: shock, distress, hysteria. Her friend suddenly thought to remind her: 'Remember what Elizabeth said to you: "When you learn of my death, you will say: My God, you gave her to me, you have taken her back from me, may your Holy Name be blessed. And you will fall on your knees"' (ETB, p. 718). On hearing this, Madame Catez immediately fell to her knees and repeated the words Elizabeth had so recently spoken to her.

'So beautiful'

In the Dijon Carmel that morning, some of the sisters designated by the prioress began moving around in a quiet hive of activity. Like scene-shifters on a stage, moving and arranging props, the nuns were preparing to lay out Elizabeth in ceremonial fashion, so that the community, and later the public, could see her one last time and pay their respects to the one they had lost. She would be in the infirmary parlour for the whole of that Friday until the next morning; then, over the weekend, in the choir where she could also be seen by her family and friends who came to the public chapel. As the funeral could not take place until the Monday, Mother Germaine savoured the 'pleasure of keeping her...among us' for three whole days (cf. PG, p. 223).

The sisters clothed Elizabeth in her full habit, with veil and white mantle; then, according to custom, they placed a little crucifix in her hands, with the face of the figure of Christ facing her own.[2] Straight after her death, they had tried to close her

---

[2] For full details of the customs which would have been observed by the monastery from the time a sister died up to her funeral, see the *Cérémonial*, # 849–889, pp. 190–201. See also the photographs of Elizabeth laid out in the infirmary cell, in De Meester & Carmel of Dijon (eds.), pp. 138–9.

eyelids; but now as they raised her body to prop her up on some high cushions, her eyes, like those of a doll when it is moved, spontaneously opened. Sister Aimée saw once more Elizabeth's gaze, clear as at the moment of death, and thought to herself: 'so beautiful, so beautiful!' (PD, p. 199). However, they could not leave her like this, so they closed her eyelids once again. On her head they placed a crown of white roses. They also framed her outline on the bed with luxuriant blossoms of several kinds, and her habit was strewn with flowers. And around the walls of the little infirmary cell, they arranged tall plants of overhanging greenery and white lilies.

Near Elizabeth's head, and to her left, was a most imposing display – one which she herself would have loved. On a small ornate table was a high crucifix, with the Christ looking down towards her. Also on the table were two candelabra, one on either side of the crucifix, each of which was bearing three candles. And standing in the centre, directly beneath the figure of the Christ, was none other than Elizabeth's beloved statue of Our Lady of Lourdes, 'Janua Coeli'. She was watching over Elizabeth but at the same time lifting her eyes to heaven, a double movement that recalls Elizabeth's final letter to Françoise de Sourdon – this beloved statue may even have influenced her words: 'It seems to me that I am like a mother bending attentively over her favourite child: I raise my eyes and look at God, and then I lower them on you, exposing you to the rays of His Love' (GV 1). Finally, everything was complete. Sister Geneviève came in with her camera and captured the beautiful scene for posterity.

The Revelation of a Saint

Yet the central figure of it all, the one who lay on the bed, had a different kind of beauty. Her face, said Sister Marie of the Trinity, had 'an austere beauty' – that of someone who had 'spent all her substance for God' (ETB, p. 718). Mother Germaine felt that Elizabeth had truly achieved resemblance to Jesus crucified – 'Her dream was realized' (PG, p. 223), she would say. But the physical reality was more a nightmare than a dream. In her final days, Elizabeth's body had seemed 'absolutely unrecognisable' (S1, p. 191), and Mother Germaine knew that the 'extreme alteration in her features' revealed nothing less than a 'martyrdom' (PG, p. 223). One sister thought of Jesus as he was taken down from the Cross: Elizabeth, she said, was 'ravaged, absolutely a skeleton, astonishing for a young sister' – but at the same time, she felt that her death was 'a triumph, an event, the revelation of a saint' (PD, p. 205).

This was the feeling both inside and outside the monastery. As soon as Elizabeth's death became known, a number of rosaries and medals were brought to the Carmel, to be touched against the dead nun and so become precious relics. As the prioress put it so well: 'Everybody thought that any souvenir of her would bring a blessing with it' (PG, p. 223). Sister Aimée had not only inherited Elizabeth's name of 'Laudem Gloriae' (cf. ESS, p. 43); she had also acquired her role of second portress! So a large number of such objects were handed to her, and later that very evening she crept into the infirmary parlour with the basket in her hand. No one else was there. She took out the objects and touched them, one by one, against Elizabeth. After this, she felt unable to tear herself away, and kept watch until midnight. When asked, years later, about her memories of Elizabeth, she would say that she still had no words to express the grace of that night (cf. PD, p. 200).

On Saturday morning, it was time for Elizabeth to be transferred to the choir. So it was now the sacristan, Mother Marie of the Heart of Jesus, who was busy with the preparations. She covered the altar in the choir and those in the public chapel with black cloth, and placed candles on them. She also erected trestle supports, covered with serge, very close to the door-sized grille that gave onto the chapel; and she put up a large black curtain in the choir, which would shield the community from view whenever the grille was open. Then, at the appointed time, the nuns processed in silence to the infirmary parlour, lit their candles, and gathered round Elizabeth. The prayers were recited, and Mother Germaine sprinkled Elizabeth with blessed water. Finally, the community began to accompany Elizabeth to the choir – the place of her many hours of prayer during her five years in Carmel.

The procession recalled, in some ways, the day Elizabeth had taken her vows. Then, all the sisters had preceded her to the chapter room, except for the prioress who, according to custom, was the last in the line, leading Elizabeth by the hand. Now, the community again went before Elizabeth in their white mantles and carrying their candles; and at the back came the coffin, carried by four sisters, with the prioress alone following behind. This would without doubt have been a moving experience for Mother Germaine, looking down at the head of her protégée; but in the wake of those gruelling nine days and nights when she had barely left Elizabeth's bedside, she must also have been physically and emotionally drained.

They entered the choir, where the candles on the altar next to them as they came in had already been lit by the sacristan. Through the grille at the far end of the long room could be seen the glow of the candles on the main altar in the chapel. Three sisters now took up position in front of the grille, one holding a large crucifix, the other two a candelabrum each – standing there as if to greet Elizabeth who was being carried in towards them.

The other sisters took their places in their choir stalls along each wall, forming two rows of light as each sister held her candle. Then the coffin was placed on the trestle supports, Elizabeth facing towards the chapel's main altar and the tabernacle. The three nuns at the grille now moved to the head of the coffin, and Mother Germaine stood at Elizabeth's feet to read out the prayers. When the final prayer ended, and the prioress and remaining sisters returned to their stalls, the community blew out their candles and the focus of light switched to Elizabeth: the candelabra were placed on a bench behind her head, as was the high crucifix; and four candles were lit, one at each corner of the coffin. Elizabeth was ready to be revealed to the public.

Dedication of the House of God

For the Offices, though, the nuns had Elizabeth to themselves for a very intimate gathering. For the three days Elizabeth was with them, she was surrounded, felt the prioress, with their 'prayers and loving veneration' (PG, p. 223); and this would have been an almost tangible experience as the Carmelites looked over to her, from their choir stalls, during the Offices. Mother Germaine was aware of the symbolism of the prayers that first day Elizabeth was in the choir, for November 10 was the feast of the Dedication of the Churches of France. She was also most struck by the significance of the date of Elizabeth's death. For within the Church's year, November 9 was the main feast of dedication: that of the Lateran Basilica in Rome.

This, and other such feasts, reflected the charism of Elizabeth herself – she who, since the evening of her First Communion at the age of ten, had understood that her name meant 'House of God'. In fact, Mother Marie of Jesus – the Carmelite who had explained it to her on that day – was herself just as conscious of how apt it was that Elizabeth had died on a feast that had been so dear to her. Mother Germaine recalled, too, that Elizabeth had not only departed from Carmel on a feast of dedication, but had also entered it on one: for August 2, the date on which Elizabeth had entered the monastery in 1901, was the feast of the dedication of Our Lady of the Angels in Assisi. These dates, it seemed to the prioress, were confirmations of Elizabeth's vocation to be a 'House of God' – the dwelling place of the Trinity. She nourished these thoughts as the 'beautiful liturgy [of the dedication of the churches] was chanted opposite this little "house of God"' (PG, p. 222).

Mother Germaine took part in the Office, that Saturday, as if in conversation with Elizabeth who was right in front of her. She drank in all the phrases that described a church dedicated to God, and spontaneously applied them to Elizabeth. Glancing over to the body, she addressed to her these words which she read out from her breviary: 'O bride! how blessed is your lot!

you are endowed with the glory of the Father, filled with the grace of the Bridegroom...' (SI, p. 195). How the liturgy that day seemed to her a perfect description of Elizabeth: 'The Lord has sanctified his tabernacle; my house is a house of prayer...' (SI, p. 195). The words even recalled the dying nun at the mercy of her harrowing illness: 'the stone hammered with many blows, polished by the chisel in the hands of the divine Sculptor' (PG, p. 223).

Finding Elizabeth Again

Mother Germaine's 'speaking' to Elizabeth in this way suggests her own sense of loss and her attempts to recapture their union – to affirm to herself that she and her protégée would never be separated. She recalled how Elizabeth had said, not long before her death, that as soon as she reached the threshold of paradise, she would 'rush there like a little rocket' (PG, p. 222) – 'into the bosom of "my Three"' (CW I, p. 32). So Mother Germaine now consciously 'sought her in the great furnace of love, the bosom of "the Three"' (PG, p. 222).

Others sought Elizabeth, too: the many, many people from the town who came to the Carmel, as soon as her death became known, to look upon her. Four sisters, at a time, were designated to keep watch at the coffin, kneeling on either side of it with their long veils lowered – two at her head, two at her feet – and praying for Elizabeth. Then finally, the large black curtain was drawn, hiding the rest of the community from view, and the tall, heavy grille was unlocked and slowly opened.

The first two faces, without any doubt, would have been those of Madame Catez and Guite, tearful and pale. Coming afterwards, possibly later in the course of the weekend, were Elizabeth's friends who, because of the monastery's parlour grilles, had not in fact 'seen' her for a few years. The last time they had seen her face to face had been when she was in good health. So the contrast for them must have been especially shocking. What struck them most was her face which bore the marks of intense suffering. Charles Hallo would later attempt to describe it by suggesting a painting by Goya. His sister and Elizabeth's best friend, Marie-Louise, noted the 'brown tint' on her face, 'as if she had been burnt' (ETB, p. 719) – which was very possibly the case, given how much Elizabeth in her final weeks had been burning up with inflammation. Françoise found the sight 'frightening' (PD, p. 190). Years later, she would describe the scene vividly: 'You felt it was a ravaged, consumed creature; a skeleton wearing clothes' (PD, p. 190); but with great insight, she would say also: 'With Elizabeth, the love of God was consuming' (ETB, p. 719). And as the weekend wore on, a stream of visitors began to pour into the chapel, to gaze with veneration upon the Carmelite who was being called 'the little saint' (PG, p. 223).

On the Sunday evening, after everyone had left, Mother Marie of the Heart of Jesus had a dizzy spell. This former prioress was now sixty-two and subject to frequent, lengthy attacks of vertigo that kept her confined to bed for as long as they lasted. This was the state she was in when the turn sisters rang for her that evening. When she didn't come, the bell rang again. Suddenly, she had an inspiration: as she knew that she was being called to help with Elizabeth's funeral arrangements, she thought that Elizabeth would help her! So, she dragged herself to the choir, rested her forehead against Elizabeth's feet – and instantly became well and returned to her work.

A Child Surrounded by Priests

In no time at all, it was Monday, November 12, and the community had to let Elizabeth go. In a final gesture which must have moved Mother Germaine to the core, she lowered Elizabeth's veil over her face before the lid of the coffin was closed. She also removed the cross from Elizabeth's hands and replaced it with a small, simple one made of pinewood with which she would be buried. The sisters then carried Elizabeth in procession to the enclosure door. There, they were met by the clergy who had come for the funeral Mass, and who lifted up the coffin and carried it into the public chapel.

With the sombre gravity of the occasion, all the altars covered in black, and the sound of the solemn chants, Madame Catez must have been even more overwhelmed with distress. But although Mother Germaine felt her own loss keenly, she would later say that the funeral was 'a genuine triumph' (PG, p. 223) – not least because there were no fewer than twenty-four priests celebrating the Mass.[3] What seems to have moved her most, though, was not seeing all these priests gathered round the altar, but seeing them gathered round the coffin. The prioress could not help noticing the paradox of this 'imposing circle' of clergy surrounding a 'humble child,...retired and silent' (PG, p. 223). Yet she also perceived the divine logic of it: they were recognising a young woman who 'had immolated herself for Holy Church and [its] consecrated [priests]' (PG, p. 223); and in this, she was expressing the hidden but fruitful vocation of the Carmelite nuns.

Elizabeth was to be buried in the nearby cemetery in town. This meant that the nuns could not go with her to the graveside, as she would be taken outside the enclosure. She would be accompanied there by the priests and people, while the sisters themselves would be in the choir, accompanying Elizabeth with their prayer. As the cortège passed along the route, with the people singing as they followed the coffin, many of them shared their thoughts; and the feedback which afterwards reached Mother Germaine suggested hope rather than mourning. This was a great consolation to the prioress, to feel that she had offered Elizabeth as a sacrifice to God that was perfectly pleasing to him (cf. PG, pp. 223–4). The mere presence of so many people and priests was eloquent witness to this.

Finally, they reached the 'Cimetière des Péjoces', about half a mile away, where Elizabeth's father had been laid to rest nineteen years earlier. A section was reserved for the Carmelite nuns, and that is where Elizabeth was buried. Her grave was marked

---

[3] While Mother Germaine gives the figure of 'twenty-four' in her biography (cf. PG, p. 223), note that the *Summarium* for the beatification Process states that there were twenty priests (cf. De Bono, p. 104, n. 501).

with a plain wooden cross. It read simply: 'Sr. Elizabeth of the Trinity, 9 November 1906'.

A Void and a Presence

The three momentous days were over. Elizabeth had left a void in the monastery. But also a presence. Mother Germaine felt aware of a presence that could only be Elizabeth's, for the convent seemed to her to be bathed in a deep peace. It was, she would say, 'both a pledge and a reflection of that [peace] into which our dearly-loved sister had entered for all eternity' (PG, p. 224).

As the prioress walked onto the terrace, the memories came flooding back. She could see Elizabeth once more, seated there with her breviary beside her. Or holding her statue of Our Lady of Lourdes in her arms. Or walking tentatively from the infirmary after yet another exhausting night of insomnia and pain, to take grateful rest in her armchair. She would smile, close her eyes, and appear lost to everything around her – except, perhaps, to the prayers of the community being recited in the choir below. In the weeks and months that followed, Mother Germaine could never cross this corridor to the infirmary without picturing Elizabeth in her mind's eye.

There was now the usual paperwork to be done, some things more painful than others. Firstly, the death had to be registered. As Elizabeth had passed away so peacefully, it was not easy to know the exact moment of her last breath. Eventually, a time of 'around' a quarter past six was agreed on as the most likely one; this information was given to Guite's husband Georges, who had the death recorded in the civil registers.

The day after Elizabeth died, the prioress wrote to inform Mother Marie of Jesus in Paray-le-Monial – obviously unaware that she knew already! This letter, though, would have been a more pleasant duty, in that it must have been a relief to write to someone with whom she could share her love of Elizabeth. Still steeped in her memories of the unforgettable last few days, Mother Germaine wrote to the Carmelite nun who had been her own prioress in Dijon:

> My very dear mother, if only I could see you to speak of our little saint! for truly she was one, our Elizabeth! What an agony of nine days, what a death! I had the happiness of not leaving her, so to speak, from October 31 to November 9; even then, for three nights I had been sleeping in the little pharmacy, at her door. It gave her so much joy! No one can say what she suffered, and suffered like a saint! (ETB, p. 716)

On the 16th, exactly a week after Elizabeth's death, Mother Germaine posted the letter to Dr Barbier (L 340), the one Elizabeth had dictated to her just over a week earlier and signed with a little cross; the prioress would also have enclosed Elizabeth's farewell gift to him of the letters of St Paul. And on the 21st, two years to the day since Elizabeth had written the *Prayer to the Trinity* – asking Christ to 'overwhelm' and 'possess' her – Mother Germaine wrote to Madame Gout de Bize with an account of Elizabeth's heroic suffering: 'I was witness to a patience, to a serenity, which did not fail her even for an instant, and which revealed the reality of that soul thoroughly possessed by God.'[4]

A Personal Gift

At some point, Mother Germaine faced the emotional task of opening Elizabeth's little writing box and sorting through her personal papers. What she found there moved her far more even than she could have expected. There was a small but bulky envelope addressed to herself with the words, 'Secrets for our Reverend Mother'. On the back was a seal of red wax. Mother Germaine broke the seal and pulled out the booklet of eight small pages which Elizabeth had folded to make it fit inside. It was in a shaky handwriting, but in ink: a sign that Elizabeth, too weak to hold a pen steady during the final weeks of her illness, was making a very special effort – creating a keepsake, a final memorable gift for her prioress.

---

[4] In Poinsenet, p. 268.

We can only begin to imagine the emotions of Mother Germaine as she read the opening words: 'My Cherished Mother, my Holy Priest, when you read these lines, your little Praise of Glory will no longer be singing on earth, but will be living in Love's immense furnace' (LL 1). It was Elizabeth's voice – her voice from heaven! 'What your child is coming to do is to reveal to you what she feels, or, to be more exact, what God…makes her understand' (LL 1) – which is that Mother Germaine should *let herself be loved*. Reading on, she felt Elizabeth to be so incredibly close: 'If you will allow her, your little host will spend her Heaven in the depths of your soul… I will do nothing before the throne of God without you' (LL 4).

Enclosed in this solemn outpouring was a smaller piece of paper. This one also was written in ink, though this time it was not her own words. It was the long quotation she had copied out for the prioress from a revelation of God to Angela of Foligno, and it contained these words, so resonant with Elizabeth's spirituality: 'I will enter into the depths of your being… Love Me! All your life will please Me, provided that you love Me!... I will be made known in you, glorified, and praised in you!...' (LL 7).

Mother Germaine took these treasures away and put them in a safe place, accessible to herself alone. As prioress, she made constant use of something called a 'Grace Book' – a collection of prayers, such as the one with which she gave the blessing at mealtimes – and at some point she slipped between its pages this revelation to Angela of Foligno. As for Elizabeth's precious letter itself, the one now known as *Let Yourself Be Loved*, Mother Germaine kept it in her office. Over the years, she would reread it often. No one knew of it until her own death in 1934, when it was found there, on her table.

'Never to be forgotten'

Mother Germaine was not the only person who felt a bond with Elizabeth that was deeply personal. Sister Aimée felt that Elizabeth's presence was with her; and it was years before she could bring herself to read the first biography – even though its author was Mother Germaine who had known Elizabeth better than anyone – 'for fear,' said Sister Aimée, 'of taking away from myself something of what was in my soul' (PD, p. 200). Guite herself felt unable to speak freely of Elizabeth, even to her children when they were grown up and would have loved to know more about their aunt. When, years later, Guite was interviewed by Father Philipon who was writing a book on Elizabeth, she opened up more, speaking about her with great love, no doubt because she knew she was conversing with someone who understood Elizabeth at the greatest depth. So it is no coincidence that this bereavement brought Guite very close to Mother Germaine.

As we have seen, when the two sisters had met for the very last time, on October 29, Elizabeth had told Guite to remain just as attached to the Carmelite convent after her death as when she had been alive. Guite now began to pay regular visits to Mother Germaine. They would meet innumerable times until the prioress died twenty-eight years later – when Guite would be overwhelmed with grief. For Mother Germaine, too, this friendship must have been a great consolation: in a way, it must have been like acquiring another Elizabeth. Indeed, Guite now, like her late sister, saw the prioress as a mother.

In March 1907, Elizabeth's own mother received an outpouring from someone whose life had been influenced by her elder daughter. Father Donin, who had given Elizabeth Communion a few times when she was dying, and had visited her after her brush with death on Palm Sunday evening, felt forever changed by these encounters. Wanting to share his experience, he spontaneously wrote to the one who had been closest to her:

> Although I saw her only for an instant, when administering Extreme Unction to her, and two or three times later on when I gave her Holy Communion, I look upon this providential meeting as one of the graces of my priestly life, and recall it as a thing precious and never to be forgotten, a deep and vivid impression, neither to be told nor to be described...

Dear Madame Catez, I have ventured to write these few lines to you concerning a past which is both your joy and grief, a Calvary that you have mounted with Christian fortitude. But all these reminiscences ought to terminate in praise to God… It is by this joy which is wholly spiritual, accompanied by resignation and hope, that you will best honour the blessed memory, and will rejoice the heart of your saintly daughter as she watches over you. As for myself, I reckon upon the help which she promised me in the name of holy obedience, the efficacy of which I have already experienced more than once. Now that she is with God she fulfils her vocation as a Carmelite by interceding for the clergy. (PG, pp. 286–8)

'Look at her gaze'

Elizabeth had made such an impact on her Carmelite sisters that for months after her death, she was the only topic of conversation when they came together at recreation. Sister Geneviève displayed the various photographs she had taken, and everyone had their own favourite. 'That one shows her smile most,' one sister would say. Or: 'That's what she gave us most in community' (PD, p. 204). But Mother Germaine would say simply: 'Look at her gaze' (PD, p. 204). Father Vallée was overjoyed with the picture he received. 'It is exactly like her,' he wrote when thanking the prioress, '…with her sweet gentleness, her peaceful recollection, her pure expression, her eyes that seem fixed with an inner gaze upon the vision of her soul, and her whole attitude, which should have forewarned you, had you thought of anything except of the happiness of having her with you, that heaven would not leave her with you long' (PG, p. xxxix).

New novices to the Carmel, who had not known her, were rather in awe of their saintly predecessor. The prioress reassured them that Elizabeth had not had it easy: 'She struggled a great deal' (PD, p. 204), she said. Words that were meant to encourage, but hopefully did not discourage! (That is: 'If *she* struggled, then what about *us*?!') Mother Germaine took obvious pride in speaking of Elizabeth: it was, said one sister, 'almost a mother's jealousy' (PD, p. 204). But while proud of her protegée, the prioress was modest in her own regard. She was especially keen to play down her own contribution to Elizabeth's formation. She would repeat forcefully that it was especially the Holy Spirit who had formed Elizabeth (cf. PD, p. 204).

Everyone had felt loved by Elizabeth. As we have seen, she gave of her best to everyone, so that each sister, to quote Mother Germaine, 'believed herself the most loved' (PD, p. 202). When the community were reminiscing one day, an elderly sister, known for her 'very, very difficult character' (!), declared that she herself was the sister Elizabeth had loved the most. The prioress was amazed – this could hardly be true! But the nun continued: 'How she loved me, we spoke of music, she drew me to God through that' (PD, p. 202).

A Lamp in the Dark

The impact Elizabeth made on all who knew her was deep and lasting. When she left the 'world' of Dijon society and entered Carmel, we have seen how her friendships continued. Now that she had left the world for good, she was never to be forgotten. Charles Hallo kept her letter in his wallet for the rest of his days. Antoinette de Bobet prayed to Elizabeth every day, and was still doing so when interviewed by Father Philipon, about thirty years later. Canon Angles, who normally burned all the letters he received, kept only the ones written by Elizabeth: he felt intuitively that they could well be needed one day for a Process of beatification or canonisation. Sister Marie-Odile of Paray-le-Monial treasured Elizabeth's last letter 'like a relic' (PD, p. 201). And Father Vallée kept Elizabeth's photograph near him for the remainder of his life.

For this Dominican priest, Elizabeth's radiant face bore eloquent witness to her spiritual life. He would recall her large eyes that 'drank in the light which she received fully and deeply, her whole soul...immersed in the peace of God' (PG, p. xlv). Peace and light are words he used more than once when describing

Elizabeth. When asked by the prioress to write an appreciation of her, he recalled especially the times of trial – precisely those moments when the light shone in the dark. He spoke of the 'darkness' of her novitiate year – a time, he did not add, when he had failed to recognise the 'dark night' and so had totally misunderstood her! This spiritual darkness, he said with insight, did not disturb her faith – because she trusted in God, and because: 'Light and peace were from the first her "dowry" from her heavenly Bridegroom. They were always hers because her faith had nothing vague or abstract about it, but was a living faith' (PG, p. xxxix). And he added that even when illness had 'almost destroyed' Elizabeth, 'her little lamp still shed its light within her' (PG, p. xl).

The Battle for the Light

With incredible irony, on the very day of Elizabeth's death the French Government was congratulating itself on having extinguished the light of faith. In the Chamber of Deputies, René Viviani, a Socialist politician and future Prime Minister, delivered an impassioned speech celebrating the work of atheism in France. He declared: 'We have torn human consciences away from belief. When a poor wretch, worn out by the weight of the day, bent his knees, we have helped him back to his feet, we have told him that beyond the clouds, there were only fantasies. Together, and in one magnificent gesture, we have extinguished lights which no one will put on again.'[5] This was the backdrop of darkness against which Elizabeth would shine.

From now on, we leave the story of Elizabeth's life and move on to that of her message. It is the record of a light that shone and was not extinguished (cf. Jn 1:5). It is still, nonetheless, the story of 'the unfolding of her message' – no longer how it evolved within Elizabeth herself, but how it took root in others, starting in Dijon and spreading throughout the world. As we shall now see, Mother Germaine would place herself at the disposal of

---

[5] Quoted by Luigi Borriello, OCD, in Clapier (ed.), p. 717.

Elizabeth's life and message. She would be the privileged witness who would take the first steps in bringing into the darkness of the world the radiance of Elizabeth's mission. We read in the book of Daniel: '[The wise] will shine as brightly as the vault of heaven, and those who have instructed many in virtue, as bright as stars for all eternity' (Dn 12:3). These words, applied in the liturgy to the Doctors of the Church,[6] apply perfectly to Elizabeth of the Trinity. As Pope John Paul II would say of her: 'a new light is shining.'[7]

---

[6] Cf. *Benedictus* antiphon at Morning Prayer, in *Divine Office*, vol. I, p. 359*.

[7] As explained in the Prologue, the titles of Chapters 24–32 and the Epilogue – those sections devoted to the spreading of Elizabeth's message after her death – are drawn from phrases in the homily given by Pope John Paul II at Elizabeth's beatification ceremony and his address to Carmelite pilgrims the following day: cf. De Meester, 'Elizabeth in the Words of the Pope'.

Chapter 25

'HER MESSAGE IS SPREADING'

A Labour of Love

At the time of her death, there is no doubt that Elizabeth was very well known, certainly in Dijon. We have only to think of the many people who had flocked to the Carmelite chapel, on hearing she had died, to look upon the body of the young nun whom everyone was calling 'the little saint' (PG, p. 223). Several had known Elizabeth personally; possibly, most of them simply knew *of* her. By word of mouth, her reputation for holiness had begun to spread. But now it was the turn of the pen and the printing press to spread her life and message.

The first written account, though, was not intended as a proper work of publication. A fortnight after Elizabeth's death, Mother Germaine began a task that was, in fact, simply a duty: to write, as prioress, the obituary notice of a deceased sister. This, we have seen before, was the piece known as the 'Circular'. The custom in the Order was that when a nun died, a brief account of her life would be sent to the other Carmelite monasteries, to tell them something about the sister they had probably never met but who was still theirs in heaven.[1]

After the sadness of the recent days, Mother Germaine found this project an unexpected delight. It was no duty but a labour of love. It must have felt like being in Elizabeth's company again: in fact, it seemed to her that she was writing the *Circular* together 'with' (CW I, p. 33) her protégée, and she must have

---

[1] For this chapter on Mother Germaine's writings on Elizabeth, I am indebted to the research of Conrad De Meester: see CW I, pp. 32–42, and his discussion in Clapier (ed.), pp. 683–94. Also very informative is the essay 'Présentation des Souvenirs' by the Carmel of Dijon, in S1, pp. 9–14.

recalled how Elizabeth had promised to help her, saying one day: 'We will do it together' (CW I, p. 31).

As we know, they had, that autumn, worked on it together – Elizabeth giving her the relevant information as she spoke of her spiritual life as a young girl and of how she had received the call to Carmel. But Mother Germaine was also keen to know about Elizabeth's youth. So she now invited Madame Catez to come and help her by filling in some more details. There, in the parlour, Elizabeth's two 'mothers' met with each other and shared their memories of this daughter whom they had each loved so much.

Guite, too, contributed to the research. She brought with her, for copying, the letters she had received from her elder sister. In the days before photocopiers, this task was given to one of the nuns to do by hand: this was most likely Sister Agnes, who at community retreats had taken down the talks of the preacher verbatim and recorded them in the convent's archives. Now, she carefully copied out Elizabeth's letters clearly and neatly – which is undoubtedly why she was given the task. In fact, it had almost certainly been Sister Agnes, with her classic, round handwriting, who had been instructed to give Elizabeth lessons in writing less like an artist and more like a nun!

It is not difficult to see why Mother Germaine felt that Elizabeth was helping her write the *Circular*: the extracts in it from her writings meant that Elizabeth's own voice was speaking while the pen of the prioress was flowing. We recall Elizabeth's knowing look when Mother Germaine had tentatively asked her, on the eve of her final retreat, to make sure to take notes! The prioress, who had been more than pleased with them, now quoted from this notebook, which today is known as the *Last Retreat*, as well as from *Heaven in Faith*, the *Diary*, some verses from the poetry of Elizabeth's youth, and from two letters.

We might wonder which two letters we ourselves might select. The passages chosen by Mother Germaine had been written in the two months before Elizabeth died, and bring to life her courage and commitment to Christ at a time of extreme suffering. They both reflect the saying of Angela of Foligno – on suffering as the dwelling place of Jesus – which had been so inspirational to Elizabeth for living with her own pain. The first of these letters was to Madame Catez, in which Elizabeth had said: 'Every soul crushed by suffering, in whatever form it may occur, can tell itself: I dwell with Jesus Christ, we are living in intimacy, the same dwelling shelters us!' (L 314). For the second piece, Mother Germaine chose this extract from a letter to Madame de Vathaire: 'David said about Jesus Christ: "His suffering is immense." I have fixed my dwelling place in that immensity, it is the royal palace where I live with my cruci-fied Bridegroom; I am keeping a rendez-vous there with you, for your soul knows how to appreciate the happiness of suffering and to regard it as the revelation of the "exceeding love" Saint Paul speaks of. Oh! how I love it! It has become my peace, my repose; pray that God might increase my capacity for suffering' (L 323a).

While it was not unusual to include notes by the sister who had died, it *was* unusual to write a very long Circular: Elizabeth's would extend to fourteen pages of small type – 'well beyond the usual limits of our circulars' (CW I, p. 33), its author would say. This very fact was likely to attract attention about the sister whose life was being related – the Circular of Thérèse of Lisieux had also been rather long! As for Mother Germaine herself, she was surprised at the 'extraordinary ease that led me to finish this work very rapidly' (CW I, p. 32). The *Circular* was completed in less than a month, and signed with the date of December 18, 1906. It came back from the printers within a week and was sent out on the 24th – just in time to be a welcome Christmas present! For its author, the whole experience had been a gift. She wrote, in her accompanying letter to Guite: 'I have found profound joys and true graces in the course of this little work done with my holy child' (CW I, p. 33).

'You have not told us all'

Also that Christmas Eve, the prioress sent a copy to Madame Catez and said: 'If I have not spoken more of her family, it was to conform to the customs of the Order, but we can make up for this in a notice' (CW I, p. 34). At first sight, we might think this was simply some nice words for the benefit of her recipient: the author had had to emphasise Elizabeth's years in Carmel, given that most of the readers of the *Circular* were Carmelites, and was apologising to the mother for not including all the childhood memories which Madame Catez had shared with her. But Mother Germaine's mention of a 'notice' – her term for a longer biographical work – was more than wishful thinking. She was in earnest about her suggestion.

Writing the *Circular* had simply shown the prioress that the confines of a few pages were hopelessly inadequate to convey everything she felt about Elizabeth. In short, her subject matter was crying out for a work that was much longer. It was not just for the sake of including Elizabeth's upbringing, or her music, or the parish work in Dijon. It was not even in order to say more about her life in Carmel. What was nagging away at Mother Germaine was Elizabeth's spiritual life – the life of her *soul*. This, she felt, was what needed to be brought into the light and given all the scope it demanded. As she said to Guite in her letter accompanying the *Circular*: 'It seems to me that I have said nothing in these [fourteen] pages, there was so much to be said; it is rather a sketch than a life of a soul' (CW I, p. 33).

The first replies from the Carmels began to arrive at the Boulevard Carnot as early as December 28 – practically by return of post. For Mother Germaine, reading these letters could not have been more rewarding. It was soon clear to her that the *Circular* had been very much appreciated and even inspirational. Several of the convents requested more copies. And more than this: her intuition about a 'notice' was confirmed: for the suggestion was made that she should write the full story of Elizabeth's spiritual life![2] The most encouraging reply was almost certainly this one from the Carmel of Anderlecht: 'I think you have not told us all... The simplicity and silence of Sister Elizabeth of the Trinity will be a valuable example for Carmel and for many souls. There is but one opinion about it here: you must write an account of it' (PG, p. xliii).

Mother Germaine would have been thrilled to read these words from Anderlecht in particular, and she would quote them in her Introduction to the biography, saying of that monastery that it 'personifies the great traditions of the Order' (PG, p. xlii). Founded in 1604 as the first French Carmel, it was often better known by the name of its Paris location, the 'Rue d'Enfer' – an unfortunate name, meaning 'Hell Street', which was later conveniently disguised as the 'Rue Denfert'! (And which has since been renamed again: as the Rue Henri-Barbusse.) Great must have been the shock waves felt in the Dijon Carmel when, in 1901, the year Elizabeth entered, this 'cradle [of the Order] in France' (PG, p. xlii) had had to go into exile. It was currently in the Belgian town of Anderlecht, and would not return to France until 1920 when the community would settle at Clamart, a few miles south-west of Paris. Given its illustrious history, it was often consulted about Carmelite customs, and a letter from Anderlecht was like the voice of authority.

Her Opposite Number

But there was another, though unofficial, authority in France: the Carmel of Lisieux. For Mother Germaine, there was already a striking parallel between Elizabeth and Thérèse. We remember that not long before Elizabeth's death, she and Mother Germaine had spoken together of her posthumous mission – a

---

[2] It is not the case that the idea of the biography occurred to Mother Germaine only after she received the feedback from the *Circular*: see CW I, p. 34. In her Introduction to the biography (cf. S1, p. 17), she does actually attribute her project to the feedback received from the *Circular*, but this would appear to be simply a means of justifying the writing of a full-length work on Elizabeth.

clear echo of Thérèse (cf. LC, p. 102) – and that the prioress had specifically asked her if she would 'come down' to help souls as 'Little Thérèse' had done (cf. CW I, p. 32). In her Introduction to a later edition of the biography, Mother Germaine would eagerly point out that her life of Elizabeth had been called a 'second "Histoire d'une Âme"' (PG, p. xliv), a second *Story of a Soul* – something we might assume that she had, from the outset, been hoping to emulate in some way: for as from the first edition, she refers, in the opening lines of her Introduction, to this 'soul' having an extraordinary 'story' (S1, p. 17). She would also have felt that the person who had brought out *Story of a Soul* – Mother Agnes of Lisieux, Thérèse's elder sister Pauline – was the one who could best advise her as she embarked on her daunting task.

Mother Agnes was, in every way, Mother Germaine's 'opposite number'. Although a blood relation of Thérèse, her relationship with her younger sister barely outweighs the bond between Mother Germaine and Elizabeth. Both of them were only a few years older than their protégées, yet fulfilled a formative maternal role towards them. As mentioned before, the lives of Thérèse and Elizabeth would have been seriously impoverished without these vital mother-cum-sister figures, who were also their closest confidantes. These two prioresses, then, were ideally placed to make their respective younger sisters better known. Thérèse had given full authority to Mother Agnes to publish her manuscripts; and Elizabeth had the same confidence in Mother Germaine. 'I'm happy to think that you will write my circular' (CW I, p. 31), she had said; and: 'Next to Him, you are everything to [me]' (L 329).

In her letter to Lisieux, Mother Germaine raised the idea of her proposed 'notice', as well as some of the difficulties she envisaged. Mother Agnes understood very well that there was a world of difference between writing a biography from scratch, and merely editing an autobiography. This is what she herself had done. She had arranged her sister's manuscripts into eleven chapters, included extracts from Thérèse's other writings, and contributed just one chapter of her own: this twelfth chapter being her account of Thérèse's illness and death. So she wrote back to Dijon on January 25, 1907, expressing solidarity but not exactly reassurance: 'I am so happy that you are thinking of the little notice. But as for all the difficulties which you have explained to me, ah! Mother, how I understand you. If Thérèse had not herself written her life, I would only ever have been able to publish her letters, her poems, and something like chapter XII [of *Story of a Soul*].'[3]

Another aspect of the letter from Mother Agnes was a kind of censorship. Today, we may regret that Mother Germaine's biography is weighted almost exclusively in favour of the spiritual, and so is lacking in anecdotal details of Elizabeth's life. Quite possibly, the letter from Lisieux set her on this course, although this was already very much in keeping with Mother Germaine's own approach. When Mother Agnes came to edit Thérèse's manuscripts, she 'rewrote'[4] them, so to speak: following Thérèse's permission to amend the text as she wished, she made more than seven thousand changes! Her purpose in this was admirable, however: to do good to souls rather than tell all. And her hopes were matched by those of Mother Germaine whose aim, in the biography of Elizabeth, was to 'facilitate *her mission*' (S1, p. 19) – that is, Elizabeth's longing to draw souls to God (cf. S1, p. 19; L 335). So the advice she received from Mother Agnes was that of a censor, or at any rate of an editor who had selected only the most edifying parts of Thérèse's writings. And we can read between the lines of Mother Germaine's own letter – which is sadly now lost – that the prioress of Dijon was on the same wavelength as the prioress of Lisieux. For Mother Agnes replied to her, saying: 'You have guessed it, yes, for Thérèse as

---

[3] Quoted by Conrad De Meester, OCD, in Clapier (ed.), p. 688, n. 11.
[4] This is the term used by Father François de Sainte-Marie, OCD, the Carmelite who published the original manuscripts of Thérèse in 1956: quoted in the Introduction to Sainte Thérèse de l'Enfant-Jésus et de la Sainte-Face, *OEuvres Complètes (Textes et Dernières Paroles)*, Paris: Cerf / Desclée De Brouwer, 1992, p. 63.

for Elizabeth, God has permitted for their sanctification things that cannot be explained other than in this sense and which cannot be quoted. If you knew, Mother, the *whole* life of Thérèse, you would be amazed.'[5]

Armed with these various pieces of encouragement and fellow-feeling, Mother Germaine set her sights on the task ahead. If she had had any doubts about her project, the continuing popularity of the *Circular* would itself have been sufficient incentive to persevere. More copies were requested; they all ran out – and by mid-January 1907, a second printing had been arranged. By the middle of April, all those copies had run out, too. 'Even the Carmel of Saigon is asking for three!' (CW I, p. 33), exclaimed Sister Agnes – a rather gratifying piece of feedback, given that the Carmel of Saigon had been founded by that of Lisieux. And there was one request for a full-length biography that simply could not be ignored: Madame Catez was impatient to have it!

Steeped in Memories

And so began the 'notice' or 'project':[6] Mother Germaine's modest working titles for what would become her worldwide bestselling biography of Elizabeth, known as the *Souvenirs*,[7] which literally means 'Memories' or 'Reminiscences'. It is a

---

[5] Quoted by Conrad De Meester, OCD, in Clapier (ed.), p. 688, n. 11.

[6] See *ibid.*, p. 688.

[7] This is actually the subtitle. The full title of the first edition translates from the French as: *Sister Elizabeth of the Trinity, Carmelite Nun, 1880–1906: Reminiscences*. It was reissued by the Carmel of Dijon in 2008 (though not as a facsimile) and is referred to here as 'S1'. In addition to the seventeen chapters, the 2008 work contains the author's Introduction and the appreciation of Elizabeth by Father Vallée, but not the introductory letters or the Appendix, consisting mostly of extracts from Elizabeth's writings. In English, the work is known as *The Praise of Glory*. The English version consulted for this book – referred to here as 'PG' – states 'Second English Edition' on the title page, and the date '1914'. Two modern editions of the work are available in English: a facsimile of the 1914 edition, brought out as one of 'Kessinger Publishing's Rare Reprints' in 2009; and a newly issued reproduction of the 1962 edition (though not as a facsimile), which appeared with Loreto Publications in 2007.

deeply personal title, chosen by an author who was steeped in memories of her subject and missing her so much. Mother Germaine may also have had an additional, specific meaning in mind: that of the book being somehow a relic of Elizabeth, a sign of her presence. For when, in the closing pages, she speaks of the rosaries and medals touched against Elizabeth's body after her death, she comments: 'Everybody thought that any souvenir of her would bring a blessing with it' (PG, p. 223).

Incredibly, it would take three years from the time of Elizabeth's death until the book could see the light of day. It was a large project and there would be several delays, not least because Mother Germaine had many demands on her time. She was still prioress, and her term would not come to an end until October 1907. But in readiness for the writing, she made use of these months to collate as much material as possible.

As early as December 30, 1906, she wrote to Mother Marie of Jesus to ask for her recollections of Elizabeth; she would publish the full reply in later editions (cf. S2, pp. 444–6). Then, possibly even on New Year's Day itself, the prioress, speaking to Guite in the parlour, asked if she might have some details of Elizabeth's childhood, holidays and education – and having received nothing by January 7, she sent her a reminder, included in a request for her to ask if Madame Catez could kindly jot down some notes about Elizabeth's family background. She also spread her net more widely: to Elizabeth's early confessor, Father Sellenet; to Canon Angles, whose reminiscences appear in the first chapter (cf. PG, pp. 12–14); to long-standing friends of Elizabeth's, such as Marie-Louise Hallo and Germaine de Gemeaux; to Louise Demoulin, to whom Elizabeth had taught catechism... The prioress sent out requests for letters Elizabeth had written. And a few people seem to have spontaneously sent theirs in, without being asked.

A biography, inevitably, would allow the space to include more of Elizabeth's writings than the short extracts that had appeared in the *Circular*. Most importantly, it was around this time that Mother Germaine, looking through Elizabeth's personal notes, discovered a prayer without a title, beginning: 'O my God, Trinity whom I adore...' Elizabeth had never spoken of this magnificent prayer which she wrote on November 21, 1904. But although it was too late for inclusion in the *Circular*, it would be reproduced in full in the *Souvenirs* as 'Prayer to the Most Holy Trinity'. As the prayer grew in fame, the title, sadly, would also gain in length – becoming, in the third edition, 'Pious Elevation of Sister Elizabeth of the Trinity'. As the convent's elections of October 1907 approached, the outgoing prioress looked forward to giving herself to her project in earnest. She did indeed begin the writing then, but the year ahead would be fraught with obstacles and distress.

We remember how the *Circular* had been completed with 'an extraordinary ease' and been a source of 'profound joys' for its author (cf. CW I, pp. 32–3). The genesis of the biography could not have been more different. To quote from the Circular of Mother Germaine herself, the one written about her after her own death in 1934: 'the works of God are brought to birth in suffering and humiliation... Also, our dear Mother needed a special grace to complete the work undertaken, for there was no lack of difficulties and trials' (CW I, p. 74, n. 21). The 'work' mentioned here by the author of the obituary – Mother Marie of St John who entered the Dijon Carmel in 1915 – is precisely a reference to the writing of the *Souvenirs*.

On her Knees, Weeping

At the October elections, Mother Germaine was duly relieved of her position – but only to encounter problems, regarding both her new role and her successor as prioress. She was appointed bursar, which was a demanding position. And the new superior was Mother Marie of the Heart of Jesus, who had been prioress three times before. Despite being cured of her dizzy spell through touching Elizabeth's feet on the eve of the funeral, she had not been close to Elizabeth. And being of a practical nature, even 'a bit rigid' (ETB, p. 578), she was not very close to Mother Germaine either, who was a sensitive and refined soul. What was relevant now was that she was not convinced of the need for the biography. She thought that it demanded too much time. Worse still, not to put too fine a point on it: she 'felt that it was a waste of time' (CW I, p. 74, n. 21)![8]

For Mother Germaine, all this must have been a shock to the system. Her grief at losing Elizabeth, with whom she had had a unique bond, had been cushioned to some extent by the sharing of memories in the convent over the last few months and the warm reminiscences of the sisters at recreation. Now she was under a superior who seemed, quite frankly, hostile to her work in spreading Elizabeth's name. While remaining humble towards the new prioress, Mother Germaine was terribly upset. Almost certainly not so much because her project was being misunderstood, as because Elizabeth herself was being misunderstood. Years later, Mother Marie of St John would speak of the 'anguish and affliction' of Mother Germaine which this painful episode had 'cost her maternal heart' (CW I, p. 74, n. 21). She knew what she was talking about, for Mother Germaine had one day confided in her about it, saying: 'I wrote the *Souvenirs* on my knees weeping' (CW I, p. 74, n. 21).[9] Probably, she had never missed Elizabeth so much as she did then. But her resolve did not waver: Mother Germaine knew that she was meant to write this book; and so, without infringing obedience, she made sure she carried on with the project.

Her Two Supports

The author's cloud, however, had not one but two silver linings. She had two people behind her who were of enormous help

---

[8] A statement by Mother Marie of St John at Elizabeth's beatification Process. The irony is that the new prioress, whose real name was Marie-Amélie Hertzog, was the sister of Monsignor Hertzog who would become the first Postulator of Elizabeth's Cause for beatification! See CW I, p. 74, n. 21.

[9] This confidence would be relayed by Mother Marie of St John at Elizabeth's beatification Process. This was more candid than in the obituary Circular of Mother Germaine, where Mother Marie of St John would give only the words 'on her knees', and in place of 'weeping' she would put: 'continually praying to obtain light from the Holy Spirit' (CW I, p. 74, n. 21).

and encouragement. One was the new Bishop of Dijon, Pierre Dadolle. He had met Elizabeth on the feast of Teresa of Avila, less than a month before she died. This meeting had been a grace for Elizabeth herself, but it could well have made a great impression on the Bishop, too. For he became an enthusiastic supporter of the biography and encouraged Mother Germaine at every step of the way. After each chapter was written, it was taken to the Bishop who would read it and give his feedback, always full of support for the author. He was extremely impressed with Elizabeth's own writings, and urged Mother Germaine to include some of Elizabeth's letters.

The second, and indispensable, support was Sister Marie of the Trinity. Between the death of Elizabeth in 1906 and that of Mother Germaine in 1934 – a period of almost thirty years – she helped Mother Germaine with the writing of the *Souvenirs*, with revising it for subsequent editions, and with drawing up the *Articles* for the diocesan Process of beatification.[10] As we have seen during Elizabeth's time in Carmel, Sister Marie of the Trinity was sub-prioress and therefore worked closely with Mother Germaine; she had also been the 'Angel' of Elizabeth up to her profession, and thereafter Elizabeth had continued to confide in her to some extent. Relieved of her position as sub-prioress at the elections of October 1907, Sister Marie of the Trinity was the ideal person to help Mother Germaine with the project of the biography. The daughter of a magistrate, she was highly intelligent and well read, endowed with a good memory and a great capacity for work. Writing came easily to her. And this is where her help proved invaluable. In fact, it was she who wrote what is undoubtedly the first-ever biography of Elizabeth. Early in 1907, Mother Germaine had asked her, as she had others, to write down her memories of Elizabeth. But rather than submitting a short piece, listing a few episodes, she produced a thirty-eight-page life, entitled, *Memoirs of her*

---

[10] On the help given by Sister Marie of the Trinity, see Conrad De Meester, OCD, in Clapier (ed.), pp. 690–4.

Angel.[11] While several other people sent in their own reminiscences, this account would be a most precious contribution, if not the basis of the *Souvenirs*, as we shall see.

A Convergence of Voices

When Mother Germaine started writing, she felt clear about her aim: to give a faithful and living portrait of Elizabeth, and let her subject speak for herself. As she wrote in January 1908 to the Abbé Jaillet, a priest whom Elizabeth herself had met and corresponded with (cf. L 193): 'we are limiting ourselves to quite simply stating the facts so that the praise can emerge on its own without us trying to praise her ourselves' (CW I, p. 35). For this, Mother Germaine had to strike a delicate balance in the book: to come across as a believable voice, and yet to efface herself sufficiently so as to allow the readers to keep their eyes fixed on Elizabeth alone. She achieved this admirably.

Firstly, Mother Germaine had known Elizabeth so well that she was incapable of describing her as if from a distance, in a factual, remote sort of way. Instead, she wrote as someone who had entered into Elizabeth's thoughts and feelings – and as her closest confidante, she was without any doubt writing from real knowledge. So, at one and the same time, Mother Germaine was able to speak with authority while letting much of the actual 'speaking' be done by her subject. An example of how she managed this can be seen where she writes, for example, about the impact on Elizabeth of a passage from St Paul (Ph 3:10): 'She was startled at the words. Was not he, whom in her simplicity she termed the "father of her soul", announcing her speedy deliverance to her? She thought so' (PG, p. 149).

Then there is a more literal 'speaking' by Elizabeth, with the use of her own words as much as possible. Mother Germaine did not just place selections of her writings in the Appendix, but

---

[11] This work, and other such accounts of Elizabeth, are among the pieces that will be contained in Conrad De Meester's forthcoming collection of documents, entitled *Élisabeth vue et entendue par les témoins* [*Elizabeth Seen and Heard by Witnesses*], which is discussed in the next chapter.

inserted extracts from her letters, or from her spoken words, into the text as it flowed along. In this way, she created an invariably seamless interweaving of the following various elements: facts; reminiscences (of the author and of others); the author's comments; Elizabeth's thoughts and feelings; Elizabeth's words, both spoken and written. So smoothly do these ingredients run together that we barely notice where one ends and another begins. In fact, they are often to be found combined in a very short space. Here, for example, are the opening words of five consecutive paragraphs concerning Elizabeth at the age of nineteen: 'It is evident from this that she was no longer forbidden to visit her longed-for convent [*author's comment*]... "It was a real trial to me," she confided to us, "to be taken during the holidays far from my Carmel" [*Elizabeth's spoken words*]... No one suspected anything of the sort; the brave girl knew how to hide her feelings [*Elizabeth's feelings and author's comment*]... Elizabeth spent the summer of 1899 in travelling [*fact*]... "Enjoy those beautiful landscapes," she writes from her little cell in Carmel [*Elizabeth's writings*]' (PG, pp. 48–9).

Along the way, Mother Germaine also introduced some spiritual lessons for the good of the readers. Yet not even these comments, general in nature, break up the tone. There is nothing impersonal about them, precisely because every lesson is linked, in this book, to the personal experience of Elizabeth whose life is being related. Here is a passage from the difficult time of the novitiate, which opens up into a lesson for everyone: 'It was well for her, humble and modest as she was, to realize by experience the weaknesses of humanity. Nature had rebelled at times in the past; there were other revolts of which she knew nothing... she was astonished at discovering sometimes that there were other states less free from temptation' (PG, pp. 80–1).

'Indispensable'

In its first edition, the biography contains seventeen chapters divided into three parts: Elizabeth's youth (Chapters 1–5), her life among the Carmelite community (6–11), and the account of her final illness (12–17).[12] They are followed by an Appendix comprising extracts from Elizabeth's writings and one letter by a priest: the *Last Retreat* (in revised form);[13] the *Prayer to the Trinity*; twenty-three letters (or extracts from them); seventeen poems;[14] and the letter written by Father Donin to Madame Catez after her daughter's death. Additionally, at the front of the book are the letter of approbation from Bishop Dadolle (cf. PG, pp. xvii–xix; CW I, p. 36) and Mother Germaine's Introduction (cf. S1, pp. 17–19); and before the beginning of the second part – the chapters devoted to Elizabeth's years in Carmel – an appreciation of her by Father Vallée which reads like a parallel preface.

Subsequent editions would be expanded at front and back: with more letters from eminent figures, and extra material in the Appendix. But of all the revisions, the most significant one to note is that, as from the edition of 1927, an eighteenth chapter would be added (cf. S2, pp. 269–307). This important addition bears witness to the impact which Elizabeth was by then having on so many people throughout the world.[15]

Conrad De Meester rightly calls the *Souvenirs* 'indispensable' (CW I, p. 39). But for the sake of modern readers, he discusses not only its positive points but also some aspects which could be seen as limitations.[16] Elizabeth's own writings, for example, are not always given in the right chronological order. However, the problem of ordering the texts is completely understandable

---

[12] The chapter numbers in the *Souvenirs* are given in Roman numerals, but for convenience are listed here as Arabic numerals.

[13] The *Last Retreat* appeared with the fifteenth 'day' missing in the first two editions (1909 and 1910), as some of this material had already been included within the life story: see CW I, p. 139, n. 13. *Heaven in Faith* would appear in the *Souvenirs* (also in revised form) as from the 1915 edition (and would remain in partial form in all editions of the biography): see CW I, p. 91, and the discussion below.

[14] A list of these is given in CW I, p. 74, n. 20, which also names the recipients of the letters quoted in the Appendix.

[15] The nature of this impact will be explored in later chapters.

[16] See his discussion of both the strengths and the weaknesses of the *Souvenirs*, in CW I, pp. 36–9.

– this point being made by Father Conrad who, for the critical edition of Elizabeth's works, carried out the most painstaking work to establish the chronology of her many, many letters. Mother Germaine, he also points out, made some amendments to Elizabeth's writings; these are, though, extremely slight, such as the omission of superfluous words – not in the same league as Mother Agnes' seven thousand or more changes!

A more important reservation – one we might notice more today than when the book was written a century ago – is that there is not as much of the human approach as might have been included in a life story. Quite apart from any 'censoring' influence that Mother Agnes of Lisieux may or may not have had on her, Mother Germaine's interests were primarily spiritual: her great merit, to quote Conrad De Meester, was 'recognizing, testing, and strengthening the gift of mystical life which the Lord granted to Elizabeth' (CW I, p. 39). But while she was less concerned with concrete details, the book is enhanced in this respect by contributions from Sister Marie of the Trinity's *Memoirs of her Angel*, which contains some anecdotes and sayings of Elizabeth[17] – and these bring the human side more to the fore.

On the whole, though, Mother Germaine's approach can make it easy to retain an *image* of Elizabeth – one that paints a halo around her. For modern readers, it certainly seems harder to relate to her, every time she is described as 'angelic' or referred to as a 'child'. With regard to this, Conrad De Meester points out that even the spiritual plane, which is so prominent in this book, could have been explored further – if, for example, the term 'child' had been discussed as part of the notion of spiritual childhood; and this is, of course, a key theme in the writings of Thérèse, with which Mother Germaine would have been extremely familiar. In short, he says: 'It seems...that Mother Germaine did not know how to bring out all the richness of her saint' (CW I, p. 39).

---

[17] See Conrad De Meester, OCD, in Clapier (ed.), p. 693.

However, if this was a limitation of the author, it did not diminish in any way the great spiritual worth of Elizabeth herself as depicted in the work. Mother Germaine would have been very pleased with Father Conrad's comment that she 'effaces herself...behind the memory of Elizabeth and her writings' (CW I, p. 37). As he points out, it was Elizabeth's life and the texts themselves that would ensure the success of the *Souvenirs*. The inclusion of so many of Elizabeth's own words, he says, means that 'the biography became, as it were, [Elizabeth's] auto-biography' (CW I, p. 37). And this is what gives the *Souvenirs* its affinity with Thérèse's *Story of a Soul*.

Alive and Beautiful

Throughout the work, Mother Germaine always says 'we' and 'us', never 'I' and 'me'. This is often a custom with books written in French. But more than this, it was almost certainly the intention of the author to show that this account came from a whole community reminiscing on Elizabeth – another reason for effacing herself. When she refers to her own role in episodes of Elizabeth's life – which is inevitable, for she truly played a role as one of the 'characters', so to speak – it is always as 'the Prioress' (cf. PG, p. 169), or even as an unnamed 'sister' (cf. PG, p. 201). The title page carries the name 'Carmel of Dijon' (S1, p. 15), and the author likewise signs her Introduction with a communal name: 'From our monastery of St Joseph' (S1, p. 19).

The word 'we' is in fact very apt: for the book is indeed a communal effort, based on the reminiscences of Elizabeth's friends, family and Carmelite sisters. As mentioned earlier, one of the main foundations of this book was the *Memoirs of her Angel* by Sister Marie of the Trinity. To a great extent, Mother Germaine used it as a template: she roughly followed the same ordering of material, retained much of the content, and her handwritten notes can be seen on the sub-prioress's manuscript. And this is how the collaboration continued, judging by the work in producing the much-revised 1927 edition. For this, Sister Marie of the Trinity wrote her own revisions onto a printed copy of a 1921 edition, so that Mother Germaine could make use of them in producing her next one.

But most of all, the 'we' includes Elizabeth herself. Not just the selections from her writings, or the quotations that appear throughout the work. The *Souvenirs* is bursting with Elizabeth's very self – the 'image' of the saint is no less fresh or full of vitality. When the book appeared, Mother Germaine would rejoice in her creation: not the book itself, so much as the person of Elizabeth who seemed to her to be miraculously brought back to life. She would write joyfully to Madame Catez: 'Our little saint is so alive and so beautiful in it! What a soul!' (CW I, p. 36).

The Final Delay

Mother Germaine completed the first draft in the middle of October 1908, a year since she had been relieved of her charge as prioress. She was now impatient to start the editing. This took another four months, not least because her checking was meticulous. Every minor point was rechecked in the cause of truthfulness, and she said: 'we must, before all, be scrupulously exact' (CW I, p. 35). Finally, she dated her Introduction on February 11, 1909, feast of Our Lady of Lourdes. Elizabeth's statue was obviously watching over her!

However, there was a delay when the book came into the hands of Bishop Dadolle. At first, things ran smoothly: he read the manuscript and approved it enthusiastically. So it was sent to the Jobard printing press in Dijon in early March, for the type to be set up. But the Bishop asked to see the first proofs before writing his letter of approbation. And now came the delay. Ironically, it was for a most positive reason: his enthusiasm! He declared Elizabeth to be 'a saint and a soul of genius' (CW I, p. 36), and he was so captivated by the *Souvenirs* that he read the book again and again! It was only on September 24 – after six months – that he gave the official approval. At which point, fifteen hundred copies were rapidly printed. The book came off the press in the first few days of October 1909 – almost three years after Elizabeth's death.

In High Demand

The Carmelites did not take on themselves any great work of promotion: 'we neglected the usual means of diffusion,' Mother Germaine would say, 'preferring to leave to God the care of making his humble servant known as he wished, according to the plans of his love and for his glory' (S2, p. 271). And it seems that he wished Elizabeth to be known all over the world! From the moment the book was published, the *Souvenirs* was in high demand and circulated rapidly. After a mere four months, Mother Germaine had the great joy of writing to the Carmel of Anderlecht, on February 10, 1910: 'Its success surpasses our expectations' (CW I, p. 40). She had good reason to say this: all fifteen hundred copies of the first edition had sold out! She immediately began to occupy herself with a second edition, which came out at the end of March. By that time, a cheaper and smaller edition was also being requested.

The modest author continued to call her book a 'modest work' (S2, p. xlii). But it was in the service of Elizabeth's posthumous mission (cf. S1, p. 19), and she was overwhelmed at being able, in this way, to help Elizabeth fulfil it. As Mother Germaine wrote, only four months after the work first appeared: 'the mission of [Elizabeth] is affirmed in a very comforting manner in all parts of the world' (CW I, p. 40). She must have been overjoyed when she heard that the *Souvenirs* was being called a second *Story of a Soul* (cf. PG, p. xliv). Perhaps she thought back to the time when batches of Thérèse's autobiography were being bought up and sold out in the Dijon Carmel's extern quarters – and how one eager young reader was Elizabeth herself! Now, piles of the *Souvenirs* were disappearing at the same rate.

More than this: even beyond the Carmel of Dijon, the *Souvenirs* was proving virtually as popular as *Story of a Soul*. By the last week of June 1910, all fifteen hundred copies of the second edition had also sold out – disappearing in under three months. Six months later, the third edition appeared, and in the space of two months eight hundred copies had already been sold. In

September 1911, the fourth edition saw the light of day, only to vanish even more rapidly than the earlier ones. And so it would continue until the last French edition of 1956, at which time sales had exceeded a hundred thousand copies.[18]

In France alone, sixteen editions were published between 1909 and 1956, ten of them by 1920 – that is, averaging almost one a year in the first decade.[19] The first eleven were printed by Jobard in Dijon. However, their equipment was unsophisticated, which made it difficult for them to insert changes without having to reset the pages. So when the *Souvenirs* began to run from edition to edition, the work was handed over in 1926 to a printing house (later publishing house) in Paris called 'St Paul' – a name with which Elizabeth would have been delighted! Mother Germaine took the opportunity of revising the whole text, which led to the important edition of 1927 which notably contained the new, eighteenth, chapter; this edition also included more unpublished material, such as new texts by Elizabeth and testimonies from her friends (cf. CW I, p. 75, n. 27).

Very quickly, the work spread beyond France, to many countries of the world. Already in 1912, Mother Germaine received requests for the work to be translated, and in her revised Introduction of October 27, 1912, was able to announce, rather

---

[18] See CW I, p. 75, n. 25. The print-runs for each edition, where known, are listed in *ibid.*, pp. 74–5, n. 24.

[19] The dates of the (known) sixteen editions are: 1909, 1910, 1911 (date on title page, though printed December 20, 1910 and referred to by the Dijon Carmel as a 1910 edition: see S1, p. 11), 1911 (again), 1912, 1915, 1917, 1918, 1919, 1920 (though with two different covers, one stating '1921'), another edition though undated, 1927, 1930, 1935, 1946 and 1956. Twelve of these appeared in the usual large format of approximately nine by five and a half inches, three in a small format of about six and a half inches by four and a quarter (1917, 1918 and 1930), and one in an intermediate-sized format of about seven inches by four and a half (1956), only slightly larger than the small format. The three in the small format omitted the letters and poems. For these details, I am indebted to the highly informative and meticulously researched note by Conrad De Meester (cf. CW I, pp. 74–5, n. 24), which has been followed in this book; it should always be borne in mind, however, and as he himself suggests, that there may be other, untraced, editions.

lyrically: 'the "Praise of glory", Sister Elizabeth of the Trinity, will soon be able to repeat afresh her song of love in seven other languages' (PG, p. xlviii). The first translation came out in England in 1912, followed by the United States, Spain and Italy the following year. Thereafter, translations snowballed: the work appeared in Brazil, Holland and Flemish-speaking Belgium – even in Austria and Germany during the First World War. The work would appear in other languages, too, including Czech, Polish, Japanese and Ruthenian, an eastern Slavonic language.[20]

The Emergence of Elizabeth's 'Works'

The *Souvenirs* gave rise to some smaller publications, in addition to two abridged versions of the biography – *Extract from the Souvenirs* and *A Praise of Glory* – both of which sold widely. The *Last Retreat* was published separately in 1911, then at least six times more up to 1968 together with *Heaven in Faith* in a short work entitled, *Reflections and Thoughts in the Form of Retreats*.[21] The retreats would also be translated into many languages, including Arabic, Korean, Vietnamese and (in an abridged version) Russian (cf. CW I, p. 41). Individual texts, too, such as Elizabeth's magnificent *Prayer*, were printed on isolated sheets, often with photographs.

Indeed, the *Prayer to the Trinity* took on a life of its own, not least because of the important commentaries on it, which were themselves printed in several editions and translations. Notable names are those of Eugène Vandeur, a Benedictine monk (1923), the Carmelite nun Marie-Amabel du Coeur de Jésus (1932), and the Redemptorist Father Maurice De Meulemeester (1942).

---

[20] For the dates of translations, see S1, p. 11.

[21] Mother Germaine had revised *Heaven in Faith*, from which she removed especially the quotations from Ruysbroeck, and it would not be read in its entirety until the edition of 1942. Note that the titles given above are direct translations of the French wording, and that the abridged work entitled, *A Praise of Glory* is not to be confused with the English translation of the original *Souvenirs*.

These were the first few in a tradition of commentaries that still continues today.

The text of the *Prayer* itself, though, ran into a few difficulties. Scrupulous theologians began to question some phrases as theologically audacious. As from the first edition of the *Souvenirs* in 1909, Bishop Dadolle had the words 'cover [me] with Your shadow' (cf. Lk 1:35) removed – as *'too strong'* an expression, in his opinion, for it concerned the Incarnation and he felt it should be applied only to the Virgin Mary.[22] Later, in 1926, the eminent Dominican theologian, Father Garrigou-Lagrange, advised Mother Germaine to delete 'whole' from the phrase 'that I may be another humanity for Him in which He can renew His whole Mystery'. His objection was not unlike that of Bishop Dadolle. The word 'whole' in this context, he felt, should be applied only to the hypostatic union, the divine and human nature of the person of Christ.

Sister Marie of the Trinity commented, with regard to this, that mystics use strong terms which 'are not always the classic expressions of theologians'![23] Elizabeth could have answered the objection easily: it was Christ himself who was living in her, and that is how he could 'renew His whole Mystery' in her – which is how she herself had once explained it (cf. L 214). Perhaps it is worth leaving the last word to St John Eudes, who would have understood Elizabeth perfectly: 'So the Son of God decided to complete and fill up all his mysteries in us. When he is born again in our souls by the holy sacraments of baptism and the blessed eucharist, and conforms us to his likeness, he wishes to complete in us the mysteries of his incarnation, birth and hidden life. He makes it possible for us to live an interior spiritual life, hidden with him in God. He intends to bring to perfec-

---

[22] See Conrad De Meester, OCD, in Clapier (ed.), p. 692.

[23] In *ibid.*, p. 692. This comment could apply equally well to Thérèse's *Act of Oblation to Merciful Love*, which was also amended by a cautious theologian: a Father Lemonnier who replaced Thérèse's 'infinite desires' with 'immense desires': cf. LT 230, n. 4. This change, unlike those made to Elizabeth's *Prayer to the Trinity*, still stands today: cf. SS, p. 276.

tion in us the mysteries of his passion, death and resurrection by causing us to suffer, to die and to rise with him and in him. Finally, he plans to complete his state of glorious immortality in us by bringing it about that we shall lead a glorious everlasting life with him and in him in heaven.'[24]

*

Today, the Carmel of Dijon, looking back over the spectacular popularity of this worldwide bestseller, has summarised its appeal as 'the universality of Elizabeth' (S1, p. 11). As pointed out in the essay prefacing the reissued first edition of the *Souvenirs* in 2008: Elizabeth belongs to all milieux – social and ecclesial; and she crosses all boundaries – linguistic, national and spiritual (cf. S1, pp. 11–12). As for Mother Germaine herself: when she saw the life and message of Elizabeth spreading throughout the world, she remarked simply, 'It is indeed the work of God alone' (S1, p. 11).

---

[24] In *Divine Office*, vol. III, p. 782.

Chapter 26

'A NEW GUIDE – CERTAIN AND SURE'

A New Wave of Publications

In 1935, two publications saw the light of day, very different in scope. One was a modest Circular on Mother Germaine who had died the previous November. The other was the fourteenth French edition of the *Souvenirs*, which by now had at least eighty thousand readers – almost all of whom would never know the name of the author. While Mother Germaine was unknown to them, it could be said that her greatest work for Elizabeth was also unknown, hidden to the human eye: the spiritual formation she had given in Carmel, enabling Elizabeth to open herself fully to the transforming action of God.

The biography, likewise, is not an achievement simply because of its publishing success, but because it continues Mother Germaine's work of forming souls. As novice mistress in the Dijon Carmel, she had shared with Elizabeth the example and writings of the Carmelite saints, especially Teresa of Avila and Thérèse of Lisieux. Now, through the *Souvenirs*, she was sharing Elizabeth's own life and spirituality with the general public. Thanks to this book, people had begun to pray to Elizabeth and there were calls for her to be beatified. But most of all, readers were helped by her spiritual teachings on silent prayer and the indwelling of God in the soul – which was precisely the 'mission' Elizabeth had hoped to fulfil after her death: 'to draw souls by helping them go out of themselves to cling to God by a wholly simple and loving movement, and to keep them in this great silence within that will allow God to communicate Himself to them and transform them into Himself' (L 335).

The impact of the *Souvenirs* on its early readers will be explored in subsequent chapters. But for now, we come to a specific influence of the work: a new wave of publications on Elizabeth, written in the wake of the *Souvenirs* and representing another huge impetus in the unfolding of her message.

At first sight, it might appear that this chapter is dealing with Elizabeth only at second remove: covering works not *by* her but *about* her – those that are generally known as 'secondary literature'. But when we trace how her message developed in posterity, these works are not of merely secondary importance: for their contribution has been directly responsible for shaping the image and impact of Elizabeth that has come down to us. And given the influence of these authors, they will, to varying degrees, be put under the spotlight: so as to examine what aspects of Elizabeth they have emphasised (and why) – and even, on occasion, distorted. The purpose of this chapter, then, is not simply to list what to read or who wrote what, but to highlight the new directions and turning-points in our understanding of Elizabeth, by exploring the different types of work and the various approaches. All these works, combined, create a picture both broad and deep – a mining along the rich seams of Elizabeth's soul.

While it is true to say that most works would defy neat labelling, they are nonetheless listed here in categories, for the sake of clarity.[1] The main publications which followed in the immediate wake of the *Souvenirs* were, unsurprisingly, not more biographies but studies of Elizabeth. So, reflecting this new direction, the first category examined here is *doctrinal works* – studies exploring the theological aspects of Elizabeth's teachings. This will then be followed by *spiritual works* – books on spirituality and prayer, together with some of the main anthologies of her writings. The third group consists of the main *biographies* of Elizabeth since that of Mother Germaine. And the fourth category is concerned

---

[1] It is not, of course, possible to do justice to the whole range of works on Elizabeth, but mention will be made of those authors or titles of special importance. In each case, it is stated whether the work in question has been written in, or translated into, English.

with the primary sources, the 'raw materials' as it were: the *critical edition of Elizabeth's writings, and related documents* including photographs – all of which, combined, allow a comprehensive picture of her to emerge.

But the starting point – after Elizabeth herself, of course – was once more Mother Germaine. Which brings us to one day in August 1933, when she went into the parlour to meet a new visitor to the Carmel of Dijon.

A) DOCTRINAL WORKS

Father Marie-Michel Philipon

The man who had come to speak with Mother Germaine was a young priest by the name of Father Marie-Michel Philipon.[2] Although neither of them knew it at the time, he would one day rank alongside her in making Elizabeth known throughout the world. Soon after entering the Dominican Order at the age of twenty-two, he came across a copy of the *Souvenirs*; and this book, he would say, brought 'an immense light' (CW I, p. 43) into his life. He then did his theology studies, culminating in a doctorate on a subject that would have delighted Elizabeth: 'The Indwelling of the Trinity in the Soul'; in his preaching, too, the mystery of the Trinity was always his preferred subject. After completing his qualifications, Father Philipon reread his beloved *Souvenirs* and decided that he, too, wanted to write about Elizabeth. So here he was, the young philosophy professor from the Dominican college of Saint-Maximin, meeting the nun whose book had brought such light into his life.

Mother Germaine was hesitant at first. Perhaps she was reticent about letting a virtual stranger have access to that most precious material in the archives: Elizabeth's own manuscripts. But when she saw how earnest he was, she readily offered him all the help he needed. As Philipon would later recall, rather vividly: as soon as Mother Germaine could see from his conversation

---

[2] See the helpful discussions of his writings by Conrad De Meester, in CW I, pp. 42–8, and in Clapier (ed.), pp. 694–703.

how much he understood Elizabeth, 'I felt the battle was won and I immediately saw, in my mind's eye, the grilles of the impenetrable enclosure open ajar, to let through the documents which were so desirable and indispensable' (PD, p. 186)!

Mother Germaine not only allowed him access to the archival material but also gave her own time generously, sharing with him her memories of Elizabeth's time in Carmel. It was also thanks to Mother Germaine that he would have the opportunity to meet members of the Carmelite community, as well as Guite and close friends of Elizabeth such as Françoise de Sourdon. It was truly providential that the idea of this book came to him then and no later. For Mother Germaine would die suddenly, just over a year after their first meeting. By then, as he said, he would have had the privilege of 'long hours of private conversation' (CW I, p. 45) with her.

As it was August, and the new teaching year was about to begin, Father Philipon soon had to return to the Dominican college. But the following summer, he came back to Dijon and devoted the month of July 1934 to going through the manuscripts with a fine toothcomb, checking the nuns' transcriptions against Elizabeth's originals, and interviewing people who had known her. To his delight, he found that he was on the same spiritual wavelength as Mother Germaine. 'She was in perfect agreement,' he would say, 'with every essential point in this book.'[3]

'This book' was *The Spiritual Doctrine of Sister Elizabeth of the Trinity*, which appeared in 1939 and which would prove to be the next great work and bestseller on Elizabeth of the Trinity. Ironically, it was one of the main reasons for the waning popularity of the *Souvenirs*.[4] When *The Spiritual Doctrine* first appeared in France, it sold out in only three months, and seven transla-

---

[3] Philipon, *The Spiritual Doctrine*, p. xxi. Quotations are taken from the 1947 English first edition (rather than the 2001 reprint of it brought out by Teresian Charism Press), as it contains the Preface by Father Reginald Garrigou-Lagrange and also numbers the introductory pages.

[4] Another reason is that the *Souvenirs* was last published in 1956, just before the 1960s which heralded a new way of thinking in the Church: cf. S1, p. 12.

tions were already being prepared. It would eventually run to twelve French editions and nine translations and is still available today; the most recent English-language reprint, the fifth, was brought out in 2001. Like the *Souvenirs*, *The Spiritual Doctrine* has the status of a classic.

Of this ground-breaking work – the first doctrinal study of Elizabeth – Conrad De Meester has said, quite rightly, that it 'gave a new impetus to the study and diffusion of Elizabeth's message' (CW I, p. 42). After the first chapter, with a brief sketch of her life, it diverges from biography completely and discusses theological themes, such as the indwelling of the Trinity, praise of glory, conformity to Christ, Mary, the priestly vocation, and the Holy Spirit. This book also contains the secret of success that we find in the *Souvenirs*: it is full of Elizabeth's own words and spiritually uplifting. Yet, as some authors today have pointed out, it is not without limitations.[5]

In the Preface, the eminent theologian Father Garrigou-Lagrange states as a positive comment on Philipon's approach: 'he has sought to explain [Elizabeth's life and writings] in the light of the principles of theology, as formulated by St. Thomas [Aquinas]'.[6] One Carmelite commentator of today, Steven Payne, makes almost the same point – only it is with dismay: 'He wants to make her into a Thomist'![7] Father Conrad himself calls the chapter divisions 'sometimes a little artificial' (CW I, p. 45), though he recognises that they are helpful to readers by their very clarity.

---

[5] Apart from the discussion which follows, it is worth pointing out – especially for anyone relying on *The Spiritual Doctrine* today – that one limitation is the erroneous dating of Elizabeth's discovery of the call to be a 'praise of glory', which has implications for charting her spiritual itinerary: cf. Philipon, *The Spiritual Doctrine*, p. 83. This has since been corrected by Conrad De Meester: see his discussion in Clapier (ed.), pp. 696–703; see also the present book, Chapter 11, nn. 6 & 8.

[6] Philipon, *The Spiritual Doctrine*, p. xiv. This, we have seen, is the theologian who recommended that the word 'whole' should be removed from the *Prayer to the Trinity*.

[7] Payne, side 1. See also the comments by Father Marie-Eugène Grialou, in Chapter 29, section 'Places of Pilgrimage'.

There is also a memorable comment in the obituary of a French Carmelite provincial, Father Louis. He had constantly read and reflected on the Carmelite saints, especially Teresa, John and Thérèse, but just could not take to Elizabeth. Why? Because, it is said, he found her 'too much of a theologian, too Dominican'![8] From this, we may just hazard a guess at which book on her he had read! Yet it should perhaps be noted that Elizabeth's own life, writings and posterity are linked with several Dominicans, as well as with Father Philipon, and each time to good effect: the spiritual guidance of Father Vallée; the inspiring retreat by Father Fages, at the end of which she wrote her *Prayer to the Trinity*; her friendship with the seminarian André Chevignard who was in the Dominican Third Order; the inspiration of some of the sayings of St Catherine of Siena; and, as we shall see later, the main work of restoring the human face of Elizabeth in a biography would be accomplished by the Dominican nun, Marie-Dominique Poinsenet.

The Spiritual Doctrine is an important book of great value, and the problem evoked here is mainly one of perspective. Had Philipon written a manual of spiritual theology, enriched by supporting quotations from Elizabeth's writings, he would have brought abstract concepts admirably to life. But this is meant to be a book first and foremost about Elizabeth, and at times he appears to be fitting Elizabeth around the doctrine instead of the doctrine around Elizabeth. This is particularly noticeable in the eighth chapter, where her writings are used to illustrate each of the seven gifts of the Holy Spirit in turn. The style is quite clinical and didactic here, and risks giving the impression that this is how Elizabeth herself wrote. Some of the jargon, too, is overly academic, foreign to Elizabeth's own temperament. In the chapter on the indwelling of the Trinity, her communion with the 'Three', as Elizabeth would have expressed it, is rendered

---

[8] See Jean-Philippe Houdret, OCD, 'Le Père Louis de Sainte-Thérèse', in *Carmel*, no. 65, 1992/3, p. 77.

by Philipon as: 'this deiform life of perfect souls admitted to the *consortium* of the life of the Trinity'.[9]

The heart of the problem – even for a doctrinal work – is the apparent over-emphasis on 'doctrine' as a goal. Philipon seems to have had a love affair with this word! He says that Elizabeth's was an 'essentially doctrinal spirituality'.[10] And reading and listening to feedback from people about the *Souvenirs*, he asserts that what had most impressed readers was the '*doctrinal character*'[11] of Elizabeth's writings – Philipon's own italics – though we should note that he quotes from the feedback of priests and theologians, who are not representative of readers as a whole. Philipon then defines his task as: 'to bring out...the *doctrinal sense* of the life and writings of Sister Elizabeth of the Trinity'.[12] And this, he says, is his method: 'to analyze and accurately and surely to indicate *the principles of mystical theology to which the movements of this privileged soul were linked*'.[13] There is, of course, much merit in this approach, so long as it does not become one-sided or give the impression that it reflects Elizabeth's self-expression and way of thinking.

However, almost thirty years after *The Spiritual Doctrine* first appeared, Father Philipon's own thinking had evolved. In 1966, he published his second study of Elizabeth's spirituality, *In the Presence of God*, which also contains a commentary on her two written retreats.[14] Near the end of this book he admits humbly: 'A veritable reversal of perspectives has taken place in my thought' (PD, p. 208). The doctrine, he explains, had previously been his 'main preoccupation' (PD, p. 208). In fact, it had been for the sake of doctrine that he had interviewed Elizabeth's family and friends! The reason for listening to their

---

[9] Philipon, *The Spiritual Doctrine*, p. 57.
[10] *Ibid.*, p. xix.
[11] *Ibid.*, p. xviii.
[12] *Ibid.*, p. xxi.
[13] *Ibid.*, p. xxii.
[14] This work has not been translated into English. Its French title, *En Présence de Dieu*, explains the abbreviation 'PD' used throughout this book.

testimonies, he says, had been to prove the authenticity of her virtue – as background for understanding the doctrinal aspects of her writings. In the later work, however, he publishes those interviews for the first time – in an appendix that gives the work perennial appeal – and explains the shift in his thinking: 'what strikes me in Elizabeth of the Trinity *still more than her doctrine is the heroism of her virtues*' (PD, p. 208) – these being his own italics for emphasis. What he has discovered, and again he emphasises this in italics, is '*the connection between her doctrine and life*' (PD, p. 210). And that, in a nutshell, is the essence of Elizabeth: a spiritual message which, first and foremost, was expressed by her own way of living and being.

In *The Spiritual Doctrine*, Elizabeth's life as such is virtually effaced. The publisher, finding the manuscript too long for a doctrinal study, was responsible for Elizabeth's life story being radically shortened – though the author seems to have had no qualms about this. For in a matter of minutes, Philipon removed seventeen pages from the opening chapter – and, in the process, much of her life as a lay person. We will never know what those pages contained, but the portrayal of Elizabeth that remains conforms exactly to the spiritual image of her in the *Souvenirs*: 'one-sidedly lofty and mystical', to quote Conrad De Meester, who adds that the 'theological digressions' on the Trinity and the Holy Spirit 'succeed in making her even more sublime' (CW I, p. 46)!

Yet Philipon's contribution is a major one: for to explore the doctrinal relevance of Elizabeth's teachings brought out a whole new dimension of her works; to quote Father Conrad once more, the book 'left an impression of solidity' (CW I, p. 45). In other words, Philipon rendered Elizabeth an immense service by enabling her to be taken seriously as a spiritual teacher; or as 'a new guide – certain and sure', to quote John Paul II.[15] And Philipon made a further important contribution by publishing an anthology of her writings, as we shall see later.

---

[15] See De Meester, 'Elizabeth in the Words of the Pope', p. 19.

Between them, the *Spiritual Doctrine* and the *Souvenirs* present the two complementary sides of Elizabeth – the doctrine and the life – though it would be years before the portrayal of the life became fully lifelike. Until the appearance of Elizabeth's *Complete Works* in 1979–1980, Mother Germaine and Father Marie-Michel Philipon would be the two main foundation stones for a lasting tradition of works on Elizabeth. For which they are owed an enormous debt of gratitude.

Hans Urs von Balthasar

A sign of just how seriously Elizabeth would be taken is nowhere more evident than in the next landmark work, where she is the subject of a study by the famous theologian Hans Urs von Balthasar. A profound and serious work, rich in theological insights, it first appeared in German in 1952 – as *Elizabeth of Dijon and Her Spiritual Mission* – and four years later in English.[16] It immediately stood out as being in a league of its own: because of both the eminence of its author and the originality of its approach. It still counts as an outstanding work among the literature on Elizabeth.

Her Spiritual Mission, as it will be referred to here, differs from its two sources. Firstly, from the *Souvenirs*, in that it is as far removed from a work of biography as it is possible to be. There is no mention of her life at all, which is deliberate in order to 'direct the reader's attention entirely to the teaching of Elizabeth of the Trinity' and 'do justice to [her] explicitly doctrinal mission'.[17] Von Balthasar diverges from Philipon's approach, too, in that he has not selected the same doctrinal themes – prayer, the gifts of the Holy Spirit, Mary, and so on. Instead, von

---

[16] This first appearance of the work in English is published as: *Elizabeth of Dijon: An Interpretation of Her Spiritual Mission*, London: The Harvill Press, 1956. The translation, by A V Littledale, is said to be 'adapted' from the original.

[17] From von Balthasar's Foreword to the second edition (1970) where the work is published jointly with his study of Thérèse in *Two Sisters in the Spirit*. The English translation of this edition (published in 1992) is the version followed here; the words just quoted are on p. 371.

Balthasar homes in on the theological aspects of what he sees as Elizabeth's 'mission' – which, as we can see from the title of the work, is the key theme of the whole book. His five chapters are devoted to: predestination, infinity ('limitlessness' in the English version followed here), adoration, praise, and service.

There is a natural progression in the author's arrangement of themes which can be summarised as follows, using von Balthasar's own words (with my own italics to highlight the chapter concerned): 'Predestination is the framework, limitlessness the destination of this movement [of worship]; adoration is its essential content, action, fullness and significance... The same movement that makes the soul simple [adoration] also makes [the soul] mirror God [praise]... In dedicating herself to praise of the Trinity, Elizabeth gives herself to praise of love... Love that serves God is always also service to God's works, the souls [service].'[18]

Von Balthasar was ideally placed to write this study, for he was a theologian most anxious to reconcile theology and spirituality.[19] He was deeply spiritual and had a genuine, insightful interest in mysticism, not least through his close collaboration with the mystic Adrienne von Speyr. But von Balthasar had more than one agenda when he came to write this book, and while he admired Elizabeth's writings greatly, he also used her for his own aims.

One of them – possibly the most innocuous – is that von Balthasar was making a specific point about holiness. At the time he was writing this book, he was fully involved in dialogue with Protestant theology, especially with Karl Barth. As one commentator on von Balthasar has written: in the Protestant view, holiness belongs to God alone; or if to human beings, then only after their death. For Catholics, however, human beings, by participating in the life of Christ, can attain holiness during

---

[18] In von Balthasar, *Two Sisters in the Spirit*, pp. 438, 463 & 479–80. See also the helpful summary and discussion by Gilbert Narcisse, OP, in Clapier (ed.), pp. 765–90.
[19] Cf. Gilbert Narcisse, OP, in Clapier (ed.), p. 769.

their life on earth.[20] So Karl Barth was quite taken aback when von Balthasar brought out a book on Thérèse in 1950 – and also, we may gather, when his work on Elizabeth appeared two years later.

Von Balthasar also had a particular interest in the Carmelite Order, which he saw as graced with a mission to 'call us back to the one thing necessary, to contemplation'.[21] He was familiar with many of its saints and wrote on three of them. In *The Glory of the Lord*, he hails John of the Cross as one of twelve people whom he considers to have conveyed 'the glory of the divine revelation' in almost two thousand years of Christian theology.[22] Then there is his study of the mission of Thérèse, to which his work on Elizabeth was intended as a sequel; today, as mentioned, they can be read together in one volume, *Two Sisters in the Spirit*, which was first published in 1970.

If, however, von Balthasar turned his sights to these two French Carmelites, it was not, first and foremost, to demonstrate Catholic notions of holiness. But rather, to follow a number of hidden (or not so hidden) agendas. Firstly, and with apparent disregard for movements of social work, he says that the graces of contemplation should counter recent trends such as 'churchly projects and campaigns' or 'Catholic action'.[23] Then he states that contemplation should be an antidote to the 'age of psychology' and adds with approval, rather worryingly: 'we are called back to anonymity...where the worshippers seem

---

[20] Cf. *ibid.*, pp. 765–6. Note, however, that there are many variations in Protestant theology, and that Father Narcisse's comments are possibly less in tune with Anglican theology, for example.

[21] From his Introduction in *Two Sisters in the Spirit*, p. 373.

[22] See Hans Urs von Balthasar, *The Glory of the Lord: A Theological Aesthetics*, vol. II: *Studies in Theological Style: Clerical Styles*, Edinburgh: T & T Clark, 1984, p. 14; see also *ibid.*, p. 18.

[23] The first phrase comes from the English translation: see *Two Sisters in the Spirit*, p. 373; the second is from the French translation of 1959 and it echoes specifically the lay social movements in the Catholic Church, especially active as from the nineteenth century, which may well have been the author's intention: cf. von Balthasar, *Élisabeth de la Trinité*, p. 21.

to be indistinguishable from each other'![24] Furthermore, he continues, the graces of contemplation, such as those received by the Carmelite Order, should also be a remedy against an 'emphasis on religious personality'.[25] This may seem a surprising statement, given that he has chosen to write on some of the shining personalities of the Carmelite tradition. Until, that is, we see how he approaches them.

In the work on Elizabeth, which is entirely focused on her 'mission', von Balthasar explains: 'we are called back into the life of a supernatural mission...that demands a readiness to sacrifice one's entire nature.'[26] These are frightening words, suggesting an annihilation of the person or personality. So we can now begin to grasp why he has omitted any biographical details of her: it was not, like Philipon's publisher, to save space! It was not even just for the sake of doing justice to Elizabeth's doctrine – which, as we have seen, is the reason he gives in his Foreword to the 1970 edition. Rather, back in 1952, his aim, in removing the 'life' aspects, was far more radical. It stemmed from one influence in particular: his close friend, the mystic Adrienne von Speyr, and her own theory of mission.

The idea for the books on Elizabeth and Thérèse was suggested by von Speyr herself, who actually drafted a few pages on what she saw as Elizabeth's mission, so as to stimulate von Balthasar's own thinking for when he came to write his Introduction.[27] The main idea could well be stated with this irony: that the person who receives a mission is the greatest *risk* to that mission. This is how Elio Guerriero, a biographer of von Balthasar, explains it: 'Adrienne, a fervent disciple of *effacement*, of annihilation in relation to the mission received from God,

---

[24] Von Balthasar, *Two Sisters in the Spirit*, p. 373.

[25] *Ibid.*, p. 373.

[26] *Ibid.*, p. 373.

[27] Von Balthasar himself, speaking of the earlier work – that on Thérèse – declares his indebtedness to Adrienne's theology of mission; without it, he says, his own book would never have seen the light of day: see Conrad De Meester, OCD, *The Power of Confidence: Genesis and Structure of the "way of spiritual childhood" of Saint Thérèse of Lisieux*, New York: Alba House, 1998, p. 369.

felt a certain aversion towards Thérèse's fixation on her own self, towards this emphasis placed so insistently on her person.'[28] An attitude, incidentally, that does not come from ignorance of Thérèse but from a close study of her writings: Adrienne von Speyr had translated *Story of a Soul* into German! Guerriero then says, astonishingly, that von Balthasar wrote on Thérèse – and by extension, we may say, on Elizabeth – 'as if for a bet'![29] It was to prove the point that even saints travel a slow and laborious path in understanding their mission: that this is a path of distancing themselves from all that is psychological and subjective, and of moving towards a vision that is theological and objective.[30]

In this light, we can again summarise von Balthasar's five chapters, but this time with an eye to the bias of his anti-personality agenda. *Predestination*, he points out, depends for Elizabeth on objective revelation, far removed from individualism. *Infinity* allows the soul to be 'swallowed up' in God. Through *adoration* the soul forgets oneself and disappears in God, though it is not annihilated. *Praise* is a means of disappearing into the Trinity which is a space into which one can be 'absorbed'. *Service* is needed as a remedy for egocentrism and psychology.[31]

If the author seems, at times, to be on a crusade against the human person, he also sometimes engages in criticism of Elizabeth herself, as when he follows slavishly the assertion of von Speyr that Elizabeth wants to 'impress' with her 'lofty' way of speaking![32] Von Balthasar's equivalent statement occurs in a

---

[28] Quoted by Gilbert Narcisse, OP, in Clapier (ed.), p. 771.

[29] In *ibid.*, p. 771.

[30] See *ibid.*, p. 771. Note also an interesting parallel with Father Philipon who gave identical titles ('*The Spiritual Doctrine of...*') to two different figures: Elizabeth of the Trinity and Dom Columba Marmion, where the book in each case is structured around doctrinal questions; cf. M-M Philipon, *The Spiritual Doctrine of Dom Marmion*, London & Glasgow: Sands & Co, 1956. With von Balthasar, too, we have a parallel pair of books: *The Spiritual Mission of Thérèse of Lisieux* and *The Spiritual Mission of Elizabeth of the Trinity* – with the figure in question being fitted around the author's area of interest, in this case mission.

[31] These points are found in von Balthasar, *Two Sisters in the Spirit*, pp. 404, 423, 449, 477 & 484.

[32] Quoted by Conrad De Meester, OCD, in Clapier (ed.), p. 708.

prominent position: his Introduction! He writes: '[Elizabeth] often seems, rather naïvely, to expect her lofty sentiments to arouse a cry of amazement... For a minute she may linger on the lofty heights, but she cannot maintain her perch with complete believability.'[33] While this judgment does not seem completely believable either, one could always reply to it with this point made by Conrad De Meester: that if Elizabeth had really wanted to impress, she would have shown around her impressive *Prayer to the Trinity*[34] – whereas she had simply left it in a drawer where it was found, after her death, buried in her notes.

Incredibly, von Balthasar puts this very prayer in the firing line. He criticises it as an example of Elizabeth's so-called 'personal satisfaction'![35] In her very first words, 'O my God, Trinity whom I adore', she has already, apparently, committed a grievous fault: she has used the word 'I'. He counts forty-three instances of 'I' and 'mine' in this text and concludes: 'It is not really a prayer of adoration but a petition for the ability to adore'.[36] This is, in part, quite true – we could say it is both of these things – but it brings us to a misunderstanding. Von Balthasar has reservations about the *Prayer to the Trinity* because, he says, it is 'a prayer that moves exclusively back and forth between the "I" and God'.[37] Yet he could not have said it better. For this is the genius of the Carmelite tradition: *relationship* with God. Or, as one commentator points out: Elizabeth bridges the objective truths of the theologian and the subjective experience of the spiritual person – '[she] is a remarkable witness to the conversion of the individualistic "subjective principle" of modern man into a true Christian interiority, according a place simultaneously to the "I" and to otherness, that of God, of Christ, of neighbour and of universal truth.'[38]

---

[33] Von Balthasar, *Two Sisters in the Spirit*, p. 382.
[34] From his discussion, in Clapier (ed.), p. 706.
[35] Von Balthasar, *Two Sisters in the Spirit*, p. 383.
[36] *Ibid.*, p. 383.
[37] *Ibid.*, p. 383.
[38] Gilbert Narcisse, OP, in Clapier (ed.), p. 789.

However, von Balthasar's study has a happy ending. For by the end of her life, Elizabeth has, apparently, 'shed all spiritual vanity'.[39] These words invite a brief comparison with his work on Thérèse of Lisieux. For when Thérèse throws herself like a 'little child' into God's arms, this, the author feels, shows frankly 'a bit too much self-consciousness'![40] But there is a happy ending for Thérèse, too. For just before her death, we are told: 'Her ego collapses, and her mission bursts through'.[41] Ultimately, Elizabeth takes the prize: the author tells us that she moves beyond Thérèse's self-consciousness 'and into the universality of the mystery of Christ' – and for good measure he adds, obviously impressed by now, that in this respect she even surpasses St Paul![42]

Had all these jarring notes appeared in a minor work, it would not have been included in this survey of books on Elizabeth. But given that it is an influential study by a renowned theological authority, it is vital to disentangle all this background so that, keeping the author's agenda in mind, we may best be able to benefit from the work which is a thought-provoking, insightful and in fact beautiful exploration of Elizabeth's message. The author was not a carping critic, but an idealist who aspired to such holiness and purity that he wanted earnestly to be divested of self and to focus on God alone. That is why he runs into unfortunate expressions, such as when he admiringly describes Elizabeth's mission as 'fully directed toward the greatest objectivity and depersonalization'.[43] But if the chapters are read in a positive way, and especially in the spirit of Elizabeth, they can be most helpful and enriching. The other merit of the publication is that it contributed yet more to Elizabeth's being taken seriously as a spiritual figure of stature; it is doubtless due to this book that she appears in a survey of notable mystics

---

[39] Von Balthasar, *Two Sisters in the Spirit*, p. 383.
[40] *Ibid.*, p. 413.
[41] *Ibid.*, p. 351.
[42] *Ibid.*, p. 413.
[43] *Ibid.*, p. 383.

of the Trinity by another great theologian of our times, Karl Rahner.[44]

Luigi Borriello

In the 1960s, especially after the Second Vatican Council, the Catholic world was immersed in new thinking and challenges. Saints were not, at this time, uppermost in most people's minds, a situation which Conrad De Meester has colourfully termed a 'hagiographical strike' (CW I, p. 48). But as he points out, there was a revival of interest during the following decade, not least because of two major centenaries: that of the birth of Thérèse of Lisieux in 1973, and the death of Bernadette of Lourdes in 1979. Then, in 1980, there was of course the centenary of the birth of Elizabeth.

To mark this anniversary, there appeared in 1980 a study by the Carmelite friar Luigi Borriello. The title translates from the original Italian as: *Elizabeth of the Trinity: A Vocation Realised according to God's Plan*. The title of the English-language edition, however, *Spiritual Doctrine of Blessed Elizabeth of the Trinity* (1986), implies straightaway that this is a direct successor to Father Philipon's classic study – updated, of course, by the addition of the word 'Blessed'! And at face value, the two books of 'spiritual doctrine' have much in common. They are medium-length, intended for the general reader; Borriello devotes several of his chapters to spiritual themes found in Philipon: conformity to Christ, Mary, the Holy Spirit, the indwelling of the Trinity, and so on. And the life story is shortened still further: replaced by a four-page chronology, so that the full focus is on the 'doctrine'.

But Borriello's original contribution, in this work, is to make Elizabeth – a spiritual figure from before Vatican II – relevant to the modern Church. His Introduction and the Preface by Cardinal Anastasio Ballestrero, OCD, not to mention the pub-

---

[44] See Karl Rahner, *Theological Investigations*, vol. IV: *More Recent Writings*, London: Darton, Longman & Todd / New York: The Seabury Press, 1974, p. 79. Rahner had consulted both this study and *The Spiritual Doctrine* by Philipon: see Rahner's note, p. 79, n. 5.

lisher's back cover blurb, make it clear that this is the purpose of the book. The themes of contemplation, the priest, and charity, for example, are all grouped together in a chapter entitled, 'In the Service of the Church'. Of special note is the final chapter, 'The Relevance of a Message', in which Borriello declares: 'the main points of Elizabeth's doctrine can be found here and there in the various documents issued by Vatican Council II';[45] and he illustrates her teachings here by quoting from six of the Council's documents. The overall accent is on 'Christian' and 'Church', rather than 'cloister' or 'monastery'. The subtitle of the English version is *'Apostolic Contemplative'* – a vital theme for lay people today, aspiring to live as contemplatives in the world. The only regrettable gap in the book – one that is quite surprising, given the author's wish to show Elizabeth's relevance in this area – is that almost nothing is said of her own life during the twenty-one years that she herself spent as a lay person.

At the end of the original Italian edition, the author includes the *Prayer to the Trinity*. It is just worth mentioning in passing that almost every work on Elizabeth includes this text, whatever the book's theme. It is a reminder that this vital prayer contains her whole 'doctrine' – and all her soul.

B) SPIRITUAL WORKS

After Scripture, especially the writings of St Paul, it was books on spirituality and prayer that Elizabeth herself loved most. And in the 1980s, there began to be a marked growth in books on the spirituality of Elizabeth herself. This renewed interest in her is not only due to her beatification in 1984, but also, in great part, to the publication of her *Complete Works* in 1979–1980. For the very first time, Elizabeth's entire spiritual output[46] was placed at the disposal of authors, and therefore gave rise to a wealth of in-depth studies on her writings, as well as a profusion of popular works on prayer. As said before, it is not possible to do justice

---

[45] Borriello, *Spiritual Doctrine*, p. 139.
[46] Other than a few small pieces found since then: see the discussion under D) below, especially n. 74.

to the whole range of works on Elizabeth, but mention will be made of those authors or titles of special importance.

Jean Lafrance

The first author considered here – and an important forerunner of the many works that were to come – wrote on Elizabeth twenty-one years before her beatification, while Vatican II was still taking place. Born in 1931, Jean Lafrance, a priest from the north of France, felt strongly called to lead a life dedicated to prayer. He spent a long period in an abbey, reflecting on his future, after which he became chaplain in a convent of religious sisters in Paris, and began a spiritual ministry of writing and giving retreats. He wrote books on such topics as prayer and the Holy Spirit, Mary, and the rosary. One of his best-known works, *My Vocation is Love*, is a study of Thérèse's message of abandonment to God's mercy. He died in 1991.

It was in 1963, the year of his ordination, that Lafrance wrote *Learning to Pray according to Sister Elizabeth of the Trinity* – a book which is still available almost fifty years later.[47] At first sight, the Foreword echoes, ominously, von Balthasar's Introduction to his own work, for the French author identifies the 'mission' of Carmel – to lead us to contemplation – as distinct from 'Catholic Action'.[48] But there is no hidden agenda informing this book: the emphasis is entirely on contemplation. In four chapters, the work describes: the Trinitarian basis of Elizabeth's spirituality; silent recollection (together with the ascetic effort of purification); aspects of Elizabeth's teachings on prayer; and 'the purifying night of trials'.

An important contribution is the Appendix entitled, 'The Present Relevance of Sister Elizabeth's Message on Prayer'. As

---

[47] It appeared, unchanged, in a new French edition in 1984, and was published in English in 2003, which is the version followed here. Another English publication by Jean Lafrance – *Elizabeth of the Trinity: The Charism of her Prayer* (undated but with an *imprimatur* of December 27, 1983) – is not identical and is said to be an 'adaptation' from the French: see *ibid.*, p. i.

[48] Lafrance, *Learning to Pray*, p. 15.

seen earlier, Luigi Borriello, in his work on doctrine, would devote a final chapter to demonstrating Elizabeth's relevance to the post-Vatican II Church. Lafrance, writing almost twenty years earlier and at the very time of the Second Vatican Council, was likewise addressing himself to people of modern times who would be fairly unlikely to respond to pious depictions of enclosed nuns that seemed a world away from their own lives. So we are told, in his chapter on recollection, that it is possible to 'aspire to a profound intimacy with God while living outside the cloister'[49] – which, as we know, is in harmony with the Council's 'universal call to holiness'. And his Appendix on her 'relevance' is devoted to proving exactly this point: that prayer, being an 'interior attitude', can be practised 'wherever we are'[50] – something, incidentally, that Elizabeth discovered for herself while waiting to enter Carmel (cf. P 43; IN 6). Today, we would take this point for granted; but in the 1960s, Lafrance did a great service by highlighting this aspect of Elizabeth's message. Drawing on the *Souvenirs* and Philipon, but addressing the readers of his own day, Lafrance may be said to have carried Elizabeth's message from the old and into the new.

Jean Rémy

We now come to an author who has been writing book after book on Elizabeth for about thirty years. Unsurprisingly, then, Father Jean Rémy is a name which, at least in France – for he is not yet published in English – immediately calls to mind Elizabeth of the Trinity. His many books on her spirituality originate from a life-changing conversion experience and bear the freshness of personal testimony. In 1983, having spent thirty years in active ministry both in France and in the missions, he was due to be sent to Upper Volta (now Burkina Faso). Just before leaving, he suffered a major heart attack. Informed by doctors that he was inoperable, he was more or less told to prepare for death, and

---

[49] *Ibid.*, p. 58.
[50] *Ibid.*, p. 129.

was offered a disused presbytery in which he could spend his time in silence and rest. At this point, he says that he could easily have succumbed to depression. But a few days before leaving for the presbytery, he happened to come across a magazine – an amazing piece of Providence – on which was printed Elizabeth's *Prayer to the Trinity*. He had never read it before or even heard of her, but he knew instantly that he was being shown his future: 'to live this prayer, to pass from a life marked by a frenzied activism to a truly contemplative life'.[51] Indeed, it is to activism – rather than to the apostolic work of 'Catholic Action' – that Carmelite spirituality is the perfect antidote.

Rémy immediately began studying and writing on Elizabeth, and within a year of his heart attack produced, in 1984, *What Elizabeth of the Trinity Believed* – the first of at least eight books on her, and the number may well grow! Of these, two in particular indicate new areas of study of Elizabeth. *Guite*, his second book which was first published in 1986, was written following a no doubt providential relapse which occurred just when he had begun to take on a heavy workload again! This biography of Elizabeth's sister, based on interviews with her surviving children and wider family, provides a powerful example of 'how the faith of Elizabeth was lived out by her sister Guite' in 'a life like millions of others'.[52]

The other book to note is *Gazes of Love* (1993), a rich source of points of contact between Elizabeth and John of the Cross, arranged according to topic: contemplation, the Trinity, love, faith, the Eucharist and so on. Rémy immersed himself in John of the Cross, simply to imitate Elizabeth. But in so doing, he may also have contributed to making John himself more accessible, for the author discovered along the way 'that the teaching of John of the Cross is nothing other than the Christian life lived to its most extreme limits and that it only, of course, clarifies the

---

[51] Rémy, *Prier 15 jours*, p. 11. See a fuller account in his autobiographical work, *Confidences d'un prêtre: Élisabeth de la Trinité m'a sauvé...* [*Confidences of a Priest: Elizabeth of the Trinity Saved Me...*], pp. 155–60.

[52] Rémy, *Guite*, p. 7.

Gospels.'[53] Implicitly, this book shows that Elizabeth belongs to both the Carmelite and the mystical tradition.

Patrick-Marie Févotte

Another author whose name is associated with Elizabeth is Father Patrick-Marie Févotte of the Sitio Fraternity near Dijon; his own books, though, like those of Jean Rémy, have not yet been translated into English. His first, in 1991, is an important contribution. Entitled, *Loving the Bible with Elizabeth of the Trinity*, it concerns this vital dimension of her life, which had been highlighted by John Paul II at her beatification seven years earlier. And it presents her as an example of how we, too, might base our lives on the riches of Scripture. While this book is the fruit of a longer, academic study, it is written in a most readable way, accessible to all. The first chapter explains how Elizabeth let herself be penetrated by Scripture, and the final one is on the Virgin Mary as her model for receptivity to the word of God. In-between, the four central chapters examine one biblical theme in turn – God's love, suffering, our destiny, and the indwelling – each of which is illustrated through Elizabeth's favourite verses from Scripture and a commentary on what these passages meant to her.

Two years later, Févotte had a similar achievement when he wrote on another relatively unexplored theme in connection with Elizabeth. In *Virginity, a Path of Love*, he presents 'virginity' not as deprivation but as an excess of love. This book, written with great beauty and freshness, concerns an interior attitude rather than the actual taking of vows: a virginity of heart which, the author points out, is as relevant to married people as to celibates and is all about 'interior silence'.[54]

Since 1993, Févotte has written at least three smaller books on Elizabeth, one of which relates her writings to the Jubilee message of John Paul II opening the third millennium, and

---

[53] Rémy, *Regards d'amour*, p. 19.
[54] Févotte, *Virginité*, p. 66.

another of which explores how to be rooted in Christ. Févotte will surely produce still more works, and hopefully continue to cast the spotlight on half-buried aspects of Elizabeth's message.

Other Works of Note

No two authors have the same style and approach, and the three listed here are very different indeed. The first book, which is written in English, is *Elizabeth of the Trinity – Her Life and Spirituality* (2011). The author, **Marian T Murphy, OCD**, who has previously produced an anthology of Elizabeth's writings, devotes three chapters to Elizabeth's life and five to her spirituality – on the call to holiness, the Eucharist, 'Praise of Glory', prayer, and faith in God's love – which she also illustrates with many references to Church documents and spiritual writers. This is an intelligent, insightful study, and one that is beautifully written.

Father **Philippe Ferlay** is the author of *Peace and Silence: In the Desert with Elizabeth of the Trinity* (1981), a study of Elizabeth's spirituality; and *O my God, Trinity whom I adore* (1985), a commentary on her famous prayer.[55] It is to be hoped that these books will one day be translated into English, for they are filled with penetrating insights – each of them, one feels, the fruit of prayer.

Another author of two substantial works on Elizabeth is Father **Marie-Michel Hostalier**, a Carmelite friar who, after years of ministry with young people, has co-founded the Carmel of the Missionary Virgin, a community in the Holy Land. He has written a biography, *A Thirst for the Infinite* (2006), discussed below; and a study of what he calls Elizabeth's 'prophetic spirituality': *Touching the Infinite* (2007). His style is enthusiastic and direct; and the second book in particular is written exactly for our times, as it presents Elizabeth's message as a remedy for the

---

[55] This book is part of a long line of commentaries on the *Prayer to the Trinity*. Three of the main commentaries from the earlier part of the twentieth century are listed in Chapter 25, section 'The Emergence of Elizabeth's "Works"'.

spiritual void in today's society, an emptiness that needs to be filled by interiority and a sense of the presence of God.

Writers on Spiritual Traditions

A great authority in the fields of theology and spirituality, **Louis Bouyer** places Elizabeth within the context of a mystical tradition. His 1989 study, published four years later in English, is entitled, *Women Mystics* and highlights the importance of some of the great women of the Church. It focuses on Hadewijch (Hedwig) of Antwerp, Teresa of Avila, Thérèse of Lisieux, Elizabeth of the Trinity, and Edith Stein.

The chapter on Elizabeth picks out the main themes of her spirituality: praise of glory, and life in the Trinity. But Bouyer's main contribution resides in the links he identifies between Elizabeth and her spiritual predecessors, both male and female: Hedwig, Ruysbroeck, John of the Cross and especially Thérèse. The chapter on Elizabeth is brief, but it nonetheless gives her full recognition as a mystic of depth whose own way of expressing herself – unlike that of an academic study, the erudite author humbly admits – 'can bring out far more of the inexpressible'.[56]

In connection with studies of more than one spiritual figure, mention should be made of a recent popular book by the Canadian academic **Shirley Darcus Sullivan** – a work written in English. In *Transformed By Love* (2002), she traces a three-stage spiritual journey which she illustrates with the teachings of three women from the Carmelite tradition. Firstly, the author describes the path of the will to the centre of the soul by exploring *The Interior Castle* of Teresa of Avila. She then explains how God trains the soul in the likeness of Jesus, as she draws on the writings of the American nun Mother Aloysius of the Blessed Sacrament. Finally, Elizabeth of the Trinity shows us what is at the centre of the soul: the indwelling Trinity. Sullivan brings out well the immediacy of Elizabeth's appeal: her writings, the author says quite rightly, give us 'not only an awareness of the

---

[56] Bouyer, p. 171.

divine presence in the soul but also a deep knowledge of what that presence is like'.[57]

Collections of Articles

One of the most important publications for the 2006 centenary is *Elizabeth of the Trinity: The Mystical Adventure*. This is an impressive collection of essays directed by the Carmelite friar Jean Clapier, consisting of twenty-nine scholarly articles by specialists in theology and spirituality – a work that is unfortunately not available in English.

Clapier has arranged the contributions into four parts: 'Sources', on the saints and writers who influenced Elizabeth; 'Theological Experience', with discussions of spiritual themes in her writings; 'Pastoral Outreach', on aspects of Elizabeth's teaching and its importance for the Church; and 'Posterity', which identifies some of the influence Elizabeth herself has had during the last century. These four areas in themselves are a testimony to the universality and relevance of Elizabeth's life and message.

Also to mark the centenary, a major conference was held in Dijon in 2006, and the talks were published the same year – as the 'Actes' of the colloquium – with the title, *Elizabeth of the Trinity, Fascinated by God, Close to All*. Of special note – though all the articles are in fact worthy of note – is the testimony of Marie-Paul Stevens, whose cure from Sjøgren's Syndrome is currently being investigated for Elizabeth's canonisation Process.

Concerning reviews, there have been several issues devoted to Elizabeth by *Mount Carmel* magazine, and by the French review *Carmel* which contains important contributions from well-known authors on Elizabeth; both publications are by the Discalced Carmelites. Another French review, *Sources Vives* (which translates as 'Living Springs'), devoted an impressive issue to Elizabeth in 2007; this is the journal published by the Fraternités Monastiques de Jérusalem, which is based in Paris.

---

[57] Shirley Darcus Sullivan, p. 93.

Anthologies

While anthologies of Elizabeth's writings are not studies in their own right, they fulfil a useful role in presenting her spiritual message, and a few are singled out here. The one compiled by the Dominican priest **Marie-Michel Philipon**, *Spiritual Writings of Elizabeth of the Trinity*, appeared in French in 1949, and in English with a similar title in 1962. For thirty years, until the publication of the *Complete Works*, it would be vastly influential in making Elizabeth better known, and in helping countless readers to engage with her teachings.[58]

More recently, there has been the substantial collection in French, *The Most Beautiful Pages of Elizabeth of the Trinity*, first published in 1991, by **Conrad De Meester**. In common with Philipon's, this compilation can be read like a biography in Elizabeth's own words. The extracts are arranged chronologically, conveying her life story closely, and the format makes this book the direct successor of Philipon's anthology; Father Conrad's, too, should hold authority status for years to come.

Another helpful arrangement – though again only in French – is that adopted in *The Experience of God with Elizabeth of the Trinity* (2004) by Father **Jean Rémy**. While the second part contains texts by Elizabeth arranged chronologically, the first part has several extracts grouped together at a time, along with comments by the author, and they are headed by exclamations such as 'Nobody loves me!' or 'Prayer bores me!' This is a collection that speaks to many people's experience today.

An anthology in English, as mentioned earlier, is that by **Marian T Murphy, OCD**. *Always Believe in Love* (2009) arranges the material chronologically within individual works, and includes the complete text of the *Prayer to the Trinity*, *Heaven in Faith* and the *Last Retreat*. This collection is a great service to English-speaking readers.

---

[58] See, for example, the testimony of Mother Marie-Michelle, OCD of the Carmel of Dijon: in *Carmel*, nos. 22–23, 1981, pp. 199–200.

C) BIOGRAPHIES

Marie-Dominique Poinsenet

For the first half of the twentieth century, the *Souvenirs* by Mother Germaine was *the* authoritative biography of Elizabeth – hugely popular right up to its sixteenth and final edition in 1956. The second half of the century saw the first of the major biographies in more recent decades: *This Presence of God in You* by the Dominican nun Marie-Dominique Poinsenet. First published in 1969, though unfortunately not in English, it is an important contribution in its portrayal of the very human face of Elizabeth.

The author was familiar with the psychology of young people, so it is not surprising that she gives special emphasis to Elizabeth's youth: to her education and upbringing, as well as to her relationship with her mother. The human face of Elizabeth that emerges is greatly enhanced by lively, concrete anecdotes based on the author's interviews with surviving childhood friends of Elizabeth, including Marie-Louise Hallo, Yvonne de Rostang, Françoise de Sourdon and Marie-Louise Maurel. Poinsenet also portrays daily community life in Carmel extremely well, as she not only interviewed the Carmelites of Dijon but also knew the monastic life from first-hand experience. In this area, too, the stress is on the humanity of Elizabeth. Conrad De Meester points out that the spiritual itinerary has not been brought out sufficiently,[59] but it is nonetheless a most valuable book: it makes Elizabeth accessible as an ordinary person, at a time when the Church was exploring new ways of thinking, relevant to men and women of modern times.

Antonio Sicari

The life of Elizabeth by Antonio Sicari (1984), an Italian Carmelite friar and theologian, is an original and valuable work,

---

[59] See his discussion of this work, in Clapier (ed.), p. 710.

sadly not translated into English. It could well be called the biographical counterpart of von Balthasar's study, to which Sicari often refers. The subtitle of this book – 'A Theological Existence' – is a conscious link with the Swiss theologian, for von Balthasar had described Elizabeth and Thérèse as 'theological existences', in that they devoted their lives to the reality of their faith.[60] Sicari intended his own work, he said, not as a simple biography but as 'the account of a lived theology'; and he comments: '[Elizabeth's] existence is entirely a reflection worthy of the best theology'.[61]

It was mentioned earlier that Philipon, in The Spiritual Doctrine, sometimes appears to be fitting Elizabeth around doctrinal issues instead of the other way around. There is less danger of this in a biography, and Sicari achieves the balance by telling the life of Elizabeth with explanatory digressions along the way. However, while Father Conrad greatly admires this work, he regrets that the author has not sufficiently explored the message contained in the writings of Elizabeth's youth, and that he follows von Balthasar in giving too much stress to the theme of predestination.[62]

Sicari draws on material submitted for the beatification Process, including one negative testimony from a Carmelite nun who had actually never known Elizabeth and which was eventually proved false. This 'witness', Mother Geneviève of St Bernard, had in 1920 exceptionally been sent from the Carmel of Anderlecht to be prioress at Dijon. Testifying in the role of 'witness of a witness', she said that in the Souvenirs Mother Germaine, due to an excessive affection for her protégée, had constructed a myth of Elizabeth's sanctity.[63] However, there is another issue worth raising here, quite independently of her jealousy of Mother Germaine. The nun in question believed Thérèse of Lisieux to have been a 'mediocre' saint and wished

---

[60] Von Balthasar, Two Sisters in the Spirit, p. 11.
[61] Sicari, pp. 7 & 8.
[62] See Conrad De Meester, OCD, in Clapier (ed.), p. 713.
[63] See Sicari, p. 256.

she could have blocked Thérèse's cause for canonisation. She likewise thought that Elizabeth had been a good Carmelite but not 'of the stature' of the great models of the tradition of the Order.[64] This is where modern biographies of saints are so valuable: by portraying the heroism of a person's struggles, they show that holiness is at the reach of ordinary people – that saints do not necessarily have ecstasies or visions but, crucially, become holy in the course of everyday life.

Recent Biographies of Note

A fairly recent biography written in English is *He is My Heaven* by **Jennifer Moorcroft** (2001). A Third Order Carmelite, she also has an understanding of the Carmelite monastic life and is aware of the spiritual thirst of lay people today. The book is readable, warm and inspiring, and perhaps comes closest in approach to being a direct successor to Mother Germaine's *Souvenirs*; but the information is up to date, thanks to the author's knowledge of recent studies and especially the *Complete Works*.

In the series 'A Brief Life of...', there is a helpful work by **Bernard Sesé**, an academic and translator who has also written lives of other Carmelite saints for the same series: Teresa of Avila and John of the Cross. His life of Elizabeth (1993), unfortunately not available in English, is small but compact – full of information on both Elizabeth and the times in which she lived.

A recent biography, in a style to enthuse young people, is *A Thirst for the Infinite* (2006), by the Carmelite friar Father **Marie-Michel Hostalier**. As said before, this author has a special ministry with the young. His book reaches out to them, conveying the dynamism of Elizabeth's character, and her enthusiasm both for life and for God. Unsurprisingly, a large proportion of the book is devoted to her youth, and in this respect the work fulfils an important role. Also, its portrayal of the spiritual life and the religious life as a love story, an exciting search for the Infinite, makes this a work that could well have a life-changing impact

---

[64] *Ibid.*, p. 256.

on young people, and hopefully both this and his other work on Elizabeth may one day be translated into English.

Not strictly a biography, but telling the story of Elizabeth's life, is a literary work entitled, *Elizabeth Catez or an Obsession with God*, first published in 1991. The author, **Didier Decoin**, is an eminent novelist and winner of the Prix Goncourt (the French equivalent of the Booker Prize). He became intrigued with Elizabeth after seeing a photograph of her as a young girl when he went into a church, simply to admire the stained-glass windows; Decoin himself was an atheist at the time. Captivated by 'the humility, the purity, the beauty' of her expression,[65] he began to read and subsequently to write about her. Perceptively, he entitles each chapter, or stage of her spiritual journey, according to a landmark in the life of Jesus.

The book is written with freshness, verve and enthusiasm. In fact, it is written so creatively that one feels it is a work of fiction, although the life story is itself accurate; the author invents conversations, as one would find in a historical novel, but nonetheless stays close to his sources, especially the *Complete Works*. The form alternates between a third-person narrative (to recount external events) and a second-person speech in which he recounts the life story of Elizabeth to Elizabeth herself, in a style that switches between dialogue and reflection. Two examples from the same stage of her life: '[your mother] decrees that you may not go to the Boulevard Carnot, to the monastery, to the Carmel. Well, almost: to Mass or vespers in the chapel, yes; but you are absolutely forbidden to have any kind of contact with the nuns whatsoever.' Then, the next paragraph, a mere two words: 'Punished, baby.'[66] A while later, in more reflective mode: 'Now, your great drama is that God lives in you, and that you live with your mother. A double passion, then, in both senses of the word'.[67]

---

[65] Decoin, p. 33. Quotations are from the 2003 French edition; the book has not been translated into English.
[66] *Ibid.*, p. 78.
[67] *Ibid.*, p. 114.

When this book first appeared, the face of the thirteen-year-old Elizabeth, on the front cover, could be seen gazing out at the general public from the window displays of the mainstream French bookshops. Decoin's contribution is not just original writing, but the bringing of Elizabeth to the notice of the secular and literary world.

Conrad De Meester

The summit of this selection of lives is reached with Conrad De Meester's *Elizabeth of the Trinity: A Biography*, which is likely to remain the definitive biography of Elizabeth and will hopefully be translated into English before long. Brought out in time for the actual centenary of her death, November 9, 2006, its original working title had been *He Loved Me* – summing up Elizabeth's life in words she so loved by St Paul (cf. Gal 2:20). In this vast book, Father Conrad has admirably fulfilled his aim of producing 'a critical biography'[68] – the word 'critical' denoting a careful sifting of material and an analysing of her writings and documentation, so as to chart Elizabeth's spiritual itinerary. But the focus, he says more than once, is that this book is first and foremost a biography, and that it would require another volume to explore thoroughly the riches of her writings (cf. ETB, pp. 17–18; 671–2).

This work, the fruit of years of research, is based on numerous sources, especially an intimate knowledge of Elizabeth's writings and the archival documents which Father Conrad, as editor of these two bodies of work, is ideally placed to use. He also has the ability to combine painstaking research with readability, warmth, humour and enthusiasm – a style of writing that conjures up the flavour of Elizabeth's own lively personality. To discover the *whole person* of Elizabeth, this is probably as close as one can get.

---

[68] See his discussion in Clapier (ed.), p. 713.

A Life in Film

Progress in technology has given rise to films in the form of DVDs – a vivid way of presenting a person's life. *Elizabeth of the Trinity: Boundless Love,* produced for the 2006 centenary by the **Carmel of Dijon** (and available in English) is an attractive and helpful documentary on Elizabeth's life and message. This impressive compilation draws on her writings, archival documents, testimonies of family and friends, and an array of visual and audio aids such as photographs, maps and music – especially that of Chopin and Liszt which she herself loved to play. The overall picture of Elizabeth is brought to life in a most memorable and moving way.

Another production for the centenary is a film-cum-documentary in a set of three DVDs, called *Sabeth.* Again brought out by the Carmel of Dijon and available in several languages including English, it is the creation of **Massimo Manservigi**, an Italian priest who is President of 'Religion Today', an international religious film festival. The emphasis in this production is on Elizabeth's relevance to people today, especially the young.

Instead of the lead role being that of Elizabeth played by an actress, *Sabeth* features a young woman who goes to stay on retreat at the new Dijon Carmel in nearby Flavignerot, and there gets to learn about Elizabeth. This is not a fictitious scenario but a true event; we do not see an actress but the young woman herself, and we also meet some of the Carmelite nuns. The first two DVDs of this film recreate the life of Elizabeth, as seen through photographs and documents being shown to the young guest. The third DVD contains testimonies, including those of Elizabeth's two surviving nephews, as well as talks by specialists on Elizabeth such as Conrad De Meester, Antonio Sicari and Patrick-Marie Févotte.

The film is itself an eloquent witness to Elizabeth's relevance to the world. Notably, the girl visiting the monastery is not a prospective applicant to the Carmel but is on retreat in preparation for her forthcoming marriage. A full menu of contents and the division into chapters show how DVDs can be an excellent tool for pastoral or vocational work, and how Elizabeth can be brought to life for church and youth groups with captivating immediacy.

D) COMPLETE WORKS AND DOCUMENTS

Complete Works

We come now to the primary sources, or the 'raw materials'. And the most important of these is the *Complete Works* of Elizabeth. Their vital importance for understanding her is summed up well by Conrad De Meester himself, who produced this critical edition: he says that, when he encountered her writings in the archives, he 'discovered Elizabeth in a new and more complete light' (CW I, p. 48).

The way in which the *Complete Works* came about is as follows.[69] One Sunday evening in early November 1977, Father Conrad made what he called a 'chance' visit to the Carmel of Dijon. There, he spoke with the prioress, Mother Marie-Lucie, as well as the sister in charge of the Elizabeth archives, Mother Marie of the Blessed Sacrament. Knowing that the centenary of Elizabeth's birth was less than three years away, he suggested producing a small anthology of quotations from her writings, to be called *Thoughts*. The two little volumes of *Thoughts* would eventually be brought out to coincide with the beatification in 1984. But right now, he realised that he had a larger and more immediate task on his hands.

One month and two days after his initial visit, on the feast of the Immaculate Conception, Father Conrad made a decision which, he says, was as 'naive' as it was 'clear'. He had seen enough of what was in the archives to realise that a complete edition was necessary. The Carmelite nuns of Dijon were delighted and in full agreement. And with the help of a good friend, the

---

[69] For Father Conrad's full description of how the *Complete Works* were produced, see CW I, pp. 48–68; see also his account of his decision to bring them out, in Clapier (ed.), pp. 710–11.

Dominican priest Bernard Bro, the way was smoothed for publication with Cerf. Now, only the hard work itself remained to be done!

While the sisters had not had time to classify the items in the archives, they had nonetheless continued to collect information and items pertaining to Elizabeth. This included, for example, the memorabilia that had belonged to Guite – photographs, letters, notebooks and so on – which had been given to the Carmel by her children after her death in 1954. Father Conrad went through storerooms, cupboards, boxes, files. He saw the habits Elizabeth wore, the books she used, and found 'little nuggets of gold for Elizabeth's history' (CW I, p. 49). The major task, though, concerned the numerous writings. There was especially the problem of the letters.

For anyone seeking to trace the evolution of Elizabeth's life and message, it is absolutely vital to have all the works in strict chronological order. Father Conrad was only too aware of this. As he says: 'to amass or mix up the documents could only lead to inexact conclusions' (CW I, p. 57). However, Elizabeth rarely dated her correspondence! When Edith Stein began work as assistant to the philosopher Husserl in 1916, she had to piece together his enormous mass of notes comprising thousands of loose pieces of paper covered in shorthand (which Edith therefore had to learn)! But if one reads Father Conrad's description of his work in dating Elizabeth's letters, his task does not seem to have been any easier than Edith's!

To date a letter, he would, for example, have to compare the quality of the paper, or the colour of Elizabeth's ink; to seek cross-references within a letter to certain events, or maybe a mention of the day of the week. He even made jigsaws – piecing together the scraps of paper, so that he could ascertain which letters came from the same large sheet of paper. One great ally was the letter 'f'! Elizabeth's handwriting, as we have seen earlier, underwent a marked evolution in Carmel. The prioress had objected to her artistic style of handwriting and provided lessons for her to write in a more religious style: forming letters that were regular and rounded, not fancy and jerky! The 'f', for example, lost its loop after April 1903, and by this fact alone became 'a priceless chronological reference' (CW I, p. 81, n. 96).

The *magnum opus* came out in time for the centenary of Elizabeth's birth – the first volume in 1979, and the remaining two in 1980 – with the title, *I Have Found God: Complete Works of Elizabeth of the Trinity*. It is technically in two volumes, the first being divided into I A and I B, but because of the size they were bound separately, so that the collection is generally thought of as 'three' volumes – three separate paperbacks.[70] Then, in 1991, all three were issued in one tome, with over one thousand pages of very thin paper. This is the edition referred to in this book with the abbreviation 'OC' (for *'Œuvres Complètes'* – *'Complete Works'*).

The fact that it took only two to three years to produce all this is quite astonishing. And not only was there the work of piecing together and ordering the writings, but every item Elizabeth wrote – whether a long treatise or a four-line poem – is accompanied, where relevant, by Father Conrad's detailed, scholarly footnotes. They identify works Elizabeth quoted, make cross-references to letters containing similar themes, point out stages of evolution on her spiritual journey, explain the dating where necessary, give biographical details of people mentioned, and even contain small essays on the importance of a given spiritual topic. In addition to this, there is a long, informative General Introduction; shorter introductions relating to each section of the works; and maps, indexes, and various other items of appendix material. It is perhaps clear by now why, for this task alone (quite apart from his other important works), every

---

[70] Volume I A = General Introduction and Spiritual Treatises; volume I B = Letters from Carmel; volume II = Diary, Intimate Notes, Letters from her Youth, Poems. This last volume, because it contains Elizabeth's earlier writings, was the one published first (1979). The English translation of volumes I A and I B have appeared as volumes 1 and 2 with ICS Publications: volume 3, corresponding to the French volume II, is still forthcoming. Twenty of the poems in that volume have been translated into English by Alan Bancroft, in his *Barb of Fire* (2001).

writer on Elizabeth owes Conrad De Meester an immense debt of gratitude – as, indeed, does every reader.

This indispensable publication renders the authentic Elizabeth in her entirety. The effect of encountering the *Complete Works* has been summed up perfectly by Mother Marie-Michelle of the Carmel of Dijon. Before entering the monastery, she had already encountered Elizabeth through the inspiring extracts from the writings in Philipon's anthology. But the *Complete Works* contained for her 'wonderful surprises'. And she says: 'Personally, the reading of these three volumes did not make me discover "another" Elizabeth, but all the intuitions from earlier times were enriched, developed, unified.' Once the extracts she had previously read were put back in their context, they took on colour and became as if 'humanised' – Elizabeth's soul, it seemed to her, now regained a body.[71] For Bishop (later Cardinal) Decourtray, the *Complete Works* were a revelation. He, who for years had loved the *Prayer to the Trinity* but known little of its author, now discovered 'a young girl astonishingly alive, with a passion for life,... in a word, wonderfully human!'[72]

Concordance

Once the *Complete Works* became available, they were at one's disposal but not at one's fingertips. If one wished to trace a particular quotation, it could be like searching for a needle in a haystack! But in 2006, the Carmel of Bourges produced a vast concordance entitled, *The Words of Elizabeth of the Trinity*; there is also a prefatory essay on Elizabeth as a writer, by Conrad De Meester. Although the work is only in French, knowledge of any key word from a quotation makes it fairly easy to trace the reference: for the word in question is italicised, and its surrounding text clearly visible due to a judicious choice of spacing and font. This valuable tool puts the *Complete Works* fully at the disposal of readers and authors.

---

[71] For this description, see her testimony in *Carmel*, nos. 22–23, 1981, p. 204.
[72] Quoted by Sister Marie-Michelle, OCD, in Clapier (ed.), p. 799.

Documentation

The writings of Elizabeth which appear in the *Complete Works* do not provide the whole story. Father Conrad found a wealth of other documentation in the archives of the Dijon Carmel that broadens the picture still further. His compilation of this voluminous material which is currently forthcoming – *Elizabeth Seen and Heard by Witnesses* – is likely to be massive and should make available all the remaining manuscript sources that are still unknown.[73]

To give an idea of the contents before the work comes out, here are some examples (though not all) from Father Conrad's own description: more than fifty biographical accounts from eyewitnesses; more than two hundred documents by Mother Germaine, including Elizabeth's *Circular*; the most important testimonies from the beatification Process; an account of the interviews carried out by Philipon and Poinsenet in the course of their research; the diary of Madame Catez as a young girl; Elizabeth's 'non-spiritual writings' – essays for her governess, for example – and some more of her spiritual writings that have come to light since the publication of the *Complete Works*.[74]

In the meantime, Conrad De Meester's vast biography (referred to throughout this work as 'ETB') is itself a valuable source of some of these documents, especially eyewitness accounts of Elizabeth.

Photographs

We may also add to the 'raw materials' the collection of photographs, produced by the Carmel of Dijon together with Conrad De Meester in 1985. It contains known and relatively unknown pictures of Elizabeth, as well as of her family, friends and places

---

[73] This work is sometimes referred to as 'EVE': an abbreviation of its title in French, *Élisabeth vue et entendue par les témoins*.

[74] For further details of the contents of this volume, see Conrad De Meester, OCD, in Clapier (ed.), p. 714. Note also two recently discovered poems – P 72 bis (P 72a) and P 72 ter (P 72b) – published in *Carmel*, no. 96, 2000, pp. 41–4.

associated with her, and it is accompanied by Father Conrad's explanatory comments. It was published in English as *Elizabeth of the Trinity: Light, Love, Life – A Look at a Face and a Heart* (1987). The original French title is *Je te cherche dès l'aurore* (*I Seek You at Daybreak*), which explains the abbreviation 'JCA' found in books on Elizabeth.

All these publications are the indispensable, lasting sources and tools which bring to life the whole person of Elizabeth, fully human and richly spiritual.

*

In this survey of works over the last hundred years, there have been two parallel strands. One is a gradual development in understanding of Elizabeth, along with various types of book and approaches. The other – to which this is linked – is the changing times and new ways of seeing in the Church throughout the twentieth century.

Up to and including the 1950s, there was a devotional climate that in many ways was a continuation of nineteenth-century piety. This is the context in which the *Souvenirs* of Mother Germaine and *The Spiritual Doctrine* of Father Philipon could flourish as bestsellers.

The 1960s and much of the 1970s heralded a modern age in the Church, following the Second Vatican Council. Saints, especially those with a pious image, were not the flavour of the day. It is revealing that the *Souvenirs* came to a sudden halt, like a steam train putting on the brakes, with the last of its sixteen editions appearing in 1956. Conrad De Meester points out that it was rare in the 1960s for Elizabeth even to be quoted by writers or preachers.[75] This makes the works of the 1960s all the more significant: so that Jean Lafrance's study of Elizabeth in 1963, which spells out strongly the relevance of Elizabeth's message of prayer and holiness to lay people in all walks of life, may be seen as ground-breaking in its own way. So, too, can Marie-Dominique

---

[75] See his discussion, in Clapier (ed.), p. 711.

Poinsenet's very human depiction of Elizabeth which she makes accessible for young people. In fact, each of her chapters opens with a different slogan that had been daubed as graffiti on the walls of campus buildings in Paris during the student riots of 1968 – the very year she was completing her biography.

The 1970s mark the beginning of a return of interest in the saints, especially with the centenaries of Thérèse in 1973 and Bernadette in 1979. This brings us to the turning-point of the next decade: the centenary of Elizabeth's birth, which was celebrated for a whole year running from November 25, 1979 to the same date in 1980, and which opened with a Mass from the Dijon Carmel, shown on French television. A major impetus to the knowledge of Elizabeth was given during those two years with the publication of the volumes of the *Complete Works*, as well as her beatification in 1984.

In the 1980s, renewed attention to Elizabeth, together with the availability of her works in their entirety, made possible the main new publications, both biographies and studies, which drew on the wealth of material in her complete works. In this respect, we might quote Father Bernard-Marie Chevignard, a nephew of Guite's husband Georges: he speaks of the *Complete Works* as such a decisive contribution to knowledge of Elizabeth that, as he expresses it, 'one may say there is a "before" and "after" Fr De Meester.'[76] This critical edition is the foundation of the many and various publications over the last three decades.

Today, at the beginning of the twenty-first century, there is a proliferation of popular books on prayer and spiritual themes on all subjects and saints; and in the case of Elizabeth, there is an emphasis on her youth and her relevance to lay people in general. This undoubtedly corresponds to the widespread interest in spirituality nowadays, which is reflected by the popularity of the retreat movement. Another major impetus for interest in Elizabeth has been the centenary of her death, which ran from Trinity Sunday 2006 until the same feast in 2007. And soon, it

---

[76] In *Carmel*, no. 40, 1985, p. 282.

is to be hoped and prayed for, Elizabeth will be canonised. Just as the *Souvenirs* introduced her to readers throughout the world a hundred years ago, Elizabeth may become officially a saint belonging to the whole Church. And the ensuing books, articles and films will continue to make known her life – as well as her life-giving message.

Chapter 27

'MAY SHE HELP MANY'

Testimonies in Abundance

As John Paul II came to the end of his homily at Elizabeth's beatification ceremony, he concluded with these words: 'may she help many men and women, in secular life or consecrated life, to receive and share the "waves of infinite charity" which she gathered up "at the Fountain of life".'[1] This is the real point about the spreading of Elizabeth's message: it is never just to make her known, but always to *help others*. As we see from reactions to the *Souvenirs*, readers tended to fall into two groups (though they could of course overlap): those who were inspired by Elizabeth's spiritual teachings, and others who received graces through her intercession. In both cases, people were *helped* – so much so that hundreds of men and women from all over the world spontaneously wrote to the Carmel of Dijon to express their gratitude.

While the previous two chapters have focused on the *writers* on Elizabeth, and their output – that is, the *Souvenirs* and later works – this chapter and the next will explore the impact made on the *readers*, so that we can begin to get an idea of the influence of Elizabeth's spiritual message throughout the years.[2] For this, we can look at two peak periods, of about thirty years each, during which testimonies were gathered in abundance. The first period covers roughly 1910 to the end of the Second World War – three and a half decades during which the *Souvenirs* saw no

---

[1] In De Meester, 'Elizabeth in the Words of the Pope', p. 19.
[2] With regard to graces received through Elizabeth's intercession, these will be covered in Chapter 29, as a prelude to the discussion of Elizabeth's beatification Process.

fewer than fifteen French editions, if we include the first edition
of 1909 and the fifteenth of 1946.[3] From the voluminous correspondence arriving each day at the Carmelite monastery, some
of these testimonies were selected and printed in subsequent
editions of the biography – our main source of knowledge as to
the impact of the *Souvenirs*.

The second peak period, starting around 1980 and continuing to the present day, corresponds to the growth of interest
following the centenary of Elizabeth's birth (together with the
publication of her *Complete Works*), and four years later her beatification. Testimonies to the impact of her message can be found
especially in magazines commemorating these events, and the
reactions of readers from this later period will be the subject of
the next chapter.

A) THE OFFICIAL TESTIMONIES

The feedback from readers of the *Souvenirs* can be roughly
divided into official and general letters. If we take a glimpse
behind the scenes, we can visualise Mother Germaine reading
the piles of incoming mail with an eye to 'front' and 'back', so to
speak. The 'front' refers to letters from bishops or other eminent
readers, which she would add to the introductory pages of the
Souvenirs, edition by edition. These include especially the 'letters
of approbation' from successive Bishops of Dijon. The 'back'
concerns the large body of testimonies from general readers in
all walks of life; these were taken from mostly unsolicited letters,
sent in by people who felt moved to do so. Selections from this
feedback concerning the *impact of Elizabeth's message* would eventually go into the new chapter, the eighteenth, which was added
to the *Souvenirs* as from the edition of 1927; while *accounts of
graces received through her intercession* would be allocated a separate
section in the Appendix.[4]

---

[3] Quotations are taken from this fifteenth edition, referred to as 'S2': see
Abbreviations.

[4] Also in the Appendix can be found significant letters which do not fit into
the categories of official correspondence or accounts of cures. These com-

The official correspondence is a useful place to begin. For these letters, combined, provide an overview of the various elements of Elizabeth's spirituality which were having the most impact. Each letter emphasises a key point or points, and this is surely no coincidence. In fact, one cannot help feeling that when Mother Germaine sent out complimentary copies, she must have slipped in a questionnaire! This might explain why certain formulas keep recurring from letter to letter, bearing an uncanny resemblance to the answers found in school essay questions. So, for example, we see these eminent people making such statements as: 'What I admire the most [is]...'; or: 'what has struck me most particularly [is]...'; and even: 'I must not omit to notice one of the most striking points...'[5] If they were indeed answering a question, it is not too difficult to guess what it was!

The First Response

The responses from the very early days – around the time the first edition came out, in early October 1909 – have a certain pristine quality. They are engaging directly with Elizabeth's spirituality while totally uninfluenced by knowledge of her fame – indeed, unaware of whether she would become well known at all. This can be seen, for example, in the very first response: the letter of September 24, 1909 by Bishop Pierre Dadolle who wrote his appreciation without even knowing if the *Souvenirs* itself would be successful; for his comments were based on a reading of the printers' proofs, delivered to him before the book was published so that his letter of approbation could appear in the first edition.

As we have seen, Bishop Dadolle knew the monastery in the Boulevard Carnot and had met Elizabeth just before her death. This fact – quite apart from not knowing how famous she

---

prise recollections of Elizabeth by Mother Marie of Jesus and Father Maurice Donin, as well as an appreciation by Father Louis de la Trinité, OCD: see S2, pp. 444–54.

[5] See S2, p. xxxii; PG, pp. xxxiv & xxvi.

would become outside the Order – may explain why he focused almost exclusively on *Elizabeth as a Carmelite nun*. She was, he said, 'a Carmelite almost from her birth' (PG, p. xvii). He listed her virtues as being prayer, mortification, vigilance and zeal – 'specific virtues of the Carmelite vocation' (PG, p. xviii), he explained. Her apostolate, too, was depicted by him in the same light: '[Elizabeth's] object, in all she wrote, was to impart a share of the light of Carmel to those she had left in the world' (PG, p. xviii).

With this approach, the letter by Bishop Dadolle sounds like one written by a religious or a Carmelite. There may be a slight difference, though, in that Carmelites immediately saw her in the context of the charism of the Order and often emphasised the affinity between Elizabeth and other saints or outstanding figures of Carmel. Benedict Zimmerman, for example, in his Introduction to the first English edition of 1912, was concerned especially with making the point that Elizabeth was likely to 'prove the peer' (PG, p. xi) of Thérèse of Lisieux.

While Thérèse was, in many ways, an obvious comparison – mentioned, unsurprisingly, by non-Carmelites as well[6] – Mother Germaine would later point out that most of the Carmels, when they first read about Elizabeth, 'spontaneously' made the connection with Teresa of Avila and her way of 'interior recollection' (S2, p. 270). Elizabeth, she said, was spoken of as 'this true Carmelite' (S2, p. 270), bearing the 'imprint' (S2, p. 271) of St Teresa.[7] Other members of the Order were struck by a similarity with John of the Cross: one correspondent described Elizabeth as a 'daughter of St John of the Cross' (S2, p. 271), as seen from Elizabeth's ascetical efforts to overcome anything that could be an obstacle to union with God. And writing in 1926, Father

---

[6] See, for example, the letter by Bishop Monestès in 1912 (cf. PG, p. xv), or the (undated) comment of a Jesuit provincial who called the *Souvenirs* 'this other "Story" of a soul' (S2, p. 277; cf. PG, p. xliv).

[7] There were, of course, non-Carmelites who were very much steeped in spiritual literature and who also saw the connection with Teresa: see, for example, the letter by Germain Foch, SJ (cf. PG, p. xxxvi).

Louis of the Trinity – not to be confused with that other Father Louis who found Elizabeth 'too Dominican'[8] – would say that Elizabeth's mission 'consists precisely in drawing souls into this great interior silence which gives free rein to the divine action, if it is authentic, according to the thinking of the *Living Flame of Love* [by John of the Cross]' (S2, p. 454).

The First Twelve Months

We turn now to the replies written in the first year after the biography appeared, and to a letter sent in almost immediately, within the first month. Henri Altmayer, the Dominican Archbishop of Sinnade, seems to have had trouble selecting any one point when answering the unspoken question as to 'which [aspect] to admire the most' (PG, p. xx). The word *'everything'* might be closest to his reaction! For he lists: virtue, warmth of her love of God, faith, her teaching, her intense union with God, sharing the life of heaven while still on earth – and his conclusion is that she is *a saint* (cf. PG, p. xx).

Writing in February 1910, Eugène Vandeur, Prior of the Benedictine Abbey of Louvain, was overflowing with an 'outburst of feeling' (PG, p. xxxii), as he expressed it, and said that he found the *Souvenirs* so 'holy' and 'full of God' that it could not fail to bring people to their knees in prayer (cf. PG, p. xxviii). For this deeply spiritual man, the best way to 'describe her adequately' was to call Elizabeth 'the perfect adorer of her God' (PG, p. xxix). The 'evidence', he said, was her *Prayer to the Trinity* (cf. PG, p. xxx), and he devoted several more paragraphs to commenting on this prayer. These were the first seeds of the book-length commentary he would publish on it in 1923, which itself would be a bestseller and make Elizabeth's spirituality ever more widely known. Ultimately, for Eugène Vandeur, the *Prayer to the Trinity* was 'a prayer which breathes forth the whole mystery of our union with God, and which reveals the secret of [Elizabeth's] sanctity' (PG, pp. xxx–xxxi).

---

[8] See Chapter 26, n. 8.

An especially important letter is that by Germain Foch, a Jesuit and author of a treatise on the interior life, who saw Elizabeth as an example of *the flowering of baptismal grace* (cf. PG, p. xxxvii) – a model for everyone, in that she followed the 'normal' path of faith and love. He answered the tacit question in this way: 'What strikes me as the particularly attractive character of the life is the fact that, upon analysis, the perfection of the soul of this nun is found to consist in the outgrowth of grace, in the progressive, normal, and logical development of the theological virtues infused into souls in their Baptism' (PG, p. xxxvii).

Foch also homed in – as did others, too – on *Elizabeth's openness to Scripture*; he thus anticipated, by over seventy years, the words of John Paul II in the beatification homily: that 'Elizabeth gives the witness of a perfect openness to the Word of God'.[9] And just as the Pope would speak of Elizabeth's assimilating Scripture into her life, so Foch pointed out that she did not just read it but 'took it to heart' – which, he added, 'many souls devoted to the interior life either forget entirely or else neglect to do' (PG, p. xxxvii). His overall picture was not simply one of admiration, but of the need to imitate Elizabeth: her life, he pointed out, shows 'what the noblest natural and supernatural qualities can produce in a frank, high-minded, upright, generous soul which is faithful to the grace it receives' (PG, pp. xxxvi–xxxvii).

Two letters in particular placed great emphasis on *doctrine*. One of these was by Charles Sauvé, former Director of the Grand Seminary of Dijon. While Elizabeth was still alive, he gave some talks entitled, 'Dogmatic Elevations' and used to publicise them by sending out lots of little green leaflets. Elizabeth had been delighted to have them as scrap paper and wrote several of her poems on the back! Sauvé defined Elizabeth's life as characterised by a '*doctrinal* spirituality' (PG, p. xxxiv) which was, he said, how the *Souvenirs* would probably 'do most good' (PG, p. xxxv).

---

[9] In De Meester, 'Elizabeth in the Words of the Pope', p. 18.

Philipon, that great lover of 'doctrine', would read this statement with delight and would comment: 'Sauvé struck the right note, and merely voiced the general impression'![10]

The other doctrinal letter of this period, by Charles Paul Sagot du Vauroux, Bishop of Agen, appreciated the person of Elizabeth in her own right – 'How lovable she was,' he exclaimed, marvelling on the harmony in her of 'human qualities and divine grace' (PG, p. xxiii). He then singled out the *conformity of her life and words with the soundest principles of mystical theology* (cf. PG, p. xxiii), an expression which Philipon would quote in *The Spiritual Doctrine*.[11] In addition, the Bishop of Agen highlighted Elizabeth's apostolic spirituality – one, he said, that would in turn inflame others with *zeal for the apostolate*; and he added by way of explanation: 'I mean, the devotion to the cause of God and His Church, which is so much needed in the present century' (PG, p. xxvi). This last phrase, written only four years after the passing of the Law of Separation of Church and State, is the first mention, in the official letters, of difficult times. As we shall see, Elizabeth's message would sometimes be suggested as a potential antidote to problems of the modern age.

The First Few Years

Jacques Louis Monestès, Dadolle's immediate successor as Bishop of Dijon, wrote his own letter of approbation on October 15, 1912, three years after the *Souvenirs* first appeared, and straight after listening to a talk in the Carmelite chapel about Teresa of Avila whose feast day it was. Fired up with a sense of the apostolate of Carmel, he was much struck by the fact that the voice of Elizabeth, a cloistered nun, was having so much influence on people at precisely a time when religious life was being persecuted (cf. PG, p. xiv). We have only to think of the innumerable religious communities which had gone into exile by that date.

---

[10] Philipon, *The Spiritual Doctrine*, p. xviii.
[11] See *ibid.*, p. xix.

Monestès' real worry was the *atheistic thinking* of the day, which he defined as the philosophy of 'positivism' – according to which the only true knowledge comes from sense experience, from the things which are on earth, and therefore belief in God and heaven is rejected. His description of this philosophy recalls, in a way, the Parliamentary speech delivered on the day of Elizabeth's death – when René Viviani, as we have seen, had boasted that the State had torn the faithful away from faith and 'extinguished lights which no one will put on again'.[12] As Monestès wrote to Mother Germaine: 'Positivism has now penetrated everywhere; it has raised for the masses a solid wall between the visible and the supernatural order of creation. It has declared that there is no real intercourse between one world and the other, for that on which man dwells alone exists; that no ray of light filters through this wall, for there is but one light – that which illumines the earth' (PG, pp. xii–xiii).

In view of this depressing scenario, the Bishop found Elizabeth a particular cause for hope. He stated that God does not leave us with this desolate situation, but dwells in us and associates us with his eternal life while we are still on earth – and that this coming of the Holy Spirit into our soul is a 'second and continual Pentecost' (PG, p. xiv). In this connection, Monestès considered Elizabeth a chosen soul, 'amid the wickedness and impiety of our times' (PG, p. xiii), who was showing people the truth of God's presence. So he saw her as fulfilling the *mission of an apostle*, and he declared: '[she] has been chosen by God as an apostle of the continual Pentecost of the Holy Ghost within souls' (PG, p. xv). Furthermore, in the light of the secular philosophy that banished belief in heaven, Monestès was particularly struck by one of Elizabeth's most central ideas: that, through faith in the indwelling presence of God, we are in *contact with heaven while we are on earth*. He therefore quoted this striking sentence of hers, indirectly making her beautiful saying into *an instrument of counter-propaganda*: 'I have

---

[12] Quoted by Luigi Borriello, OCD, in Clapier (ed.), p. 717.

found heaven on earth, since heaven is God, and God is in my soul' (PG, p. xv; cf. L 122).

From this time on, whether always because of the Bishop's letter or not, the notion of *apostle* would sometimes occur in the official correspondence. Monestès' own successor as Bishop of Dijon, Maurice Landrieux, wrote in 1918 that Elizabeth was an *apostle for the whole Church* and that she was being 'called...to spread the fire [of divine love]' (S2, p. xviii). Nine years later, the Dominican Juan-G Arintero – editor of the second Spanish edition of the *Souvenirs* – repeated the point made by Monestès when he said that Elizabeth was 'an apostle of the permanent Pentecost in souls' (S2, p. xxxii). Arintero most admired in Elizabeth 'her profound sense of the great mysteries of the Christian life' which, he felt, she shared with 'the Apostle', St Paul (S2, p. xxxii). Meanwhile, a letter (undated) from another religious spoke of Elizabeth as having *a formative influence on the apostles of the Church* (cf. S2, p. xxxvii). As we shall see, feedback from seminaries would amply bear this out.

'The modern world'

After the anti-religious persecution of the early decades of the twentieth century, the 1940s brought in unprecedented evils: the horrors of war, as well as the Nazi occupation. In April 1944, the then Bishop of Dijon, Guillaume Sembel, pointed out three ways in which Elizabeth was a help to people of modern times. She was, he wrote, *a sign of light in darkness, and of peace in disorder*: 'Coming into contact with this privileged soul, our contemporaries seek light in the midst of the darkness which seems to get thicker every day, calm in the midst of the discord which is throwing the world into unrest' (S2, p. vii).

Sembel also considered that Elizabeth, like Thérèse, was *an antidote to the modern world that placed a value on appearances and loud actions*. Her life, he said, was 'a brilliant revelation to the modern world...of the true source of all supernatural fruitfulness' (S2, p. vii). And he felt the need to highlight the *value of the religious vocation*. With regard to those who thought that entering a convent was a waste of a person's life, he pointed to Elizabeth as an example of what God can do in someone who places herself at the disposal of the divine action: God, he said, 'resolved to use [Elizabeth], during her life and still more after her death, to carry out great plans of love and of sanctification in many souls' (S2, p. ix).

To the official letters by eminent men of the Church Mother Germaine would append three others – from a priest, a monk, and a missionary. These, grouped together, provided a fitting conclusion to the official correspondence introducing the *Souvenirs*, for all three made an important suggestion: they *called for Elizabeth's canonisation* (cf. S2, pp. xxxiv–xxxvii).

B) TESTIMONIES FROM THE GENERAL READER

While the bishops and theologians were sending in their comments – most of them, possibly, in response to Mother Germaine's request – a far larger number of unknown people needed no such invitation. The Carmelites of Dijon must have been astonished as letters poured in from Europe, Africa, America, the Far East, Australia; from priests and missionaries, seminarians and novices, lay men and women from all walks of life. Overflowing with what the *Souvenirs* had done in their own lives, these people felt compelled to express their thanks. So, for the edition of 1927, benefiting from the transfer to the St Paul printing house in Paris with its more sophisticated equipment, Mother Germaine took the opportunity of adding an eighteenth chapter. This, as previously mentioned, contains selections from many of these letters, illustrating how Elizabeth was carrying out her mission after her death.

The sheer variety of people, of different nationalities and life situations, is itself ample testimony to *Elizabeth's relevance for all people in all places*. This point was made explicitly by an English canon, a priest of eighty-four, when he congratulated the author of the *Souvenirs*: '[Elizabeth's] great merit is that she is…imitable, even though it is the height of perfection. You show clearly that this perfection is proposed to all souls without exception, and can be attained in any profession' (S2, p. 278). Likewise, a Benedictine monk was struck by Elizabeth's *ordinariness*, so to speak: the fact that her supernatural life was the *normal development of her baptismal grace*. And he added: 'Her life is what God would like for all of us... It is the simple programme of all Christian life' (S2, p. 279).

One person writing from Poland, however, suggested that Elizabeth would be helpful to 'elite souls' (S2, p. 272) – a somewhat less democratic expression! It was one that Elizabeth herself had used, when a teenager – though as the word occurs only in her poems, and each time to rhyme with 'Carmélite', it seems to have been mostly a rhyming device for her! Nonetheless, it was an expression of the times, and an explanation of it was given by someone writing to the Dijon Carmel from Brussels: as denoting generous souls who are given to the interior life (cf. S2, p. 303). In this sense, Elizabeth is indeed a model for everyone: it all depends on how much a person wishes to have the same generous dispositions that she did.

Priests and Religious

Of the vast number of people writing to the Carmel, Mother Germaine would have been especially struck by one particular group. Elizabeth, she could see, was having a marked influence on priests. This gave great joy to the author of the *Souvenirs*, for it is an integral part of the Carmelite vocation to help priests; and in this connection she called Elizabeth 'a true child of St Teresa' (S2, p. 284). Especially interesting is the fact that it was not just a case of Elizabeth's spiritual message itself being inspiring to priests (or future priests). More than this: Elizabeth, it seems, was helping them understand their very *vocation as priests*. This was nothing less than an extension of Elizabeth's own life, as we recall from her inspiring letter on contemplation and the apostolate to the missionary Abbé Beaubis, in which she had written: 'how powerful over souls is the apostle who remains always at the Spring of living waters; then he can overflow without his soul ever becoming empty... "Apostle, Carmelite", it is all one!' (L 124).

The director of one seminary wrote to tell Mother Germaine that he had made himself an 'apostle' of Elizabeth's spirituality. His reason was profound: 'I have the joy, the greatest possible joy for a priest, of seeing the souls entrusted to me taking great strides, thanks to Sister Elizabeth, on the path of divine love' (S2, p. 286). Another director of a seminary gave this astounding testimony: 'According to a very frequent experience, I feel I can say that reading the book of Sister Elizabeth is a great event in the life of a seminarian or a priest!' (S2, p. 287).

This is superlative praise, but his observation is well borne out by letters from the seminarians themselves – again, expressing the help they had received for their priestly vocation. One of them wrote: 'Sister Elizabeth...has made me understand how I must live my life as a priest, with an immense love for the supreme glory of the Holy Trinity' (S2, p. 285). Another took to heart Elizabeth's words – from her letter to the Abbé Beaubis, just mentioned – describing how to be a true apostle: 'Like Sister Elizabeth,' wrote the young man, 'I too want to live in the heaven of my soul, convinced that in order to give Jesus to others later, I must be filled unceasingly at the "divine springs"' (S2, p. 285; cf. L 124). Another seminarian understood Elizabeth in the light of the priestly prayer of Jesus, and he said: 'Elizabeth truly has a *priestly heart*; for after sanctifying herself by assimilating the writings of St Paul, she sanctifies others' (S2, p. 285; cf. Jn 17:19). Philipon himself was profoundly marked by Elizabeth's writings on the priesthood, and he would devote a chapter of *The Spiritual Doctrine* to 'Sister Elizabeth of the Trinity and the Souls of Priests'.

Philipon would also point out that the *Souvenirs* was often the bedside reading of Cardinal Mercier, who recommended the book warmly to his priests.[13] One man who received this advice from him was the future Cardinal Suenens. He would later say how, when he was a seminarian, the *Souvenirs* 'revealed to [him] in an instant the present relevance of the letters of

---

[13] See Philipon, *The Spiritual Doctrine*, p. xviii.

St Paul' and helped him take on board, for his own life, the rich implications of this verse from Galatians, much loved by Elizabeth: 'It is no longer I who live, it is Christ who lives in me' (Gal 2:20).[14] From the letters sent to the Dijon Carmel, we can see that Joseph Suenens was far from being the only priest or seminarian struck by Elizabeth's grasp of St Paul (cf. S2, p. 277). Meanwhile, the English canon, mentioned earlier, went so far as to give Elizabeth an equivalent status to Thomas Aquinas! She was, he said, his *angelic doctor* of the Carmelite life and the priestly life' (S2, p. 278).

In Novitiates and Seminaries

One Carmelite friar informed the Dijon Carmel that he had placed his theology classes under Elizabeth's protection (cf. S2, p. 290). Meanwhile, the prioress of a Carmelite monastery wrote to say that her novices were to be formed in the 'school' of Elizabeth, because it was a school of *simplicity, peace and recollection* – qualities, she said, that would help *unite people with God* (cf. S2, p. 270). We remember how Mother Germaine, as novice mistress, had a picture of Thérèse on the wall of her novitiate and referred to the Carmelite of Lisieux as the novice mistress of Dijon (cf. L 179, n. 16). It must have been extremely moving for her to know that Elizabeth herself was now the unofficial novice mistress in another Carmel!

As Mother Germaine read letter after letter from young men studying theology, she noticed that some of them spoke of how they appreciated Elizabeth's *practical help in the interior life,* as a complement to the theoretical dogma they were studying (cf. S2, p. 286). The irony here is that the doctrine so beloved by Elizabeth – that of the Trinity – can sometimes be one of the driest and most obscure subjects to read about when discussed in works of theology! The Dominican writer, Father Ambroise-Marie Carré, would point out that the very word 'Trinity', which does not figure in the New Testament, 'has rendered the mystery

---

[14] See his testimony, in *Carmel*, nos. 22–23, 1981, p. 181.

of God abstract'.[15] By contrast, what Elizabeth was giving the students, in the words of one director of a seminary, was a 'life-giving' spirituality (S2, p. 286), while a novice master spoke of Elizabeth *transforming the lives* of several of his novices (cf. S2, p. 290). Meanwhile, Raoul Plus, a Jesuit spiritual writer, made this succinct and impressive comment: 'St Paul for the theory, Sister Elizabeth of the Trinity for the practice: with them you have the whole substance of the interior life' (S2, p. 279).

One extract from a seminarian's letter begins with the words: 'At the moment we are studying the mystery of the Holy Trinity' (S2, p. 284). We can imagine the awesome tomes on his desk! But thanks to a more modest volume, the *Souvenirs*, we see that he had taken the whole subject into his life: 'How Elizabeth makes me understand it, or rather *see it within myself!*' (S2, p. 284). For another seminarian, the subject had taken on life in a palpable way: he was, he said, grateful to Elizabeth 'for having made me taste better the dogma of the indwelling of the Holy Spirit in us, for having made me touch with my finger, so to speak, this presence in the deepest part of my soul' (S2, p. 284).

In short, Elizabeth was *turning theory into practice, and academic students into men of prayer.* But perhaps the most moving letter on the subject came from a missionary in South Africa. He wrote: 'I felt an emptiness which I could not fill: I needed, not *something*, but *someone* to make [God] tangible for me, so to speak' (S2, p. 291). So he set about studying the Trinity. He found it a profound subject but he could not see how to apply it in a practical way. Then came the moment of revelation: 'One day, I opened the dear book of the *Souvenirs*: night gave way to sunlight, cold to warmth, emptiness to plenitude' (S2, p. 291). What had been hidden from him, he said, was now revealed.

He also spoke explicitly of what he saw as Elizabeth's ground-breaking contribution – not just for the general reader, but also for members of religious Orders who, he felt, obviously from his own experience, actually needed help even more. He

---

[15] From his testimony, in *ibid.*, p. 185.

wrote: 'The mystery of the Holy Trinity may be adapted to the simplest souls, even in the world, but especially in religious life, where so many souls grow weak, due to lack of solid nourishment. Elizabeth of the Trinity has given the impetus in this direction' (S2, p. 292).

In All Places

Thanks to reading the *Souvenirs*, this missionary no longer felt alone. God had become real for him, and he was able to write: 'since that blessed hour, I never feel so much in company as when I am alone and far from all creatures' (S2, p. 291). He had, we can see, taken to himself Elizabeth's message that being alone in prayer is actually to live *in communion with the three Divine Persons*, as she used to express it.[16] Solitude is perhaps the most obvious 'place' for prayer. But Elizabeth had learned, too, from the time before she entered Carmel, that 'even in the midst of the world one can listen to Him in the silence of a heart that wants to belong only to Him' (L 38). *Peace and happiness* are what one priest discovered through reading the life of Elizabeth: 'Since I met her...I have always been happy,' he wrote; '...and especially I have realised the dream of my soul: "To find solitude in the midst of the multitude", and divine peace in the midst of a life incredibly full of commotion' (S2, p. 289).

The extent of Elizabeth's impact is brought home when we discover that the 'commotion' from which he was writing was nothing less than the horrendous circumstances of the First World War. Letter after letter arrived at the Dijon Carmel, revealing this amazing fact: the *Souvenirs* was being read in the trenches! One chaplain at the front expressed it powerfully: 'Faith in the divine Indwelling in our souls, which Sister Elizabeth has revealed to [the soldiers], is a powerful comfort to them when, under the hail of bullets and gunshot, they see themselves deprived even of the assistance of their chaplain' (S2,

---

[16] See, for example, L 223. As seen earlier, the English translation of her letters has the word 'communion'; in French, Elizabeth writes 'société', which literally means 'fellowship'.

p. 289). Mother Germaine would exclaim in amazement: 'From the front, we received letters which one would have thought had come from a cloister, rather than a battlefield' (S2, pp. 287–8).

One letter, from a Carmelite novice on active service, suggests that he was being helped to realise more than ever that he could be a *Carmelite in spirit*, even outside the cloister. He wrote: 'The Life of our holy Sister Elizabeth of the Trinity has found me in the trenches; she has already obtained for me heavenly joys and will make me spend these long days more intimately united to God... What especially pleases me in her is her entirely *Carmelite* way of sanctifying herself: living continually in her soul with God, through silent prayer, so as to allow God to carry out there his work of transformation into himself... her life is a living example for me to sanctify myself according to the true means of Carmel' (S2, p. 288).

Naturally, not all the readers in the trenches were novices or seminarians. They were ordinary soldiers – mostly just young men who had found themselves there by force of circumstance. And the help they received from reading the *Souvenirs* was incalculable. It is summed up here in a moving testimony from a military chaplain on the Belgian front: 'When one succeeds in getting a serious young man to read the *Souvenirs*, he finds in it a pleasure, a comfort, a life which he did not suspect. I have experienced this: they are admirable, the little soldiers, in their interior life, after reading [this book]' (S2, p. 289).

Quite apart from such terrible situations, though, everyday life has its own uncomfortable 'places'. Readers were *strengthened in their suffering* when they encountered the life of Elizabeth, and especially the account of her illness. Mother Germaine, who knew just how heroic Elizabeth had been, chose this letter, for example: 'what heroism... To go beyond all suffering, to smile when everything is broken, soul and body, with God alone as a witness!' (S2, p. 294). Another reader began to *love sacrifice*; she also found herself *submitted to God's will*, and *confidently surrendered to him in times of trial* – all of which she attributed to Elizabeth (cf. S2, p. 294). A deep insight was given to a missionary in Africa, struck by Elizabeth's suffering as a self-offering in love: 'if I had such a soul,' he exclaimed, 'what an apostle I would be!' (S2, p. 294).

'What preachers should be teaching'

The words of this missionary are akin to the reaction of an English religious who said of Elizabeth: 'Where will one find a more powerful preacher of love?' (S2, p. 280). Indeed, many people were quite simply astonished by Elizabeth's message, their eyes opened for the first time. 'I did not know that the good God loved us so much and that he was so close to us' (S2, pp. 280–1), wrote one woman whom Mother Germaine described as 'a humble person, simple in the eyes of the world' (S2, p. 281). And with simple directness, this reader added: 'yet that is what preachers should be teaching' (S2, p. 281).

Perhaps the reason, above all else, for the huge impact of Elizabeth's message is that *she answers our needs*. A Sacred Heart sister expressed it succinctly: Elizabeth's teaching, she said, 'satisfies so fully our need of intimacy with God' (S2, p. 283). There were other letters, too, saying that Elizabeth's mission responded to 'present needs of souls' (S2, p. 273), while still more described her as 'made for our times' (S2, p. 275) or 'admirably suited to the needs of our era' (S2, p. 290).

Statements of this kind underline so well just how inspirational Elizabeth can be for everyone. Her teaching tells people just how much they are loved by God, it satisfies their thirst for an intimate relationship with him, and it draws them into a life of deep contemplation. All these things are as necessary today as they always were and always will be, so long as there is a human heart.

Chapter 28

'PRESENTED TO OUR WORLD'

'The dwelling place of God'

In August 1933, a young Dominican friar was visiting the Carmel of Dijon. Ambroise-Marie Carré had been ill for several months, and during the enforced break from his studies had drawn great strength from reading the *Souvenirs*. Now, a few days after his ordination to the priesthood, he was filled with gratitude and came to give thanks at the Carmel. There, he met a fellow Dominican, Father Philipon, who was going to write a book on Elizabeth and who conveyed to him some of his passion for her message. Father Carré also found himself invited to meet the prioress, the very author of the *Souvenirs*. So he went into the parlour to have a conversation about the one person uppermost in both their minds: Elizabeth.

The young priest was most impressed by Mother Germaine. He found her 'simultaneously reserved and vibrant'. The vibrancy, it seemed to him, was especially noticeable when he asked what she thought Elizabeth's influence would be like in years to come. The prioress replied that she expected it to be 'intense'. Why? Because, she explained, 'many [Christians] were waiting for someone to tell them that they were the dwelling place of God.'[1]

Around fifty years later, the Dijon community wrote these words: 'Scarcely a day passes at the Carmel of Dijon without a visitor or the mail bringing proof of devotion to [Elizabeth], of the strong spiritual impact made by contact with her writings,

---

[1] See his testimony in *Carmel*, nos. 22–23, 1981, pp. 184–6; the quotations are from p. 184.

of people who confide their problems or priestly difficulties to the intercession of "the Praise of Glory".[2] Yes, Mother Germaine had been right when she said that Elizabeth's influence would be intense, and also when she highlighted what is without doubt the core of Elizabeth's message: the indwelling of God in the soul of each person. Again half a century after the conversation with Father Carré, a young woman of twenty-one, a student by the name of Marie-Gabrielle, sent this heartfelt, passionate testimony to the Carmel of Dijon: 'It is to Elizabeth that I owe…the overwhelming and marvellous encounter with JESUS… Not the fairly rigid and distant Christ whom I thought I knew, but the Christ who is very close "who lives IN YOU", says Paul, and who lovingly waits for us so as to teach us everything: "REMAIN in Me, AND I IN YOU".'[3]

A similar outpouring around this time came from a widow who had felt the crushing burden of loneliness after the death of her husband. But then something changed, as she wrote in a letter to the Dijon Carmel: 'Your little sister led me gently to the only truth of the Christian life: the Triune God who dwells in the heart of each one'. In this way, she explained, 'the Lord entered my life' – and now, 'there is no place for loneliness'.[4] In the words of a testimony years earlier, 'emptiness' had given way to 'plenitude' (cf. S2, p. 291).

The Reality of God

The transformation of these two lives, and of countless others, is immeasurable. Just as with early readers of the *Souvenirs*, these two women already believed in God. However, through Elizabeth they discovered *the reality of his presence* for the first time ever. The same has been true of Elizabeth's influence on priests: all priests know the doctrine of God's indwelling in the soul, and all of them surely pray – yet the sad irony is that these spiritual

---

[2] From a 1980 article by the Carmel of Dijon, republished (in revised form) in *Mount Carmel*, vol. 32/4, 1984, p. 243.

[3] In *Carmel*, no. 40, 1985, p. 324.

[4] In *Mount Carmel*, vol. 32/4, 1984, p. 244.

leaders are precisely the people for whom everything seems to conspire against prayer and recollection: namely, the exhausting demands of constant apostolic activity, not to mention a crushing workload of administration.

In order to mark the end of the centenary year commemorating Elizabeth's death, a priest of St Patrick's Missionary Society in Ireland wrote an article about her influence on his life.[5] Michael Golden had been ordained in 1959 and immediately afterwards thrown into demanding jobs: as a headmaster, a manager of a college, and a parish priest – not to mention other, lesser roles! But in 1966, when he had been a priest for only seven years, he found himself sitting in a convent chapel, desolate, and pondering leaving the priesthood. In hindsight, he would say that he had been 'successful as a priest', 'busy and efficient', but 'little more than a civil servant of the Church'. And crucially, he added: 'I felt I had never met God.'

So he began to read spiritual books, in the hope of finding some help. Then, three months later – which shows just how true are the words, 'seek and you will find' (Mt 7:7) – he came across a book on Elizabeth of the Trinity. It brought instant enlightenment. What he discovered was what he would later call 'realisation' or '*Reality*'. '[Elizabeth's] great insight,' he would write, 'was that what we experience through supernatural faith is real.' He became aware of God's presence and *knew* that it was real. 'One day I believed in a notional way. The next day I believed in a real way.' From this time on, the Mass and prayer became truly *real* for him. And he summed up his conversion experience with these words, forty years after the event: 'I believe I owe my priesthood today to [Elizabeth].'

We can hardly fail to think of another priest, Jean Rémy, whose story has already been evoked in the survey of books on Elizabeth. For ten years, he had been so absorbed by his ministry and all its activities that he had completely lost the taste for

---

[5] In *Spirituality*, vol. 13, no. 73, 2007, pp. 195–7; the quotations are from pp. 195–6.

prayer – he had, he said, lost 'the way to "the source"'.[6] But when a serious heart attack took away his ministry and threatened to take his life, too, he was about to succumb to depression – until, as if by chance, he encountered Elizabeth and found himself brought back to the source. And he rediscovered – this time from 'the inside', as he expressed it – the things he knew and had preached about hundreds of times. Most of all, he began to pray – 'long hours of silent prayer which became a mysterious need, the means I had discovered for an authentic spiritual and apostolic life'. All this left him bemused and amazed: 'I didn't understand what was happening to me: it was a metamorphosis.' His life would indeed be transformed – from frenzied activity to deep contemplation and even a new ministry: that of promoting the message of Elizabeth. During the 2006 centenary, he published a work of autobiography. The title says everything: *Confidences of a Priest: Elizabeth of the Trinity Saved Me...*

Beginning an Adventure

In the case of these two priests, their discovery of Elizabeth's message brought about a conversion and a whole new start in life. But even if the encounter is less dramatic, and there is no *new* direction but a continuation along the same familiar path, Elizabeth always seems to deepen that path and widen the horizons. She herself was conscious of a never-ending journey into God: 'you can always go farther in infinity!' (L 192), she said in one letter. Or, as she wrote in her *Prayer to the Trinity*: 'may each minute carry me further into the depths of Your Mystery.'

Bernard Card describes, in his testimony, being on retreat at the Dijon Carmel in the summer of 1979 when he was a seminarian. While there, he decided he would learn something about Elizabeth – one reason being that he knew the Carmel well, but the other being more a question of 'duty': as a future priest of the diocese of Dijon, he felt he ought to know a bit about her! He

---

[6] See Rémy, *Regards d'amour*, pp. 16–17, from which the quotations here are taken.

began with Philipon's anthology and in no time was captivated by Elizabeth. He now adopted into his spiritual life her writings and especially the *Prayer to the Trinity*. Revealingly, none of this gave him the sense of having reached a goal; rather, as he said: 'I have the impression of still being only at the beginning of a long adventure.'[7]

Part of his journey involved an inevitable questioning. Where, he wondered, did Elizabeth find such great strength when living with her terrible suffering? What gave her such deep, unshakable peace? On reflection, he came to realise that it was 'the profound and permanent certainty of the indwelling of the Trinity in the deepest part of herself'.

Encountering this message of the indwelling God was, for Bernard Card, 'a veritable illumination'. His experience echoes Elizabeth's own – one which she bequeathed to her friend Antoinette de Bobet in a farewell letter about a fortnight before her death, and which is her bequest to us today: 'I leave you my faith in the presence of God, of the God who is all Love dwelling in our souls. I confide to you: it is this intimacy with Him "within" that has been the beautiful sun illuminating my life, making it already an anticipated Heaven; it is what sustains me today in my suffering. I do not fear my weakness; that's what gives me confidence. For the Strong One is within me and His power is almighty' (L 333).

The *Prayer to the Trinity*

The *Prayer to the Trinity* has always played a unique role in drawing people into the heart of Elizabeth's spirituality. It would be much loved by Albert Decourtray who would later become Cardinal Archbishop of Lyon. He discovered this prayer, as well as other writings of Elizabeth, thanks to reading *The Spiritual Doctrine* by Philipon in the early 1940s. But for the next thirty years, it never occurred to him to find out anything about its

---

[7] See his testimony in *Carmel*, nos. 22–23, 1981, pp. 196–7; the quotations are from both pages.

author. However, Albert Decourtray soon began to learn about Elizabeth when he was appointed Auxiliary Bishop of Dijon in 1971 (he would become titular Bishop of Dijon three years later). He visited the Carmel, and it was there that he discovered the author of the prayer as a person in her own right; he also had the joy of discerning, from the *Complete Works*, the very human face of the one whom he would call '*my saint*'. But he never lost sight of the *Prayer to the Trinity*, and every day devoted twenty minutes of his hour of prayer to pondering a phrase from it. He confided to one of the Carmelite sisters: 'I try to say slowly, steadily, while bringing into it what I am, the Prayer of Elizabeth, a privileged [text] for me. Yesterday, I remained as if in total amazement when saying: O my beloved Christ...'[8]

What is without doubt the most moving testimony of the influence of this famous prayer comes indirectly through Decourtray himself. When a young priest studying in Rome, he made friends with a Chinese Jesuit. Naturally, he was only too happy to introduce him to the riches of this prayer. Then disaster struck. For when the Jesuit was later back in China, he was imprisoned for his faith – and remained in prison for the next eighteen years. During the entire time, he was allowed neither visits nor books. But most providentially, he had memorised the *Prayer to the Trinity*. So he regularly recited it to himself, as well as the verses he could remember from John's Gospel. And that, he said later, was what enabled him to survive.[9]

One Message, Many Themes

Father Philipon described Elizabeth's *Prayer to the Trinity* as 'the synthesis of her interior life'.[10] Within that synthesis, however, there are many different elements. As Mother Germaine had foreseen, there would be countless people who welcomed with joy the message of the *indwelling of God in the soul*. For academ-

---

[8] From the article on Elizabeth's presence in Decourtray's life by Sister Marie-Michelle, OCD, in Clapier (ed.), pp. 791–806; this quotation is from p. 803.
[9] See *ibid.*, pp. 793–4.
[10] Philipon, *The Spiritual Doctrine*, p. 190.

ics, or for bishops with their sound theological training, it is often the case that one doctrinal topic stands out for them in Elizabeth's writings.

Inevitably, the theme most associated with her is that of the *Trinity*. As mentioned earlier, the theologian Karl Rahner named Elizabeth as one of the most outstanding mystics of the Trinity, and he placed her among such figures as Bonaventure, Ruysbroeck, Ignatius of Loyola and John of the Cross.[11] Von Balthasar, on the other hand, highlighted *predestination* as 'the core of Elizabeth's message', and he commented: 'These two texts [Eph 1:4–6; Rm 8:29–30]...made up the load-bearing framework of Elizabeth's spiritual edifice until her death.'[12]

Yet it is clear from von Balthasar's study that Elizabeth did not just broaden the horizons of his thinking but was also quite inspirational for his own spiritual life. This is especially noticeable when he writes of *adoration,* as in the following passage: 'Adoration filled [Elizabeth] to the limit with the mystery she contemplated: the indisputable present-ness of God, before her and in her, in the nakedness, surrender and self-sacrifice of eternal love.'[13]

For Albert Bundervoert, who in 1980, the centenary of Elizabeth's birth, became Archbishop of Rabaul in Papua New Guinea, the notion of being a *praise of glory* made enormous impact on him, as he felt that the only way to explain the 'phenomenon' of Elizabeth was the Holy Spirit. As a result, he took as his episcopal motto: 'To the praise of the glory of his grace'.[14] As a missionary priest, he was also drawn to what he saw as the *apostolic nature of her charism,* especially the *Prayer to the Trinity* in which she asks that Christ may renew his 'Mystery' in her. 'I know,' the Archbishop commented, 'that she understood that this Mystery was one of Redemption, bringing salvation to

---

[11] See Chapter 26, n. 44.

[12] The quotations are from von Balthasar, *Two Sisters in the Spirit,* pp. 402 & 386.

[13] *Ibid.,* p. 440.

[14] In *Carmel,* nos. 22–23, 1981, p. 182.

everyone. It is an apostolic prayer right to its deepest roots...
In the perspectives of this charism of praise and assimilation
to Christ, her rootedness in Christ is profoundly apostolic and
missionary.'[15]

Finally, we might quote these words written in the visitors'
book of the Dijon Carmel by a future Cardinal, Edward Pironio
of Argentina: 'Sr. Elizabeth, from you I learned the secret of
an authentic interior life, according to the phrase of St Paul:
"He predestined us for adoption as sons in Christ Jesus...for the
praise of his glory"... I [have] prayed for three graces through
your intercession: To be aware of the "indwelling" of the Trinity
in my soul, to grow in self-forgetfulness and to be daily more
conformed to Christ crucified.'[16]

Those Luminous Eyes

We could well assume that contact with Elizabeth comes solely
through the written word. But the impact of photographs should
never be underestimated. For Elizabeth to attract people in this
way is not entirely surprising, since her radiant gaze had always
captivated those who knew her when she was alive. Cardinal
Decourtray had a poster of her on the wall facing his desk, so
that every time he raised his eyes he could see the thirteen-year-
old Elizabeth seated at the piano and looking back at him with
those deep, luminous eyes. Later, after a visit to Auschwitz, he
gave her a companion: a picture of a young Jewish boy, with his
hands raised, in the Warsaw ghetto. After the Cardinal's death,
one journalist described these pictures as representing 'the two
poles of [Decourtray's] vocation: prayer and commitment'.[17]

Perhaps unsurprisingly, artistic and creative people seem
to be especially touched by encountering Elizabeth through
visual means. The famous novelist Julien Green had spent his
life devoted to words, yet said that the photograph he saw of

---

[15] In *ibid.*, p. 183.
[16] In *Mount Carmel*, vol. 32/4, 1984, p. 247.
[17] See the article on Cardinal Decourtray by Marie-Michelle, OCD, in Clapier
(ed.), p. 804.

Elizabeth 'tells us more than any book could, because there is such depth in her gaze'. And the picture had such an impact on him that he expressed this wish, discerning a need for our times: 'I would like to write a book about her, a very simple book accessible to the public at large.'[18]

We have already come across another well-known novelist who did actually write on Elizabeth: Didier Decoin. In an interesting coincidence with Julien Green, Decoin also encountered her for the first time through seeing a photograph of her as a young girl. What is very striking (quite apart from the fact that he was an atheist at the time) is that this writer was captivated by the picture – but not, at first, by the words! When he came across the photograph of Elizabeth in the church he was visiting, he saw a nun in a blue habit standing nearby, so he asked her who was in the picture. She gave him the name and then quoted what she must have felt would be pleasing to hear: the first line of the *Prayer to the Trinity*. Decoin, however, was not too impressed! He had no desire to 'forget himself entirely' and couldn't understand why anyone could possibly want to be 'immobile'![19] However, he liked pictures. So he bought the card and decided that one day he would come back to Elizabeth. Which, of course, he did – and he became something of an apostle of Elizabeth to the literary world.

Reaching Out

The experience of Didier Decoin reveals another dimension of Elizabeth's influence: that she reaches beyond Carmel and beyond the Church, making direct contact with people who feel they are on the outside in any way. This was something she had done during her lifetime, too, as when she would bend over backwards to help the extern sisters, for she was acutely aware that they were not permitted to enter the enclosure. Quite apart from her qualities of kindness and charity, she must have been

---

[18] In *Mount Carmel*, vol. 32/4, 1984, p. 244.
[19] See his testimony, in Decoin, pp. 32–4. The phrase 'as still and as peaceful' in the *Prayer to the Trinity* is, in the French, 'immobile et paisible'.

sensitised to outsiders from the pain of her own long years of waiting to enter Carmel, and even thinking she might *never* be able to enter Carmel – that monastery tantalisingly in view from her balcony, a constant aching reminder of her exile.

One person who unexpectedly found himself an outsider from religious life was greatly helped by Elizabeth. Signing his testimony anonymously as a 'lay man', he wrote of how he had been a Trappist monk, only to be sent away at the end of his novitiate. This rejection from the monastic life, which meant everything to him, nearly destroyed him: he developed nervous troubles and an addiction to alcohol. So we might well assume that to think of an enclosed Carmelite nun could only revive the wound and make matters worse. On the contrary: he thought of Elizabeth as his 'little Mother'. He was eventually able to give up alcohol and return to prayer, and felt certain that Elizabeth had had a hand in his recovery. He also surrendered himself to Jesus and was finally able to say: 'I am happy'.[20]

The Closeness of Elizabeth

Something that shines through many testimonies on Elizabeth is a sense of her closeness. Elizabeth was a warm and protective friend to all who knew her during her lifetime, and there appears to be the same experience for people who become her friends after her death. A vivid and memorable account is given by Sister Marie-Michelle of the Dijon Carmel. Reminiscing on her first visit there as an eighteen-year-old student, she was struck by how the parlour – the very one that Elizabeth herself had known – felt so obviously from 'another age'; and yet Elizabeth, for her, transcended all barriers of time and place, and felt as 'close' to her as the parlour was old! Recalling how she first encountered Elizabeth's writings in the anthology by Father Philipon, Sister Marie-Michelle would say: 'More than a reading, this was a *meeting*, the birth of a *friendship*. Elizabeth came to me, and my heart was given warmth, light, wonderment. She took me

---

[20] In *Carmel*, no. 40, 1985, p. 328.

by the hand...'[21] In the years to come, she would deepen that relationship, referring to Elizabeth as her 'friend', 'companion' and 'guide'. After she entered the monastery, it was a special joy for her – as we can well imagine! – whenever she was able to go into Elizabeth's cell, and there she felt the grace of a 'Presence'.

This sense of nearness – of Elizabeth communicating directly, beyond time and place – is often mentioned in testimonies. Here are just two examples. Whenever Father Jean Rémy read Elizabeth's works, he said: 'It was to me that she was speaking.'[22] And a lay man, described as the 'father of a family', wrote to the Carmel of Dijon, saying: 'I feel her Love, her presence at my side... I feel that she is guiding me from within.'[23] It always seems, though, to be in the nature of Elizabeth's influence that she does not want people to focus on herself but, as an instrument and a channel, she draws them to her teaching only so that she might draw them to God. One woman states this well: 'Elizabeth of the Trinity is transparent to God. She will never capture a soul, but quite on the contrary she will lead it gently, teaching [that person] to love as she did'.[24] But there is another aspect to Elizabeth's closeness: it is her proximity to our times – her relevance specifically to people of today.

A Time of Searching

Again and again, when people speak of the impact of Elizabeth on their lives, they mention her relevance to modern times. This fact alone is quite interesting, because it seems that we are not just aware of our need of *God* today; we are also aware of our *today*. There appears to be a heightened consciousness of the nature of our very era, as well as a sense of being marked by it. And often of wanting to rise above it, or go beyond it.

---

[21] See her article, 'Élisabeth, ma sœur et mon amie...' ['Elizabeth, My Sister and My Friend...'], in *Carmel*, nos. 22–23, 1981, pp. 199–205; this quotation is from p. 199.
[22] Rémy, *Regards d'amour*, p. 16.
[23] In *Carmel*, no. 40, 1985, p. 325.
[24] In *ibid.*, p. 330.

In this age when the notion of God is absent from many lives, it is no coincidence that numerous people today are searching for 'the truth'. When the novelist Julien Green wrote to thank the Carmel of Dijon for a photograph of Elizabeth, he remarked: 'Her message becomes increasingly more important... She has so much to say in today's world to souls in search of the truth!'[25] Given his mention of 'the truth', he would doubtless have had agnostics in mind, as well as people seeking for a deeper meaning to their lives.

But even for believers, the world today is a confusing place, sometimes beguiling and always full of flux. It is a time of 'great change', to quote a professor who wrote to the Dijon Carmel, saying: 'It is a real joy for me to read Sr. Elizabeth; in these times of great change it is good to have points of reference, sources of life, to help us remain faithful...'[26] His words reflect Elizabeth's own understanding of God as the 'Unchanging One' (PT); or, as she wrote to her sister Guite: 'What does it matter what we feel; *He*, He is the Unchanging One, He who never changes: He loves you today as He loved you yesterday and will love you tomorrow' (L 298).

Unrest and Revival

In 1980, Cardinal Anastasio Ballestrero, himself a Carmelite friar, wrote that Luigi Borriello's book presenting Elizabeth's message 'is very appropriate in this time of spiritual unrest and revival, of interior searching and experience'.[27] This 'unrest', however, is not always a negative thing: it can be the stirring that initiates an awakening, the search for an authentic way of relating to God. One recent testimony is from a wife and mother, Claude Gillot-Schappler, who felt that something 'profound' and 'vital' was going wrong within herself. Unable to put her finger on the problem, she even worried that she might be suffering from a psychological disorder. Confused, she turned to a parish

---

[25] In *Mount Carmel*, vol. 32/4, 1984, p. 244.
[26] In *ibid.*, p. 244.
[27] From his Preface in Borriello, *Spiritual Doctrine*, p. viii.

priest and received this swift reply: 'Madame, you have your husband, your children, that ought to be enough for you!'

While this priestly 'father' was of little help to her, thankfully her own father was full of enthusiasm for a book he had just read by a certain novelist called Didier Decoin! And in this way, Elizabeth entered her life. Suddenly, Claude saw a way out of her emptiness: ironically, to remain exactly where she was in the humdrum of daily life, but with this overwhelming difference: 'to try to live deeply and fully this life which is ours'. 'In Elizabeth,' she would say, 'I discovered a girl who resembled me…in a desire for an extraordinary life'.[28]

'Here and now'

Elizabeth's message is so healthy, precisely because it is never about retreating from life – not even for those entering the cloister – but rather, it is all about *transforming* life, which can often seem a treadmill of never-ending activity, leaving little space for a person to live from the depths. Our times are often referred to as the 'hectic pace of modern life', an expression so true that it has become a cliché.

Dr Max Sheithauer, who wrote to the Dijon Carmel at the time he was Director of the Austrian National Bank as well as being a university professor – presumably a busy man! – was a great devotee of Elizabeth. A number of similar phrases occur in his letter – ones which will resonate with many people: 'in the midst of the world', 'the multiple tasks…of each day', 'the din of this world'.[29] With these potential obstacles to inner peace, Dr Sheithauer delighted in Elizabeth's message of living 'in the midst of the world…*with God in the centre of one's soul*' – his words echoing her own (cf. L 38; L 233).

The challenge, here, is to unite prayer and activity. Even Elizabeth found this difficult at times, when in Carmel she was rushing through her sewing work so as to keep up with deadlines

---

[28] See her testimony, in *Actes du Colloque*, pp. 123–39; the quotations are taken from p. 124.
[29] In *Carmel*, nos. 22–23, 1981, p. 189.

– and then found that recollection eluded her during the hour of silent prayer. She confided to one of the nuns: 'it has happened to me once or twice to do my work hurriedly when seeing my officer in a rush, I wanted to please her, and I became feverish about it; but God does not want that from his brides. So when I went to prayer afterwards, I tried in vain to pray, I could not raise myself higher than *my rags*' (ETB, p. 534).

One man wrote to the Dijon Carmel, explaining how activity and the spiritual life had always been a 'conflict' for him until he encountered Elizabeth. Perceptively, he took her for his spiritual guide, not only through following her teaching but also by asking her to help him. He wrote: 'I can well see that Elizabeth's words are real when she says that we must forget ourselves... I say to Elizabeth what she said to her sisters in Carmel: "I love you so much, you must therefore love me as well"... Yes, she really does draw my soul into interior recollection and that seems to happen quite naturally'.[30]

Two other people, both in their twenties, followed Elizabeth's example of turning the concrete happenings of everyday life into opportunities for an encounter with God. Marie-Gabrielle, the student mentioned earlier, spoke of going to him 'through everything' – 'everything in daily life, and especially every person'.[31] And a young man by the name of Emmanuel admired what he called Elizabeth's 'realism'. Rather touchingly, he even wrote her a letter to tell her so. He was impressed by the fact that Elizabeth's prayer was not an escape from the difficulties of life. As he said to her: 'you meet God here and now, not elsewhere and in the past, or tomorrow... Your realism is the best antidote to our desire to get away from the dullness of our lives by taking refuge in sweet dreams.' And he ended: 'Sister Elizabeth, help us to keep our feet on the ground.'[32]

---

[30] In *Carmel*, no. 40, 1985, pp. 324–5.
[31] In *ibid.*, p. 324.
[32] In *ibid.*, p. 323.

The Deepest Source of Healing

As all these testimonies reveal, Elizabeth's message shows us that there is a meaning – a very deep meaning – to every moment of our existence: even the 'here and now' that can seem so empty and commonplace. An important account has been given by Philippe Madre, a spiritual teacher and psychiatrist whose work has made him particularly aware of anxiety, which he describes in terms of a general feeling of angst at the apparent meaninglessness of life. He is also acutely conscious of the importance for people to find meaning in their lives, a concern which is doubtless at the heart of his many retreats on the discernment of vocation, as well as his book *The Call of God*.[33] This is an extract from the part of his testimony given from a psychological viewpoint: 'the life of Sr. Elizabeth of the Trinity is an excellent remedy for one of the worst and most recent ills of modern civilization: [anxiety]…which proposes the spectre of an existence without meaning, left at the mercy of "fate". I am profoundly convinced – as a doctor – that this liberating truth [of the indwelling of God in the soul], lived so intensely by Sr. Elizabeth, has much to contribute today, not only to souls who are seeking God, but also to despairing temperaments, embittered by successive failures, tormented and unbalanced by the multiple traumas of modern living.'[34]

Dr Madre's testimony on Elizabeth also lays an emphasis on healing. Perhaps this is to be expected, given that he is both a doctor and a member of the Charismatic Renewal movement, in which the healing ministry is of great importance. But he sees Elizabeth's message not as a sudden cure, but as a going back to the deepest source of healing, which is *love*: the intimate friendship with God dwelling within us – which, he says, can turn an anxious person into an 'adorer'. He writes: 'Can an

---

[33] See Philippe Madre, *L'Appel de Dieu: Discernement d'une vocation*, Nouan-le-Fuzelier: Éditions du Lion de Juda, 1991.
[34] From his testimony in *Mount Carmel*, vol. 32/4, 1984, pp. 245–6; this quotation is from p. 246.

authentic fulfilment of the human person really take place without approaching this mystery of Life: the three divine persons, loving each other in us, and leading us into their eternal movement of Love?... This luminous witness of Sister Elizabeth of the Trinity opens up a path for healing, accessible to all, offered to all, for every man needs to be healed by the discovery of Love, whose temple he is.'[35]

Also quite revealing is the fact that it is often illness that brings people to Elizabeth and to inner healing. We have already come across individuals who have been taken out of the 'rat race', as it were: Father Carré, who avidly read the *Souvenirs* when ill-health had interrupted his studies, and who had drawn strength from it; Father Jean Rémy, whose heart attack nearly killed him but whose rest cure led him to Elizabeth and to a new springtime in his life. There is also the testimony of a woman about her visits to cancer sufferers and who described Elizabeth as her 'irreplaceable friend'. She would read passages from Elizabeth's writings to the patients – and, she said: 'How the faces light up then!' She then explained further: 'You could say that [Elizabeth] liberates in them a new joy of believing by turning them away from themselves so as to direct them to God. This liberation is even more visible if they discover, at the same time, Rublëv's icon of the Trinity: Elizabeth's message then becomes deeply moving, giving a more profound peace.'[36]

All these people, due to circumstance if not choice, have stopped and listened to the silence. We could express their state of vibrant stillness in the beautiful prose of Julien Green: 'What [Elizabeth] says about silence is a spring of living water for me.'[37]

'A landmark of light'

This brings us back full circle to Father Carré, with whom this chapter began. When he read the *Souvenirs* in his illness, he

---

[35] In *Carmel*, nos. 22–23, 1981, p. 195. The English translation of Dr Madre's testimony (cf. n. 34) is an abridged version and does not contain this quotation.
[36] In *Carmel*, no. 40, 1985, p. 324.
[37] In *Mount Carmel*, vol. 32/4, 1984, p. 244.

was given 'light, strength, wonderment'. And this led him to the Dijon Carmel where, for a second time, his eyes were opened. For Mother Germaine had to 'insist' to him – it seems he had not fully believed the biography – that Elizabeth had known terrible trials: 'the darkness of faith' at the time of her novitiate; and later, during her harrowing illness, 'an abandonment of her whole being'. This Dominican, who would have a ministry to actors, many of whom were sensitive, tormented souls, would exclaim of Elizabeth: 'What a model for so many men and women of these times!'[38]

Ambroise-Marie Carré would live for another seventy years after meeting Mother Germaine and would become one of the most eminent priests of the twentieth century: recipient of the Legion of Honour, preacher at the Vatican, and author of numerous spiritual books, including one entitled, *Holiness*. He never forgot Elizabeth: in fact, just weeks before his death, he wrote these words: 'Elizabeth of the Trinity borne away by the Trinity'.[39]

With his broad culture and deep spirituality, it was with an informed view that Father Carré pondered on Elizabeth's importance for our modern age – not just in a spiritual or psychological light, but in terms of theological vision. One day, he was sponsor of a candidate at a confirmation ceremony. It was a small, intimate affair, and a brief talk was given by Jean Guitton, an eminent philosopher and spiritual writer. Guitton spoke of how, throughout the ages, the three divine Persons – Father, Son and Holy Spirit – had been progressively revealed. 'In my eyes,' he summed up, 'the meaning of history consists in revealing the Trinity.' And Father Carré, thinking of the milestones along the long road of revelation, said to himself: 'In the history of the People of God, and in the history of many, Sister Elizabeth is, forever, a landmark of light.'[40]

---

[38] The quotations are from his testimony in *Carmel*, no. 40, 1985, pp. 184–6.
[39] See http://www.donecponam.org/index.php?option=com_content&task=view&id=106&Itemid=76. The quotation is taken from a lecture of December 6, 2004 by Daniel Pannier.
[40] In *Carmel*, nos. 22–23, 1981, p. 186.

Chapter 29

'WE INVOKE HER'

'Our Saint'

'While your [Elizabeth] lived here on earth, she was "your Carmelite"; now she is in glory, she is "our Saint"' (S2, p. 303). These words, sent to the Dijon Carmel in 1925, open up for us a new stage in the posthumous life of Elizabeth: of how she was raised to the altars of the Church – becoming, almost sixty years after that letter, 'Blessed Elizabeth of the Trinity'. But long before this event, long before her Cause for beatification was even opened, the foundations were being laid: the many years in which the people were already turning to Elizabeth, spontaneously praying to her whom they recognised as a saint.

This unofficial veneration – traditionally known as 'the voice of the people'[1] – began even while Elizabeth was still alive. It was the case both inside and outside the Carmel. 'The whole community saw her as a saint, already during the time of her illness' (ETB, p. 717, n. 1), Sister Marie of the Holy Spirit would say. Sister Marthe would relate how she herself had kissed Elizabeth's hands 'with the same faith, the same respect, as if I had kissed those of Jesus crucified' (ETB, p. 714). Another of the nuns would recall: 'It had started during her illness... She was surrounded by sisters, they didn't stop kissing her, making her touch objects' (PD, p. 205) – these 'objects' becoming souvenirs or relics. Then, when Elizabeth's body was laid out in the choir, Mother Marie of the Heart of Jesus, believing that Elizabeth could take away her vertigo, had dragged herself there and rested her forehead against Elizabeth's feet – and the dizziness instantly left her.

---

[1] The phrase *vox populi*; cf. Molinari, p. 55.

As for the people of the town, it seems that even before she had died, they, too, considered Elizabeth a saint. For as soon as news of her death became known, people crowded to the Carmel, bringing rosaries and medals so that these might be touched against the body of 'the little saint' (PG, p. 223), as everyone was calling her. After the burial, visitors would come to her tomb, and it often proved to be something of a religious experience: several people were struck by an extraordinary sense of recollection that was so strong they found difficulty in tearing themselves away (cf. S2, p. 299).

But without a doubt, it was the biography of Elizabeth, published three years after her death, that unleashed the massive waves of veneration. Mother Germaine had captured, above all, the great sanctity of her protégée, and readers readily turned to Elizabeth for help. As early as November 1909 – only a month after the *Souvenirs* first appeared – Elizabeth's grave began to be decorated by unknown hands. White flowers were laid there; and the plain wooden cross, inscribed simply with her name and the date of her death, was soon covered with what Mother Germaine described as 'touching inscriptions' (S2, p. 299). Before long, there were too many of them to fit on the large cross, so visitors began to leave pieces of wood in the earth, carrying their urgent appeals to Elizabeth or their thanks for graces received. And souvenirs were taken away from the graveside: a little flower, for example, or a handful of earth would be carefully picked up and treasured.

Places of Pilgrimage

It was not long before both the Carmelite monastery and Elizabeth's grave became, to some extent, places of pilgrimage. Situated in the eastern half of France, Dijon was particularly well placed to receive visitors returning from Rome on their way home to Paris or many other parts of the country. Mother Germaine noted with delight how young priests, who had just finished their studies in Rome, would come to kneel at Elizabeth's tomb and place their future ministry under her protection. They also wished to celebrate Mass in the Carmelites' chapel, knowing that Elizabeth herself had prayed there (cf. S2, p. 286).

One notable visitor returning from Rome was Cardinal Mercier. He came in 1920, directly after the canonisation ceremony of Joan of Arc. He was taken around parts of the monastery, and in the chapter room was shown a picture of Elizabeth. He asked how long she had spent in Carmel. On hearing that it was only five years, he smiled and remarked: 'You become holy quickly here!'[2] He was also taken to her cell, which by that time had been turned into an oratory. Here, he made a similar comment: '*She* became a saint in no time, while we drag along.'[3] And the Cardinal recommended to all the clergy in his diocese that they should read and own a copy of the *Souvenirs*.

Another noteworthy visitor in the 1920s was Father Marie-Eugène Grialou. He came in June 1927, as a young Carmelite who at that time had been in the Order for only five years. But even before entering Carmel, he had been known to recommend Elizabeth's writings for her insights into the letters of St Paul. Now, he prayed at her tomb and had a long conversation with Mother Germaine, aware that this was Elizabeth's own prioress. When he was based in Rome in the late 1940s, working for the government of the Order, he would be actively involved in helping promote her Cause for beatification, which he referred to as a 'dear Cause'.[4] And in his important book of 1949, *I Want to See God*, he would speak of Elizabeth's prayer of recollection and love of Scripture, and would especially redress the balance with regard to those who saw doctrine as the focus of her spirituality instead of merely its 'point of departure'.[5] As he wrote: 'Let theologians learn from Sister Elizabeth to make use of the

---

[2]   In Philipon, *The Spiritual Doctrine*, p. xvii.
[3]   In *ibid.*, p. xviii.
[4]   See the article by Louis Menvielle, Notre-Dame de Vie, in the newsletter *Père Marie-Eugène de l'Enfant-Jésus: Cause de canonisation*, Letter 16, June 2006, p. 2.
[5]   Father Marie-Eugène of the Child Jesus, OCD, *I Want to See God – A Practical Synthesis of Carmelite Spirituality*, vol. 1, Notre Dame, IN: Ave Maria Press (Christian Classics), 1998, p. 515.

truths of dogma in order to be recollected in God: they will thus help her to fulfil her mission, which is to attract souls to recollection'.[6]

A Time of Miracles

As the years went by, the *Souvenirs* played an ever more pivotal role. The numerous editions were not just a *sign* of existing interest in Elizabeth: they inevitably *caused* her popularity to increase. By 1927, the time of the major revised edition, there had been twelve French editions in eighteen years – a remarkable average of one every eighteen months – as well as translations into several languages.

As we have seen, many people wrote to the Carmel to say how much they had been helped by Elizabeth's spiritual message. But there was a parallel stream of incoming mail, concerned with veneration for Elizabeth. Frequently, relics were requested. One priest, for example, feeling he was probably asking quite a lot, tentatively asked if he might have a lock of Elizabeth's hair for himself, and another for a female parishioner (cf. S2, p. 300). And a Carmelite novice, during the First World War, wrote from the trenches to say that he had sewn his relic of Elizabeth into his scapular – so that, even in the difficulties of war, 'I may always remain a Carmelite with all my soul' (S2, p. 288).

The requests for relics, and prayers for Elizabeth's help, reveal the utmost confidence people had in her. Such faith was amply rewarded. So, another type of letter began to arrive at the Carmel: accounts of *graces received*. Several of these were physical cures. This may strike us as surprising today, when for years after her beatification there was no sign of another miraculous cure – and it is only now, almost three decades later and a century

---

[6] *Ibid.*, p. 516. See further comments by him on Elizabeth, in the section 'Elizabeth Among the Saints'. I would like to acknowledge, here, an article which indicates the passages on Elizabeth in *I Want to See God*: Lucy O'Sullivan, 'Fr Marie-Eugène, Founder of Notre-Dame de Vie: Taking Carmel into the Post-Millennium World', in *Mount Carmel*, vol. 55/3, 2007, pp. 57–64; see especially p. 58, n. 1.

after her death, that a miracle for her canonisation is being investigated.[7] But, as one author has pointed out: 'Knowledge leads to imitation, devotion, and prayer. God answers prayers through miracles.'[8] In the early years when the *Souvenirs* was being read by thousands, there was ample evidence of the power of Elizabeth's intercession.

One example, from 1912, concerns the cure of a Belgian nun (cf. S2, pp. 456–9). She had cysts in her neck so serious that she could hardly breathe, and after an operation she continued to have a raging fever and was told to expect an imminent death. Her spiritual director, however, suggested that she pray a novena to Elizabeth. The next morning, which was actually November 9, the anniversary of Elizabeth's death, the symptoms suddenly disappeared; and the nun was later seen by doctors who declared her cured. Another healing reported to the Carmel was of a little French girl who had a serious disease of the ear (cf. S2, p. 471). She underwent an operation, but it left her in great pain with her head swollen and a fever of forty degrees. Her mother, who had received a relic from the Carmel of Dijon – a single hair of Elizabeth – placed it on her daughter's head. 'Immediately,' we are told, 'the head took on its normal appearance, the pain disappeared, and so did the fever' (S2, p. 471).

The cure, in October 1926, of a two-week-old baby with jaundice is of interest for another reason. The doctor considered that death would be imminent, but a novena to Elizabeth was suggested by the curate of the family's parish, a certain 'Abbé Ch.' of the diocese of Dijon. Although the name is not given in full in the *Souvenirs*, the initials immediately suggest Elizabeth's priest friend, the brother of Guite's husband: André Chevignard. A further clue is given by the curate's familiarity with Elizabeth's spirituality. With the family kneeling around the baby, who looked more dead than alive, he offered up the child to Elizabeth and asked her 'to intercede with "her Three"'

---

[7] For details, see Chapter 31, section 'The pain has gone…!'.
[8] Sheldon, p. 62.

(S2, p. 475) – Elizabeth's way of speaking of the Persons of the Trinity, which André Chevignard would surely have heard her say during their conversations in the parlour. Immediately, the child gave a sign of life; and two days later, the jaundice had completely disappeared.

As needs changed, so did the prayers and the favours. In the First World War, a widow who had two sons in active service lost her elder one at the Battle of the Marne. Terrified of losing her second son, she gave him a relic from Elizabeth's clothes. When he twice narrowly escaped death, his mother was convinced that this had happened miraculously through Elizabeth's intercession (cf. S2, pp. 476–7). Another grace attributed to Elizabeth was when a hospital at Nancy, sheltering six hundred casualties of war, was placed under her protection: every house in the town suffered some damage in the bombardment, but the hospital itself was left intact: 'not one window pane was broken' (S2, p. 477), a witness reported to the Carmel of Dijon.

Vocations and Conversions

Perhaps because of Elizabeth's long, painful years of waiting to enter Carmel, young people, uncertain of the future of their own vocation, turned to her for help. So one group of testimonies is concerned with vocation. Mother Germaine heard from postulants and novices who had health problems that threatened to jeopardise their continuing in the Order to which they belonged. These people entrusted themselves to Elizabeth and found themselves able to persevere in their vocation (cf. S2, p. 476).

Another grace given to someone in religious life concerns not a cure but inner enlightenment. In 1919, a letter was received from a Redemptorist lay brother in England. For over four years, he had felt an intense desire for more silence and solitude, and wished to join the Carthusians at Parkminster. Two confessors confirmed that he had the dispositions for a contemplative life, but pointed out wisely that this did not mean he should necessarily leave the Redemptorists. The man took a five-day retreat in the hope of finding discernment; and during these days it occurred to him how much Elizabeth had loved her own vocation, and he thought she would be interested in his as well: 'so,' he said, 'I placed the affair in her hands with great trust' (S2, p. 466). By the end of the five days, he was given a 'clear inspiration' that he was meant to stay with the Redemptorists, and he received 'a wonderful peace and a happiness that I had never experienced before in my holy vocation' (S2, p. 467). He never again felt the need to leave.

This gift of peace and enlightenment is also characteristic of conversions, and several are attributed to Elizabeth. Her old friend and confidant, Canon Angles, the elderly priest in the south of France, was one of the first to experience her power in bringing others to God. In 1907, just the year after her death, he entrusted to her intercession someone considered 'a hardened sinner'. This man was apparently near death, yet refused to have a Christian burial. Canon Angles prayed to Elizabeth: the man converted and 'died a good Christian' (S2, p. 271).

During her final agony, Elizabeth had said, 'I would willingly spend my eternity near [those who are dying] to help them' (PG, p. 218). So Mother Germaine, once more recalling these words (cf. S2, p. 296), could not have been surprised that there were testimonies about people converted on their deathbed through Elizabeth's intercession. A young Carmelite friar from Italy was worried when a dying man refused to go to confession. So he attached a picture of Elizabeth to the man's shirt – we are not told what the wearer himself thought of this! – and the man subsequently decided to receive the sacraments and died 'in the Lord's peace' (S2, p. 296).

Without doubt the most extraordinary intervention of Elizabeth concerns nothing less than an apparition. A chaplain to one of the state hospitals in Paris was trying to attend to a young girl 'whose moral life,' wrote Mother Germaine colourfully, 'called for a resurrection' (S2, p. 297)! The young girl was dying, and like the man in Italy at first refused to receive the sacraments. As it happens, the chaplain had the opportunity to visit Dijon, and to pray at both the Carmel and Elizabeth's grave where he entrusted the dying girl to her entirely. When he returned to the hospital, the young girl spontaneously asked him to hear her confession; and she made it, he said, 'in the best dispositions' (S2, p. 297). But the real surprise of the story occurred after he left the room. The girl turned to the nurse and asked: 'Who, then, was that nun who came in with [the priest] and who told me to make my confession?' (S2, p. 298). Naturally, the nurse was lost for an answer!

An Ever-Increasing Crescendo

For the Dijon Carmel, it must have been overwhelming to hear about these and other graces received, and to know that their Carmelite sister was becoming known in countries all over the world. There was, for example, a missionary sister in Turkey who said that she was obtaining conversions and healings by distributing pictures and souvenirs of Elizabeth (cf. S2, p. 297). A Spanish Dominican on missions to the east expressed 'a very great confidence in her intercession' (S2, p. 304). And a priest in Australia wrote to say that he was advising people who came to him for spiritual direction to invoke Elizabeth's help (cf. S2, p. 305). It was becoming clearer and clearer, like an ever-increasing crescendo, that people throughout the world were looking on her as a saint. They often used the word 'saint' (cf. S2, p. 305), and called openly for Elizabeth to be raised to the altars of the Church.

An impetus came in May 1925 with the canonisation of Thérèse of Lisieux. This event, as well as her beatification two years earlier, must surely have given great hope to Mother Germaine. It certainly did to other people, for Elizabeth was often associated with her near-contemporary from Lisieux. Some pilgrims returning from the Vatican after the canonisation stopped off at Dijon to pray at Elizabeth's grave and also to visit the Carmel. There, they said that during the ceremonies for Thérèse in Rome, they had felt impelled to pray that the same honours would be given to Elizabeth (cf. S2, p. 303). Many other people, as well, were expressing this desire. Requests were even received for Masses in honour of Thérèse, entrusting to the new saint the Cause of her younger sister in Carmel.

A Self-Evident Phenomenon

By the following year, Mother Germaine was engrossed in a new writing project. Surrounded by the hundreds of testimonies, accounts of graces received and cures obtained, not to mention all the requests for pictures and relics, she began to write what would become Chapter 18 of the *Souvenirs*. The story she had told up to that point had concluded straight after Elizabeth's funeral. But this new chapter which, as said before, would appear as from the edition of 1927, tells of Elizabeth's posthumous mission. Here, Mother Germaine included carefully selected extracts from the letters people had sent in, testifying to the impact on them of Elizabeth's life and writings; the new chapter also included some early examples of veneration of Elizabeth, and accounts of conversions obtained through her intercession. This eighteenth chapter, then, is primarily concerned with the impact of Elizabeth's message or with cures that were *spiritual* in nature, such as conversions.[9] But another important addition to the *Souvenirs* was a separate section in the Appendix, which recounted the *physical* cures that had allegedly taken place through Elizabeth's intercession.[10]

Obviously, all this new material represented far more than just the case of a biographer extending her book after new information had come to light. It was, rather, an attempt to demonstrate that Elizabeth was a fitting candidate for

---

[9] The eighteenth chapter (cf. S2, pp. 269–307) is entitled, 'To Light, to Life, to Love'. Note the word order which corresponds to a change within the biography itself when giving Elizabeth's last spoken words: cf. S2, p. 263. The *Circular* and the first edition of the *Souvenirs* both have the order: 'light', 'love', 'life': cf. ETB, p. 716, n. 1; S1, p. 194.

[10] The section containing accounts of physical cures and other graces (cf. S2, pp. 455–77) – which could not be called 'miracles' as they had not been officially approved as such – is called, 'Some Reports of Favours Attributed to the Intercession of Sister Elizabeth of the Trinity'.

canonisation. A beatification Process – the most detailed and difficult part of a Cause – carefully scrutinises a number of elements. These are to decide on, and confirm: a person's holiness – a life that has been lived according to the 'heroic practice of virtue'; spread of 'fame of sanctity' (veneration that must not at this stage be organised publicly but must arise spontaneously from the people) – as with visits to the tomb, for example, or prayers for intercession; and, the most crucial outcome of these prayers – miracles obtained.[11]

All these ingredients can be found in later editions of the *Souvenirs*. Even the mention of the 'touching inscriptions' (S2, p. 299) placed on Elizabeth's grave are more than just touching! They are a pointedly stated proof of veneration by the people. Mother Germaine also made a point of following up reports of cures by writing back to ask for further details. And from the replies, we can see that she was asking such questions as: Was the cure a lasting one? Had a doctor verified the healing? Some of the answers are printed in the *Souvenirs* along with the original letters she received (cf. S2, pp. 459, 463, 464 & 473). She frequently pointed out that a cure was 'sudden', and sometimes highlighted this in italics (cf. S2, pp. 455 & 470). Again, there is nothing accidental here: any cure accepted as a miracle must not only be beyond medical help, but also 'rapid, complete and permanent'.[12]

It is important to keep in mind, though, that Mother Germaine was not setting out to prove Elizabeth's sanctity at all costs. The author was scrupulously truthful, and she felt she must relate what was now a self-evident phenomenon: that hundreds if not thousands of people, all over the world, believed in

---

[11] See Molinari, pp. 55–8. Note that the canonisation Process, as such, is concerned only with a miracle or miracles occurring after a person has already been beatified; all the work that goes into investigating a person's life and writings is therefore part of the beatification Process.

[12] This is the formula used in the decree approving a miracle: 'rapida, perfecta et constanti sanatione' ('the rapid, complete and permanent cure'): see *Acta Ordinis*, 1984, p. 46. See also Simeone, *Indice*, pp. 38 & 124; Keeffe, pp. 21 & 41–2.

Elizabeth's genuine holiness and were praying to her as a saint – often receiving confirmation of her intercession through the graces and healings which they obtained.

Calls for Canonisation

Finally, another important element of the new chapter is the extracts from letters calling for Elizabeth's canonisation. These, too, are well selected so as to highlight the various reasons given. A seminarian summed her up in this way: 'Sister Elizabeth is surely a saint; her great love suffices to give her this beautiful title' (S2, p. 285). A Dominican prelate spoke of Elizabeth's holiness as her 'eminent virtue' and said that everyone with whom he had discussed her in Paris hoped to see Elizabeth raised to the altars (cf. S2, p. 300). One person wrote to Mother Germaine from Brussels: 'If your dear Carmelite did not practise virtue to a heroic degree, then who is heroic?' (S2, p. 303). The superior of a seminary considered Elizabeth a saint because, he said, 'sanctity consists in *hearing* and *doing* the word of God' (S2, p. 277).

A woman from Mexico suggested that Elizabeth should become '*the patron saint of interior souls*': and she considered Elizabeth to be '*the simplest and easiest model for reaching the most intimate union with God*' (S2, p. 304). Another lay person testified to the impact of Elizabeth's message, but in addition spelt out the implications – the proof of her sanctity: 'I have met many people,' he wrote, 'whose lives have been transformed by Sister Elizabeth; it is only saints to whom God gives such an influence' (S2, pp. 300–1). This point was likewise made by Father Vallée, whose words provided a fitting conclusion to the many testimonies in the new chapter of the *Souvenirs*. Here, he described the fact of Elizabeth's bringing souls into union with God as 'a gift that reveals sanctity' (S2, p. 306). He then recalled her presentiment that she would one day have this mission in heaven. And he ended, with regard to this mission: 'I do not know of any more impressive proof of sanctity' (S2, p. 307).

With Elizabeth's holiness recognised far and wide, and the calls for her canonisation ever more numerous, some people were themselves actively trying to contribute to her Cause. A Portuguese priest, for example, offered Mass for this intention on the ninth day of every month, in memory of the date of her death (cf. S2, pp. 301–2). A prayer was circulating for Elizabeth's beatification, and one letter came from a missionary who enclosed his translation of it into English: this prayer, he said, was being recited more and more in Africa (cf. S2, pp. 304–5). It was now time for action to be taken towards the official recognition of Elizabeth as a saint.

Chapter 30

'RICH IN PROMISE FOR THE FUTURE'

The First Signs

One Friday morning in October 1930, visitors to the public cemetery in Dijon could not fail to notice that something was afoot: a tent was being erected over the burial area set aside for the graves of the Carmelite nuns. There was no doubt in their minds that it had something to do with the sister known as the 'little saint' (S2, p. 479). Word spread quickly, and people began to gather. By the time of the ceremony which was to be held there later that day, around three hundred people would have stationed themselves around the tent.

On this date, October 10, Elizabeth's remains were exhumed and identified, then placed in a more secure coffin to ensure that they were preserved as well as possible. The ceremony was presided over by the then Bishop of Dijon, Pierre Petit de Julleville, together with a number of priests, including Monsignor François-Xavier Hertzog, the 'Postulator' of Elizabeth's Cause, a role which will be explained later. While the crowds had spontaneously gathered there, just a small group of Elizabeth's family and friends had been invited. Her mother was no longer alive, having died in 1914. But Guite was there: she was now forty-seven, widowed, and the mother of nine children.

The whole procedure was carried out with solemnity, beginning with a hymn to the Holy Spirit, the *Veni Creator,* and some other liturgical prayers. After this, three doctors and the official helpers took an oath before beginning their work. Then, for the first time in almost twenty-four years, Elizabeth's grave was opened. It immediately became clear that the simple wooden coffin was in a bad state of repair. In fact, it could not even be lifted out of the ground, as it was intertwined with large roots which were holding it down.

So, one by one the contents were carried out. And the first thing that appeared was the little pinewood cross which Mother Germaine had placed between Elizabeth's hands just before the coffin had been closed and taken out of the enclosure for the funeral. On hearing of this, the author of the *Souvenirs* could not help thinking it symbolic of Elizabeth's 'supreme desire: to be transformed into Jesus crucified' (S2, p. 480). The remains had been lying directly on a thick bed of small tangled roots, and when her skull was picked up, its clear imprint could be seen on them. Once everything was removed, the people spontaneously touched pious objects and even jewellery against Elizabeth's remains. The spirit of veneration was almost tangible.

Now began the official inspection, with the doctors carefully identifying all the bones. Once this was done, they wrote up their report there and then, on parchment bearing the Bishop's coat of arms. Meanwhile, another report was drawn up by the ecclesiastical notary, on identical parchment, this one being an account of the ceremony. Then, both documents were enclosed in a protective metal tube.

Elizabeth now received her new coffin: a more robust and splendid affair than the first one. It was made of oak lined with lead, and this in turn was lined with white satin. Her remains were placed in it, together with the metal tube containing the documents. The lid was closed, the coffin was secured with canvas straps, and the Bishop's seal was marked upon it. After this, Monsignor Petit de Julleville said the concluding prayers, the coffin was placed in the earth, and the ceremony was completed. It had taken three hours, during which the crowds had remained quiet and reverent throughout. Before he left, the Bishop spoke a few words to express his satisfaction with the whole atmosphere of veneration. Upon which, everyone dispersed in silence.

Opening the Process

In 1917, when the *Code of Canon Law* brought together the various protocols and procedures for someone to be beatified or canonised, one of the rules (canon 2149) stated that the Process could not be opened by the Bishop until thirty years after the person had died.[1] But it was possible to waive this, as sometimes happened with very popular figures, such as Thérèse of Lisieux or Pope Pius X. And for Elizabeth, too, the timescales were waived.

The event in the Dijon cemetery that October in 1930 took place before the Process had been opened, but it was a clear sign of what the Bishop was intending to do.[2] The date on which the opening was announced in the diocesan newspaper was May 23, 1931, vigil of the feast of Pentecost (cf. CW I, p. 41); but Mother Germaine appreciated his thoughtfulness in choosing the feast of the Trinity for it to be announced in all the churches and chapels in the diocese of Dijon (cf. S2, p. 481).[3] From the moment a bishop opened a Process, the candidate was known as the 'Servant of God'; this explains why later editions of the *Souvenirs* carry these words on the front cover: as the first line

---

[1] Or fifty years for the discussion in Rome of the candidate's virtues (canon 2101): see Sheldon, p. 56, n. 12. The procedures for Causes would be modified in the second half of the twentieth century, as we shall see, with the most major changes being introduced by John Paul II. However, almost all of Elizabeth's Cause for beatification, right up to just before the final stages, would be conducted according to the 1917 *Code of Canon Law*. In recounting Elizabeth's path towards beatification, this chapter will attempt to explain the various stages and terminology as much as possible, so as to put her Cause into context and to clarify some of the technical terms.

[2] The local bishop would open a Process either on his own initiative or at the request of interested parties (called the 'Actors' of the Cause), most often a religious Order. In Elizabeth's case, the request was made to the Bishop of Dijon by the Discalced Carmelite Order: see Simeone, *Indice*, p. 37.

[3] These dates do not entirely tally, as Mother Germaine also speaks of the announcement being *published* on the feast of the Trinity (cf. S2, p. 481). But as this feast was on May 31 in 1931, and the date of the newspaper was May 23, the answer may well be that the announcement was *read out* on the feast of the Trinity.

of the title, in pride of place – while the more modest epithet, 'A Carmelite Nun', has disappeared.

Also read out on Trinity Sunday was a request for anyone who had anything written by Elizabeth to submit it to the ecclesiastical tribunal of the Process which was now being set up: 'that is,' the announcement continued, 'everything that she wrote with her own hand, that she dictated to others, or that had been written at her direction: whether it concerns printed works or manuscripts or simple opuscules, short writings, meditations, personal notes, intimate diaries, letters, notes to others, and the like; whether these writings refer to the period that preceded her entrance into Carmel or to that which followed this entrance' (CW I, p. 41). In short, every single word would be scrutinised.

In those days, most of the investigations for a Cause belonged to two main stages, called the 'Ordinary Process' and the 'Apostolic Process'.[4] What the Bishop of Dijon had just opened was the former, so called because this stage of the proceedings came under the authority of the 'Ordinary' (that is, the Bishop). As part of the Ordinary Process, he would conduct three separate investigations, themselves known as 'Processes'. The most important was the 'Informative Process': a gathering of information from the testimonies of people who had known Elizabeth and could speak of the degree to which she had practised the *virtues*. Secondly, her *writings* would be examined. And thirdly, it was necessary to determine that there had been *no public cult* of veneration towards her. The examination of these three areas would help establish whether or not a case could be made for Elizabeth's sanctity to be properly investigated by

---

[4] These two stages would be streamlined by Paul VI into one 'Cognitional Process', conducted by the bishop but with previous permission from the Holy See: see his Apostolic Letter *Sanctitas Clarior*, # I.1 (March 19, 1969). Fourteen years later, '[in the] light of the doctrine of the Second Vatican Council on collegiality', John Paul II would place this whole process under the authority of the bishop: see his Apostolic Constitution *Divinus Perfectionis Magister* (January 25, 1983). For background to the procedures, I have drawn especially on Woodward, pp. 77–86, and the articles by Molinari and Sheldon.

the Holy See (and therefore go through to the second stage, the 'Apostolic Process'). The other word which can easily be overlooked is 'Process', which also has the meaning of 'legal proceedings' and therefore denoted the juridical character of a Cause for beatification.[5] Indeed, 'Cause' is itself taken from the Latin word 'causa', which can mean 'case', 'judicial process' or 'lawsuit'.[6] In a real sense, Elizabeth's holiness was to be put on trial!

So, too, were her writings. They would eventually be examined with a fine toothcomb, to make sure that everything she had said was in line with Church teachings (also known as having 'purity of doctrine').[7] Anyone who owned anything in writing by Elizabeth now submitted it to the Bishop's tribunal, which in turn passed it on to the Dijon Carmel for transcribing. Four sisters were set to work on the project. It was no easy task, given Elizabeth's almost illegible writing at the time of her illness, not to mention her paper-saving habit of often continuing letters in the margins of earlier pages. But the Carmelites willingly added to their workload: they took advantage of having Elizabeth's writings under their roof by making transcripts for their own archives as well. They filled up one notebook after another.

Apart from the writings and the testimonies, there was, as mentioned earlier, one more thing to be examined. This was to make sure that Elizabeth had never been the subject of a 'public cult', also called an 'ecclesiastical cult'.[8] While 'fame of sanctity' was a most promising sign of a candidate's holiness, veneration had to come spontaneously from the people, rather than being organised in any formal way or incorporating the kind of honours paid to established saints or blesseds.

---

[5] See William Little (et al.), *The Shorter Oxford English Dictionary on Historical Principles*, Oxford: Clarendon Press, 1959, p. 1590. As explained here, the verb 'to process' can also mean 'to institute a process or action against' or 'to prosecute'.

[6] See Charlton T Lewis & Charles Short, *A Latin Dictionary*, Oxford: Clarendon Press, 1907, p. 304.

[7] See Molinari, p. 56; cf. Woodward, p. 80.

[8] Cf. Langlois, p. 64.

At the Tribunals

Meanwhile, the witnesses presented themselves at the tribunals which were being held in various places and gave their testimonies, known as 'depositions'. The Ordinary Process was held in Dijon; and for more than three years, the nuns would be interviewed at the Carmel, while people outside the monastery were seen at the Bishop's Palace. Interviews were also held in Paris, Toulouse, Agen and Carcassonne: these were known as 'Rogatory Processes', set up for the convenience of people who lived in those areas and where there were several depositions to be recorded.[9]

There were seventy sessions in all, and the Ordinary Process would last for ten years. However, in 1933 it suffered a blow, due to the negative testimony of an unworthy witness. As mentioned earlier, Mother Geneviève of St Bernard had been sent from Anderlecht in 1920, to be prioress at Dijon. She had never known Elizabeth but testified as the 'witness of a witness': that is, speaking about Mother Germaine who, as author of the *Souvenirs*, had given the greatest testimony of all about Elizabeth's holiness. It has already been mentioned that this nun from Anderlecht was opposed to Elizabeth's Cause, considering her a good Carmelite but nothing more, and that she even considered Thérèse of Lisieux a 'mediocre' saint – for this prioress expected saints to conform to the models of sanctity in the ancient traditions of the Order.[10] By this, she no doubt meant Carmelites who had had mystical experiences such as visions, or perhaps those who had founded new monasteries.

However, no doubt more to the point is that this sceptical nun seems to have been motivated by jealousy of Mother Germaine. In the three years that Mother Geneviève was prioress at Dijon, she could see that her predecessor was still highly

---

[9] It was normal practice for an Ordinary Process as such to be held only in the diocese where the candidate had died: cf. Molinari, p. 56. A later Apostolic Letter on Elizabeth mentions 'four' Rogatory Processes: cf. *Acta Ordinis*, 1987, p. 11; and the places are named in Larkin, p. 79.

[10] See Sicari, p. 256.

thought of in the community, and she wrongly considered Mother Germaine a rival. At the same time, the new prioress began to oppose Elizabeth's reputation for holiness and even influenced some of the sisters, especially the unstable Sister Anne-Marie, the unofficial patient in the infirmary. Mother Geneviève left Dijon in 1923, and ten years later was called to give evidence at the Ordinary Process. Here, she took every opportunity to undermine both Elizabeth's reputation for holiness and Mother Germaine's account of it. Mother Geneviève claimed that the author of the *Souvenirs* had exaggerated Elizabeth's virtues, concealed her defects, imposed her own judgment on the community, and in the biography constructed what was no more than a myth of sanctity.[11] So serious were these allegations that the Cause for beatification would be held up for about two decades. Mother Germaine died suddenly the following year, on November 30, 1934, and it is to be hoped that Mother Geneviève never let her know that she had done her best to try and scupper Elizabeth's Cause. Mother Germaine would have been heartbroken.

Before the Legal Battles

In 1941, after ten years of gathering evidence, the Ordinary Process was closed, and a copy of the records sent to Rome. While it might be assumed that almost all the work had now been completed to investigate the case of Elizabeth's holiness, this was virtually only the beginning! Much documentation would need to be produced – known as the *Positio* – on the basis of which the Vatican would decide whether the Cause could be formally 'introduced'. And if the Cause was allowed to resume, investigations would begin all over again – this time even more thoroughly than before! The 'Apostolic Process' was the stage of detailed, probing examination, with the aim of proving whether a *reputation* for holiness was based on *fact*.[12] And while

---

[11] See *ibid.*, p. 256.
[12] Cf. Woodward, p. 82.

the investigations would take place in Dijon and elsewhere outside the Vatican, this second stage was always directly under the authority of the Holy See which appointed the judges.

At this point, it is worth mentioning the main people involved. The 'Postulator', responsible for the Cause at every stage of the way, was literally the one who would 'ask for' the candidate's beatification. In fact, even before a Cause was opened, a Postulator would already have been appointed.[13] As has previously been mentioned, the first man to have held the post was Monsignor Hertzog; his sister who had died in 1926, Mother Marie of the Heart of Jesus, had been a member of the Dijon Carmel – though unfortunately, this was the very nun who had succeeded Mother Germaine as prioress and had thought that writing the *Souvenirs* was a waste of time! We can be sure that her brother had been rather more enthusiastic about it.

There were three other main roles. As and when evidence was discussed in Rome, a cardinal would present it to successive Vatican committees known as 'Congregations'.[14] This was the role of the 'Relator' – that is, one who 'relates' information; he is sometimes referred to by his Latin title of the 'Cardinal *ponens*' (since he 'posits' an argument and 'presents' a Cause). The person appointed for Elizabeth's Cause in November 1942 was, like herself, a Discalced Carmelite: Cardinal Raffaele Carlo Rossi. Then – for the legal battles were now about to come into their own – the Postulator selected an 'Advocate' from among the canon lawyers registered with the Vatican to handle Causes; rather like a barrister for the defence, he would argue the case for sanctity and refute objections. And these objections or 'Animadversiones' (literally, 'Observations') would be made by the famous 'Devil's Advocate', a popular name for the official who held the position of 'Promoter of the Faith'.

When the evidence from the Ordinary Process reached Rome after it was closed in 1941, a public copy was made and then

---

[13] Cf. Langlois, p. 62.
[14] See n. 33 below.

given to the Postulator as the basis for future work. Meanwhile, Elizabeth's writings were considered by two theological censors, and on January 28, 1944 a 'Decree on the Writings' was issued. This part, at least, had gone smoothly. But her virtues had a much rougher ride. Normally, the Advocate would now draw up the document known as the *Positio*, setting out the evidence and petitioning the Holy See for the formal 'Introduction of the Cause'. But the testimony of Mother Geneviève of St Bernard had raised serious concerns about whether Mother Germaine's claims for Elizabeth's holiness could be believed. And it was backed up by the testimony of Sister Anne-Marie who would repeatedly declare in community that after what she herself had said at the diocesan tribunal, Elizabeth could not possibly be beatified (cf. ETB, p. 586, n. 1)!

Putting Things Right

So, from 1948 to 1950, a 'Supplementary Process', under the authority of the Bishop, was held in Dijon and Toulouse. The focus now was not so much on investigating Elizabeth's holiness as on ascertaining Mother Germaine's credibility (cf. ETB, p. 577, n. 1). The core of Mother Geneviève's false testimony, as we have seen, was to try and undo Elizabeth's reputation for holiness. The way in which she did this was to discredit Mother Germaine by claiming that she had had a disordered affection for her protégée which had led her, in the *Souvenirs*, to construct a myth of Elizabeth's sanctity.[15] Those sisters from Dijon who were still alive were now confronted with the negative testimonies given at the Ordinary Process in the 1930s. They must have been shocked in the extreme.

Sister Agnes, whom Mother Geneviève had sent to the Carmel of Toulouse in 1920, was one of the chief witnesses, ardently defending Elizabeth against each unjust suspicion. On being asked about the so-called disordered affection or, more specifically, 'particular friendship' – that oft-used phrase

---

[15] See Sicari, p. 256.

in religious life – Sister Agnes retorted that one simply could not call the 'benevolence' and 'maternal affection' of a prioress towards one of her dying daughters evidence of this. And she added, hitting the nail on the head: 'to imagine that is pure jealousy' (ETB, p. 700, n. 2).

In fact, she may well, at this point, have been responding to a criticism made by Sister Anne-Marie who, as previously mentioned, had been influenced by Mother Geneviève. This unofficial patient was a most unstable character who had spoken both well and ill of Elizabeth at the Ordinary Process. When testifying to Elizabeth's charity towards her sisters in Carmel, she had described her in glowing terms (cf. ETB, p. 531). However, the key problem seems to have been jealousy: as seen from her deposition, it was this sister who had taken umbrage at Elizabeth's visits to the prioress' office in the last few weeks of her life (cf. ETB, p. 705, n. 1) – a time, we recall, when Elizabeth was providing Mother Germaine, as requested, with some background to her life for the writing of the *Circular*. As well as this, Sister Agnes had to counter the statement by Mother Geneviève that Elizabeth had had few opportunities to practise patience. In response, she spoke of how Elizabeth had, for years, moved around silently in her cell, out of consideration for her neighbour, Sister Aimée, who suffered from headaches and could not bear the slightest noise (cf. ETB, p. 535).

In addition to the jealousy, Mother Geneviève seems to have had a sick mind. In her interview in 1933, she had given a startlingly different account of the morning of Elizabeth's death. She had drawn a vivid picture, saying that Elizabeth had died on a commode (!) and that she had then been put back into bed; so, when the community were summoned to recite the prayers for the dying, they were therefore being deceived into thinking they were witnessing Elizabeth's final moments, when in fact they were gathered round a dead body! Fortunately, Sister Marie of the Holy Spirit – the strong nun who had helped carry Elizabeth – was still alive. Known by her civil name of Marthe Billotte, as she had by this time left the Carmel for health reasons, she was utterly indignant at the suggestion that she and Mother Germaine had deceived the community by putting a dead body into the bed! She said that Elizabeth could possibly have lost consciousness by that time, but that she had definitely still been alive (cf. ETB, p. 717, n. 1).

Other than responses to specific criticisms, personal judgments were given – both now and at the Apostolic Process – as to the reliability of the witnesses. Mother Marie-Pia of Toulouse, also originally from Anderlecht, had turned against Mother Geneviève completely, and at the Apostolic Process would describe her as 'hostile' towards Elizabeth's reputation for holiness; she would also assert that Sister Agnes' positive declarations about Elizabeth had never wavered (cf. ETB, p. 592). Mother Marie of St John, prioress of Dijon at the time of the Supplementary Process, testified there and gave the true picture of Sister Anne-Marie: as feeble-minded, unwilling to do any work or obey any prioress, and a false mystic wrongly believing herself favoured with the highest mystical graces; this sister, who had died in 1944, had also, the prioress said, been harbouring a certain motive: 'jealous of the veneration which people had for Sister Elizabeth of the Trinity, she did not want the cause to succeed' (ETB, p. 586, n. 1). Finally, it is worth quoting a most apposite account of Mother Germaine's character which would be given later, at the Apostolic Process, by the then prioress Mother Thérèse: 'After my entrance into Carmel [in 1917]...I was immediately much struck by Mother Germaine, due to her very sound judgment, a great balance in her way of speaking about Sister Elizabeth, not seeking to influence anyone' (ETB, p. 590).

A Miracle!

The 1940s also saw an occurrence which would be of crucial importance: a miraculous cure through Elizabeth's intercession. However thorough the tribunals investigating a person's holiness, all this work is nonetheless carried out by human endeavour. That is why, for beatification and canonisation, miracles are needed: for then it is no longer people but God himself who is seen to be proving the candidate's holiness. At the time, two miracles were needed for beatification. And in 1943, a cure took place which would eventually be selected for presentation through all the official channels.

Father Jean-Marie Chanut was a monk at Cîteaux, the great abbey of the Cistercians. He was born in 1909, the year the *Souvenirs* was first published, and entered the Order in 1926 at the age of seventeen. Twelve years later, he began to suffer severe pain and was diagnosed with tuberculosis of the kidneys, especially the right kidney. On September 24, 1938, he had an operation to remove the right kidney, yet this brought no improvement at all. Worse still, the surgeon's prognosis was that his patient was heading towards total kidney failure and certain death. Examinations over the next four years confirmed that the TB was not only still present but had spread. The pain was now violent, and Father Chanut was often confined to bed in the infirmary. Heroically – somewhat like a candidate for beatification himself! – he would drag himself along, with great fatigue, doing his best to continue carrying out his role as novice master.

Then, in January 1943, Monsignor Catherinet, Rector of the Grand Seminary of Langres, came to the abbey to preach a retreat. On learning of the plight of Father Jean-Marie, who by that time had been suffering for nearly five years, he felt inspired to begin a novena to Elizabeth of the Trinity; and at his initiative, the whole community took part, as did many other communities as well. At the end of the nine days of prayer, Father Jean-Marie suddenly felt his energy return, and in no time was following the Trappists' austere monastic rule in its entirety. As from that very month, his medical examinations showed that the tuberculosis had completely disappeared.[16]

---

[16] My thanks to the Carmel of Dijon for sending me the 'Account of the Miracle obtained through the Intercession of Elizabeth of the Trinity for Father Jean Chanut, ocso'; this contains details of both the cure and the life of Father Chanut.

This cure looked likely to fulfil all the criteria. In medical terms, it had to be inexplicable: a healing that could not have occurred by natural means; this was all the more evident as it was a case of terminal illness, where all medical treatment had been tried and had failed. In theological terms, it had to be not only a sign of divine action but also performed by Elizabeth alone (which could not have been proved to be the case if prayers had been made to other saints at the same time). Also, it had to be in the nature of a miraculous healing that it was rapid, complete, and permanent.[17] As for its being permanent, only time would tell – which is why the cure of Father Chanut in 1943 could not be considered officially for quite a while.

Introducing the Cause

In 1953, a new Relator was appointed for Elizabeth's Cause. Cardinal Rossi had died five years earlier, and his successor was another Discalced Carmelite, Cardinal Adeodato Giovanni Piazza.[18] And with the Supplementary Process completed, a formal request could now be made to Rome for the 'Introduction of the Cause'. The Postulator would present and defend this request, and the Advocate would prepare a brief, stating the case for Elizabeth's sanctity and the reason why the Cause should be introduced. The documentation would contain an *Informatio* presenting the case, and a *Summarium* which was a summary of the depositions made by the witnesses at the Ordinary Process. Once the Promoter of the Faith had studied this and drawn up his *Animadversiones*, and the Postulator and Advocate had produced a *Responsio* to these objections, all four documents would be collated together and submitted as a *Positio* – or, to quote the English title in full, a *Position on the Introduction of the Cause*. This large volume, which could run to hundreds of pages, would then

---

[17] See Chapter 29, n. 12.

[18] For the appointments of Relators, and for the main stages of Elizabeth's Cause, see the chronology in Simeone, *Indice*, pp. 37–8. For details of the cardinals involved, I have drawn on the website http://www.catholic-hierarchy.org.

be discussed by the cardinals and official prelates of the Sacred Congregation of Rites.[19] And provided the vote was in favour, the Pope would then approve the Introduction of the Cause.

By 1956, all the documentation was ready,[20] but a delay occurred when the new Relator, Cardinal Piazza, died the following year. He was replaced, in January 1959, by a French Cardinal, André Jullien, and the case was finally discussed in Rome in October 1961. The next day, October 25, Pope John XXIII signed the 'Decree on the Introduction of the Cause'.

Before the next stage could begin, though, it had to be established that Elizabeth had never received a public cult, or else the whole Cause could be jeopardised. This investigation was no mere formality, as there is a thin dividing line between fame of sanctity and 'public' veneration. Specifically, veneration could be made by *individual members* of the public, but not *organised* publicly – by an official such as a priest or a prioress, for example.[21] And, as previously mentioned, the form of veneration must not be of the nature of honours given only to an established saint or blessed. So, people could kneel at Elizabeth's tomb, for example, but not light a candle there – one of many rules to be observed, and to be proved as having been observed.[22] However, Elizabeth passed the next hurdle, and the 'Decree of No Cult' was signed on June 22, 1962. Now at last – over thirty years since

---

[19] Until 1969, this Congregation was responsible both for regulating divine worship and for dealing with Causes for beatification and canonisation. In that year, Paul VI split them into two departments or 'dicasteries', calling the one on Causes the 'Sacred Congregation for the Causes of Saints': see his Apostolic Constitution *Sacra Rituum Congregatio* (May 8, 1969), as well as the explanation in John Paul II, *Divinus Perfectionis Magister*. A further change to the title occurred in 1985 when the word 'Sacred' was omitted from the names of Vatican Congregations: see Sheldon, p. 52, n. 6.

[20] Cf. Larkin, p. 79.

[21] Cf. Langlois, p. 65.

[22] A recent article by Claude Langlois on the Cause of Thérèse of Lisieux shows the thoroughness of the investigations in determining whether a 'Decree of No Cult' could be approved; see Appendix III: Works Consulted. A list of rules can be found in Langlois, pp. 64–5, and the probing questions to be asked of witnesses on pp. 69–71.

the Ordinary Process had opened in Dijon – it was time for the Apostolic Process to begin.

A Probing Inquiry

While the Second Vatican Council was taking place in Rome, the Apostolic Process on Elizabeth's virtues was being held in Dijon, Paris and Toulouse from 1963 to 1965.[23] As already mentioned, this stage of the proceedings was under the direct authority of the Holy See, and it was a thorough examination to probe deeply into the case for Elizabeth's heroic virtues. Questions were drawn up by the Promoter of the Faith (the 'Devil's Advocate'), and witnesses were called to answer them. About halfway through this investigation, in September 1964 instructions were received from the Vatican, allowing the Bishop of Dijon to begin a 'Process on a presumed Miracle'.[24] So, beginning that year, and running concurrently with the examination of Elizabeth's virtues, the cure of Father Jean-Marie Chanut was deliberated. It was now twenty-one years since the event, and he was still in excellent health. In fact, he had been appointed Abbot in 1963, a position involving frequent visits to affiliated Cistercian communities in France and Africa. This allowed him little time for rest and gave him many preoccupations, but his health was not at all affected.

In 1965, the examinations of the virtues and the miracle were both completed, and all the evidence was sent to Rome. The remaining stage – for the climax, though not the end (!), was now in sight – was to prepare the documentation to be discussed in the Vatican itself. The case for Elizabeth's virtues would normally have been presented by Cardinal Jullien as Relator, but he had died at the beginning of 1964 while the Apostolic Process was taking place; so in June 1966, a successor was appointed: a Spanish missionary priest, Cardinal Arcadio María Larraona Saralegui.

---

[23] Dijon (1963–1965), Paris (1963–1964) and Toulouse (1964): cf. *Acta Ordinis*, 1987, p. 11.
[24] Cf. Simeone, *Indice*, p. 37.

Meanwhile, in readiness, the dossier of Elizabeth's writings, which had been painstakingly transcribed by the four Carmelites of Dijon over thirty years earlier, was reassembled in a better order, in view of the beatification, and translated into Italian by a man with a most literary name: Dante! Entitled *Scritti*, or *Writings*, it was published in 1967; and while nothing less than a critical edition could be fully accurate, Dante's compilation nonetheless served the overall purpose of allowing a judgment to be made on Elizabeth's faith and virtues (cf. CW I, p. 42).

There was one last staging post, a juridical one, before the discussions reached the Vatican committees: to confirm that the Processes up to that point had been conducted with proper procedure. This led to the 'Decree on the Validity of the Ordinary and Apostolic Processes', issued on July 5, 1969; and it was confirmed, by another decree of that title, on March 13, 1970 once it could be established that a full examination of the writings attributed to Elizabeth had been completed by the theological censors.[25] A new decade was about to begin, together with another stage in this seemingly never-ending Cause for beatification. And yet, compared with many other Causes, Elizabeth's was not unusually slow!

A Quiet Hive of Activity

The 1970s could be characterised as a time of busy hiddenness: when nothing obvious seemed to be happening, yet a hive of activity was quietly taking place behind the scenes. It was time to prepare the important document known as the *Position on the Virtues*. Rather like the earlier *Position on the Introduction of the Cause* – both of which are often referred to simply as the *Positio* – it would contain four main parts with the same titles: the *Informatio* (a clear exposition of Elizabeth's life and virtues); the *Summarium* (a summary of the testimonies regarding these specific points); the *Animadversiones* (objections by the Promoter of the Faith); and the *Responsio* (a response to them by the

---

[25] The decree of 1970 is reproduced in *Acta Ordinis*, 1967–1970, p. 141.

Postulator and the Advocate). A few other sections would also be included, as we shall see.

On December 5, 1973, the Discalced Carmelites appointed a new Postulator General for the Order: Father Simeón Tomás Fernández, perhaps better known by his religious name of Father Simeón of the Holy Family. Formerly the long-standing librarian of the Order's theology faculty in Rome, for the last eighteen months he had been assistant to the previous Postulator General, Father John of Jesus Mary, who had held the post since 1947.[26] It was Father Simeón who would oversee Elizabeth's Cause right through to beatification.

Just two months after his appointment, the new Postulator lost no time in visiting the Dijon Carmel, both to assure the nuns of his interest in the Cause, and also to gather together documents and other pieces of information for the drawing up of the *Positio*, as well as for compiling a *Bibliography* of publications relating to Elizabeth. This second document would also be needed for the Cause – as the number of editions and translations of her works, for example, would be more evidence of her influence and fame of sanctity. Father Simeón completed it that same year, when it was also published.[27]

The following year, 1975, the main sections of the *Positio* were completed. In April, the Advocate finished the *Summarium*, the most fundamental part of the *Positio*, bringing together the main testimonies and documents from the Processes on Elizabeth's virtues; and in June, the *Tabella* or *Index* of the testimonies was ready. In October, the Advocate and Postulator jointly produced the *Informatio*, presenting Elizabeth and her Cause, and petitioning the Holy See for her heroic virtues to be proclaimed. Also to be included was a study, in Italian, on Elizabeth's life and spiritual experience by the archivist of the Order, Father Valentino Macca. It was entitled, *Elizabeth of the*

---

[26] See *ibid.*, 1973–1974, p. 196; also, on Father Simeón's appointment in May 1972 as Vice-Postulator, see *ibid.*, 1971–1973, p. 190.

[27] For an account of the work that took place in preparing the documents from 1974 to 1979, see *Acta Postulationis*, pp. 158–62.

Trinity, an Experience of Grace in the Heart of the Church,[28] and copies
reached the Postulator at the beginning of April. The very next
month, all four sections were collated into the provisional *Positio*,
and the large document was sent to Rome so that the Promoter
of the Faith could begin producing his objections – without
which (and without the corresponding response), the document
would be incomplete.

After this marathon of about two years' solid work, in July
1976 Fathers Simeón and Valentino paid a three-day visit to the
Carmel of Dijon, to inform the nuns, the Bishop, and friends of
Elizabeth who were still alive, about the progress of the Cause.
It must have been most encouraging for them to know that
things really were moving. Indeed, the 'Devil's Advocate' would
spend an entire year, from the summer of 1977 to August 1978,
studying the *Positio* and formulating thirty-six pages of objections! Six months later, on February 18, 1979, the Postulator
and Advocate completed eighty-eight pages of a 'Response'! This
written exchange was appended to the first four documents,
which meant that the *Position on the Virtues* was finally complete.
Copies were sent for discussion to the Sacred Congregation for
the Causes of Saints, and yet another decade was ending – and
beginning. This time, the change of decade marked a special
anniversary, and the Order waited in anticipation for a successful outcome: 'If only this could happen before 1980, by the first
centenary of [her] birth', ran an entry in the chronicles of the
Postulator's department.[29]

The First Centenary

The celebrations began on November 25, 1979 and lasted
a whole calendar year. But firstly, a major change had taken
place: a few months earlier, the Carmelite nuns had moved. The
Boulevard Carnot, so quiet in Elizabeth's day, had become a
noisy, overpopulated quarter of a busy modern city. So the hard

---

[28] Cf. *ibid.*, p. 160.
[29] Cf. *ibid.*, p. 162.

and very sad decision had been taken to leave that monastery, rich in tradition and in memories of Elizabeth, and to move to a new one on the outskirts of Dijon.

Already in January 1978, Father Simeón, having learnt of this plan, had paid his third visit to the Boulevard Carnot, staying there for six days. He had been accompanied by Father Girolamo Salvatico, director of the Italian review *The Messenger of the Holy Infant of Prague*, as he had great expertise in photography. Father Girolamo now took colour photographs of all the places and objects associated with Elizabeth in the monastery and in the convent church and garden, so as to create a visual historical record.

So, when the centenary celebrations began at the end of 1979, the nuns were already in the new convent, on a hill about eight miles south-west of Dijon near the village of Flavignerot. The new monastery would be described by the community as 'beautiful and simple, half-hidden in the woods and enveloped in an extraordinary silence'.[30] But while the buildings were hidden away, the events for Elizabeth's anniversary were high-profile. The opening Mass of the centenary, held in the new convent, was televised and presided over by the Bishop of Dijon. It would again be Monsignor Decourtray who would close the centenary year, giving the last in a series of talks,[31] many of which took place in the prestigious Palace of the Dukes of Burgundy – where Bishop Gaidon of Paray-le-Monial also gave a piano recital, accompanied with readings from Elizabeth's works.

---

[30] In *Mount Carmel*, vol. 32/4, 1984, p. 248.

[31] See Decourtray, *Présence d'Élisabeth de la Trinité* [*The Presence of Elizabeth of the Trinity*]; the Bishop could not read it aloud himself, having been completely mute since September 1980, following an operation for cancer of the vocal cords. On the very day of the lecture – the closing of the centenary – his voice began to return, which was seen as a sign of Elizabeth's intercession: see the account by Marie-Michelle, OCD, in Clapier (ed.), p. 797. The lecture is also reproduced in *Carmel*, nos. 22–23, 1981, pp. 11–43. For his pastoral letter (dated November 9, 1979), opening the centenary, see Decourtray, *Élisabeth de la Trinité: Un Prophète de Dieu pour notre temps* [*Elizabeth of the Trinity: A Prophet of God for Our Times*].

Two other things happened during the centenary year, quietly advancing Elizabeth's Cause. On August 17, 1980, Father Chanut died in Africa at the age of seventy-one, having never had a relapse from the tuberculosis. This proved, beyond the shadow of a doubt, that the cure through Elizabeth's intercession had been permanent. Also, just before the celebratory year was over, another decree was issued on Elizabeth's writings: this time, that of November 7, 1980 on writings which had been 'recently discovered'. The centenary ended in style, but unfortunately the cure of Father Chanut could not yet be taken any further. This was possibly because it was normal practice for the virtues to be discussed in Rome before the miracles, but also because two miracles were needed for beatification and were considered together at the Vatican committees. So it appears that there was nothing to do except wait and pray for a second miracle.[32]

The next year, 1981, came and went. Or rather, it had almost disappeared when, in November, things started moving again – and for once, they moved fairly rapidly. In fact, the success of the Cause for beatification was not far off. It was actually closer than anyone could realise.

'Venerable Elizabeth of the Trinity'

In the Vatican, on November 24, 1981, there took place the 'Particular Congress of Theologians on the Virtues'.[33] This was

---

[32] While there was evidence of earlier cures, as recounted in the Appendix to the *Souvenirs*, for example (cf. S2, pp. 455–77), that of Father Chanut appears to have been the only one which had been considered as fulfilling all the criteria, as this was the cure selected for investigation when in 1964 the Vatican had given permission to open a 'Process on a presumed Miracle': cf. Simeone, *Indice*, p. 37. Note, however, that other healings which suggested Elizabeth's intercession had also been discussed at the diocesan tribunal as they are alluded to in later Vatican documents: cf. *Acta Ordinis*, 1967–1970, p. 141; *ibid.*, 1984, p. 45.

[33] For most of the twentieth century, and according to the 1917 *Code of Canon Law*, the virtues were discussed at three Vatican committees known as 'Congregations', which were called the 'Antepreparatory', 'Preparatory' and 'General': see Molinari, p. 58. Following the reforms of Paul VI, these were

a meeting of one official prelate and six consultors to discuss the *Position on the Virtues* and to vote on whether Elizabeth had practised all the virtues to a heroic degree. At this point, it is worth noting the meaning of the phrase 'heroic virtues'. As all Christians are called to practise the virtues, the criterion for a candidate for beatification is that they have been practised to a 'heroic' or exceptional degree. Regarding the word 'virtues' in the plural, it denotes the three theological virtues (faith, hope and charity) and the four cardinal virtues (prudence, justice, temperance and fortitude). These virtues had been a specific focus of the diocesan tribunals.[34]

The vote on Elizabeth's virtues was positive, and the case went forward to be considered at the 'Plenary Congregation of Cardinals on the Virtues'. Firstly, though, on December 4, Cardinal Mario Luigi Ciappi, a Dominican, was appointed as Relator since his predecessor had died eight years earlier. The Plenary Congregation was held on April 6, 1982, and the cardinals voted unanimously in favour. Finally, the 'Decree on the Heroic Virtues' was read in the presence of Pope John Paul II who then promulgated it. This was on July 12, 1982. From now on, Elizabeth could be called 'Venerable' – a title which indicated that her heroic virtues had been proved, but that she was still awaiting approval of miracles for beatification.[35]

---

reduced to two – the 'Particular Congress' and the 'Plenary Congregation': see Simeone, *Indice*, pp. 40–1. In 1983, John Paul II changed the name of the second one to the 'Ordinary Congregation': see *ibid.*, p. 130.

[34] See, for example, the extracts from the depositions given on Thérèse at the Ordinary Process, in Christopher O'Mahony (ed. & tr.), *St Thérèse of Lisieux by those who knew her: Testimonies from the Process of Beatification*, Dublin: Veritas, 1975. As explained in this work, questions to the witnesses concerning the virtues were generally arranged under the headings of the seven just listed, with 'charity' divided into 'love of God' and 'love of neighbour'; also included were the 'evangelical counsels': 'poverty', 'chastity' and 'obedience', together with 'humility' (cf. pp. 14–16).

[35] There are, however, some exceptions to this: before the rescript of Pope Pius X of August 26, 1913, this title could be applied to a candidate after the decree formally introducing his or her Cause. Hence, the 'Venerable Anne of Jesus': cf. Simeone, *Indice*, p. 10.

In describing a legal document, which this decree undoubtedly is, one would not normally expect to apply to it the word
'beautiful'.[36] But everything is touched with beauty when coming
into contact with Elizabeth and her writings. And as the decree
gives an overview of her life and message, it cannot help but
convey the beauty of her spirituality. It opens with her much-
loved verse from John's Gospel on the indwelling presence of
God (Jn 14:23), then evokes her contemplation of and communion with the Trinity; her life as a praise of God's glory and in
the image of Christ; her search for, and adoration and love of
God; and her help to the Church through her prayers, works
and self-sacrifice while 'carrying her universal brothers in her
heart with maternal love'.[37]

Next, there is a brief account of her life, though still very
beautiful and deeply spiritual – as when the document describes
her at worldly gatherings as having 'turned her eyes full of spiritual joy to God, to whom she was singing in her heart'.[38] The
short biography is then followed by an overview of the main
aspects of Elizabeth's charism, and this section stands very much
as a complement to the evocation of points in the opening of the
document. Mentioned this time are: her meditation of Scripture,
especially St Paul; her love of Mary; her contemplation of God's
word; her hope of being transformed into Christ through the
cross; her great love of Christ and the Church which she proved
by her works; her following of the will of God; her contemplation of the divine face; her influence in drawing innumerable
Christians to intimacy with the Trinity.[39]

After this, comes a summary of the stages of her Cause
for beatification, beginning with the opening of the Ordinary
Process in 1931, and ending with the formal statement of
Elizabeth's heroic virtues. The formula is all-embracing: that
she practised the theological virtues of faith, hope and charity,

---

[36] For the full text of the decree, see *Acta Ordinis*, 1982, pp. 70–4.
[37] Cf. *ibid.*, p. 70.
[38] Cf. *ibid.*, p. 71.
[39] Cf. *ibid.*, p. 72.

both to God and to her neighbour; also, the cardinal virtues of prudence, justice, temperance and fortitude; and finally, that she practised all these virtues to a heroic degree, both in her deeds and in her dispositions.[40]

'At last!'

This major milestone had been reached: Elizabeth's heroic virtues had now been proved. Yet there was still the long wait for a second miracle before she could be considered for beatification. Then, in 1983, a change in Vatican procedure proved to be virtually a miracle in itself. On January 25 of that year, John Paul II published his Apostolic Constitution *Divinus Perfectionis Magister* (*Divine Teacher of Perfection*), which simplified the over-lengthy procedures for Causes. And one of the effects of his reforms was that only one miracle was needed for beatification![41] Crucially, too, the document made clear that Causes already pending could now proceed according to the new rules.

Almost immediately, the cure of Father Chanut, which had already been investigated in Dijon, was presented to the relevant Vatican committees. Firstly, to the 'Medical Council on the Miracle' on June 10, 1983. This was made up of doctors who had the task of determining whether the healing was indeed of

---

[40] Cf. *ibid.*, p. 74.

[41] Or none, in the case of a martyr, as the requirement is waived: cf. Keeffe, p. 44; also, only one additional miracle was now required for canonisation. The most far-reaching changes (although these particular ones came too late for Elizabeth's own Cause) concerned the procedure for proving heroic virtues. Much of the juridical aspect was now omitted, as proving the virtues would henceforth depend in great part on a long, critical biography using historical methods in place of the long-running objections and responses on the part of lawyers: see the discussion of the changes, in Woodward, pp. 90–9 & 223–8. The reorganising and renaming of the Ordinary and Apostolic Processes have been referred to earlier: see n. 4 above. Possibly the best account of all the changes can be found in *Divinus Perfectionis Magister*, in which John Paul II also summarises the reforms of his predecessors; see, too, the norms which implement it: Sacred Congregation for the Causes of Saints, *Norms to be Observed in Inquiries made by Bishops in the Causes of Saints* (February 7, 1983).

supernatural character, inexplicable by human standards. As the vote was in favour, the case progressed to the next stage: to the 'Particular Congress of Theologians on the Miracle'. They met on November 29, and their task was to discern whether the healing had taken place by divine action, and also through the intercession of Elizabeth. Another positive decision was given, and the miracle passed through to the third and final stage of discussion. This, the 'Ordinary Congregation of Cardinals and Bishops on the Miracle', took place on January 24, 1984, and again the vote was in the affirmative. Finally, on February 17, 1984, the 'Decree on the Miracle' was read in the presence of the Pope who promulgated it.[42] Naturally, this text concentrated on the miraculous healing of Father Chanut, but it also acknowledged the existence of other cures indicating Elizabeth's intercession. The decree concluded with the formal declaration on the miracle. It asserted 'the rapid, complete and permanent cure of Father Jean-Marie Chanut from tuberculosis of the right kidney, in a subject affected with advanced Potts' Disease'.[43]

And now, almost a century after Elizabeth had died, there came the final stage – the end of what must have seemed like the labours of Hercules! For the beatification to go ahead and a date to be set, there was one final meeting of the cardinals in the presence of the Pope. He himself would determine 'whether it is possible safely to proceed to the beatification of the Servant of God'.[44] On Tuesday, February 21, 1984, four days after the Decree on the Miracle, Father Simeón received notification from the Vatican's Secretariat of State that 'the Holy Father

---

[42] See the full text of the decree, in *Acta Ordinis*, 1984, pp. 44–6. This decree, like that on the heroic virtues, was signed by the Prefect of the Congregation for the Causes of Saints, Cardinal Pietro Palazzini; the role of the Pope at this stage was to approve it and order its publication.

[43] Cf. *ibid.*, p. 46.

[44] Cf. Molinari, p. 59. Sometimes, even though a Cause had reached this final stage, beatification was considered 'inopportune' at the time – in the case of a controversial figure, for example, or a martyr who had died at the hands of a Government still in power: cf. Woodward, p. 85.

had decided to proceed with the beatification on November 25, the solemnity of Christ the King'.[45] The news was immediately relayed to the General of the Order, Father Felipe Sáinz de Baranda, who exclaimed: 'Elizabeth: at last! We've been waiting for that...!'[46]

---

[45] Cf. *SIC*, vol. XVII, no. 3, 1984, p. 41.
[46] In De Meester, 'Een grote Vreugde' ['A Great Joy'], p. 265.

Chapter 31

'JOY OF THE WHOLE CHURCH'

Precious Relics

Up until now, the story of Elizabeth's path towards beatification has been a seemingly unending round of documents, bureaucracy and committees – like a black and white film where all the main characters, so to speak, take the form of dossiers, paper and ink! But with the beatification itself, all that changes – and with an infusion of colour, the paperwork gives way to excited gatherings, moving ceremonies, and explosions of joy.

But firstly, an episode two months before the great event brings us back full circle to the beginning of Elizabeth's Cause for beatification. As we recall, the first signs that something was happening was the opening of her tomb, presided over by the then Bishop of Dijon, on October 10, 1930. That was seven months before the Ordinary Process was officially opened. And now, on September 10, 1984, two months before her beatification in Rome, a parallel ceremony took place.

At the first exhumation, there had been two purposes: to identify Elizabeth's remains, and to preserve them more securely in a robust coffin. This time, there were again two purposes: the first was the identification of the remains, which was a necessary stage before a person was beatified;[1] but the second was their removal, known as their 'translation', for they would soon be kept in a shrine in her former parish church of St Michael's. Already at the beginning of the year – just four days after the miracle had been approved by the Cardinals and Bishops – permission had been received from Rome to do

---

[1] Cf. Woodward, p. 83.

this.[2] The remains, though, could not be venerated publicly until after the beatification – when, at long last, the rules of 'no cult' would no longer apply!

While the people present at the exhumation in 1930 were mostly locals who had spontaneously gathered to pay their respects, in 1984 there was a prominent presence of civil and religious authorities: the former were represented by a deputy mayor and a high-ranking police officer; the latter included Bishop Jean Balland of Dijon, Carmelite friars from Paris and Rome, and some of the Carmelite nuns from the monastery of Flavignerot. Mother Germaine had once paid tribute to the 'discreet hands' which were continually placing white flowers on Elizabeth's tomb, and she had mentioned the 'touching inscriptions' (S2, p. 299) left there. Now, in 1984, one of the prayers was equally touching: Bishop Balland prayed for 'those innumerable families of poor and anonymous people who have not ceased to place flowers on this tomb'.[3]

After the opening prayers, and the lifting up of Elizabeth's coffin from the ground, the civil authorities handed it to their religious counterparts. Three urns were to be filled with her remains – these most precious relics. The main urn was destined, as mentioned, for St Michael's Church in Dijon; the second one would go to the Carmel at Flavignerot; and the third would be taken to St Peter's Basilica in Rome.[4]

At the Side of the King

It was here, inside the Basilica – rather than in St Peter's Square, more suited for warmer weather! – that Elizabeth would be beatified on November 25, 1984. By a curious coincidence, that same

---

[2] For the Decree granting permission, dated January 28, 1984, see *Acta Ordinis*, 1984, p. 53. In fact, in 1965, the year when the Apostolic Process was completed, the remains had, then also, been identified in view of a future beatification: cf. Huvet, p. 151; Rémy, *Guite*, p. 107.

[3] Quoted in Huvet, p. 152.

[4] See *ibid.*, p. 152. Most of the remains would be kept at St Michael's, with one relic at the Carmel: see http://www.saint-michel-dijon.com/elisabeth-trinite/vie/.

date had been chosen to begin her centenary year in 1979, which in that year had been the Sunday of Christ the King. Now, five years later, and thanks to two leap years in-between, Elizabeth was to be beatified on the same date and the same feast. And as we shall see, her beatification would, to some extent, be presented by the Pope within the framework of this feast. Instituted by Pius XI in 1925, to counteract the growing secularism and atheism of his time, the 'Feast of Christ the King' – the last Sunday of the liturgical year, bringing it to completion – affirms Christ's sovereignty over the whole universe. It also shows him to be the Redeemer King, paradoxically obtaining his kingship by the shedding of his blood (cf. Lk 23:35–43).[5]

There is no doubt that Elizabeth would have been delighted with the choice of this feast. For wherever Christ was to be found, Elizabeth as his bride was with him – and as her illness had progressed, she had in fact seen herself more and more as the 'queen' who was walking the path to Calvary at the side of her suffering King. 'The queen stood at your right hand' (Ps 44:10; cf. LR 13). Elizabeth had commented on these words from the Psalm, when racked with pain during her last retreat: 'such is the attitude of this soul [who shares in His work of redemption]; she walks the way of Calvary at the right of the crucified, annihilated, humiliated King' (LR 13). When Elizabeth contemplated Jesus on his way to the Cross, she saw his courageous, silent dignity in suffering, and she aspired to emulate it. 'My Master,' she had said in the painful last months of her illness, 'asks me to go to my passion with the majesty of a queen' (ESS, p. 40). So, for Elizabeth, to be the queen by the side of the King was nothing other than to be the bride of Christ – occupying a privileged place by his side, where she would 'draw numerous graces from His Heart' (ESS, p. 41). And these graces – as seen so often from records of her posthumous influence – are mostly concerned with how she drew people towards God and

---

[5] See W J O'Shea, 'Feast of Christ the King', in *New Catholic Encyclopedia*, vol. III, 1967, p. 627. The passage from Luke's Gospel is read at Mass on the feast in Year C of the Church's liturgy.

the interior life.[6] In fact, this too was linked with how Elizabeth understood God's kingdom: for she had always thrilled to these words in Luke's Gospel, 'The kingdom of God is within you' (Lk 17:21; cf. HF 3), which she saw as a statement of the presence of God within the soul.[7]

Among Saints and Blesseds

Two other people were to be beatified with Elizabeth, both of them priests from religious congregations. One was Joseph Manyanet y Vives from Catalonia who was born in 1833 and died in 1901, the year Elizabeth entered Carmel. He was outstanding for his ministry to families and founded two religious congregations, one for men and one for women: the Sons, and the Missionary Daughters, of the Holy Family. Like Elizabeth, he had been declared 'Venerable' in 1982; more recently, he was canonised on May 16, 2004.

The other person had special links to Carmel, especially to Thérèse of Lisieux. Daniel Brottier, born in 1876, was a French missionary priest from the Congregation of the Fathers of the Holy Spirit. Sent first to Senegal, he conducted a fundraising campaign to build a cathedral in Dakar. Then, when the First World War broke out, while he was not enlisted due to poor health, he nonetheless volunteered to be a chaplain on the battlefield, and he positioned himself at the front line so as to help those who were suffering most or dying. Awarded the Legion of Honour for his bravery, he attributed his survival – during fifty-two perilous months – to the intercession of his beloved St

---

[6] There are passages on Elizabeth's posthumous spiritual influence in S2, pp. 269–307; also, in Vatican documents such as the Decree on the Heroic Virtues (cf. *Acta Ordinis*, 1982, pp. 72–3), and, as we shall see, the Apostolic Letter on Elizabeth (cf. *ibid.*, 1987, p. 11).

[7] The impact of these words on Elizabeth may first have come to her through reading a passage near the opening of *The Spiritual Canticle* (SC 1:7), where they are quoted by John of the Cross in connection with God's indwelling in the soul. These same words would later be quoted by John Paul II when writing of Elizabeth in his Apostolic Letter: see the discussion later in this chapter.

Thérèse. And it was under her protection that he placed his next project, for which he is perhaps best known of all: the orphanage in Paris, known as the Orphan Apprentices of Auteuil, which he expanded tenfold and where he worked tirelessly for the welfare of the orphans. It was there that he built a chapel for Thérèse when she was canonised, the first place of worship ever dedicated to her, and her picture appears just above his own in the official portrait of him for the beatification.[8]

Of the three candidates, though, it was Elizabeth who held a special place in the heart of Pope John Paul II who would preside over the ceremony. As it happens, his visit to France in 1980 coincided with her centenary year. On June 1, in his homily at a Mass held at Le Bourget near Paris, he addressed the people of France and listed those 'sons and daughters of your nation' who, he said, had exerted 'the greatest influence on my life'. It would have come as no surprise to many when he mentioned such famous saints as François de Sales, Vincent de Paul, Louis-Marie Grignion de Montfort and Jean-Marie Vianney. But suddenly, came the name: 'Sr Elizabeth of the Trinity'. On hearing this, Albert Decourtray, who at the time was Bishop of Dijon, was – to use his own word – 'stupefied'.[9] Yes, he himself was a great admirer of Elizabeth. But he had had no idea that her influence extended to the Pope himself!

The previous day, John Paul II had addressed a meeting of women religious at the Rue du Bac in the heart of Paris. This was where the Virgin Mary had appeared in 1830 and revealed the Miraculous Medal. Urging the sisters to 'follow Christ', he offered them the example of Elizabeth who had wished to be 'another humanity' for Christ. On October 11 of that year, in Rome, the

---

[8] See Ufficio per le Cerimonie Pontificie, p. 15. Details of the life of Joseph Manyanet y Vives and Daniel Brottier are taken from this official booklet, used at the beatification ceremony (cf. pp. 5–21), and from the website http://en.wikipedia.org/wiki/Daniel_Brottier.

[9] See Decourtray, *Présence d'Élisabeth de la Trinité*, p. 4, a lecture reproduced in *Carmel*, nos. 22–23, 1981 (cf. p. 11); the passage is also quoted by Marie-Michelle, OCD, in Clapier (ed.), p. 798. The names listed by the Pope are given in *SIC*, vol. XVII, no. 3, 1984, p. 42.

Pope would address the major superiors of women's congregations based in Italy. To them he again spoke of Elizabeth, and
quoted from one of her letters (cf. L 122), so giving a brief but
powerful synthesis of her message: to treat God as a friend, to
strive for a living faith, and to recognise that heaven is within
us because, as she had written, 'heaven is God and God is in my
soul'. Elizabeth had called this her 'secret', one that she wanted
to convey to others; and, the Pope added: 'You, also, should
live this secret and proclaim it to families... It is a secret that
illuminates, strengthens and saves.' Two years later, speaking in
Segovia on November 4, 1982, John Paul II referred to Elizabeth
as one of 'the most outstanding sons and daughters of Carmel'.[10]

The Mass of Beatification

It was now four years since the Pope's visit to France, and he was
almost certainly delighted that Elizabeth could now be beatified.
The ceremony took place in the morning, and St Peter's Basilica
was a magnificent sight, as always for such an event. All eyes were
on the centre: the large main altar, framed by the four curved
Bernini columns, which was ready for the celebration of Mass
by John Paul II and fourteen prelates and priests. Among them,
the most significant names were those of the prelates representing their own blesseds: Cardinal Arnau of Barcelona, Cardinal
Lustiger of Paris, and Bishop Balland of Dijon. Also invited were
a number of Carmelite priests, including Conrad De Meester,
who was already rightly considered *the* authority on Elizabeth,
as his critical edition of her works had appeared around four
years earlier.[11]

The procession of priests made their way to the main altar,
and the Mass began with the opening hymns and prayers, the

---

[10] The quotations from these three talks given by John Paul II are in *ibid.*,
p. 42.
[11] For accounts of Elizabeth's beatification ceremony, I have drawn on Ufficio
per le Cerimonie Pontificie, pp. 43–115; *Acta Ordinis*, 1984, pp. 15–18; Huvet,
pp. 152–4; and an article by Madame Jean Dardau, in *Carmel*, no. 40, 1985,
pp. 276–9.

Confiteor and the *Kyrie*. But instead of the *Gloria* coming next, there now took place the Rite of Beatification itself. It fell into three parts, the first being the request. This was where the prelates from the relevant dioceses formally requested that the Pope beatify the candidates. Bishop Balland stepped forward with Father Simeón, the Postulator of Elizabeth's Cause, as well as their counterparts representing the other two candidates. Cardinal Arnau, speaking on behalf of all three, read out the petition: 'Most holy Father: the Bishops of Barcelona, of Paris and of Dijon humbly ask Your Holiness to enrol the Venerable Servants of God, Joseph Manyanet, Daniel Brottier and Elizabeth of the Trinity, among the Blessed.'[12]

At this point, each of the three prelates read out a short summary of the life of his own particular candidate. In a voice that was audibly moved, Bishop Balland spoke of Elizabeth and said why the diocese of Dijon desired that she be beatified: 'Humble and simple, Elizabeth Catez fully lived adoration in spirit and truth. She reached the highest summits of perfect charity and we believe that her beatification will help her fulfil her promise to take care, from heaven, of the souls who do not yet know themselves dwelt in by the love of the Trinity.'[13]

As soon as the formal request had been made, everyone stood up. All except for the Pope, who alone remained seated. He now replied with the 'Formula of Beatification': 'Acceding to the request of our brothers Narcís Jubany Arnau, Archbishop of Barcelona, Jean-Marie Lustiger, Archbishop of Paris, Jean Balland, Bishop of Dijon, and also of many of our other brothers in the Episcopate, and of many of the faithful, after consultation with the Sacred Congregation for the Causes of Saints, by Our Apostolic Authority we declare that the Venerable Servants of God, Joseph Manyanet, Daniel Brottier and Elizabeth of the Trinity, may henceforth be called Blessed, and that their feast

---

[12] Cf. Ufficio per le Cerimonie Pontificie, p. 53. As can be seen, Elizabeth was the only candidate not referred to by her surname, so much was she identified with the Trinity.

[13] Quoted in Huvet, p. 153.

may be celebrated every year, on the day of their birth in heaven: on December 17 for Joseph Manyanet, on February 23 for Daniel Brottier, and on November 9 for Elizabeth of the Trinity, in the places and according to the norms juridically laid down. In the name of the Father, and of the Son, and of the Holy Spirit.'[14]

As from this very moment, the three Venerables were officially 'Blessed', and the whole assembly acclaimed them by singing an 'Amen'. Immediately, three veils which had been suspended at the front of the Basilica were lifted up, revealing behind them a large banner, each depicting one of the new blesseds. While those of the two priests faced out towards the people, that of Elizabeth was facing the main altar. It was a picture showing her in full Carmelite habit and white mantle, next to a building that was recognisably the monastery of the Boulevard Carnot in Dijon; she was depicted standing on a globe representing the earth, while her head was within a cloud in which could be seen the three Persons of the Trinity, towards whom she was gazing. In the bottom right-hand corner were the words: 'IN LAUDEM GLORIAE'. Her image would be constantly before the eyes of the Pope as he continued with the celebration of Mass.[15]

Firstly, though, it is worth noting the meaning of the 'places and...norms juridically laid down'. This formula determines the nature of the veneration given to someone who has been beatified but not yet canonised: the 'places' are restricted to a specified city, diocese, region, nation or religious institute (whereas a saint is venerated throughout the universal Church); and the 'norms' refer to a Mass liturgy and Proper Office in the person's honour.[16] As for Elizabeth's appointed feast day, the 'day of her birth in heaven': November 9 coincided with the great feast of

---

[14] Cf. Ufficio per le Cerimonie Pontificie, pp. 54–5.

[15] For a photograph of the banner, see Furdzic (ed.), p. 157.

[16] For these details, see A E Green, 'Beatification', in *New Catholic Encyclopedia*, vol. II, 1967, p. 193, and Molinari, p. 59. In addition, veneration of a blessed is only permitted, whereas for a saint it is commanded: see A E Green, 'Canonization of Saints (Theological Aspect)', in *New Catholic Encyclopedia*, vol. III, 1967, p. 61.

the Dedication of the Lateran Basilica; so the nearest free day would subsequently be chosen, which is why Elizabeth is celebrated by the Carmelites on November 8.[17]

The request had been made, and the Pope had responded by beatifying the candidates. All that remained was for Cardinal Arnau, again speaking in the name of the three prelates, to give his formal vote of thanks: 'Most holy Father: the Bishops of Barcelona, Paris and Dijon give heartfelt thanks to Your Holiness for having today conferred the title of Blessed on the Venerable Servants of God Joseph Manyanet, Daniel Brottier and Elizabeth of the Trinity.'[18] The Pope then intoned the *Gloria*, and the liturgy continued – this Mass representing the first act of veneration towards the new blesseds.[19]

In 1984, the readings were taken from Year A of the three-year cycle of the Church's liturgy. While Year B lays the stress on Christ's universal kingdom, and Year C on the King on Calvary, the readings on the day of the beatification focused in particular on God as the Shepherd King (cf. Ez 34:11–12.15–17) and also on the last judgment (cf. Mt 25:31–46). So we might wonder what John Paul II would choose to comment on in that part of his homily devoted to the Sunday of Christ the King, which would be the framework for his presentation of the new blesseds. Would he take the Old Testament reading – and speak of Christ as the Shepherd who saves his sheep? Or the Gospel reading – and focus on the end of time when the sheep are separated from the goats? We cannot help recalling the terrifying talk Elizabeth had heard on the last judgment during the Mission to Dijon! Instead, John Paul II highlighted a phrase from the second reading (1Cor 15:20–26.28), which would have delighted Elizabeth because it came from St Paul: 'those who belong to Christ' (1Cor 15:23). In his introductory words, given in Italian, he described the three blesseds as those whose lives had clearly

---

[17] Cf. *Carmelite Missal*, pp. 99–100 & 346–8; *Discalced Carmelite Proper Offices*, pp. 211–13.

[18] Cf. Ufficio per le Cerimonie Pontificie, p. 56.

[19] Cf. Molinari, p. 59.

been a 'sign of belonging to Christ'.[20] He then spoke of each of them in turn, using their respective languages.

The Words of the Pope

The part of the homily devoted to Elizabeth is a small master-piece in itself: brilliantly concise, and flooded with richness and beauty.[21] In five brief paragraphs, which exude a genuine enthusiasm for Elizabeth, John Paul II conveyed what it is that makes her so memorable and her message so inspiring. Imbued with her own spirit, he focused on love and especially on being loved; on Elizabeth's self-giving; on a complete openness to Scripture; and on the great influence of her message.

The Pope began by recalling Elizabeth's *abundant gifts*. He mentioned her intelligence and sensitivity, her musical accomplishment, her capacity for friendship, and even her delicacy of affection. He spoke, too, of how she blossomed 'in the silence of contemplation'. And, as if capturing a picture of her in action, he described her as 'radiant with the happiness of a total forgetfulness of self'. Evoking her openness to God, he showed this gifted person welcoming 'without reserve…the gift of God' as well as the sacraments: those of baptism, of reconciliation, and of the Eucharist. But both the first and the last sentences of this paragraph contain the most essential statements of all: 'Elizabeth of the Trinity had a profound experience of the presence of God'; and: 'To an exceptional degree, she was aware of the communion offered to every creature by the Lord'. The point being made here was that any person who is completely

---

[20] In *Acta Ordinis*, 1984, p. 17.

[21] The section of the homily relevant to Elizabeth – as well as the Pope's addresses about her the next day – are published together in *Acta Ordinis*, 1984, pp. 17–20. They were translated into French by Father Conrad, who also included his own commentary on them (cf. *Carmel*, no. 40, 1985, pp. 272–5), and his whole article was subsequently translated into English: see De Meester, 'Elizabeth in the Words of the Pope'. In the English translation, which is the one quoted here (with one small amendment), the homily itself is on pp. 18–19, the speech to French pilgrims on p. 19, and the address to Carmelite visitors on pp. 19–20.

open to God, and aware of his presence through a lively faith, can be totally permeated by him.

In the next paragraph, John Paul II depicted Elizabeth as *a witness to love*. Almost feeling the need to justify himself, he said: 'We dare, today, to present to the world this cloistered religious' – doubtless because the world and the cloister might at first sight seem like opposites. He then immediately explained the reason for presenting her to the world: because she is a 'witness'. He would use this word twice more about Elizabeth – once more in the homily, and once in a speech he would give the next day. Referring, at this point, to a passage much loved by Elizabeth from the Letter to the Ephesians, he specified: 'she is a brilliant witness to the joy of being rooted and grounded in love' (cf. Eph 3:17). And in lyrical language, he commented that she 'celebrated the splendour of God', for she was aware of 'the reality of love that is infinitely alive' – the reality, he explained, that she recognised in the Father, Son and Holy Spirit dwelling in her inmost self.

The Pope then passed onto Elizabeth's *suffering*. He began by suggesting how closely we can relate to her: for, he said, 'Elizabeth, too, was no stranger to physical and mental suffering.' Here, he spoke of her union with Christ crucified, and again we see the theme of unreserved self-giving: 'she offered herself totally'. At the same time, he stressed the primacy of love – love both given and received: she was, said John Paul II, 'always sure of being loved and of being able to love'. And he completed this point with powerful words: 'In peace, she made the gift of her wounded life.'

The homily then moved onto Elizabeth's *outreach to others today*. The people most in need of her help, he said, were: 'our disorientated humanity which no longer knows how to find God or which disfigures him, which searches for a word on which to found its hope'. This 'word', explained the Pope, is the 'Word of God', on which Elizabeth nourished herself in her thoughts, her prayer, and her life. Moreover, he said, she 'gives the witness of a perfect openness' to the Word of God. As we can see, the

Pope was directing his focus to this essential characteristic of Elizabeth: a person *totally open*, who put up no barriers to God's action. And this is why her reflection and prayer were 'truly nourished' by Scripture – 'to the point that she found in it all her reasons for living and for consecrating herself to the praise of his glory'.

Finally, John Paul II showed that Elizabeth was *a natural teacher*: 'this contemplative,' he said, 'far from being isolated, knew how to communicate to her sisters, and to those close to her, the riches of her mystical experience.' Her message, he said, was today spreading rapidly – 'with a prophetic force'. He then called to mind the potential field of her influence: he hoped that she would 'inspire and sustain the whole family of Carmel'; and that she would 'help many men and women, in secular life or consecrated life'. And the help he envisaged, echoing one of her memorable letters to the seminarian André Chevignard, was that people might 'receive and share the "waves of infinite charity" which she gathered up "at the Fountain of Life"' (cf. L 191). With these words, he concluded the part of the homily devoted to Elizabeth.

The Mass now continued. Of particular note is that, at the offering of the gifts, two religious sisters came up towards the Pope, bearing a chasuble: these were in fact Guite's two daughters in the Dominican Order, Chantal and Geneviève Chevignard. They had at last seen their famous aunt beatified.

When the Mass ended, there was a rush to find a place in St Peter's Square, and in no time there was almost nowhere left to stand. All eyes were fixed on the window where John Paul II would appear and lead the Angelus prayers. Banners depicting the new blesseds were displayed on the façade of the Basilica, with Elizabeth's – a full-length photograph of her in habit and white mantle – descending from the balcony of the central loggia.[22] While the crowds were looking on, the Pope

---

[22] For a photograph of the façade of the Basilica showing the three banners, see De Meester (ed.), *La Giovinezza di una Santa*, p. 31.

appeared and was greeted with prolonged applause. In a brief address, he once more linked the beatifications and the feast of Christ the King: the three blesseds, he said, were 'members of [Christ's] Kingdom, from which no one will take them away.'[23]

'She helps us in our turn'

A prominent place in the Vatican is the Nervi Hall, also known as the Paul VI Hall – the great hall of papal audiences with its impressive large statue of the Risen Christ. It was here, at eleven o'clock on the Monday morning, that John Paul II greeted pilgrims who had come to Rome for the beatifications, and gave some short speeches of only a few lines. Speaking to the French visitors in their own language, he gave an address on Elizabeth which contained the main points of his beatification homily, and as such it is a miniature gem. It is quoted here in full:

> Yesterday we celebrated Blessed Elizabeth of the Trinity. It is striking that, when very young, in a secular life similar to that of her many friends, she had a very strong experience of the presence of God within her, of the greatness of the love of God. In Carmel, she offered her life totally, even in harsh trials, while radiating around her the happiness of being loved by God and of being dwelt in by the divine persons whom she loved to call, in a familiar way, 'my Three'. An admirable witness to the grace of baptism which blossoms in a being who welcomes it without reserve, she helps us in our turn to find the ways of prayer and of giving ourselves.

Here, then, in a nutshell, is the Pope's message: Elizabeth is relevant to us, as we have a similar life situation in the world; she experienced God's presence and his love; she gave her life totally in Carmel; she suffered; she was radiant with the happiness of knowing herself loved by God and dwelt in by the Trinity; and

---

[23] In *Acta Ordinis*, 1984, p. 18.

because of her openness to God, the grace of baptism could blossom in her and she became a spiritual guide to others.

An Important Mission

John Paul II now switched to Italian, to greet pilgrims from closer to home, and addressed himself to Carmelites in particular. So whereas his previous speech had been tailored to the general public, this time he presented Elizabeth in the light of the Carmelite tradition. He called her beatification 'the sign of how your ancient spiritual family is more than ever, today, alive and rich in promise for the future'. Against 'our world so full of uncertainty and darkness', Elizabeth, he said, is shining for us as 'a new light' and 'a new guide – certain and sure'.[24] Her role, he said, is 'to show us, in the name of the Mystery of the Trinity, the way of salvation and the means of reaching it'.

John Paul II had always been close to the Discalced Carmelite Order. As a young man, he had wanted to enter, but the Carmelites had told him they were not accepting anyone during the war, and his own Bishop did not want to lose his most talented seminarian to a monastery. He also wrote a long contemplative poem which was published in a Carmelite magazine – his adult debut in print – and a doctoral thesis on John of the Cross.[25] Extremely conscious of Carmel's vital importance for the Church, he now described Elizabeth as a stimulus to Carmelites for taking on board their vocation 'for the good of the Church and the salvation of the world'. Their active apostolate he saw as one of spiritual teaching – of passing on a much-needed message: Carmelites, he said, surely inspiring his listeners, are called 'to teach the people of today to hunger and thirst for this very lofty Mystery [of the Trinity]'.

---

24 The word he used for 'sure' – the Italian 'sicura' – has, like the French 'sûr' or the English 'secure', the additional meaning of 'safe': that is, a safe guide in an uncertain world.

25 See Tad Szulc, *Pope John Paul II*, New York: Scribner, 1995, pp. 17, 127, 130–1 & 151–2. His thesis has been published as: Karol Wojtyla, *Faith according to St. John of the Cross*, San Francisco: Ignatius Press, 1981.

John Paul II had an abiding concern for the dignity of the human person. In fact, he had concluded his address to the French pilgrims by saying: 'I wish you all a future worthy of human beings, worthy of the children of God which you are through the grace of Christ.'[26] But to the Carmelite audience, he stressed the importance of the Order's mission of passing on that message to others – not least by teaching the people of today to 'hunger and thirst' for the mystery of the Trinity, and by teaching them 'the paths of true contemplative experience'. To do this, he continued, Carmelites need to highlight the truth that contemplation itself is related to the deepest aspirations of every person, and that it has 'an extraordinary fruitfulness' in transforming the world – in raising up human beings 'to their condition as children of God'.

From Rome to Home

When, the previous day, John Paul II had given his blessing from his balcony in St Peter's Square, a group of Spanish acrobats in green waistcoats had climbed onto each other's shoulders to form a human pyramid of at least six levels, and a little child had clambered to the top to blow kisses at the Pope. Afterwards, they had dismounted, level by level.[27] In the immediate aftermath of Elizabeth's beatification, the celebrations for her were a little like this dismounting. The top of the pyramid represented St Peter's Basilica, where she had been raised to the altars of the Church by John Paul II. Thereafter, the celebrations and events continued, but moving down level by level: firstly to Rome itself, and then to her home town of Dijon.

On the morning after the beatification, as we have seen, pilgrims met John Paul II in the hall for papal audiences. Then, in the afternoon, a Mass of thanksgiving was held at the Basilica of St Maria Maggiore, during which Father Jean Rémy carried aloft

---

[26] These concluding remarks of the Pope to the French pilgrims are in *Acta Ordinis*, 1984, p. 19.

[27] See the article by Madame Jean Dardau, in *Carmel*, no. 40, 1985, p. 279.

an icon of Elizabeth.[28] From that Monday until the Wednesday, a solemn triduum was held in her honour at the Carmelite Basilica of St Teresa, also in Rome.[29] We recall how, almost sixty years earlier, visitors returning from Rome after attending the canonisation of Thérèse of Lisieux had stopped off at Dijon to pray at Elizabeth's tomb and in the chapel of her monastery (cf. S2, pp. 302–3). Now, there were about a thousand people from the Dijon area returning from Rome after Elizabeth herself had been raised to the altars.

On the evening of Saturday, December 1, the General of the Order, the Postulator of the Cause and other Carmelite friars in senior positions celebrated Mass at the Carmel of Flavignerot, which was presided over by the Bishop of Dijon; members of Guite's family were among the congregation. In the homily, the General of the Order, Father Felipe Sáinz de Baranda, proposed Elizabeth as a 'model of Carmelite fidelity in this post-Vatican II era.'[30]

Now that Elizabeth was beatified, her relics could at long last be venerated. So at eight o'clock that evening, when the Mass was ended, the Carmelite nuns greeted her relics which were contained within their wooden repository. Then, Fathers Felipe and Simeón, accompanied by ten other Carmelite friars, took the relics to St Michael's parish church in Dijon, where Elizabeth had made her First Communion. There, a crown of white flowers was placed on the wooden shrine, and the veneration by many, many young people lasted throughout the night. The next day, December 2, the relics would find their home in the side chapel dedicated to the Virgin Mary, where Elizabeth herself had loved to pray; there was a niche in the wall, and there they would be enshrined.

That Sunday morning, the church was crowded for a solemn Mass which was also attended by representatives from

---

[28] See *ibid.*, p. 279.
[29] For an account of the celebrations which took place in the week following the beatification, see *Acta Ordinis*, 1984, pp. 20–1; and Huvet, pp. 154–5.
[30] Cf. *Acta Ordinis*, 1984, p. 20.

the nearby monastery of Cîteaux – due to the miraculous cure of the Cistercian Father Chanut who had been a monk there – and from the Congregation of the Holy Spirit, to which Daniel Brottier had belonged; in a reciprocal gesture, the Carmelite General, before returning to Rome, would visit the grave of Blessed Daniel in Paris. At this Mass, Bishop Balland would give an important homily, showing Elizabeth's relevance to the people of today, and speaking of how she had taken an active part in the parish and blossomed through it. Notably, he described parish life in terms of the very ordinary, humdrum daily life of Nazareth: 'This,' he said, 'was Elizabeth's Nazareth where we all are: too often we think that God is absent.' But he then added: 'It is however already Bethany'. As we recall, Bethany was a place with which Elizabeth had identified her soul – as the dwelling place of the presence of God, in which she gave him hospitality (cf. IN 5; Jn 12:1–2). And the Bishop continued: 'The first and the great lesson is that we are Nazareth, the parish of every day, the soil on which each person is called to listen to the call and respond to it. May Elizabeth's destiny make us believe in the daily Nazareth where we live, in this maturing of God among us, especially with regard to the young.'[31]

Bishop Balland also brought to mind some familiar names from Elizabeth's youth, when recalling her experience at St Michael's Church. He mentioned the organist, Monsieur Diétrich, who had taught her the piano; and he even named Monsieur Chapuis – the landlord for whose conversion Elizabeth had prayed so much – as this man, the Bishop said, had given Elizabeth a sense of 'the mystery of personal faith and of the mercy of God'.[32] Lastly, before his final blessing he thanked the Carmelite nuns of Flavignerot for the gift of the relics to St Michael's parish church.

---

[31] Quoted in Huvet, p. 155.
[32] In *ibid.*, p. 155.

'As an everlasting remembrance'

After every beatification, the Pope issues an Apostolic Letter (or Brief) on each new blessed, entitled, *As an Everlasting Remembrance of the Event*.[33] This is not merely a record confirming his or her new status in the Vatican chronicles, but a spiritual essay in its own right: it details the person's charism and life story, and the history of the Cause, ending with the solemn formula of beatification pronounced by the Pope at the ceremony earlier that day. As such, this document resembles the structure of the Decree on the Heroic Virtues – only, in Elizabeth's case at least, the Apostolic Letter is longer and even more beautiful.

Evident from the opening words is the Pope's great love for John of the Cross, and he begins by quoting a paragraph of *The Spiritual Canticle* (SC 1:7). This particular extract goes to the heart of the charism of the indwelling of God in the soul, and can be summed up with one phrase from it: 'you yourself are [God's] dwelling'. The Pope then explains that the soul which shares in the divine nature, and lives in love and obedience of Christ, is the place where God dwells, the temple chosen by the divine Persons, and the tabernacle in which they manifest their glory. And Elizabeth, he continues, was the dwelling place of the Trinity.

John Paul II who, as mentioned earlier, felt called to Carmel as a young man, speaks of the nature of Elizabeth's own calling: it was, he says, a 'vocation to sacred silence, to continual adoration, to praise of the Beloved, to self-offering'.[34] He then speaks of her likeness to Christ, and of how she suffered in her own flesh what was lacking in the passion of Christ for the sake of the Church (cf. Col 1:24) – but he also makes clear that in her

---

[33] *Ad perpetuam rei memoriam.* The Apostolic Letter on Elizabeth – while signed on the day of the beatification, according to usual practice – was not published by the Apostolic See until 1987. It was reproduced in the chronicles of the Discalced Carmelite Order that same year; for the full text, see *Acta Ordinis*, 1987, pp. 7–12.

[34] In *ibid.*, p. 7.

bitter pains she did not interrupt her converse of love with the divine Guest, nor did her soul fail in carrying the cross with her Master. The Pope then describes her as a brilliant light who could stay no longer in the narrow confines of the monastery but disappeared into the Church in heaven, like St Clare who was radiant with the light.

After this deeply spiritual opening, the letter moves onto the account of Elizabeth's life. While the factual contents are familiar, the Pope's comments on them shed new light, not least in view of who it is who is writing. One could apply to them the remark of a Carmelite visitor to another beatification: 'The biographical profile...contains nothing that is new, but it acquires for us a special meaning when we hear it from the lips of the Supreme Pastor of the Church.'[35] But while this is true of the Apostolic Letter to some extent, in fact the words of John Paul II *do* contain something new: in that everything he says or writes about Elizabeth is fresh with insight and comes from a contemplative depth that resembles her own.

Beginning the account of Elizabeth's life with her childhood, the Pope notes in particular the 'vehement appetite for holiness' which arose in her especially after her First Communion; her 'forgetting herself for Jesus and for others'; her withdrawing into the 'little heaven of her soul'; and her success in containing her 'lively and impulsive' natural disposition.[36] Then, moving onto her early teenage years, John Paul II mentions how she followed St Teresa of Avila in living with Christ as with a friend. But with regard to this stage of her life, the Pope especially focuses on the years in which Elizabeth had to wait to enter Carmel, due to her mother's opposition. A weaker will might have given in to pressure, he points out – but as for Elizabeth, by contrast, 'the fire of love...was ablaze in her spirit'.[37] He recalls, too, the spiritual progress she made during

---

[35] Maria Pilar Resa, CM, in Carmelite Missionaries, *Francisco Palau Beatified*, Rome: Carmelite Missionaries, 1988, p. 47.
[36] In *Acta Ordinis*, 1987, p. 8.
[37] In *ibid.*, p. 9.

this time: in her life of prayer, and her apostolic work in teaching catechism and helping the poor.

The letter discusses Elizabeth's time in Carmel: her formation under the wise and prudent Mother Germaine; her growing experience of the divine as she listened to the still, small voice of God (cf. 1Kgs 19:12) and lived 'with a great openness of heart, in a measure which we can define as cosmic'.[38] Another aspect highlighted by the Pope is Elizabeth's sense of the apostolate: her wish to 'proclaim the goodness which God wants to pour out into souls',[39] and her prayer and sacrifice reaching the whole world. Considering now her posthumous mission, he quotes from a letter she wrote just before her death, in which she envisaged helping people to go out of themselves so as to cling to God, and keeping them in an interior silence which would allow him to transform them into himself (cf. L 335). The Pope also points out that while Elizabeth cultivated silence, contemplation and study, this did not prevent her from following faithfully and attentively the monastic observances and community life. (He presumably knew nothing of how her absorption in prayer caused her to forget messages and lose keys!)

The letter then moves onto Elizabeth's illness; and it states, without exaggeration, that she lived the paschal mystery in both soul and body. Unable to witness to Christ with her blood 'as she wished', she instead witnessed to him through her 'authentic joy' in the most bitter of sufferings. And despite acute pain, she retained her tranquillity and her smile, and 'was content that she was being consumed by the fire of divine love, so that she might become fully a praise of glory and a sacrifice of praise.'[40]

John Paul II then brings Elizabeth's life story to a close by saying that she was an example of fervour for religious life, of self-offering, of lofty meditation, of constant prayer, of adoration full of love; and that she always imitated the Virgin Mary who herself was a model of adoration of God and of coopera-

---

[38] In *ibid.*, p. 9.
[39] In *ibid.*, p. 10.
[40] In *ibid.*, pp. 10–11.

tion in the work of redemption. Finally, before recounting the stages of Elizabeth's Cause and giving the solemn formula of beatification, the Pope states that the fame of her sanctity, which was already apparent while she was alive, 'has, since her death, continually increased'.[41]

On a Global Scale

When Elizabeth became 'Blessed', she in fact had the profile of a canonised saint: for even if no public veneration of her was prescribed beyond a specific region or the Carmelite Order, she continued to be much loved throughout the whole Church, just as she had been in the wake of the bestselling *Souvenirs*. The centenary of her birth had been an important event, especially in Dijon. That of her death – running from Trinity Sunday 2006 until the same feast in 2007 – was celebrated on a truly global scale.[42]

A few examples are mentioned here, giving the general flavour. And while many of the events were organised by the Carmelite Order, the participation extended far beyond it. In El Salvador, there was a six-day congress on the spirituality of Elizabeth, with one hundred and forty participants from Latin America, the Caribbean and the United States. Conferences and public lectures were held in many other places, too, including Spain, northern Italy, Argentina, Madagascar, Mauritius and the Democratic Republic of Congo. In Kerala, southern India, there was a huge gathering of the Carmelite family with around thirteen hundred participants; events included an enactment of Elizabeth's life, and a symbolic presentation of her *Prayer to the Trinity*. And in the Central African Republic, the centenary opened with a solemn Mass in Bouar Cathedral, attended by

---

[41] In *ibid.*, p. 11.

[42] Coinciding more closely with the actual date of Elizabeth's death, the centenary year was celebrated in Africa – or certainly in some African countries – from November 2006 until November 2007. For the worldwide centenary events, I have drawn especially on the newsletter of the Discalced Carmelites: *Communicationes* (issues from June 2006 to December 2007).

more than seven hundred people. The celebratory year in that country then saw: a public lecture on Elizabeth every three months; the broadcasting of her message on 'Radio Siriri'; the translation into Sango of a work on her life and teachings; a concert and dances; and a theatrical work by a Carmelite student, entitled, *The Spiritual Combat of Elizabeth.*

In France, the locations of most of the events were places associated with Elizabeth. As she had been born and baptised at Avord, the nearby city of Bourges held a huge concert in the cathedral, where more than three hundred choristers sang their homage to her, and where representatives from the army camp of Avord presented her baptismal certificate.

Meanwhile, in November 2006, Carlipa in the south of France, where Elizabeth had often stayed with her Rolland 'aunts', had the unusual experience of becoming a popular centre of attraction. Coachloads of pilgrims descended on the tiny village, bringing children, the handicapped, religious of the diocese, and devotees of Elizabeth from all walks of life. The parish church had been redecorated, there was a concert devoted to Elizabeth's poems – for it was in Carlipa that she first began to write verse – and an exhibition featuring her visits to her relations. There were even some people who shared their own memories at the celebrations. One was a man to whom the Rolland sisters had given a bed, telling him to take good care of it because it had been slept on by Elizabeth and she would one day be a saint! And the parish priest spoke of a lady he had known, Angeline Mons, whom Elizabeth had one day been accompanying on the harmonium for a solo which the young girl would be performing at a concert. Angeline had been very stubborn, and as she didn't like part of the music, she refused to sing a note at the rehearsal. The priest asked her, in her old age, what Elizabeth had said to her. Angeline replied: 'She said nothing! she remained silent! that silence! it is the response of the saints!'[43]

---

[43] See http://elisabeth-dijon.org/archives/centenaire_carlipa.html. For the centenary events discussed below, see the webpages at: http://elisabeth-dijon. org/archives/.

Throughout France during the centenary year, a troupe of actors travelled from town to town, performing a musical show portraying Elizabeth's life. But without any doubt, the main centre for all the celebrations was the place where she had spent that life: Dijon itself. The centenary opened with a solemn Mass at St Michael's on Trinity Sunday, June 11. Immediately afterwards, hundreds of balloons were released into the air, each one bearing four lines: 'God loves you today / As he loved you yesterday / As he will love you tomorrow / Elizabeth of the Trinity' – encouraging words taken from a letter Elizabeth had once written to her sister (cf. L 298). The parish church and the Carmel, combined, organised days for children and young people, prayer vigils, night walks, and televised concerts; there was also veneration of Elizabeth's relics.[44]

The most moving event must surely have been the one that took place overnight from the 8th to the 9th of November 2006, when the relics were loaned to the Carmel of Flavignerot to coincide with the exact anniversary of Elizabeth's last night on earth. While the nuns and friars kept vigil, so too did her inseparable companion from the time of her illness: the statue of Our Lady of Lourdes, 'Janua Coeli', whose gaze now rested on the shrine of the relics, just as it had on Elizabeth herself in 1906. Then, at six o'clock on the morning of the 9th, the whole community, as well as the Carmelite friars, gathered around the relics – just as an earlier community had gathered around Elizabeth's bed a hundred years before – and the account of her final moments was read aloud from Mother Germaine's *Souvenirs*.

'The pain has gone...!'

Of the many people who gave talks during the centenary year, one person deserves special mention: Marie-Paul Stevens, who testified to a cure received through Elizabeth's intercession.

---

[44] Cf. *Communicationes*, no. 67, October 15, 2006. Six days after the opening of the centenary at St Michael's, a Mass was held at the Carmel of Flavignerot to open the centenary there: see the homily of June 17, 2006, by the General of the Order, Luis Aróstegui, in *Acta Ordinis*, 2006, pp. 44–50.

In 1997, when nearly forty, she was diagnosed with Sjøgren's Syndrome: a debilitating auto-immune disease in which her body began to dry up. Medical interventions failed to bring any improvement to the condition – or even alleviate the atrocious pain – and she was given to understand that she must prepare for a fairly imminent death.

Sustained all this time by her love for Elizabeth, whose message of union with Jesus she now tried to live with intensity, she had one last wish before dying: to visit the Carmel of Flavignerot, despite the long and painful journey from her native Belgium, so as to thank Elizabeth for everything she had taught her during the illness. Up to two hundred people were praying for her to Elizabeth, and at the beginning of April 2002 Marie-Paul set off, driven there by friends. By that time, she had been ill for five years.

On arrival, and in excruciating pain, she firstly spent time praying in the chapel and visiting Elizabeth's reconstructed cell. She then came out into the convent car park where she and her friends had something to eat – and suddenly she leapt up, exclaiming: 'The pain has gone...!' Instantly, all the symptoms disappeared, including an atrophied left leg! On her return to Belgium, the doctors were astounded – it simply wasn't medically possible. The following year, in a pilgrimage of thanksgiving, Marie-Paul, together with a friend, returned to Flavignerot on foot – walking about two hundred and thirty miles in twelve days, and sharing Elizabeth's message with everyone they met along the way.[45]

At the time of writing, this tremendous healing can still only be called a 'presumed miracle' while it has not yet been approved by the Vatican as an official miracle. But the Process has now been initiated – with the opening in Dijon, on July 11, 2011, of the diocesan enquiry so as to gather information. The cure is mentioned here, as it has already been documented

---

[45] See her testimony, in *Actes du Colloque*, pp. 141–50, as well as an interview reproduced in Rémy, *Confidences d'un prêtre*, pp. 168–74.

in the press, both national and Catholic.[46] And there will be rejoicing, the world over, if and when Sister, Venerable, Blessed Elizabeth finally becomes 'St Elizabeth of the Trinity'.

Gift to the Church

In 1984, four months before Elizabeth was raised to the altars of the Church, Conrad De Meester made the following point: that to beatify someone is not primarily about veneration of a person. It is more about service to the people: Elizabeth's beatification, he remarked, is 'a gift of the Church to the Church'.[47] These words would be partly echoed twenty-two years later in a note addressed to all who would take part in the centenary celebrations, and it thanked the Lord for having 'given the Church such a great disciple of the Gospel'. This note was in fact a telegram from the Secretary of State in the Vatican, Cardinal Angelo Sodano, who was writing to the Carmelites to convey the blessings of Pope Benedict XVI for Elizabeth's centenary year.[48]

But perhaps this 'gift' of Elizabeth to the Church is expressed best of all by a woman from Paris, Madame Jean Dardau, who attended the beatification ceremony in Rome and afterwards wrote these words in her diary:

> The proclamation of the Beatifications is very moving and truly received as a grace given *for us, to our Church of today*. They are our contemporaries. And it is the Lord who is calling all of us: 'Be holy'.[49]

---

[46] See the announcement of the opening of the enquiry, as well as details of the cure, in *Le Bien Public*, July 7, 2011: http://www.bienpublic.com/cote-d-or/2011/07/07/elisabeth-bientot-canonisee; *La Croix*, July 6, 2011: http://www.la-croix.com/Religion/Urbi-Orbi/France/Le-diocese-de-Dijon-etudie-un-miracle-presume-d-Elisabeth-de-la-Trinite-_NP_-2011-07-06-686509. See also *Communicationes*, no. 179, July 13, 2011.

[47] De Meester, 'Een grote Vreugde' ['A Great Joy'], p. 266.

[48] See the text of the telegram in *Acta Ordinis*, 2006, p. 19, and in *Communicationes*, no. 64, June 30, 2006. The letter from the General of the Order, informing the Pope of the forthcoming centenary, is in *Acta Ordinis*, 2006, pp. 37–8.

[49] In *Carmel*, no. 40, 1985, p. 278.

Chapter 32

'TEACHING THE PATHS
OF CONTEMPLATION'

A Popular Manual of Holiness

'Let us be holy, little sister' (L 245), wrote Elizabeth to her sister Guite in October 1905. As we have seen throughout her life, Elizabeth's letters are energised with both the warmth of her affection and the ardour of her teachings. The two are inseparable: for without the teachings, the letters would lack their essential richness; and without the affection, the message would be less personal and possibly less effective. So Guite is not only invited to be 'holy' – she is, at the same time, receiving this invitation as Elizabeth's dear 'little sister'.

John Paul II knew that Elizabeth had a natural gift for teaching. In his homily at the beatification, he said of her: 'this contemplative, far from being isolated, knew how to communicate to her sisters, and to those close to her, the riches of her mystical experience.' Likewise, in a speech the next day, he pointed to her as an inspiration for '[teaching] the people of today...the paths of true contemplative experience'.[1] In these statements the Pope was stressing two important points: that Elizabeth was *teaching from her own experience,* and also that she was *able to make this profound message accessible to others.*

One of the early readers of the *Souvenirs,* a Canon from England, was struck by exactly 'this twofold character' of Elizabeth's writings. His reaction can be seen from a letter he

---

[1] Both passages are in De Meester, 'Elizabeth in the Words of the Pope', p. 19; the second quotation provides the phrase from which the title of the current chapter has been drawn.

wrote to the Dijon Carmel about the *Souvenirs,* and about *Heaven in Faith* in particular: 'The magnificent doctrine contained in the chapter *Heaven on Earth* makes so tangible what we will find in heaven, that one believes oneself to be there already... I will ask Cardinal X...to draw the attention of the Sovereign Pontiff to this twofold character of this marvellous little Sister, who combined with such a perfect practice of the interior life a teaching that is so profound and so realisable, even in the world. It is a true popular manual of holiness' (S2, p. 278). And here we have a third point about Elizabeth's writings: not only does she teach from lived experience, but hers is a spirituality that can be *practised by anyone, in whatever life situation.*

A Work of Many Titles

The '*Heaven on Earth*' which the Canon singled out is the spiritual work, written for Guite in August 1906, known today as *Heaven in Faith*; and it is the subject of the present chapter, drawing the book to a close with this synthesis of Elizabeth's spirituality – or, to borrow the words of the English Canon: 'a true popular manual of holiness'. Elizabeth herself did not give a title to the work. It was published in the *Souvenirs* for the first time in the 1915 edition, where it appeared in a shorter form, especially without the ample quotations from Ruysbroeck.[2] The Canon was referring to it by the short title which the publishers had printed above it as a header, prominently at the top of every odd-numbered page; but Mother Germaine had in fact entitled the work: '*How One Can Find Heaven on Earth*' (cf. S2, p. 311). A still further abridged version appeared in Father Philipon's *Spiritual Doctrine* (cf. pp. 219–31); but he, wishing to have a shorter title, simply

---

[2] This abridged version also appeared as from the second edition of *Réflexions et Pensées sous forme de Retraites* [*Reflections and Thoughts in the Form of Retreats*], with the date believed to be between 1911 and 1915; the first edition of 1911 had contained the *Last Retreat* only: cf. CW I, p. 92, nn. 10–11. As Madame Catez had given Elizabeth an anthology of Ruysbroeck, Elizabeth wished to share his writings with Guite – hence the many quotations from Ruysbroeck in *Heaven in Faith* which was written for her.

retained the words '*Heaven on Earth*'. The definitive title was given by Conrad De Meester in his critical edition of Elizabeth's *Complete Works*. He combined the best of the two approaches: he was quite happy to have a shorter title, as Father Philipon had done, but he wanted to keep Mother Germaine's sense of 'how one can find': for the main focus of the work is the means of *finding heaven* while still on earth. And the means, he could see, was *faith*. So he changed the title to *Heaven in Faith*, which also has the merit of being a phrase which Elizabeth herself often used – as, for example, when she recalled the night before her vows: 'I understood that my Heaven was beginning on earth; Heaven in faith...' (L 169).

Elizabeth, as we have seen, wrote this piece as a surprise for her younger sister (cf. CW I, p. 85). It was indeed a surprise – coming from beyond the grave! For Guite knew nothing about it until two months after Elizabeth's death. Mother Germaine had held on carefully to the little black notebook, so as to include extracts from it in the obituary *Circular*. Two weeks after this appeared at Christmas 1906, the prioress wrote to Guite on January 7, to tell her about the existence of the notebook; and in a letter to Madame Catez the same day, she explained the delay in sending it and spoke of the work as follows: 'I am going to send you a little retreat notebook that [Elizabeth] prepared during the last days of her exile for her dear Marguerite. She asked me to send it to her as a last souvenir. She had in mind her sister's soul and that of her nieces but she thought that the soul of her beloved mother would also joyfully find in it this wholly profound movement of faith and love' (CW I, p. 90).

'The object of this retreat'

As the letter to Madame Catez makes clear, *Heaven in Faith* was written, not for Elizabeth herself but for her sister and family, so as to share with them some of her spiritual ideas. This makes it somewhat different from the *Last Retreat*, even though both works were written in the same month and at first sight bear considerable resemblance to each other in both format and themes. But as we have seen, the *Last Retreat* is a personal notebook from Elizabeth's own retreat, recording her quest to explore every possible way in which she might live her vocation as a praise of glory; whereas *Heaven in Faith* is a treatise, as it were – expressing ideas which Elizabeth had already formulated and was passing on to others. This difference can be seen from the language, too: the *Last Retreat* generally uses the first person singular, as with 'my Master' (LR 28); while *Heaven in Faith* invariably uses the plural form, referring, for example, to 'our God' (HF 41). A striking parallel is when Elizabeth asks, in each work, how one might be a praise of glory. In the *Last Retreat*, she begins the question with the words: 'How can I...' (LR 20); and in *Heaven in Faith*: 'How do we...' (HF 41).

While many of the themes overlap – which is inevitable, as both works are the expression of Elizabeth's own spirituality – there are nonetheless differences of emphasis. These often reveal how Elizabeth tailors *Heaven in Faith* to her sister's life situation which was more socially active than her own. Describing the Visitation, for example, Elizabeth highlights Mary's charity in going to help her cousin (cf. HF 40); while in the *Last Retreat*, the focus is on Mary's beauty, calmness and interior recollection as Elizabeth contemplates her making the journey there alone (cf. LR 40).

Finally, each work has a specific aim. The *Last Retreat* is concerned, throughout, with how to live the call to be a praise of glory. But in *Heaven in Faith*, Elizabeth states the overall aim as how to be in the likeness of Christ and in union with him: 'The object of this retreat,' she writes, 'is to make us more like our adored Master, and even more, to become so one with Him that we may say, "I live no longer I, but He lives in me"' (HF 28; cf. Gal 2:20). However, there is no essential difference between these two aims, as is only too clear from the climax to *Heaven in Faith* where the portrait of a 'praise of glory' is also that of a person who is in union with Christ and in his likeness (cf. HF 43).

While Elizabeth speaks here of a 'retreat' (HF 28), *Heaven in Faith* was not the outcome of a retreat as such. She did, however, write it from an atmosphere of relative solitude and produce it as a retreat notebook, dividing the work into ten 'days' – the usual length of a Carmelite's private retreat. Elizabeth then subdivided each 'day' into two essays or meditations called 'prayers', which gives a total of twenty short sections. We can now consider them in turn, reflecting on their relevance to us all, just as they were intended for Guite who lived out her own spiritual life 'in the midst of life's cares' (cf. HF 16).

We shall also observe, along the way, how Elizabeth's teaching is rooted in the Carmelite tradition. In his address to Carmelite pilgrims to the Vatican on November 26, 1984, John Paul II described 'the joy of the whole Church' – the joy about Elizabeth's beatification, which had taken place the previous day – as 'the sign of how your ancient spiritual family is more than ever, today, alive and rich in promise for the future'.[3] And he pointed to the relevance for the world of the Carmelite charism which Elizabeth embodied:

> Blessed Elizabeth stimulates you now to become still more keenly aware of your particular charism for the good of the Church and the salvation of the world: to teach the people of today to 'hunger and thirst' for this very lofty Mystery [of the Trinity], to teach them the paths of true contemplative experience, its relationship with the deepest aspirations of people and its extraordinary fruitfulness in view of the transformation of the world, according to the demands of justice and of the elevation of human beings to their condition as children of God.[4]

FIRST 'DAY'

Christ's Last Wish

Elizabeth was a true Carmelite: she knew that the Christian life is the story of a *relationship*, one that is initiated by God himself.

---

[3] In De Meester, 'Elizabeth in the Words of the Pope', p. 19.
[4] In *ibid.*, pp. 19–20.

And this conviction is expressed in the opening words of *Heaven in Faith*:

> 'Father, I will that where I am they also whom You have given Me may be with Me, in order that they may behold My glory which You have given Me, because You have loved Me before the creation of the world.' Such is Christ's last wish, His supreme prayer before returning to His Father. He wills that where He is we should be also, not only for eternity, but already in time, which is eternity begun and still in progress. (HF 1; cf. Jn 17:24)

It is very characteristic of Elizabeth – and indeed of the Carmelite saints – to see things as much as possible from God's point of view, so alive was she to his desire to be loved.[5] Taking Scripture as her privileged source of information, Elizabeth knew that it was Christ's 'last wish' to have us live with him (cf. Jn 17:24). She will speak again of his 'wish' (HF 3) – and also of 'His divine dream' (HF 1) or the 'great dream of the Heart of our God' (HF 41). The genius of Elizabeth was to intuit that this 'last wish' of Jesus, uttered the night before he left this earth, is not that we should be with him only when we, too, have left this earth, but that we might be with him *now* – 'in time', as Elizabeth expresses it. And she defines 'time' as 'eternity begun and still in progress' (HF 1). As Mother Germaine could well see, this was Elizabeth's central idea: *to live, while still on earth, the life of heaven* – a life of union with God (cf. CW I, p. 136).

At her beatification, John Paul II spoke of Elizabeth's 'perfect openness' to the word of God.[6] It is an attitude that has much of the candour of the Virgin Mary, who asked the Angel Gabriel: 'How can this be?' (Lk 1:34). Mary's was not a doubting question like Zechariah's 'How can I be sure of this?' (cf. Lk 1:18), but a simple request for an explanation of what she believed but did not yet understand. This is the candid way

---

[5] This is true, for example, of Teresa, John and Thérèse, to name only the most famous: cf. BL 13:22; LF 3:28; SS, pp. 180–1.

[6] In De Meester, 'Elizabeth in the Words of the Pope', p. 18.

in which Elizabeth, too, asked questions – simply seeking to be instructed. So she continues: 'It is important then to know where we must live with Him' (HF 1).

Elizabeth saw that the ground was already prepared through baptism (cf. HF 2). This itself shows how much she knew her teaching to be relevant to all Christians, and not just to Carmelite nuns. John Paul II would say of Elizabeth: 'To an exceptional degree, she was aware of the communion offered to [everyone]'; and he added that she was an 'admirable witness to the grace of baptism'.[7] In this opening section of *Heaven in Faith*, Elizabeth says that baptism unites us to Jesus (cf. Rm 6:4–5) and that we belong to the 'House of God' (cf. Eph 2:19). So she is now able to provide the answer to *where* we must dwell with Christ: 'The Trinity – this is our dwelling, our "home", the Father's house that we must never leave' (HF 2).

'Remain in Me'

Like many Carmelite writers, perhaps especially Teresa of Avila, Elizabeth had a wish to convey her ideals practically, so as to make them accessible to others. Ideals are irrelevant to us if we cannot connect them with the reality of our own lives. So she now asks, not the *where* but the *how*: how, in concrete terms, can we live with Jesus? As so often, Elizabeth turned to Scripture to find the answer. And in John's Gospel she discovered it in these words of Jesus: 'Remain in Me' (Jn 15:4; HF 3).

Elizabeth calls this not just a 'wish' but an 'order' (HF 3)! It seems, too, that she may have had a wish of her own: that Jesus might have said a bit more! Because at this point, she helps him to express his 'wish', and to explain what he might have said, had he elaborated! Elizabeth had a gift for opening up the riches of Scripture. She was formed to do this, we might say, through her daily pondering of short passages – the way in which she would have practised *lectio divina* in Carmel – for she so often breaks down a concept or extends an image so as to explore its

---

[7] In *ibid.*, pp. 18 & 19.

every dimension and apply it to daily life. So, having recalled the words 'Remain in Me' (Jn 15:4), she extends them, still keeping the 'speaker' as Jesus: 'Remain in Me, not for a few moments, a few hours which must pass away, but "*remain...*" permanently, habitually...' (HF 3).

We recall that when Elizabeth was in her final agony and in so much pain that she could barely control her thoughts, they still expressed her love of God; they showed, as the prioress noted, the extent to which union with God had become 'habitual' to Elizabeth (PG, p. 214). This, then, was the result of remaining in God 'permanently, habitually' (HF 3). Elizabeth's words on remaining in God could also be expressed as 'the practice of the presence of God', to use the famous phrase associated with Brother Lawrence, a Carmelite of the seventeenth century. There is no evidence that Elizabeth knew his writings, but she has great affinity with this lay brother who practised awareness of God in his every waking moment. It was said of him after his death that 'his fidelity [to this practice] was rewarded with a continuous awareness of God' – so much so that it had become almost impossible for him *not* to think of God.[8]

Elizabeth now extends the words of Jesus still more, but this time in an extremely practical and specific way. She gives six examples of how Jesus might ask us to remain in him: 'Remain in Me, pray in Me, adore in Me, love in Me, suffer in Me, work and act in Me' (HF 3). Prompted by these examples, we could continue Elizabeth's approach yet further, so that the whole of our lives might be covered with prayer. Instead of saying: 'work in Me', we could think: every time we pick up a pen, or dig the garden, or sit down to write – we could do this in Jesus. Or 'suffer in Me': each time we swallow a pill, or feel pain – we are invited to experience it in union with him. Such a strategy, both practical and simple, would allow us to acquire the *habit* of keeping Jesus in our mind and heart at every moment.

---

[8] Cf. *The Ways of Brother Lawrence*, # 9, in Brother Lawrence of the Resurrection, OCD, *Writings and Conversations on the Practice of the Presence of God*, Washington, DC: ICS Publications, 1994, p. 115.

Apart from the obvious enrichment to the spiritual life, Elizabeth was also showing Guite how remaining in Jesus is a means of coping with the demands of everyday life. She again extends the quotation: 'Remain in Me so that you may be able to encounter anyone or anything' (HF 3). In other words: simply as a matter of survival! This recalls something Elizabeth had learned from harsh experience at the age of eighteen and a half. As we know, she had been going through a very difficult time for over a year, believing she could never enter Carmel because of her mother's opposition and subsequently her mother's ill health as well. Elizabeth was in great distress and often used to stand on her balcony in the evening, looking over to the monastery garden and weeping. Then, she attended a retreat which proved to be a true turning-point. She experienced that by entering within herself, she had greater strength to suffer (cf. P 66). She had previously discovered that by looking at the worrying situation – in her case, *literally* looking: at the unattainable monastery buildings – all we do is get distressed, and weakened by the minute. But if we look within – which has nothing to do with self-preoccupation, and everything to do with gazing on the indwelling God – then we become stronger.

There is still one more aspect to this important quotation – 'Remain in Me' – which is again rich in Carmelite resonances. The word 'Remain' is, in French, 'Demeurez'. This would have brought to mind, for Elizabeth, Teresa of Avila's *Interior Castle* which is commonly known as the '*Book of the Mansions*' – notably, in French: the '*Livre des Demeures*'. These 'demeures' are literally 'dwelling places'; and as Teresa shows, these are the places within our soul where we encounter God's presence. Further on in *Heaven in Faith*, Elizabeth will once more take up the theme of where to remain, and make a conscious link with Teresa: 'It is in "this little heaven" that He has made in the centre of our soul that we must seek Him and above all where we must remain' (HF 32). Those three quoted words, 'this little heaven', come straight from *The Way of Perfection*, where Teresa writes: 'Those who by [recollection] can enclose themselves within this little heaven of our soul, where the Master of heaven and earth is present,...will journey far in a short time' (WP 28:5).[9]

So far, then, Elizabeth has explained that we can live with Jesus by remaining in him. But what she knew fully for herself, she needed to make crystal clear to Guite for whom she was writing. In other words: what must we *do* to be able to remain in him? The answer Elizabeth gives – in line with Teresa, as just seen – is the prayer of 'recollection' (HF 4; cf. WP 28:5). Elizabeth now quotes St Paul: 'I pursue my course' (Ph 3:12; HF 4). And she adds, drawing on an image from Ruysbroeck: 'let us slide down the slope' (HF 4)! As Elizabeth explains: we need to descend into 'the very depths' of our soul; there we will meet God, and 'the divine impact takes place': the encounter of our 'nothingness' with God's 'mercy' – and once we meet him, truly encounter him, we will be given the 'strength to die to ourselves' (HF 4). If this sounds arduous, Elizabeth reminds us that the stakes are high: 'losing all vestige of self, we will be changed into love...' (HF 4).

SECOND 'DAY'

In Our Deepest Centre

Elizabeth begins her second 'day' by continuing her answer to 'where' we may live with God. Her approach is the hallmark of Carmelite prayer: it is an interior place, our innermost depths – the centre of our soul where we will meet the indwelling God. We remember how Mother Germaine said to the young Father Carré, in 1933, that Elizabeth's influence was likely to be intense because many people 'were waiting for someone to tell them that they were the dwelling place of God'.[10] This is what Elizabeth tells us – not just at this point in *Heaven in Faith*, but throughout her writings.

---

[9] Confirmation that Elizabeth is making a conscious link with Teresa here comes from the fact that both of them, with these words, are commenting on the opening line of the Our Father: cf. HF 32, n. 11.

[10] In *Carmel*, nos. 22–23, 1981, p. 184.

There is a verse in Luke that Elizabeth particularly loved and now quotes at the beginning of this new section: 'The kingdom of God is within you' (HF 5; cf. Lk 17:21). Modern translations of the Bible often render this as 'among you' (*Jerusalem Bible*) or 'in the midst of you' (*Revised Standard Version*). The version Elizabeth was using, from her *Manual*, has 'au-dedans de vous', which means 'within you' or, even more physically, 'inside you'.[11] So Elizabeth makes a crucial statement about prayer as she reads the message contained in this verse from Luke: '[God] reveals to us that we do not have to go out of ourselves to find Him: "The kingdom of God is within"!...' (HF 5). This is again a vital lesson on indwelling prayer from St Teresa, who also expresses it with humour: 'Within oneself, very clearly, is the best place to look [for God]' (BL 40:6; cf. IC IV:3:3); and as God is 'within' ourselves, there is no 'need to shout' – 'Neither is there any need for wings to go to find Him' (WP 28:2)!

Importantly, Elizabeth is not speaking about prayer in isolation from life. When Teresa of Avila was asked by her Carmelite sisters to write a book about prayer – which would become her *Way of Perfection* – she firstly explored how to *live* so as to become a person of prayer: so she discussed the virtues of love of neighbour, detachment and humility (cf. WP 4–10; 4:4). Elizabeth will likewise stress the importance of these virtues (cf. HF 9–10; 7; 37) – though with the emphasis on love of *God* – and especially the elimination of selfishness (cf. HF 12) that is an obstacle to encountering God. But at this point in the work, she quotes John of the Cross, to say that it is love that will take us to the centre of the soul: 'Since love is what unites us to God, the more intense this love is, the more deeply the soul enters into God and the more it is centred in Him' (HF 6; cf. LF 1:13).

When the seminarian André Chevignard looked back on his conversations with Elizabeth after her death, he realised that

---

[11] This rendering corresponds to the Latin Vulgate: 'intra vos' ('inside you'). The Greek New Testament has 'entòs humôn', meaning both 'within you' and 'among you'; the *New Revised Standard Version* indicates that either can be used.

this great teacher of prayer had never even spoken to him about prayer! She had only ever spoken about God. 'LUI' – 'HIM' – she used to say with emphasis (cf. PD, p. 196). Elizabeth was a true person of prayer, precisely because she recognised that prayer was only a means of relating to the divine Persons whom she loved.

Solitude of Spirit

'Hurry and come down, for I must stay in your house today' (HF 7; Lk 19:5). Elizabeth now quotes these words which Jesus spoke to Zacchaeus who, being short, had climbed up into a sycamore tree to get a proper look at Jesus when he walked past. Elizabeth loved these words: she was drawn to the notion of *descent*, as it evoked for her the movement into the depths of her soul. And she shows that this communing with God is not for enclosed nuns alone, but for all who embrace the true *spirit of enclosure*, which has nothing to do with monastic buildings:

> what is this descent that He demands of us except an entering more deeply into our interior abyss? This act is not 'an external separation from external things', but a 'solitude of spirit', a detachment from all that is not God. (HF 7)

Elizabeth had recently made this same point to a young friend, Germaine de Gemeaux, whom she invited to live '*alone and set apart*'. But in case there was any misunderstanding, Elizabeth explained to her the real sense of her words: 'I am not speaking of religious life, which is a great separation from the world, but of the detachment, the purity that places a veil over all that is not God and allows us to adhere constantly to Him through faith' (L 278).

One of the impressive things about *Heaven in Faith* is how Elizabeth had so many Scripture texts at her fingertips, which she wove effortlessly into her narrative. And like John of the Cross (cf. 1A 6:2–3), she often interpreted them symbolically, to bring out a spiritual sense. This is very enriching, but we might wonder how valid it is to explain biblical verses in a completely different context. It may seem fanciful to interpret Zacchaeus' climbing down a sycamore tree as a soul descending into its depths. And yet, for all that the literal meaning of the text is different, Elizabeth is drawing out a level of truth that is equally valid, if not more so. Zacchaeus descends in order to meet Jesus. We descend into the centre of our soul for precisely the same reason. In both cases, the encounter leads to a conversion: this tax collector leaves behind his worldly values and his dishonesty as he decides to give half his property to the poor and to repay, four times over, the people he had exploited. In the same way, Elizabeth speaks of just such a conversion: when God has consumed every imperfection, she says, quoting Ruysbroeck, 'he leads us with no turning back' (HF 8). This encounter with Christ brings to mind the words of Père Jacques, a great contemplative and Carmelite priest: 'We cannot see Christ and remain as we are.'[12] Interestingly, this was his comment on the conversion of Zacchaeus.

THIRD 'DAY'

Each Event a Sacrament

Elizabeth begins the third 'day' of *Heaven in Faith* with a classic biblical verse on God's indwelling presence in our soul: 'If anyone loves Me, he will keep My word and My Father will love him, and We will come to him and make our home *in him*' (Jn 14:23).[13] These italics are Elizabeth's own emphasis, and we know how powerfully she had experienced the reality of this verse. For less than three months earlier, on Ascension Day, she had had a vision of the Trinity dwelling in her soul and had heard these very words spoken within her – though in the account of this in

---

[12] In Murphy (ed. & tr.), *Listen to the Silence, op. cit.*, p. 15.

[13] As with her discussion of Luke 17:21 (cf. HF 5), this is another case of Elizabeth's version of Scripture containing an expression ('in him') which denotes the indwelling of God. The standard translations have 'with him', following the Latin and Greek sources ('apud eum', 'par' autô'), although the *New Jerusalem Bible* does in fact have 'in him'.

the *Souvenirs*, the phrase about keeping God's word is omitted.[14] In like manner, Elizabeth now interprets this verse by showing that the first thing that matters is love. So she comments on the verse in this way:

> The Master once more expresses His desire to dwell in us. 'If anyone loves Me'! It is love that attracts, that draws God to His creatures... (HF 9)

Elizabeth is not, of course, suggesting that we do not need to keep God's word! Her own life is an eloquent witness to how she herself kept it. Rather, she is emphasising that love is the priority – and that love will inevitably lead a person to keep God's word. Combining two verses from John's Gospel, she now quotes Jesus as saying: 'Because I love My Father, I do always the things that are pleasing to Him' (HF 10; cf. Jn 14:31; 8:29). Again, Elizabeth gives practical advice: for the notion of pleasing God and doing his will are fairly abstract so long as we do not recognise how to do this in concrete ways. She explains this by showing that we need to see that *everything* that happens is the expression of God's will – and indeed of his presence. So she says:

> Each incident, each event, each suffering, as well as each joy, is a sacrament which gives God to [the soul]; so it no longer makes a distinction between these things; it surmounts them, goes beyond them to rest in its Master, above all things. (HF 10)

We do not know if Elizabeth ever read or knew of the eighteenth-century Jesuit, Jean-Pierre de Caussade, but she writes in the spirit of de Caussade who describes the present moment in terms of the sacrament of the Eucharist when he speaks of 'the real presence of the divine love...in all the events of life'.[15] In fact, even before entering Carmel, Elizabeth knew how to receive the presence of God at all times. One day, unable to walk

---

14 See Chapter 16, n. 3.
15 Jean-Pierre de Caussade, SJ, *Self-Abandonment to Divine Providence*, London: Collins (Fontana), 1971, p. 65.

to Mass because of a bad knee, she wrote to Canon Angles: 'the good God has no need of the Sacrament to come to me' (L 62). She was not diminishing the importance of the Eucharist, which was the highlight of her life, but rather extending the Eucharist into her entire life. God comes to us, Elizabeth is saying in *Heaven in Faith*, because of his presence in the daily events of our lives. In this way, as de Caussade expresses it, the present moment contains the real presence. Elizabeth makes this explicit in a letter which again speaks of the sacrament of daily life: 'Be devoted…to the will of this adorable Master; look at every suffering as well as every joy as coming directly from Him, and then your life will be a continual communion, since everything will be like a sacrament that will give God to you. And that is very real, for God does not divide Himself, His will is His whole Being' (L 264).

Another modern Carmelite saint, Teresa of the Andes, once wondered how it could be possible to love a God whom she could not physically touch or hug. One day, it became clear to her: every event was giving God to her and was an embrace from God, for it was a revelation of his presence. 'Believe me,' she wrote to a friend. 'I'm speaking to you sincerely: I used to believe it was impossible ever to fall in love with a God who is unseen; with someone who can't be hugged and touched. But today I can affirm with my hand over my heart that God completely makes up for that sacrifice. You feel that love so much and those caresses from Our Lord, that it seems God is there by your side.' And she explained: 'We can't touch God with our hands, but we see Him clearly in each of His works.'[16]

Set Apart

Both Elizabeth and Teresa of the Andes are calling us to faith: to see all the incidents and events of our days not simply as they appear on the surface, but as containing the presence of God.

---

[16] In *Letters of Saint Teresa of The Andes*, Hubertus, WI: Teresian Charism Press, 1994, Letter 40, p. 71.

For as long as we are alive, we live in this passing world, and it can command all our attention. The senses tell us that everything we see, hear, touch, taste and feel are real. It is very easy to live as if the invisible God were less real – or even unreal if we lose him from view altogether. Yet God is infinitely more real than all the rest. And Elizabeth, with the eye of faith, urges us to switch from the natural to the supernatural perspective: we need, she says, to transcend things which pass away and to seek God alone (cf. HF 11). She speaks of this as a *dying* to the world and to self as she draws inspiration from a verse of St Paul which always thrilled her: 'You have died, and your life is hidden with Christ in God' (Col 3:3; cf. HF 11).

As we have seen in the account of her last days, Elizabeth gave the phrase 'Hidden in God' – 'Abscondita in Deo' – to one of the sisters in Carmel as a new name (cf. L 339). And a few days later, although weak in the extreme, Elizabeth managed to explain it to her: 'Oh, what a vocation! *Abscondita in Deo* means separation from all earthly things, a continual ascension to Him. What mortification, what prayer, what self-effacement that name requires!' (PG, p. 217). To speak of 'mortification' is religious terminology with which the nuns in Carmel would have been very familiar. But for Guite, Elizabeth uses instead the language of John of the Cross – of being 'set apart, stripped, and withdrawn from all things' (HF 11; cf. SC 40:2); and notably, Elizabeth adds '*in spirit*' after this, in brackets. As with her letter to Germaine de Gemeaux (cf. L 278), Elizabeth is speaking of a separation, not behind convent walls but within the soul. It is still, of course, a 'mortification' – literally, a *dying* to self. But there is nothing negative about this: for the result, Elizabeth knew, is *life*. As she says, coming towards the end of this section: '"I die daily." ...for I want to make room for my Master. I live no longer I, but He lives in me' (HF 12; cf. 1Cor 15:31; Gal 2:20).

FOURTH 'DAY'

Transformed into God

'God is a consuming fire' (Hb 12:29; Dt 4:24; HF 13), writes Elizabeth, in Latin, at the beginning of her fourth 'day'. She speaks with enthusiasm in this section about the Holy Spirit: the 'fire of love' which 'transforms into itself everything it touches' (HF 13). Here, she is quoting from *The Living Flame* – from John's own comment on this phrase from Scripture (cf. LF 2:2). Then, borrowing a passage from Ruysbroeck, she points out that this is 'a renewal that takes place at every moment' (HF 13). These are words to awaken faith in the invisible reality of God's continuous action. At one retreat, Père Jacques said to his audience: 'Creation is actually continuing while I speak to you.'[17] He was not referring here to the growth of plants and trees, for example, but to the transformation that takes place within human beings at every moment through the creative action of God. And once our eyes are fixed on this inner reality, we can no longer be daunted by thinking of the effort that dying to self will entail. This is how Elizabeth explains it:

> For these souls, the mystical death of which St. Paul spoke yesterday becomes so simple and sweet! They think much less of the work of destruction and detachment that remains for them to do than of plunging into the Furnace of love burning within them which is none other than the Holy Spirit, the same Love which in the Trinity is the bond between the Father and His Word. (HF 14; cf. Col 3:3)

This 'bond' is a most exciting concept, and it occurs in another chapter from John of the Cross where he speaks of the transformation of the soul in God. Here, he describes this bond as 'spiration' (cf. SC 39:3): the Holy Spirit being the means by which the Father and the Son communicate with each other, and by which

---

[17] In Murphy (ed. & tr.), *Listen to the Silence, op. cit.*, p. 35.

we ourselves communicate with God – breathing in God and breathing God back to himself. This is the reality of prayer that thrilled Elizabeth's heart (cf. L 185). And combining terms from the Letter of St John and from Ruysbroeck, Elizabeth shows how people can, in this way, become truly contemplative: 'They live, in St. John's expression, in "communion" with the Three adorable Persons, "sharing" their life, and this is "the contemplative life"' (HF 14; cf. 1Jn 1:3).

Transformed into Fire

In the second part of the fourth 'day', Elizabeth brings in a new biblical quotation on fire: 'I have come to cast fire upon the earth and how I long to see it burn' (HF 15; Lk 12:49). She comments: 'It is the Master Himself who expresses His desire to see the fire of love enkindled... Nothing pleases Him so much as to see [our soul] "grow"' (HF 15).

We feel how Elizabeth longs for everyone to fulfil this desire of Jesus: to be consumed by God's fire and transformed into him. In *Story of a Soul*, with which Elizabeth was very familiar, Thérèse says of Jesus (referring to him here as 'Love'): 'in order that Love be fully satisfied, it is necessary that It lower Itself, and that It lower Itself to nothingness and transform this nothingness into *fire*' (SS, p. 195). Elizabeth may have been thinking of that passage now, as she moves from the image of fire to the theme of the equality between lovers. Here, she quotes John of the Cross: '[God] demands from the soul the tribute of its love, as the property of love is to make the lover equal to the beloved as much as possible' (HF 15; cf. SC 28:1). Elizabeth then shows how this is rooted in the Gospels as she recalls the words of Jesus to his disciples: 'I have called you My friends because all things that I have heard from My Father I have made known to you' (HF 15; cf. Jn 15:15). Here, she is firmly in the school of Teresa of Avila who defined mental prayer as 'nothing else than an intimate sharing between friends' (BL 8:5). To be able to live this relationship with Jesus, says Elizabeth, we must be filled with love – making every action of our life an act of love. And she repeats, in the words of John of the Cross: 'My only occupation is loving' (HF 16; cf. SC, stanza 28).

FIFTH 'DAY'

The Inner Sanctuary

A contemplative has sharpened interior senses: the 'eyes' of the soul with which to gaze on God, and the 'ears' of the soul with which to hear his voice. 'I want to spend my life in listening to You,' Elizabeth had written in her *Prayer to the Trinity*. It requires a hearing that can pick up the slightest sound as she shows now in *Heaven in Faith*:

> 'Behold, I stand at the door and knock. If any man listens to My voice and opens the door to Me, I will come in to him and sup with him, and he with Me.' Blessed the ears of the soul alert enough, recollected enough to hear this voice of the Word of God; blessed also the eyes of this soul which in the light of a deep and living faith can witness the 'coming' of the Master into His intimate sanctuary. (HF 17; cf. Rv 3:20)

Elizabeth thrills to this 'coming' of God, which she expresses in the words of Ruysbroeck: 'He is continually coming, always for the first time as if He had never come; for His coming, independent of time, consists in an eternal "*now*", and an eternal desire eternally renews the joys of the coming' (HF 17).

Yet at the same time, the God who comes is already within us. Elizabeth saw the implications of this and was overawed. As she reads in Ruysbroeck with delight: 'a phenomenon occurs: God, who is in our depths, receives God coming to us, and God contemplates God!' (HF 17).

Giving and Receiving

'He who eats My flesh and drinks My blood remains in Me and I in him' (HF 18; cf. Jn 6:56). Beginning with these words to describe the encounter with Jesus in the Eucharist, the second section of the fifth 'day' – which consists almost entirely of passages from Ruysbroeck – conveys the dynamic, all-consuming love which makes Jesus pour himself into us: 'The property of love,' writes Elizabeth, quoting the Flemish mystic, 'is to be always giving and always receiving.' But as Ruysbroeck shows, God wants something back: he longs, more than anything, to receive *us* in return for his love. Again quoting Ruysbroeck, Elizabeth writes of a giving which we ourselves are incapable of making:

> All that He has, all that He is, He gives; all that we have, all that we are, He takes away. He asks for more than we of ourselves are capable of giving. He has an immense hunger which wants to devour us absolutely. (HF 18)

When receiving Communion, we focus on receiving Jesus; we forget that he is also receiving *us*. Like Elizabeth, Edith Stein was aware, with the eyes of faith, that nothing of the Blessed Sacrament is a one-way process. When we gaze at Jesus in the tabernacle, says Edith Stein, he gazes back at us. And when he comes to us in Holy Communion, he forms us into himself, so that we can say: 'I am no longer what once I was'.[18]

SIXTH 'DAY'

'Believe in His Love'

Faith is the vital theme of the important sixth 'day'. It is, says Elizabeth, the way to approach God. And she recalls a delightful image from John of the Cross (cf. SC 1:11): faith is the 'feet' which take us to God!

If there is one thing we can pinpoint which Elizabeth learnt most of all in Carmel, it is the role of *faith*. As we have seen, during her novitiate she was devoid of consolations in prayer and assailed with distressing thoughts. But she came through this extremely difficult time because she was helped by her prior-

---

[18] Stein, *The Hidden Life, op. cit.*, p. 137; this is the same reference for Edith Stein's point about Jesus gazing back at us from the tabernacle.

ess to see with the eyes of faith. She applied herself so well that it became her second nature, as it were – with the result that, seeing with the eyes of faith, she was able to see far into the infinite, into the mystery of God.

Faith, Elizabeth would say, is what made her happy (cf. L 236). But her faith, revealingly, was not concerned most with belief in God's *existence* – rather, it was belief in his *love*. She writes in *Heaven in Faith*:

> '"We have come to know and to believe in the love God has for us." That is our great act of faith, the way to repay our God love for love; it is "the mystery hidden" in the Father's heart, of which St. Paul speaks, which, at last, we penetrate and our whole soul thrills!' When it can believe in this 'exceeding love' which envelops it, we may say of [the soul] as was said of Moses, 'He was unshakable in faith as if he had seen the Invisible.' It no longer rests in inclinations or feelings; it matters little to the soul whether it feels God or not, whether He sends it joy or suffering: it believes in His love. (HF 20)[19]

The Virtue of Simplicity

People sometimes speak about being 'integrated' – possibly as wishful thinking, for life so often seems compartmentalised, complicated, even 'all over the place'! Elizabeth, perhaps more than many, saw the importance of *simplicity*. In the *Last Retreat*, she praises it in connection with the soul's inner unity (cf. LR 3–4); and here, in *Heaven in Faith*, she expresses her thoughts about it in the words of Ruysbroeck:

> '[Simplicity] is the principle and end of virtues, their splendour and their glory. I call simplicity of intention that which seeks only God and refers all things to Him.' 'This is what places man in the presence of God...' (HF 21)

---

[19] Cf. 1Jn 4:16; Col 1:26; Eph 2:4; Hb 11:27. The first two sentences of this extract are in quotation marks as Elizabeth was quoting (from memory) from a letter she received at this time from Father Vallée: cf. HF 20, n. 11a.

Elizabeth herself practised this 'simplicity of intention', seeing it as all the more vital because it 'gathers into unity all the scattered forces of the soul and unites the spirit itself to God' (HF 21) – again, a quotation from the Flemish mystic. To refer once more to the *Last Retreat*, Elizabeth would write there, a few days later: 'A soul that debates with its self, that is taken up with its feelings, and pursues useless thoughts and desires, scatters its forces, for it is not wholly directed toward God' (LR 3). An image that comes to mind is that of a rocket: its streamlined design allows it to ascend high and fast; but if, on the contrary, it had pieces sticking out at various angles, they would work against its flight by trying to take it in other directions. Elizabeth would have been thinking of these 'feelings' and 'useless thoughts and desires' when she wrote in this sixth 'day' of *Heaven in Faith* – combining passages from Ruysbroeck which resonated with her own soul – that simplicity 'gives peace' and 'imposes silence on the useless noises within us' (HF 21); and, moreover, that simplicity 'hourly increases the divine likeness' as the soul that is simple enters within itself and is 'touched' by God (HF 21). This, comments Elizabeth, is 'the touch of the Holy Trinity' (HF 21).

SEVENTH 'DAY'

A Thought in his Heart

'Let us be holy, little sister' (L 245), Elizabeth had written to Guite, as we have seen at the beginning of this chapter. And in the seventh 'day' of *Heaven in Faith*, she explains why. It is because God has given us this vocation: 'God chose us in Him before creation, that we should be holy and immaculate in His presence, in love' (HF 22; cf. Eph 1:4).

Nothing could so fill Elizabeth with joy as looking back to the time before she was born, when God himself was *thinking of her* and *choosing her.* As she once wrote to Canon Angles: 'when I look back I see a divine pursuit of my soul; oh! what love, as if I were crushed beneath its weight, then I am silent and adore!' (L 151). So her heart must have leapt with joy when she first read the opening chapter of Ephesians – this chapter from Scripture that seems to have marked her more than any other. There, Elizabeth learned that God chose us, *even before creation*, to live in his presence! And there, too, she read that we have been chosen to be the praise of his glory.

As we have seen so often, to be a praise of glory is, for Elizabeth, to praise God with our whole self – by being conformed to his likeness. That is why the theme of resemblance to God is so crucial to her. And we will see it becoming ever more prominent in the closing pages of *Heaven in Faith* which will culminate with what might be termed a 'hymn' to being a praise of glory. But here – and speaking of being in the image of the Trinity – Elizabeth looks back once more to the love God had for us before creation: 'The Holy Trinity created us in its image,' she writes, quoting Ruysbroeck, 'according to the eternal design that it possessed in its bosom before the world was created' (HF 22). And Elizabeth herself comments: 'In the beginning was the Word; and we could add: in the beginning was nothing, for God in His eternal solitude already carried us in His thought' (HF 22).

While this and other sections of *Heaven in Faith* contain numerous quotations from Ruysbroeck, Elizabeth is so finely attuned to his thinking and style that we could easily believe she is not quoting at all. Only the quotation marks tell us otherwise, as well as one or two theological terms and a few striking images. She uses one of these now, to show that Christ is our model; it is a dynamic image, expressing a reaching out towards union: 'God wills that, freed from ourselves, we should stretch out our arms towards our exemplar and possess it' (HF 23). But how can we do this? Elizabeth (with Ruysbroeck) explains: 'by His dwelling in us and by our dwelling in Him'. Most of all, it is thanks to love: love draws us into our innermost sanctuary, and there God 'imprints on us a true image of His majesty' (HF 23). In this way, Elizabeth sums up, it is 'thanks to love and through love, as the Apostle says, that we can be holy and immaculate in God's presence' (HF 23; cf. Eph 1:4).

The Desire of God's Heart

Following the words of Scripture, 'Be holy for I am holy' (1Pt 1:16; Lv 11:44–45), Elizabeth says explicitly that this is a call to everyone, regardless of whether we wear a habit or not (cf. HF 24) – this being her one and only reference, in this work, to the religious life. Resonating as always with Ruysbroeck, she defines holiness with his contemplative definition; and we can see, as so often, how his words resonated with her own contemplative soul. The holiest person, she says, is the one 'who is most loving, who gazes longest on God and who most fully satisfies the desires of His gaze' (HF 24). With her ever-lively faith, Elizabeth knew that contemplation is a two-way movement: we gaze at God, and he gazes back at us. But that alone is not enough: Elizabeth knows that he wants to be pleased with what he sees.

So she asks how we may 'satisfy the desires of God's gaze' (HF 24). And her answer shows that gazing on God is actually the *means* by which we can be changed into his likeness. If we open ourselves to his gaze – if, that is, we make ourselves fully receptive to his action – then God will transform us into himself. All we need to do, she says, is to remain '"simply and lovingly" turned towards Him so that He may reflect His own image as the sun is reflected through a pure crystal' (HF 24). The image of the soul as a crystal calls to mind Teresa of Avila (cf. IC I:1:1) and John of the Cross (cf. LF 1:13), perhaps both of them at the same time: for in this connection John speaks of the soul as being indistinguishable from the light, and Teresa writes of us being made in the image and likeness of God, which is Elizabeth's next point.

So Elizabeth now quotes the verse from Genesis which surely spoke most to her from that book: 'Let us make man in our own image and likeness' (Gn 1:26). And she comments: 'such was the great desire in the Heart of our God' (HF 24). With these poignant words, we see that Elizabeth wishes to satisfy the desires of God's gaze, quite simply because it will satisfy his desires. She also recognises that we need to prepare ourselves before he can transform us. Here, she quotes a passage from Ruysbroeck that is extremely important. It shows that while God does all the work of transformation, we must contribute towards the work of preparation for it:

> 'When God sees that we are prepared to receive His grace, His generous goodness is ready to give us the gift that will give us His likeness. Our aptitude for receiving His grace depends on the inner integrity with which we move towards Him.' (HF 24)

When pondering these words of Ruysbroeck, Elizabeth may have been thinking of 'integrity' as truthfulness of character, but she possibly had more in mind its sense of the unified wholeness of a person, with all its parts gathered together and ready to be offered to God (cf. HF 21; LR 3). For she now speaks of uniting the soul's 'faculties' of reason, memory and will – which is technical terminology found in John of the Cross and in the 'pious author' (HF 25) from whom she now borrows. At this point, she copies out the passage she took as her retreat devotion of 1904, which in her day was attributed to Albert the Great but has since been proved to be by Jean de Castel (cf. HF 25, n. 20). A Benedictine monk, he was evidently of a contemplative nature, as we can see from his description of the three faculties when they bear the image of God, which Elizabeth now quotes: 'the intellect is completely enlightened by knowledge of God, the will captivated by love of the supreme good, and the memory fully absorbed in contemplation and enjoyment of eternal happiness' (HF 25).[20] Elizabeth would have been even more thrilled when the same author described this state as 'the glory of the blessed' (HF 25) – she who longed to live the life of heaven while still on earth. And she saw that he said, too, that God imprints his image on us 'like the seal on wax' (HF 25).

---

[20] In the scholastic terminology used by both this author and John of the Cross, 'memory' is a storehouse which applies not just to the past but also to the present and future: cf. Cummins, *Freedom to Rejoice, op. cit.*, p. 106.

As we know, for an impression to be made on wax, it must firstly be heated up, softened, even melted. In the same way, Elizabeth sees, the whole of our self can be offered to God if it is supple and malleable, ready for him to transform us into himself:

> To 'realise this ideal' we must 'keep recollected within ourselves', 'remain silently in God's presence', 'while the soul immerses itself, expands, becomes enkindled and melts in Him, with an unlimited fullness.' (HF 25)

EIGHTH 'DAY'

Predestined in Love

After this intensely contemplative writing, Elizabeth moves onto the eighth 'day' of *Heaven in Faith* and focuses on the theme of our predestination to be in the likeness of Christ. The previous 'day', she had begun by speaking of being chosen to be in the image of the Trinity (cf. HF 22). But now, she speaks of being 'conformed to the image of [God's] divine Son' (HF 26; cf. Rm 8:29) – a notion from St Paul that was sustaining her, day after day, during her terrible illness and pain, at the very time she was writing *Heaven in Faith*. There are, as it were, two faces of God: the contemplative beauty of the Trinity; and the harrowing torments inflicted on the crucified Son. Yet both belong to the face of God: both are the sign of his love.

Elizabeth begins by recalling the passage from Romans which tells us that God has predestined us, called us, justified us, and wishes to glorify us (cf. Rm 8:30). She writes firstly of *predestination*, not from a Jansenistic point of view – which would have more to do with condemnation – but as the story of an immense love. Here, she selects a moving passage from Ezekiel:

> Cannot God say to our soul what He once said through the voice of His prophet: 'I passed by you and saw you. I saw that the time had come for you to be loved. I spread my garment over you. I swore to you to protect you, and I made a covenant with you, and you became mine.' (HF 26; cf. Ez 16:8)

This covenant of *love* comes straight from the writings of the Carmelite saints. When quoting Ezekiel here, Elizabeth was using the translation in her copy of John of the Cross (cf. SC 23:6), but she may also have known the passage – in slightly different wording – from Thérèse (cf. SS, p. 102). Elizabeth sees this predestination itself as a *call*. So, commenting on the quotation from Ezekiel, she continues: 'Yes, we have become His through baptism, that is what [Saint] Paul means by these words: "He called them"; yes, called to receive the seal of the Holy Trinity' (HF 27).

Elizabeth moves on now to how we are *justified*. Her mind seems to race so fast that she lists one means of justification after another. But so as not to read her at a similar pace, and risk over-looking each item, it helps to ponder on each one. Especially as Elizabeth is issuing an invitation to incorporate them seriously into our lives as we become aware of the hidden work God is carrying out in us. One of these vital means is the *sacraments*, and Elizabeth singles out baptism which makes us belong to Christ (cf. HF 27). Another is *contemplation* – which is where God 'touches' us in the 'depths of our soul' (HF 27; cf. SC 19:4–5). *Faith*, too, is utterly essential – and Elizabeth specifies that this is 'faith in the redemption that Jesus Christ has acquired for us' (HF 27).

Finally, Jesus wants to *glorify* us. But he can do this, says Elizabeth, only to the extent that we are in his own image. And as she points out, this requires much contemplation:

> So let us contemplate this adored Image, let us remain unceasingly under its radiance so that it may imprint itself on us; let us go to everything with the same attitude of soul that our holy Master would have. Then we will realise the great plan by which God has 'resolved in Himself to restore all things in Christ'. (HF 27; cf. Eph 1:9–10)

Identified with Christ

The words just quoted, on Christ's 'attitude of soul', give us an insight into how Elizabeth meditated on the Gospels. She looked *beyond* the events of his life, the literal content of his spoken words, and the physical image of his person, to try and *penetrate into his heart and soul*. In this second part of the eighth 'day', she exclaims: 'I want only to be identified with Him... Oh! Let us study this divine Model' (HF 28). Elizabeth now shows us what her 'study' consists in, as we see what she learns of his dispositions. And one, in particular, holds everything together for her:

> when He first came into the world what did He say? 'You no longer delight in holocausts; so I have assumed a body and I come, O God, to do Your will.' During the thirty-three years of His life this will became so completely His daily bread, that at the moment of handing over His soul into His Father's hands, He could say to Him: 'All is accomplished', yes, all Your desires, *all* have been realised, that is why 'I have glorified You on earth.' (HF 29)

Everything in the life of Jesus gave glory to the Father. This is why, as Elizabeth will say, Jesus is 'the perfect praise of His Father's glory' (LR 2; cf. LR 38).

In the *Last Retreat*, Elizabeth would apply to herself Christ's final words while he was *on the Cross*, especially concerning those times which she terms the 'hour of humiliation, of annihilation... the hour of abandonment, of desertion, and of anguish' (LR 39). But in *Heaven in Faith*, writing for Guite who is about to lose her elder sister and would have to face many life challenges, Elizabeth instead focuses on the words of Christ while he was *on his way* to Calvary, so as to give her courage for the hard times ahead: 'If sometimes His will is more crucifying, we can doubtless say with our adored Master: "Father, if it is possible, let this cup pass me by", but we will add immediately: "Yet not as I will, but as You will"; and in strength and serenity, with the divine Crucified, we will also climb our calvary singing in the depths of our hearts and raising a hymn of thanksgiving to the Father' (HF 30).

Here, Elizabeth shows us a helpful and effective way of identifying ourselves with Jesus: *making his words in the Gospels our own*, as we apply them to the various situations of our own life. Then, it is a short step to *making his thoughts and dispositions our own*, so that we end up with a very intimate reading of the word of God where no nuance is overlooked. And we can also ask Christ to help us with this, as Elizabeth did when she asked him: 'identify my soul with all the movements of Your Soul' (PT).

NINTH 'DAY'

Children of God

In the previous two 'days', Elizabeth had spoken of being predestined to be in the image of the Trinity, and then in the likeness of Christ. Now, she explains the third element of our predestination: to be children of God. We remember that two days before she died, she would move her listeners to tears when explaining to the community's physician, Dr Barbier, the meaning of our destiny as children of God – or, as she sometimes expressed it, 'the mystery of the divine adoption' (L 239).

Elizabeth draws, here, on the riches of Scripture, especially St Paul and St John, to show that we, chosen as God's children, are 'moved by the Holy Spirit' (HF 31; cf. Rm 8:14; LF 2:34) and must make ourselves holy, just as God himself is holy (cf. HF 31; 1Jn 3:3). But how? Again, it is with the insight of contemplation that Elizabeth gives us the answer, and her words carry strong echoes of the writings of Teresa of Avila and John of the Cross:

> we do this by living close to Him in the depths of the bottomless abyss 'within'... 'Then the soul seems in some way to resemble God'... It is in 'this little heaven' that He has made in the centre of our soul that we must seek Him and above all where we must remain. (HF 32; cf. SC 20 & 21:12; 1:6–10; WP 28:5)

As children of God, there is something else to which we are invited: 'to do always what is pleasing to the Father' (HF 33; cf. Jn 8:29). And this, Elizabeth points out, means adoring the Father in spirit and in truth – which is, she says, to adore him '*through* Jesus Christ and with Jesus Christ, for He alone is the true Adorer in spirit and truth' (HF 33). Then, she continues, we will have a direct experience of the truth of these words of Isaiah: 'You will be carried at the breast and He will caress you on His knees' (HF 34; cf. Is 66:12). Elizabeth would have encountered this passage in two of her favourite Carmelite books: *The Spiritual Canticle* (cf. SC 27:1), and *Story of a Soul* (cf. SS, p. 208). It had a vital impact on Thérèse when she was discovering the notion of spiritual childhood; Thérèse would have endorsed Elizabeth's significant phrase 'experiential knowledge...of these words' (HF 34), for such knowledge goes far deeper, and is more life-transforming, than anything we can learn from books. 'Oh!' Elizabeth exclaims, adapting a line from Scripture so that 'son' becomes 'daughter' with relevance to Guite. 'Let us be attentive to the mysterious voice of our Father! "My daughter," he says, "give me your heart"' (HF 34; cf. Pr 23:26).

From Sin to Humility

In the second part of the ninth 'day', Elizabeth touches on the doctrine of sin and redemption. In the first part, she had quoted with delight these words from Genesis: that we are 'created... in His image and likeness' (HF 31; cf. Gn 1:26). Now, she highlights the next stage, the more sorrowful part of the story – the damage done by creatures: 'all have sinned and have need of the glory of God' (HF 35; cf. Rm 3:23).

This is particularly moving when we remind ourselves that Elizabeth was writing just before her death and would have been looking back on her own life at the time. It becomes all the more fraught with emotion, when she quotes Ruysbroeck on the person who considers how poorly he or she has responded to God's love:

When the soul 'considers deep within itself, its eyes burning with love, the immensity of God, His fidelity, the proofs of His love, His favours which can add nothing to His happiness; then, looking at itself it sees its crimes against this immense Lord, it turns to its own centre with such self-contempt that it does not know how it can endure its horror.' (HF 36)

What can be done? Again quoting from Ruysbroeck, as she does throughout the rest of this section, Elizabeth considers that sins themselves can have a positive side, in that they are potentially 'a source of humility' (HF 35). This has nothing to do with discouragement or self-loathing. Rather, it is the beautiful virtue of humbling ourselves completely before God. 'The humble,' she says, quoting another choice passage, 'can never rank God high enough [or] themselves low enough. But here is the wonder: their weakness turns into wisdom, and the imperfection of their acts, always insufficient in their eyes, will be the greatest delight of their life' (HF 37).

The words are Ruysbroeck's but the teaching is pure Thérèse who had so much confidence in God's mercy that she declared herself 'happy' to be weak (cf. SS, p. 199); and it also recalls these words of St Paul: 'I shall be very happy to make my weaknesses my special boast so that the power of Christ may stay over me' (2Cor 12:9). To this, Elizabeth adds her own contemplative approach; it echoes her earlier invitation to plunge in a downward movement into the deep place of our meeting with God, a place which she had called 'our interior abyss' (HF 7). So she says now, in the words of the Flemish mystic: 'to be plunged into humility is to be plunged into God, for God is the bottom of the abyss. That is why humility, like charity, is always capable of increasing' (HF 37).

TENTH 'DAY'

Mary, 'so luminous'

The climax of *Heaven in Faith*, the tenth 'day', is a small master-piece in its own right or, rather, two miniature gems. The first of these is an extended portrait of the Virgin Mary – a lyrical and deeply contemplative piece. Elizabeth's starting-point is a longing to enter into the mystery of God – or, as she expresses it, to know his 'gift' (HF 38; cf. Jn 4:10). And she quotes John the Baptist as saying: 'There is one in the midst of you, "*in you*", whom you do not know' (HF 38; cf. Jn 1:26; Lk 17:21). This leads into her portrayal of Mary – because it is Mary, Elizabeth adds, who knew the gift of God:

> There is one who knew the gift of God, one who did not lose one particle of it, one who was so pure, so luminous that she seemed to be the Light itself: 'Speculum justitiae' ['Mirror of justice']. One whose life was so simple, so lost in God that there is hardly anything we can say about it. (HF 39)[21]

Notably, this does not mean that there is nothing about Mary worth speaking of! Rather, she passed into God so totally that she became utterly transparent, a reflection of his own holiness.

Mary, who knew the gift of God, 'kept all these things in her heart' (HF 39; cf. Lk 2:19.51). And as Elizabeth shows, it was in proportion to Mary's 'lowliness' (HF 39; cf. Lk 1:48), and to her recollection in God, that she attracted into herself the greatest gift of God imaginable:

---

[21] Titus Brandsma writes about Mary in almost identical terms when discussing the image, found in John of the Cross, of the sun shining through a window pane (cf. SC 26:17; 2DN 12:3; LF 3:77): 'If the pane of glass be clean and spotless, the sunbeam will light it up and change it in such a way that it seems to be the light itself and gives out light itself. That is the reason why Our Lady deserved to become the Mother of God; because she offered not the slightest hindrance to the divine indwelling. Like Our Lady we must absorb the divine light': in Titus Brandsma, O Carm, *The Beauty of Carmel*, Dublin: Clonmore & Reynolds / London: Burns, Oates & Washbourne, 1955, p. 93.

She remained so little, so recollected in God's presence, in the seclusion of the temple, that she drew down upon herself the delight of the Holy Trinity... The Father bending down to this beautiful creature, who was so unaware of her own beauty, willed that she be the Mother in time of Him whose Father He is in eternity. (HF 39)

Elizabeth now turns her gaze to Mary in the period between the Annunciation and the Nativity. This is no coincidence in that she was writing for Guite who, being a mother, would identify with Mary carrying the Christ Child within her. But we also see here the hallmark of Elizabeth herself: for at this time in Mary's life, the Blessed Virgin was the supreme example of a contemplative gazing on the *God dwelling within her*. So Mary, writes Elizabeth, 'is the model for interior souls, those whom God has chosen to live within' (HF 40).

We now get a glimpse of how Elizabeth saw Mary when looking on her with the gaze of contemplation: 'In what peace, in what recollection Mary lent herself to everything she did! How even the most trivial things were divinised by her! For through it all the Virgin remained the adorer of the gift of God!' (HF 40). This touches on one of Elizabeth's constant ideals: to 'make something divine' (cf. P 106) out of the ordinary events of everyday life. It also reveals the importance of contemplating models, for their influence then becomes infectious. When Sister Marie-Odile reflected on Elizabeth after her death, she described her in similar terms to Elizabeth's description of the Virgin Mary: she remarked that Elizabeth did the same things as everyone else and yet differently, infusing them with 'something of greatness' (CG, p. 37); and she said: 'you feel in her the presence of Our Lord' (ETB, p. 411).

Finally, Elizabeth depicts Mary as a model of charity in 'spending herself outwardly' when she went to the aid of her cousin. Here, Elizabeth shows encouragingly that active work does not have to take our eyes away from the God who dwells within us: 'Never did the ineffable vision that she contemplated within herself in any way diminish her outward charity' (HF 40). Elizabeth now gives a very helpful explanation, adapting a passage from Ruysbroeck, of how to simplify the relationship between contemplation and action. Contemplation, she points out, is turned towards praise and eternity. However: 'If an order from Heaven arrives, contemplation turns towards men, sympathises with their needs, is inclined towards all their miseries'. Then, when the works of charity have been done, it 'rises, burning with its fire, and takes up again the road on high' (HF 40). The key to all this is that it is contemplation itself that is engaged in active works – 'it possesses unity and will not lose it' (HF 40).[22]

A Hymn to Glory

We come now to the climax of *Heaven in Faith*, the second part of the tenth 'day', and the theme which holds together all the others: a *praise of glory*. This, for Elizabeth, is the perfect expression of our ultimate predestination. As we have seen, she was first struck by this expression around Christmas 1903,[23] when another sister pointed it out to her in Ephesians. Elizabeth now quotes the relevant lines in the opening of this section: 'We have been predestined by the decree of Him who works all things according to the counsel of His will, so that we may be *the praise of His glory*' (HF 41; cf. Eph 1:11–12). And she comments, with joy and awe, that this is the 'great dream of the Heart of our God, this immutable will for our souls' (HF 41); she speaks in the plural ('our souls'), because she knows from Ephesians that this is God's will for everyone – his call to everyone. So she asks: 'how do we correspond to our vocation and become perfect *Praises of Glory* of the Most Holy Trinity?' (HF 41). The remainder of the work is devoted to answering this question.

---

[22] In these quotations from Ruysbroeck, Elizabeth is adapting his passage on 'freedom' (or free will) and replacing the word with 'contemplation': see HF 40, n. 11.

[23] See Chapter 11, n. 6.

These concluding paragraphs to *Heaven in Faith* are also a climax to the central theme: of how to find heaven on earth. In heaven, she says, 'each soul is a praise of glory of the Father, the Word, and the Holy Spirit'. The reason is that, in heaven, 'each soul is established in pure love and "lives no longer its own life, but the life of God"' (HF 41; cf. SC 12:8). Each soul, then, will be in the perfect likeness of God – not that this is something achieved by these souls themselves: 'In reality,' Elizabeth says, quoting here as before from *The Spiritual Canticle*, 'it is the Spirit of love and of strength who transforms the soul... He works in it this glorious transformation' (HF 42; cf. SC 38:2).

And this brings us to Elizabeth's central idea: this state of the blessed in heaven can be lived 'even here below!' (HF 42). For it is not only the souls in heaven who are transformed by the Holy Spirit. Elizabeth had once described John of the Cross as 'incomparable' (ETB, p. 628) in his teachings on the transformation of the soul in God. And she now quotes again from his discussion of spiritual marriage towards the end of *The Spiritual Canticle*: 'the soul surrendered to love, through the strength of the Holy Spirit, is not far from being raised to the degree of which we have just spoken' (HF 42; cf. SC 38:3). This 'degree' or state, which can be lived even here below, is, she exclaims, 'a perfect praise of glory!' (HF 42).

At this point, we reach the real climax: Elizabeth's definition of a praise of glory. It admirably captures how the attempt to live the life of heaven is to live our essential Christian vocation to be in the likeness of God and rooted in love. This passage includes the memorable image of the lyre, but Elizabeth was not writing for the sake of beauty alone: the strings of the lyre are perfectly suited to illustrate the point she is making about the soul being moved by the Holy Spirit. We cannot help thinking once more of the words of Dr Barbier, who said of Elizabeth: 'what intelligence and what poetry!' (S1, p. 153). In her, always we see the two combined.

Given the musical quality of this passage, however, and the fact that it all holds together like a poem, it seems best to quote it here in full. If it were dissected point by point, it would lose in flavour and even in impact. But firstly, it is worth noting that in terms of style, Elizabeth's description of a praise of glory is reminiscent of St Paul's hymn to love (cf. 1Cor 13), from which she has just quoted (cf. HF 42; 1Cor 13:12). For just as St Paul frequently states there, 'Love is...', so Elizabeth begins almost every paragraph with the words, 'A praise of glory is...' And this climax of *Heaven in Faith* (HF 43) is itself as lyrical as a hymn; like her *Prayer to the Trinity*, it is a gem in its own right:

> A praise of glory is a soul that lives in God, that loves Him with a pure and disinterested love, without seeking itself in the sweetness of this love; that loves Him beyond all His gifts and even though it would not have received anything from Him, it desires the good of the Object thus loved. Now how do we *effectively* desire and will good to God if not in accomplishing His will since this will orders everything for His greater glory? Thus the soul must surrender itself to this will completely, passionately, so as to will nothing else but what God wills.
>
> A praise of glory is a soul of silence that remains like a lyre under the mysterious touch of the Holy Spirit so that He may draw from it divine harmonies; it knows that suffering is a string that produces still more beautiful sounds; so it loves to see this string on its instrument that it may more delightfully move the Heart of its God.
>
> A praise of glory is a soul that gazes on God in faith and simplicity; it is a reflector of all that He is; it is like a bottomless abyss into which He can flow and expand; it is also like a crystal through which He can radiate and contemplate all His perfections and His own splendour. A soul which thus permits the divine Being to satisfy in itself His need to communicate 'all that He is and all that He has', is in reality the praise of glory of all His gifts.
>
> Finally, a praise of glory is one who is always giving thanks. Each of her acts, her movements, her thoughts,

her aspirations, at the same time that they are rooting her more deeply in love, are like an echo of the eternal Sanctus.

And now, Elizabeth comes to her concluding words (HF 44) – her final invitation to Guite to live on earth the vocation which Elizabeth herself will continue in heaven. This had been Elizabeth's solemn gift to her sister around the end of April 1906, when she was expecting death to be imminent. Elizabeth had written to her then: 'you will be "the praise of His glory" I dreamed of being on earth. You will take my place; I will be "Laudem Gloriae" before the throne of the Lamb, and you, "Laudem Gloriae" in the centre of your soul' (L 269). Indeed, the final two paragraphs of *Heaven in Faith* will highlight the parallel between 'the Heaven of glory' (cf. Rv 4:8) and 'the heaven of [the] soul' (cf. WP 28:5) – and these, as we shall see, are not *essentially* different. Elizabeth also reminds Guite not to be discouraged by 'the weakness of nature' and its 'distractions' – for there is a deeper, uninterrupted prayer in each of us, of which we are often not even aware:

> In the Heaven of glory the blessed have no rest 'day or night, saying: Holy, holy, holy is the Lord God Almighty... They fall down and worship Him who lives forever and ever...'
>
> In the heaven of her soul, the praise of glory has already begun her work of eternity. Her song is uninterrupted, for she is under the action of the Holy Spirit who effects everything in her; and although she is not always aware of it, for the weakness of nature does not allow her to be established in God without distractions, she always sings, she always adores, for she has, so to speak, wholly passed into praise and love in her passion for the glory of her God. In the heaven of our soul let us be praises of glory of the Holy Trinity, praises of love of our Immaculate Mother. One day the veil will fall, we will be introduced into the eternal courts, and there we will sing in the bosom of

infinite Love. And God will give us 'the new name promised to the Victor'. What will it be?

LAUDEM GLORIAE

GUITE – THE RECIPIENT OF *HEAVEN IN FAITH*

'She drew life from her sister'

Guite would read and reread, throughout the rest of her life, every word that her elder sister had sent her. So concerned was she that these writings might go astray, that every time she went away she carried the precious box of letters for safekeeping to the Carmelite monastery – depositing it like a pot of gold in a banker's safe! Then, on her return, one of the first things she did was to go to the Carmel and collect it again – together with 'Janua Coeli', Elizabeth's beloved statue of Our Lady of Lourdes, which in Guite's household was treasured like a precious relic. Her eldest daughter – Sabeth, who would follow her aunt into the Carmel of Dijon – would say of Guite: 'She drew life from her sister Elizabeth, from everything she had told her, from everything she had given her, from all the advice she had received'. Then Sabeth immediately added: 'but she kept everything for herself.'[24]

By temperament, Guite was extremely discreet and reserved. And the union between the two sisters had been so intimate and close that, perhaps for this reason too, Guite felt unable to show the correspondence to her own children when they were older. More than this: she could not even speak to them about her, so instead they read Mother Germaine's *Souvenirs* to learn about their famous aunt! It may also have been the case that Guite felt she could only share Elizabeth with someone on the same spiritual wavelength, someone who truly understood her sister. When she was being interviewed by Father Philipon, the

---

24 In Rémy, *Guite*, p. 124. The information about Guite is taken from this book unless otherwise stated.

Dominican priest preparing his book on Elizabeth, she spoke with great love about her sister and confided to him: 'It is she who initiated me into the interior life.'[25]

Guite, too, was an interior soul. Her inner life permeated the whole of her existence: both the demands of daily life 'in the midst of life's cares' (HF 16), to quote again from *Heaven in Faith*, and the major crises of which there were many. Guite had her first two children during Elizabeth's lifetime and went on to have another seven; but when the youngest was only eight months old, her husband Georges Chevignard died suddenly. So in 1925, Guite was left a widow at the age of forty-two, with nine children to bring up; there were five girls and four boys, and the five youngest children were aged ten or under.

Much impoverished, the family moved to a smaller apartment;[26] and as no one was earning a living, two of the daughters now began to give music lessons. In the coming years, Guite's children would cause her worries, too: Sabeth had health problems and at one point became so ill she nearly died; Pierre caught tuberculosis, from which he fortunately recovered; and Jacques was a prisoner of war for five years – all three crises occurring at the same time. There were also distressing separations. For while one daughter, Marie, left home to get married, the remaining four girls all entered convents. Guite, who had been devastated when her own sister entered Carmel, had acquired an inner self-possession as an adult that would have done credit to Elizabeth. But when Geneviève was about to leave home to join the Dominicans, the Carmelite eldest daughter saw Guite break down in tears. 'I was hoping,' she said to Sabeth, 'that the good God would leave me my last daughter.'[27] Her situation calls to mind the father of St Thérèse. Louis Martin saw four of his five children enter enclosed monasteries; after his death, all five

---

[25] In *ibid.*, p. 123.
[26] At no. 48, rue Chaudronnerie, behind Notre-Dame Church: cf. Huvet, p. 148; De Bono, p. 57, n. 222.
[27] In Rémy, *Guite*, p. 112.

daughters would in fact be nuns. Like the widowed Guite, Louis had lost his spouse when relatively young – and the children's religious vocations speak reams about the spiritual influence of their surviving parent.

'Aunt Elizabeth will come'

The worst crisis of all, however, tells us a great deal about Elizabeth's mission in heaven. Guite's son Xavier, born in 1922, was as if set apart for God from his earliest years. At the age of six, he wanted to be a missionary and go to China. When his eldest sister Sabeth asked him why, he replied with touching candour: 'The Chinese don't know the good God. If someone goes and tells them, they will know him and they'll be nice...'[28] But at the age of ten he contracted meningitis, and he would die from it after a terrible agony lasting three weeks.

During this time of such appalling pain that it recalls the sufferings of Elizabeth herself, someone tried to encourage him by saying that he would go to heaven and see Jesus. At which, Xavier answered in surprise: 'But I always have him with me. He comes every day!'[29] All this time, Guite, torn apart with distress, had the uncanny feeling, nonetheless, that Elizabeth was remarkably close. She said at one point: 'I so feel the presence of his Aunt who is watching over this little bed of suffering...'[30]

One day, Xavier suddenly announced: 'In five days' time, Aunt Elizabeth will come at five o'clock in the morning.'[31] And that is exactly what happened: he died at precisely the moment he had predicted. Which means that we should not doubt that Elizabeth really did come to fetch her little nephew. Guite had not forgotten how her sister had told Madame Catez to say a certain prayer, the moment she heard of Elizabeth's death (cf. PG, p. 209). Now it was Guite's turn to lose a child, and she

---

28 In *ibid.*, p. 100.
29 In *ibid.*, p. 102.
30 In *ibid.*, p. 104.
31 In *ibid.*, p. 102.

prayed in similar words: 'You gave him to me, you have taken him back, may your will be done.'[32]

While Xavier could never fulfil his dream of being a missionary to China, his life and prayers almost certainly had an impact within his immediate surroundings. Just before his death, he had been sharing a desk at school with a boy called Jean Chalmandrier who was one of many praying to Elizabeth for the cure of her little nephew. This boy would later make contact with the Carmelite monastery and himself become a missionary priest in 1948. During the war, he had been imprisoned by the Gestapo and deprived of everything in his cell. However, 'there remained to me,' he would say, 'one treasure which no one could take away from me: "*O my God Trinity whom I adore*".'[33]

'Living the same ideal'

Throughout her life, Guite followed Elizabeth's teaching of the presence of God in both her prayer and her daily life. In *Heaven in Faith*, Elizabeth had said to her: 'we must...enter ever deeper into the divine Being through recollection' (HF 4). We have the testimony of Guite's children to know that their mother did exactly this. Marie would say, after Guite's death: 'Mama really prayed a great deal... she was recollected all the time... I can still see her, her eyes closed...'[34] And the novice mistress in Geneviève's convent told her charges: 'When Madame Chevignard is in the chapel, you can watch her, you will see someone who is truly praying, someone who is totally absorbed by the Lord.'[35]

In her climax to *Heaven in Faith*, Elizabeth had described a praise of glory as one who embraces the will of God. She had said forcefully: 'the soul must surrender itself to this will completely, passionately, so as to will nothing else but what God wills' (HF 43). Guite was radical in putting this advice into practice.

---

[32] In *ibid.*, p. 105.
[33] From his testimony in Krikorian (ed.), p. 14.
[34] In Rémy, *Guite*, p. 156.
[35] In *ibid.*, p. 156.

As Geneviève would say: '[My mother] made a cult of the will of God. In everything that happened, she encountered God. It was the will of God. You had to cling to it with love and that was everything.'[36]

Elizabeth and Guite had different life situations and different temperaments. As we know, the Carmelite nun was vivacious and a born leader, the wife and mother gentle and reserved. But Guite followed the teachings of Elizabeth with the same absoluteness as her elder sister had done; and it was said that Guite was, 'in the world, what her sister was in the cloister'.[37] In fact, after her death in 1954, at the age of seventy-one, people who had known Guite – just like others who had known Elizabeth half a century earlier – called this remarkable woman a 'saint'. Marie-Louise Hallo, who had been Elizabeth's best friend, would say: 'I considered [Marguerite] a true saint in the world.'[38] And Marie's husband, Armand Cartron, would give this beautiful testimony: 'My mother-in-law, for me, was obviously a saint, but not the image of a saint, a saint in the true sense of the word. She was holy, as much in her daily life as in her spiritual life, and in both at the same time. They were inseparable. She was extraordinary.'[39]

There is a curious, perhaps prophetic, letter which Elizabeth wrote to her sister on the eve of Guite's marriage to Georges Chevignard. At the time, Elizabeth herself was preparing for the vows that would make her the bride of Christ. She wrote to Guite: 'you'll see that both of us are blessed, each in the way our Master calls us and wishes us to be' (L 140). But when Elizabeth said that both of them would be 'blessed', she did not write 'bénies', which would have been the more usual term. Instead, referring to the fact that Guite had received a painting which featured St Elizabeth and St Margaret, she spontaneously wrote the word 'béatifiées'! Elizabeth was beatified

---

[36] In *ibid.*, p. 148.
[37] In De Bono, p. 57.
[38] In Rémy, *Guite*, p. 156.
[39] In *ibid*, p. 143.

before the end of the century; will it be the turn of Guite in our own?

Guite's life has great implications for Elizabeth's teachings. It is clear proof, if any were needed, that Elizabeth's message is of benefit for everyone – in the world as much as in the cloister – to attain to the holiness which Vatican II has proclaimed a 'universal call'.[40] Guite's son-in-law Armand expressed it well: the two sisters, he said, were 'truly living the same ideal'.[41] Different life situations, but parallel paths of contemplation.

This brings to mind another letter of Elizabeth. It dates from when she was preparing to enter Carmel, and she was writing to a friend, Marie-Louise Maurel, who was engaged to be married: 'Jesus...has chosen two different paths for us, but the goal must be the same. Oh, let us belong wholly to Him, let us love Him very much, He loves us so much!' (L 36).

---

[40] Cf. *Lumen Gentium* (*Dogmatic Constitution on the Church*), # 39–42.
[41] In Rémy, *Guite*, p. 160.

Epilogue

'A BRILLIANT WITNESS'

As Natural as Being Alive

Elizabeth of the Trinity, said John Paul II at her beatification, 'is a brilliant witness to the joy of being rooted and grounded in love.'[1] In fact, he called her a 'witness', not just once but three times.[2] Here, he was expressing something fundamental about Elizabeth, who since her youth had spontaneously given witness to God, speaking about him with great warmth – quite simply because she loved him so much and wanted others to love him, too. It was possibly, though, with her life, even more than with her words, that Elizabeth wished to draw people close to Jesus: 'Ask Him,' she wrote to a friend about a forthcoming social event, 'that He may be in me so much that people may feel Him when coming close to [me] and that they may think of Him!... may everything in us reflect Him, may we give Him to souls' (L 54). Bearing witness, then, was as natural to Elizabeth as being alive.

In Carmel, she would continue to radiate God, whether to her sisters in the convent, to visitors in the parlour, or when writing her letters as she continually invited her family and friends to live in God's presence. Even on her deathbed, just two days before she died, she explained to the doctor that we have been adopted by God as his children (cf. S1, p. 194). This outpouring exhausted her so much that she never recovered her ability to communicate – she was truly a witness right to the end. And *after* the end, too, as she had envisaged a posthumous

---

[1] In De Meester, 'Elizabeth in the Words of the Pope', p. 18; cf. Eph 3:17.
[2] Cf. *ibid.*, pp. 18–19. The third occasion was in a speech on Elizabeth the day after the beatification.

mission of drawing people close to God, so that they might cling to him and live in communion with him as she had done (cf. L 335).

Elizabeth's witnessing had an impact on all who met her. Far from trying to convert or convince people by argument, she simply overflowed with her own love of God and conveyed it with the genuine affection she had for everyone. Her personal warmth and the ardour of her faith have always made themselves felt, even when her written words are being read by people who have never met her. We have previously quoted this testimony from a missionary in South Africa, when he first encountered Elizabeth's teachings in the *Souvenirs*: 'night gave way to sunlight, cold to warmth, emptiness to plenitude' (S2, p. 291).

But that is not to overlook the other, most vital, ingredient of Elizabeth's witnessing: the things themselves to which she gives witness. This Epilogue, then, will take some final glimpses of Elizabeth – this 'brilliant witness' – as we look at some of the aspects of the spiritual life to which her example and her writings bear testimony.

A Witness to the Certainty that we are Loved

Through all her difficulties, whether trials in life or dryness in prayer, Elizabeth did not waver for one instant in her belief that God loved her – and that he loves each one of us individually. She knew, from Scripture, that before the world was created, God chose us to be holy and to live, through love, in his presence (cf. Eph 1:4). And that at every moment, he is thinking of us, loving us and wanting us for himself: 'when I look back I see a divine pursuit of my soul' (L 151), she wrote in awe. Her first and primary response was quite simply to *let herself be loved*.

A Witness to Loving God

And her second response, simultaneous with the first, was to love God in return and to be with him all the time. We might say that Elizabeth could not get enough of prayer! Like any person in love, she stole away to spend every spare moment with him.

'It is so good to be close to Jesus... / Can one wish for anything more?' (P 12); 'To rest near His Heart / Gives me my happiness here below' (P 24). Elizabeth wrote these words as a young teenager, and her constancy in prayer never changed – not even years later, when at times she no longer felt his presence.

'He loved me, he gave himself for me' (Gal 2:20), she would often repeat. Even as a very young child, Elizabeth instinctively responded to his love by blowing kisses at the crucifix. Over ten years later, she wrote: 'For me you wanted to die! / For you, Jesus, can I not suffer?' (P 18). And after another ten years: 'I wish to love You... even unto death!' (PT). And she did.

A Witness to Loving Others

Elizabeth had firm premises: never to speak one word against her neighbour; never, it seems, even to entertain a thought against her neighbour. So she approached each and every person with the same positive feelings. If someone expressed annoyance with her, she countered it with such genuine affection that peace was immediately restored. When she was asked for help, she gave it with a radiant smile, however tired or unwell she might be. She even made it seem that the other person was doing her a favour by asking. She was gracious to everyone, but she did not fight shy of correcting people where necessary – she was able to 'tell the truth in love' (Eph 4:15). She gave her full attentiveness to the person before her, so that after her death it seemed that every sister in the Carmel felt that she herself was the one Elizabeth had loved the most. And the more she loved, the more she became able to love: 'You see,' she once said, 'in Carmel the heart expands' (L 90).

A Witness to Faith

The whole of Elizabeth's life could be summed up as *faith*. She believed God had chosen her before creation and destined her to live with him in eternity. She believed he loved her – with a love that was 'excessive' (cf. Eph 2:4) – and she would urge others, again and again, to believe in his love (cf. 1Jn 4:16). She believed he was lovingly directing her life, and she wrote of the soul who trusts him: 'she does not look at the paths on which she is walking; she simply gazes at the Shepherd who is leading her' (LR 14). She believed that he willed that she become a Carmelite, so despite her continuing spiritual trials, she took her vows for life – 'in pure faith' (ETB, p. 522), she would later admit.

She believed in his real presence in the tabernacle; and even when prayer became so difficult she wanted to run out of the oratory, she stayed there in every spare hour – because 'He was there...' (ETB, p. 564). She believed in his presence in *everything*, and that each event was 'a sacrament which gives God to [the soul]' (HF 10). She believed he was at work in her, transforming her constantly: all she had to do was open herself up to his creative action – remaining still and supple, to be moulded as he willed. It was in this disposition that she went to her prayer.

A Witness to Prayer

Elizabeth was so much a person of prayer that to say 'Elizabeth' is to say 'prayer'. Or, as she was told at the age of ten, 'Elizabeth' meant 'House of God'. A light went on for her: God himself was dwelling within her! 'I'm never alone,' she would say: 'my Christ is always there praying in me, and I pray with Him' (L 123). Hers was a prayer of intimate contact, of deep recollection, of loving and listening.

Later, she came to realise that the God within her was the Trinity. So now she found she had *three* divine Friends living within her! She related to each of them in their own way: to the Father, bending lovingly over her; to the Son, her beloved confidant and Bridegroom; and to the Holy Spirit transforming her into the divine likeness, the way the breeze moves the strings of a lyre. As she placed herself in stillness under his action, she became an instrument on which the Spirit played the divine harmonies – her whole life singing out the praise of God.

A Witness to taking Scripture Seriously

'Elizabeth,' said John Paul II, 'gives the witness of a perfect open-ness to the Word of God'.[3] She went to the Bible to discover the heart of Jesus and to fathom the mystery of God; to learn of his plan of salvation for us and of how we must respond. When she read that we are chosen to be a praise of glory (cf. Eph 1:12), she took it seriously. It set her future on course; and right to the end, she was continually exploring how to praise God with her whole life. 'Be holy for I am holy' (Lv 11:44–45), she read with delight. Her search for how to reflect the holiness of God brought her to the point where she could even rejoice in resembling Christ crucified, as she pondered again and again this phrase from her beloved St Paul: that we must be 'conformed to the image of [the] Son' (Rm 8:29).

The prioress would say of Elizabeth that she had a remark-able talent for discovering the deep meaning of Scripture and of identifying with its teachings (cf. PG, p. 94). When Elizabeth felt weak, whether in spiritual trials or when almost too ill to take a step, she clung to the word of God and it gave her the strength to keep going: 'I can do all things in him who strengthens me' (Ph 4:13; cf. PG, p. 146), she would say. John Paul II would say powerfully: 'she assimilated [Scripture] to the point...that she found in it all her reasons for living'.[4]

A Witness to the Life of the Church

Another vital source of life for Elizabeth was the sacraments of the Church. Elizabeth, said John Paul II, was an 'admirable witness to the grace of baptism which blossoms in a being who welcomes it without reserve'.[5] When her niece was baptised, Elizabeth felt like falling on her knees before her, to adore the Trinity who had come to dwell within this young child (cf. L 197).

---

[3] In *ibid.*, p. 18.
[4] In *ibid.*, p. 18.
[5] In *ibid.*, p. 19.

Baptised on the feast day of Mary Magdalene – the saint who 'loved much' (Lk 7:47) – Elizabeth, who would become an angry young girl throwing tantrums almost every day, began to change her ways at the early age of seven when preparing for her first confession. Taking it seriously – as she did everything, with her upright and generous nature – she examined her conscience and opened herself fully to the grace of God, enabling him to begin the process of change. At her First Communion, Elizabeth felt drawn to give herself to God forever, and Confirmation made her love of God increase even more. The sacrament of the Eucharist meant everything to her, and she lived from one Communion to the next.

Elizabeth loved the Church. She was overwhelmed at the divine transformation wrought in the priest in the sacrament of ordination. She received with gratitude each priestly blessing. She felt keenly that Christ himself was being hurt when the French State was rejecting the Church. And she offered up her terrible sufferings, 'drop by drop for [His] Church' (ESS, p. 39).

A Witness to Loving the Will of God

Embracing the will of God does not come naturally. But if it seems like the hardest thing in the world, that is only if we think that what God wants is to make us unhappy! Elizabeth never fell into that trap.

Still, she struggled a great deal to accept circumstances. As a teenager, she was impatient to enter Carmel as soon as possible and suffered deep distress at her mother's opposition to the idea. At seventeen, she even begged her patron saint: 'tell [Jesus] to give in to my desire' (P 42)! But not long afterwards there came a turning-point. Generously, she prayed: 'May your will be done' (P 44) – even if she could never enter the monastery.

She then had to face the torment of her mother's ill health which at one point was so serious that it looked as though the dream of entering Carmel was gone for good. Then one day Elizabeth realised, through faith, that it was not *her mother* standing in the way of her entering Carmel, but *Jesus himself,* for he has control of all events and circumstances. At once, she accepted this fate: 'I would so love, O my Master, to live with you in silence,' she wrote at the age of nineteen. 'But what I love more than anything is to do your will, and since you still want me to be in the world, I submit with all my heart *out of love for you*' (IN 5). And as life's events continued to unfold, Elizabeth learned to read in them the will of God – and was in perfect peace.

A Witness to Peace

'There must be peace' (LR 26), wrote Elizabeth. Peace, she knew, begins with the inner self. For if our feelings and emotions are like a river in full spate, we will always be agitated. Elizabeth shows us that we are *not* at the mercy of our emotions: that we must, and can, *forget ourselves*, and *remember the silent but powerful presence of Jesus within us*. When one day an unjust remark was making her 'blood boil', as she wrote in her *Diary*, she was just about to retort angrily when: 'I heard His voice in the depths of my heart' (D 1). It was a silence more powerful than the surge of emotion. This forgetting ourselves, and remembering God, allows the cause of inner turmoil to *disappear from view*, and the faculties of our soul – with all our thoughts, our memories, our desires – to rearrange themselves, so to speak, into the harmony for which they were created. Our inner life must be *unified*, Elizabeth tells us. She cultivated this state of soul as a beautiful but indispensable ideal, praying: 'that I may be established in You as still and as peaceful as if my soul were already in eternity' (PT).

A Witness to being Fully Alive

There was nothing dour or stern in Elizabeth's pursuit of holiness. She contemplated God in prayer and *radiated* his light, as in the words of the Psalm she so loved: 'Look towards him and be radiant' (Ps 33:6). The more Elizabeth grew in love of Jesus, the more she blossomed, so that she could say to a young friend: 'We must become aware that God dwells within us and do everything with Him, then we are never commonplace' (GV 8).

Elizabeth herself was far from commonplace. Dressing with style, graceful and vivacious, she was the life and soul of every gathering. Yet she stood out just as much even when she put herself in the background, so as to let others be the centre of attention. She was vibrant with life, had a number of very good friends, and enjoyed walking, dancing, picnics and holidays. She especially enjoyed music: she was not only a virtuoso pianist, enthralling her audiences with both skill and expression; she played for Jesus, bringing out her most sonorous chords for him alone. Her life and prayer were seamless. As she said one day of the piano: 'When I can no longer pray, I play. I do so for the good God' (ESS, p. 7).

A Witness to Coping with Suffering

Few people have ever suffered as much as Elizabeth did during her final illness – her whole body racked in torment, and with not a single painkiller. She was constantly nauseous, unable to eat more than a few tiny mouthfuls a day, could hardly ever sleep, had relentless headaches which were sometimes crippling in intensity, and eventually burned up with a generalised inflammation that made it too painful even to drink a drop of water. Yet right to the end, she retained her smile, her affection and her kindness towards others. How? It seems impossible.

There is no answer but Christ. A letter she wrote at the time shows what was giving her strength: 'Every soul crushed by suffering, in whatever form it may occur, can tell itself: I dwell with Jesus Christ, we are living in intimacy' (L 314). The *joy* she radiated – which, under such circumstances, could never be feigned by an effort of will – bears ample testimony to just how much she truly desired to resemble Christ. She contemplated him on the Cross. And as if by osmosis, she took on the same dignity in suffering, and the disposition of willingly giving oneself for others. She could offer up her pain because she knew there was a purpose in it. Again, Scripture was her teacher: 'In my own flesh I fill up what is lacking in the passion of Christ for the sake of His body, which is the Church' (Col 1:24; GV 7).

Anyone in that amount of pain would, as a *natural* response, resist and rebel. But to do this would weaken and divide us, sapping us of our remaining strength. Instead, utterly emaciated, deprived almost completely of food and sleep for months on end, Elizabeth was inwardly strong. When she felt herself waver and fall into distress, she seemed to hear God calling to her: 'where are you?' (ESS, p. 36); and she returned at once to her inmost centre, the place of her tranquillity. She did not perceive herself as one to be pitied in her suffering. Instead, she willingly surrendered herself to the process of transformation. For she knew that God was creating her in the likeness of Christ, and drawing her ever closer to heaven: 'faith tells me,' she wrote a few weeks before she died, 'that it is love...who is slowly consuming me; then I feel a tremendous joy' (GV 7).

A Witness to Heaven on Earth

We often have a tendency to compartmentalise our lives. But nowhere is this more evident than in the distinction we make between life and death. We turn them into extremes: either the happiness of being alive contrasted with the tragedy of death; or the cares and worries of this life contrasted with a longed-for never-ending bliss.

Not so for Elizabeth: she immersed herself in the Book of Revelation to learn about the life of the saints in heaven. She saw them standing before the face of God, continually praising and adoring him; and she recognised that we, too, even here below, can stand before the face of God, praising and adoring him constantly. There is no *essential* difference!

Elizabeth defined 'time' as 'eternity begun and still in progress' (HF 1). She lived constantly in the presence of God. 'I do everything with Him,' she wrote, 'so I go to everything with a divine joy' (L 139). In this way, her whole life, even those things that she might naturally have found difficult or boring, or even excruciatingly painful, still contained for her the joy of knowing that she was with God. She is a witness to this truth, which we often forget: that being in pain does not have to make us unhappy. With just days to live, Elizabeth wrote movingly to a friend: 'I confide to you: it is this intimacy with Him "within" that has been the beautiful sun illuminating my life, making it already an anticipated Heaven; it is what sustains me today in my suffering' (L 333).

Life was a joy; and heaven, she saw, was its continuation. Death, for Elizabeth, was a door opening onto the fullness of joy.

A Witness and Doctor?

'People today,' said Pope Paul VI in 1974, 'listen more willingly to witnesses than to teachers, and if they do listen to teachers, it is because they are witnesses.'[6] But is every witness a teacher? And could Elizabeth ever be considered a potential Doctor of the Church?

As her life evolved, she listened ever more keenly to the slightest inspirations of the Holy Spirit. And her insights were combined, and refined, into a vital and original message. It began with her knowledge that she was a 'House of God', a soul within whom God was *dwelling*. It was a short step to realising that Christ was *living* in her. From there, she progressed to desiring with all her heart that she might become *another humanity* for him – not wanting to replicate just one or two aspects of his life, but to be a person in whom Jesus could, as she said, 'renew His whole Mystery' (PT).

Longing to be *holy as God is holy*, Elizabeth strove to resemble him: both the Christ in the wretchedness of his Passion, and the Trinity in its beautiful stillness and silence. She knew that these may be opposites in appearance, but that there was no real difference between them because both are expressions of the God who is love. *Rooted in love*, she could reflect his holiness, and her whole life would then become a continual *praise of his glory*. It would mirror the life of the saints in heaven.

---

[6] From Paul VI, 'Address to the Members of the *Consilium de Laicis*' (October 2, 1974), quoted in his Apostolic Exhortation of December 8, 1975, *Evangelii Nuntiandi* (*Evangelisation in the Modern World*), # 41.

So, ultimately, she found that she could live the life of heaven *already on earth*.

Every aspect of Elizabeth's charism of union with God is contained in the heavenly life as lived by faith. And this is what she constantly teaches us. She is a doctor of *how to find heaven on earth*.

ELIZABETH AMONG THE SAINTS

The Influence of the Saints

I have met many people whose lives have been transformed by Sister Elizabeth; it is only saints to whom God gives such an influence. (S2, pp. 300–1)

A lay person, reader of the _Souvenirs_

You remember that Sister Elizabeth had a presentiment of this role [of uniting people with God] which would be given to her in heaven: I do not know of any more impressive proof of sanctity. (S2, p. 307)

Father Gonzalve Vallée, OP

*
*   *

'I'll imitate her and become a saint'

I'm reading Elizabeth of the Most Holy Trinity. She enchants me. Her soul is like mine. Though she was a saint, I'll imitate her and become a saint. I want to live with Jesus in the intimate depths of my soul. I want to defend Him from His enemies. I want to live a life of heaven, as Elizabeth says, by being a praise of His glory: 1. By living a divine life. By loving God with pure love. By giving myself to Him without reserve. By living in intimate communion with the Spouse of my soul. 2. By fulfilling the will of God in all things. How? By fulfilling my obligations joyfully at every moment. Nothing must disturb me. All must be peace, like the peace that inundates the angels in heaven. 3. By living in silence, because in this way the Holy Spirit will draw forth from me harmonious sounds and the Father, together with the Spirit, will form the image of the Word in me. 4. By suffering, since

Christ suffered His whole life long and was the praise of the glory of His Father. I'll suffer with joy for my sins and for sinners. 5. By living a life of faith. By considering all things from a supernatural point of view. By reflecting Christ as if in a mirror in our actions. 6. By living in a continual state of thanksgiving, that our thoughts, desires and acts may be a perpetual thanksgiving. 7. Living in continual adoration, like the angels, by repeating: 'Holy, holy', etc. And since we can't be constantly in prayer, at least let's renew our intention before each exercise, and thus we'll be a praise of glory and we will live a life of Heaven. What is more, we must become more and more inflamed with zeal for the divine glory.[1]

St Teresa of the Andes, OCD

A Temple of the Trinity

Do you know the little sister who in her heart
Built a temple for the Trinity
And did not want to leave this temple any more?
But think of this: her name was 'the House of Bread'!
We carry the Triune God in our heart
If we nourish ourselves with the living Bread
Which has come down from heaven,
If our heart is one with the divine Heart,
A true temple of the most holy Trinity.
Do you know where I learnt this wisdom?
I found it in the heart of our Mother,
The pure heart of the most pure Virgin.
This heart, ah, never did it go away

---

[1] In Michael D Griffin, OCD, *God, the Joy of My Life: A Biography of Saint Teresa of Jesus of The Andes with the Saint's Spiritual Diary*, Hubertus, WI: Teresian Charism Press, 1995, pp. 235–6. This passage, which she wrote in her diary at the age of seventeen, is based on Elizabeth's description of a 'praise of glory' in the climax of *Heaven in Faith*: cf. HF 43–44. The correspondence also contains numerous references to Elizabeth as well as many echoes of her writings: cf. *Letters of Saint Teresa of Jesus of The Andes*, op. cit., especially pp. 12–13, 22, 62–3, 71, 140–1 & 202. Teresa of the Andes was canonised in 1993.

From the divine Heart, the Heart of her dear Child.
So [her heart] was always one with the Trinity
And simply rested in deep peace.[2]

St Edith Stein, OCD

Penetrating the Mystery

Silence is a necessity for a contemplative soul, and there can
be no prayer without it. To each of us is given the obligation to
make our cloister and our souls a House of Prayer, the Home of
the Blessed Trinity, a Sanctuary of God where we may pass our
life listening to Him and learning all from Him.[3]

Mother Aloysius of the Blessed Sacrament, OCD

I already know of Elizabeth of the Blessed Trinity... This holy
soul, Sister Elizabeth, understood the mystery of Our Lord. She
learnt it in the school of the great St Paul, and the Holy Spirit
filled her soul with admirable lights for penetrating into the
divine obscurity of the Holy of Holies.[4]

Blessed Columba Marmion, OSB

---

[2] In *Edith Stein Gesamtausgabe*, vol. 20 – *Geistliche Texte II* [*Complete Works of Edith Stein*, vol. 20 – *Spiritual Texts II*], Freiburg, Basle & Vienna: Herder, 2007, p. 255. These words are spoken by 'Elizabeth of the Trinity' who is a character, based on the real Elizabeth, in *St Michael*, the last play Edith wrote in Carmel (June 1942, two months before her death). The theme of 'House of Bread' fits in well with that of the indwelling God, although the real translation of Elizabeth's name from the Hebrew is 'My God swears an oath' or 'My God is Seven' (a number symbolising perfection): cf. *ibid.*, p. 255, n. 82. Edith Stein also translated Elizabeth's poem 'The Carmelite' (P 83): cf. *ibid.*, pp. 211–2. She was canonised in 1998 and was named one of the patron saints of Europe the following year.

[3] A passage which echoes Elizabeth's *Prayer to the Trinity*, in *Fragrance from Alabaster: Thoughts of Reverend Mother Aloysius of the Blessed Sacrament, Discalced Carmelite*, Concord, NH: The Discalced Carmelite Nuns of Concord, 1999, p. 51. The Cause of beatification of Mother Aloysius was opened in 1963 by Bishop Ernest J Primeau of Manchester, New Hampshire: cf. *ibid.*, pp. 67–8.

[4] In Bancroft (ed. & tr.), p. 45. Columba Marmion was beatified in 2000.

Hidden in Delightful Darkness

It is in the company of Saint Paul that Sister Elizabeth of the Trinity lives, in her silent and hidden contemplation.

Sister Elizabeth of the Trinity...seems to lower her gaze before the dazzling light.

Sister Elizabeth draws us to silent recollection in the splendours of the most sublime mysteries of Christianity... For Sister Elizabeth, dogma furnished a point of departure or a confirmation of a state already lived, and always serves her as support, in surrendering herself to the inflowings of divine light, or entering into supernatural contemplation and resting in serene tranquillity in the darkness which is its fruit. Sister Elizabeth goes beyond all distinct lights, deep into the night: '*Nescivi*', I know nothing, she will say on returning from her contemplation. This contemplative, of whom some want to make a theologian, is above all a daughter of Saint John of the Cross. Her contemplation is more Dionysian, more in the negative way, than positive, more thick with delightful darkness than clear with light. Most often she lives in an atmosphere without light or breeze, without perfumes or images, and is sustained only by faith and by silence.[5]

Father Marie-Eugène of the Child Jesus, OCD

A Disciple of St Teresa and St John

A near-contemporary of Thérèse of the Child Jesus, Elizabeth of the Trinity had a profound experience of the presence of God, which she nurtured in an impressive way during a few years of life in Carmel... To an exceptional degree, she was aware of the communion offered to every creature by the Lord... She celebrated the splendour of God because she knew that, in her

---

[5] In Father Marie-Eugène of the Child Jesus, OCD, *I Want to See God, op. cit.*, pp. 226, 302 & 515. Father Marie-Eugène was declared 'Venerable' in 2011.

innermost self, she was dwelt in by the presence of the Father, the Son and the Spirit in whom she recognised the reality of love that is infinitely alive... Elizabeth gives the witness of a perfect openness to the Word of God which she assimilated to the point that she truly nourished her reflection and her prayer with it; to the point that she found in it all her reasons for living and for consecrating herself to the praise of his glory. And this contemplative, far from being isolated, knew how to communicate to her sisters, and to those close to her, the riches of her mystical experience. Her message is spreading today with a prophetic force. We invoke her: a disciple of Teresa of Jesus and of John of the Cross, may she inspire and sustain the whole family of Carmel; may she help many men and women, in secular life or consecrated life, to receive and share the 'waves of infinite charity' which she gathered up 'at the Fountain of Life'.[6]

Blessed John Paul II

*
*   *

At the School of the Saints

Ask the Queen of Carmel, *our Mother*, to teach you to adore Jesus in profound recollection... Pray also to our seraphic Mother Saint Teresa, who loved so much that she died of love! Ask her for her passion for God, for souls, for the Carmelite must be apostolic... Are you familiar with Saint John of the Cross? He is our Father who went so far into the depths of the Divinity! Before him, I should have spoken to you of Saint Elijah, our first Father; you can see that our order is very ancient since it goes back to the prophets. Ah, I wish I could sing all its glories! Let us love our Carmel, it is incomparable! (L 136)

---

[6] From the homily which John Paul II gave at Elizabeth's beatification ceremony on November 25, 1984: in De Meester, 'Elizabeth in the Words of the Pope', pp. 18–19; the two phrases quoted are from L 191. Pope John Paul II was beatified in 2011.

Saint Paul says that 'we are no longer guests or foreigners, but we belong to the City of saints and the House of God'. (L 237; cf. Eph 2:19)

This is the measure of the holiness of the children of God: 'to be holy as God, to be holy with the holiness of God'; and we do this by living close to Him in the depths of the bottomless abyss 'within'. (HF 32; cf. 1Jn 3:3; SC 1:6–10)

My God,...you who know everything, you know at least that I love you! Help me...for I want to become a saint for you. (D 138)

APPENDICES

Appendix I

OVERVIEW OF THE CHAPTERS

Chapter 1   A Passion Within

Dates: July 18, 1880 – April 19, 1891
Content: Early years. Birth of sister. Bereavements. House moves. Elizabeth's terrible temper. Catechism and music lessons. Attraction to religious life. First Communion.

Chapter 2   A Girl Fully Alive

Dates: April 19, 1891 – c. July 1896
Content: Confirmation and spiritual growth. Elizabeth's personality. Holidays. Piano prizes and end of music studies. Vow of virginity. Call to Carmel. Confiding in mother about her vocation.

Chapter 3   Crossing the Wilderness

Dates: Summer 1896 – Autumn 1898
Content: Feeling exiled from Carmel. Acceptance of will of God: frustration replaced with peace. Holidays. Spiritual growth and new insights.

Chapter 4   'Merci'

Dates: November 1898 – March 26, 1899
Content: Mother's illness. Elizabeth's trial of believing she can never enter Carmel. Retreat by Father Chesnay. Elizabeth's reading of Teresa of Avila. Redemptorists' Mission to Dijon. Permission from mother to enter Carmel in two years' time.

Chapter 5   In Training

Dates: March 26, 1899 – c. June 1900
Content: Elizabeth in training for becoming a Carmelite. Accepted by Carmel: joins group of 'postulants outside the

485

walls'. Holidays. Society life. Apostolic work. Retreat by Father Hoppenot. First meeting with Father Vallée.

Chapter 6   Departures

Dates: July 1, 1900 – August 2, 1901
Content: Final holiday. Health problems. Tension at home. Two more meetings with Father Vallée. Friendship with Marguerite Gollot. Aridity in prayer. Foundation of the Carmel of Paray-le-Monial. Elizabeth learns, at the last minute, that she may enter Carmel at Dijon rather than at Paray.

Chapter 7   A Corner of Heaven

Dates: August 2 – December 8, 1901
Content: Settling into the convent. Elizabeth's dispositions. The postulant's questionnaire. Community elections. Intimation of the date of her clothing. Formation in the novitiate. Clothing ceremony.

Chapter 8   The Trial Begins

Dates: December 9, 1901 – c. end of July 1902
Content: Beginning of Elizabeth's year as a novice. Spiritual themes of: vision and faith; transformation in God; powerlessness; 'prisoners' of Jesus; finding 'Heaven on earth'; and wanting to see God. Transition from first to second stage of trial of faith. Description and analysis of her difficulties. Celebrating feasts. Friendship with a missionary brother and a seminarian. Guite's engagement. Elizabeth considers her own vocation in the light of those of the apostle, bride, mother and Carmelite nun.

Chapter 9   The Night Preceding the Day

Dates: August 1902 – January 21, 1903
Content: Fruits of the ongoing trial of faith. Retreat by Father Vallée and distressing interview with him. Government hostility towards religious congregations. Mother Germaine inspects a property in Switzerland, in case of exile. Elizabeth's meeting with mother and sister on day of canonical examination. Retreat

preceding profession. Anguish. Meeting with Father Vergne. Ceremony of profession. Trial of faith finishes. Veiling ceremony.

Chapter 10   Always Belonging to Others

Dates: January 12 – December 25, 1903
Content: Life and work in Carmel after taking her vows. First letter to André Chevignard. Government persecution of the Church. Theme of 'giving God'. Elizabeth as a spiritual teacher through her letters and parlour visits. Themes of love and holiness. A new Pope. Frictions in community life. Testimonies on Elizabeth's charity. Her dispositions for living by love. Fruits of reading *The Spiritual Canticle*. Christmas poem on penetrating the Mystery of God.

Chapter 11   Into the Silence of the Trinity

Dates: December 30, 1903 – November 21, 1904
Content: Elizabeth's love of silence. Daily liturgy. Important letter on St Paul. Her discovery of the phrase 'praise of glory'. Turmoil in the Dijon diocese, with rebellion against the Bishop. The nature of Elizabeth's prayer, and difficulties in prayer. Elizabeth becomes an aunt. Hostilities between Church and State. Reflections on the priestly role. Poem inspired by encyclical of Pius X. Bishop Le Nordez is asked to resign. Grace-filled private retreat. Community elections. Retreat by Father Fages. Writing of the *Prayer to the Trinity*; analysis of the *Prayer*.

Chapter 12   Immersed in the Word of God

Dates: November 29, 1904 – c. end June 1905
Content: Letter on the Carmelite and priestly soul. Christmas poem. Increasing knowledge of the New Testament. Biblical figures and writers. Old Testament and Psalms. Theme of living 'in communion' ('en société') with the Trinity. Forgetfulness as portress. First signs of illness. Birth of second niece. Theme of predestination. Studying St Paul. Reflections on the sacrament of priestly ordination.

Chapter 13 'In Him who strengthens me'

Dates: July – December 1905
Content: Worsening health. Poem on love. Addison's Disease and consultation with Dr Martignoli. Taking a rest. Letter on motherhood. Being a 'sacrifice of praise to His glory'. Private retreat, and receiving light on her vocation. Fruits of the retreat. New postulants. Letter on suffering. Defines vocation as being a praise of glory. Elizabeth's first use of the Latin phrase 'Laudem Gloriae'. Christmas poem on Christ's coming.

Chapter 14 Waiting for St Joseph

Dates: January 1 – c. March 20, 1906
Content: Letter on her vocation to be a praise of glory. Divine Office overtakes silent prayer for her. Elizabeth's influence on new postulants. Effects of Law of Separation of Church and State. Encyclical of Pius X denouncing that Law. Impact on Elizabeth of Philippians 3:10. Severe sufferings and feelings of vulnerability. Letter on coping with suffering. Illness becomes evident: Elizabeth is told to move to the infirmary.

Chapter 15 Preparing for Eternity

Dates: c. March 20 – c. end April 1906
Content: Layout of Elizabeth's new surroundings and description of her infirmary cell. Her new companions and regular doctors. Palm Sunday attack: appears to be at point of death. The visit of Father Donin. Letters written in the aftermath of the attack.

Chapter 16 The Host, the Altar, the Priest

Dates: May – June 15, 1906
Content: Consultation with three doctors. Second attack: death again appears imminent. Worsening of symptoms. The 'priesthood' of Mother Germaine towards Elizabeth. Ascension Day: vision of the indwelling Trinity. Important spiritual letters. Poems for Trinity Sunday. Celebrations for feast day of Mother Germaine.

Chapter 17 Walking to Heaven

Dates: Mid-June – August 2, 1906
Content: Prayer in the infirmary tribune. Reading Ruysbroeck. Hears interiorly that she will not be cured. Letter to console a former postulant about the difficulties with her vocation. Regains use of legs through intercession of Thérèse. Renewed love for Mary. Seeing the positive aspects of suffering. New consultation with the three doctors. Important poem containing the main themes of Elizabeth's spirituality.

Chapter 18 The Song of the Lyre

Dates: August 2 – August 15, 1906
Content: The writing of *Heaven in Faith*; summary of its broad outlines. Essay, in the form of a 'retreat devotion', on Ruysbroeck (possibly written in July). Intense prayer and pain. Correspondence with Father Vallée. Further conflict between Church and State. Important poem on going out of herself and into God's presence. Preparing for her private retreat or 'novitiate for heaven'.

Chapter 19 The Last Retreat

Dates: August 15 – August 31, 1906
Content: The conditions in which Elizabeth lived her final retreat and wrote the *Last Retreat*. Grace of embracing suffering and going beyond its bitterness. Overview of the *Last Retreat*: aim; style; structure; discussion of the work, section by section.

Chapter 20 The Home of the House of God

Dates: August 31 – c. beginning October 1906
Content: Increased love for the *Rule* and monastic customs, and the Office of Lauds. Faith and dispositions allowing her to cope with intense suffering. Her spiritual influence on the sisters. *The Greatness of Our Vocation*: discussion of main points. Immersion in the Passion through the writings of Bl Angela of Foligno.

Celebrating the anniversary of Mother Germaine's profession. The 'palace of pain and bliss'.

Chapter 21   Clothed for a New Life

Dates: October 4 – October 22, 1906
Content: Renewal of clothing ceremony. An attempt at matchmaking. Last poem for Mother Germaine: on their relationship as priest and sacrificial offering. Triduum at the Dijon Carmel in honour of the Carmelites of Compiègne. Inspiring final meeting with Father Vallée. Worsening of symptoms. Rendering service to the community. Clothing ceremony of a new novice. Elizabeth's final poem: on living the Carmelite vocation.

Chapter 22   The Fire of Love

Dates: October 22 – October 30, 1906
Content: Coping with intense suffering. Recounting her youth to Mother Germaine, to help her write the obituary *Circular*. Elizabeth's future mission. Temptation to suicide and a strengthening by God: a mystical experience of God's fire. Letters expressing anticipation of heaven. *Let Yourself Be Loved*: discussion of the work, section by section. Testament letters and envisaging her posthumous mission. Final meeting with her family. The last day Elizabeth is able to get up.

Chapter 23   Through Darkness into Light

Dates: October 30 – November 9, 1906
Content: Prelude to her final agony. Joy on feast of All Saints. Dictation of two letters while expecting to enter heaven that very day. Final trial: overwhelming pain, with physical and spiritual darkness. Identification with Jesus on the Cross. Spiritual help from chaplain, community, and especially Mother Germaine. Elizabeth's final letter. Veneration of the sisters towards her. Spiritual darkness giving way to light: Elizabeth's glimpses into heaven. Final meeting with Dr Barbier. Her last night. The morning of her death.

Chapter 24   'A new light is shining'

Dates: November 9, 1906 – aftermath of Elizabeth's death
Content: The news of Elizabeth's death. Her body displayed in the infirmary and the choir. Liturgy of the Dedication of the Churches of France. Elizabeth's body is viewed by the public. Funeral and burial. Community and friends remembering her.

Chapter 25   'Her message is spreading'

Dates: Late November 1906 – 1956
Content: The obituary *Circular* and feedback. Correspondence between Mother Germaine of Dijon and Mother Agnes of Lisieux, regarding the former's proposed biography of Elizabeth. The writing of the *Souvenirs*. Style and content of the biography. Popularity of the work. Related publications. Amendments to the *Prayer to the Trinity*.

Chapter 26   'A new guide – certain and sure'

Dates: August 1933 – c. 2006
Content: First meeting between Mother Germaine and Father Marie-Michel Philipon. Doctrinal works on Elizabeth: by Philipon, von Balthasar and Borriello. Spiritual works on Elizabeth: by Lafrance, Rémy, Févotte and others, including books situating her within spiritual traditions; also, collections of articles. Anthologies of her writings. Biographies of Elizabeth: by Poinsenet, Sicari, De Meester and others, both books and DVDs. Primary sources: *Complete Works*, concordance, documents, and photographs. Summary of the main trends in literature on Elizabeth in the century following her death.

Chapter 27   'May she help many'

Dates: 1909 – 1946
Content: The impact on readers of the *Souvenirs*: official testimonies from eminent men of the Church, arranged chronologically; unsolicited feedback from the general public, arranged according to readers' life situations.

Chapter 28 'Presented to our world'

Dates: c. 1980 – c. 2006
Content: The impact on general readers of Elizabeth's message, arranged according to theme.

Chapter 29 'We invoke her'

Dates: November 1906 – c. 1927
Content: Veneration of Elizabeth at her death and following the appearance of the *Souvenirs*. Letters sent to the Dijon Carmel requesting relics and reporting on cures, as well as spiritual help with regard to vocations and conversions. Addition of an eighteenth chapter to the *Souvenirs*. Calls for canonisation.

Chapter 30 'Rich in promise for the future'

Dates: October 10, 1930 – February 21, 1984
Content: First exhumation of Elizabeth's body. The Ordinary Process for beatification. A false testimony, and its dismantling. Miracle for the beatification. The Apostolic Process. Work behind the scenes. Centenary of Elizabeth's birth. Declaration of 'Venerable', and the Vatican document on Elizabeth's heroic virtues. Approval of the miracle, and authorisation for beatification.

Chapter 31 'Joy of the whole Church'

Dates: September 10, 1984 – July 11, 2011
Content: Final exhumation of Elizabeth's body. Feast of Christ the King. Mass of beatification. Discussion of the homily by John Paul II. The Pope's addresses on Elizabeth the next day. Celebrations in Rome and in Dijon. Discussion of the Pope's Apostolic Letter on Elizabeth. Centenary of Elizabeth's death. Opening of the investigation into a presumed miracle for the canonisation.

Chapter 32   'Teaching the paths of contemplation'

Dates: N/A

Content: *Heaven in Faith*: title; purpose; differences from the *Last Retreat*; discussion of the work, section by section. Guite, the recipient of *Heaven in Faith*: her closeness to Elizabeth; her children and hardships; death of her ten-year-old son, and the tangible presence of Elizabeth; comparison of Elizabeth and Guite, and the relevance of Elizabeth's teachings for all.

Appendix II

DETAILED CHRONOLOGY

IN THE WORLD

1880

Jul 18	Elizabeth Catez is born at Avord, near Bourges
Jul 22	Baptism at Avord: 'Marie-Elizabeth-Josephine'

1881

Jan 18	Her father, an army captain, is named a Knight of the Legion of Honour
May	Catez family moves to Auxonne

1882

End Apr	Elizabeth's first letter
May 8	Death of Josephine Rolland, Elizabeth's grandmother
Nov	Family moves to Dijon: no. 1, Route de Paris, opposite railway station

1883

Feb 20	Birth of Elizabeth's sister Marguerite ('Guite')

c. 1884

	Family moves to the Rue Lamartine

1885

Jun 12	Elizabeth's father, Joseph Catez, retires from the army

1886

'Age 6'	Noted for recollection and fervent prayer in church

1887

Jan 24	Death of Raymond Rolland, Elizabeth's grandfather, from heart trouble
c. Jul	Begins attending Sunday Mass (customary for seven-year-olds)
Oct 2	Death of Joseph Catez from a heart attack
Nov 1	Begins attending catechism classes (again, customary for her age)
c. Christmas	First Confession
'Age 7'	Elizabeth feels called to the religious life

1888

Spring	Family moves to no. 10, Rue Prieur de la Côte d'Or, overlooking the Carmelite monastery on the Boulevard Carnot
'Age 8'	First visit to Carmel: Elizabeth afraid of voice behind grille!
Summer	During holiday in south of France, tells Father (later Canon) Angles she wants to be a nun
Oct	Mother enrols her at Dijon's Music Conservatory

1889

Summer	Holiday at army camp of Châlons-sur-Marne
Oct	Adolphe Diétrich, a well-known local composer, becomes her piano teacher

c. Dec	Following an ultimatum from Madame Catez, threatening to postpone the date of First Communion, Elizabeth works hard to control her temper

1890

Summer	Holiday in south of France and first visit to Lourdes
c. Dec (or Jan 1891)	Arrival in Dijon of Marie-Louise Hallo, soon to become Elizabeth's best friend

1891

Apr 18	Elizabeth makes a general confession (customary before First Communion)
Apr 19	First Communion at St Michael's Church: aware of Jesus dwelling within her, wishes to live for him alone, and will later say that her religious vocation began on this day
	Later that day, second visit to Carmel: is told that her name means 'House of God'
'After First Communion'	A period of scruples (length unknown), eventually cured by trust in God
Jun 8	Sacrament of Confirmation at Notre-Dame Church: much spiritual growth from now on, especially love of Eucharist; she will also attend 'Catechism of Perseverance' classes (possibly up to age 18)
Summer	Holiday, possibly in northern or eastern France

1892

Summer	Probably spends summer holidays staying with relatives in the south of France (the usual destination in alternate years)

1893

Apr 3	Pilgrimage to shrine of Notre-Dame d'Étang at Velars-sur-Ouche, where Elizabeth asks to die young
Jul 18	Awarded First Prize for music theory
Jul 25	Awarded First Prize for piano
Summer	Holiday in Gemeaux, Mirecourt and Jura mountains

1894

c. Jan	Marie-Louise Hallo moves to Bourges
Apr 8	Elizabeth performs Liszt's *Second Hungarian Rhapsody* at a concert attended by Gabriel Fauré
c. May	Elizabeth writes her first poem
c. Jul 16	Vow of virginity, during thanksgiving after receiving Communion: from now on, she is absorbed in God and ever more resolved to give herself to Jesus
c. 10 days later	Receives call to Carmel, again after receiving Communion
End Jul	Unanimously voted winner of prestigious Prize of Excellence for piano; the prize is unjustly withheld due to behind-the-scenes rivalry and machinations
Summer	Holiday in south of France

1895

Apr 23	Visits Avord, where she was born and baptised, while spending Easter holidays with the Hallo family in Bourges

Jul	End of music studies
Summer	Holiday in Vosges region and Jura mountains

1896

Apr	Easter holidays with the Hallo family in Bourges
Between c. Jun 4 & c. Jul 16	Tells mother about call to Carmel: Madame Catez opposed to the idea, and Elizabeth is now forbidden even to speak to the nuns; from now on, carrying a hidden sadness, longing to enter Carmel
Jul	Guite is awarded Prize of Excellence for piano
Summer	Holiday in south of France and (in October) second visit to Lourdes

1897

c. spring	The Hallo family moves back to Dijon
Jul	Elizabeth's confessor, Father Sellenet, before leaving Dijon tries to urge Madame Catez to let her enter Carmel: Elizabeth's mother protests
Summer	Holiday in eastern France
Sep	Elizabeth gazing at monastery from her balcony in sad longing; Father Golmard is now her confessor, but she misses Father Sellenet
	Wishes to 'share' (P 34) Jesus' sufferings – the first mention of this term in her writings
2nd half of Oct	A reversal of perspectives, in that despite her longing for heaven, Elizabeth wishes to remain alive and share Jesus' agony (P 39)
Nov	Acute frustration at exile from Carmel

Dec 8	Important turning-point: she accepts the will of God, even if it is his will that she may never enter Carmel (P 44)
Dec 25	Writes for the first time about being 'in [the] image' of Jesus (P 45)

1898

Apr–Jun	More poems reflecting spiritual growth and new insights: trust in divine Providence (P 51); union (P 54); being a bride of the Trinity (P 54); being in the image of Christ crucified and a victim for sinners (P 55); Jesus as 'all Love' (P 57)
Summer	Holiday in the south of France and third visit to Lourdes; beginning of friendship with Marie-Louise Maurel
Nov–Dec	Madame Catez ill: Elizabeth afraid of never being able to enter Carmel

1899

Jan	Her mother's health begins to improve
Jan 24–28	Elizabeth attends a retreat given by Father Chesnay, SJ: receives strength to suffer and graces of prayer – 'regions unknown', 'a union' (P 66)
Jan 30	Beginning of Elizabeth's (surviving) *Diary*
Jan or Feb	Madame Catez refuses Elizabeth permission to have Father Chesnay as her confessor
Feb	Reading Teresa of Avila's *Way of Perfection*
Spring	Reading Thérèse of Lisieux' *Story of a Soul* (in its first edition)

Feb 18	Émile Loubet becomes President of France
Mar 4–Apr 2	Attends Mission at St Michael's, given by Redemptorists
Mar 12	Madame Catez recovers from her illness
Mar 15	Father Lion, one of the Redemptorists, affirms Elizabeth in her Carmelite vocation
Mar 26	Madame Catez gives Elizabeth permission to enter Carmel at the age of 21; Elizabeth immediately considers how to prepare herself for becoming 'a bride less unworthy' (D 105)
Mar 31	Madame Catez presents a marriage proposal
Jun 20	Elizabeth's interview with Mother Marie of Jesus: accepted as a future postulant
Jun 22	Pierre Waldeck-Rousseau is elected Prime Minister
Summer	Holiday in the Jura Mountains, in Switzerland and in the Vosges region
Oct	Elizabeth now part of the group of 'postulants outside the walls' preparing for Carmel; around this time, begins to be involved in apostolic works
Nov	Writes an important self-offering (IN 4)
1900	
Jan 23–27	Attends a retreat given by Father Hoppenot, SJ
Jan 27	Wants to be a Carmelite within her soul, realising she can still belong to Jesus even in the world
May 9	Day pilgrimage to Paray-le-Monial

May or Jun	Inspirational first meeting with Father Vallée, OP: he speaks on God's great love
Jul 1	Signs her name for the first time 'Marie-Elizabeth of the Trinity', the religious name given to her by Mother Marie of Jesus
Summer	Holiday in south of France; Madame Catez is tempted to withdraw permission for entering Carmel; Elizabeth in distress; visits Carmel of Tarbes; fourth and final visit to Lourdes
Sep 8	Takes definitive farewell from Canon Angles
c. Oct	Second meeting with Father Vallée: it is probably on this occasion that he speaks on the Trinity
'Age 20'	After two years of headaches, reveals to Mother Marie of Jesus that she has been praying for suffering and wearing a hair shirt: she is ordered to stop, and her health returns
c. Nov	As Elizabeth's 21st birthday gets ever-nearer, Madame Catez is increasingly torn apart by the future departure for Carmel; Elizabeth suffers from the tension at home
c. Dec	Third meeting with Father Vallée: he speaks on St Paul
1901	
Jan	Father Vallée moves to Paris
Feb	Beginning of friendship with Marguerite Gollot, one of the group preparing for Carmel
Mar–Apr	Teaches catechism to Louise Demoulin
Apr–May	God seems absent in prayer; Elizabeth goes to him in 'pure faith'

Apr 16	Visits the Carmel of Beaune where she kisses St Teresa's staff
Jun 2	For the first time, speaks with real enthusiasm about God as Trinity
Early Jun	Has to rest up because of water on the knee: deprived of the sacraments, but aware she still has God's presence with her
Jun	Family moves to smaller apartment in the same house, in view of Elizabeth's imminent departure
Jun–Jul	Farewell visits from friends; tension with Marguerite Gollot who wants an exclusive friendship with Elizabeth
Jun 29	Official founding of the Carmel of Paray-le-Monial by Mother Marie of Jesus
c. end Jun	Madame Catez and Elizabeth agree to the request of Mother Marie of Jesus that Elizabeth should enter Carmel at Paray-le-Monial
Jul 1	Law of Associations comes into force
Jul 10–12	Is given the third volume of the works of John of the Cross: *Ascent* (Book 3) and *Dark Night*; there is no evidence that she ever read these two works
Jul 14–19	Learns the date of her entrance to Carmel: August 2
c. Jul 28	Madame Catez writes to Mother Marie of Jesus to ask if Elizabeth may enter at Dijon instead of at Paray
Jul 30	Elizabeth receives the news of permission to enter at Dijon

c. Aug 1–2	Is given the fourth volume of the works of John of the Cross: *Spiritual Canticle* and *Living Flame*; as from January 1903, Elizabeth will read this volume thoroughly, and John of the Cross will become a major inspiration for her

IN COMMUNITY

Aug 2	Enters the Carmel of Dijon on the Boulevard Carnot
Aug 5	Group photographs taken of the sisters in the community which are sent, the next day, to Lisieux with a description of Elizabeth as a future saint
c. Aug 9	Fills in the postulant's questionnaire (IN 12)
Aug 13	Performs a poem to the community which she has been asked to write (P 73) – the first of several
c. Sep	Elizabeth learns that the Carmel of Dijon is not going into exile, despite Government persecution of religious communities: Elizabeth inspired by thoughts of martyrdom, which will be a recurrent theme in her spirituality
Oct 9	Community elections: Mother Germaine becomes prioress and remains novice mistress; Sister Marie of the Trinity is the new sub-prioress
Oct 10	Mother Marie of Jesus moves definitively to Paray, taking three sisters from the 'novitiate' group; Elizabeth is now the only postulant
Oct 16	Mother Germaine's inaugural speech as prioress

Oct 16–23	One evening, praying before a relic of St Teresa, Elizabeth is informed 'interiorly' that she will receive the Carmelite habit on December 8, feast of the Immaculate Conception
Oct–Nov	Madame Catez is tempted to force Elizabeth to return home
Nov	Eight-day community retreat given by Father Edmond Vergne, SJ, on the *Exercises* of St Ignatius
Nov, 3rd or 4th week	Elizabeth is accepted unanimously to receive the habit
Dec 5–7	Elizabeth's three-day private retreat in preparation for receiving the habit
Dec 8	Clothing ceremony: a 'Tabor' experience characteristic of her whole postulancy
c. Dec 10	Beginning of first phase of trial of faith (lasting about four months): aridity in prayer, scruples, inner turmoil

1902

c. early Apr	Beginning of second phase of trial of faith (lasting eight to nine months): problems intensify to become 'cruel sufferings'
Apr 27 & May 4	National elections: the Republicans retain power
May 25	Deeply contemplative poem for feast of the Trinity (P 79)
Jun 7	The anticlerical Émile Combes becomes Prime Minister, following the resignation of Pierre Waldeck-Rousseau

c. mid–Jun	Elizabeth speaks of finding 'Heaven on earth' (L 122)
Jun 21	Sister Hélène leaves: Elizabeth is now the one remaining novice
Jun 22	First letter to the missionary brother, Henri Beaubis, whom Mother Germaine must have put in touch with Elizabeth: theme of Carmelite as apostle (L 124)
Jun 27	Government closes 135 Catholic schools
Jul 15	Government closes over 3000 Catholic schools
Jul 22	Guite becomes engaged to Georges Chevignard; that summer, after reflecting on the nun's vocation as bride, Elizabeth writes a magnificent meditation on being a bride of Christ (IN 13)
Jul 29	Important poem on the vocation of the Carmelite nun (P 83)
Summer	Living by faith is increasingly bearing fruit: aware of dependence on God; understanding the trial as God's action as she sees with the eyes of faith
Aug 11	A law is passed, bringing about the closure of many teaching congregations, one of which had been responsible for a network of primary schools in the diocese of Dijon
c. Sep	Beginning of friendship with Guite's brother-in-law, the seminarian André Chevignard; this will lead Elizabeth to reflect on the priestly vocation
Oct 6–15	Community retreat, with eight days of talks (October 7–14) by Father Vallée, on Jesus

Christ; during the retreat, Elizabeth has a distressing interview with him as he fails to understand her dark night experience

Oct 15   Guite's wedding to Georges Chevignard on the feast of Teresa of Avila

The bishops of France protest against the Government closure of religious congregations, especially in the light of the law of August 11; Albert Le Nordez is one of only two bishops refusing to sign the petition; he is by now very unpopular in the Church because of his Republican sympathies

Nov 11   Mother Germaine travels to Switzerland to inspect a property in case her community is forced to leave France

Dec 22   'Canonical examination' before being admitted to take vows

c. late Dec   Accepted unanimously by the community to take her vows

Dec 25   Elizabeth learns of the good news: her profession to take place at Epiphany

Christmas   Sister Geneviève leaves 'novitiate' group, as three years have elapsed since taking her vows: Elizabeth is now the only member of the 'novitiate'

1903

Jan 1–10   Retreat preceding profession; from this time on, she begins to read John of the Cross thoroughly (*Spiritual Canticle* and *Living Flame*), having previously only dipped into his works

Jan 10	Height of anxiety; reassuring interview with Father Vergne, SJ and a providential misunderstanding
Jan 11	Epiphany Sunday: ceremony of profession (perpetual vows)
c. Jan 12	Trial of faith comes to a sudden end
Jan 21	Elizabeth receives the black veil
c. Jan	Elizabeth becomes 'second habit sister' and 'second portress'
Feb 24	First letter to the seminarian André Chevignard: theme of apostolate of Carmelite and priest (L 158)
Mar 18–24	Government refuses authorisation to 134 religious congregations to teach or preach
Apr 16	Golden Jubilee celebrations of Sister Marie of the Incarnation; following Government measures (and during a service in chapel), the convent chapel is ordered to be closed to the public indefinitely
May 20	In case of exile, Mother Germaine leaves for Belgium to inspect possible accommodation in Noiseux; Elizabeth, throughout, is conspicuously calm about the situation because of her trust in Providence
Jul 15	Elizabeth writes of her wish to become holy (L 169), a theme which becomes prominent in her writings this year
Jul 20	Death of Pope Leo XIII
Aug 4	Pius X becomes Pope
Aug 20	Elizabeth writes of her vocation as living by love (L 172)

c. Aug 27	Elizabeth writes of love as letting oneself be loved (L 177)
Oct	Huge wave of closures by Government, affecting 10,000 religious establishments
Oct 4	First encyclical of Pius X (*E Supremi Apostolatus*), with the theme (also his motto) of 'restoring all things in Christ' (Eph 1:10)
Nov 19	Death of Elizabeth's former landlord, Henri Chapuis, for whom she had continued to pray
Nov 21	Elizabeth renews her vows with the community for the first time
Nov	Theme, in her letters, of belonging to heaven; by now, she is reading the final chapters of *The Spiritual Canticle* by John of the Cross: she is especially struck by theme of transformation into the three divine Persons
Dec	Elizabeth is allowed to keep the statue of Our Lady of Lourdes, which she had left at home when entering Carmel, in her cell during Advent
Christmas	Poem on penetrating the Mystery of God (P 88)
c. Christmas	It is probably now that Sister Aimée speaks to Elizabeth about the phrase 'praise of glory'; at this time, Elizabeth has been reading St Paul thoroughly for a while

1904

| c. Jan | Increasingly drawn into deep silence |
| Jan 25 | Important letter to André Chevignard, with her first mention of being 'the praise of His glory' (L 191) |

Feb	The seminarians refuse ordination from Bishop Le Nordez as he is close to the Government and rumoured to be a Freemason
Feb 23	Beginning of 'seminarians' strike'
Mar 11	Guite's first child is born and named after Elizabeth
c. Mar	Disagreement between Church and State as to which of them should appoint bishops; Pius X refuses to consecrate the unsuitable candidates put forward by Prime Minister Émile Combes
Apr	Pius X refuses to receive French President, Émile Loubet, after the latter visits the King of Italy; French ambassador to the Holy See is now recalled to France
May 28	Henri Beaubis is ordained priest
Jun 2	Important letter to Beaubis (L 202), reflecting on the priestly vocation which Elizabeth relates to her own calling
Jun 13	Over 200 children are kept away from Confirmation in Dijon, in protest against the Bishop; noisy crowds demonstrate against him
Jul 7	Government bars all members of religious congregations from teaching; 2000 schools are closed with immediate effect
Jul 9	Bishop Le Nordez is summoned to Rome
Jul 27	Bishop Le Nordez leaves for Rome
Jul 30	French Government breaks off diplomatic relations with the Vatican

Mid-Aug	Elizabeth wishes to have a 'passion for sacrifice' (L 207)
Sep 4	The See of Dijon becomes vacant after Le Nordez is asked to resign
Sep 25 (p.m.)– Oct 6 (a.m.)	Elizabeth's ten-day private retreat (the first since the one preceding her profession) with the writings of St Paul; great graces, especially that of understanding that she can remain in God's love through everything; as from this retreat, Elizabeth's soul becomes unified
c. Autumn	Arrival of Sister Madeleine, a new postulant
Oct 10	Community elections: Mother Germaine is re-elected prioress; Sister Marie of the Trinity remains sub-prioress
Nov	Émile Combes sets out a plan for the Separation of Church and State
Nov 12–21	Community retreat, with eight days of talks (November 13–20) by Father Fages, OP, on the Incarnation; Elizabeth is especially struck by his focus on the Annunciation
Nov 21	Renews vows in community: has a sense of transformation in God
	Elizabeth writes her *Prayer to the Trinity*, the same day, at the end of the retreat
Dec 8	Golden Jubilee of dogma of Immaculate Conception; Elizabeth helps carry a large statue of Mary in procession through the cloisters

1905

Jan	Elizabeth's letters contain the themes of God's love and living for his glory; by now, she already has many Scripture passages at her fingertips
Jan 8	Beatification of Jean-Marie Vianney, the Curé d'Ars
c. Jan 20	First appearance in her letters of the expression 'in communion' ('en société') with the Trinity (L 223)
Jan 24	Maurice Rouvier takes over as Prime Minister after the fall of Émile Combes
Jan–Feb	First signs of Elizabeth's health deteriorating, such as fatigue and feeling the cold more
Mar	French Government begins to discuss plans for Separation of Church and State
Early Mar	Beginning of stomach pains and difficulty with eating; Elizabeth is disappointed not to be allowed to fast during Lent
c. Mar 8	Speaks of a sense of spiritual wretchedness (L 225)
Apr 8	Ordination of André Chevignard to the diaconate: Elizabeth has been reflecting on the anointing of the Holy Spirit
Apr 19	Birth of Elizabeth's second niece, Odette
c. Apr 30	First mention, in her writings, of 'predestination' (L 228; cf. Eph 1:11–12; Rm 8:29–30)
Jun	By now, studying St Paul's letters: making indexes and noting favourite passages

Jun 1–11	Community's annual 'Cenacle' retreat: Elizabeth applies herself to standing beneath the anointing of the Holy Spirit (L 226)
Beg. Jun & c. Jun 25	Important letters to André Chevignard on the priestly ordination (L 231 & L 232)
Jun 29	André Chevignard is ordained priest
Jun 30	His First Mass: at the Dijon Carmel
c. Jul	Elizabeth's health rapidly worsens: pain, weakness and exhaustion; also, around this time, a feeling of God's absence
Jul 3	Law of Separation of Church and State is passed by the Chamber (first stage of voting)
Jul 29	Important poem on love (P 94)
Early Aug	Around this time, Elizabeth is seen by an Italian specialist, Dr Martignoli, who prescribes rest and fresh air
Mid-Aug	Elizabeth is given a month's break from her portress duties (which she will never be well enough to resume)
Aug 13–c. 17	Letter to Guite on motherhood (L 239)
Oct 6	Law of Separation of Church and State is passed by the Senate (second stage of voting)
Oct 8	Writes, for the first time, about being 'a sacrifice of praise to His glory' (L 244)
Oct 8 (p.m.)– 19 (a.m.)	Elizabeth's ten-day private retreat, described by Mother Germaine as 'the crown of all the rest': receives light on her vocation and feels unable to reach, and remain on, the heights; asks not to live long

Oct 19–	As from her retreat, community perceives Elizabeth as having 'passed into God' or dwelling 'in higher regions'
c. Nov 26	Long, insightful letter on coping with suffering (L 249)
c. Nov 29	Important letter to André Chevignard, on understanding her vocation to be a 'praise of glory'; also, her first use of the phrase in Latin, 'Laudem Gloriae' (L 250)
Dec 9	Law of Separation of Church and State is promulgated as law, and published two days later
Dec 15	Arrival of postulant Sister Thérèse
c. Dec–c. Jan	Arrival of postulants Clémence Blanc and Sister Marie-Joseph; Elizabeth is given the role of 'Angel' for both of them – one of these postulants arrives before Sister Thérèse, the other shortly afterwards
Dec 20	Decree of Pius X allowing daily Communion
Advent	Elizabeth, preparing crib, is overheard whispering to the baby Jesus: 'we'll see each other closer up next year'
Dec 25	Christmas poem on Christ's coming (P 96)
Dec 29	State decrees that all Church goods must be recorded in inventories before being handed over to 'associations of worship'; by now, 38 of the 117 French Carmels have left France
End Dec	Elizabeth considers how to live her vocation to be a praise of glory (L 256)

1906

Jan 1	Elizabeth draws St Joseph as her patron for 1906; since he is the 'Patron of a Good Death', she sees this as a good sign
c. Jan	From the time of her vocation to be a praise of glory, the Divine Office actually overtakes silent prayer for her
Jan 7	Epiphany Sunday: third anniversary of Elizabeth's profession; she is asked, around this time, to remain in the 'novitiate', to help the new postulants
Jan 15–23	Community retreat by Father Rollin, SJ: Elizabeth becomes yet more resolved to unite her will to God's and walk the way of the Cross
Jan–Mar	Elizabeth still managing to hide most of her sufferings; the pain, weakness and exhaustion are by now a torture
Jan 26	Letter on coping with suffering (L 263)
Feb 11	Encyclical, *Vehementer Nos*, of Pius X, denouncing the Law of Separation
Feb 18	Armand Fallières becomes President of France, succeeding Émile Loubet
Feb 25	Pius X consecrates 14 new French bishops, including Pierre Dadolle for the diocese of Dijon which has been without a bishop for nearly 18 months
Early Mar	At beginning of Lent, Elizabeth reads the words 'communion with his suffering and conformity with his death' (Ph 3:10) and feels called to live this

Mar 6	A demonstrator against inventories of Church goods is killed in violent clashes at Boeschèpe
Mar 12	As a result of the violence at Boeschèpe, Maurice Rouvier falls from power and is replaced by Ferdinand Sarrien as Prime Minister
Mar 15	Bishop Dadolle enters his cathedral
Mar 19	Feast of St Joseph: probably Elizabeth's last full day in community

IN THE INFIRMARY

Mar 20	Probable date of Elizabeth's move to the infirmary
Apr 8	Palm Sunday; first attack: loses consciousness for a while; Mother Germaine prepares her for death; Extreme Unction and Viaticum from Father Donin, summoned from the parish church
Apr 9	Madame Catez is informed for the first time of Elizabeth's serious illness; that week, she writes a letter, saying she is resigned to God's will, which much consoles Elizabeth who will read it often
Apr 14	Holy Saturday: after acute sufferings in Holy Week, Elizabeth's health shows a sudden improvement
Apr 21	Catholic newspaper of Dijon publishes Pius X's decree of December 20, 1905, allowing daily Communion; it will soon be applied in the Dijon Carmel but as Elizabeth is usually too weak to be carried to the grille, she receives Communion only five times in her first 50 days in the infirmary

End Apr	Elizabeth's recent brush with death leaves her remembering the prospect of meeting 'Divine Beauty' (L 270) and feeling as if she is 'coming out of a beautiful, luminous dream' (L 268); she is very much disappointed; from now on, she is also keen to make use of every moment in preparing for eternity
End Apr– beg. May	First visit to infirmary parlour from Madame Catez and Guite; future visits will be roughly one a fortnight
May 4	Consultation with three doctors, including a stomach specialist, sent to the convent by Elizabeth's brother-in-law (this is probably the first of their two visits): an operation is decided on, then rejected a few days later
May 12	Catholic newspaper of Dijon announces the reopening of the Carmelite chapel to the public (made possible by Law of Separation, as Church is no longer under State control); in this month, national elections retain the anticlerical majority in power
May 13	Second attack: again loses consciousness and appears to be close to death; from now on, symptoms are very severe: inflammation of the stomach which makes drinking acutely painful and leads to a scorching thirst
May 17	Visit from Madame Catez and Guite; they all expect this to be their final meeting
May 24	Ascension Day: vision of the indwelling Trinity; Elizabeth also hears the words of John 14:23 spoken in her soul; from now on, she is overwhelmed by God's love

c. May 27	Important spiritual letter to Madame Catez (L 273)
May 27	Beatification of the Carmelites of Compiègne
Beg. Jun	Elizabeth feeling slightly stronger and is able to be carried to the first-floor Communion grille each morning; also, she is often now carried to the open-air 'terrace'
Early Jun	From around this time, the Scripture verse 'God is a consuming fire' (Hb 12:29) becomes important to her, possibly because of her symptoms of inflammation
c. Jun 10	Important spiritual letter to Germaine de Gemeaux (L 278)
Jun 11–13	Madame Catez attends a triduum of celebrations in Paris for the newly beatified Carmelites of Compiègne
Jun 14	Carried to chapter room for eve of Mother Germaine's feast day: Elizabeth's first time with the whole community since entering the infirmary
Jun 15	Feast day of Mother Germaine: Elizabeth writes poems for the occasion and prepares a display of gifts and celebrations; she calls Mother Germaine 'Priest' for the first time in her writings (P 100)
c. Jun 16	Elizabeth is allowed to write one letter a day if she feels able
Jun 19	Feeling stronger; able to attend the whole of Mass in the infirmary tribune and spend an hour there in prayer afterwards; her voice, though, is becoming weaker

Jun 23	Madame Catez brings Elizabeth an anthology of Ruysbroeck (as suggested by Mother Germaine) and the *Maxims* of John of the Cross (a gift from Madame Hallo); a few days earlier, Elizabeth had received a small book on the Carmelites of Compiègne from Madame Hallo
Jun 24	Already writing enthusiastically about Ruysbroeck (L 288)
End Jun– early Jul	Letters are marked with a sense of imminent death and a longing for heaven
c. beg. Jul	Letter to console Clémence Blanc, who has recently left the monastery and is upset about the difficulties with her vocation (L 293)
Early Jul	Around this time, Mother Germaine tells Elizabeth to pray to be cured; Elizabeth obeys, but is happy when she hears an interior voice saying: 'Earthly offices are no longer for you.'
Jul 8 or 9	Regains use of legs on praying to Thérèse; had asked for this as a sign that she would not be cured!
c. 2nd week of Jul	On looking at a picture of Our Lady of Sorrows, Elizabeth receives a renewed love of Mary; she soon asks for her statue of Our Lady of Lourdes to be returned from home: the inseparable 'Janua Coeli'
c. mid-Jul	Feels increasingly drawn towards suffering as the gift of herself – 'the culmination of love' (L 298)
c. end Jul	Another consultation with the three doctors

Jul 29	Important poem containing the main themes of her spirituality (P 106)
Jul–Aug	Essay in the form of a 'retreat devotion', on Ruysbroeck (IN 17)
Aug	Intensifying of stomach pains and headaches; pain now dominates her nights of insomnia; Elizabeth draws strength from prayer in the infirmary tribune which is close to the tabernacle
	Some time during this month, important poem on going out of herself to live in God's presence (P 109); around this time, Elizabeth speaks of having a greater sense of inner freedom
Aug 2	Writes to Father Vallée for advice on being conformed to Christ Crucified; his reply, a few days later, will direct her primarily to love
1st half of Aug	Writes *Heaven in Faith* for Guite
Aug 10	Pius X rejects the possibility of 'associations of worship' (as well as the compromise suggestion of canonico-legal associations), in his encyclical *Gravissimo Officii Munere*
Aug 15–31	Elizabeth's final retreat, which Mother Germaine calls her 'novitiate for heaven'; during this time, has her last meeting with Mother Marie of Jesus; Elizabeth is by now almost overcome with violent pain
c. Aug 16–31	Elizabeth writes her *Last Retreat*, exploring how to live fully her vocation to be a praise of glory
c. Aug 20	Receives the grace to embrace suffering and go beyond its bitterness

Sep	With onset of cooler weather, has to give up her nocturnal prayer vigils at cell window; but she will continue to rise for her much-loved Office of Lauds until the last week of her life
c. Sep	Elizabeth has an ever-increasing ardour for observing the Carmel's *Rule* and customs, as a way of giving herself; she feels that this would reconcile her to being cured, despite her continued longing for heaven
	Having previously drawn other sisters to recollection, Elizabeth's influence now leads them primarily to practise heroic virtue; in this month, the postulant Sister Thérèse leaves because of health reasons
	Treatments with the stomach pump
Early Sep	Writes *The Greatness of Our Vocation* for Françoise de Sourdon over several days, finishing by about September 9
c. Sep 14	Elizabeth discovers a phrase by Bl Angela of Foligno which will be inspirational for her: 'Where then did He dwell but in suffering?'
Sep 14	Feast of the Exaltation of the Cross: Elizabeth gives Mother Germaine a cardboard 'Citadel of suffering and of holy recollection', which she has made, and an important poem inspired by the words of Bl Angela (P 113)
c. Sep 21	Elizabeth's desire for suffering – as a means of conformity to Christ – by now almost surpasses her longing for heaven
Sep 24	12th anniversary of Mother Germaine's profession: Elizabeth gives her poems, presents, and especially the manuscript of the *Last Retreat*

End Sep	Still 'absorbed in the passion' (L 317) through the writings of Bl Angela of Foligno
End Sep– beg. Oct	Note to Mother Germaine from 'the palace of pain and bliss' (L 320)
Oct 4	Elizabeth receives new (warmer) habit and renews her clothing ceremony; in the evening, is carried downstairs to the choir (for the first and last time) to renew her self-offering: her second time with the whole community
Oct 7	Writes secretly to Madame Gout de Bize, to try matchmaking her daughter with Mother Germaine's brother!
Oct 9	Elizabeth's last poem for Mother Germaine, on their relationship as priest and sacrificial offering (P 122)
Oct 13–15	Triduum of celebrations at the Dijon Carmel in honour of the Carmelites of Compiègne; during these days, Elizabeth has an inspiring final meeting with Father Vallée: as with his letter in early August, he again urges her not to focus solely on suffering, this time telling her simply to surrender herself to whatever Christ wills for her
Oct 15	Bishop Dadolle gives her his blessing; Elizabeth looks on this as her 'final consecration to the Trinity'
c. Oct 20	By now, has continual nausea; just able to eat some chocolates, but struggles to eat eight a day as instructed by Mother Germaine
3rd week of Oct	Despite her extreme exhaustion, Elizabeth renders many services to the sisters, especially helping to make the white bridal outfit for the clothing ceremony of Sister Marie-Joseph

Oct 22	Elizabeth's final poem, written for the new novice: an important one as Elizabeth, at the end of her life, is here summing up how to live the Carmelite vocation (P 123)
	Later that evening, the pain becomes so intense that Elizabeth feels at screaming point: inflammation is now raging throughout her body
c. 4th week of Oct	Elizabeth recounts her youth to Mother Germaine, who will need the information for writing the obituary *Circular*; at some point during these exchanges, Elizabeth describes her posthumous mission, in response to questioning by Mother Germaine
Oct 25	Georges Clémenceau becomes Prime Minister; he will put an end to the inventories of Church goods and pursue a policy of conciliation
c. last week of Oct	One night, Elizabeth feels tempted to throw herself out of the window because of the level of pain
c. Oct 27	Elizabeth is strengthened by a mystical experience: 'a fire of infinite sweetness'
Last days of Oct	Writes *Let Yourself Be Loved* for Mother Germaine
	After Elizabeth has kept her eyes for so long on the crucified Christ, the image of the risen Christ now also holds its place in her mind; her letters at the end of October (as from the 28th) are pervaded by the themes of light and beauty
Oct 28	Describes her posthumous mission in a letter to Sister Marie-Odile (L 335); also around the end of October, writes an inspiring spiritual letter to Antoinette de Bobet (L 333)

Oct 29	Final meeting with Madame Catez and Guite; Elizabeth takes her crucifix and gives a solemn blessing to her two nieces
Oct 30	The last day that Elizabeth is able to get up; she has 'her last meal on earth' (moistening her tongue with ice) – she can no longer eat or drink; Elizabeth gives Sister Marie-Xavier the name 'Abscondita in Deo' ('Hidden in God')
Oct 31	Receives Extreme Unction and Viaticum for the second time
Nov 1	Feast of All Saints: Elizabeth receives Communion for the last time (from now on, her tongue will be too dried up to swallow even a particle of the Host)
	Full of joy, expecting to go to heaven before the end of the day; it is very probably on this day that she dictates (to Mother Germaine) her letters to Madame Hallo and Charles Hallo (L 341 & L 342)
Nov 2	Final trial begins: for the next few days, overwhelming pain and spiritual darkness; also, physical darkness due to her eyes becoming almost impossible to open
Early days of Nov	Elizabeth's letter (dictated to Mother Germaine), addressed to Dr Barbier (L 340); this is almost certainly her final letter
Nov 5	Manages to explain to Sister Marie-Xavier the meaning of being 'hidden in God'
c. Nov 6 or 7	Spiritual darkness gives way to light; Elizabeth seems to glimpse into heaven

Nov 7	Joyful outburst to Dr Barbier about going to heaven; she also speaks to him of the meaning of being children of God; from now on, has no more energy to speak, and will be heard only to murmur: 'I am going to Light, to Love, to Life!...'
Nov 8–9	Very difficult final night, with the added new symptom of asphyxiation
Nov 9	Elizabeth dies peacefully at around a quarter past six in the morning

AFTER HER DEATH

1906

Nov 9	The day of Elizabeth's death, René Viviani declares triumphantly in the Chamber of Deputies: 'We have torn human consciences away from belief.'
Nov 12	Elizabeth's funeral in Carmelite chapel; burial at the 'Cimetière des Péjoces', the public cemetery of Dijon, in the section reserved for the Carmelite nuns
Dec 18	Mother Germaine completes the writing of Elizabeth's obituary *Circular*
Dec 24	Mother Germaine mentions her wish to write a 'notice': a longer biographical piece on Elizabeth (this will be the *Souvenirs*); in the next few days, she begins requesting information for it

1907

Jan 2	Government's response to Pius X's encyclical of August 10, 1906, *Gravissimo Officii Munere*: the threats contained in the Law of

	Separation are carried out completely, and the Church's property passes to the State
Jan 7	Encyclical of Pius X, *Une Fois Encore*, addressed to the Church in France to sustain them during their trials
c. Jan	Mother Germaine discovers, among Elizabeth's papers, the *Prayer to the Trinity*
c. mid-Jan	The *Circular* has to be reprinted; the second print-run will run out by mid-April

1909

Early Oct	First edition of the *Souvenirs*, Mother Germaine's biography of Elizabeth; it will sell out rapidly and, by 1956, have run to at least 16 French editions as well as numerous translations
Nov	Already, only a month after the appearance of the *Souvenirs*, flowers and inscriptions are left at Elizabeth's grave; over the next few years, ever-increasing numbers of pilgrims will visit her grave and the monastery
1912	First English edition of the *Souvenirs*; this is also the first translation to appear

1914

Mar 10	Death of Madame Catez

1917

Pentecost	Promulgation of the *Code of Canon Law*, which brings together the protocols and procedures for beatification and canonisation

1925

May 17   Canonisation of Thérèse of Lisieux

Nov 18   Death of Georges Chevignard, Elizabeth's
          brother-in-law; Guite is now a widow with
          nine children

1927   Addition of an 18th chapter to the *Souvenirs*;
          the work is now in its 12th French edition,
          and from now on is brought out by the St Paul
          printing house (later publishing house) in
          Paris

1928

Dec 8   Elizabeth Chevignard, Elizabeth's niece,
          enters the Carmel of Dijon

1930

Oct 10   Elizabeth's remains are exhumed, identified,
          and placed in a more secure coffin

1931

May 23   Opening, in Dijon, of the Ordinary Process
          for beatification, which will last until 1941;
          Rogatory Processes will also be held: in Paris,
          Toulouse, Agen and Carcassonne

1934

Nov 30   Death of Mother Germaine

1939

Beg. of year   First edition (in French) of *The Spiritual
          Doctrine of Sister Elizabeth of the Trinity* by Father
          Marie-Michel Philipon, OP (first English
          edition = 1947); this bestselling publication is
          the first doctrinal work on Elizabeth and will
          bring her to the attention of theologians

1943

Jan   Cure of Father Jean-Marie Chanut, OCSO
                  from tuberculosis of the right kidney and
                  advanced Potts' Disease, following prayer of
                  intercession to Elizabeth

1944

Jan 28   Decree on the Writings

1948   Opening, in Dijon and Toulouse, of a
                  Supplementary Process, which will last until
                  1950

1949   First edition (in French) of *Spiritual Writings of
                  Elizabeth of the Trinity,* edited by Father Marie-
                  Michel Philipon, OP (first English edition
                  = 1962); this anthology will be extremely
                  influential in making Elizabeth's writings
                  known

1952   First edition (in German) of *Elizabeth of Dijon
                  and her Spiritual Mission* by Hans Urs von
                  Balthasar (first English edition (adapted) =
                  1956; first French edition = 1959)

1954

May 7   Death of Guite

1961

Jan 25   John XXIII signs the Decree on the
                  Introduction of the Cause

1962

Jun 22   Decree of No Cult

Oct 11   Opening of the Second Vatican Council,
                  which will end in 1965

1963	Opening of the Apostolic Process on Elizabeth's virtues, which will be completed in 1965 (Dijon = 1963–1965; Paris = 1963–1964; Toulouse = 1964)
	First edition (in French) of *Learning to Pray according to Sister Elizabeth of the Trinity* by Father Jean Lafrance (first English edition = 2003); this is a forerunner of many spiritual works on Elizabeth
1964	Opening, in Dijon, of the Process on a presumed Miracle, investigating the cure of Father Jean-Marie Chanut; this will be completed in 1965
1965	Elizabeth's remains are exhumed and identified, in view of a future beatification
1966	Publication (in French) of *In the Presence of God* by Father Marie-Michel Philipon, OP (not translated into English); this book is of special importance in that it includes an appendix containing eyewitness accounts of Elizabeth
1969	First edition (in French) of *This Presence of God in You* by Sister Marie-Dominique Poinsenet, OP (not translated into English); this noteworthy biography shows the very human face of Elizabeth and makes her accessible to the modern Church
Mar 19	Apostolic Letter, *Sanctitas Clarior,* by Paul VI, amending the procedures for beatification and canonisation

1970

Mar 13   Decree on the Validity of the Ordinary and
                Apostolic Processes; the decree of that title of
                July 5, 1969 is now confirmed, as Elizabeth's
                writings have now been fully examined by
                theological censors

1973

Jan 2   Centenary of the birth of St Thérèse of
                Lisieux

Dec 5   Father Simeón Tomás Fernández is appointed
                Postulator General of the Discalced
                Carmelites

1979

Apr 16   Centenary of the death of St Bernadette of
                Lourdes

Nov 25   Sunday of Christ the King: opening of the
                centenary of Elizabeth's birth, which will last
                until November 25, 1980; a few months before
                the opening of the centenary, the Carmelite
                nuns of Dijon had moved to the nearby new
                monastery of Flavignerot

1979–1980   First edition (in French) of the *Complete Works
                of Elizabeth of the Trinity*, edited by Father
                Conrad De Meester, OCD (English edition
                of the first two volumes = 1984 and 1995; the
                third is forthcoming); this is a vastly influential
                publication, making Elizabeth's complete
                writings available for the first time, and
                showing her in 'a new and more complete light'

1980   Publication (in Italian) of *Elizabeth of the
                Trinity: A Vocation Realised according to God's*

Plan by Father Luigi Borriello, OCD (first English edition, *Spiritual Doctrine of Blessed Elizabeth of the Trinity* = 1986); this work shows Elizabeth's relevance to the modern Church, in the light of the teachings of Vatican II

Aug 17   Death of Father Jean-Marie Chanut, aged 71, having never had a relapse since his miraculous cure

Nov 7   Decree on the 'recently discovered' Writings

1982

Jul 12   John Paul II promulgates the Decree on the Heroic Virtues, by means of which Elizabeth becomes 'Venerable'

1983

Jan 25   Apostolic Constitution, *Divinus Perfectionis Magister*, by John Paul II, reforming the procedures for beatification and canonisation

1984   Publication (in Italian) of *Elizabeth of the Trinity: A Theological Existence* by Father Antonio Sicari, OCD (not translated into English); this is an important biography, exploring Elizabeth's life as a 'lived theology'

Jan 28   Permission granted by Rome for Elizabeth's remains to be transferred from the public cemetery of Dijon to St Michael's parish church

Feb 17   Decree on the Miracle for beatification, concerning the cure of Father Jean-Marie Chanut in 1943

Feb 21	News is received from Rome that John Paul II authorises Elizabeth's beatification
Sep 10	Elizabeth's remains are exhumed, identified, and removed in readiness for transferral to St Michael's parish church in Dijon once Elizabeth is beatified; one relic will also be given to the new Dijon Carmel at Flavignerot
Nov 25	Sunday of Christ the King: Elizabeth is beatified by John Paul II in St Peter's Basilica, Rome
	Apostolic Letter (or Brief) of the Beatification, by John Paul II
1985	Publication (in French) of *I Seek You at Daybreak*, edited by the Carmel of Dijon and Father Conrad De Meester, OCD (English edition, *Elizabeth of the Trinity: Light, Love, Life* = 1987); this is a collection of photographs of Elizabeth and of significant people and places in her life
1989	First edition (in French) of *Women Mystics* by Louis Bouyer (first English edition = 1993); this work places Elizabeth in the context of a mystical tradition
1991	First edition (in French) of *Elizabeth Catez or an Obsession with God* by Didier Decoin (not translated into English); this highly original work, by an eminent novelist, brings Elizabeth to the attention of the secular and literary world
Oct 17	Death of Elizabeth Chevignard, Elizabeth's niece who was a nun in the Carmel of Dijon

2006	Publication (in French) of *Elizabeth of the Trinity: A Biography* by Father Conrad De Meester, OCD (not yet translated into English); this is a major biography based on years of research
	Publication (in French) of *The Words of Elizabeth of the Trinity* by the Carmel of Bourges; this is a major concordance of Elizabeth's writings
	Publication (in French) of *Elizabeth of the Trinity: The Mystical Adventure*, edited by Father Jean Clapier, OCD (not translated into English); this is an important collection of 29 scholarly articles
Jun 11	Trinity Sunday: opening of the centenary of Elizabeth's death, which will last until Trinity Sunday, June 3, 2007
2011	
Jul 11	Opening, in Dijon, of the diocesan enquiry into a presumed miracle for the canonisation: the cure of Marie-Paul Stevens from Sjøgren's Syndrome after prayer of intercession to Elizabeth in April 2002; the Postulator of the Cause is now Father Ildefonso Moriones, OCD who had succeeded Father Simeón as Postulator General of the Discalced Carmelites

Appendix III

WORKS CONSULTED

A NOTE ABOUT REFERENCES

Abbreviations in Text

The main works referred to in this book are indicated by abbreviations in brackets directly after the quotation or passage concerned: see Abbreviations section, at the end of each volume, for a full list. These works include: Elizabeth's writings, her spoken words, testimonies by people who knew her, and the major biographies; also, the writings of those Carmelite saints whom Elizabeth often quoted.

Footnote References

All other works are referred to in footnotes. For those which are listed below – that is, works specifically relevant to Elizabeth or her times – just the surname of the author is given in the footnote (together with page numbers), except that: (i) where there is more than one author of that surname, the Christian name is also given; and (ii) where an author has more than one title listed below, the work's short title is also supplied.

WORKS BY ELIZABETH

De Meester, Conrad, OCD (ed.), *I Have Found God: Complete Works of Elizabeth of the Trinity*, vol. 1: *General Introduction [&] Major Spiritual Writings*, Washington, DC: ICS Publications, 1984 [includes: *Heaven in Faith, The Greatness of Our Vocation, Last Retreat, Let Yourself Be Loved, Prayer to the Trinity*].
-----, vol. 2: *Letters from Carmel* [= L 84–L 342], Washington, DC: ICS Publications, 1995.

-----, *J'ai trouvé Dieu – Œuvres complètes d'Élisabeth de la Trinité*, vols. I/A, I/B, II, Paris: Cerf, 1979–1980.

-----, *Œuvres complètes d'Élisabeth de la Trinité*, Paris: Cerf, 1991. [In addition to the works contained in the English volumes, this includes: *Diary, Intimate Notes, Letters from her Youth* [= L 1–L 83], *Poems* – the contents of the 1979 French vol. II.]

POEMS

Bancroft, Alan (ed. & tr.), *Barb of Fire*, pp. 49–181 [see full reference under 'Works Relevant to Elizabeth and her Times'].

SPOKEN WORDS OF ELIZABETH AND EYEWITNESS ACCOUNTS

Curia Generalis OCD, *To be a Carmelite*, pp. 36–40 [see full reference under 'Works Relevant to Elizabeth and her Times'].

Office for the Promotion of Causes [OCD] (ed.), *Elizabeth Still Speaks... – In the Processes of Beatification and Canonization: Words of the Servant of God Reported by Witnesses*, Eugene, OR: Carmel of Maria Regina, 1982.

Philipon, Marie-Michel, OP, *En Présence de Dieu*, pp. 185–205 [see full reference under 'Works Relevant to Elizabeth and her Times'].

ANTHOLOGIES OF QUOTATIONS OF ELIZABETH

De Meester, Conrad, OCD (ed.), *Les plus belles pages d'Élisabeth de la Trinité*, Paris: Cerf, 2000.

-----, *Pensées I: Vous êtes la Maison de Dieu*, Paris: Cerf, 1984.

-----, *Pensées II: Pour son amour j'ai tout perdu*, Paris: Cerf, 1984.

Moorcroft, Jennifer (ed. & tr.), *Elizabeth of the Trinity: Her Message and Spirituality*, London: Catholic Truth Society, 2005.

Murphy, Marian T, OCD (ed.), *Elizabeth of the Trinity: Always Believe in Love*, Hyde Park, NY: New City Press, 2009.

Philipon, Marie-Michel, OP (ed.), *Sister Elizabeth of the Trinity: Spiritual Writings – Letters, Retreats, and Unpublished Notes*, London: Geoffrey Chapman, 1962.

Rémy, Jean (ed.), *L'Expérience de Dieu avec Élisabeth de la Trinité*, Quebec: Fides, 2004.

CONCORDANCE

Carmel of Bourges, *Les Mots d'Élisabeth de la Trinité: Concordance précédée d'un Essai sur Élisabeth écrivain par Conrad De Meester o.c.d.*, Bourges: Carmel of Bourges / Moerzeke: Carmel-EdiT, 2006.

COLLECTIONS OF PHOTOGRAPHS

De Meester, Conrad, OCD (ed.), *La Giovinezza di una Santa: Elisabetta della Trinità* [supplement to the review *Il Messagero del S. Bambino Gesù di Praga*], Arenzano, 1985.

De Meester, Conrad, OCD & Carmel of Dijon (eds.), *Elizabeth of the Trinity: Light, Love, Life – A Look at a Face and a Heart*, Washington, DC: ICS Publications, 1987.

Furdzik, Paweł Piotr, OCD (ed.), *Błogosławiona Elżbieta od Trójcy Świętej: O świcie Ciebie szukam – Wspomnienie pewnego oblicza i pewnego serca*, Kraków: Wydawnictwo Karmelitów Bosych, 2006.

WORKS RELEVANT TO ELIZABETH AND HER TIMES

Acta Ordinis Carmelitarum Discalceatorum, Rome: Curia Generalis OCD, Ann. 12–15, Fasc. 8–12, 1967–1970.

-----, Ann. 16–18, 1971–1973.

-----, Ann. 18–19, 1973–1974.

-----, Anno 25, 1980.

-----, Anno 26, vol. 2, 1981.

-----, Anno 27, 1982.

-----, Anno 29, 1984.

-----, Anno 32, 1987.

-----, Anno 51, 2006.

Acta Postulationis Generalis et Status Causarum Beatificationis et Canonizationis Ordinis Carmelitarum Discalceatorum [December 1973–end of March 1979], Rome: Postulatio Generalis OCD, 1979.

Actes du Colloque de Dijon 2006: Élisabeth de la Trinité, fascinée par Dieu, proche de tous, Toulouse: Éditions du Carmel, 2007.

Allchin, A M, *The Gift of Theology: The Trinitarian Vision of Ann Griffiths and Elizabeth of Dijon*, Fairacres, Oxford: SLG Press, 2005.

Ardens, *Un Balzo nel Divino: Vita e pensieri di Suor Elisabetta della Trinità*, Rome & Milan: Editrice 'Regnum Dei', 1983.

Attwater, Donald (revised and updated by Catherine Rachel John), *The Penguin Dictionary of Saints*, London: Penguin, 1983.

Bancroft, Alan (ed. & tr.), *Barb of Fire: Twenty Poems of Blessed Elizabeth of the Trinity, with Selected Passages from Blessed Columba Marmion*, Leominster: Gracewing, 2001.

Benedictines of Solesmes (ed.), *The Liber Usualis with Introduction and Rubrics in English*, Tournai: Desclée & Co., 1953.

Borde, Marie-Bruno, OCD, Thierry-Joseph de Marie Mère de Dieu, OCD, Guillaume Dehorter, OCD & Benoit-Marie Langlois, OCD, *Élisabeth: Une âme de prière*, Toulouse: Éditions du Carmel, 2006.

Borriello, Luigi, OCD, *Elisabetta della Trinità: Una vocazione realizzata secondo il progetto di Dio*, Naples: Edizioni Dehoniane, 1980.

-----, *Spiritual Doctrine of Blessed Elizabeth of the Trinity: Apostolic Contemplative*, New York: Alba House, 1986.

Bouyer, Louis, 'Elizabeth of the Trinity', in his *Women Mystics: Hadewijch of Antwerp, Teresa of Avila, Thérèse of Lisieux, Elizabeth of the Trinity, Edith Stein*, San Francisco: Ignatius Press, 1993, pp. 155–71.

Burton, Katherine, *The Great Mantle: The Life of Giuseppe Melchiore Sarto, Pope Pius X*, Dublin: Clonmore & Reynolds, 1951.

Carmel, nos. 22–23 (issue: *Sr Élisabeth de la Trinité: Une soif d'infini – Cahier du centenaire 1880–1980*), 1981.

-----, no. 40, (issue: *Merveilleusement humaine: Actualité d'une béatification – Élisabeth de la Trinité*), 1985.

-----, no. 96 (issue: *Élisabeth louange de la Trinité*), 2000.

-----, no. 122 (issue: *Élisabeth de la Trinité: L'intériorité au service du monde – Numéro spécial Centenaire*), 2006.

Carmelite Missal, [Oxford: Carmelite Priory], 2005, pp. 99–100 & 346–8.

Carmel of Dijon, *Élisabeth de la Trinité: Un amour excessif / Elizabeth of the Trinity: Boundless Love / Elisabeth von der Dreifaltigkeit: Eine Liebe ohne Maß* [DVD], Dijon: Carmel of Dijon, [2006].

-----, 'Présentation des Souvenirs', in [Saint-Seine, Mother Germaine de, OCD], *Élisabeth de la Trinité*, pp. 9–14 [see full reference below].

[Carmel of Paray-le-Monial], *A Carmelite of the Sacred Heart: The Life of Mère Marie de Jésus, Foundress of the Carmel of Paray-le-Monial, 1853–1917*, London: Burns, Oates & Washbourne, 1923.

Cérémonial pour les Religieuses de l'Ordre de N.-D. du Mont Carmel de la première Règle selon la Réformation de sainte Thérèse de l'Observance de France, Clamart: Carmel of Clamart, 1935.

Clapier, Jean, OCD (ed.), *Élisabeth de la Trinité: L'Aventure mystique – Sources, expérience théologale, rayonnement*, Toulouse: Éditions du Carmel, 2006.

Cobban, Alfred, *A History of Modern France*, vol. 2: *From the First Empire to the Fourth Republic, 1799–1945*, Harmondsworth: Penguin, 1961.

Communicationes [Information Service of the Discalced Carmelite Curia], no. 63, June 15, 2006.

-----, no. 64, June 30, 2006.

-----, no. 67, October 15, 2006.

-----, no. 72, January 2, 2007.

-----, no. 75, February 20, 2007.

-----, no. 89, October 29, 2007.

-----, no. 91, December 1, 2007.

-----, no. 179, July 13, 2011.

Curia Generalis OCD (Secretariatus pro Monialibus), *To be a Carmelite with the Blessed Elizabeth of the Trinity* [Chapter 18 of the series *Guidelines for study following the order contained in the Declarations*], Rome: Discalced Carmelite Order, no date.

Daniel-Rops, Henri, *A Fight for God, 1870–1939*, London: J M Dent & Sons / New York: E P Dutton & Co., 1966.

De Bono, Juan, OCD, *La Sofferenza nella Vita e negli Scritti della Beata Elisabetta della Trinità*, Rome: Teresianum, 2001.

Decoin, Didier, *Élisabeth Catez ou l'obsession de Dieu*, Paris: Cerf, 2003.

Decourtray, Cardinal Albert, *Élisabeth de la Trinité: Un prophète de Dieu pour notre temps*, Flavignerot: Carmel of Dijon, 1979.

-----, *Présence d'Élisabeth de la Trinité*, Flavignerot: Carmel of Dijon, 1980.

De Meester, Conrad, OCD, *Dans le Ciel de notre âme: 'Dernière retraite' avec Élisabeth de la Trinité*, Paris: Cerf, 1992.

-----, 'Een grote Vreugde: De Zaligverklaring van Elisabeth van de Drieeenheid op 25 november 1984', in *Innerlijkleven: Een Tijdschrift van de Teresiaanse Karmel*, vol. 38/4, 1984, pp. 264–76.

-----, *Élisabeth de la Trinité: Biographie*, Paris: Presses de la Renaissance, 2006.

-----, *Élisabeth de la Trinité racontée par elle-même*, Paris: Cerf, 1988.

-----, 'Elizabeth in the Words of the Pope: "A New Guide – Certain and Sure"', in *Mount Carmel*, vol. 55/2, 2007, pp. 16–20.

-----, 'Essai sur Élisabeth écrivain', in Carmel of Bourges, *Les Mots*, pp. VII–XXIV [see full reference under 'Concordance'].

-----, *Your Presence is My Joy!: Life and Message of Blessed Elizabeth of the Trinity*, Darlington: Darlington Carmel, no date.

Discalced Carmelite Proper Offices: A Supplement to the Divine Office, Oxford: Carmelite Priory, 2006, pp. 211–13.

Dorgan, Margaret, DCM, *Elizabeth of the Trinity: Life in the Trinity*, Washington, DC: ICS Publications Cassettes, ref. TLT, no date.

Ferlay, Philippe, *Ô mon Dieu, Trinité que j'adore: La prière d'Élisabeth de la Trinité*, Paris: Cerf, 1992.

-----, *Paix et silence: Au désert avec Élisabeth de la Trinité*, Paris: Cerf, 2010.

Févotte, Patrick-Marie, *Aimer la Bible avec Élisabeth de la Trinité*, Paris: Cerf, 1991.

-----, *Enraciné dans le Christ: À la suite de la Bienheureuse Élisabeth de la Trinité*, Toulouse: Éditions du Carmel, 2005.

-----, *Le Jubilé 2000 avec Élisabeth de la Trinité*, Toulouse: Éditions du Carmel, 1999.

-----, *'Prends-la chez toi.': Chemin de vie avec Élisabeth de la Trinité*, Toulouse: Éditions du Carmel, 2002.

-----, *Virginité, chemin d'amour: À l'école d'Élisabeth de la Trinité*, Paris: Cerf, 1993.

Gaughran, Michael, SSC, *The Spirit and Message of Blessed Elizabeth of the Trinity*, Darlington: Darlington Carmel, no date.

Golden, Michael, SPS, '"I Felt I Had Never Met God..."': Story of a Conversion through the Writings of Bl Elizabeth of the Trinity', in *Spirituality*, vol. 13, no. 73, 2007, pp. 195–7.

Hales, E E Y, *Revolution and Papacy, 1769–1846*, London: Eyre & Spottiswoode, 1960.

Hampden Jackson, J, *Clemenceau and the Third Republic*, London: The English Universities Press, 1946.

Heyer, Friedrich, *The Catholic Church from 1648 to 1870*, London: Adam & Charles Black, 1969.

[Hostalier], Marie-Michel, OCD, *Toucher l'Infini: Élisabeth de la Trinité – Une spiritualité prophétique*, Paris: Éditions du Jubilé, 2007.

-----, *Une soif d'infini: Élisabeth de la Trinité – Sa vie, son visage*, Paris: Éditions du Jubilé, 2006.

Houdret, Jean-Philippe, OCD, 'La belle lumière de foi', in *Actes des Assemblées fédérales des Carmélites de France-Nord: 'Marchons ensemble, Seigneur!' – Femmes à la suite du Christ au Carmel*, Toulouse: Éditions du Carmel, 2004, pp. 127–42.

Huvet, Michel, *Élisabeth de Dijon*, Dijon: Éditions de Bourgogne, 2006.

John of the Cross, *The Collected Works of Saint John of the Cross*, Washington, DC: ICS Publications, 1991.

John Paul II, *Ad perpetuam rei memoriam* (Apostolic Letter (or Brief) of Beatification), November 25, 1984, in *Acta Ordinis*, Anno 32, 1987, pp. 7–12 [see full reference above].

-----, *Divinus Perfectionis Magister* (Apostolic Constitution), January 25, 1983.

-----, [For the Pope's homily and addresses on Elizabeth at her beatification, see De Meester, Conrad, OCD, 'Elizabeth in the Words of the Pope', pp. 18–20 – see full reference above.]

Keeffe, Christopher, *How Saints are Canonised*, London: Catholic Truth Society, 2008.

Kelly, J N D, *The Oxford Dictionary of Popes*, Oxford & New York: Oxford University Press, 1988.

Krikorian, Jean-Claude Y (ed.), *Élisabeth de la Trinité: Musique et silence du Carmel*, Sainte-Maxime: Éditions C.I.F., 1983.

Lafrance, Jean, *Elizabeth of the Trinity: The Charism of her Prayer* ('adapted from the French by a nun of the Carmel du Pater Noster, Jerusalem'), Darlington: Darlington Carmel, [c. 1983].

-----, *Learning to Pray according to Sister Elizabeth of the Trinity*, Sherbrooke, QU: Médiaspaul, 2003.

Langlois, Claude, 'Un Centenaire oublié. Le Procès de non-culte (1911–2011)', in *Vie Thérésienne*, no. 204, 2011, pp. 61–92.

Larkin, Thomas, OCD, *Sister Elizabeth of the Trinity, A Carmelite Nun of Dijon, 1901–1906: An Introduction to her Life and Spirituality*, Dublin: Carmelite Centre of Spirituality, 1984.

Leo XIII, *Au Milieu des Sollicitudes* (Encyclical), February 16, 1892.

-----, *Immortale Dei* (Encyclical), November 1, 1885.

-----, *Nobilissima Gallorum Gens* (Encyclical), February 8, 1884.

Manservigi, Massimo, *Sabeth: Élisabeth de la Trinité, 1880–1906* [3 DVDs, in French, English, Italian, Spanish, German and Polish], Dijon: Carmel of Dijon, 2006.

Marie Amabel du Cœur de Jésus, OCD, *A Soul of Silence: Sr Elizabeth of the Trinity*, Cork & Liverpool: The Mercier Press, 1949.

-----, *The Doctrine of the Divine Indwelling: A Commentary on the Prayer of Sister Elizabeth of the Trinity*, Cork & Liverpool: The Mercier Press, 1950.

Marie-Michelle, OCD, 'Élisabeth de la Trinité', in *Actes des Assemblées fédérales des Carmélites de France-Nord: 'Marchons ensemble, Seigneur!' – Femmes à la suite du Christ au Carmel*, Toulouse: Éditions du Carmel, 2004, pp. 103–25.

McCaffrey, Eugene, OCD, *Let Yourself Be Loved: Elizabeth of the Trinity*, Oxford: Teresian Press, 2008.

McCaffrey, James, OCD, 'Elizabeth of the Trinity: Prophet of the Presence of God', in his *Captive Flames: A Biblical Reading of the Carmelite Saints*, Dublin: Veritas, 2005, pp. 98–128.

Molinari, Paolo, SJ, 'Canonization of Saints (History and Procedure)', in *New Catholic Encyclopedia*, vol. III, Washington, DC: The Catholic University of America, 1967, pp. 55–9.

Moorcroft, Jennifer, *He is My Heaven: The Life of Elizabeth of the Trinity*, Washington, DC: ICS Publications, 2001.

Mount Carmel: A Review of the Spiritual Life, vol. 32/4 (issue: *Beatification of Elizabeth of the Trinity*), 1984.

-----, vol. 52/1 (issue devoted to Elizabeth of the Trinity), 2004.

-----, vol. 54/3 (issue: *Elizabeth of the Trinity Centenary Issue*), 2006.

-----, vol. 55/2 (issue: *Elizabeth of the Trinity – End of Centenary Issue*), 2007.

Murphy, Marian T, OCD, *Elizabeth of the Trinity: Her Life and Spirituality – The Vast Triangled Heart*, Leominster: Gracewing, 2011.

New Catholic Encyclopedia, 19 vols., Washington, DC: The Catholic University of America, 1967–1996.

O'Donnell, Christopher, O Carm, 'The Eucharist and Elizabeth of the Trinity (1880–1906)', in Eltin Griffin, O Carm (ed.), *Hidden Riches: The Eucharist in the Carmelite Tradition*, Dublin: Columba Press, 2005, pp. 44–68.

Paul VI, *Sacra Rituum Congregatio* (Apostolic Constitution), May 8, 1969.

-----, *Sanctitas Clarior* (Apostolic Letter), March 19, 1969.

Payne, Steven, OCD, *Bl. Elizabeth of the Trinity: Her Message*, Washington, DC: ICS Publications Cassettes, ref. TE 108, no date.

Philipon, Marie-Michel, OP, *En Présence de Dieu: Élisabeth de la Trinité*, Bruges: Desclée De Brouwer, 1966.

-----, *La Doctrine spirituelle de Sœur Élisabeth de la Trinité*, Bruges: Desclée De Brouwer, 1954.

-----, *The Spiritual Doctrine of Sister Elizabeth of the Trinity*, Cork: The Mercier Press, 1947.

Pierami, Don Benedetto, OSB, *The Life of the Servant of God Pius X*, London: Burns, Oates & Washbourne, 1929.

Pius X, *E Supremi Apostolatus* (Encyclical), October 4, 1903.

-----, *Gravissimo Officii Munere* (Encyclical), August 10, 1906.

-----, *Sacra Tridentina Synodus* (Decree), December 20, 1905.

-----, *Une Fois Encore* (Encyclical), January 6, 1907.

-----, *Vehementer Nos* (Encyclical), February 11, 1906.

Poinsenet, Marie-Dominique, OP, *Questa Presenza di Dio in te...: Elisabetta Catez, Suor Elisabetta della Trinità o.c.d., 1880–1906*, Milan: Editrice Àncora / Rome: Postulazione Generale dei Carmelitani Scalzi, 1971.

Postulazione Generale dei Carmelitani Scalzi, *Cause di Beatificazione e Canonizzazione dell'Ordine dei Carmelitani Scalzi, degli Istituti ad esso affiliati, del suo Ordine Secolare*, Rome: Postulazione Generale dei Carmelitani Scalzi, 1995.

Rémy, Jean, *Confidences d'un prêtre: Élisabeth de la Trinité m'a sauvé*, Paris: Éditions du Jubilé, 2006.

-----, *Élisabeth de la Trinité et la prière: Commentaire de la prière de la Bienheureuse Élisabeth de la Trinité*, Paris: Desclée De Brouwer, 2003.

-----, *Élisabeth de la Trinité: Le secret du Bonheur*, Montreal & Paris: Médiaspaul, 2003.

-----, *Guite: La sœur d'Élisabeth de la Trinité*, Toulouse: Éditions du Carmel, 2003.

-----, *Prier 15 jours avec Élisabeth de la Trinité*, Montrouge: Nouvelle Cité, 2000.

-----, *Regards d'amour: Élisabeth de la Trinité et Jean de la Croix*, Paris: Cerf, 1993.

Rule of Saint Albert, in John Malley, O Carm, Camilo Maccise, OCD & Joseph Chalmers, O Carm, *In Obsequio Jesu Christi:*

The Letters of the Superiors General O.Carm. and O.C.D. 1992–2002, Rome: Edizioni OCD, 2003, pp. 133–9.

Sacred Congregation for the Causes of Saints, *Norms to be Observed in Inquiries made by Bishops in the Causes of Saints*, February 7, 1983.

[Saint-Seine, Mother Germaine de, OCD], *Élisabeth de la Trinité, 1880–1906: Souvenirs*, Flavignerot: Carmel of Dijon, 2008 [reproduction of first edition of 1909].

-----, *La Servante de Dieu: Élisabeth de la Trinité, 1880–1906 – Souvenirs*, Paris: Éditions St-Paul, [1946].

-----, *The Praise of Glory: Reminiscences of Sister Elizabeth of the Trinity, A Carmelite Nun of Dijon, 1901–1906* ('Second English Edition'), London: R & T Washbourne / New York: Benziger Brothers, 1914.

Sesé, Bernard, *Petite vie d'Élisabeth de la Trinité*, Paris: Desclée De Brouwer, 1993.

Sheldon, William W, CM, 'Canonization of Frederick Ozanam: History of the Cause', in *Vincentian Heritage Journal*, vol. 17, issue 1, 1996, pp. 51–62.

SIC [*Servitium Informativum Carmelitanum*], vol. XV, no. 7, 1982.

-----, vol. XVII, no. 3, 1984.

Sicari, Antonio, OCD, *Elisabetta della Trinità: Un'Esistenza teologica*, Rome: Edizioni OCD, 1984.

Simeone della Sacra Famiglia, OCD [Simeón Tomás Fernández], *Indice delle Cause di Canonizzazione della Postulazione Generale dei Carmelitani Scalzi*, Rome: Postulazione Generale OCD, 1991.

-----, *La Postulazione Generale dei Carmelitani Scalzi: Sguardo panoramico dal 1973 al 1990*, Rome: Postulazione Generale OCD, 1990.

Sources Vives – La revue des Fraternités Monastiques de Jérusalem, no. 132 (issue: *Élisabeth de la Trinité*), 2007.

Sullivan, Emmanuel, OCD, *Bl. Elizabeth of the Trinity: Mary in Her Interior Life*, Washington, DC: ICS Publications Cassettes, ref. TEI 122, no date.

Sullivan, Shirley Darcus, *Transformed By Love: The Soul's Journey to*

God in Teresa of Avila, Mother Aloysius of the Blessed Sacrament, Elizabeth of the Trinity, Hyde Park, NY: New City Press, 2002.

Teresa of Avila, *The Collected Works of St. Teresa of Avila*, 3 vols., Washington, DC: ICS Publications, 1987, 1980 & 1985.

Thérèse of Lisieux, *General Correspondence*, 2 vols., Washington, DC: ICS Publications, 1982 & 1988.

-----, *Story of a Soul: The Autobiography of Saint Thérèse of Lisieux*, Washington, DC: ICS Publications, 1996.

-----, *St. Thérèse of Lisieux: Her Last Conversations*, Washington, DC: ICS Publications, 1977.

-----, *The Poetry of Saint Thérèse of Lisieux*, Washington, DC: ICS Publications, 1996.

Ufficio per le Cerimonie Pontificie, *Beatificazione dei Servi di Dio José Manyanet, Daniel Brottier, Elisabetta della Trinità, Basilica Vaticana, 25 Novembre 1984*, Vatican: Tipografia Poliglotta Vaticana, 1984.

Valabek, Redemptus Maria, O Carm, 'Patroness of Contemplatives: Our Lady in the Life and Writings of Blessed Elizabeth of the Trinity', in his *Mary, Mother of Carmel: Our Lady and the Saints of Carmel*, vol. II, Rome: Institutum Carmelitanum (Carmel in the World Paperbacks), 1988, pp. 101–18.

Von Balthasar, Hans Urs, *Élisabeth de la Trinité et sa mission spirituelle*, Paris: Seuil, 1959.

-----, *Elizabeth of Dijon: An Interpretation of Her Spiritual Mission* [adapted by A V Littledale], London: The Harvill Press, 1956.

-----, *Two Sisters in the Spirit: Thérèse of Lisieux & Elizabeth of the Trinity*, San Francisco: Ignatius Press, 1992.

Woodward, Kenneth L, *Making Saints – Inside the Vatican: Who Become Saints, Who Do Not, and Why…*, London: Chatto & Windus, 1991.

ABBREVIATIONS

(*Note:* See Appendix III, 'Works Consulted', at the end of this volume, for full details of the works listed below)

The Writings of Elizabeth: Complete Works

CW I   *Complete Works of Elizabeth of the Trinity*, vol. I
CW II *Complete Works of Elizabeth of the Trinity*, vol. II
OC   *Œuvres complètes d'Élisabeth de la Trinité* (1991 edition)

The Writings of Elizabeth: Individual Works

D   *Diary*
GV   *The Greatness of Our Vocation*
HF   *Heaven in Faith*
IN   *Intimate Notes*
L   *Letters*
LL   *Let Yourself Be Loved*
LR   *Last Retreat*
P   *Poems*
PT   *Prayer to the Trinity* ('O my God, Trinity whom I adore')

Spoken Words of Elizabeth and Eyewitness Accounts

CG   Curia Generalis OCD (Secretariatus pro Monialibus), *To be a Carmelite with the Blessed Elizabeth of the Trinity*
ESS Office for the Promotion of Causes [OCD] (ed.), *Elizabeth Still Speaks…*
PD   Marie-Michel Philipon, OP, *En Présence de Dieu*

The Major Biographies of Elizabeth

ETB Conrad De Meester, OCD, *Élisabeth de la Trinité: Biographie*
PG   Mother Germaine de Saint-Seine, OCD, *The Praise of Glory* (English translation of the *Souvenirs* – the 1914 'Second English Edition' is used here)

547

S1   Mother Germaine de Saint-Seine, OCD, *Souvenirs* (first edition of 1909, reproduced in the 2008 edition)

S2   Mother Germaine de Saint-Seine, OCD, *Souvenirs* (the 1946 edition consulted here, containing the eighteenth chapter added as from edition of 1927)

Writings of Teresa of Avila

BL   *The Book of Her Life*
C   *The Constitutions*
F   *The Book of Her Foundations*
IC   *The Interior Castle*
Sol   *Soliloquies*
ST   *Spiritual Testimonies*
WP   *The Way of Perfection*

Writings of John of the Cross

A   *The Ascent of Mount Carmel*
DN   *The Dark Night*
LF   *The Living Flame of Love* (second redaction)
SC   *The Spiritual Canticle* (second redaction)
SLL   *The Sayings of Light and Love*

Writings of Thérèse of Lisieux

LC   *Her Last Conversations*
LT   Letters (in *General Correspondence*)
PN   Poems
SS   *Story of a Soul*

Carmelite *Rule*

See *Rule of Saint Albert*, in Works Consulted; this edition follows the numbering of points agreed in 1999.

Psalms

Numbering and text follow the Grail version, in *The Psalms: A New Translation*, London & Glasgow: Fontana, 1963.

ACKNOWLEDGEMENTS

I would like to express my thanks for the following permissions received:

To the Carmel of Dijon:

for permission to reproduce photographs *E pastel, 128.jpg* and *E 65b.jpg* on the front cover of volumes 1 and 2 respectively; and photographs *E 05.jpg, Elis 63.jpg, E 68.jpg* and *Mère Germaine, 147. jpg* within the book itself.

To Les Éditions du Cerf:

for permission to quote from Conrad De Meester, OCD (ed.), *Œuvres complètes d'Élisabeth de la Trinité*, Paris: Cerf, 1991; specifically, from the works contained in *J'ai trouvé Dieu – Œuvres complètes d'Élisabeth de la Trinité*, vol. II, Paris: Cerf, 1979.

To ICS Publications:

for permission to quote from the writings of Elizabeth of the Trinity, Teresa of Avila, John of the Cross, Thérèse of Lisieux and Edith Stein © Washington Province of Discalced Carmelites ICS Publications 2131 Lincoln Road, N.E. Washington, DC 20002-1199 U.SA. www.icspublications.org

To Presses de la Renaissance:

for permission to quote from Conrad De Meester, OCD, *Élisabeth de la Trinité: Biographie*, Paris: Presses de la Renaissance, 2006.

TERESIAN PRESS
SOME FORTHCOMING TITLES

John of the Cross: Seasons of Prayer
Iain Matthew, OCD

A Moment of Prayer – A Life of Prayer
Conrad De Meester, OCD

The Writings of St Teresa of Avila
Eugene McCaffrey, OCD

St Teresa on Prayer
Jerome Lantry, OCD

How Do I Pray Today?
Edited by James McCaffrey, OCD & Joanne Mosley

Teresian Press
Carmelite Priory
Boars Hill
Oxford OX1 5HB

www.carmelitebooks.com

Also published by the Discalced Carmelites:
Mount Carmel: A Review of the Spiritual Life